East-West Perspectives on International Law
A Selection of Papers from Conferences in Beijing and Hangzhou (2015-2017)

东西方的国际法观
北京和杭州会议论文选集

East-West Perspectives on International Law
A Selection of Papers from Conferences in Beijing and Hangzhou (2015-2017)

-主编-

刘大群 [英] 苏珊娜·林顿 朱利江

Liu Daqun, Suzannah Linton, Zhu Lijiang eds.

中国政法大学出版社

2019·北京

China University of Political Science and Law Press

声 明　　1. 版权所有，侵权必究。

　　　　　2. 如有缺页、倒装问题，由出版社负责退换。

图书在版编目（ＣＩＰ）数据

　东西方的国际法观:北京和杭州会议论文选集/刘大群,(英)苏珊娜·林顿，朱利江主编.—
北京:中国政法大学出版社，2019.10
　ISBN 978-7-5620-9263-6

　Ⅰ.①东…　Ⅱ.①刘…　②苏…　③朱…　Ⅲ.①国际法－学术会议－文集　Ⅳ.①D99-53

中国版本图书馆CIP数据核字(2019)第227647号

出 版 者　　中国政法大学出版社
地　　址　　北京市海淀区西土城路 25 号
邮寄地址　　北京 100088 信箱 8034 分箱　邮编 100088
网　　址　　http://www.cuplpress.com (网络实名：中国政法大学出版社)
电　　话　　010-58908289(编辑部) 58908334(邮购部)
承　　印　　固安华明印业有限公司
开　　本　　720mm×960mm　1/16
印　　张　　31.5
字　　数　　580 千字
版　　次　　2019 年 10 月第 1 版
印　　次　　2019 年 10 月第 1 次印刷
定　　价　　139.00 元

Editors' Foreword

East-West Perspectives on International Law is a collection of some of the papers addressing international justice, international humanitarian law at sea and the principle of effective control that were originally presented at conferences in Beijing (2015), Hangzhou (2016) and Beijing (2017). These events have been made possible through the Collaborative Innovation Center of Judicial Civilization ("CICJC") initiated by China University of Political Science and Law ("CUPL"), the CUPL Sub-Center of Collaborative Innovation Center on State Sovereignty and Maritime Right (CICSSMR) and Zhejiang University. They have been the hosts of the conferences from which this collection draws.

Inspired by the over-arching project's vision of cross-cultural dialogue and exchange of expertise, the conferences have regularly gathered together outstanding Chinese academics, professional and young talents, to engage with distinguished practitioners and renowned academics around the world. The annual conferences, conducted entirely in English, are intensive and highly demanding events, held over a three day period. Participants at each conference are carefully selected for their competence and outstanding work. They present papers and dialogue with other participants in relation to presentations made. The gatherings have contributed towards the creation of a lively intellectual community of international lawyers in China, and a network of friends abroad. These fora also provide a venue for young Chinese talent to gain exposure; in a number of instances, this has led to international careers.

East—West Perspectives on International Law is a collection of excellent papers by an elite community of global citizens sharing a common vision of justice, expressed through the technical tools of the legal discipline. It is not a comprehensive compilation of writings on international justice, international humanitarian law at sea and the principle of effective control; that would be impossible to achieve. Nor do we claim it is a collection exploring a uniquely sophisticated theoretical framework that will change the world. The papers have been selected for publication because of their fine quality, and because they have the common feature of contributing towards a balanced appreciation of critical issues in international law. They address important developments, ongoing and pressing matters of controversy, as well as new institutions and emerging issues. The papers have all been strengthened by an inter—active process of dialogue and debate, and have been revised and updated for this publication. They have been written by Chinese and international participants.

East—West Perspectives on International Law is divided into three Parts: East—West Perspectives on International Justice, East—West Perspectives on International Humanitarian Law at Sea, and East—West Perspectives on The Principle of Effective Control.

East—West Perspectives on International Justice as Part I offers fine contemporary insights into international criminal law and procedure, and weighty perspectives on controversial issues. Within the unifying concept of international justice, the topics and approaches taken by the authors are varied, and multi—dimensional. The editors strongly believe that the mix of world—renowned, experienced, established and up—and—coming authors from different countries is not just refreshing but leads to a multi—dimensional collection.

Eminent senior Chinese scholar, Professor Ma Chengyuan of the CUPL, has kindly opened East—West Perspectives on International Justice with reflections on the project that has made this possible, and also the impact of international justice and cross—cultural intellectual exchanges on the development of a globally—minded legal community in China.

The contributions begin with Judge Howard Morrison's reflections, drawn from rich experience both as a judge and practitioner at domestic and international trials. His thoughtful and insightful perspective sets the tone for the seven remaining papers that form the core of this particular collection.

In "The pre-trial phase of international criminal proceedings—give the investigating judge a chance", Göran Sluiter reflects on whether we should give judges a stronger role in the pre-trial phase in international criminal proceedings. He begins with a comparative overview of national and international investigative practice, including that of France, the Netherlands, the Extraordinary Chambers in the Court of Cambodia and the International Criminal Tribunal for the former Yugoslavia, and the International Criminal Court. He concludes that wholesale import of a national system with full judicial investigations is, at present, not in the interests of the international criminal justice system. His contribution ends with three recommendations for developing a stronger judicial role in the pre-trial phase of international criminal proceedings.

Diana Tseng examines one of the most complicated and protracted cases at the International Criminal Tribunal for Rwanda ("ICTR"), the *Butare* case, and the issue of undue delay in international criminal proceedings. The delays in this case were so egregious that the Appeals Chamber held the Prosecution and, for the first time in the ICTR's history, the authorities of the Tribunal, accountable for the delay caused. Her chapter on "The *Butare* Case - Examining Undue Delay Through the ICTR's 'Swan Song'" demonstrates how the ICTR Appeals Chamber moved the jurisprudence of the ICTR closer to international human rights and regional standards in relation to the protection of an accused for his fair trial rights and, particularly, undue delay.

The decision of the majority of the judges of the Appeals Chamber of the International Criminal Tribunal for the former Yugoslavia ("ICTY") in the *Perišić* case generated a tsunami of legal commentary, as did the initial acquittal (followed by the order of retrial and then appeal hearing) of the former state security chief Jovica Stanišić, and the former paramilitary leader Franko Simatović. The furore turned on whether a conviction for aiding and abetting crime requires specific direction of an accused's aid and assistance towards the crimes. Marina Aksenova tackles the controversial flux in the jurisprudence over 2013—2016 in her contribution "On The 'Specific Direction' requirement for aiding and abetting: "refining the modes of liability or setting the threshold too high?". She expertly demonstrates how interpreting the *actusreus* of aiding and abetting as containing a requirement that assistance must be specifically directed towards the crimes and not just geared to the general war effort is problematic on several levels.

In "Indirect Co – Perpetration before The International Criminal Court: The 'Cheops' approach to collective criminal action", William St—Michel takes on another contested issue in international criminal proceedings. His paper on "indirect co—perpetration", one of the forms of group criminality recognized at the International Criminal Court ("ICC"), visualizes the construction of the concept at the Court in terms of pyramids. His contribution analyses the roots and constitutive elements of "indirect co—perpetration", studies concrete applications of "indirect co—perpetration" and examines the interplay between "indirect co—perpetration" and other similar modes of liability. He argues that indirect co—perpetration "has proven to be a flexible and suitable approach for addressing criminal responsibility in context of mass crimes".

The ICC's unique approach to victim participation has now been tried and tested many times since the Court became operational. Despite significant challenges of implementation, Ines Peterson points out that "ICC jurisprudence has come a long way to fill the gaps in the ICC Statute and the Rules of Procedure as to how exactly victim participation should look like in practice". In her paper on "Participation of victims in proceedings of the International Criminal Court", she provides a balanced and insightful overview of the statutory framework and the experiences at various ICC procedural stages ranging from investigations, pre-trial, trial and appeal.

Two contributions engage in a comparative survey of the landscape of international courts and tribunals. Yang Lijun's chapter considers some of the legal issues surrounding the disqualification of judges that have arisen at the ICC, ICTY and ICTR. The concrete situations that the tribunals have had to deal with include leaked personal emails, blogging, potential judicial contamination from hearing related cases and whether legal advisors and consultants should be subject to the same rules that apply to judges. She reveals how, in their many years of existence, the procedure at the ICTY and ICTR for disqualification was changed several times to address problems that arose in practice. Suzannah Linton delves into the issue of whether sentencing of convicted accused at the ICC is an improvement on the ICTY and ICTR. She finds that sentencing has certainly evolved, most obviously in the ICC's statutory regime, although much is still left undefined or unaddressed, notably the absence of meaningful sentencing ranges to help guide the judges and indeterminate concepts such as gravity. The ICC judges have used what they have been given in the legal framework and have built on the rich heritage of existing practice. What emerges is also not conveyer-belt justice; the practice is not uniform, but is broadly consistent and follows several regularly emphasised principles. ICC judges, like those before them have done, are trying to create a legitimate sentencing framework that blends traditional sentencing approaches with the unique purposes of international justice, and the specificities of their particular institution.

Finally, Roman Boed takes us into the future with a concluding reflection—"From the Legacy of the International Criminal Tribunal for Rwanda to the new model of dispensing International Criminal Justice: The International Residual Mechanism for Criminal Tribunals". He concludes on an optimistic note, arguing that the Mechanism, operating on two continents and in an more efficient way than its predecessors, "is poised to ensure the legacy of the Rwanda and Yugoslavia Tribunals and serve as a model for further developments in the effective and efficient administration of international criminal justice".

We will not make detailed introduction to the excellent contributions in Part II and Part III. The appreciation and study of these papers are left to the interested readers themselves.

We sincerely thank all our authors for their wonderful contributions and very much appreciate the efforts of all who have taken part in the conferences in Hangzhou and Beijing, and those who have made the gatherings possible. In this regard, the support and contributions of Professor Ma Chengyuan have been exceptional, and we are deeply grateful to him. We are also indebted to Vice-Dean Zhao Jun of Zhejiang University School of Law. We would also like to thank Jiayi Li, PhD candidate of international law in CUPL, and Qifan Wang, previously at the School of Law, Trinity College Dublin and now with UNCHR in Beijing, for their fine editorial assistance and support. We also thank Professor Nina H. B. Jørgensen, professor at the Faculty of Law, the Chinese University of Hong Kong.

Finally, we must show our appreciation to the CUPL Sub-Center of CICSSMR with Professor Ma Chengyuan as the director for its publication funding.

The Editors

8 August 2018

The Hague, Beijing and Hangzhou

Contents

Part I   East–West Perspectives on International Justice

REFLECTIONS

Judge Sir Howard Morrison [*]

I start by emphasising that the views I express are mine alone from the standpoint of a concerned jurist and an observant senior citizen. I do not suggest that my views are necessarily those of any other judge or judges of the International Criminal Court nor that they represent any aspect of official policy for or of that court. I am not setting out to make any form of political statement. That is not for a judge to do. The hard reality is that throughout all aspects of international law, politics and both conflict and peace are intertwined. It is impossible to deal with one without illustrating another.

When I became a lawyer in the UK in 1977, after brief military service and working in international development in Africa, I had no idea where the law was going to lead me. I started practising criminal, civil and family law with excursions into courts martial defence, employment law and construction law, indeed anything to make a living in a highly competitive legal environment.

After working in the UK, and then Fiji and the Caribbean [those are stories in themselves], I started doing defence work at both the UN International Criminal Tribunals for the Former Yugoslavia ("ICTY") and Rwanda ("ICTR") based in The Hague and Tanzania respectively. That was my real initiation into international criminal and humanitarian law and, of course, international human rights law. That led in turn to being a judge in the UK and the Sovereign Base Areas of Cyprus, and then briefly at the Special Tribunal for the Lebanon, and then the ICTY as a trial judge in

---

[*] Judge of the International Criminal Court.

the case of Radovan Karadžić and other trial and appellate cases, and latterly and currently, the International Criminal Court where I am now in the Appeals Division.

I had always been a very strong supporter of the International Criminal Court, having attended some of the preparatory commissions of what was to become the Rome Statute in my private capacity as a practising international criminal case lawyer in order to lobby for the defence to be an organic part of the court structure. It had not been so, in the early days of the Yugoslav and Rwanda tribunals, and that had made for significant difficulties for the defence. They were resolved by forward thinking individuals.

I mention all this simply to illustrate how I personally became so acutely aware of what is in fact self—evident, that international criminal and humanitarian law and the maintenance of the rule of law at both domestic and international levels are absolutely crucial to the building, and furtherance, of peaceful societies. Moreover, that peace through the rule of law must be recognized as an essential goal for lawyers and judges as part of the fabric of domestic and international society. The rule of law is fragile and requires constant nurturing and care. When it breaks down it usually does so rapidly and with serious consequences. I am not just talking about, for instance, small failing states. Look what happened to civil society in New Orleans after Hurricane Katrina. Robbery, looting, rape and other violence exploded and there were reports of the police abandoning their duties and even committing criminal acts. There are a host of other examples, past and present. Perhaps Syria is the saddest and most potent that we currently have to face.

I am now more aware than ever of the problems we face before and the unacceptable consequences of not finding solutions. I teach and lecture extensively on international law principles and issues as much and as widely as judicial duties allow because these are concerns that the new generations of politicians, scientists, lawyers and other academics are going to have to grapple with and solve. But we cannot sit back and say that these are simply problems for the next generation. They are very much our problems, here and now. We need to be aware and active and determined. And, we need to be finding solutions now. Some of the truths are uncomfortable.

It is fortunate that, as a species, humans generally have an innate sense of what is fair. That is apparent from a very early age. Walk past any elementary school playground and listen to children at play. Sooner or later some aggrieved participants in a game or joint activity will complain of behaviour and the complaining cry will go up "that's not fair".

Organised sport, a very human activity and one in which we participate unlike other living species, is predicated upon fairness ranging from formalised rules and referees to a ban of drugs giving offending athletes an unfair advantage. Breaches generate sanctions from individual red cards to the banning of offending teams of even nations. Fairness is thus ingrained in our collective and individual psyche. That, for me at least, is the basis of the rule of law.

The world faces a plethora of challenges to any maintained order or fairness amongst nations. Let me outline some, but only some, of those I consider as being the most urgent.

There have been wars ever since man became societal. Historically, we have seen territorial wars, dynastic wars, political and theological wars and wars of simple aggression. We still see them worldwide today. Warfare is widespread and the technology of weaponry advances at an alarming rate. My fear is that the list of causation or excuse to wage war is going to expand.

There are, at the very least, two global factors that will generate further conflicts. The first is a rapidly expanding world population, and the second, and very closely connected, is climate change and associated environmental damage.

It is estimated that by the year 2050, the global human population will have expanded from the present 7 plus billion to 10 billion. It went from less than 5 billion to our current number since 1975. That means, in each decade from now to 2050, something approaching the current population of China will have to be absorbed into the global society.

Uncontrolled population growth, and I see no obvious signs of organized and rational control being undertaken on any substantial scale anywhere in the world, is bound to lead to huge social problems, domestically and internationally. It is inevitably, through those social and practical pressures and discords, going to generate grave challenges to the rule of law and universal justice and peace. How might these challenges arise?

More people means more pressure on all resources, particularly finite resources such as oil and minerals in general. The greater the number of consumers, the faster non—renewable resources are depleted, the higher the price and the greater the temptation to use political and/or military means to secure supplies.

The larger the population becomes, the more desperate people will become for living space, and the larger urban centres will become, increasing pressure for housing, food, water, electricity and other requirements. Add resultant conflict to the equation, which will reduce the possibility of settling or staying in certain areas, and the growing population and emigration pressures expand rapidly. We see it now in North Africa and the desperate flight to Europe, and the growth in human traffickers.

Globally increasing population means the greater need for sustainable water supplies for human use and farming. Water wars are no longer just the province of fiction writers. They are likely come about. We already have examples of international tensions when cross border rivers are dammed in upstream territories for hydroelectric production or irrigation reducing the downstream flow.

Oil wars, living space wars, food wars, fishing limit wars. All and more can be the product of unrestrained population growth and will be fertile ground for exploitation by political and religious extremists.

Population growth and pollution in turn generate climate change and environmental damage and disaster. Take just two examples. Rising sea levels permanently flooding low—lying coastal agricultural land, for instance in Bangladesh. Add rising temperatures affecting plant growth cycles and torrential rain washing away fertile soil. More people, less food, less water, less viable food growing and living space. Add blind nationalism and intolerance and bigotry into the algorithm and what do we have?

The stark answer is an obvious recipe for serious social unrest and conflict domestically and internationally, and a very real threat to the rule of law and peace on the widest scale. States will become more inward looking, nationalism and intolerance will spread and, almost inevitably, human rights, both individual and collective, will be early victims of self—interest and isolationism, political and religious extremism and the erosion of liberal democratic systems.

All of this is readily foreseeable and, without timely restraints, more than likely. We see it some of it already. I do not need to name the places or worst offenders. We know where they are.

What can we do? Indeed, can anything be done to resolve or counter these potential and, frankly, largely man—made disasters? Well of course many thousands of intelligent and concerned people, scientists, medical professionals, agronomists and engineers amongst others have already started to construct protocols and solutions in the fields of pollutants, energy, food and disease control.

Can we change the social and legal architecture, which of course involves legal order as an essential ingredient, to run in parallel to the climate and resource solutions? I very firmly believe we can, but it is going to take brave political, religious, academic and not least legal leaders to galvanise and coordinate resolutions and create fair and sustainable peace preserving social and legal architecture. It is on any analysis a massive task. More than that, it is a very urgent one.

How do we start? Well of course many have started already. None of us as individuals can change the world. Take for instance Martin Luther King. He did not set out to change the world or create a perfect one. Indeed, it would probably be impossible to agree upon what a perfect world should look like. Instead, Martin Luther King set out to publicise and eradicate institutionalised racism in the United States of America by raising awareness, and mobilising those who recognised the evil and wanted to do something about it. So what did he do, how did he start? Well, simply by using his talents to do the very best he could. That is surely the key to successful human endeavour; doing the very best that is possible and, vitally, motivating others to do the same. And that is the answer to my reflective question; how do we start? We start and we continue by doing the very best we can as individuals with the abilities we possess and by pursuing our goals with courage and tenacity. Vitally, we also motivate and encourage others to do the same, at very least by example. That brings results both individually and collectively. It empowers those who do not yet have power and it gives duty and direction to those already fortunate enough to have positions of influence in whatever sphere they operate. But, it is actions and not aspirations that count.

So, now I turn more specifically to the challenges that brings for universal justice and peace in a globalised world. Inevitably, as an international law judge, I look specifically at the role of international law and, in particular, international criminal and humanitarian law and, not least, the International Criminal Court.

Globalisation is a process that has radically changed the way in which States and international institutions interact with one another. Economies are more than ever before interdependent and damage to the environment caused by the activities of one State can have profound effects on others. Technology has made information available to a mass of people who 20 or 30 years ago would have been struggling to find access to it, and it now travels virtually instantly around the globe and via television and the internet to millions if not billions of people. The value of that information is measured by its accuracy and quality. Misleading or dishonest information, more accurately described as propaganda, can be particularly damaging as it is often the first information that arrives concerning a particular issue or event that shapes the views and reactions of the recipient thereafter. It also feeds conspiracy theories that often damage real and effective resolutions.

States, which mostly evolved to consolidate dynastic control and common cultures with degrees of individual and collective wealth, at the same time had to provide basic protections to citizens via some species of social contract. This balance was necessary to maintain social order and political stability. Those same States are now being forced to confront newer and more effective ways to maintain power structures and peace. At the international level, until the 20th century, international relations operated for the most part in the classic Westphalian scheme. After the establishment of the League of Nations and the dramatic effects of two world wars leading to the creation of the United Nations, structures had to be established to both maintain and institutionalise the classic balance of power amongst States as well as between States and their citizens.

Individual States inevitably seek to maintain national, sovereign and cultural characteristics and ambitions. There is no doubt that globalization presents significant challenges to those existing power structures, and the authority of the state itself. As a result, the defects inherent in them become more obvious and the tensions greater. As populations grow and information spreads faster and wider, the tensions can only increase. Old structures based upon increasingly archaic power dynamics and *Realpolitik* feel threatened and insecure. One classic diversion is a military excursion to divert attention from economic failure or corruption within a given system. Often that gives rise to breaches, or at least allegations of breaches, of international law, specifically international humanitarian law and the tensions spread from the domestic to the international scene.

Globalization, although often viewed through the lens of the economist, is actually far more than economic cooperation or control. It embraces the extension of social relationships through the transmission of ideas, meanings and values into what might be termed a "common consumption" of values more recently fuelled by the internet and relative ease of international travel.

Cultural globalization encompasses the transmission of ideas and values around the world in such a way as to extend and intensify intercultural and international social relations including inter−faith dialogue. In a world marked by savage and apparently irrational religious intolerance and extreme violence, the latter may prove to be of exceptional value and necessity in the maintenance of the rule of law. Religious movements and faiths were amongst the earliest cultural elements to globalize, being spread by evangelism, migration and sometimes the force of military occupation. Christianity, Islam and Buddhism are amongst those faiths which have influenced endemic cultures in places far from their origins. The convergence and interaction between belief systems and law is obvious.

We can see globalization in the movement of musical tastes. Young people especially worldwide find commonality in genres spread far from their roots such as reggae and blues. Cuisine now crosses boundaries more than ever, whether it be a result of migration or travel or publicity. Chinese and Indian restaurants abound worldwide. It is almost as easy to find sushi in Germany as it is in Japan.

The creation and expansion of social relations are thus not observed on solely a material level. It is more than some vague notion of multi−culturalism. It involves sharing norms and knowledge with which peoples associate their individual and collective cultural identities. Of course that may dilute the uniqueness of once isolated communities, but the alienation of individuals from their traditions is likely to be of modest effect compared to the overall impact of modernity itself.

In general globalization tends to reduce the importance of individual nation states. International institutions such as the United Nations, the European Union, the World Trade Organisation, the World Bank, the G8 or the International Criminal Court replace or extend national functions to facilitate international agreement.

Increasingly, non−governmental organisations influence public opinion and policy across national boundaries including humanitarian aid and development efforts. This extends to the protection of environments especially flora and fauna. Private philanthropy is of increasing moment through charities such as the Bill and Melinda Gates Foundation which contributes, for example, multi—billion dollar commitments to immunization programmes. Associations such as the Global Philanthropy Forum provide multi—million dollar aid to poorer communities that would otherwise be reliant upon scarce national aid programmes.

The hard truth, however, is that the international or global community has, more often than not, been unable to effectively respond to threats to peace and security, violations of human rights, grinding poverty and health issues or even natural disasters. One of the more obvious reasons is that the mechanisms established to react to those disorders are politically—based bureaucratic entities that are slow to implement, or even reluctant to pursue, what may be the most effective remedial policies. Recent illustrations, and there are many, include Syria and Libya and, more historically but with continuing effects, Rwanda and Cambodia.

Power and self—interest struggles between major States only add to the delay and confusion and create opportunities for extreme groups to exploit and extend the violence. So called "Islamic State" is a prime example.

On a narrower, but nonetheless worrying scale, are the tensions that exist between States seeking to preserve their sovereignty [or naked self—interest and often quasi—xenophobic policies under the emotive cloak of sovereignty] and those individuals and NGOs seeking to protect human rights in particular, and democratic freedoms in general. The rise of populist political movements, not least in Europe, is all too obvious.

Another hard but self—evident truth is that focus has been dominant on punishment of perpetrators after the fact, where breaches of human rights treaties and mechanisms by high ranking state officers have occurred, rather than the diligent prevention of such abuses at a very early stage.

That is, perhaps, almost inevitable as most States have been hesitant to risk violating the actual or purported sovereignty of another State, absent some political or economic interest or benefit for itself. In that regard, and as but one of many examples, I recommend reading *Shake Hands with the Devil* by General Romeo Dallaire, a book that provides valuable and powerful insight into the manifest and avoidable failings that surrounded the horrors in Rwanda.

Even basic study illustrates that almost every human rights mechanism that exists is contingent upon the political will of States rather than solely a commitment to justice and the peace that engenders. At present we need look no further than Syria.

Although the doctrine of the "responsibility to protect" has gained traction it is still widely agreed between States that only the UN Security Council may authorize the use of force, even in obvious cases of crimes against humanity and war crimes. The widely accepted reality is that the Security Council is primarily and inevitably a highly political body with the real power being vested in the permanent membership and the end–game power of veto.

Cynics would argue that it is naïve to accept that the inefficiencies embedded in the system are simply inadvertent.

If human rights enforcement mechanisms are to regulate the potentially hostile acts of States, or state officials, against individuals or selected groups then it appears foundationally irreconcilable that the mechanisms should also be controlled solely by States.

Some greater cynics are also likely to be of the view that those bureaucracies that have been established by States to apparently protect the interests of individuals under the rule of law, contain within their structures a regulatory matrix designed, not to prevent, but to slow down and curtail the ability of human rights organisations, and international criminal justice systems, to develop to a level which could seriously undermine the ability of states to pursue their interests both domestically and internationally.

That view would maintain that ineffective, or at least inefficient, mechanisms

form to this international convention. According to the Report of the Secretary General to the UN Security Council pertaining to the establishment of the ICTY:

> [i]t is axiomatic that the (ICTY (must fully respect internationally recognized standards regarding the rights of the accused at all stages of its proceedings. In the view of the Secretary-General, such international recognized standards are, in particular, contained in Article 14 of the International Covenant on Civil and Political Rights. [27]

Indeed, the language of Article 14 (3)(c) is almost identical to that found in Article 20 (4)(c) of the ICTR Statute and Article 21 (4)(c) of the Statute of the ICTY ("ICTY Statute"). [28] Furthermore, in interpreting Article 21 (4)(c) of the ICTY Statute, the Appeals Chamber has explicitly referenced "major international human rights instruments", including Article 14 (3)(c) of the ICCPR and the European Convention on Human Rights ("ECHR"). [29]

Returning to the *Butare* case, and as will be discussed below, the Appeals Chamber explicitly referenced and relied on the views of the UN Human Rights Com-

---

[27]   Security Council, Report of the Secretary-General Pursuant to Paragraph 2 of Security Council Resolution 808 (1993), UN Doc. S/25704, 3 May 1993, para. 106.

[28]   Statute of the International Criminal Tribunal for the Former Yugoslavia, 25 May 1993, established by Security Council Resolution 827 (1993) and last amended by Security Council Resolution 114 (2002). The language of Article 20 (4)(c) of the ICTR Statute is: "4. In the determination of any charge against the accused pursuant to the present Statute, the accused shall be entitled to the following minimum guarantees, in full equality: (c) To be tried without undue delay." The language of Article 21 (4)(c) of the ICTY Statute is: "4. In the determination of any charge against the accused pursuant to the present Statute, the accused shall be entitled to the following minimum guarantees, in full equality: (c) to be tried without undue delay."

[29]   *See* ICTY, *Prosecutor v. Sefer Halilović*, Decision on defence motion for prompt scheduling of appeal hearing, Appeals Chamber, IT-01-48-A, 27 October 2006, para. 17, fn. 44 (http://www.legal-tools.org/doc/e79d4d/) ("*Halilović* Decision") and references cited therein; European Convention for the Protection of Human Rights and Fundamental Freedoms, adopted on 4 November 1950, entered into force on 3 September 1953.

mittee regarding the interpretation of undue delay. [30] Beyond the ICCPR, the Appeals Chamber further relied on findings of the European Court of Human Rights, the African Commission on Human and People's Rights, and the Inter—American Court of Human Rights. [31] As the final appeal judgement at the ICTR, this appears to send a strong indication that the Appeals Chamber is interested to ensure its jurisprudence is consistent with international standards in relation to matters of undue delay.

3. Duty and role of the tribunals

Based on the founding documents of the Tribunals, the UN Security Council decided to establish the ICTR and ICTY for the sole purpose of prosecuting persons responsible for genocide and other serious violations of international humanitarian law committed in the related territories. [32] In addition to this mandate, the UN Security Council inserted provisions in the statutes of both Tribunals for the protection of an accused's fair trial rights. Pursuant to Article 19 (1) of the ICTR Statute and Article 20 (1) of the ICTY Statute:

> The Trial Chambers shall ensure that a trial is fair and expeditious and that proceedings are conducted in accordance with the Rules of Procedure and Evidence, with full respect for the rights of the accused and due regard for the protection of victims and witnesses. [33]

This duty to ensure the protection of fair trial rights is bolstered by Article 20 of

---

[30] *See Butare* Appeal Judgement, para. 376, fn. 916 and references cited therein, see *supra* note 2.

[31] *See Butare* Appeal Judgement, para. 376, fn. 916 and references cited therein, see *supra* note 2. See also ICTY, *Prosecutor v. Nikola Šainović et al.* , Judgement, Appeals Chamber, IT–05–87–A, 23 January 2014, para. 100 (http: //www. legal–tools. org/doc/81ac8c/) ("*Šainović et al.* Appeal Judgement"). At the time of this paper, the *Šainović et al.* Appeal Judgement appears to be the most recent ICTY Appeal Judgement dealing with undue delay.

[32] Security Council Resolution 827, UN Doc. S/RES/827, 25 May 1993, para. 2; Security Council Resolution 955, UN Doc. S/RES/955, 8 November 1994, para. 1.

[33] ICTY Statute, art. 20 (1).

the ICTR Statute and Article 21 of the ICTY Statute, which set out the "bundle of rights" or "minimum guarantees" bestowed upon an accused before the Tribunals. [34] The right to be tried without undue delay is within this "bundle of rights." [35] Accordingly, within the language of both ICTY and ICTR Statutes, a significant positive obligation is placed on the Tribunals to ensure the rights of the accused are protected. [36]

This obligation to ensure a fair trial is ever-present within the jurisprudence of the Tribunals. As stated in the ICTY *Šainović et al.* Appeal Judgement:

[t]he Appeals Chamber recalls that the primary duty of the trial chamber is to safeguard the fairness of the trial, ensuring that the proceedings are conducted with full respect for the rights of the accused. In this context, the Appeals Chamber also recalls that the right to be tried without undue delay is provided under Article 21 (4) (c) of the [ICTY] Statute and embodied in numerous international human rights instruments and is 'an inseparable and constituent element of the right to a fair trial.' Accordingly, the trial chamber has a duty to be proactive in ensuring that the accused is tried without undue delay, regardless of whether the accused himself asserts that right. [...] [37]

The Appeals Chamber in the *Butare* case reiterated the existence of a proactive duty on the part of the Trial Chamber to ensure that the accused is tried without undue delay. [38]

---

[34] See also Patrick L. Robinson, "Ensuring Fair and Expeditious Trials at the International Criminal Tribunal for the Former Yugoslavia", in *European Journal of International Law*, 2002, vol. 11, no. 3, p. 583 ("Robinson").

[35] *See* Article 20 (4) (c) of the ICTR Statute, and Article 21 (4) (c) of the ICTY Statute.

[36] Robinson, p. 583, see *supra* note 35.

[37] *Šainović et al.* Appeal Judgement, para. 100 (internal references omitted), see *supra* note 32.

[38] *Butare* Appeal Judgement, para. 346, fn. 843, see *supra* note 2.

While the jurisprudence of the Tribunals affirms the achievement of a fair and expeditious trial as a fundamental purpose of their respective statutes and rules of procedures, the case law also states that:

The fulfilment of this purpose cannot, however, be separated from the broader purpose and context in which the Tribunal [s] operate, that is, the prosecution of persons for serious violations of international humanitarian law. [39]

This balancing responsibility of the Tribunals is also reflected in the jurisprudence. The Appeals Chamber in the *Butare* case recalled that the ICTR Statute protects against "*undue* delay" and that the length of an accused's detention, including the years he or she has been detained at the time a trial judgement is issued, does not in itself demonstrate or constitute undue delay. [40] In the Appeals Chamber's view, because of the Tribunal's mandate and the inherent complexity of the cases tried, it is "not unreasonable to expect that the judicial process will not always be as expeditious as before domestic courts. " [41]

According to the *Šainović et al.* Appeal Judgement:

[t]he Appeals Chamber is mindful, however, that in cases of significant scope and complexity [...] , the trial chamber's duty to ensure the expeditiousness of the trial will often entail a delicate balancing of interests. In upholding the overall fairness of proceedings, while the trial chamber must ensure that the proceedings do not suffer undue delays and that the trial is completed within a reasonable time, it must equally ascertain that the proceedings are not compromised by the imposition of excessive time constraints. [...] [42]

---

[39] Robinson, p. 572, see *supra* note 35.

[40] *Butare* Appeal Judgement, paras. 346, 359 (emphasis in the original), see *supra* note 2.

[41] *Butare* Appeal Judgement, para. 359, see *supra* note 2.

[42] *Šainović et al.* Appeal Judgement, para. 101 (internal references omitted), see *supra* note 32.

It is within this context of inherent complexity concerning the alleged commission of the most heinous crimes that potentially involve multiple accused, numerous geographical locations, or various timeframes that the question of undue delay must be examined. Regarding the six accused in the *Butare* case, the question is: does complexity of the case fully justify detaining the accused for up to or more than 20 years before a final judgment? With this in mind, it is important to examine the test at the Tribunals for establishing undue delay.

4. Test for undue delay at the tribunals

In interpreting Article 14 (3)(c) of the ICCPR, the Human Rights Committee stated that what constitutes reasonable delay has to be assessed in the circumstances of each case, taking into account mainly the complexity of the case, the conduct of the accused, and the manner in which the matter was dealt with by the administrative and judicial authorities. [43] According to the Human Rights Committee, exceptional reasons must be shown to justify delay, [44] and furthermore the burden of proof rests with the State party. [45]

Regarding the jurisprudence of the ICTR, as stated most recently in the *Butare* Appeal Judgement, the Appeals Chamber recalled that the right to be tried without undue delay is enshrined under Article 20 (4)(c) of the ICTR Statute and that undue delay is determined on a case-by-case basis. [46] This is equally reflected in the

---

[43] General Comment No. 32, para. 35, see *supra* note 23. See also Human Rights Committee, *Tatyana Krasnov v. Kyrgystan*, Communication No. 1402/2005, UN Doc. CCPR/C/101/D/1402/2005, views adopted on 29 March 2011, para. 8. 7.

[44] Human Rights Committee, *José Antonio Martínez Muñoz v. Spain*, Communication No. 1006/2001, UN Doc. CCPR/C/79/D/1006/2001, views adopted on 30 October 2003, para. 7. 1 and references cited therein.

[45] Human Rights Committee, *Aleksander Smanster v. Belarus*, Communication no. 1178/2003, UN Doc. CCPR/C/94/D/1178/2003, views adopted on 23 October 2008, para. 10. 4 and references cited therein.

[46] *Butare* Appeal Judgement, para. 346, see *supra* note 2.

ICTY *Šainović et al.* Appeal Judgement and other ICTY cases. [47] Relying on established jurisprudence, the ICTR Appeals Chamber in *Butare* stated:

> [a] number of factors are relevant to this assessment, including: the length of the delay; the complexity of the proceedings; the conduct of the parties; the conduct of the relevant authorities; and the prejudice to the accused, if any. [48]

The Appeals Chamber further stated that trial chambers have a duty to be proactive in ensuring that the accused is tried without undue delay, regardless of whether the accused himself asserts that right, echoing the Appeals Chamber in the *Šainović et al* case. [49]

Turning to the assessment of undue delay in the *Butare* case, the Trial Chamber set out the following factors: the length of the delay, the complexity of proceedings, the conduct of parties, the conduct of relevant authorities, and any prejudice suffered by the accused. [50] It considered the Defence teams' arguments that the delay was not attributable to them, and was caused by, *inter alia*, the Prosecution's conduct and late disclosures of evidence and documents, the joinder of the trials with

---

[47] *Šainović et al.* Appeal Judgement, para. 100, see *supra* note 32, *referring to* Article 21 (4)(c) of the ICTY Statute, *Halilović* Decision, 2006, para. 17, see supra note 30, citing ICTY, *Prosecutor v. Miroslav Kvočka et al.* , Decision on Interlocutory Appeal by the Accused Zoran *Žigić* Against the Decision of Trial Chamber I Dated 5 December 2000, Appeals Chamber, IT-98-30/1-AR73. 5, 25 May 2001, para. 20 (http: // www. legal-tools. org/doc/f28d47/). See also ICTY, *Prosecutor v. Jadranko Prlić et al.* , Decision on Joint Defence Interlocutory Appeal Against the Trial Chamber's Oral Decision of 8 May 2006 Relating to CrossExamination by Defence and on Association of Defence Counsel's Request for Leave to File an *Amicus Curiae* Brief, Appeals Chamber, IT-04-74-AR73. 2, 4 July 2006, p. 4, fn. 18 (http: //www. legal-tools. org/doc/2f8dbc/).

[48] *Butare* Appeal Judgement, paras. 346, 363 and references cited therein, see *supra* note 2.

[49] *Butare* Appeal Judgement, para. 346, see *supra* note 2. See also *Šainović et al.* Appeal Judgement, para. 100, see *supra* note 32.

[50] *Butare* Trial Judgement, para. 137, see *supra* note 3.

co-accused, and the Rwandan government's lack of cooperation. [51] Focusing primarily on complexity of the case, the Trial Chamber found that the pre-judgement detention, ranging from between 12 to 15 years, did not amount to undue delay. [52] The Trial Chamber also considered the "gravity of the charges", which is not necessarily an explicit factor in the undue delay test, to find that the delays were not unreasonable. [53] More significantly and contrary to the Human Rights Committee's standard, the Trial Chamber seems to have placed the burden of proving delay and of prejudice predominantly upon the Defendants. [54] For example, the Trial Chamber stated that because "the Accused have not demonstrated that they suffered any legal prejudice, the Chamber need not consider the conduct of the Prosecution or other legal authorities. "[55] There is also no clear indication that the Trial Chamber mandated the Prosecution or relevant authorities to justify the delays.

The Appeals Chamber in the *Butare* case found that the Trial Chamber erred in its conclusions regarding undue delay. [56] In making this finding, the Appeals Chamber examined first the length of delay. [57] It considered that by the time the Trial Judgement was delivered, the Defendants had already been detained between 13 and up to 16 years, and that some will have waited more than 20 years for a final appeals determination in their case. [58] According to the Appeals Chamber, it was

---

[51] *Ibid.* , para. 135.

[52] *Ibid.* , paras. 135–139, 141–143.

[53] *Ibid.* , para. 141.

[54] *Ibid.* , paras. 134–137, 140–143. See also ICTR, *Prosecutor v. Arsène Shalom Ntahobali*, Decision on Ntahobali's Motion for a Stay of Proceedings for Undue Delay, Trial Chamber II, ICTR-97-21T, 26 November 2008, paras. 56–62 (http: //jrad. unmict. org/webdrawer/webdrawer. dll/webdrawer/rec/227108/view/) ; ICTR, *Prosecutor v. Pauline Nyiramasuhuko*, Decision on Defence Motion for Stay of Proceedings and Abuse of Process, Trial Chamber, ICTR-97-21-T, 20 February 2004, para. 21 (http: //www. legal-tools. org/doc/9ebc26/).

[55] *Butare* Trial Judgement, paras. 143, 348 – 378, 397, 3521, 3524, 3527, 3530, 3533, 3536, 3539, see *supra* note 3.

[56] *See Butare* Appeal Judgement, see *supra* note 2.

[57] *Ibid.*, paras. 357, 358, see *supra* note 2.

[58] *Ibid.*, para. 357.

therefore "indisputable" that the proceedings in this case have been of an "unprecedented and considerable length. " [59] Furthermore, given the "extraordinary length" of the proceedings and the interests of justice, the Appeals Chamber exercised its discretion to consider one Defendant's arguments on undue delay, despite his failure to raise the matter at trial, and to consider *proprio motu* the impact of its findings on another Defendant's rights regardless of the fact that he did not raise allegations in this regard at trial or on appeal. [60] This exercise of discretion is consistent with the Appeals Chamber's statement that the Tribunal has a proactive duty to ensure that an accused is tried without undue delay.

Regarding the complexity of the case, the Appeals Chamber agreed with the Trial Chamber: [61]

The Appeals Chamber is satisfied that the Trial Chamber did not err in considering that the instant proceedings were complex. With six accused, this case is the largest ever heard before the Tribunal. The six accused were prosecuted on the basis of numerous allegations with regard to crimes that occurred in several locations and on different dates. The Trial Chamber also had to rule on a particularly broad scope of counts, from conspiracy to commit genocide, genocide, direct and public incitement to commit genocide, to several crimes against humanity and serious violations of Article 3 common to the Geneva Conventions and of Additional Protocol II, as well as to consider a wide range of modes of liability. As noted in the Trial Judgement, the Trial Chamber heard numerous witnesses and had to consider an exceptionally large amount of tendered evidence

---

[59]　*Ibid.*

[60]　*Ibid.* See also paras. 390, 398. Nteziryayo's arguments on undue delay were not raised at trial and the Prosecution argued that he thus waived his right to challenge the issue on appeal. Nsabimana did not raise arguments on undue delay in his appeal. *See Butare* Appeal Judgement, paras. 355, 358, see *supra* note 2.

[61]　*Butare* Appeal Judgement, paras. 360–362, see *supra* note 2.

and trial transcripts. [62]

However, the Appeals Chamber found that the Trial Chamber erred in solely relying on complexity of the case to justify the extraordinary length of
proceedings. [63]

The Appeals Chamber proceeded to consider other factors, including, *inter
alia*, the conduct of other parties and of relevant authorities. [64] In examining the
Prosecution's conduct, the Appeals Chamber noted the Prosecution's repeated failure
to comply with its disclosure obligations towards the Defence, and its lack of readiness to start trial causing a delay of several months. [65] The Appeals Chamber also
noted that the Prosecution provided no explanation as to why it did not disclose relevant materials despite the Trial Chamber's orders, or why the Prosecution repeatedly
changed the date for its readiness to commence trial. [66] In light of these considerations, the Appeals Chamber found that the Prosecution's conduct created unjustified
delays. [67] This finding is significant, as, unlike the Trial Chamber's silence, the
Appeals Chamber seems to signal the Prosecution's responsibility to justify its delays,
which is in line with the position of the Human Rights Committee on undue delay.

As to the conduct of authorities, the Appeals Chamber assessed, in particular,
the Trial Chamber judges' assignment to other simultaneous proceedings at the Tribunal. [68] The Appeals Chamber observed that the judges' obligations in other cases

---

[62]   *Ibid.* , para. 362 (internal references omitted).

[63]   *Ibid.*, paras. 378, 390.

[64]   *Ibid.*, paras. 363–390.

[65]   *Ibid.* , paras. 369–372.

[66]   *Ibid.*, para. 372.

[67]   *Ibid.*, para. 372.

[68]   *Ibid.*, paras. 374–376, 378.

prevented them from sitting in the *Butare* case for approximately 36 weeks. [69] Beyond taking time away from the *Butare* case, the Appeals Chamber considered that these other cases also required the judges' time to dispose of motions, deliberate on their merits, and write the judgements. [70] In the Appeals Chamber's view, it was "unquestionable that the pace of the trial was affected by the judges' obligations in other cases. " [71] In examining this factor of delay, the Appeals Chamber was cognizant that: (i) given the workload of the ICTR, it was common practice for judges to sit in multiple proceedings; and (ii) significant efforts were made by authorities, including the President of the ICTR and the UN Security Council, to obtain necessary resources to complete its mandate while ensuring respect for accused rights. [72] Nevertheless, the Appeals Chamber determined that given the specific circumstances of this case, [73] additional delays from the judges' assignment to other cases caused undue delay. [74] In no unclear terms, the Appeals Chamber stated that:

---

[69]　*Ibid.*, paras. 374, 375. The Appeals Chamber explicitly considered that: (i) from 4 to 25 July 2001, to 5 October 2001, 26 November to 13 December 2001, 16 September to 9 October 2002, 18 November to 12 December 2002, and 31 March to 24 April 2003 because all three judges of the Trial Chamber were seised of the *Kajelijeli* case; and (ii) from 3 to 25 September 2001, 28 January to 19 February 2002, 6 to 14 May 2002, 19 August to 12 September 2002, 13 January to 30 April 2003, and 5 to 15 May 2003 because all three judges of the Trial Chamber were seised of the *Kamuhanda* case. Moreover, the Appeals Chamber notes that: (i) Judge Bossa, who was assigned to the case on 20 October 2003, was also at the time assigned to the *Ndindabahizi* case, which was in session notably from 27 October to 28 November 2003 and on 1 and 2 March 2004; (ii) all three judges of the Trial Chamber were also seised of the *Bisengimana* sentencing case, in which they sat on 17 November 2005, 7 December 2005, 19 January 2006, and 20 April 2006; and (iii) all three judges of the Trial Chamber were seised of the *Nzabirinda* sentencing case, in which they sat on 14 December 2006, 17 January 2007, and 23 February 2007. *Butare* Appeal Judgement, para. 374 (internal references omitted), see *supra* note 2.

[70]　*Butare* Appeal Judgement, para. 375, see *supra* note 2.

[71]　*Ibid.*

[72]　*Ibid.*, para. 376, fns. 912, 913. The Appeals Chamber was aware that at the time of the *Butare* trial, the ICTR's trial chambers were seized of 38 cases involving 53 accused. *Butare* Appeal Judgement, p. 135, fn. 912, see *supra* note 2.

[73]　The Appeals Chamber noted that the Defendants had been in pre-trial detention for nearly 4 to 6 years due to, *inter alia*, the Prosecution's lack of readiness and the replacement of a trial judge. *See Butare* Appeal Judgement, para. 376, see *supra* note 2.

[74]　*Ibid.*, para. 376.

[...] logistical considerations should not take priority over the trial chamber's duty to safeguard the fairness of the proceedings. In the same vein, the Appeals Chamber is of the view that organisational hurdles and lack of resources cannot reasonably justify the prolongation of proceedings that had already been significantly delayed. [75]

This finding is significant to the protection of the right of an accused from undue delay in several ways. First, this appears to be the first time that the ICTR Appeals Chamber has placed the responsibility of undue delay on the authorities of the Tribunal. [76] Furthermore, in coming to this conclusion, the Appeals Chamber explicitly referred to cases from the Human Rights Committee, as well as from the European Court of Human Rights, the Inter-American Court of Human Rights, and the African Commission on Human and People's Rights. [77] In this regard, the Appeals Chamber made explicit reference to other tribunal findings that: (i) authorities have the responsibility to organize themselves and their legal systems in such a way as to ensure the protection of an accused right to be tried without undue delay; [78] (ii) excessive workloads cannot justify unreasonable delays; [79] and (iii) that 'excuses, impediments and substitution of judges' and resulting delays are insufficient to justify

---

[75]   *Ibid.* , para. 376 (internal references omitted). See also *Šainović et al.* Appeal Judgment, 2014, para. 101, fn. 331 and references cited therein, see *supra* note 32.

[76]   *Butare* Appeal Judgement, para. 376, see *supra* note 2.

[77]   *Ibid.* , para. 376, fn. 916. See also *Šainović et al.* Appeal Judgement, p. 38, fn. 328, see *supra* note 32.

[78]   *Butare* Appeal Judgement, see *supra* note 2, para. 376, fn. 916, see *supra* note 2, referring to, *inter alia* , *Haregewoin Gabre-Selassie and IHRDA (on behalf of former Dergue Officials) v. Ethiopia* , African Commission on Human and People's Rights, Communication No. 301/05, 12 October 2013, para. 235; European Court of Human Rights, *EKO - Energie, SPOL. S. R. O v. The Czech Republic* , No. 65191/01, Judgment, 17 May 2005, para. 33.

[79]   *Butare* Appeal Judgement, see *supra* note 2, para. 376, fn. 916, see *supra* note 2, referring to European Court of Human Rights, *Mansur v. Turkey* , No. 16026/90, Judgment, 8 June 1995, para. 68; European Court of Human Rights, *Dobbertin v. France* , No. 13089/87, Judgment, 25 February 1993, para. 44; European Court of Human Rights, *Vocaturo v. Italy* , No. 11891/85, Judgment, 24 May 1991, para. 17.

excessive delays. [80] Based on the above, the ICTR Appeals Chamber seems to be a-ligning its jurisprudence with that of international and regional human rights tribunals and institutions while shifting the burden from defendants onto authorities, and even the Tribunal itself, to justify delay.

As to prejudice, the Appeals Chamber noted the Trial Chamber's consideration that the Defence provided no specific assertion of "legal prejudice" beyond the general complaint that the trial was unfair and that the Defence did not demonstrate that any "legal prejudice" resulted from the delay. [81] According to the Appeals Chamber, *"any form of prejudice"* [82] that a party suffers because of undue delay ought to be considered. [83] The Appeals Chamber found that, in failing to expressly address the entirety of the Defence's arguments on prejudice and conduct a comprehensive assessment, Trial Chamber infringed the Defendant's right to a reasoned opinion under Article 22 of the ICTR Statute and Rule 88 (C) of the ICTR Rules of Procedure and Evidence. [84]

Turning to specific allegations of prejudice, the Appeals Chamber found that the Defence did not substantiate the existence of prejudice in relation to, *inter alia*, witnesses and their testimonies, pecuniary losses as a result of detention, site visits, or Nyiramasuhuko's *de facto* "solitary confinement" as the only female detainee. [85] Nevertheless, given the undue delay resulting from the conduct of ICTR authorities and the Prosecution, the Appeals Chamber determined that the delays and the resul-

---

[80] *Butare* Appeal Judgement, para. 376, fn. 916, see *supra* note 2, referring to Inter—American Court of Human Rights, *Jean Paul Genie-Lacayo v. Nicaragua*, Judgment, 29 January 1997, paras. 39, 80.

[81] *Butare* Appeal Judgement, para. 382, see *supra* note 2, referring to *Butare* Trial Judgement, paras. 140, 143, see *supra* note 3.

[82] According to the Appeals Chamber, the meaning of 'legal prejudice' in the Trial Judgement is not clear. *Ibid.*, para. 385.

[83] *Ibid.* , para. 385.

[84] *Ibid.*, para. 385.

[85] *Ibid.*, paras. 386, 387, 389.

ting prolonged detention constituted "prejudice *per se*", [86] and ultimately found that the Trial Chamber erred in concluding that the Defendants suffered no prejudice. [87] This finding on prejudice is significant, as the Appeals Chamber has clearly signalled the Trial Chamber's duty to examine and comprehensively assess all allegations of prejudice. Furthermore, even if allegations of prejudice are not proven, once there is undue delay and prolonged detention, prejudice is established. [88]

Based on the foregoing, the *Butare* Appeal Judgement signals the alignment of ICTR jurisprudence with international standards on an accused's right to be tried without undue delay. In this regard, the Appeals Chamber departed from its earlier appeal judgements in significant ways.

- *Théoneste Bagosora and Anatole Nsengiyumva v. The Prosecutor*: The Appeals Chamber noted that the Trial Chamber "considered numerous factors" to decide that the Defendant's right to a fair trial had not been infringed. [89] The factors enumerated pertained to the complexity of the case (i. e. number of accused, number of infringements, scope and gravity of crimes charged, amount and scope of evidence and disclosures). [90] The Appeals Chamber did not list factors such as conduct of parties or authorities. Despite the fact that the Defendant in question (Nsengiyumva) had been detained for almost 13 years at the time of the trial judgement and 15 years at the time of the appeal judgement, the Appeals Chamber and the Trial Chamber, focusing mainly on complexity of the case, found that no undue delay had been prov-

---

[86]　*Ibid.*, para. 388, referring to ICTR, *Jean—Baptiste Gatete v. Prosecutor*, Judgement, Appeals Chamber, ICTR—00—61—A, 9 October 2012, paras. 44, 45 (https: //www. legal—tools. org/doc/1d0b08/) ("*Gatete* Appeal Judgement").

[87]　*Butare* Appeal Judgement, paras. 388, 390, see *supra* note 2.

[88]　*Ibid.* , para. 388; *Gatete* Appeal Judgement, paras. 44, 45, see *supra* note 87.

[89]　ICTR, *Théoneste Bagosora and Anatole Nsengiyumva v. Prosecutor*, Judgement, Appeals Chamber, ICTR—98—41—A, 14 December 2011, para. 37 (http: //www. legal—tools. org/doc/52d501/) ("*Bagosora and Nsengiyumva* Appeal Judgement").

[90]　*Ibid.*, para. 37.

en. [91]

The Butare Appeal Judgement departs from this as it clearly notes the Trial Chamber's duty to examine all factors of undue delay, even when the defendant in question does not raise it, and shifts the full weight of the burden of proof away from the defendants.

- *Édouard Karemera and Matthieu Ngirumpatse v. The Prosecutor*: Defendant Ngirumpatse had been detained for more than 13 years at the time of the trial judgement and 16 years at the time of the appeal judgement. [92] The Appeals Chamber, while setting out the law and the factors for undue delay, [93] appeared to focus mainly on the complexity of the case. [94] It noted that the Trial Chamber correctly assessed numerous considerations pertaining to the case complexity, and stated that " (except for a general allegation that his case was not complex, Ngirumpatse merely claims that the Trial Chamber erred in dismissing his challenges to the length of the proceedings but he has failed to discuss any of these factors, or to challenge their assessment by the Trial Chamber. " [95] The Appeals Chamber found that given "the circumstances of this case, which is among the largest ever heard by the Tribunal, the period of time which elapsed during these proceedings can be reasonably explained by the size and complexity of the case. " [96]

---

[91] *Ibid.*, para. 38. Nsengiyumva was arrested on 27 March 1996, the trial judgement in that case was delivered and signed on 18 December 2008, and the appeal judgement rendered on 14 December 2011. See *Bagosora and Nsengiyumva* Appeal Judgement, p. 1, see *supra* note 90.

[92] Ngirumpatse was arrested on 5 June 1998, the trial judgement in his case was delivered in public on 21 December 2011, and the appeal judgement rendered on 29 September 2014. See ICTR, *Édouard Karemera and Matthieu Ngirumpatse v. Prosecutor*, Judgement, Appeals Chamber, ICTR-98-44-A, 29 September 2014, paras. 1, 65 (http://www.legal-tools.org/doc/372a64/).

[93] *Ibid.*, para. 69.

[94] *Ibid.*, paras. 70, 71.

[95] *Ibid.*, para. 70.

[96] *Ibid.*, para. 71.

The Butare Appeal Judgement departs from this by again noting the Trial Chamber's duty to examine all factors of undue delay, even when the defendant in question does not raise it, and shifts the full weight of the burden of proof away from the defendants.

- *Justin Mugenzi and Prosper Mugiraneza v. The Prosecutor*: Both Defendants had been detained for more than 12 years at the time of the trial judgement and almost 14 years at the time of the appeal judgement. [97] Both were eventually acquitted on appeal. [98] In examining undue delay, the Appeals Chamber laid out the jurisprudence and the factors. [99] It noted that the Trial Chamber assessed various factors, including complexity of the case, Prosecution's alleged disclosure violations, as well as delays caused by "organizational failings" of the ICTR. [100] Regarding "organization failings" of the ICTR, the Appeals Chamber stated:

The Appeals Chamber is also not convinced that the Trial Chamber erred in rejecting the allegation that organizational failings resulted in undue delay in the context of the pre-trial and trial phases of the proceedings. [...] (T (he Appeals Chamber observes that it is not unusual for judges of the Tribunal to participate in multiple proceedings, impacting the pace of those respective proceedings. In any event, Mugenzi and Mugiranze have not show the relative significance of the judges' workload distribution, overlapping duties, and outside activites, or the relative sig-

---

[97]   Both Defendants were arrested on 6 April 1999, the trial judgement was pronounced on 30 September 2011, and the appeal judgement on 4 February 2013. ICTR, *Justin Mugenzi and Prosper Mugiraneza v. Prosecutor*, Judgement, Appeals Chamber, ICTR9950-A, 4 February 2013, para. 18 (http://www. legal-tools. org/doc/c16ca2).

[98]   *Ibid.*, para. 144.

[99]   *Ibid.*, para. 30.

[100] *Ibid.*, paras. 31–35.

nificance of any related staffing issues, for the conduct of this case. [101]

The *Butare* Appeal Judgement is a significant departure from this finding as the Appeals Chamber explicitly found that organizational hurdles amounted to unjustified delays, and that the burden did not rest with the accused to show that the delay was justified or that they were prejudiced. Indeed, had this case been assessed after the *Butare* Appeal Judgement, there could have been findings of undue delay and prejudice.

Despite the holdings in the *Butare* Appeal Judgement aligning the ICTR's jurisprudence with international standards on the right to be tried without undue delay, the Appeals Chamber could have taken a more critical and concrete approach vis-à-vis the issue of joinder of trials. In assessing this matter as part of undue delay, the Appeals Chamber stated:

[…] The Appeals Chamber recalls that the joinder of trials is provided for by the Rules and that it had found no error in the Trial Chamber's decisions to join the trials of the co-accused and to reject their requests for separate trials. The argument that the excessive length of the proceedings in this case was an unavoidable and clearly foreseeable consequence of the joinder decision is not substantiated. Accordingly, the Appeals Chamber finds that, notwithstanding that the joinder added some degree of complexity to the proceedings, the mere contention that separate trials would have proceeded faster is insufficient to substantiate a claim that undue delay occurred as a result of the joinder. The Appeals Chamber rejects the arguments made in this respect. [102]

---

[101]   *Ibid.*, paras. 34, 35 (internal references omitted).

[102]   *Butare* Appeal Judgement, para. 365, see *supra* note 2.

Given that the *Butare* case is the final matter before the ICTR Appeals Chamber and having the benefit of hindsight, the Appeals Chamber could have used the opportunity to examine the factual circumstances of how the joinder in fact prolonged trial and appeal proceedings for individual Defendants in this case. Rather, the Appeals Chamber opted to stay close to the law and dismissed the Defence arguments as unsubstantiated and/or hypothetical.

In her declaration at the end of the *Butare* Appeal Judgement, Judge Khalida Rachid Khan did look at the issue of joinder by examining empirical and anecdotal data and using it to challenge theoretical justifications for joinders. [103] Considering first the "judicial efficiency theory", which states that joint trials require less court time and resources, she observed that joint proceedings at the ICTR required on average more trial days to hear witnesses than single accused trials. [104] She then considered and rejected the theory that joint proceedings minimize hardship to witnesses, who may need to testify multiple times if there are several single-accused cases dealing with the same facts or events. [105] In her view, "we must not blindly fear that hardship on witnesses will prevent them from testifying more than once" and that the

---

[103] *Butare* Appeal Judgement, Dissenting Opinion and Declaration of Judge Khan, paras. 27–36, see *supra* note 2.

[104] *Ibid.* , para. 28. In this regard, Judge Khan noted that "trials with one defendant, on average, have used 53 trial days to hear around 46 witnesses" while trials with "multiple defendants have, on average, required around 343 trial days to hear only around 154 witnesses. " She specifically noted that "not a single multi-accused case had more witnesses testify than trial days, standing in marked contrast to several single-accused cases. " See also para. 28 and references cited therein. According to Judge Khan, reasons for this "comparative inefficiency" include, *inter alia*, the greater complexity of cases, and that the examinations of witnesses tend to be "less focused and unnecessarily lengthy because the size of cases can prevent the parties–the prosecution in particular– from fully grasping what evidence is and is not crucial to their case. " She further noted the proceedings with multiple defendants "present weighty, practical and legal challenges that would not otherwise arise in a single accused case", and further that disputes or procedural matters that arise with one co-accused will affect and delay proceedings for all other codefendants. Also see paras. 29, 30.

[105] *Ibid.* , paras. 31, 32. Judge Khan noted that this theory is not necessarily true as the proceedings related to Tharisse Muvunyi, Ildéphonse Nizeyimana, and Ildephonse Hategekimana, originally joined but subsequently severed, required that the same witnesses be called several times. According to Judge Khan, prosecution and defence teams were able to produce evidence on the same or related events in successive proceedings and witnesses testified in more than one proceeding. See also paras. 31, 32.

ICTR is equipped with a witness and victim support section to mitigate hardships faced by witnesses. [106]

Most significant is Judge Khan's examination and challenge to the theory that joined trials avoid undue delays. [107] Considering empirical data from the ICTR, Judge Khan noted the following:

[A] single accused proceeding from opening statement to the issuance of a trial judgement will last on average 641 days, whereas the length for a multiple accused trial is on average 2,026 days. On average, the time between closing arguments to the issuance of trial judgements in single accused cases before the Tribunal is 196 days, where in multiple accused cases it is 479 days. From notice of appeal to appeal judgement, the duration for a case involving a single convicted person is 556 days, where it is 973 days when it involves multiple convicted persons. The average length from the date of arrest to final judgement on appeal for a single accused proceeding before the Tribunal is 2395 days (or around six and a half years), while the length of multiple accused proceedings is approximately 4825 days (or just over 13 years). [108]

Her conclusions highlight the " staggering difference" that, compared to a Defendant tried in a single accused case, "an accused convicted at trial in a joined proceeding might expect to spend around *six and a half years more in preventative detention* before receiving a final verdict than an accused who proceeds at trial and appeal alone. " [109]

While proceedings for other cases do not necessarily have direct impact, never-

---

[106] *Ibid.* , para. 32.

[107] *Ibid.* , paras. 33–35.

[108] *Ibid.* , para. 33 (internal references omitted). For more information, see fns. 85–90.

[109] *Ibid.* , para. 34 (emphasis added).

theless, had the Appeals Chamber in the *Butare* case considered the empirical data regarding joinder of trials, perhaps it would have found that the joinder of the six accused in this case indeed contributed to undue delays.

5. Remedies

The right to an effective remedy is enshrined in Article 2 (3) (a) of the ICCPR, which states that: "[a] ny person whose rights or freedoms as herein recognized are violated shall have an effective remedy, notwithstanding that the violation has been committed by persons acting in an official capacity. " [110] According to the Human Rights Committee, this provision needs to be respected whenever Article 14 of the ICCPR has been violated. [111]

This is reflected in the *Butare* Appeal Judgement, where the Appeals Chamber, in citing ICTR jurisprudence and Article 2 (3)(a) of the ICCPR, stated that " any violation, even if it entails a relative degree of prejudice, requires a proportionate remedy. " [112] The Appeals Chamber further stated that the nature and form of the effective remedy needs to be proportionate to the gravity of harm that is suffered. [113] In determining the scope of an effective remedy for the violation of the right to undue delay and the prejudice suffered, the Appeals Chamber considered the following remedies: (i) a stay or termination of proceedings; (ii) formal recognition of the viola-

---

[110] ICCPR, Article 2 (3)(a), see *supra* note 22.

[111] General Comment No. 32, para. 58, see *supra* note 23. See also Human Rights Committee, General Comment No. 31 (80 (: The Nature of the General Legal Obligation Imposed on States Parties to the Covenant, UN Doc. CCPR/C/21/Rev. 1/Add. 13, 29 March 2004, paras. 15, 16.

[112] *Butare* Appeal Judgement, para. 391, see *supra* note 2, referring to ICTR, *André Rwamakuba v. Prosecutor*, Decision on Appeal Against Decision on Appropriate Remedy, Appeals Chamber, ICTR–98–44C–A, 13 September 2007 (http: //www. legal–tools. org/doc/370307/) ("*Rwamakuba* Appeal Decision"); *Gatete* Appeal Judgement, para. 286, see *supra* note 87; ICTR, *Juvénal Kajelijeli v. Prosecutor*, Judgement, Appeals Chamber, ICTR–98–44A–A, 23 May 2005, para. 255, (http: //www. legal–tools. org/doc/2b7d1c) ("*Kajelijeli* Appeal Judgement").

[113] *Butare* Appeal Judgement, para. 391, see *supra* note 2, referring to *Rwamakuba* Appeal Decision, 2007, para. 27, see *supra* note 113.

tion; (iii) financial compensation; and (iv) reduction of sentence. [114]

Regarding a stay or termination of proceedings, the Appeals Chamber considered jurisprudence that to allow this remedy, it must be shown that the "violations of the accused's rights would prove detrimental to the court's integrity"; for example, instances where the accused was "very seriously mistreated, maybe even subject to inhuman, cruel or degrading treatment, or torture." [115] According to ICTR jurisprudence, these cases are exceptional, and the termination of proceedings would be disproportionate in most circumstances. [116] Additionally, the Appeals Chamber of the ICTR and ICTY have emphasized that there needs to be a balance between "the fundamental rights of the accused and the essential interests of the international community in the prosecution of persons charged with serious violations of international humanitarian law." [117] The Appeals Chamber in *Butare* eventually found that the violation of the Defendants' right to be tried without undue delay and the prejudice they suffered was not "so serious or egregious" to justify this remedy. [118]

As for formal recognition of violation, jurisprudence holds that this remedy is appropriate where the violation did not materially prejudice the accused. [119] The Appeals Chamber in *Butare* found that given the length of the undue delay, and that material prejudice was suffered, it was not convinced that this was an effective reme-

---

[114] *Butare* Appeal Judgement, paras. 392–396. See also *Butare* Appeal Judgement, paras. 3521, 3523–3524, 3526–3527, 3529–3530, 3532–3533, 3535–3536, 3538.

[115] *Butare* Appeal Judgement, para. 394, fn. 943, see *supra* note 2, referring to *Kajelijeli* Appeal Judgement, para. 206, see *supra* note 113.

[116] See *Butare* Appeal Judgement, see *supra* note 2, para. 394, fn. 943, referring to *Kajelijeli* Appeal Judgement, para. 206, see *supra* note 113.

[117] *Kajelijeli* Appeal Judgement, para. 206, see *supra* note 113; ICTY, *Prosecutor v. Dragan Nikolić*, Decision on Interlocutory Appeal Concerning Legality of Arrest, Appeals Chamber, IT-94-2-AR73, 5 June 2003, para. 30 (http://www.legal-tools.org/doc/61711b/).

[118] *Butare* Appeal Judgement, paras. 392, 394, see *supra* note 2.

[119] See *Rwamakuba* Appeal Decision, 2007, para. 27, see *supra* 113. See also Basic Principles and Guidelines on the Right to a Remedy and Reparation for Victims of Gross Violations of International Human Rights Law and Serious Violations of International Humanitarian Law, G. A. Res. 60/147, 16 December 2005, para. 22 (noting that reparations can take the form of official recognition of the violation).

dy. [120]

Concerning financial compensation, the Appeals Chamber noted that this remedy was used in "limited situations where the accused was ultimately not found guilty." [121] For example, USD 2000 per month was granted in the *Rwamakuba* Appeal Decision where Rwamakuba was acquitted of all charges, and he was financially compensated for the violation of Rwamakuba's right to legal assistance and initial appearance without delay. [122]

In respect to a reduction of sentence, the *Butare* Appeals Chamber noted that pursuant to ICTR jurisprudence, this was an effective remedy where the breach of fair trial rights resulted in an individual being detained impermissibly or for a longer period than necessary. [123] For example, the Appeals Chamber in the *Gatete* case found that a pre—trial delay of seven years was unjustified, that Gatete suffered prejudice as a result, and accordingly reduced his sentence from life imprisonment to 40 years. [124] In the *Kajelijeli* case, the Appeals Chamber found that Kajelijeli was impermissibly detained for 306 days and accordingly set aside two life sentences and the fifteen—year sentence he was serving concurrently while sentencing him to a single sentence of 45 years' imprisonment. [125]

The Appeals Chamber in *Butare* stated that to determine whether a reduction of

---

[120] *Butare* Appeal Judgement, para. 394, see *supra* note 2.

[121] *Ibid.*, para. 395, referring to, inter alia, ICTR, *Jean—Bosco Barayagwiza v. Prosecutor*, Decision (Prosecutor's Request for Review or Reconsideration), Appeals Chamber, ICTR9719—AR72, 31 March 2000, para. 75 (http://www.legal—tools.org/doc/1c0fe7/) ("*Barayagwiza* Review Decision"); *Rwamakuba* Appeal Decision, 2007, paras. 24—30, see *supra* note 113.

[122] *Rwamakuba* Appeal Decision, 2007, paras. 31, 32, see *supra* note 113. See also *Butare* Appeal Judgement, para. 395, see *supra* note 2.

[123] *Butare* Appeal Judgement, para. 395, see *supra* note 2, referring to *Gatete* Appeal Judgement, paras. 45, 286, 287, see *supra* note 87; *Kajelijeli* Appeal Judgement, paras. 323, 324, see *supra* note 113; *Barayagwiza* Review Decision, 2000, para. 75, see *supra* note 122; *Semanza* Appeal Decision, 2001, p. 34, see *supra* note 122.

[124] *Gatete* Appeal Judgement, paras. 45, 286, 287, see *supra* note 87.

[125] *Kajelijeli* Appeal Judgement, paras. 323, 324, see *supra* note 113.

sentence or granting of financial compensation was appropriate and effective, it had to consider the gravity of offences the Defendants were finally convicted of and their individual circumstances. [126] In assessing the impact of its findings on the sentences of each individual Defendant, the Appeals Chamber noted many of the crimes were eventually upheld on appeal. [127] The Appeals Chamber chose reduction of sentence as the appropriate remedy in all cases and accordingly lowered the years of imprisonment for each Defendant to the following:

- Nyiramasuhuko: Life sentence reduced to 47 years' imprisonment;
- Ntahobali: Life sentence reduced to 47 years' imprisonment;
- Nsabimana: 25 years imprisonment reduced to 18 years;
- Nteziryayo: 30 years imprisonment reduced to 25 years;
- Kanyabashi: 35 years imprisonment reduced to 20 years; and
- Ndayambaje: Life sentence reduced to 47 years imprisonment. [128]

Given that Nsabimana had already spent more than 18 years in prison and Kanyabashi more than 20 years, both were ordered to be immediately released. [129]

6. Conclusion and looking forward

In its Swan Song, the ICTR Appeals Chamber moved the jurisprudence of the ICTR closer to international human rights and regional standards in relation to the protection of an accused's fair trial rights and, particularly, undue delay. As discussed above, the ICTR Appeals Chamber was not only focused on its mandate to prosecute the most heinous crimes, but was also aware of its equally important duty, and positive obligation, to ensure the rights of the accused are protected. In the *Butare* Appeal Judgement, the Appeals Chamber was critical of the Trial Chamber's analysis and found that the Trial Chamber's focus on complexity of the case was insuf-

---

[126]   *Butare* Appeal Judgement, para. 396, see *supra* note 2.
[127]   *Ibid.* , paras. 3522, 3525, 3528, 3531, 3534, 3537.
[128]   *Ibid.* , paras. 3523, 3526, 3529, 3532, 3535, 3538, 3539.
[129]   *Ibid.*, p. 1214.

ficient to encapsulate the scope of the delay suffered by the accused, some more than 20 years of detention prior to the appeal judgement. The Appeals Chamber also held the Prosecution and, for the first time in the ICTR's history, the authorities of the Tribunal accountable for the delay caused. Indeed, while the Appeals Chamber in *Butare* missed an opportunity to scrutinize the trackrecord of joined cases, it cannot be disputed that this final case, the longest and largest in ICTR history, has left a mark on the jurisprudence of international criminal tribunals. This judgement not only has an impact on future trial and appeal judgements at the ICTY and at the UN Mechanism for International Criminal Tribunals, the residual institution mandated to finish the work of the ICTR and ICTY. The *Butare* Appeal Judgement reiterates and reinforces an important message to existing and future international criminal tribunals and domestic trials of international crimes–the prosecution of the most heinous crimes is important, but it must be done so in accordance with the highest standards of fair trial rights and, indeed, international human rights.

THE "SPECIFIC DIRECTION" REQUIREMENT FOR AIDING AND ABETTING: REFINING THE MODES OF LIABILITY OR SETTING THE THRESHOLD TOO HIGH?

Professor Marina Aksenova [*]

1. Introduction

This chapter critically assesses a trend that persisted in the case law of the International Criminal Tribunal for the Former Yugoslavia ("ICTY") between 2013 and 2016 manifesting itself with the acquittals of the general Momčilo Perišić, and the initial acquittal (followed by the order of retrial) of the former state security chief Jovica Stanišić, and the former paramilitary leader Franko Simatović on the basis of the lack of the specific direction of their aid and assistance towards the crimes. [1] The novel interpretation of the conduct requirement of aiding and abetting as containing the element of the 'specific direction' quickly became a contentious issue. [2] The

---

* Professor, Law School, International University in Spain.

[1] ICTY, *Prosecutor v. Momcilo Perišić*, Judgment, Appeals Chamber, IT-04-81-A, 28 February 2013, para. 44 (http://www. legal-tools. org/doc/f006ba/) ("*Perišić* Appeal Judgment"); ICTY, Judgment, *Prosecutor v. Jovica Stanišić and Franko Simatović*, Judgement, Trial Chamber, IT-03-69-T, 30 May 2013, para. 131 (http://www. legal-tools. org/doc/066e67/) ("*Stanišić and Simatović* Trial Judgement"); ICTY, *Prosecutor v. Jovica Stanišić and Franko Simatović*, Appeals Chamber, IT-03-69-A, 9 December 2015, para. 131 (https://www. legal-tools. org/en/doc/198c16/) ("*Stanišić and Simatović* Appeal Judgement"). *Cf.* SCSL, *Prosecutor v Charles Ghankay Taylor*, Judgement, Appeals Chamber, SCSL-03-1-A, 26 September 2013, para. 473 (http://www. legal-tools. org/doc/3e7be5/) ("*Taylor* Appeal Judgement").

[2] Kevin Jon Heller, "Why the ICTY's 'Specifically Directed' Requirement Is Justified", Opinio Juris Blog, 2 June 2013, available at http://opiniojuris. org/2013/06/02/why-the-ictys-specifically-directed-requirement-is-justified/, last accessed at 1 May 2014. *Cf.* Jens Ohlin, "Why did the ICTY Acquit Stanisic and Simatovic?", Lieber Code Blog, 1 June 2013, available at http://www. liebercode. org/2013/06/why-did-icty-acquit-stanisic-and. html, last accessed at 1 May 2014; James Stewart, "The ICTY Loses its way on Complicity", Opinio Juris Blog, 3 April 2013, available at http://opiniojuris. org/2013/04/03/guest-post-the-icty-loses-its-way-on-complicity-part-1/, last accessed at 1 May, 2014.

words of Judge Picard—the dissenting voice in the *Stanišić and Simatović* case—reflect the level of controversy attached to the new restrictive formulation of accessory liability: "If we cannot find that the Accused aided and abetted those crimes, I would say we have come to a dark place in international law indeed. "[3] Concerns about the new enhanced standard translated into its ultimate rejection by the majority in *Šainović et al.* and later in *Popović et al.* [4] The Appeals Chamber held that 'specific direction' is not an element of aiding and abetting liability under customary international law. [5]

There is merit in briefly tracing the evolution of the problem. The "specific direction" saga started in the *Perišić* case, when the Appeals Chamber interpreted the *actus reus* of aiding and abetting as requiring that the assistance is specifically directed towards the crimes. [6] The justification for this additional element was the need to address the situations where the accused's individual assistance is remote from the actions of principal perpetrators or when such assistance could be used for both lawful and unlawful activities. [7] In such circumstances, the Chamber reasoned, it is necessary to establish "a *direct link* between the aid provided by an accused individual and the relevant crimes committed by principal perpetrators. "[8] In line with this restrictive formulation of accessory liability, the Appeals Chamber overturned Perišić's conviction for aiding and abetting the Army of the Republika Srpska ("VRS") in his capacity as Chief of the Yugoslav Army General Staff. This is not-

---

[3] *Stanišić and Simatović* Trial Judgement, Dissenting Opinion of Judge Michèle Picard, para. 2406, see *supra* note 1.

[4] ICTY, *Prosecutor v. Šainović et al.* Judgement, Appeals Chamber, IT-05-87-A, 23 January 2014, para. 1649 (http: //www. legal-tools. org/doc/81ac8c/) ("*Šainović et al.* Appeal Judgment") ; ICTY, *Prosecutor v. Popović et al.* , ICTY Case No. 05-88-A, Appeal Judgment, 30 January 2015, paras. 1749, 1751 ("*Popović et al.* Appeal Judgement").

[5] Judge Tuzmukhamedov dissented on this point. Dissenting Opinion of Judge Tuzmukhamedov, *Šainović* et al. Appeal Judgment, paras. 43, 47, see *supra* note 4.

[6] *Perišić* Appeal Judgment, para. 44, see *supra* note 1.

[7] *Ibid.*, paras. 44, 73.

[8] *Ibid.*, para. 44, emphasis added.

withstanding the fact that Perišić, as the most senior figure in the Yugoslav Army, was held to have knowingly provided logistical and personnel assistance to the VRS, which was committing crimes in Sarajevo and Srebrenica. [9] The rationale for the acquittal in *Perišić* was the Chamber's reluctance to find that the accused's assistance was specifically directed at supporting the criminal activities, and not just geared towards the general war effort. [10] In particular, the VRS was conceptualized as "an army fighting a war" rather than an organization whose actions were criminal *per se*. [11] The judges thus concluded that since not all of the VRS activities were criminal in nature, the policy of providing assistance to the VRS's general war effort did not, in itself, demonstrate that assistance facilitated by Perišić was specifically directed to aid the crimes. [12]

The same type of reasoning surfaced in the *Stanišić and Simatović* trial judgment. [13] The accused in this case organized and directed a special unit within the Serbian state security service, which they knew committed crimes of murder, deportation, forcible transfer, and persecution. [14] The Chamber fell short, however, of declaring this unit a criminal organization, despite the fact that it operated covertly and was engaged in numerous crimes. [15] The extensive involvement of the accused with the operation of the unit led the judges to conclude that their contributions assisted the commission of the crimes by the unit members. [16] However, the fact that the accused were not physically present in the field during operations resulted in the finding that their assistance may have been directed towards the legitimate military

---

[9] *Ibid.*, paras. 2, 62, 68.

[10] *Ibid.*

[11] *Ibid.*, para. 53.

[12] *Ibid.*

[13] *Stanišić and Simatović* Trial Judgement, para. 2360, see *supra* note 1.

[14] *Ibid.*, paras. 2318, 2323.

[15] *Ibid.*, paras. 1421, 1423.

[16] *Ibid.*, para. 2359.

objective of establishing and maintaining Serb control and not the criminal goals. [17]

The new strict standard of aiding and abetting liability quickly re-emerged in the work of the ICTY Appeals Chamber: the defence team of Vladimir Lazarević in the *Šainović et al.* case contested his conviction for aiding and abetting deportation and forcible transfer on the basis of the lack of determination by the Trial Chamber of whether his alleged acts and omissions were specifically directed to assist the commission of these crimes. [18] The Appeals Chamber subsequently rejected the "specific direction" requirement finding a clear divergence between the *Perišić* standard and the previous jurisprudence of the ICTY. [19]

The "specific direction" saga did not end with the dismissal of the contentious criterion in the *Šainović et al.* appeal judgment. The Office of the Prosecutor attempted to reverse the acquittal in *Perišić* by filing a motion seeking reconsideration. [20] The Appeals Chamber denied the request failing to find "cogent reasons in the interests of justice" for the reconsideration of a final judgment. [21] It is disappointing that this brief decision does not elaborate on what constituted "cogent reasons in the interests of justice" and why this test was not met in circumstances of the case. The rejection of the "specific direction" requirement in the case law of the ICTY was confirmed by two subsequent appeal judgments: *Stanišić and Simatović* and *Popović et al.* In the latter case, the defence of Vinko Pandurević argued that purposeful assistance is an essential part of aiding and abetting liability, regardless of whether it is incorporated into *mens rea* or *actus reus.* The Appeals Chamber refuted this claim

---

[17] *Ibid.*, para. 2360.

[18] *Šainović et al.* Appeal Judgment, para. 1617, see *supra* note 4.

[19] *Ibid.*, para. 1621.

[20] Statement of Prosecutor Serge Brammertz in relation to the motion for reconsideration submitted by the Prosecution in the *Perišić* case, 3 February 2014, at http://www.icty.org/sid/11447, last accessed at 3 April 2014.

[21] ICTY, *Prosecutor v. Momcilo Perišić*, Decision on Motion for Reconsideration, Appeals Chamber, IT-04-81-A, 20 March 2014 (https://www.legal-tools.org/en/doc/6cdbd5/).

holding that it has been established that the "specific direction" is *not* an element of aiding and abetting liability under customary international law. [22]

The appeal judgment in *Stanišić and Simatović* overturned the acquittals in this case and ordered a retrial because the Trial Chamber erred in two major points: first, it did not examine in sufficient detail the nature of the agreement required to prove the existence of the joint criminal enterprise, and, secondly, it erroneously required that the acts of the aider and abettor be specifically directed to assist the commission of the crime. [23] The new trial is currently taking place before the Mechanism for International Courts and Tribunals. Despite the seeming finality of the 'specific direction saga', it seems prudent for the sake of conceptual and legal clarity to furnish a comprehensive set of arguments against such narrow vision of aiding and abetting.

The aim of this chapter is thus to test the validity of the restrictive interpretation of *actus reus* of aiding and abetting. The inquiry is undertaken on two levels: the first part answers the question as to whether the additional requirement of the "specific direction" has any foundation in the sources of international law, while section two outlines several conceptual problems with the latest approach. It follows that the enhanced standard for aiding and abetting presents difficulties both in terms of legality and application. Moreover, if not checked, this development could have far-fetched implications that go beyond mere difficulties with attaching liability to the accused removed from the scene of the crime. It raises an important question: what are the legal boundaries of the "general war effort"?

2. The "specific direction" requirement in the sources of international law

The approach of the *Perišić* Appeals Chamber and the *Stanišić and Simatović* Trial Chamber solicited a number of distinct concerns. One of the most worrying characteristics was the feeble legal foundation. It is for this reason the majority in *Šainović et al.* Appeals Chamber rejected "specific direction" as an element of *actus reus* of

---

[22] *Popović et al.* Appeal Judgment, see *supra* note 4, paras. 1756, 1758.

[23] *Stanišić and Simatović* Appeal Judgement, paras. 90, 106, see *supra* note 1.

aiding and abetting. [24] Indeed, the new criterion can hardly be traced in any of the primary sources of international law listed in the Article 38 (1) of the Statute of the International Court of Justice, which are also relevant to international criminal law. [25]

2. 1 Lack of recognition in treaty and custom

Article 7 (1) of the ICTY Statute dealing with individual criminal responsibility reads as follows:

A person who planned, instigated, ordered, committed or otherwise aided and abetted in the planning, preparation or execution of a crime referred to in articles 2 to 5 of the present Statute, shall be individually responsible for the crime.

The Statute is thus silent on the legal requirements for each form of responsibility. The ICTY Appeals Chamber clarified that the Statute only provides an *a priori* jurisdictional framework *ratione personae*, and the existence of a particular form of liability as well as its legal requirements will be determined by customary international law. [26] Custom is a notoriously ambiguous source when it comes to defining human rights obligations and international criminal law provisions. [27] In fact, the tribunals often avoid making a distinction between the two constituent elements of custom—

---

[24] *Šainović et al.* Appeal Judgement, para. 1650, see *supra* note 4.

[25] These are international conventions, international custom, and the general principles of law recognized by civilized nations. See United Nations, Statute of the International Court of Justice, 18 April 1946.

[26] ICTY, *Prosecutor v. Vlastimir Đorđević et al.*, Decision on Dragoljub Ojdanić 's Motion Challenging Jurisdiction—Joint Criminal Enterprise, Appeals Chamber, IT−99−37−AR72, 21 May 2003, paras. 9−10 (http: //www. legal−tools. org/doc/d51c63/), quoting Report of the Secretary−General Pursuant to paragraph 2 of Security Council Resolution 808, 1993, para. 21. See also ICTY, *Prosecutor v. Zdravko Mucić et al.*, Judgement, Appeals Chamber, IT−96−21−A, 20 February 2001, para. 178 (http: //www. legal−tools. org/doc/051554/) ("*Čelebići* Appeal Judgement"), as quoted by Guénaël Mettraux, *International Criminal and Ad Hoc Tribunals*, Oxford University Press, Oxford, 2005 ("Mettraux, 2005"), p. 270.

[27] Bruno Simma and Philip Alston, "The Sources of Human Rights Law: Custom, *Jus Cogens*, and General Principles", in *Australian Yearbook of International Law*, 1988−1989, vol. 12, pp. 82, 91−92.

opinio juris and state practice. [28] It is understandable because international criminal law is a peculiar field of law—the state practice element of custom often points to an undesirable outcome (i. e. a violation). [29]

Has the "specific direction" component of *actus reus* of aiding and abetting ever been part of customary international law? The *Perišić* Appeals and the *Stanišić and Simatović* Trial Chambers appear to have answered this question in the affirmative, while in the *Šainović et al.* the Appeals Chamber strongly rejected this proposition. [30] In *Perišić*, the judges ruled that there are no cogent reasons to depart from the first appeal judgment setting out the parameters of aiding and abetting liability, namely the *Tadić* appeal judgment. [31] *Tadić* held that "[t]he aider and abettor carries out acts *specifically directed* to assist, encourage or lend moral support to the perpetration of a certain specific crime...". [32] It is true that the interpretation of "aiding and abetting" contained in this and other early judgements such as *Furundžija* judgments proved to be authoritative, with the subsequent jurisprudence merely clarifying the elements initially set out by the first two cases. [33] It seems, however, that the understanding of *actus reus* of aiding and abetting furnished in *Perišić* differs from

---

[28] Boas *et al.* argue that the most worrying characteristic of the *Tadić* is the methodology used to establish the rules of customary international law. International judgments pursuant to Control Council Law No. 10—supporting in *Tadić* the existence of common purpose liability—do not amount to state practice. See Gideon Boas et al, *International Criminal Law Practitioner Library*: *International Criminal Procedure*, Cambridge University Press, 2007, pp. 21—22.

[29] *First report on formation and evidence of customary international law by Michael Wood*, *Special Rapporteur*, 17 May 2013, UN Doc. A/CN. 4/663, para. 70. See also Larissa van den Herik, "Using Custom to Reconceptualise Crimes Against Humanity", in Shane Darcy and Joseph Powderly (eds.), *Judicial Creativity at the International Criminal Tribunals*, Oxford University Press, 2010, p. 101.

[30] *Perišić* Appeal Judgment, para. 28, see *supra* note 1; *Stanišić and Simatović* Trial Judgement, para. 1264, see *supra* note 1; *Šainović et al.* Appeal Judgement, para. 1649, see *supra* note 4. See also Kai Ambos and Ousman Njikam, "Charles Taylor's Criminal Responsibility", in *Journal of International Criminal Justice*, 2013, vol. 11, p. 807.

[31] *Perišić* Appeal Judgment, paras. 26, 28, see *supra* note 1.

[32] ICTY, *Prosecutor v. Duško Tadić*, Judgement, Appeals Chamber, IT-94-1-A, 15 July 1999, para. 229 (http: //www. legal-tools. org/doc/8efc3a/) ("*Tadić* Appeal Judgement").

[33] Boas et al, 2007, pp. 303—304, see *supra* note 28.

that of the original *Tadić* appeal judgment. In the *Šainović et al.* the Appeals Chamber pointed exactly to this inconsistency, concluding that the *Perišić* approach significantly diverges from the previous jurisprudence. [34]

Due to their authoritative value in international criminal law and for the sake of clarity, it is worth summarizing the elements of aiding and abetting as established by the *Tadić* and *Furundžija* judgments: an aider or abettor is the one who provides "practical assistance, encouragement, or moral support" to the principal. [35] These actions must have had a substantial effect on the perpetration of a crime. [36] In the *Tadić* the Trial Chamber borrowed this element of aiding and abetting from the formulation of the ILC Draft Code of Crimes Against the Peace and Security of Mankind, which called for criminal responsibility of the individual who "knowingly aids, abets or otherwise assists, directly and substantially, in the commission of such a crime [...]. "[37] The commentary to the ILC Draft Code did not define "substantially", but provides a hint: assistance of the accomplice must facilitate the commission of a crime in some *significant* way. [38] Based on these considerations, the *Tadić* Chamber clarified that substantial contribution requirement presupposes a contribution that in fact has an effect on the commission of the crime. [39] The *Furundžija* Chamber further elaborated on the effect of assistance, holding that the acts of the accomplice need not "bear a causal relationship to, or be a *conditio sine qua non* for, those of

---

[34] *Šainović et al.* Appeal Judgement, para. 1621, see *supra* note 4. See also *Stanišić and Simatović* Appeal Judgement, paras. 104–106, see *supra* note 1, and *Popović et al.* Appeal Judgment, see *supra* note 4, para. 1758.

[35] ICTY, *Prosecutor v. Anto Furundžija*, Judgment, Trial Chamber, IT–95–17/1–T, 10 December 1998, para. 235 (http: //www. legal–tools. org/doc/e6081b/) ("*Furundžija* Trial Judgment"); *čelebić i* Appeal Judgement, para. 352, see *supra* note 26; *Tadić* Appeal Judgment, para. 229, see *supra* note 32.

[36] *Furundžija* Trial Judgment, paras. 223, 224, 249, see *supra* note 35.

[37] The Draft Code of Crimes Against the Peace and Security of Mankind adopted by the International Law Commission in 1996, U. N. A/51/10 (1996), Article 2 (3)(d) ("ILC Draft Code").

[38] ILC Commentary to the ILC Draft Code 1996, p. 21, para. 11, emphasis added.

[39] ICTY, *Prosecutor v. Duško Tadić et al.* , Judgement, Trial Chamber, IT–94–1–T, 7 May 1997, para. 688 (http: //www. legal–tools. org/doc/0a90ae/) ("*Tadić* Trial Judgement").

the principal. "[40] This finding underlines the derivative nature of aiding and abetting: an accomplice can only influence the conduct of the principal perpetrator to a certain extent; and the final decision to commit or not to commit a crime rests with the perpetrator and not with the accomplice. [41]

According to the ILC, the contribution of an aider and abettor need not only be "substantial", but also "direct". [42] The commentary to the ILC Draft Code did not explain the exact meaning of "direct contribution". Lack of clarity as to the content of this qualifier was therefore partially to "blame" for the confusion that followed. The *Tadić* Trial Chamber seemed to have embraced the requirement of directness treating the accused as culpable where his participation "directly and substantially affected the commission of the offence. "[43] In *Furundžija*, however, the court rejected the term "direct" in describing the proximity between the assistance and the principal act as misleading because "it may imply that assistance needs to be tangible, or to have a causal effect on the crime. "[44]

It is noteworthy that the post-Nuremberg trials of war criminals, cases that informed *Furundžija* and *Tadić* along with the provisions of the ILC Draft Code, do not seem to support any requirement that aid has to be specifically directed towards the crimes. For example, in the trial of *Gustav Becker, Wilhelm Weber and Eighteen Others*, the Permanent Military Tribunal at Lyon convicted the former German customs

---

[40] *Furundžija* Trial Judgment, para. 233, see *supra* note 35. See also ICTY, *Prosecutor v. Milan Simić*, Judgment, Appeals Chamber, IT-95-9-A, 28 November 2006, para. 85 (http: //www. legal-tools. org/doc/ e6081b/); ICTY, *Prosecutor v. Tihomir Blaskić*, Judgment, Appeals Chamber, IT-95-14-A, 29 July 2004, para. 48 (http: //www. legal-tools. org/doc/88d8e6/).

[41] Sandford H. Kadish, "Complicity, Cause and Blame: A Study in the Interpretation of Doctrine", in *California Law Review*, 1985, vol. 73, issue 2, p. 334.

[42] ILC Commentary to the Draft Code 1996, p. 21, para. 11. For the discussion of this provision see also *Šainović et al.* Appeal Judgment, para. 1647, see *supra* note 4.

[43] *Tadić* Trial Judgment, .para. 692, see *supra* note 39. The *Tadić* Appeal Chamber later used the "specific direction" criterion to delimit aiding and abetting and participation in the joint criminal enterprise. See *Tadić* Appeal Judgment, para. 229, see *supra* note 32.

[44] *Furundžija* Trial Judgment, para. 232, see *supra* note 35.

officers in French Savoy for the illegal arrest and ill treatment of French citizens, which later resulted in the death of the three victims in Germany. [45] The tribunal found the accused responsible. Their actions were instrumental in the death of the victims; this was regardless of whether the injuries sustained in France were the direct cause of their deaths in Germany. [46] In the other widely cited case, *Zyklon B*, the British Military Court in Hamburg convicted the owner and the second-in-charge of war crimes for supplying poison gas to concentration camps. The Court disregarded the arguments that the gas was to be used for lawful purposes. [47]

While the *Tadić* trial judgment set out the elements of aiding and abetting, the *Tadić* appeal judgment focused primarily on defining the notion of the joint criminal enterprise (common design). [48] The *Tadić* appellate panel used the phrase "acts *specifically directed* to assist..." in order to compare responsibility for aiding and abetting and that pursuant to the joint criminal enterprise that presupposes acts in *some way directed* to the furtherance of common design. [49] Thus, the emphasis was not on the physical proximity of the accomplice's aid to the offence in question, but rather on the existence of the crime-specific relationship between the aider and abettor and the principal perpetrator as opposed to the group-specific situation, characteristic of the joint criminal enterprise.

In contrast, *Perišić* employed the terminology to stress the directness of the link between the aid and the crime. [50] To support of the specific direction requirement, *Perišić* cited a number of judgments emanating from the ICTY and the International

---

[45]   Permanent Military Tribunal at Lyon, *France* v. *Becker et al.*, in *Law Reports of Trial of War Criminals*, 1948, vol. 7, pp. 67-70.

[46]   *Ibid.*

[47]   British Military Court, *United Kingdom v. Tesch et al.*, in *Law Reports on Trial of War Criminals*, 1947, vol. 1, pp. 93-101 ('*Zyklon B* Case"). This case is referenced in the *Perišić* Appeal Judgment, fn. 115, see *supra* note 1 and the *Šainović et al.* Appeal Judgment, para. 1628, see *supra* note 4.

[48]   *Tadić* Appeal Judgment, para. 229, see *supra* note 32. The same point is being made in the *Šainović et al.* Appeal Judgment, para. 1623, see *supra* note 4.

[49]   *Ibid.*, emphasis added.

[50]   *Perišić* Appeal Judgment, para. 44, see *supra* note 1.

Criminal Tribunal for Rwanda ("ICTR") that either reproduced the wording of the *Tadić* appeal judgment verbatim or followed it closely. [51] Yet, none of these judgments elaborated on the original *Tadić* pronouncement. [52] It appears that the requirement of specific direction was inferred by the *Perišić* Appeals Chamber from the wording of the *Tadić* appeal judgment, and was taken out of context. [53] Moreover, on at least two occasions, the ICTY Appeals Chambers expressly rejected the idea that the "specific direction" is an essential ingredient of *actus reus* of aiding and abetting. [54]

The majority of the *Šainović et al.* Appeals Chamber highlighted exactly this problem with interpreting the sources of law in *Perišić*. The judges acknowledged that there is a clear divergence on the "specific direction" issue between the *Perišić* ap-

---

[51] *Ibid.* , paras. 28−29.

[52] For example, the *Blagojević* Appeals Chamber simply acknowledged that the Trial Chamber did not err in restating the formulations and principles of aiding and abetting contained in the previous ICTY judgments. Also, *Kvočka et al.* and *Blagojević* discussed the difference between perpetration by means of the joint criminal enterprise and aiding and abetting; *Simić* specified that the accused need not know "either the precise crime that was intended or the one that was, in the event, committed"; *Orić* merely reiterated the minimum basic elements of aiding and abetting for the purposes of conviction for omission. See also ICTY, *Prosecutor v Vidoje Blagojević et al.* , Judgement, Appeals Chamber, IT−02−60−A, 9 May 2007, paras. 127−128 (http://www. legal−tools. org/doc/c32768) ("*Blagojević et al.* Appeal Judgement"); ICTY, *Prosecutor v. Milorad Kvočka et al.* , Judgment, Appeals Chamber, IT−98−30/1−A, 28 February 2005, paras. 89−90; ICTY, *Prosecutor v. Mitar Blagojević* Judgment, Appeals Chamber, IT−98−32−A, 25 February 2005, para. 102 (http://www. legal−tools. org/doc/e35d81/); ICTY, *Prosecutor v. Blagoje Simić*, Judgement, Appeals Chamber, IT−95−9−A, 28 November 2006, paras. 85−86 (http://www. legal−tools. org/doc/28524b/); ICTY, *Prosecutor v Naser Orić*, Judgment, Appeals Chamber, IT−03−68−A, 3 July 2008, para. 43 (http://www. legal−tools. org/doc/e053a4/).

[53] To that effect see *Taylor* Appeal Judgment, para. 475, see *supra* note 1.

[54] ICTY, *Prosecutor v. Mile Mrkšić and Veselin Šljivančanin* Judgment, Appeals Chamber, T−95−13/1−A, 5 May 2009, para. 159 (http://www. legal−tools. org/doc/40bc41/); *Blagojević et al.* Appeal Judgement, para. 189, see *supra* note 52; See also *Furundžija* Trial Judgment, para. 232, see *supra* note 35; ICTY, *Prosecutor v. Naser Orić*, Judgement, Trial Chamber, IT−03−68−T, 30 June 2006, para. 285 (http://www. legal−tools. org/doc/37564c/) . Judge Liu argued to this effect in his partially dissenting opinion: 'Given that specific direction has not been applied in past cases with any rigor, to insist on such a requirement now effectively raises the threshold for aiding and abetting liability. ' Partially Dissenting Opinion of Judge Liu, *Perišić* Appeal Judgment, para. 3, see *supra* note 1.

proach and the previous jurisprudence. [55] The *Šainović et al.* judges solved the legal conundrum by assessing accurately where the law stands on the issue of specific direction. [56] Their extensive review of ad hoc tribunal jurisprudence and that of the post Second World War cases demanded the conclusion that specific direction is not an element of aiding and abetting liability under customary international law or the Statute of the Tribunal. [57]

In the *Taylor* Appeal judgment, the Special Court for Sierra Leone ("SCSL") also displayed little enthusiasm about the alleged specific direction requirement. [58] In that case, the Appeals Chamber attempted to circumvent the controversy by framing the discussion about the specific direction in terms of the non-binding nature of ICTY precedent, rather than one of custom. [59] The judges concluded that the definition of the *actus reus* of aiding and abetting under customary international law is established by assistance that has a substantial effect on the crimes, not the particular manner in which such assistance is provided. [60] The *Taylor* judges found no reason to depart from the settled principles of law and refused to introduce the novel element of the specific direction in the definition of *actus reus* of aiding and abetting because the requirement that the acts of the accused have substantial effect on the commission of the crime establish sufficient causal link. [61] The judges further noted that the question of physical proximity between the accused and the crimes may be relevant

---

[55] *Šainović et al.* Appeal Judgement, para. 1621, see *supra* note 4.

[56] *Ibid.*, para. 1622.

[57] *Ibid.*, para. 1649. *Cf.* Judge Tuzmukhamedov argued that the case at hand did not merit consideration of the issue of the 'specific direction' for factual reasons. Lazarević's assistance was not remote—and reasons of legal certainty, stability and predictability—the majority did not provide cogent reasons for deviating from the *Perišić* judgment. See Dissenting Opinion of Judge Tuzmukhamedov, *Šainović et al.* Appeal Judgment, paras. 43, 45, 47, see *supra* note 4.

[58] *Taylor* Appeal Judgment, para. 486, see *supra* note 1.

[59] *Ibid.*, para. 476.

[60] *Ibid.*, para. 475.

[61] *Ibid.*, para. 490.

on a case-by-case basis, but it is not a legal requirement. [62]

In modern international criminal law, a uniform approach by different courts and tribunals to a particular issue may serve as the evidence of consensus on a given topic, and, thus, allow one to consider the formation of a customary rule. The judgments referred to in the *Perišić* case do not seem to support customary status of a specific direction component of *actus reus* of aiding and abetting. Moreover, it appears that the *Šainović et al.*, the *Taylor*, the *Popović et al.* and, finally, the *Stanišić and Simatović* Appeals Chambers certainly weakened (if not disposed of) any emerging customary rule requiring the "specific direction" element as a part of *actus reus* of complicity.

2.2 Failure to qualify as a "general principle of law"

The remaining question is whether the purported requirement of specific direction finds support in the third source of international law: the general principles of law. This source of law appears promising in the light of the problematic nature of custom within international criminal law. [63] This is not to suggest that the meaning of the expression "general principles of law" is crystal clear in public international law. The term has been attributed different meanings depending on the context, but there seems to be some form of convergence in understanding that reference has to be made to various domestic legal systems.

The *Šainović et al.* Appeals Chamber engaged in a praiseworthy initiative to "probe" this third source of international law in order to establish whether domestic law may be of assistance in resolving the issue of the "specific direction". [64] The Chamber made a brief reference to national law, correctly observing that the varia-

---

[62] *Ibid.*

[63] See Malcolm Shaw, *International Law*, 6th edn, Cambridge University Press, Cambridge, 2008, p. 99; Bin Cheng, *General Principles of Law as Applied by International Courts and Tribunals*, Cambridge University Press, Cambridge, 1987, p. 2 ("Cheng, 1987"); Fabián O. Raimondo, *General Principles of Law in the Decisions of International Criminal Courts and Tribunals*, Martinus Nijhoff, Leiden, 2008, p. 1.

[64] *Šainović et al.* Appeal Judgement, para. 1643, see *supra* note 4.

tions among national jurisdictions did not allow deducing a common principle. [65] The Chamber's substantive conclusion about the lack of the uniform rule in respect of this particular aspect of aiding and abetting also appears correct. The methodology employed for assessing domestic law, was, however, far from clear. The judgment a-dopted a reductionist approach, i. e. grouping the countries together, without taking into account the specific features of different legal families and individual legal systems. [66] It would have been more convincing to explain the features of the law on aiding and abetting in respect of each country; such an individualised approach would have added credibility to the argument that the "specific direction" is not root-ed in domestic law. The following paragraph addresses this by looking at six examples.

Methodologically speaking, international law does not require a fixed number of countries that need to recognize a certain principle in *foro domestico* in order for it to qualify as a source of international law. [67] The jurisprudence of the ad hoc tribunals does not seem to require universal acceptance of the rule by all states, but it is essential that the "general principle" is *representative* of the variety of nations. [68] The six legal systems that will be considered are the United States, England, Germany, France, Italy, and Poland. They represent some of the major parent legal systems in the world. [69] The aim is to establish whether they require specific direction as part

---

[65] *Ibid.*, para. 1644.

[66] The overview of national case law is cramped together in three paragraphs and several lengthy foot-notes. See *Šainović et al.* Appeal Judgement, paras. 1643–1646, see *supra* note 4.

[67] Cheng, 1987, p. 25, see *supra* note 63; Hans Kelsen, *The Law of the United Nations: A Critical A-nalysis of its Fundamental Problems*, Stevens, London, 1950, p. 533.

[68] Fabián O. Raimondo, "General Principles of Law, Judicial Creativity, and the Development of International Criminal Law", in Shane Darcy and Joseph Powderly (eds.), *Judicial Creativity at the International Criminal Tribunals*, Oxford University Press, Oxford, 2010, p. 52.

[69] Konrad Zweigert and Hein Koetz, *An Introduction to Comparative Law*, 3rd edn., Clarendon Press, Oxford, 1998, pp. 40–41. For more empirical data see James Stewart, " 'Specific Direction' is Unprecedented: Results from Two Empirical Studies," EJIL Blog, 4 September 2013, available at http://www.ejiltalk.org/specific-direction-is-unprecedented-results-from-two-empirical-studies/, last accessed at 1 May 2014.

of the *actus reus* of aiding and abetting. [70]

US criminal law originally started as the "common law" of England, as adopted by the American colonies in the eighteenth century, but it has evolved ever since. [71] In more recent times, a large number of states introduced or reformed their criminal codes on the basis of the 1962 Model Penal Code, promulgated by the American Law Institute as a part of the major criminal law revision ("MPC"). [72] Neither American common law nor the MPC supports the requirement of the 'specific direction' as part of *actus reus* of complicity. Pursuant to the common law, an accomplice is a person who, with the requisite *mens rea*, assists the primary party in committing an offence by physical conduct, psychological influence or omission (assuming there is duty to act). [73] Once it is determined that the accomplice assisted the primary perpetrator, the degree of aid or influence is immaterial. [74] A secondary party is accountable for the conduct of the primary party even if the assistance was causally unnecessary and the offence would have been committed without it anyway. [75] The required *mens rea* is "dual intent" —the intent to assist the primary party and the intent that the primary party commits the offence charged. [76]

The MPC provides that the accomplice satisfies the objective element of an offence through the perpetrator's conduct by facilitating it via solicitation, aiding or

---

[70]　Historically, domestic law nurtured international criminal justice, making resort to national law provisions relevant even outside the context of the discussion on the sources law. See Richard Overy, "The Nuremberg trials: international law in the making", in Philip Sands (ed.), *From Nuremberg to the Hague: The Future of International Criminal Justice*, Cambridge University Press, Cambridge, 2003, pp. 1-29.

[71]　Paul H. Robinson, "Comparative Summary of American Criminal Law" in Marcus Dubber and Kevin J. Heller (eds.), *The Handbook of Comparative Criminal Law*, Stanford Law Books, Stanford, 2011 ("Dubber and Heller, 2011") p. 564.

[72]　*Ibid.*, p. 565.

[73]　Joshua Dressler, *Understanding Criminal Law*, 4th edn., Lexis Nexis, 2006 ("Dressler, 2006") p. 506.

[74]　*Ibid.*, p. 508.

[75]　Dressler, 2006, p. 509, see *supra* note 73.

[76]　*Ibid.*, p. 511.

failing the legal duty to prevent the commission of the offence. [77] From the wording of the MPC, it follows that the mere knowledge of the crime is not sufficient to satisfy the fault requirement for complicity; it is essential that an accomplice intends to participate in it. [78] In *United States v. Peoni*, the court held that the complicity doctrine requires the defendant to "in some sort associate himself with the venture, that he participate in it as something that he wishes to bring about, that he seek by his action to make it succeed." [79] The MPC adopted the higher standard of *Peoni*. Conduct requirement for complicity under the MPC is less stringent than the fault requirement. An accomplice's assistance need not be necessary for the successful completion of the offence, nor it need be substantial; even the smallest degree of assistance suffices. [80]

The Polish Penal Code defines aiding and abetting as facilitating the commission of the prohibited act by providing the instrument, means of transport, or giving counsel or information, or failing to act when there exists a duty to act. [81] It is necessary that the accomplice acts with intent that another person commits a prohibited act (*zamiar*). [82] The objective element is expressed as "facilitates by his behavior the commission of the act". [83] With regard to the subjective element, aiding and abetting may be only intentional, yet in contrast with instigation, the intention may be

---

[77] Model Penal Code Section 2. 06 (2)(c) and (3)(a).

[78] Model Penal Code Section 2. 06 (2)(3)(a) provides that an accomplice acts with "the purpose of promoting or facilitating the commission of the offence. " The same standard had been previously confirmed in U. S. Supreme Court, *U. S. v. Nye and Nissen*, 336 U. S. 613, 1949.

[79] U. S. Court of Appeals for the Second Circuit, *United States v. Peoni*, 100 F. 2d 401, 402 (2d Cir. 1938), 12 December 1938.

[80] U. S. Supreme Court of California, *People v. Durham*, 70 Cal. 2d 171, 185, 21 January 1969; U. S. Supreme Court of Pennsylvania, *Commonwealth v. Murphy*, 844 A. 2d 1228, 1234, 22 March 2004; U. S. Pennsylvania Superior Court, *Commonwealth v. Gladden*, 665 A. 2d 1201, 1209 (Pa. Super. 1995), 26 September 1995.

[81] Art. 18 (3), Polish Penal Code.

[82] *Ibid.*

[83] T. Bojarski *et al.* (eds.), *Kodeks karny. Komentarz* do cz. OGóLNA roz. II art. 18, 2013, wydanie VI, LexisNexis, Warszawa, 2013.

expressed as direct and indirect intent. [84] Even if the aider is not fully informed about the intent of the primary perpetrator but only foresees the possibility of the crime, the aider agrees to that crime by virtue of providing assistance. [85] In this regard, the Polish Supreme Court held in a 2013 case that forging invoices with the knowledge that they will be used to obtain an unlawful tax refund amounts to complicity in fraud. [86] The judges clarified that the aider and abettor need not want to commit an offence; it is sufficient that he reconciles himself with the idea. Thus, the aider and abettor must be aware of the legal characteristics of the offence, intend to facilitate it by a non-causal contribution, and have the awareness of the impact of his behavior in particular, that it facilitates the commission of the offence by the primary perpetrator. [87]

In French law, the accomplice either facilitates the preparation or commission of the crime by aid and assistance, or incites its commission by means of a gift, promise, threat, order, or an abuse of authority or powers, or gives the directions to commit it. [88] Criminal liability of accomplices presupposes that the underlying act is objectively punishable. [89] Complicity requires a positive act, and inaction is not sufficient. [90] The aid of the accomplice does not need to be indispensable for the commission of the offence. [91] The emphasis of French law is on the mental element: it must be established that aid was furnished with the knowledge that this supports the crime. [92] The commentaries specify that while knowledge of the illegal enterprise

---

[84] *Ibid.*

[85] L. Tyszkiewicz Leon *et al.* (eds.), *Kodeks karny. Komentarz* do cz. OG6LNA roz. II art. 18 2012, wydanie III, LexisNexis, Warszawa, 2012.

[86] Wyrok Są̆du Najwy szego-Izba Karna (Judgment of the Supreme Court), III KK 184/2013, available at https: //mojepanstwo. pl/dane/sn_ orzeczenia/23391, iii-kk-184-13 last accessed at 1 May 2014.

[87] *Ibid.*

[88] Art. 121. 7, French Penal Code.

[89] Hervé Pelletier et Jean Perfetti (eds.), *Code Penal* (14 *edn.*), Litec, 2002, p. 29.

[90] *Ibid.*, pp. 30-31.

[91] *Ibid.*, p. 32.

[92] Yves Mayaud et Emmanuelle Allain (eds.), *Code Penal* (104 *edn.*), Dalloz, 2007, p. 126.

and voluntary participation are essential, it matters little whether the objectives of the accomplices are different from those of the primary perpetrator. [93]

German law defines an aider and abettor (*Gehilfe*) as " any person who intentionally assists another in the intentional commission of an unlawful act. " [94] Intent must be at minimum in the form of indirect intent, or the knowledge of the risk or likelihood for the effect to occur and the will to bring it about—at least in the form of the acceptance. [95] The intent of the aider and abettor is " double" (*doppelter*) —it embraces two elements: first, the act of assistance must have the supportive effect on the commission of the offence, and, secondly, the act must be directed towards the illegal action, without the need to concretize every detail of the offence. [96] Because the aider and abettor does not have the will to exercise certain influence on the principal offence, the requirement for the specificity of his knowledge about the offence is less stringent as compared with instigation. [97] The standard linking the act of the aider and the offence is quite low. German courts are of the view that it is sufficient that the aider furthers in some way the actions of the principal. [98] Commentaries define assistance of and aider and abettor as a causal contribution that enables, enhances, or facilitates the commission of the offence and that *does not* amount to a perpetration or incitement; it is irrelevant, however, whether the act would have been committed without the help of the aider and abettor. [99]

The accomplice in English law (sometimes called " an accessory" or a seconda-

---

[93]   *Ibid.* , p. 123.

[94]   Art. 27 (1), German Penal Code.

[95]   Michael Bohlander, *Principles of German Criminal Law*, Hart Publishing, Oxford, 2009 ("Bohlander, 2009"), p. 169.

[96]   Karl Lackner und Kristian Kühl, *StGB, Kommentar* (25th ed.), Verlag C. H. Beck, München, 2004, ("Lackner und Kühl, 2004") p. 195.

[97]   *Ibid.*

[98]   Bohlander, 2009, p. 172, see *supra* note 96.

[99]   Lackner und Kühl, 2004, p. 191, see *supra* note 97.

ry party) is anyone who aids, abets, counsels or procures a principal. [100] "Procuring" implies bringing about an offence, such as by deceiving another in order that the other commits an offence. [101] This is the only term out of the four, which embraces some form of causal relationship between the act of procurement and the execution of the offence. [102] The remaining three categories do not require such connection. The word "counsels" presupposes that the accused is responsible if he persuades the principal to commit an offence, not by threats or bribes, but by pointing to the advantages of the proposed course of action or by giving advice to the principal offender. [103] Abetting entails encouragement of the principal to commit the offence. [104] There must be some connection between abetting or counseling and the execution of the crime, but it does not have to be causal in the sense of being *conditio sine qua non* for the crime. [105] Complicity requires proof of intention, not purpose; and *dolus eventualis* (or "adverted recklessness") may be sufficient. [106] The test of specificity of accessorial knowledge is whether the offence committed was within the contemplated range of offences, if not, then was it of the same type as any of those offences contemplated. [107]

---

[100]   Andrew Ashworth, *Principles of Criminal Law* (2nd edn.), Clarendon Law Series, Oxford, 1995 ("Ashworth, 1995"), p. 410. See also Accessories and Abettors Act 1861, as amended by s. 65 (4) Criminal Law Act 1977.

[101]   Andrew Ashworth, "UK Criminal Law", in Dubber and Heller, 2011, p. 539, see *supra* at 71.

[102]   J. C. Smith and Brian Hogan, *Criminal Law* (10th edn.), Butterworths, Oxford, 2002, p. 145; Ashworth, p. 422, see *supra* note 101.

[103]   Herbert L. A. Hart and Tony Honoré, *Causation in the Law*, Oxford Scholarship Online, 1985, p. 380.

[104]   Ashworth, 1995, p. 414, see *supra* note 101.

[105]   UK Divisional Court, *Wilcox* v. *Jeffery*, [1951] 1 All England Law Reports 464, 26 January 1951, cited in Ashworth, 2011, p. 416, see *supra* note 102.

[106]   UK Divisional Court, *Blakely and Sutton* v *Chief Constable of West Mercia*, [1991] R. T. R. 405, 23 May 1991, cited in Ashworth, 2011, see *supra* note 102, p. 539.

[107]   Keith J. M. Smith, *A Modern Treatise on the Law of Criminal Complicity*, Clarendon Press, Oxford, 1991 ("Smith, 1991"), pp. 167 – 169, referring to the UK House of Lords in *Maxwell v. DPP*, [1978] 1 Weekly Law Reports 1350, 19 October 1978 and the UK Court of Appeal in *R v. Bainbridge*, [1959] 1 Queens Bench 129, 8 June 1959.

In Italy, the all—encompassing term "participation" (*concorso di persone*) ex-presses the notion that any involvement whatsoever on the part of an actor in any of-fence establishes his connection to the crime. [108] The acts of each co—participant are their own acts, which are attributed to all the others. The latter statement is true only if two conditions are met: first, an objective condition: there must be a causal link between the acts and the criminal result; and, second, a subjective condition: each participant must be aware of the final purpose of all the actions. In other words, each of them must deliberately and consciously give his or her contribution, material or in-tellectual, to the commission of the crime (wanted by everyone). [109] Thus, for a person to qualify as a party to crime in Italy, it is sufficient that the person willingly contributes to the commission of the offence with the general knowledge about the factual situation, and his input constitutes necessary support for carrying out the crime. [110] The contribution need not be *conditio sine qua non* for carrying out the crime and may take different forms. [111]

Even this brief survey of several national laws on complicity shows that they do not embrace the idea that the aid must be directed towards the specific offence in the meaning that the *Perišić* Appeals Chamber attributed to it. When it comes to the spe-cificity of the assistance furnished by the accessory, the emphasis of the domestic law provisions is on *mens rea* rather than *actus reus*. The link between the assistance and the offence is established via the mental state of accomplices, rather than the direct-ness of their aid. The level of contribution required to attract responsibility for com-plicity varies depending on the legal system in question. Yet, none of the reviewed countries require that the assistance is a precondition for the predicate offence. It

---

[108]   Art. 110, Italian Penal Code.

[109]   CCC, 1st division (Supreme Court of Cassation), n. 8084, 4 July 1987 (Cass. pen. sez. I° 4/7/ 1987 n° 8084).

[110]   Codice penale: annotato con la giurisprudenza, a cura di Sergio Beltrani, Raffaele Marino, Rossana Petrucci, p. 429.

[111]   See *supra* note 110.

seems that the higher is the threshold for *mens rea* for aiding and abetting, the looser is the conduct requirement.

3. Conceptual problems

In addition to the lack of a solid foundation in international law, the specific direction requirement as part of *actus reus* of aiding and abetting presents a number of conceptual difficulties. First, the new requirement undermines the whole idea of accomplice liability targeting the situations where the accused is removed from the scene of the crime. The new enhanced version of aiding and abetting purports to bridge the temporal and/or spatial gap between the accomplice and the principal perpetrator. The justification for the introduction of the "specific direction" element in the *actus reus* of aiding and abetting in *Perišić* was the need to expressly establish the link between accomplices' contribution and the wrongdoing in cases when the accused is removed from the offence. The judgement contrasted this situation with instances when the accomplice is physically close to the crime and where the link is implied. [112] However, physical proximity is often a false friend for establishing this connection; even if an accomplice is present at the scene of the crime, he is not directly perpetrating it, thus his contribution to the offence is often inferred from the evidence. [113]

Linking the assistance and the crime via the directness and the specificity of aid is somewhat misplaced. This type of argumentation partially stems from the lack of the well-defined causation standard for complicity in international criminal law. [114] The causal link between the accomplice and the crime is always constructed; the connection stems more from the risk that the secondary party envisages and undertakes rath-

---

[112] *Perišić* Appeal Judgment, para. 38, see *supra* note 1. *Cf.* ICTY, *Prosecutor v. Radoslav Brđanin*, Judgement, Appeals Chamber, IT – 99 – 36 – A, 3 April 2007, paras. 151, 273, 277, esp. 348 (http: // www. legal–tools. org/doc/782cef/).

[113] For example, *Furundžija*'s contribution was inferred from his position of authority. *Furundžija* Trial Judgment, para. 209, see *supra* note 35.

[114] Mettraux, 2005, p. 281, see *supra* note 26.

er than the actual harm produced by that their actions. [115] Hence, it is the mental state of the accomplice that grounds his or her relationship to the offence rather than the conduct. If one accepts that distance is not dispositive for establishing the effect of accessory's contribution on the offence, then the whole raison d´être for the specific direction fails. There is no longer need to compensate for the distance by adding additional requirements to the *actus reus* of complicity, i. e. that aid is specifically directed towards the crime. The enhanced specific direction standard may lead to impunity gaps, where culpable assistance with the substantial effect on the crime does not attract liability for the mere lack of the physical proximity between the crime and the assistance.

Secondly, the additional criterion requiring a direct link between the contribution and the crime brings aiding and abetting in the dangerous vicinity of commission because it conflates assistance with performing part of *actus reus* of the offence itself. The former, in contrast with the latter, need not be the direct cause of the crime. Judge Liu, who partially dissented in *Perišić*, pointed out this problematic aspect of the specific direction requirement. [116] The essence of "committing" the offence (as opposed to being an accomplice thereto) is bringing about its material elements. [117] This is done by the direct engagement in the crime. Thus, the qualitative criterion of "direct contribution" is better suited to describe the *actus reus* of co−perpetration, while the quantitative criterion of "substantial contribution" serves to assess the impact of the accomplice's aid, which does not need to be a precondition for the offence. [118]

---

[115] Christopher Kutz, "The Philosophical Foundations of Complicity Law", in John Deigh and David Dolinko (eds.), *The Handbook of Philosophy of Criminal Law*, Oxford University Press, Oxford, 2011, p. 157.

[116] Partially Dissenting Opinion of Judge Liu, *Perišić* Appeal Judgment, fn. 9, see *supra* note 1.

[117] See ICC, *Prosecutor v. Mathieu Ngudjolo Chui*, Judgment Pursuant to Article 74 of the Statute—Concurring Opinion of Judge Christine Van den Wyngaert, Trial Chamber II, ICC−01/04−02/12−4, 18 December 2012, para. 44 (http: //www. legal−tools. org/doc/7d5200/).

[118] *Ibid.*

Thirdly, the specific direction requirement appears superfluous and lacking its independent standing. One can view it either as: (1) an implied element of substantial contribution, in the sense of the accomplice's actions having some impact on the conduct of the principal, and, thus, being *directed* towards the crime; or (2) as part of the accused's *mens rea* for aiding and abetting, which in the ICTY's jurisprudence is the knowledge that the accomplice's acts assist in the commission of the offence. [119] If the accused knew about the crime and still provided assistance, then logically his acts are directed towards the offence. [120] The short survey of domestic laws on complicity, provided in the previous section, supports the idea that it is the specificity of accomplice's knowledge rather than the specific direction of his acts that establishes his connection to the offence.

Fourthly, the two constituent elements of aiding and abetting are interconnected. The *actus reus* and *mens rea* are part of one mechanism and cannot be assessed independently of each other, something that the *Perišić* Appeals Chamber attempted to do by stressing exclusive focus on the *actus reus* of aiding and abetting. [121] A more solid approach appears to lie in balancing the two elements based on the facts of the particular case. [122] It seems that making the requirements for the conduct element

---

[119] For example, *Furundžija* Trial Judgment, para. 249, see *supra* note 35; *Blagojević et al.* Appeal Judgement, para. 127, see *supra* note 52; ICTY, *Prosecutor v. Ante Gotovina and Mladen Markač*, Judgment, Appeals Chamber, IT – 06 – 90 – A, 16 November 2012, para. 127 (http: //www. legal – tools. org/doc/ 03b685/) ("*Gotovina* and *Markač* Appeal Judgement").

[120] Judges Meron and Agius, in their joint separate opinion in *Perišić*, noted "whether an individual specifically aimed to assist relevant crimes logically fits within our current *mens rea* requirement": Joint Separate Opinion of Judges Meron and Agius, *Perišić* Appeal Judgment, paras. 2–3, see *supra* note 1. See also Partially Dissenting Opinion of Judge Liu, *Perišić* Appeal Judgment, fn. 7, see *supra* note 1.

[121] *Perišić* Appeal Judgment, para. 48, see *supra* note 1: "[t]he Appeals Chamber also underscores that its analysis of specific direction will exclusively address *actus reus*."

[122] Keith J. M. Smith, who studied complicity in depth, noted that "complicity's derivative quality must convincingly reside *at least* in either *mens rea* or *actus reus* components [...] diminution in demands on the *mens rea* side have repercussions for the causal element as part of the *actus reus*; and vice–versa": Smith, 1991, p. 195, see *supra* note 108, emphasis added. See also Concurring Opinion of Justice Shireen Avis Fisher on Aiding and Abetting Liability, *Taylor* Appeal Judgment, para. 715, see *supra* note 1.

more stringent, without simultaneously lessening the fault requirement or getting rid of the requirement that the contribution of the accused must be substantial, skews the construction of complicity. The *Taylor* Appeal judgment adopted a more balanced approach to the two elements of aiding and abetting by drawing on the example of the US MPC that requires "purpose": instead of a more widely accepted "knowledge" -as a mental element for aiding and abetting. The enhanced mental element is balanced out by the lighter contribution requirement. US MPC allows for *any*-instead of significant or substantial-contribution to crime to qualify as a conduct element. [123]

Finally, the requirement that the aid is specifically directed towards the crime, and not just to the establishing military control or other fighting objective (even in the circumstances when the assistance is provided with the knowledge and facilitates the commission of offences) brings to the surface an uncomfortable question that goes beyond the legal technicalities of a particular liability mode. This is, what are the conditions that turn the "general war effort" into a "crime" attracting individual criminal responsibility? Also, what is the standard of behavior that we expect from the senior leadership in the context of war?

In this regard, the 2012 acquittals on appeal of the general Ante Gotovina and the operations commander of Croatian police Mladen Markac? are relevant. [124] The rationale for their acquittal was the reversal of the Trial Chamber's finding that the artillery attacks planned and ordered by the accused were unlawful. The Prosecution in this case maintained that even if the attacks were lawful, the Appeals Chamber should find Gotovina and Markač guilty of aiding and abetting deportation and persecution for their role in these attacks because they ordered them knowing that this would substantially contribute to deportation of civilian population. [125] The Appeals

---

[123] *Taylor* Appeal Judgment, para. 447, see *supra* note 1. Smith pointed out that American jurisdictions requiring purposeful accessorial attitudes experience less problems with specificity. Smith, 1991, p. 171, see *supra* note 107.

[124] *Gotovina and Markač* Appeal Judgement, see *supra* note 119.

[125] *Ibid.* , para. 111.

Chamber rejected this argument, claiming that departures of civilians concurrent with lawful artillery attacks cannot be qualified as deportation. [126]

The grounds for the acquittals of Perišić, Stanišić and Simatović at trial, on the one hand, and Gotovina and Markač? on the other, are undeniably different. Nonetheless, it seems that the underlying logic is analogous, that is the adoption of the objective approach to military activities, while shifting the emphasis from the mental state of the accused to the objective and gruesome reality of war. The acquittals share in common the expansive view of the "general war effort" that does not attract individual criminal responsibility. Accepting that war is an ugly affair that inevitably affects the civilians or results in some level of criminality is a valid policy consideration, one that appears to have framed the legal discourse around the controversial ICTY acquittals. The question remains whether the focus of international criminal law should be on the individual contribution and the state of mind of those in charge or the externalities accompanying military activities. Depending on the answer to this question, one forms their expectations of persons vested with authority during the war.

4. Conclusion

The interpretation of the *actus reus* of aiding and abetting as containing the requirement that assistance must be specifically directed towards the crimes and not just geared to the general war effort is problematic on several levels. This requirement is disconcerting from the point of view of the principle of legality because it does not find support in the sources of international law: it cannot be traced back to a custom or a general principle of law from national laws of legal systems of the world. The specific direction requirement seems to be rather the product of judges creatively interpreting the wording of the early *Tadić* appeal judgment, which dealt with contrasting aiding and abetting responsibility with that of the common design.

---

[126] *Ibid.* , para. 114.

Moreover, the narrow view of *actus reus* undermines the idea of accomplice responsibility as the form of liability that targets the situations where the accused is removed from the scene of the crime. The idea of the novel element was to bridge the temporal or spatial gap between the accomplice and the principal perpetrator by requiring the directness and specificity of contribution. The emphasis should be, however, not on compensating for the distance by adding additional requirements to the *actus reus* of complicity, but on the level of knowledge of the accused and the effect that his assistance has on the crime. Calling for the directness of the accessory's contribution brings aiding and abetting in the dangerous vicinity of commission. Finally, restrictive interpretation of aiding and abetting liability exemplifies the broader policy concern of international criminal law—lowering the expectations of persons vested with authority in the context of war.

"INDIRECT CO-PERPETRATION" BEFORE THE INTERNATIONAL CRIMINAL COURT: THE "CHEOPS" APPROACH TO COLLECTIVE CRIMINAL ACTION

William St-Michel *

1. Introduction

"From the heights of these pyramids, forty centuries look down on us. "

—Napoléon Bonaparte

International criminal law punishes a wide range of criminal behaviours. While theoretically possible, international criminal jurisdictions will usually not try individual perpetrators of crimes falling within their jurisdiction. Rather, for reasons pertaining to costs, but also with a view to empowering national jurisdictions by leaving them the primary responsibility of prosecuting perpetrators, [1] the investigative and prosecutorial efforts of the international tribunals will focus on those who are suspected to bear the most responsibility for such crimes. [2]

Adequately assessing criminal liability of leaders in the context of mass and collective criminality is, to say the least, quite challenging. First and foremost, interna-

---

   * Associate Legal Adviser, Presidency, International Criminal Court.

  [1] International Criminal Court ("ICC"), Office of the Prosecutor, "Policy Paper on Case Selection and Prioritisation", 15 September 2016, para. 5, available at https: //www. icc－cpi. int/itemsDocuments/20160915_OTP－Policy_Case－Selection_Eng. pdf, last accessed at 14 June 2017.

  [2] ICC, *Situation in the Republic of Kenya*, Decision Pursuant to Article 15 of the Rome Statute on the Authorization of an Investigation into the Situation in the Republic of Kenya, Pre－Trial Chamber II, ICC－01/09－19, 31 March 2010, para. 188 (http: //www. legal－tools. org/doc/338a6f/) ("Decision on the opening of an investigation in Kenya").

tional criminal law is meant to sit at the confluence of two major legal traditions – common law and civil law – which approach criminal responsibility in different ways. But more significantly, participation in the commission of genocide, crimes a-gainst humanity and war crimes is less tangible than participation in the commission of domestic crimes. International crimes do not involve "one perpetrator, one inci-dent, one victim" as domestic crimes do; [3] rather, international crimes often result from the coordinated action of several individuals, who bring varying, yet comple-mentary, contributions to the commission of the crimes. Attributing individual crimi-nal responsibility in such circumstances, in particular to the top leadership, requires international criminal jurisdictions to be innovative, while at the same time ensuring due respect for the cornerstone principle of legality.

The *ad hoc* international criminal tribunal for the former Yugoslavia ("ICTY") has somehow resolved the issue by resorting to *inter alia* a doctrine of collective crim-inality not expressly provided for in its statute, but stemming from post–World War II case–law—the so–called "joint criminal enterprise". With a different statute, fram-ing criminal responsibility in different terms, the International Criminal Court ("ICC") has also adopted a doctrine of collective criminality not found in its consti-tutive text. A doctrine which, like joint criminal enterprise, pushes the boundaries of "commission" beyond its ordinary meaning to encompass all those who did not physi-cally perpetrate the crime but who nonetheless played a vital role. Bearing testimony to the organized nature of mass criminality, "indirect co – perpetration", as it is known, envisages criminal responsibility through the prism of pyramids—with direct perpetrators forming a hierarchical apparatus of power under the control of master-minds acting in concord.

The doctrine of "indirect co–perpetration" has already been examined in vari-

---

[3] Stefano Manacorda, "Foreword to the Symposium 'The Principles of Individual Criminal Responsi-bility: A Conceptual Framework' ", in *Journal of International Criminal Justice*, 2007, vol. 5, no. 4, p. 913.

ous academic contributions. [4] The present Article aims to discuss the increasing importance of this theory in ICC jurisprudence, its adaptability to a wide range of situations, but also some of its shortcomings. The Article will first analyse the roots and constitutive elements of "indirect co–perpetration", proceed to outline concrete applications of "indirect co–perpetration", and conclude by examining the interplay between "indirect co–perpetration" and other similar modes of liability.

2. "Indirect co–perpetration" as a *sui generis* form of liability

The letter of Article 25 (3)(a) of the Rome Statute provides for three forms of "commission": (i) commission as an individual; (ii) commission with another person, or known as "co–perpetration"; and (iii) commission through another person, or known as "indirect perpetration". Through a reading–in of this provision, the jurisprudence of the ICC has found there to be a fourth form of commission, which merges "co–perpetration" and "indirect perpetration" into a *sui generis* form of liability called "indirect co–perpetration". Pre–Trial Chamber I found this mode of liability to be "in accordance with the Statute", as per Article 25 (2) of the Rome Statute, based on an inclusive understanding of the disjunction "or" as used in Article 25 (3)(a). [5] The present section proposes a brief overview of the factual situation which prompted Pre–Trial Chamber I to consider incorporating a new mode of liability into the ICC's legal framework, a further detailed analysis of the constitutive elements of "indirect co–perpetration" as well as a critical discussion of its legal

[4] See *inter alia*: Héctor Olásolo Alonso, *Tratado de autoría y participación en derecho penal internacional*, Tirant Lo Blanch, Valencia, 2013, pp. 585 *et ss*; Shachar Eldar, "Indirect Co–Perpetration", in *Criminal Law and Philosophy*, 2014, vol. 8, pp. 605 *et ss*.

[5] ICC, *The Prosecutor v. Germain Katanga and Mathieu Ngudjolo*, Decision on the confirmation of charges, Pre – Trial Chamber I, ICC – 01/04 – 01/07 – 717, 30 September 2008, para. 491, (http://www. legal–tools. org/doc/67a9ec/) ("*Katanga and Ngudjolo* Confirmation Decision"): "Two meanings can be attributed to the word "or" —one known as weak or *inclusive* and the other strong or *exclusive*. An inclusive disjunction has the sense of "either one or the other, and possible both" whereas an exclusive disjunction has the sense of "either one or the other, but not both". Therefore, to interpret the disjunction in art. 25 (3)(a) of the Statute as either "inclusive" or "exclusive" is possible from a strict textualist interpretation" (emphasis in the original, footnotes omitted).

soundness.

2.1 The factual background which gave rise to considering a combination of "co-perpetration" and "indirect perpetration"

The concept of "indirect co-perpetration" was first raised in the decision on the confirmation of charges in the case of *The Prosecutor v. Germain Katanga and Mathieu Ngudjolo Chui*. The respective cases of Mr. Katanga and Mr. Ngudjolo, which first proceeded separately, were joined by Pre-Trial Chamber I for the purposes of the confirmation of charges. It is the very specific facts of this case that prompted the pre-trial chamber to have recourse to a new theory of liability, not expressly contemplated in the Rome Statute. Mr. Katanga and Mr. Ngudjolo were both charged for crimes committed as part of an attack directed against the village of Bogoro in the eastern Democratic Republic of the Congo. According to the Prosecution's theory at the time of the confirmation of charges, the groups respectively led by Mr. Katanga and Mr. Ngudjolo (both non-State armed groups) launched a coordinated attack against Bogoro. However, the evidence before Pre-Trial Chamber I showed that due to ethnical loyalties within the respective organizations, some members of these organizations accepted orders only from leaders of their own ethnicity. [6] To ensure an adequate assessment of the blameworthiness of senior leaders, Pre-Trial Chamber I found appropriate to combine individual responsibility for committing crimes through other persons together with the mutual attribution among the co-perpetrators at the senior level. [7] Crimes committed by one's organization would then be attributed to the other, and vice versa. On this basis, Pre-Trial Chamber I committed Mr. Katan-

---

[6] *Katanga and Ngudjolo* Confirmation Decision, para. 493, see *supra* note 5.

[7] *Ibid.*, para. 492.

ga and Mr. Ngudjolo for trial. [8]

2. 2 The elements of "indirect co-perpetration"

As its name implies, "indirect co-perpetration" combines the relevant constitutive elements of both "co-perpetration" (commission jointly with another person) and "indirect perpetration" (commission through another person). Both modes have been extensively analysed in the jurisprudence of the Court. Before setting out the constitutive elements of "indirect co-perpetration", the present sub-section will briefly examine, in turn, the elements of co-perpetration and indirect perpetration as they have been defined in ICC jurisprudence.

(i) Co-perpetration

The commission of a crime jointly with another person, also known as "co-perpetration", was the first mode of liability considered in detail by the jurisprudence of the ICC, namely in the *Lubanga* case, which dealt with charges of enlistment, conscription and use of child soldiers. It is also, at the time of writing, the only mode of liability that has received full appellate scrutiny.

In essence, co-perpetration requires the proof of a contribution on the part of the accused to a common plan agreed upon with one or more other persons.

According to the Appeals Chamber, the common plan need not have been spe-

---

[8] Yet, while proceeding on the basis of the charges as confirmed by Pre-Trial Chamber I, the trial against Mr. Katanga and Mr. Ngudjolo went in a different direction. In November 2012, during the deliberations phase, the cases of Mr. Katanga and Mr. Ngudjolo were severed for a second time (that time, by Trial Chamber II), as an examination of the evidence had revealed that Mr. Katanga's participation could be considered from a different perspective than that underlying the *Katanga and Ngudjolo* Confirmation Decision, namely, under art. 25 (3)(d): ICC, *The Prosecutor v. Germain Katanga and Mathieu Ngudjolo*, Decision on the implementation of regulation 55 of the Regulations of the Court and severing the charges against the accused persons, Trial Chamber II, ICC – 01/04 – 01/07 – 3319 – tENG, 21 November 2012 (http://www. legal – tools. org/doc/f5cbd0/). The severance was the logical outcome as 'indirect co-perpetration' requires at least two co-perpetrators. Mr. Ngudjolo was ultimately acquitted (ICC, *The Prosecutor v. Mathieu Ngudjolo Chui*, Judgment pursuant to Article 74 of the Statute, Trial Chamber II, ICC-01/04-02/12-3-tENG, 18 December 2012, (http://www. legal-tools. org/doc/2c2cde/), while Mr. Katanga was convicted of certain charges pursuant to art. 25 (3)(d). The latter judgement is further discussed below: *infra*, sub-section III B.

cifically directed at the commission of a crime—it is sufficient that it presented a "critical element of criminality". [9] This requirement is intended to be consonant with the way "intent" and "knowledge" are conceptualized in the Rome Statute. [10] As per Article 30 of the Rome Statute, "intent" to commit a crime can be established, in addition to intending the crime, by awareness that the crime "will occur in the ordinary course of events". [11] In the very same way, a person can be deemed to have had "knowledge" of the commission of the crime if he or she was aware that such crime would occur in the ordinary course of events. [12] Yet, even though it is not necessary for the common plan to be designed to further a specific crime, it results from the above reading of Article 30 that there must have been at least a virtual certainty that a crime would be committed in the course of implementing the common plan. In the *Lubanga* case, the agreement entered into by Mr Lubanga with the other co-perpetrators was not aimed at the commission of any specific crime—the common plan was to build an effective army in order to ensure political and military control over the region where Mr Lubanga's organization was active. [13] Yet, the war crimes of enlistment, conscription and use of children under the age of 15 were found to be a consequence of the implementation of the common plan at hand, which occurred in the ordinary course of events. The Appeals Chamber referred in particular to the fact that the recruitment and training of children under the age of 15 was already ongoing

---

[9] ICC, *The Prosecutor v. Thomas Lubanga Dyilo*, Judgment on the appeal of Mr. Thomas Lubanga Dyilo against his conviction, Appeals Chamber, ICC-01/04-01/06-3121-Red, 1 December 2014, para. 446 (http://www. legal-tools. org/doc/585c75/) ("*Lubanga* Appeals Judgement"), approving the approach followed at the pre-trial and trial phases.

[10] *Lubanga* Appeals Judgement, para. 446, see *supra* note 9.

[11] Art. 30 (2)(b).

[12] Art. 30 (3).

[13] ICC, *The Prosecutor v. Thomas Lubanga Dyilo*, Judgment pursuant to Article 74 of the Statute, Trial Chamber I, ICC - 01/04 - 01/06 - 2842, 14 March 2012, para. 1136 (http://www. legal - tools. org/doc/677866/) ("*Lubanga* Trial Judgement"), as upheld by the Appeals Chamber: *Lubanga* Appeals Judgement, para. 455, see *supra* note 9.

at the time the common plan materialized. [14]

Furthermore, it is not required that the plan be express or previously arranged; it can be implied or materialize extemporaneously. [15]

Turning to the contribution to the implementation of the common plan, it was long debated whether the accused co-perpetrator must have executed himself or herself the incriminated conduct. The Appeals Chamber observed that under Article 25 (3)(a), it is not required for a perpetrator to be identified as such to have personally carried out the underlying crime. In particular, Article 25 (3)(a) regards the individual who commits a crime through another person as a perpetrator, even though the incriminated conduct is perpetrated by a third person. [16] The Appeals Chamber found no reason to treat co-perpetrators differently. [17] In the Appeals Chamber's view, the central issue is rather the nature of the contribution, in particular how this contribution must distinguish itself from accessory contributions under Articles 25 (3)(b) (ordering, soliciting or inducing a crime), (c) (aiding, abetting or otherwise assisting in the commission of a crime) and (d) (in any other way contributing to the commission of a crime by a group of persons acting with a common purpose). The Appeals Chamber concurred with the common holding of Pre-Trial Chamber I and Trial Chamber I that what differentiates perpetrators from accessories is the control that the former exerts over the crimes. [18] As a result, the Appeals Chamber reasoned that the contribution of a co-perpetrator must be essential to the commission of

---

[14] *Lubanga* Trial Judgement, paras. 1135–1136, see *supra* note 13, as upheld by the Appeals Chamber: *Lubanga* Appeals Judgement, para. 455, see *supra* note 9.

[15] *Lubanga* Appeals Judgement, para. 445, see *supra* note 9.

[16] *Ibid.* , paras. 465–466.

[17] *Ibid.* , para. 466.

[18] *Ibid.* , para. 469.

the crime, with the resulting power to frustrate its commission. [19]

"Co-perpetration" was recently at stake in the *Al Mahdi* case. [20] Mr Al Mahdi, a prominent figure of a splinter group of Al-Qaeda in the Islamic Maghreb, was convicted as a co-perpetrator under the charges of war crimes for the destruction of a number of religious buildings in Timbuktu, Mali. [21] Trial Chamber VII pointed out to a split in the ICC's case-law as to whether the contribution must be to the crime itself or to the common plan. [22] Confusion on the matter is indeed apparent from certain decisions dealing with co-perpetration (or the "co-perpetration" component of indirect co-perpetration). Some do refer to the contribution being made to the common plan, [23] while others link such contribution to the commission of the crime. [24] The Appeals Chamber seems to have favoured the latter approach. [25]

That being said, the question is irrelevant when the common plan is aimed at a specific crime, as was the case in *Al Mahdi*. And even if the common plan is not criminal in nature, it is doubtful that the question would become relevant: since the commission of the crime must be a virtual certainty of the implementation of the common plan, any contribution to the common plan is in reality a contribution to the

---

[19]   *Ibid.* , paras. 467–473. One of the trial judges in the *Lubanga* case expressed different views on the matter. According to Judge Fulford, determining whether a contribution has been essential to the commission of a crime is a hypothetical exercise: "Separate Opinion of Judge Adrian Fulford", para. 17, as appended to the *Lubanga* Trial Judgement, 2012, see *supra* note 13. Yet, with a view to ensuring fairness to the defence as well as ensuring jurisprudential consistency, Judge Fulford did not record a formal dissent: "Separate Opinion of Judge Adrian Fulford", para. 2, as appended to the *Lubanga* Trial Judgement, 2012, see *supra* note 13.

[20]   It has also been applied in the recent *Bemba et al.* case, which concerns offences against the administration of justice. At time of writing, the trial judgement is currently being appealed before the Appeals Chamber.

[21]   Mr. Al Mahdi's conviction was entered further to a guilty plea.

[22]   ICC, *The Prosecutor v. Ahmad Al Faqi Al Mahdi*, Judgment and Sentence, Trial Chamber VIII, ICC-01/12-01/15-171, 27 September 2016, p. 11, fn. 31 (http://www.legal-tools.org/doc/042397/).

[23]   See *e. g. Lubanga* Trial Judgement, para. 1006, see *supra* note 13.

[24]   See *e. g. Katanga and Ngudjolo* Confirmation Decision, para. 524, see *supra* note 5.

[25]   *Lubanga* Appeals Judgement, para. 473, see *supra* note 9 ("The Appeals Chamber considers that the most appropriate tool for conducting such an assessment is an evaluation of whether the accused had control over the crime, by virtue of his or her essential contribution *to it* and the resulting power to frustrate its commission, even if that essential contribution was not made at the execution stage of the crime.") (emphasis added).

commission of the crime.

However, the issue could be of relevance if the common plan aims at, or results in, more than one category of crimes being committed. Say murders on the one hand, and forcible displacement, on the other hand, are committed as a result of the implementation of a common plan to take political and armed control over a region. While one could argue that forcible displacement is a consequence that will occur in the normal course of events when intending to exert control over a region, the same would not necessarily hold true in respect of murder. In such circumstances, whether the contribution is directed towards a specific crime or the common plan is a matter of great significance in the assessment of the accused's liability. In the end, what will most probably be decisive is the intent with which the contribution is carried out.

With respect to the mental elements of co—perpetration, it is required that the accused intended to commit the crime (in case the common plan was about a specific crime) or was aware that the commission of the crime would occur in the ordinary course of events (in case the common plan was not criminal in nature). It must additionally be established that the accused was aware that his or her contribution was essential to the commission of the crime. [26]

(ii) Indirect perpetration

In addition to committing a crime jointly with another person, the Rome Statute punishes those who commit a crime *through* another person. "Indirect perpetration" as a mode of liability in and of itself has rarely been applied in the ICC jurisprudence. Its first interpretation was in fact made as part of an analysis of "indirect *co*—perpetration".

It must first be emphasized that the word "person" in the context of "indirect perpetration" has been given a specific meaning by the ICC jurisprudence. In the *Katanga and Ngudjolo* Confirmation Decision, Pre—Trial Chamber I noted that crimes

---

[26] *Lubanga* Trial Judgement, paras. 1007—1013, see *supra* note 13.

falling under the jurisdiction of the Court—which, as per the Rome Statute, are the most serious crimes of concern to the international community as a whole and which threaten the peace, security and well-being of the world[27]—will almost inevitably concern collective or mass criminality. [28] As a result, Pre-Trial Chamber I found that "indirect perpetration" within the meaning of Article 25 (3)(a) targets cases which involve a perpetrator's control over an *organization*. [29] This approach to "indirect perpetration" is in line with what the German legal theory calls *Organisationsherrschaft* ("control over an organization"). [30] In its final judgment in the *Katanga* case, Trial Chamber II held that the organization is one of the possible forms of committing crimes through another person. Trial Chamber II observed that Article 25 (3)(a) does not rule out the possibility of having two or a limited number of intermediaries. [31]

Indirect perpetrators are punished as principals, and not accessories, because they do not merely order the commission of a crime; through their control over the organization, they essentially decide *whether* and *how* the crime will be committed. [32] In such circumstances, it is immaterial whether the perpetrators could also be held

---

[27] See preamble to the Rome Statute, third paragraph ("Recognizing that such grave crimes threaten the peace, security and well-being of the world"), fourth paragraph ("Affirming that the most serious crimes of concern to the international community as a whole must not go unpunished ... "). See *also*, Rome Statute, art. 5 ("The jurisdiction of the Court shall be limited to the most serious crimes of concern to the international community as a whole ... ").

[28] *Katanga and Ngudjolo* Confirmation Decision, para. 501, see *supra* note 5.

[29] *Ibid.*, paras. 500-510, see *supra* note 5.

[30] *Ibid.*, para. 498, see *supra* note 5.

[31] ICC, *The Prosecutor v. Germain Katanga*, Judgment pursuant to article 74 of the Statute, Trial Chamber II, ICC-01/04-01/07-3436-tENG, 7 March 2014, paras. 1403-1406 (http://www.legal-tools.org/doc/f74b4f/) ("*Katanga* Trial Judgement").

[32] *Katanga and Ngudjolo* Confirmation Decision, para. 518, see *supra* note 5.

criminally responsible for their acts. [33] Ultimately, what distinguishes the order[34] issued by an indirect perpetrator from an order giving rise to accessorial liability[35] is the almost automatic compliance with the order issued by the indirect perpetrator. To quote Professor Claus Roxin, whose work has inspired Pre-Trial Chamber I in setting out the elements of "indirect perpetration", the organization is "a mere gear in a giant machine". [36] In contrast, orders attracting accessory liability only

---

[33]　Art. 25 (3)(a) specifies that those who commit a crime through another person incur criminal liability *regardless of whether that other person is criminally responsible*. Pre-Trial Chamber I observed that in national jurisdictions, the direct perpetrator who is being used as a mere instrument will usually not be fully criminally responsible for his/her actions, as he/she may have acted under a mistaken belief, acted under duress and/or not have had the capacity for blameworthiness: *Katanga and Ngudjolo* Confirmation Decision, para. 495, see *supra* note 5. Yet, as further noted by Pre-Trial Chamber I, in certain scenarios, it is possible for both the direct and the indirect perpetrator to be criminally liable as principals: the direct perpetrator for his fulfilment of the subjective and objective elements of the crime, and the indirect perpetrator for his/her control over the crime via his/her control over the will of the direct perpetrator: *Katanga and Ngudjolo* Confirmation Decision, para. 497, see *supra* note 5. In this author's view, in cases of mass or collective criminality, it is hardly conceivable that direct perpetrators, even though used as mere instruments, will not fulfil the *actus reus* and *mens rea* elements of the crimes charged, with the notable exception of crimes committed by children, who are not liable before the ICC (see Rome Statute, art. 26). In any event, in most of the cases brought before the international criminal jurisdictions, the existence of crimes (including whether the direct perpetrators bear or not full criminal responsibility for their acts) will rarely be challenged in its entirety, the most contentious issue being whether there is a culpable link between the accused and the crimes.

[34]　While it is settled jurisprudence that "co-perpetration" requires an essential *contribution* to the common plan, the nature of the act that incurs liability under "indirect perpetration" is not clearly defined. From the very few decisions dealing with this mode of responsibility, it would seem that the nature of the act which must be performed by the indirect perpetrator is an order. In the *Gaddafi et al.* case, Pre-Trial Chamber I refers to Abdullah Al-Senussi, head of the Military Intelligence, as having played an essential role in the commission of the crimes "by *giving orders* to the armed forces under his control (…) "; ICC, *Situation in the Libyan Arab Jamahiriya*, Decision on the "Prosecutor's Application Pursuant to Article 58 as to Muammar Mohammed Abu Minyar GADDAFI, Saif Al-Islam GADDAFI and Abdullah AL-SENUSSI", Pre-Trial Chamber, I, ICC-01/11-01/11-1, 27 June 2011, para. 89 (emphasis added) (http://www.legal-tools.org/doc/094165/) ("*Gaddafi et al.* Arrest Warrant Decision"). An "order" has been defined in the ICC jurisprudence as an instruction to either: (i) commit a crime; or (ii) perform an act or omission in the execution of which a crime is carried out. See ICC, *The Prosecutor v. Bosco Ntaganda*, Decision Pursuant to Article 61 (7)(a) and (b) of the Rome Statute on the Charges of the Prosecutor Against Bosco Ntaganda, Pre-Trial Chamber II, ICC-01/04-02/06-309, 9 June 2014, para. 145 (http://www.legal-tools.org/doc/5686c6/) ("*Ntaganda* Confirmation Decision").

[35]　Art. 25 (3)(b).

[36]　*Katanga and Ngudjolo* Confirmation Decision, para. 515 (referring to Claus Roxin, *Täterschaft und Täterherrschaft*, De Gruyter, Berlin, 2006, p. 245), see *supra* note 5.

require that the order had a *direct* effect on the commission of the crime. [37]

To ensure "almost automatic compliance" with the order issued by the indirect perpetrator, the organization must be: (i) based on hierarchical relations between the indirect perpetrator and the direct perpetrators; and (ii) composed of sufficient individuals to guarantee that the indirect perpetrator's orders will be carried out, if not by one, then by another. [38] This ensures that the successful execution of the order will not be compromised by any particular member's failure to comply with the order. The supply of individuals must be such that any one individual who does not comply with the order may be replaced by another who will. [39] In sum, the organization must have a life of its own and be independent from the individuality of its members. [40]

For the purpose of "indirect perpetration", the organization need not be a State body—it could well be an organization driven by non—State actors, such as a rebel group. [41] The application of "indirect co—perpetration" to both categories of perpetrators is reflective of modern mass violence, which no longer involves State perpetrators only. [42]

Interestingly, the applicability of "indirect perpetration" to crimes committed by non—State actors has been less controversial than the possibility for crimes against humanity to be perpetrated by non—State actors. Article 7 of the Rome Statute, which punishes crimes against humanity, requires the widespread or systematic attack (as part of which such crimes are committed) to be launched "pursuant to or in further-

---

[37]   *Ntaganda* Confirmation Decision, para. 145, see *supra* note 34.

[38]   *Katanga and Ngudjolo* Confirmation Decision, para. 512, see *supra* note 5.

[39]   *Ibid.* , para. 516.

[40]   *Ibid.* , para. 517.

[41]   For example, the trial of *Bosco Ntaganda*, a former figure of rebel armed group in eastern Democratic Republic of the Congo, proceeds on the basis of charges of indirect co—perpetration.

[42]   For a discussion of the phenomenon of non – State actors as addressed at the ICC, see: Silvia Fernández de Gurmendi, "Non—State actors in the law and practice of the International Criminal Court", in *Israel Yearbook on Human Rights*, 2017, vol. 47 (to be published).

ance of a State or *organizational* policy to commit such attack" (emphasis added). A minority view has been expressed that the organization must partake some characteristics of a State. [43] The prevailing view, however, is that the organization within the meaning of Article 7 must only have the capability to commit a widespread or systematic attack. [44] Yet, that is not to say that a group launching a widespread or systematic attack will automatically qualify as an "organization" for the purposes of "indirect perpetration". For example, Germain Katanga was found guilty of crimes against humanity, [45] but the group he headed—which launched the widespread/systematic attack[46]—was found not to be an organized apparatus of power, as required for 'indirect perpetration. [47] This resulted in Mr Katanga's liability to be considered under another provision. [48]

With respect to the mental elements of "indirect perpetration", as a form of principal liability, the accused must fulfil the subjective elements of the crimes he or she is charged with as well as be aware of the factual circumstances enabling him or her to exercise control over the crime through another person. [49]

(iii) Indirect co-perpetration

It follows from the above that "indirect co-perpetration" is established when:

i. The suspect/accused is part of a common plan with one or more persons;

ii. The suspect/accused and the other co-perpetrators carry out essential contri-

---

[43]   "Dissenting opinion of Judge Hans—Peter Kaul", para. 51, as appended to the Decision on the opening of an investigation in Kenya, 2010, see *supra* note 2.

[44]   See *e. g.* ICC, *The Prosecutor v. Jean—Pierre Bemba Gombo*, Judgment pursuant to Article 74 of the Statute, Trial Chamber III, ICC – 01/05 – 01/08 – 3343, 21 March 2016, para. 158 (http://www. legal – tools. org/doc/edb0cf/).

[45]   *Katanga* Trial Judgement, para. 870 and p. 658, see *supra* note 31.

[46]   *Ibid.* , see *supra* note 31, paras. 1139–1141.

[47]   *Ibid.* , para. 1420.

[48]   *Ibid.* , paras. 1596 *et ss.*

[49]   *Gaddafi et al.* Arrest Warrant Decision, 2011, para. 69, see *supra* note 34.

butions in a coordinated manner which result in the fulfilment of the materials elements of the crime;

iii. The suspect/accused has control over an organization;

iv. The organization consists of an organized and hierarchical apparatus of power; and

v. The execution of the crimes is secured by almost automatic compliance with the orders issued by the suspect/accused. [50]

Co-perpetration and indirect co-perpetration are mutually exclusive, in the sense that the former requires an element (*i. e.* adherence of the perpetrators to the common plan) which the latter does not require. It is noteworthy that in the *Ntaganda* case, Pre-Trial Chamber II declined to confirm alternative charges of co-perpetration after having confirmed charges of indirect co-perpetration. [51]

2. 3 The debatable legal foundation of "indirect co-perpetration"

"Indirect co-perpetration" is not expressly provided for in Article 25 (3)(a). Yet, the absence of a legislative reference to a given mode of liability does not preclude it from having a legal existence. For example, the theory of joint criminal enterprise, as applied by the *ad hoc* tribunals in a significant number of cases, is a purely jurisprudential creation. This theory is derived from a reading-in of the word "committed" as encompassing the participation in a so-called joint criminal enterprise. After an examination of the purpose of its statute as well as the very nature of the crimes falling under its jurisdiction, the Appeals Chamber of the International Criminal Tribunal for the former Yugoslavia ("ICTY") reasoned that the "commission" of a crime is not limited to mere physical perpetration, but can also occur

---

[50]   See *e. g. Ntaganda* Confirmation Decision, para. 104, see *supra* note 34.

[51]   *Ibid.* , para. 102.

through the participation in the realization of a common design. [52] The ICTY Appeals Chamber found support for this form of liability in international customary law, in particular post—World War II case—law, certain international instruments as well as in some national jurisdictions. [53] The extensive interpretation of the notion of commission has attracted criticism, even judicial, [54] but has nonetheless remained routinely relied upon in the jurisprudence of both *ad hoc* tribunals. [55] The conceptual interrelations between joint criminal enterprise and indirect co—perpetration are further addressed below.

The gap between the letter of Article 25 (3)(a) and the concept of "indirect co—perpetration" is less wide than the one filled in by the *ad hoc* tribunals in relation to joint criminal enterprise. As explained above, Article 25 (3)(a) expressly contains the two constitutive limbs of "indirect co—perpetration" —commission "jointly with another" and "through another". Yet, the existence in law of "indirect co—perpetration" is not authoritatively settled. No case involving this mode of liability has yet been subject to appellate consideration—all appeals against convictions have so

---

[52] ICTY, *Prosecutor v. Duško Tadić*, Judgement, Appeals Chamber, 15 July 1999, IT—94—1—A, paras. 188—193 (http://www. legal—tools. org/doc/8efc3a/) ("*Tadić* Appeals Judgement"). See *also* ICTY, *The Prosecutor v. Milan Milutinović et al.* , Decision on Dragoljub Ojdanić 's Motion Challenging Jurisdiction—*Joint Criminal Enterprise*, Appeals Chamber, IT—99—37—AR72, 21 May 2003, para. 20 (http://www. legal—tools. org/doc/d51c63/).

[53] *Tadić* Appeals Judgement, paras. 194—226, see *supra* note 52. Interestingly, the ICTY Appeals Chamber refers to art. 25 (3)(d) of the Rome Statute as an example upholding the doctrine of joint criminal enterprise: *Tadić* Appeals Judgement, paras. 222—223, see *supra* note 52. As will be further developed below, despite similar wording, the form of liability envisaged under art. 25 (3)(d) of the Rome Statute (contributing in any other to the commission of a crime by a group of persons acting with a common purpose) differs from the theory of joint criminal enterprise. It bears mentioning that the Rome Statute was not in force at the time of the *Tadić* Appeals Judgement and had therefore not received any judicial interpretation.

[54] See *e. g.* ICTY, *Prosecutor v. Milomir Stakić*, Judgement, Trial Chamber II, IT—97—24—T, 31 July 2003, paras. 431 *et ss* (http://www. legal—tools. org/doc/32ecfb/) . The trial judgement was quashed on appeal on this aspect: ICTY, *Prosecutor v. Milomir Stakić*, Judgement, Appeals Chamber, 22 March 2006, IT—97—24—A, paras. 58 *et ss* (http://www. legal—tools. org/doc/09f75f/).

[55] The theory of joint criminal enterprise has also been applied before other internationalized criminal jurisdictions, such as the Extraordinary Chambers in the Courts of Cambodia and the Special Court for Sierra Leone, the statutes of which did not mention expressly this form of liability.

far concerned modes of liability other than "indirect co-perpetration".[56] In the *Lubanga* Appeals Judgement, which dealt with *direct* co-perpetration, the ICC Appeals Chamber noted *en passant*, by way of a footnote, that "[v] iews have also been expressed in the Court's jurisprudence that Article 25 (3)(a) of the Statute provides for a fourth form of commission liability, whereby a perpetrator may commit a crime jointly with another person, where that other person commits the crime 'through [yet] another person' ",[57] without pronouncing on the existence of such a fourth mode of commission liability. The three ongoing ICC trials at the time of writing all include charges of "indirect co-perpetration" .[58] This may ultimately result in the ICC Appeals Chamber ruling on whether "indirect co-perpetration" is a proper mode of liability under the Rome Statute. But for the time being, relevant jurisprudence on "indirect co-perpetration" is essentially found in pre-trial decisions.

The above being said, in cases subsequent to the *Katanga and Ngudjolo* Confirmation Decision, challenges have been raised as to the existence of "indirect co-perpetration" under the Rome Statute at the pre-trial stage. Such challenges have consistently been rejected. In the *Ruto and Sang* case, Pre-Trial Chamber II opined that the *Katanga* decision "merely provided a dynamic or effective interpretation of the provision by way of merging the two modes of participation", which is, in the opinion of the pre-trial chamber, "consistent with the rules of treaty interpretation envisaged by article 31 of the Vienna Convention on the Law of Treaties".[59]

---

[56]   In addition, the current appeals before the Appeals Chamber involve command responsibility (*Bemba* case) and direct co-perpetration (*Bemba et al.* case).

[57]   *Lubanga* Appeals Judgement, p. 168, fn. 863, see *supra* note 9.

[58]   They are: the *Ntaganda* trial; the *Gbagbo and Blé Goudé* trial; and the *Ongwen* trial.

[59]   ICC, *The Prosecutor v. William Samoei Ruto, Henry Kiprono Kosgey and Joshua Arap Sang*, Decision on the Confirmation of Charges Pursuant to Article 61 (7)(a) and (b) of the Rome Statute, Pre-Trial Chamber II, ICC-01/09-01/11-373, 23 January 2012, para. 289 (http: //www. legal-tools. org/doc/96c3c2/). See *also* ICC, *The Prosecutor v. Dominic Ongwen*, Decision on the confirmation of charges against Dominic Ongwen, Pre-Trial Chamber II, ICC-02/04-01/15-422-Red, 23 March 2016, paras. 37-41 (http: //www. legal-tools. org/doc/74fc6e/).

Yet, "indirect co-perpetration" does not achieve full unanimity amongst the judges. Judge Christine Van den Wyngaert, who was a member of the trial bench seized of the *Katanga and Ngudjolo* case, has forcefully criticized the inclusion of "indirect co-perpetration" as a mode of liability under the Court's legal framework, albeit in an *obiter*. [60] In addition to expressing disagreement with the interpretative approach adopted by Pre-Trial Chamber I, [61] Judge Van den Wyngaert also warned against the possibility of "indirect co-perpetration" resulting in someone being held responsible for crimes committed by persons over whom he or she did not exert any form of control or without sharing their intent. [62] Yet, Judge Van den Wyngaert accepted that "co-perpetration" and "indirect perpetration" can be combined, "as long as all elements of each form are proven", giving the example of two individuals jointly subjugating a third one's will to commit a crime. [63] As described below, such a configuration—with one pyramid instead of two—has been found to fall within the realm of "indirect co-perpetration".

3. "Indirect co-perpetration" in ICC case-law: a multiplicity of situations

As explained above, the theory of "indirect co-perpetration" came into existence to ensure that two leaders, heading two distinct organizations while acting in concord, could be mutually attributed the wrongful acts committed by those under the control of one another [figure 1].

Yet, indirect co-perpetration is not limited to such a double-pyramidal configuration with a double-headed leadership. Recent cases dealing with other forms of

---

[60] Judge Van den Wyngaert expressed her views as part of a concurring opinion to the judgement acquitting Mathieu Ngudjolo after his case had been severed from that of Germain Katanga: ICC, *The Prosecutor v. Mathieu Ngudjolo Chui*, Concurring Opinion of Judge Van den Wyngaert, Trial Chamber II, ICC-01/04-02/12-4, 18 December 2012 (http://www.legal-tools.org/doc/7d5200/) ("Judge Van den Wyngaert's Concurring Opinion"). "Indirect co-perpetration" was no longer an issue in this judgement.

[61] Judge Van den Wyngaert's Concurring Opinion, para. 60 and fn. 76, see *supra* note 60.

[62] *Ibid.*, para. 61, see *supra* note 60.

[63] *Ibid.*, para. 62.

structuralized violence have been found to be adequately covered by "indirect co-perpetration", at least to proceed with trial. The ongoing *Ntaganda* case[64] revolves around a *single* pyramidal organization (a rebel armed group) allegedly controlled by a *single* group of persons, including the accused [figure 2]. [65] In contrast, the ongoing *Gbagbo and Blé Goudé* case[66] involves a single group of persons allegedly controlling a number of different sub-organizations, yet collectively referred to as "pro-Gbagbo forces". [67] These two examples illustrate the flexibility of the theory of "indirect co-perpetration" and its adaptability to a wide range of collective and mass criminality.

[**Figure 1**]

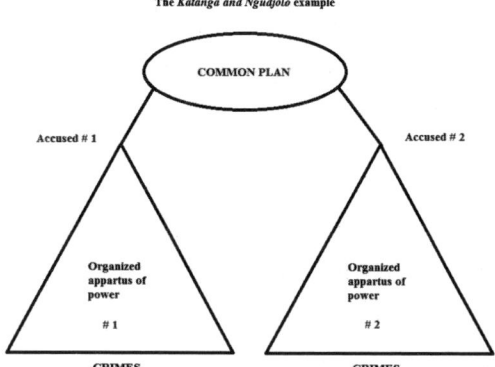

The *Katanga and Ngudjolo* example

COMMON PLAN

Accused # 1

Accused # 2

Organized
appartus of
power
1

Organized
appartus of
power
2

CRIMES

CRIMES

---

[64] This was a single-accused case relating to events which took place in eastern DRC in 2002-2003. The *Ntaganda* case concerns the events that were at stake in the *Lubanga* case, but involves more charges than the child soldier-related crimes with which Mr. . Lubanga was charged.

[65] *See*, generally: *Ntaganda* Confirmation Decision, see *supra* note 34.

[66] A multiple-accused case relating to the post-electoral violence which took place in Côte-d' Ivoire in 2010-2011.

[67] *See*, generally: ICC, *The Prosecutor v. Laurent Gbagbo and Charles Blé Goudé*, Prosecution's pre-trial brief, Office of the Prosecutor, ICC-02/11-01/15-148-Anx1, 16 July 2015 (http: //www. legal-tools. org/doc/eb7d8f/). The cases of Mr. Gbagbo and Mr. Blé Goudé were joined after charges had been confirmed in the respective cases.

[Figure 2]

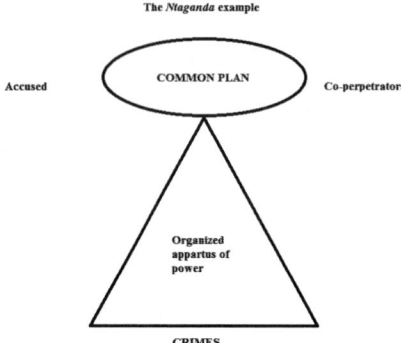

The *Ntaganda* example

Accused　　　COMMON PLAN　　　Co-perpetrators

Organized
appartus of
power

CRIMES

4. Interrelation with other modes of liability

As stated above, the Rome Statute, and international criminal law more generally, provides for a wide array of modes of liability, which sometimes overlap in their
constitutive elements. "Indirect co-perpetration" does not operate in isolation; it is
frequently alleged in the alternative to other modes of liability. The present section
will analyse the interplays between "indirect co-perpetration" and two other forms of
liability that are akin to it. The first sub-section will put "indirect co-perpetration"
in perspective and compare it with "joint criminal enterprise" as found in the jurisprudence of the *ad hoc* tribunals. The second sub-section will then examine the
convergences and divergences between "indirect co-perpetration" and a mode of liability often charged in the alternative, namely contribution "in any other way" to the
commission of a crime by a group of persons sharing a common purpose, as enshrined in Article 25 (3)(d) of the Rome Statute.

4. 1 "Indirect co-perpetration" and "joint criminal enterprise"

Indirect co-perpetration and the theory of joint criminal enterprise as applied by
the *ad hoc* tribunals have in common a number of features. In the first place, both
modes of liability extend the word "commission" beyond its ordinary meaning by
holding accountable, as principals, individuals who did not physically commit the

crime. Both modes are also premised on the existence of a "common plan" designed by the accused and one or more other individuals. More significantly, under both theories, direct perpetrators need not be adherents to the common plan. The ICTY Appeals Chamber found, upon examination of the way participation in a joint criminal enterprise had been approached in both post – World War II case – law and the tribunal's jurisprudence, that the physical perpetrator need not be a member of the joint criminal enterprise, provided that it can be shown that the crime can be imputed to one of the members of the joint criminal enterprise. [68]

Yet, "indirect co-perpetration" distinguishes itself from "joint criminal enterprise" in certain respects. Significantly, the purpose of the common plan giving rise to "indirect co-perpetration" differs from that of the joint criminal enterprise. As explained above, the common plan for "indirect co – perpetration" need not target a specific crime; it suffices that it contains a "critical element of criminality", understood as involving the virtual certainty that a crime will be committed in the normal course of events. On the contrary, joint criminal enterprise requires that the participants agreed to the commission of a crime. [69] That being said, one could reasonably argue that the common plan for "indirect co – perpetration" resembles a subsidiary form of joint criminal enterprise, the so-called third form, [70] whereby a participant to a joint criminal enterprise aimed at a specific crime can be held liable for crimes committed outside the agreed plan if such crimes were a natural and foreseeable con-

---

[68] ICTY, *Prosecutor v. Radoslav Brđanin*, Judgement, Appeals Chamber, IT-99-36-A, 3 April 2007, paras. 410–414 (http: //www. legal-tools. org/doc/782cef/) ("*Brđanin* Appeals Judgement").

[69] *Tadić* Appeals Judgement, para. 227, see *supra* note 52.

[70] There is a second form, but it is beyond the scope of this contribution to address its ins and outs. The third form does not meet universal approval in the jurisprudence and the doctrine. See *generally* Extraordinary Chambers in the Court of Cambodia, *Case No.* 002, Supreme Court Chamber Judgement Appeal, Supreme Court Chamber, 002/19-09-2007-ECCC/SC, 23 November 2016, in particular para. 791 (http: //www. legal-tools. org/doc/e66bb3/).

sequence of the execution of the plan. [71] Furthermore, and more importantly, "indirect co−perpetration" and "joint criminal enterprise" do not require the same type of contribution. While the former involves, as seen above, an *essential* contribution, the latter can be established with an *important* contribution. [72] As per the relevant jurisprudence, the indirect co−perpetrator retains the possibility to frustrate the commission of the crime by not performing his or her contribution. Conversely, for joint criminal enterprise, it is not necessary to prove that the crime would not have been committed had it not been of the accused's contribution. [73] This is so, because the focus of joint criminal enterprise is on the accused's state of mind and not so much on the level of contribution to the common plan, whereas indirect co−perpetration is characterized by control over the crime rather than by intent to commit the crime. [74]

Nevertheless, without speculating, it would be hardly conceivable that a person convicted by one of the *ad hoc* tribunals for having taken part in a joint criminal enterprise would avoid the same fate should the same charges be brought before the ICC through the prism of "indirect co−perpetration". The differences between "indirect co−perpetration" and "joint criminal enterprise" are more a matter of semantics and preferred conceptual approaches than radically diverging stances on criminal liability for mass crimes.

---

[71] *Tadić* Appeals Judgement, para. 204, see *supra* note 52. For a discussion of the similarities between "indirect co−perpetration" and the third form of "joint criminal enterprise", see Thomas R. Liefländer, "The *Lubanga* Judgement of the ICC: More than just the First Step?", in *Cambridge Journal of International and Comparative Law*, 2012, vol. 1, pp. 206−208.

[72] *Brđanin* Appeals Judgement, 2007, para. 430, see *supra* note 68.

[73] ICTY, *Prosecutor v. Miroslav Kvočka*, Judgement, Appeals Chamber, IT−98−30/1−A, 28 February 2005, para. 98 (http://www. legal−tools. org/doc/006011/).

[74] See ICC, *The Prosecutor v. Thomas Lubanga Dyilo*, Decision on the confirmation of charges, Pre−Trial Chamber I, ICC−01/04−01/06−803−tENG, 29 January 2007, in particular paras. 329, 330 (http://www. legal−tools. org/doc/b7ac4f/).

4.2 "Indirect co-perpetration" and contribution "in any other way" to a common purpose (Article 25 (3)(d))

Article 25 (3)(d) provides for a supplementary form of liability complementing those found in articles 25 (3)(a) to (c). Under this provision, the Rome Statute holds accountable those who contribute *in any other way* to the commission of a crime by a group of persons acting with a common purpose. This mode of liability shares with "indirect co-perpetration" a notable feature: the requirement of a common plan. The "common purpose" referred to in Article 25 (3)(d) has been regarded as "functionally identical" to the notion of "common plan" as required for "indirect co-perpetration".[75] This means that the group of individuals must share a common purpose which contains, at minimum, a critical element of criminality, without necessarily envisaging the commission of any crimes. In addition, it is not necessary for the accused to have been part of the group.[76]

The main difference between "indirect co-perpetration" and Article 25 (3) (d) lies in their respective nature. In contrast with "indirect co-perpetration", Article 25 (3)(d) provides for a form of accomplice liability. This is reflected, in particular, in the required culpable state of mind. As per Article 25 (3)(d)(ii), contributions made with mere knowledge of the intention of the group to commit the crime suffice for the purposes of Article 25 (3)(d).[77]

With respect to the contribution level ("in any other way"), the accessorial

---

[75]   ICC, *The Prosecutor v. Callixte Mbarushimana*, Decision on the confirmation of charges, Pre-Trial Chamber I, ICC-01/04-01/10-465-Red, 16 December 2011, para. 271 (http://www. legal-tools. org/doc/63028f/) ("*Mbarushimana* Confirmation Decision").

[76]   *Mbarushimana* Confirmation Decision, paras. 272-275, see *supra* note 75. Pre-Trial Chamber I observed that art. 25 (3)(d) liability is the only way a person can be held criminally responsible for acting merely with knowledge of the intention of others (with the exception of command responsibility pursuant to art. 28 of the Rome Statute); hence the need not to distinguish between members and non-members of the group.

[77]   Art. 25 (3)(d) provides for two different mental elements (intent and knowledge), but in the alternative. Since knowledge of the group's criminal intentions is sufficient for criminal responsibility to be triggered, it is therefore not required for the contributor to have the intent to commit any specific crime: *Mbarushimana* Confirmation Decision, para. 289, see *supra* note 75.

nature of Article 25 (3) (d) implies a level of contribution necessarily lower than that required for forms of principal liability. [78] Hence, the necessary contribution under Article 25 (3) (d) must be less than essential, as required by "indirect co-perpetration". Yet, it would be absurd to accept that any and all contributions can trigger the application of Article 25 (3) (d). The contribution must bear, at a minimum, some importance. As eloquently observed by Pre—Trial Chamber I :

[w] ithout some threshold level of assistance, every landlord, every grocer, every utility provider, every secretary, every janitor or even every taxpayer who does anything which contributes to a group committing international crimes could satisfy the elements of 25 (3) (d) liability for their infinitesimal contribution to the crimes committed. [79]

Given the similarities between "indirect co-perpetration" and Article 25 (3) (d), it is not surprising that both modes are charged, and eventually confirmed, in the alternative. [80] A further example of the close interplay between "indirect co-perpetration" and Article 25 (3) (d) is the conviction of Germain Katanga under the latter mode while having been charged on the basis of the former mode. It must be recalled that Mr. Katanga and Mr. Ngudjolo had been committed jointly for trial as indirect co-perpetrators. During the deliberations phase, an examination of the evidence had revealed that Mr. Katanga's participation could be considered from a different perspective than "indirect co – perpetration", as a result of which Mr.

---

[78] *Mbarushimana* Confirmation Decision, paras. 278–279, see *supra* note 75.

[79] *Ibid.* , para. 277. Pre—Trial Chamber I's finding rests on art. 17, pursuant to which cases brought before the ICC must be of sufficient gravity. In Pre—Trial Chamber I's view, this provision results in not only crimes, but also *contributions* to crimes needing to reach a certain threshold of significance in order to be within the Court's ambit : *Mbarushimana* Confirmation Decision, para. 276, see *supra* note 75.

[80] See *e. g.* ICC, *The Prosecutor v. Charles Blé Goudé*, Decision on the confirmation of charges against Charles Blé Goudé, Pre—Trial Chamber I, ICC–02/11–02/11–186, 11 December 2014, para. 194 (http : // www. legal–tools. org/doc/0536d5/).

Katanga's case was severed from the case of Mathieu Ngudjolo. [81] Trial Chamber II could not find beyond reasonable doubt that the organization headed by Mr. Katanga was an organized apparatus of power, nor that Mr. Katanga wielded control over the organization such as to exert control over the crimes committed. [82] Yet, after having re—characterized the facts, [83] Trial Chamber II found the militia group headed by Germain Katanga to be a group sharing a common purpose, within the meaning of Article 25 (3)(d), [84] with Mr. Katanga having made a contribution that had a significant influence on the commission of the crimes charged. [85]

5. Conclusion

The present Article has attempted to outline the fundamentals of a mode of liability which gains increasing importance in ICC jurisprudence. "Indirect co—perpetration", despite not being expressly provided for in the Rome Statute, has been applied in a number of cases involving different types of organized criminality. "Indirect co—perpetration" has proven to be a flexible and suitable approach for addressing criminal responsibility in context of mass crimes. It has yet to be subject to appellate scrutiny.

As described above, "indirect co—perpetration" is conceptualized in the form of pyramids. The ICC does not have the longevity of the Cheops pyramids, and one would hope it never does. Notwithstanding, to address chaos, ICC jurisprudence has drawn inspiration from the remarkable architecture of pyramids: structure, linearity, consistency. The theory of "indirect co—perpetration", as embraced by the ICC jurisprudence, is no exception.

---

[81] See *supra* note 8.

[82] *Katanga* Trial Judgement, para. 1420, see *supra* note 31.

[83] Reg. 55 (1) of the Regulations of the Court: "In its decision under article 74, the Chamber may change the legal characterisation of facts to accord with the crimes under articles 6, 7 or 8, or to accord with the form of participation of the accused under articles 25 and 28, without exceeding the facts and circumstances described in the charges and any amendments to the charges. "

[84] *Katanga* Trial Judgement, para. 1665, see *supra* note 31.

[85] *Ibid.* , para. 1681.

PARTICIPATION OF VICTIMS IN PROCEEDINGS OF THE INTERNATIONAL CRIMINAL COURT

Judge Ines Peterson [*]

1. Introduction

Victims of crimes under international law enjoy unique rights of participation in criminal proceedings before the International Criminal Court ("ICC" or "Court"). The fundaments are laid down in the Rome Statute of the International Criminal Court ("ICC Statute") [1] and the ICC Rules of Procedure and Evidence ("Rules of Procedure"). [2] These provisions mirror recent trends on the international and national level according victims a more prominent voice in criminal proceedings. [3] Within this broad principle, however, most of the details on how exactly victims should be involved is unspecified and has been left to jurisprudential development.

Over the years, the Court has issued numerous decisions in this regard. [4] It has changed direction several times as to the scope and modalities of victim participation. The present contribution addresses some issues that have arisen in practice and

---

[*] Research Fellow, Humboldt-Universität Zu Berlin.

[1] Rome Statute of the International Criminal Court (adopted 17 July 1998, entered into force 1 July 2002), 2187 UNTS 90 ("ICC Statute").

[2] ICC Rules of Procedure and Evidence, ICC − ASP/1/3, at 10, and Corr. 1 (2002), U. N. Doc. PCNICC/2000/1/Add. 1 (2000) (https://www.icc−cpi.int/iccdocs/pids/legal−texts/rulesprocedureevidenceeng.pdf).

[3] See Elisabeth Baumgartner, "Aspects of Victim Participation in the Proceedings of the International Criminal Court", in *International Review of the Red Cross*, 2008, vol. 90, no. 870 ("Baumgartner"), pp. 409−410.

[4] See the following for a most instructive overview, which remains valid even in light of more recent ICC decisions: Baumgartner, see *supra* note 4, pp. 414−431; Christine Van den Wyngaert, "Victims before International Criminal Courts: Some Views and Concerns of an ICC Trial Judge", in *Case Western Reserve Journal on International Law* 2011, no. 1, pp. 481−486 ("Van den Wyngaert").

highlights the different degrees to which victims may take part in judicial activities at various ICC procedural stages ranging from investigations, pre—trial, trial and appeal.

2. Involvement of victims in providing information about crimes

Articles 15 (2) and 42 (1) of the ICC Statute allow victims of crimes potentially falling into the jurisdiction of the ICC to bring information concerning such crimes to the attention of the Court. This does not require a formal recognition by a decision of the Court regarding their victim status or right to participate. [5] In this respect, victims are treated no different from any other source of information that the ICC Prosecutor can rely on in order to assess whether there is cause for further action.

3. Involvement of victims at the investigatory and pre—trial Stage

The ICC Prosecutor can conduct investigations before and after authorization by the competent pre—trial chamber under Article 15 (4) of the ICC Statute: those before are called "preliminary examinations"[6] whereas those afterwards are formally called "investigations." The former are initiated *proprio motu* "on the basis of information of crimes within the jurisdiction of the Court."[7] The Prosecutor, "*shall* analyse the seriousness of the information received" and "*may* seek additional information" from various sources, including any "other reliable sources that he or she deems appropriate."[8] A formal investigation, on the other hand, is regulated by Articles 53 and 54 of the ICC Statute.

Article 15 (3) of the ICC Statute confers on victims the right to make submis-

---

[5]   ICC, *Situation in the Democratic Republic of the Congo*, Judgment on Victim Participation in the Investigation Stage of the Proceedings in the Appeal of the OPCD against the Decision of Pre—Trial Chamber I of 7 December 2007 and in the Appeals of the OPCD and the Prosecutor against the Decision of Pre—Trial Chamber I of 24 December 2007, Appeals Chamber, ICC-01/04 OA4 OA5 OA6, 19 December 2008, ("Appeals Chamber Decision of 19 December 2008"), para. 53 (http://www. legal—tools. org/doc/dca981/).

[6]   ICC Statute, see *supra* note 1, art. 15 (6).

[7]   *Ibid.*, art. 15 (1).

[8]   *Ibid.*, art. 15 (2); emphasis added.

sions to the pre-trial chamber concerning the transition from a "preliminary examination" to a formal "investigation" but, paradoxically, does not regulate how victims may influence prosecutorial investigations before or after that formal recognition. If at all, any participation rights of victims at the investigatory stage could only be found in Article 68 (3) of the ICC Statute, according to which "the Court shall permit their views and concerns to be presented and considered at stages of the proceedings determined to be appropriate by the Court. "

In 2006 and 2007, ICC pre-trial chambers issued a number of decisions granting victims potentially far-reaching rights to participate in investigations. The judges considered that the "personal interests" of victims—a term used in Article 68 (3) of the ICC Statute to denote a precondition for their participation in proceedings before the Court—were affected in a general manner at the investigatory stage because the expression of their views and concerns at this stage could serve to clarify the facts, identify and punish the perpetrators of crimes as well as request reparations for the harm suffered. [9] Consequently, victims would be entitled to present their views and concerns during investigations and file documents in this respect, which the Court would have to examine. [10] In principle, this would not only apply to victims in relation to a specific case, but also to victims affected by the investigation of an entire situation. [11]

---

[9] See, *e.g.*, ICC, *Situation in the Democratic Republic of the Congo*, Decision on the Applications for Participation in the Proceedings of VPRS 1, VPRS 2, VPRS 3, VPRS 4, VPRS 5 and VPRS 6, Pre-Trial Chamber I, ICC-01/04, 17 January 2006, ("Pre-Trial Chamber I Decision of 17 January 2006"), paras. 63, 72 ("http: //www. legal-tools. org/doc/2fe2fc/"). See also ICC, *Situation in the Democratic Republic of the Congo*, Decision on the Requests of the OPCD on the Production of Relevant Supporting Documentation Pursuant to Regulation 86 (2)(e) of the Regulations of the Court and on the Disclosure of Exculpatory Materials by the Prosecutor, Pre-Trial Chamber I, 7 December 2007, ICC-01/04, paras. 2-4 (http: //www. legal-tools. org/ doc/27da16/).

[10] Pre-Trial Chamber I Decision of 17 January 2006, see *supra* note 9, para. 71. However, this would not entail a right of victims to access "the record of the investigation. " Also see para. 59.

[11] Pre-Trial Chamber I Decision of 17 January 2006, see *supra* note 9, paras. 65-66, 68. For details on the distinction between cases and situations before the ICC: see Baumgartner, see *supra* note 4, p. 414.

In its decision of 19 December 2008, the Appeals Chamber rejected this interpretation. Notably, the Appeals Chamber held that the term "proceedings" used in Article 68 (3) of the ICC Statute requires a judicial cause pending before a chamber and would thus exclude investigations because the latter only amounted to "an inquiry conducted by the Prosecutor into the commission of a crime with a view to bringing justice to those deemed responsible. "[12] Provisions in the Rules of Procedure could not extend the scope of Article 68 (3) of the ICC Statute. [13] Investigations fell exclusively within the province of the ICC Prosecutor so that a chamber's acknowledgement of victims' rights to participate in investigations would unduly interfere with powers only vested in the prosecution. [14]

While the Appeals Chamber therefore declined to grant victims a general say in investigations, it did not rule out entirely that they could become involved at that stage. Notably, the Appeals Chamber confirmed that victims may take part in judicial proceedings arising in the course of investigations. [15] This finding is in line with its previous decision of 30 June 2008 allowing victims to present their views and con-

---

[12]   Appeals Chamber Decision of 19 December 2008, see *supra* note 5, para. 45.

[13]   *Ibid.* , paras. 46-49.

[14]   *Ibid.* , para. 52. See also ICC, *Situation in Darfur*, Judgment on Victim Participation in the Investigation Stage of the Proceedings in the Appeal of the OPCD against the Decision of Pre-Trial Chamber I of 3 December 2007 and in the Appeals of the OPCD and the Prosecutor against the Decision of Pre-Trial Chamber I of 6 December 2007, Appeals Chamber, ICC-02/05 OA OA2 OA3, 2 February 2009 ("Appeals Chamber Decision of 2 February 2009"), paras. 45-49, 52 (http: //www. legal-tools. org/doc/dca981/).

[15]   Appeals Chamber Decision of 19 December 2008, see *supra* note 5, paras. 56 ("[V] ictims are not precluded from seeking participation in any judicial proceedings, including proceedings affecting investigations, provided their personal interests are affected by the issues arising for resolution. "), 57 ("[T] he Appeals Chamber is not in a position to advise the Pre-Trial Chamber as to how applications for participations in judicial proceedings at the investigation stage should generally be dealt with in the future, in the absence of specific facts. It is for the Pre-Trial Chamber to determine how best to rule upon applications for participation, in compliance with the relevant provisions of the Court's texts. "). See also Appeals Chamber Decision of 2 February 2009, see *supra* note 14, paras. 56-57.

cerns with respect to the appeal in question. [16] In response to the Appeals Chamber Decision, Pre—Trial Chamber I concluded that it would not grant participatory rights to victims unless there was a specific judicial proceeding in which they would be able to participate. [17]

The ICC Statute itself expressly mentions one such proceeding. Articles 13 and 17 of the ICC Statute establish specific requirements for the Court's exercise of jurisdiction and the admissibility of a case. Article 19 (3) sentence 2 of the ICC Statute stipulates that victims may submit observations to the Court in proceedings with respect to its jurisdiction or challenges to the admissibility of a case. Another prominent example is the confirmation of charges hearing, which the competent pre—trial chamber shall hold pursuant to Article 61 (1) of the ICC Statute in particular once a suspect has been arrested and surrendered to the Court or makes a voluntary appearance. After the hearing, the pre—trial chamber is called upon to decide whether to confirm the charges contained in the prosecution's "indictment" [18] and to proceed with the case against the accused. According to Rule 92 (3) of the Rules of Procedure, the Court shall notify victims regarding its decision to hold a hearing on the confirmation of charges. In practice, victims have been allowed to attend these hearings and make statements there as well as to receive access to relevant public docu-

---

[16] ICC, *Situation in the Democratic Republic of the Congo*, Appeals Chamber, Decision on Victim Participation in the Appeal of the Office of Public Counsel for the Defence against Pre—Trial Chamber I's Decision of 7 December 2007 and in the Appeals of the Prosecutor and the Office of Public Counsel for the Defence against Pre—Trial Chamber I's Decision of 24 December 2007, ICC—01/04 OA 4 OA 5 OA6, 30 June 2008 ("Appeals Chamber Decision of 30 June 2008"), in particular paras. 88 – 103 (http: //www. legal – tools. org/doc/ 6aacb4/).

[17] ICC, *Situation in the Democratic Republic of the Congo*, Decision on Victims' Participation in Proceedings Relating to the Situation in the Democratic Republic of the Congo, Pre—Trial Chamber I, ICC—01/04, 11 April 2011 ("Pre—Trial Chamber I Decision of 11 April 2011"), para. 9 http: //www. legal—tools. org/doc/ bb2a9b/). See also ICC, *Situation in the Republic of Kenya*, Decision on Victims' Participation in Proceedings Related to the Situation in the Republic of Kenya, Pre—Trial Chamber II, ICC – 01/09, 3 November 2010, para. 9 (http: //www. legal—tools. org/doc/0e64a3/).

[18] At the ICC, an indictment is designated as "document containing the charges. "

ments. [19]

ICC jurisprudence still leaves a number of questions open, of which three command particular attention. The first concerns participatory rights enjoyed by victims of crimes that ultimately do not become the subject of a case before the ICC. In its decision of 30 June 2008, the Appeals Chamber was mindful of the fact that, at that time, the proceedings under consideration were still "in the situation phase", meaning that a specific suspect had yet to be identified. [20] This indicates that the Appeals Chamber does not have an issue *per se* with granting participatory rights to "situation victims" even if it is still unclear whether crimes from which they suffered will eventually be prosecuted. At time of writing, the Appeals Chamber has not yet had to decide whether this would also apply to preliminary examinations.

There are also no definitive appeal decisions on how to deal with victim applications once the situation phase transforms into a case against a particular accused. Where an arrest warrant was issued against an accused, some pre—trial chambers have accorded victim status only to individuals who could demonstrate a sufficient link between the harm they allegedly suffered and crimes contained in the arrest

---

[19] See, *e. g.*, ICC, *Situation in the Democratic Republic of the Congo in the Case of The Prosecutor v. Bosco Ntaganda*, Decision on Victims' Participation at the Confirmation of Charges Hearing and in the Related Proceedings, Pre—Trial Chamber II, 15 January 2014, ICC—01/04—02/06 ("Pre—Trial Chamber II Decision of 15 January 2014"), paras. 85—96 (http: //www. legal—tools. org/doc/0fdd1e/); ICC, *Situation in the Republic of Côte D'Ivoire in the Case of The Prosecutor v. Laurent Gbagbo*, Decision on Victims' Participation and Victims' Common Legal Representation at the Confirmation of Charges Hearing and in the Related Proceedings, Pre—Trial Chamber I, ICC—02/11—01/11, 4 June 2012 ("Pre—Trial Chamber I Decision of 4 June 2012"), paras. 48—60 ("http: //www. legal—tools. org/doc/0fdd1e/"); ICC, *Situation in the Democratic Republic of the Congo in the Case of The Prosecutor v. Thomas Lubanga Dyilo*, Decision on the Arrangements for Participation of Victims a/0001/06, a/0002/06 and a/0003/06 at the Confirmation Hearing, Pre—Trial Chamber I, ICC—01/ 04—01/06, 22 September 2006, pp. 7—8. For further details, in particular with respect to different sets of rights granted to anonymous and non—anonymous victims, see Héctor Olásolo and Alejandro Kiss, "The Role of Victims in Criminal Proceedings before the International Criminal Court", in *Revue Internationale de Droit Pénal* 2010, vol. 81 ("Olásolo and Kiss"), pp. 140—144.

[20] Appeals Chamber Decision of 30 June 2008, see *supra* note 16, para. 91.

warrant. [21] Other chambers took a broader approach by only requiring that applicants show *prima facia* harm they sustained as a result of a crime falling within the
jurisdiction of the Court. [22] The Appeals Chamber has been very clear that, after
the confirmation of charges against an accused, victim status and accompanying participatory rights could not be granted to individuals affected by matters unrelated to
the specific charges because from then on, the charges would define the issues to be
determined at trial. [23] It remains to be seen whether the Court will extend this finding *mutatis mutandis* to situations where only an arrest warrant or a summons to ap-

---

[21] See, *e. g.*, ICC, *Situation in the Democratic Republic of the Congo in the Case of The Prosecutor
v. Thomas Lubanga Dyilo*, Decision on the Applications for Participation in the Proceedings of a/0001/06, a/
0002/06 and a/0003/06 in the Case of the Prosecutor v. Thomas Lubanga Dyilo and of the Investigation in the
Democratic Republic of the Congo, Pre – Trial Chamber I, ICC – 01/04 – 01/06, 28 July 2006 (" Pre – Trial
Chamber I Decision of 28 July 2006"), pp. 8–9 (http: //www. legal–tools. org/doc/0f3b26/) ; ICC, *Situation
in the Democratic Republic of the Congo in the Case of The Prosecutor v. Thomas Lubanga Dyilo*, Decision on the
Applications for Participation in the Proceedings Submitted by VPRS 1 to VPRS 6 in the Case The Prosecutor
v. Thomas Lubanga Dyilo, Pre – Trial Chamber I, ICC – 01/04 – 01/06, 29 June 2006, pp. 6 – 8 (http: //
www. legal–tools. org/doc/431820/).

[22] See, *e. g.*, ICC, *Situation in the Democratic Republic of the Congo in the Case of The Prosecutor
v. Thomas Lubanga Dyilo*, Decision on Victims' Participation, Trial Chamber I, ICC–01/04–01/06, 18 January 2008 ("Trial Chamber I Decision of 18 January 2008"), paras. 93–95 (http: //www. legal–tools. org/doc/
4e503b/) ; ICC, *Situation in Uganda*, Decision on Victim's Participation in Proceedings Related to the Situation
in Uganda, Pre–Trial Chamber II, ICC–02/04, 9 March 2012, para. 26 (http: //www. legal–tools. org/doc/
26b39a/) ; ICC, *Situation in Uganda*, Decision on Victims' Applications for Participation 1/0010/06, a/
0064/06 to a/0070/06, a/0081/06 to a/0104/06 and a/0111/06 to a/0127/06, Pre–Trial Chamber II, 10
August 2007, ICC–02/04, paras. 12–14 (http: //www. legal–tools. org/doc/8f9181/). It has correctly been
pointed out that these different schools would most likely not lead to different outcomes in practice because even
chambers adopting the broader approach would ultimately limit victim participation by requiring that the personal
interests of the victim be affected by the specific proceedings. Olásolo and Kiss, p. 129, see *supra* note 19.

[23] ICC, *Situation in the Democratic Republic of the Congo – The Prosecutor v. Thomas Lubanga Dyilo*,
Judgment on the Appeals of The Prosecutor and The Defence against Trial Chamber I's Decision on Victims' Participation of 18 January 2008, Appeals Chamber, ICC–01/04–01/06 OA 9 OA 10, 11 July 2008, paras. 58,
62–65 (http: //www. legal–tools. org/doc/75cf1a/).

pear has yet been issued. [24]

The second and third issues are interrelated because they both concern the question as to whether victims can force the ICC to prosecute crimes. For victims affected by the investigation of a situation, this question could arise in general if the prosecution or the Court—the latter at the stage of the confirmation of charges—decides to exclude from a case crimes from which the victims suffered harm. Victims of crimes included in a case might also have an interest to have the charges extended, for example, by adding additional incidents or with respect to the legal qualification of the crimes charged.

Expressis verbis, the ICC Statute and the Rules of Procedure stop short of providing victims with a right to force a prosecution. Article 15 (6) of the ICC Statute requires the ICC Prosecutor only to inform those who provided information of a potential crime of a decision not to proceed with a formal investigation. Rule 92 (2) of the Rules of Procedure likewise only requires the Court to notify victims of any decision by the Prosecutor not to initiate an investigation or to prosecute. Articles 53 and 54 of the ICC Statute, governing investigations, mandate no participatory rights for victims.

The ICC regime differs in this respect from regulations in some national criminal

---

[24] In this respect, see ICC, *Situation in the Central African Republic in the Case of The Prosecutor v. Jean-Pierre Bemba Gombo*, Fourth Decision on Victims' Participation, Pre-Trial Chamber III, ICC-01/05-01/08, 12 December 2008 ("Pre-Trial Chamber III Decision of 12 December 2008"), paras. 62-64 (http://www. legal-tools. org/doc/1652d9/); finding that even before the confirmation of charges, the document containing the charges (*i. e.* indictment) limits the scope of the case and thus requires a link of victims applying for participation with respect to the charges. Similarly, ICC, *Situation in the Democratic Republic of the Congo in the Case of The Prosecutor v. Callixte Mbarushimana*, Decision on the 138 Applications for Victims' Participation in the Proceedings, Pre-Trial Chamber I, ICC-01/04-01/10, 11 August 2011, para. 21 (http://www. legal-tools. org/doc/17ef31/).

procedure codes. [25] Victims have been allowed, however, to file submissions at the confirmation of charges stage suggesting that the charges against the accused should be amended to include additional crimes and counts. [26] Such requests have, in practice, always been dismissed. [27] This may change in the future since recent decisions have expressed the view that, after the submission of an "indictment" for confirmation, it is the pre-trial chamber, not the prosecution, that is the custodian of the charges against an accused. [28] This concept, if it prevails, could imply a greater openness to submissions by victims as a legitimate aspect of the pre-trial chamber's authority to determine the scope of the charges.

4. Participation of victims in trial proceedings

The question of who qualifies as a victim, what specific rights of participation victims have and how such rights can be exercised becomes most prominent and con-

---

[25]　See Baumgartner, see *supra* note 3, pp. 426–427. See also, *e. g.*, *Strafprozessordnung in der Fassung der Bekanntmachung vom 7 April* 1987, Bundesgesetzblatt I, S. 1074, 1319 ("German Criminal Procedure Code (StPO)"), Section 172, which allows victims of a crime to request a court decision against prosecutorial decisions not to bring charges; available at: http: //www. gesetze-im-internet. de/englisch_ stpo/englisch_ stpo. html#p1436, accessed at 1 August 2017.

[26]　ICC, *Situation in the Republic of Kenya in the Case of The Prosecutor v. William Samoei Ruto, Henry Kiprono Kosgey and Joshua Arap Sang*, Decision on the "Renewed Request by the Victims' Representative for Authorisation by the Chamber to Make Submissions on Specific Issues of Law and / or Fact", Pre-Trial Chamber II, ICC-01/09-01/11, 22 September 2011, paras. 5–6, 10–12 (https: //www. legal-tools. org/uploads/tx_ltpdb/doc1235754_06. pdf).

[27]　See, *e. g.*, ICC, *Situation in the Republic of Kenya in the Case of The Prosecutor v. William Samoei Ruto, Henry Kiprono Kosgey and Joshua Arap Sang*, Decision on the "Request by the Victims' Representative for Authorisation to Make a Further Written Submission on the Views and Concerns of the Victims", Pre-Trial Chamber II, ICC – 01/09 – 01/11, 9 December 2011, paras. 16 – 19 (http: //www. legal – tools. org/doc/c092ce/); ICC, *Situation in the Democratic Republic of the Congo*, Decision on the Request of the Legal Representative of Victims VPRS 3 and VPRS 6 to Review an Alleged Decision of the Prosecutor not to Proceed, Pre-Trial Chamber I, ICC-01/04, 25 October, 2010 (http: //www. legal-tools. org/doc/6897f0/).

[28]　ICC, *Situation in the Central African Republic in the Case of The Prosecutor v. Jean – Pierre Bemba Gombo et al.*, Decision on the Submission of Auxiliary Documents, Trial Chamber VII, ICC-01/05-01/13, 10 June 2015, para. 12 (http: //www. legal-tools. org/doc/6a4ba2/): "the Statute foresees a shift of authority to define the factual scope of the case: while at the stage of submitting the [document containing the charges] this authority rests squarely with the Prosecution, at the confirmation stage, such authority passes over to the Pre-Trial Chamber. In other words, at the confirmation stage the Pre-Trial Chamber has the sole authority to define the parameters of the case for the purpose of ensuing trial proceedings. "

troversial once a case has been confirmed.

4. 1 Victim definition, identification and application procedure

The ICC Statute does not contain a definition of the term "victim" because the drafters could apparently not agree on such a definition at the Rome Conference in 1998. [29] Instead, the matter was left to the Rules of Procedure, which in Rule 85 stipulate that victims are "natural persons who have suffered harm as a result of the commission of any crime within the jurisdiction of the Court" and may further include organizations or institutions that have sustained direct harm to any of their property dedicated to religion, education, art or science or charitable purposes or to their historic monuments, hospitals and other places and objects for humanitarian purposes. This notion of victims is largely based on existing definitions in international law. [30]

ICC case law has so far mainly focused on natural persons as victims. In this context, the Court has encountered problems in particular regarding the proper identification of victim applicants. This is easily understandable given that ICC cases have to date concerned African countries where it may be difficult to obtain official documents proving identity. Accordingly, various forms of identification have been accepted, including documents pertaining to medical treatment, rehabilitation or education, church membership cards, employee identity cards, political party membership cards, pension booklets or even a signed declaration from two credible witnesses attesting to the identity of the applicant. [31] Victims under age are not *per se* excluded from applying for participation themselves but, depending on their maturity, may

---

[29]   See Baumgartner, see *supra* note 3, p. 417 with further references.

[30]   *Ibid.* , p. 417 with further references.

[31]   See, *e. g.* , ICC, *Situation in the Democratic Republic of the Congo in the Case of The Prosecutor v. Bosco Ntaganda*, Decision on Victims' Participation in Trial Proceedings, Trial Chamber VI, ICC-01/04-02/06 6 February 2015 ("Trial Chamber VI Decision of 6 February 2015") , para. 45 (https: //www. icc-cpi. int/pages/record. aspx? uri = 1915167) ; Trial Chamber I Decision of 18 January 2008, see *supra* note 23, paras. 87-88.

need to be represented by an adult acting for them. [32] ICC jurisprudence appears to be divided as to whether participatory rights may be granted on behalf of deceased victims. While some decisions have assumed so, [33] others have required applying relatives to demonstrate personal harm from the victim's death. [34]

Any participation of victims in ICC proceedings further requires their demonstration of relevant "harm". While Rule 85 (1) of the Rules of Procedure broadly refers to harm as a result of the commission "of any crime within the jurisdiction of the Court", it has already been mentioned that, after the confirmation of charges, only persons who potentially suffered harm from a crime, with which the accused is charged, could qualify as victims. This excludes, in particular, individuals that merely have an interest in evidence produced at trial because that evidence might be relevant to incidents not charged. [35] The Appeals Chamber has confirmed that "harm" within the meaning of Rule 85 (1) of the Rules of Procedure may encompass physical injuries, economic loss and emotional suffering—the latter potentially even stemming indirectly from harm suffered by others victims—provided that the ap-

---

[32] See, e. g. ICC, *Situation in the Democratic Republic of the Congo in the Case of The Prosecutor v. Germain Katanga and Mathieu Ngudjolo Chui*, Decision on the Treatment of Applications for Participation, Trial Chamber II, ICC-01/04-01/07, 26 February 2009 ("Trial Chamber II Decision of 26 February 2009"), paras. 38-39 (http://www.legal-tools.org/doc/1691ec/); ICC, *Situation in the Democratic Republic of the Congo in the Case of The Prosecutor v. Thomas Lubanga Dyilo*, Decision on the Applications by Victims to Participate in the Proceedings, Trial Chamber I, ICC-01/04-01/06, 15 December 2008 ("Trial Chamber I Decision of 15 December 2008"), paras. 94-95 (http://www.legal-tools.org/doc/9551a4/). See also Rule 89 (3) of the Rules of Procedure.

[33] See, e. g., ICC, *Situation in the Central African Republic in the Case of The Prosecutor v. Jean-Pierre Bemba Gombo*, Decision on 772 Applications by Victims to Participate in the Proceedings, Trial Chamber III, ICC-01/05-01/08, 18 November 2010 ("Trial Chamber III Decision of 18 November 2010"), para. 43 (http://www.legal-tools.org/doc/ccfc38/); Pre-Trial Chamber III Decision of 12 December 2008, see *supra* note 24, paras. 39-49.

[34] See, e. g., Trial Chamber VI Decision of 6 February 2015, see *supra* note 31, para. 48; ICC, *Situation in the Democratic Republic of the Congo in the Case of The Prosecutor v. Germain Katanga and Mathieu Ngudjolo Chui*, ICC, Public Redacted Version of the "Decision on the 97 Applications for Participation at the Pre-Trial Stage of the Case", Pre-Trial Chamber I, ICC-01/04-01/07, 10 June 2008 ("Pre-Trial Chamber I Decision of 10 June 2008"), paras. 62-63 (http://www.legal-tools.org/doc/87f4c3/).

[35] See Appeals Chamber Decision of 11 July 2008, see *supra* note 23, para. 64.

plicant demonstrates *personal* harm. [36] In line with this decision, victim status could probably be granted also to individuals injured while attempting to assist direct victims of crimes charged or to prevent such crimes. [37] In contrast, it would be too far-fetched to include persons who suffered harm from crimes committed by direct victims, for example child soldiers. [38]

ICC chambers have only required victims applying for participation in trial proceedings to show *prima facie* that they suffered harm sufficiently linked to the crimes with which the accused was charged. [39] The same test has been applied in relation to pre-trial proceedings. [40] This apparently means that the Court will normally not further assess the veracity of victim accounts, but grant participatory rights as long as

---

[36]   *Ibid.* , paras. 32–39 (finding, in particular, that, for example, parents of a child soldier could qualify as victims because they suffered personal harm from the recruitment of the child due to their close relationship). See also, *e. g.* , Pre-Trial Chamber II Decision of 15 January 2014, see *supra* note 19, paras. 28–32, 47–50. In the Darfur situation, the ICC was confronted with applications for participation by individuals who claimed to have suffered indirect economic harm from an attack allegedly attributable to the accused against a peace keeping mission in North Darfur because, as a result of this attack, the mission left the area and they lost their employment at the base. Pre-Trial Chamber I rejected these applications since it was not established that the attack led to the withdrawal of the peace keeping mission and, in any event, the harm suffered by the applicants was too remote from the alleged crimes to meet the requirements of Rule 85 (1) of the Rules of Procedure. See ICC, *Situation in Darfur, Sudan in the Case of The Prosecutor v. Abdallah Banda Abakaer Nourain and Saleh Mohammed Jerbo Jamus*, Decision on Victims' Participation at the Hearing on the Confirmation of the Charges, Pre-Trial Chamber I, ICC–02/05–03/09, 29 October 2010, paras. 4, 13–15 (http: //www. legal-tools. org/ doc/fbf657/).

[37]   See, *e. g.* , ICC, *Situation in the Democratic Republic of the Congo in the Case of The Prosecutor v. Thomas Lubanga Dyilo*, Public Redacted Version of "Decision on 'indirect victims' ", Trial Chamber I, ICC–01/04–01/06, 8 April 2009 ("Trial Chamber I Decision of 8 April 2009"), para. 51 (https: // www. legal-tools. org/doc/c1cf65/pdf/); Pre-Trial Chamber I Decision of 28 July 2006, see *supra* note 21, p. 9; Pre-Trial Chamber I Decision of 10 June 2008, see *supra* note 34, para. 66.

[38]   Trial Chamber I Decision of 8 April 2009, see *supra* note 37, para. 52.

[39]   See, *e. g.* , Trial Chamber VI Decision of 6 February 2015, see *supra* note 31, paras. 30, 36, 44, 50; ICC, *Situation in the Republic of Côte D'Ivoire in the Case of The Prosecutor v. Laurent Gbagbo*, Decision on Victim Participation, Trial Chamber I, ICC–02/11–01/11, 6 March 2015 ("Trial Chamber I Decision of 6 March 2015"), paras. 30, 36 (http: //www. legal-tools. org/doc/a62e6b/); Trial Chamber III Decision of 18 November 2010, see *supra* note 34, para. 38; Trial Chamber I Decision of 18 January 2008, see *supra* note 22, para. 99.

[40]   See, *e. g.* , Pre-Trial Chamber I Decision of 4 June 2012, see *supra* note 19, paras. 21, 31; Pre-Trial Chamber I Decision of 10 June 2008, see *supra* note 34, para. 67.

the information provided in the application seems to be generally plausible. [41] In particular, the defence can hardly succeed with challenging the participation of victims on the basis that their applications are not supported by evidence or hard to evaluate due to redactions for reasons of confidentiality. [42] This approach is understandable in light of constrained ICC resources as well as the general idea implemented in the ICC Statute that victims should have broad access to the Court. However, it creates the risk of allowing individuals official access to trial proceedings—along with providing them specific participatory rights set out in more detail below—without properly establishing that they actually meet the requirements of Rule 85 (1) of the Rules of Procedure. [43]

Rule 89 of the Rules of Procedure establishes the general procedure by which victims may be admitted to present their views and concerns in the proceedings. According to Rule 89 (1) of the Rules of Procedure, victims are supposed to

---

[41]　See, *e. g.*, Trial Chamber I Decision of 6 March 2015, see *supra* note 40, para. 36; Trial Chamber VI Decision of 6 February 2015, see *supra* note 31, para. 36; Trial Chamber III Decision of 18 November 2010, see *supra* note 33, para. 48; Trial Chamber I Decision of 18 January 2008, see *supra* note 23, para. 99; ICC, *Situation in Uganda in the Case The Prosecutor v. Dominic Ongwen*, Decision on Contested Victims' Applications for Participation, Legal Representation of Victims and Their Procedural Rights, Pre-Trial Chamber II, ICC-02/04-01/15, 27 November 2015 ("Pre-Trial Chamber II Decision of 27 November 2015") , para. 11 (http: // www. legal-tools. org/doc/95f763/) ; Pre-Trial Chamber II Decision of 15 January 2014, see *supra* note 19, paras. 19, 62. In the *Ntaganda* case, some victim applications have been rejected because it was found that the applicants "provided highly inconsistent information in the narrative of the events that cast doubts on the veracity of their applications and on the credibility of the victim applicants" : Pre-Trial Chamber II Decision of 15 January 2014, see *supra* note 19, para. 67.

[42]　See, *e. g.*, Pre-Trial Chamber II Decision of 27 November 2015, see *supra* note 41, paras. 10–14; Trial Chamber VI Decision of 6 February 2015, see *supra* note 31, para. 30; Trial Chamber III Decision of 18 November 2010, see *supra* note 33, paras. 49–61; Pre-Trial Chamber II Decision of 15 January 2014, see *supra* note 19, paras. 40–46, 51–57; Pre-Trial Chamber I Decision of 4 June 2012, see *supra* note 19, paras. 32–34.

[43]　For example, in the *Lubanga* case, the trial chamber retroactively revoked in the trial judgement several victim applicants' right to participate because the original assessment of their statements was found to have been incorrect. See ICC, *Situation in the Democratic Republic of the Congo in the Case of The Prosecutor v. Thomas Lubanga Dyilo*, Judgment Pursuant to article 74 of the Statute, Trial Chamber I, ICC-01/04-01/06, 14 March 2012, para. 484 (http: //www. legal-tools. org/doc/677866/) .

make a written application to the Registrar, who shall transmit it to the competent chamber. Rules 89 (2) and (4) of the Rules of Procedure quite clearly indicate that any decision on the acceptance or rejection of victim applications lies with the chamber. Nonetheless, in some instances, chambers have outsourced the assessment of whether the conditions under Rule 85 (1) of the Rules of Procedure were met to a common legal representative appointed for the applicants. [44] This approach has been criticized for unduly shifting responsibilities, which the ICC Statute assigns to the judges. [45]

ICC chambers have also taken different views on the need to revisit decisions granting victim status at the pre-trial stage. In some decisions it was held that victims authorized to participate in pre-trial proceedings would, as a rule, automatically be considered victims at trial. [46] In other cases, trial chambers conducted their own a-nalysis. [47]

4. 2 General restrictions on victims' participation

Pursuant to Rule 90 (2) of the Rules of Procedure, a chamber may, for the purpose of ensuring the effectiveness of the proceedings, request victims to choose a

---

[44]   See, e. g. , ICC, *Situation in the Republic of Kenya in the Case of The Prosecutor v. Francis Kirimi Muthaura and Uhuru Muigai Kenyatta*, Decision on Victims' Representation and Participation, Trial Chamber V, ICC-01/09-02/11, 3 October 2012 ("Trial Chamber V Decision of 3 October 2012 in Kenyatta"), paras. 22-24, 27-32, 36-37, 48-52 (http: //www. legal-tools. org/doc/535eee/); ICC, *Situation in the Republic of Kenya in the Case of The Prosecutor v. William Samoei Ruto and Joshua Arap Sang*, Decision on Victims' Representation and Participation, Trial Chamber V, ICC-01/09-01/11, 3 October 2012, paras. 23-25, 28-33, 37-38, 49-53 (http: //www. legal-tools. org/doc/e037cc/).

[45]   See David Donat-Cattin, "Article 68", in Otto Triffterer and Kai Ambos (eds.), *Rome Statute of the International Criminal Court*, 3rd edn. , Beck, Munich, 2016, marginal no. 8 fn. 13 ("Donat-Cattin").

[46]   See, e. g. , Trial Chamber I Decision of 6 March 2015, see *supra* note 39, para. 41; Trial Chamber II Decision of 26 February 2009, see *supra* note 32, paras. 10-12.

[47]   See, e. g. , Trial Chamber III Decision of 18 November 2010, see *supra* note 33, para. 38; ICC, *Situation in the Democratic Republic of the Congo in the Case of The Prosecutor v. Germain Katanga and Mathieu Ngudjolo Chui*, Decision on the Modalities of Victim Participation at Trial, Trial Chamber II, ICC-01/04-01/07, 22 January 2010 ("Trial Chamber II Decision of 22 January 2010"), paras. 57, 62 (http: //www. legal-tools. org/doc/8b6e01/); Trial Chamber I Decision of 15 December 2008, see *supra* note 32, paras. 54-59, 137. Similarly, Pre-Trial Chamber I Decision of 11 April 2011, see *supra* note 17, para. 16.

common legal representative. The ICC has mostly interpreted this rule to mean that victims do not have a right to present their views and concerns before the Court in person. [48] In practice, victims applying for participation have normally been assigned a legal representative of their choice or it was decided that they should be represented by the Office of Public Counsel for Victims ("OPCV"), which is a section acting under the authority of the ICC Registry. [49]

Moreover, it seems that the case law has come to distinguish between a victim's general admission to participate in the proceedings and his or her right to take action with respect to a specific procedural issue arising in the course of such proceedings. As regards the latter, victims should normally set out in a discrete written application the nature and detail of the proposed intervention and describe the way in which their personal interests are affected by the issue at stake. [50]

In line with Article 68 (3) sentence 1 of the ICC Statute, decisions on victim participation usually underscore that participation in the manner requested needs to be appropriate and consistent with the rights of the accused to a fair and expeditious

---

[48] See, e. g., Trial Chamber I Decision of 6 March 2015, see *supra* note 39, para. 60; Trial Chamber V Decision of 3 October 2012 in Kenyatta, see *supra* note 44, para. 20; Pre—Trial Chamber I Decision of 4 June 2012, see *supra* note 19, para. 35. But see ICC, *Situation in Uganda in the Case of The Prosecutor vs. Joseph Kony et al.* , Decision on Legal Representation, Appointment of Counsel for the Defence, Protective Measures and Time—Limit for Submission of Observations on Applications for Participation /0010/06, a/0064/06 to a/0070/ 06, a/0081/06 to a/0104/06 and a/0111/06 to a/0127/06, Pre—Trial Chamber II, ICC—02/04—01/05, 1 February 2007, para. 10 (http: //www. legal—tools. org/doc/03e64f/).

[49] See, e. g., Trial Chamber VI Decision of 6 February 2015, see *supra* note 31, paras. 52—54; Trial Chamber I Decision of 6 March 2015, see *supra* note 40, paras. 61—63; Pre—Trial Chamber II Decision of 15 January 2014, see *supra* note 19, para. 10; Pre—Trial Chamber I Decision of 4 June 2012, see *supra* note 19, paras. 42—45. It has been pointed out that the permanent appointment of the OPCV to represent victims in court proceedings deviates from the tasks originally envisaged for this unit under ICC regulations. See Donat—Cattin, see *supra* note 45, para. 28.

[50] See, e. g., Trial Chamber I Decision of 18 January 2008, see *supra* note 22, paras. 96, 101— 104. See also Trial Chamber III Decision of 18 November 2010, see *supra* note 33, para. 46; ICC, *Situation in the Democratic Republic of the Congo in the Case of The Prosecutor v. Thomas Lubanga Dyilo*, Judgment on the Appeal of Mr. Thomas Lubanga Dyilo against the Decision of Pre—Trial Chamber I entitled " Décision sur la demande de mise en liberté provisoire de Thomas Lubanga Dyilo", Appeals Chamber, ICC—01/04—01/06 (OA 7), 13 February 2007 ("Appeals Chamber Decision of 13 February 2007") , para. 44.

trial. [51] In particular, it has been held that victims are not parties to the proceedings and care should be taken to prevent them from taking on the role of a second prosecutor. [52] However, to date there seems to be no ICC decision which has specifically rejected victims' applications for participation due to potential detriments to the accused or the trial as such.

4.3 Specific participatory rights of victims

Victims have been granted various specific rights of participation in trial proceedings in particular with respect to access to documents and filings, appearance in court, examination of prosecution or defence witnesses, the making of statements during trial, and the presentation of own evidence.

Victims have been permitted access not only to public case material, but also information classified as confidential by the prosecution, defence or the Court provided they could demonstrate a material relevance of the information to their personal interests. [53] In principle, this regime has also been applied to victims appearing as witnesses in trial proceedings. [54] While direct access to ICC materials will normally be granted only to the victims' legal representative, some decisions have expressly allowed the legal representative to discuss even confidential information obtained from such access with their clients despite the fact that this could create the risk of dispersing it to a broader audience because some victims may not be aware of or feel bound by confidentiality requirements. [55]

---

[51] See, e.g. , Trial Chamber I Decision of 18 January 2008, see *supra* note 22, para. 104.

[52] See, e.g. , Trial Chamber II Decision of 22 January 2010, see *supra* note 47, para. 75.

[53] See, e.g. , Trial Chamber VI Decision of 6 February 2015, see *supra* note 31, para. 55; Trial Chamber V Decision of 3 October 2012 in Kenyatta, see *supra* note 44, paras. 63, 65-67; Trial Chamber I Decision of 18 January 2008, see *supra* note 22, para. 106.

[54] See, e.g. , Trial Chamber II Decision of 22 January 2010, see *supra* note 47, paras. 108-125.

[55] See, e.g. , Pre-Trial Chamber II Decision of 27 November 2015, see *supra* note 42, paras. 29-31; Trial Chamber II Decision of 22 January 2010, see *supra* note 47, paras. 111-112; ICC, *Situation in the Democratic Republic of the Congo in the Case of The Prosecutor v. Germain Katanga and Mathieu Ngudjolo Chui*, Decision on Limitations of Set of Procedural Rights for Non-Anonymous Victims, Pre-Trial Chamber I, ICC-01/04-01/07, 30 May 2008, paras. 21-26, pp. 12-13 (http: //www. legal-tools. org/doc/e53882/).

Victims generally admitted for participation at trial have been allowed to present their views on the case in court especially through opening or closing statements, normally to be given by their legal representative. [56] Depending on the demonstration of personal interests and a specific request to the trial chamber, legal representatives of victims have also been permitted to make submissions on evidence produced by the parties at trial or to put questions to a witness. [57] Participation of victims may extend to closed and *ex parte* hearings or confidential / *ex parte* written submissions. [58]

In addition, victims have been allowed to tender evidence, including evidence pertaining to the guilt or innocence of the accused. [59] Accordingly, victim participants may, for example, present their own witnesses at trial. In some decisions it was stressed, however, that this should not lead to a duplication of prosecution evidence. [60] The *Lubanga* case provides an example of how difficult it can be in this respect to reconcile victim participation with the rights of the accused. In that case, the trial chamber allowed victims to present evidence regarding facts and circumstances—as well as arguably charges—not contained in the "indictment." [61] This

---

[56] See, *e. g.*, Trial Chamber V Decision of 3 October 2012 in Kenyatta, see *supra* note 44, para. 72; Trial Chamber II Decision of 22 January 2010, see *supra* note 47, para. 68; Trial Chamber I Decision of 18 January 2008, see *supra* note 22, para. 117.

[57] See, *e. g.*, Trial Chamber V Decision of 3 October 2012 in Kenyatta, see *supra* note 44, paras. 73-75; Trial Chamber II Decision of 22 January 2010, see *supra* note 47, paras. 72-78; Trial Chamber I Decision of 18 January 2008, see *supra* note 22, paras. 108-109. *See also* Rule 91 (3) of the Rules or Procedure and Evidence.

[58] See, *e. g.*, Trial Chamber V Decision of 3 October 2012 in Kenyatta, see *supra* note 44, para. 70; Trial Chamber I Decision of 18 January 2008, see *supra* note 22, paras. 113-114.

[59] See, *e. g.*, Trial Chamber V Decision of 3 October 2012 in Kenyatta, see *supra* note 44, para. 76; Trial Chamber II Decision of 22 January 2010, see *supra* note 47, paras. 81-101; Trial Chamber I Decision of 18 January 2008, see *supra* note 22, para. 108. The Appeals Chamber has confirmed this jurisprudence in general terms. See Appeals Chamber Decision of 11 July 2008, see *supra* note 23, paras. 93-105.

[60] See, *e. g.*, Trial Chamber II Decision of 22 January 2010, see *supra* note 47, para. 96.

[61] For examples, *see* Luke Moffett, "Meaningful and Effective? Considering Victims' Interests Through Participation at the International Criminal Court", in *Criminal Law Forum*, 2015, vol. 26, pp. 269-270 (with further references) ("Moffett").

practice apparently continued even after the Appeals Chamber had found that the allegations against the accused could not be broadened based on such evidence. [62] Ultimately, the trial chamber therefore heard evidence that it was not allowed to include in its determination on the responsibility of the accused. This begs the question of whether this evidence should have been admitted at all.

ICC chambers have acknowledged that participation of victims who wish to remain anonymous, for example due to security concerns, could be prejudicial to a fair trial for the accused. [63] Nonetheless, it has not yet been expressly ruled out that any of the above-mentioned rights could also be granted to victims whose identity remains undisclosed in particular to the defence. [64]

5. Participation of victims in appeal proceedings

Victims have been granted the right to join appellate proceedings, provided that the issue under litigation affected their personal interests and it seemed appropriate to allow their participation. [65] The Appeals Chamber has stressed that it will assess such requirements on a case-by-case basis without being bound by previous deter-

---

[62] See ICC, *Situation in the Democratic Republic of the Congo-The Prosecutor v. Thomas Lubanga Dyilo*, Judgment on the Appeals of Mr Lubanga Dyilo and the Prosecutor against the Decision of Trial Chamber I of 14 July 2009 entitled "Decision giving notice to the parties and participants that the legal characterisation of the facts may be subject to change in accordance with Regulation 55 (2) of the Regulations of the Court", Appeals Chamber, ICC-01/04-01/06 OA 15 OA 16, 8 December 2009, paras. 88-98 (http://www.legal-tools.org/doc/40d015/). See also ICC Statute, Art. 74 (2) sentence 2. For examples from the trial proceedings, see Moffett, see *supra* note 61, p. 270. In the aforementioned *Lubanga* decision, the Appeals Chamber arguably left open any further discussion on bringing additional charges with respect to crimes based on evidence heard at trial (paras. 99-111).

[63] See, *e. g.*, Trial Chamber I Decision of 15 December 2008, see *supra* note 32, paras. 123-132; Trial Chamber I Decision of 18 January 2008, see *supra* note 22, para. 131.

[64] *Ibid.* Also, ICC, *Situation in Uganda in the Case The Prosecutor v. Dominic Ongwen*, Decision on Disclosure of Victims' Identities, Trial Chamber IX, ICC-02/04-01/15, 17 June 2016, paras. 11-14 (http://www.legal-tools.org/doc/71978c/).

[65] See Appeals Chamber Decision of 30 June 2008, see *supra* note 16, paras. 88-103; ICC, *Situation in the Democratic Republic of the Congo in the Case of The Prosecutor v. Thomas Lubanga Dyilo*, Decision of the Appeals Chamber on the Joint Application of Victims a/0001/06 to a/0003/06 and a/0105/06 concerning the "Directions and Decision of the Appeals Chamber" of 2 February 2007, Appeals Chamber, ICC-01/04-01/06 OA 8, 13 June 2007, paras. 23-29 (http://www.legal-tools.org/doc/b3dad9/).

minations made at first instance. [66]

Arguably the most important question is whether victims may appeal a trial judgment on the merits if it results in a full or partial acquittal of the accused or leads to a sentence considered too lenient. However, victims have been granted the right to participate in proceedings before the Appeals Chamber following appeals launched by the parties in order to present their views and concerns. [67]

6. Conclusion

The express acknowledgement in the ICC Statute of victim participation in criminal proceedings before the Court was initially hailed as an important instrument of giving victims a proper voice in the prosecution of most heinous crimes. The general idea behind this applause appears to be that involving victims in criminal proceedings may move them out of the corner of being treated simply as a source of evidence, thereby enhancing their position as individuals and ultimately promote justice and reconciliation by providing a more meaningful avenue for victims and accused to interact before the court.

ICC jurisprudence has come a long way to fill the gaps in the ICC Statute and the Rules of Procedure as to how exactly victim participation should look like in practice. Many but not all issues have been resolved. Most importantly, it needs to be noted that given the macro-criminality that the ICC is dealing with, there are normally hundreds if not thousands of victims wishing to participate in proceedings. The timely assessment of their applications not only puts a strain on the limited court re-

---

[66] See Appeals Chamber Decision of 30 June 2008, see *supra* note 16, para. 88; Appeals Chamber Decision of 13 February 2007, see *supra* note 50, paras. 40, 43.

[67] See ICC, *Situation in the Central African Republic in the Case of The Prosecutor v. Jean-Pierre Bemba Gombo*, Decision on the Participation of Victims in the Appeal against Trial Chamber III's "Judgment pursuant to article 74 of the Statute", Appeals Chamber, ICC-01/05-01/08 A, 15 April 2016 (http://www.legal-tools.org/doc/7a9d04/); ICC, *Situation in the Democratic Republic of the Congo in the Case of The Prosecutor v. Thomas Lubanga Dyilo*, Decision on the Participation of Victims in the Appeals against Trial Chamber I's Conviction and Sentencing Decisions, Appeals Chamber, ICC-01/04-01/06 A4, A 5, A6, 13 December 2012 (https://www.icc-cpi.int/Pages/record.aspx? docNo=ICC-01/04-01/06-2951).

sources, but may impact on the rights of the accused, in particular where applications are redacted for reasons of confidentiality. [68] This creates the risk of allowing participation of individuals unknown to the defence who should perhaps not be given access to the proceedings.

Whether or not victim participation in criminal proceedings in general or as interpreted in ICC case law truly provides victims with a meaningful role or better understanding of a case still remains to be seen. [69]

---

[68] For further considerations in this regard, Van den Wyngaert, see *supra* note 4, p. 488.

[69] *Ibid.*, pp. 489–496.

SOME LEGAL ISSUES ON DISQUALIFICATION OF JUDGES IN INTERNATIONAL CRIMINAL TRIBUNALS

Associate Professor Yang Lijun *

1. Brief history and the legal framework

The possibility to secure disqualification or recusal of judges or arbitrators is not only a long established right of the parties to a litigation, but it also promotes public trust in the judicial system and facilitates fair trial. Judicial disqualification can be traced back to ancient times. In 530 A. D. , the Justinian Code was amended to state:

It is the clearest right under general provisions laid down from the exalted seat, that before hearings litigants may recuse judges. A judge being so recused, the parties have to resort to chosen arbitrators, before whom they assert their rights. Although a judge has been appointed by imperial power yet because it is our pleasure that all litigations should proceed without suspicion, let it be permitted to him, who thinks the judge under suspicion to recuse him before issue be joined, so that the cause go to another; the right to recuse having been held out to him [...]. [1]

---

* Senior Research Fellow at the Erasmus China Law Centre, Rotterdam, Netherlands, a board member of the Forum on International Criminal Law and Humanitarian Law, Brussels, Belgium, Associate Professor of International Law at the International Law Institute of the Chinese Academy of Social Science.

[1] Codex of Justinian, lib. III, title 1, No. 16.

It is clear that the threshold for disqualification at that time was very low. Therefore, so long as the judges or arbitrators were "under suspicion", the litigants could exercise their right to disqualify them.

The common law legal system follows the principle of natural justice whereby "*Nemo iudex in causa sua*", that is, no person can judge a case in which they have an interest. In 1609, Sir Edward Coke in *Dr. Bonham's Case* claimed: "No man shall be a judge in his own case". [2] In the common law legal system, a judge may be removed for having an "interest" in the outcome of a case. In judicial practice, an "interest" includes but is not limited to situations where the judge was (is) a counsel or witness for either party, if he is a relative to either party, if he has a financial benefit from the outcome of a case, etc.

At the present time, almost all domestic laws or regulations in the world have incorporated the right to seek disqualification or recusal of judges as a basic requirement of due process for a fair trial. The same is true for international criminal tribunals. Although the standards in different jurisdictions vary, the threshold for disqualification of a judge is rather high in international judicial practice.

Rule 15 (A) of the Rules of Procedure and Evidence ("RPE") of the International Criminal Tribunal for the former Yugoslavia ("ICTY") provided that:

A Judge may not sit on a trial or appeal in any case in which the Judge has a personal interest or concerning which the Judge has or has had any association which might affect his or her impartiality. The Judge shall in any such circumstance withdraw, and the President shall assign another Judge to the case. [3]

---

[2] *Dr. Bonham's Case*, 77 Eng. Rep. 646, 652 (1609).

[3] Rule 15 (A), Rules of Procedure and Evidence ("RPE") of the International Criminal Tribunal for the former Yugoslavia, IT/32/Rev. 50, 8 July 2015 (http: //www. icty. org/x/file/Legal%20Library/Rules _ procedure_ evidence/150710-it-282-en. pdf).

The ICTY Appeals Chamber in *Furundžija* observed, in respect of Rule 15 (A), that a judge is not impartial if it is shown that actual bias exists. Further, there is an unacceptable appearance of bias if:

i) A Judge is a party to the case, or has a financial or proprietary interest in the outcome of a case, or if the Judge's decision will lead to the promotion of a cause in which he or she is involved, together with one of the parties. Under these circumstances, a Judge's disqualification from the case is automatic; or

ii) The circumstances would lead a reasonable observer, properly informed, to reasonably apprehend bias. [4]

Turning to the International Criminal Court ("ICC"), Article 41 (2) of the Rome Statute stipulates that:

(a) A judge shall not participate in any case in which his or her impartiality might reasonably be doubted on any ground. A judge shall be disqualified from a case in accordance with this paragraph if, *inter alia*, that judge has previously been involved in any capacity in that case before the Court or in a related criminal case at the national level involving the person being investigated or prosecuted. A judge shall also be disqualified on such other grounds as may be provided for in the Rules of Procedure and Evidence. [5]

In addition, Rule 34 of the Rules of Procedure of the ICC ("ICC Rules") provides that grounds for disqualifying a judge include, *inter alia*:

---

[4] ICTY, *Prosecutor v Anto Furundžija*, Judgement, Appeals Chamber, IT-95-17/1-A, 21 July 2000, para. 189 (https://www.legal-tools.org/en/doc/660d3f/) (*"Furundžija* Appeal Judgement").

[5] Rome Statute of the International Criminal Court (adopted 17 July 1998, entered into force 1 July 2002), 2187 UNTS 90 ("ICC Statute").

(a) Personal interest in the case, including a spousal, parental or other close family, personal or professional relationship, or a subordinate relationship, with any of the parties;

(b) Involvement, in his or her private capacity, in any legal proceedings initiated prior to his or her involvement in the case, or initiated by him or her subsequently, in which the person being investigated or prosecuted was or is an opposing party;

(c) Performance of functions, prior to taking office, during which he or she could be expected to have formed an opinion on the case in question, on the parties or on their legal representatives that, objectively, could adversely affect the required impartiality of the person concerned;

(d) Expression of opinions, through the communications media, in writing or in public actions, that, objectively, could adversely affect the required impartiality of the person concerned. [6]

2. High threshold: presumption of impartiality

The ICTY's Appeals Chamber has always held that there is a presumption of impartiality which attaches to any judge of the Tribunal; this has been consistently upheld and emphasized in the Tribunal's jurisprudence. [7] Thus, it cannot be easily

---

[6] Rule 34, Rules of Procedure and Evidence, the International Criminal Court (ICC), ICC–ASP/1/ 3 and Corr. 1 ("ICC RPE").

[7] *Furundžija* Appeal Judgement, para. 196, see *supra* note 5; ICTY, *Prosecutor v. Radovan Karadšić*, Decision on Motion to Disqualify Judge Picard and Report to the Vice–President Pursuant to Rule 15 (B)(ii), Chamber Convened by Order of Vice – President, IT – 95 – 05/18 – PT, 22 July 2009, para. 17, (http: // www. icty. org/ x/ cases/ karadzic/ custom4/ en/ 090722. pdf).

rebutted. [8] Consequently, the party moving for disqualification bears the burden to adduce sufficient and reliable evidence that the judge is not impartial. [9] It is crystal clear that there is a high threshold to reach in order to rebut the presumption of impartiality, and therefore to disqualify a judge. The reasonable apprehension of bias must be "firmly established". [10] This high threshold is required as "while any real or apparent bias on the part of a Judge undermines confidence in the administration of justice, so too would disqualifying Judges on the basis of unfounded allegations of bias": no judge may be disqualified on the basis of sweeping or abstract allegations that are neither substantiated nor detailed to rebut the presumption of impartiality. [11]

This presumption is based on the following considerations. First, requirements

---

[8] ICTR, *Prosecutor v. Tharcisse Renzaho*, Judgement, Appeals Chamber, ICTR-97-31-A, I April 2011, para 21 (https://www.legal-tools.org/en/doc/0abb32/) ("*Renzaho* Appeal Judgement"); ICTR, *Prosecutor v. Ferdinand Nahimana*, Judgement, Appeals Chamber, ICTR-96-11-A, 28 November 2007, para. 48 (https://www.legal-tools.org/en/doc/04e4f9/) ("*Nahimana* Appeal Judgement"); ICTY, *Prosecutor v. Stanislav Galić*, Judgement, Appeals Chamber, IT-98-29-A, 30 November 2006, para. 41 (https://www.legal-tools.org/en/doc/c81a32/) ("*Galić* Appeal Judgement"); ICTR, *Prosecutor v. Jean-Paul Akayesu*, Appeal Judgement, Appeals Chamber, ICTR-96-04, 1 June 2001, para. 91 (http://jrad.unmict.org/webdrawer/webdrawer.dll/webdrawer/search/rec&sm_ncontents=ictr-96-4&sm_udf4 = * english * &sortd1 = rs_datecreated&count&template=reclist) ; ICTY, *Prosecutor v Zejnil Delalić et al*, Judgement, Appeals Chamber, IT-96-21-A, 20 February 2001, para. 707 (https://www.legal-tools.org/en/doc/051554/) ("*Delalić et al* Appeal Judgement") ; *Prosecutor v. Furundžija*, Appeal Judgement, paras. 196-197, see *supra* note 5.

[9] ICTR, *Prosecutor v. Renzaho* Appeal Judgement, para. 23, see *supra* note 8; ICTR, *Prosecutor v. Francois Karera*, Judgement, Appeals Chamber, ICTR-01-74-A, 2 February 2009, para. 254 (http://unictr.unmict.org/sites/unictr.org/files/case-documents/ictr-01-74/appeals-chamber-judgements/en/090202.pdf) ; ICTR, *Prosecutor v. Nahimana* Appeal Judgment, para. 48, see *supra* note 8; ICTR, *Prosecutor v. Eliézer Niyitegeka*, Judgement, ICTR-96-14-A, 9 July 2004, para. 45, (http://unictr.unmict.org/sites/unictr.org/files/case-documents/ictr-96-14/appeals-chamber-judgements/en/040709.pdf) ; ICTR, *Prosecutor v. Georges Rutaganda*, Judgement, Appeals Chamber, ICTR-96-3, 26 May 2003, para. 42 (http://unictr.unmict.org/sites/unictr.org/files/case-documents/ictr-96-3/appeals-chamber-judgements/en/030526.pdf) ("*Rutaganda* Appeal Judgement") ; *Prosecutor v. Furundžija*, Appeal Judgement, para. 197, see *supra* note 4.

[10] *Prosecutor v. Furundžija* Appeal Judgement, para. 197, see *supra* note 4.

[11] *Prosecutor v. Renzaho* Appeal Judgement, para. 23, see *supra* note 9; *Rutaganda Appeal Judgement*, para. 43, see *supra* note 12; ICTY, *Prosecutor v. André Ntagerura et al*, Judgement, Appeals Chamber, ICTR-99-46-A, 7 July 2006, para. 135, (http://www.legal-tools.org/doc/816b44/).

for candidates chosen to become international judges are very demanding. For example, under Article 36 (3) (a) of the Rome Statute of the ICC, "The judges shall be chosen from among persons of high moral character, impartiality and integrity who possess the qualifications required in their respective States for appointment to the highest judicial offices. "[12] Second, an international judge is nominated, among all the other domestic candidates, by his or her country after very careful scrutiny. While nominees do not represent their countries politically, their performances reflect the highest academic and judicial level of their respective states. Third, the election of judges involves complex procedures. We can take the example of the election of judges in the ICTY. After nomination by States, a list of the candidates was submitted to the UN Security Council for review. Thereafter, the President of the Security Council transmitted the list of candidates to the General Assembly for election. The candidates who received an absolute majority of the votes were declared elected. [13] Fourth, the judicial candidate is expected to have established competence and extensive professional experience in relevant areas of criminal law and/or international law, such as international humanitarian law and human rights law. [14] All of this indicates not merely that candidates should be experts in legal norms and have practical experience, but also implies a deep understanding and adherence to professional ethics. For instance, judges should not discuss their ideas with persons not involved in their case; they should not disclose discussions arising from judicial deliberation to third parties; and they should not meet with members of the media unless duly authorised. Finally, after being elected, international judges, before taking up their duties, are required to make solemn declarations that they will perform their duties

---

[12]　Art. 36 (3) (a) of the ICC Statute, see *supra* note 5.

[13]　Art. 13 *bis*, the Statute of the International Criminal Tribunal for the former Yugoslavia as amended (http://www. icty. org/x/file/Legal%20Library/Statute/statute_sept09_en. pdf) ("ICTY Statute"). Art. 13 *bis* was added on 14 August 2002, through UN Security Council Resolution 1431 (2002), S/RES/1431 (2002).

[14]　For example, Art. 13 of the Statute of the ICTY, see *supra* note 13.

and exercise their powers honourably, faithfully, impartially and conscientiously. [15]
This was affirmed in *Galić*:

> Judges' training and professional experience engrain in them the capacity to
> put out of their mind evidence other than that presented at trial in rendering a
> verdict. Judges who serve as fact−finders may often be exposed to information a-
> bout the cases before them either in the media or, in some instances, from con-
> nected prosecutions. The Bureau is not of the view that Judges should be dis-
> qualified simply because of such exposure ... The need to present a reasoned
> judgement explaining the basis of their findings means that Judges at the Tribu-
> nal are forced to confine themselves to the evidence in the record in reaching
> their conclusions. [16]

With such a high standard of impartiality, the instances of success in motions to
disqualify the judges of international criminal tribunals are rare. In *Hadšić*, one of the
last ICTY cases, the Defence filed a "Motion for Voluntary Withdrawal or Disqualification of Judges from Adjudication of Motion to Proceed with the Defence case" alle-
ging that the three judges of Trial Chamber II hearing the case had the appearance of
bias. [17] The Defence argued that the Motion to Proceed had "a substantial impact
on the continuation of the present proceedings and, in turn, on the Judges' own ten-

---

[15]　For example, Rule 14 of the RPE of the ICTY, see *supra* note 3.

[16]　ICTY, *Prosecutor v. Stanislav Galić*, Bureau's Decision on Galić's Application Pursuant to Rule 15
(B), Bureau, IT−98−29−T, 28 March 2003, para. 16 (http://www. icty. org/case/galic/4). This paragraph was referred to in *Prosecutor v. Ratko Mladić*, Order Denying Defence Motion pursuant to Rule 15 (B)
seeking Disqualification of Presiding Judge Alphons Orie and for a Stay of Proceedings, President, IT−09−92−
T, 15 May 2012, para 23 (Public Redacted Annex) (http://www. icty. org/x/cases/mladic/presord/en/
120515. pdf).

[17]　ICTY, *Prosecutor v. Goran Hadšić*, Motion for voluntary withdrawal or disqualification of Judges from
Adjudication of Motion to proceed with the Defence Case, Trial Chamber II, IT−04−75−T, 24 March 2015, paras. 15, 16 (https://www. legal−tools. org/doc/a0df78/pdf/).

ure. "[18] This, the Defence asserted, created in the judges a financial, economic, and professional interest in the disposition of the Motion to Proceed. [19] The matter was heard by Trial Chamber II, without changes in composition. The judges rejected the motion and pointed out that judges enjoy a presumption of impartiality, and that there is a high threshold to reach in order to rebut this presumption. [20] This high threshold is required because:

> just as any real appearance of bias [on] the part of a judge undermines confidence in the administration of justice, it would be as much of a potential threat to the interests of the impartial and fair administration of justice if judges were to disqualify themselves on the basis of unfounded and unsupported allegations of apparent bias. [21]

As for the alleged interest of those judges, the Chamber recalled the findings in *Brđanin* that:

> All Judges have, as a matter of course, an interest in ensuring the integrity of the proceedings in which they are involved. Such an interest is not . . . a personal interest, but a professional interest. It includes the interest to ensure that all proceedings before the Tribunal are conducted impartially and in accordance with international standards of due process and fair trial rights. The interest of

---

[18] *Ibid.*, para. 14.

[19] *Ibid.*, paras. 1, 15-16.

[20] ICTY, *Prosecutor v. Goran Hadšić*, Trial Chamber Decision on Motion for voluntary withdrawal or disqualification of Judges from adjudication of Motion to proceed with the Defence Case, Trial Chamber, IT-04-75-T, 21 April 2015, para. 11 fn 35 (http: //www. icty. org/x/cases/hadzic/tdec/en/150421. pdf); see also ICTY, *Prosecutor v. Nikola Šainović et al*, Judgement, Appeals Chamber, IT-05-87-A, 23 January 2014, para. 181. (https: //www. legal-tools. org/en/doc/81ac8c/); *Furundžija* Appeal Judgement, paras. 196-197, see *supra* note 5.

[21] *Delalić et al* Appeal Judgement, para. 707, see *supra* note 8.

Judges is not just to get the trial done, but rather to get it done fairly ... It is expected that Judges will not shy away from making the appropriate finding whatever it may be. [22]

Thus, it is well established in the jurisprudence of international criminal tribunals that there is a "presumption of impartiality" which attaches to a judge, and that in the absence of evidence to the contrary, it must be assumed that the Judges of the International Tribunal "can disabuse their minds of any irrelevant personal beliefs or predispositions"; in short "[t] here is a high threshold to reach in order to rebut the presumption of impartiality". [23]

3. Unacceptable appearance of bias

According to the jurisprudence of the ICTY, there is a two—pronged test for judicial bias. One is the actual bias and the other is unacceptable appearance of bias. Actual bias is a matter of evidence. As for what is the unacceptable appearance, it should be examined on a case by case basis. However, the Appeals Chamber provided some guidance on this issue. In *Furundžija*, the Appeals Chamber explained that there is an unacceptable appearance of bias if:

i) a judge is a party to the case, or has a financial or proprietary interest in the outcome of a case, or if the Judge's decision will lead to the promotion of a cause in which he or she is involved, together with one of the parties; Under these circumstances, a Judge's disqualification from the case is automatic. or ii) the circumstances would lead a reasonable observer, properly informed, to reasonably apprehend bias.

In terms of the second branch of the second principle, the Appeals Cham-

---

[22] ICTY, *Prosecutor v. Radoslav Brđanin*, Decision on Application for Disqualification, Bureau, IT—99-36-R77, 11 June, 2004, para. 19 (http: //www. icty. org/x/cases/brdanin/tdec/en/040611. htm).

[23] *Furundžija* Appeal Judgement, para. 188, see *supra* note 4.

ber adopts the approach that the 'reasonable person must be an informed person, with knowledge of all the relevant circumstances, including the traditions of integrity and impartiality that form a part of the background and apprised also of the fact that impartiality is one of the duties that Judges swear to uphold. [24]

As to the "circumstances" that may lead to a disqualification, the Appeals Chamber has held that "a Judge should not only be subjectively free from bias, but there should also be nothing in the surrounding circumstances which objectively gives rise to an appearance or a reasonable apprehension of bias".

3. 1 Promotion of a cause

One of the indicia of unacceptable bias is when the judge's decision will lead to the promotion of a cause in which he or she is involved, together with one of the parties. The Appeals Chamber of the ICTY upheld a strict standard in its judicial practice. In *Furundžija*, the appellants challenged Judge Mumba's impartiality in a case involving rape. The complaint was that because Judge Mumba had acted as a representative of her country on the United Nations Commission on the Status of Women (UNCSW), this evidenced bias on the issue; the defence sought her disqualification. The Appeals Chamber stated that:

> even if it were established that Judge Mumba expressly shared the goals and objectives of the UNCSW ... in promoting and protecting the human rights of women, that inclination ... is distinguishable from an inclination to implement those goals and objectives as a Judge in a particular case. It follows that she could still sit on a case and impartially decide upon issues affecting women.
>
> Even if Judge Mumba sought to implement the relevant objectives of the

---

[24] *Ibid.*, paras. 189–190.

UNCSW, those goals merely reflected the objectives of the United Nations, and were contemplated by the Security Council resolutions leading to the establishment of the Tribunal.

[...]

Concern for the achievement of equality for women, which is one of the principles reflected in the United Nations Charter, cannot be taken to suggest any form of pre−judgement in any future trial for rape. To endorse the view that rape as a crime is abhorrent and that those responsible for it should be prosecuted within the constraints of the law cannot in itself constitute grounds for disqualification. [25]

In *Delalić et al*, the appellants filed a motion to disqualify Judge Odio Benito on the grounds that she used to be a member on the Board of Trustees of the United Nations Voluntary Fund for the Relief of Victims of Torture. The Appeals Chamber held that:

the apprehension of bias must be a reasonable one. Such circumstances within the knowledge of the fair−minded observer would include the traditions of integrity and impartiality which a judge undertakes to uphold in the solemn declaration made when assuming office, that he or she will perform the duties and exercise the powers of such an office "honourably, faithfully, impartially and conscientiously." By accepting a position on the Board of Trustees, Judge Odio Benito undertook in her personal capacity to further the mandate of the Victims of Torture Fund ... As noted in the *Furundzija* Appeal Judgement, personal convictions and opinions of judges are not in themselves a basis for inferring a lack of impartiality. The Appeals Chamber has already emphasised that, as there

---

[25] *Ibid.*, paras. 200−202.

is a high threshold to reach in order to rebut the presumption of impartiality and before a judge is disqualified, the reasonable apprehension of bias must be "firmly established. " The reason for this high threshold is that, just as any real appearance of bias of the part of a judge undermines confidence in the adminis-tration of justice, it would be as much of a potential threat to the interests of the impartial and fair administration of justice if judges were to disqualify them-selves on the basis of unfounded and unsupported allegations of apparent bi-as. [26]

3. 2 Publicising of the personal views of judges

There have been two cases of relevance, where parties requested the disqualifi-cation of judges based on, *inter alia*, personal views of judges that were publicised.

The first concerned pre-appointment blogging. On 2 April 2012, the Defence in *Banda and Jerbo* filed a request to the ICC President to request that the Presidency convene a special plenary session in accordance with Rule 4 (2) of the ICC Rules to disqualify a judge assigned to that case. The Defence's challenge to Nigerian Judge Chile Eboe-Osuji was based on three grounds: (i) the challenged judge's nationali-ty; (ii) the endorsement of his candidacy as a judge by a regional body and by his state of nationality; and (iii) comments he wrote in a blog prior to his election as a judge. [27] On 5 June 2012, a special plenary session of the ICC, by majority of the judges in the session (eleven for, two disagreeing and three abstaining), decided the Defence's request to be without merit. The majority considered that the content of the blog, which focused on the African Union's request to the UN Security Council for a deferral in the case against Sudanese President Al Bashir, was insufficiently

---

[26] *Delalić et al* Appeal Judgement, paras. 697-699, 707, see *supra* note 8.

[27] ICC, *The Prosecutor v. Abdallah Banda Abakaer Nourain and Saleh Mohammed Jerbo Janus*, Defence Request for the Disqualification of a Judge, Presidency, ICC-02/05-03/09, 2 April 2012, paras. 3, 4 (ht-tps: //www. icc-cpi. int/CourtRecords/CR2012_ 04486. PDF).

connected to the issues in the *Banda and Jerbo* case. The majority explicitly stated that "in the absence of a genuine link between the blog commentary and the case, no reason to doubt the judge's impartiality was demonstrated". In support of its determination, the majority specified that the blog commentary: (i) made no mention whatsoever of the *Banda and Jerbo* case, let alone to the guilt or innocence of the accused; and (ii) did not take any substantive position on the deferral request regarding Al Bashir, but merely offered an assessment concerning the international response. The majority further considered that the blog commentary did not demonstrate any appearance of favouring the African Union as the commentary was general in nature, calling for acceptance of the good faith of the organisation's position in requesting an Article 16 deferral. According to the majority, merely expressing an opinion on an issue generally concerning the African Union and the situation in the Sudan, could not lead to a reasonable observer to believe that the judge in question would be unable to impartially determine the case. The majority ultimately found that the blog commentary was not contrary to any position taken by the ICC, considering that it in no way questioned the decision of the ICC to issue a warrant of arrest against President Al Bashir. [28]

The two ICC judges who did not agree found that a "strong nexus" existed between the opinion in the blog commentary and the *Banda and Jerbo* case. The minority stated that both the cases of *Al Bashir* and *Banda and Jerbo* stemmed from the same situation and concerned similar actors. More specifically, the African Union, through its mission in Sudan, was directly implicated in the facts under prosecution in *Banda and Jerbo*. The minority also highlighted the fact that there was an allegation in *Banda and Jerbo* that the African Union Mission in Sudan did not act impar-

---

[28] ICC, Decision of the plenary of the judges on the "Defence Request for the Disqualification of a Judge" of 2 April 2012, Plenary, ICC–02/05–03/09–344–Anx, 5 June 2012, paras. 17–20 (https://www. icc–cpi. int/RelatedRecords/CR2012_ 06628. PDF).

tially, as required of a peacekeeping mission. According to the minority, while the judge in question, in his 2010 blog, did not and could not express an opinion on the individual criminal responsibility of the two accused, "he did create the impression of acceptance of the African Union's viewpoints and expressed the need (and the will) not to 'alienate' the AU from the ICC". On this basis, the minority determined that a reasonable observer could apprehend that the judge's impartiality was affected. [29]

The second incident concerned leaking of correspondence at the ICTY. On 6 June 2013, Judge Frederik Harhoff circulated an e–mail letter ("Letter") to 56 of his friends and associates. In this, he alleged that the ICTY President applied "tenacious pressure" on his fellow judges in such a way that it "makes you think he was determined to achieve an acquittal", and challenging the jurisprudence of the ICTY. The Letter was leaked to the media and was eventually published online. [30] In July 2013, an accused, Vojislav Šešelj, filed a motion seeking the disqualification of Judge Harhoff from all further proceedings in his ongoing trial. Šešelj submitted that the Letter showed a strong inclination on the part of the judge to convict accused persons of Serbian ethnicity. In particular, Šešelj underlined sections of the Letter in which the judge criticised a departure from the previous "set practice" of convicting military commanders. [31] In the Letter, the judge had criticised a number of recent ICTY Appeals Chamber and Trial Chamber judgements, which he argued diluted the doctrine of Joint Criminal Enterprise ("JCE"). In this regard, Judge Harhoff stated

---

[29]   *Ibid.*, paras. 23, 26.

[30]   Sections of the Letter were published in the Danish newspaper *Berlingske* on 13 June 2013. The Letter is now widely available on the internet: see http://www. vaseljenska. com/english/orginal – private – letter – judge–frederik–harhoff/ last accessed at 26 January 2018.

[31]   ICTY, *Prosecutor v Vojislav Šešelj*, Professor Vojislav Šešelj's Motion for Disqualification of Judge Frederik Harhoff, IT – 03 – 67 – T, 9 July 2013, para. 10 (http://www. legal – tools. org/en/browse/record/a7ccdc/).

that it was "more or less set practice" at the ICTY until Autumn 2012 to convict military commanders for crimes committed by their subordinates. He further alleged that the change in the JCE doctrine came as a result of pressure that the ICTY President exerted over his colleagues in deliberations. [32] Šešelj pointed out that Judge Harhoff further stated in the Letter that he had always "presumed that it was right to convict leaders for the crimes committed with their knowledge ... " and ended the Letter by stating that he is confronted by "a deep professional and moral dilemma not previously faced". [33]

On 25 July 2013, the vice—president of the ICTY appointed a special chamber of three judges ("Special Chamber") to decide on the motion and to report its decision to him. [34] On 28 August 2013, the Special Chamber delivered a decision disqualifying Judge Harhoff from the *Šešelj* case. [35] This is the first and the only successful motion of disqualification before an international criminal tribunal.

Unlike the majority in the ICC decision, the Special Chamber majority in this case did not consider the response of the challenged judge, nor the substance of his allegation (eg. the allegations about the ICTY President, the alleged "set practice" of convicting military commanders, nor his dissatisfaction with his perceived change in the ICTY's direction in this regard). The majority simply concluded that the judge's reference to a "set practice" of convicting accused persons without reference to an evaluation of the evidence in each individual case demonstrated grounds to conclude that a reasonable observer, properly informed, would reasonably apprehend bias on the part of challenged judge in favour of conviction. The majority found that this

---

[32] *Ibid.*

[33] Sections of the Letter were published in the Danish newspaper Berlingske on 13 June 2013. The Letter is now widely available on the internet.

[34] ICTY, *Prosecutor v Vojislav Šešelj*, Order Pursuant to Rule 15, President, IT−03−67−T, 25 July 2013, p. 2. (http: //www. icty. org/x/cases/seselj/presord/en/130725. pdf).

[35] ICTY, *Prosecutor v. Vojislav Šešelj*, Decision on Defence Motion for Disqualification of Judge Frederik Harhoff and Report to the Vice−President, Chamber convened by order of the Vice−President, IT−03−67, 28 August 2013 (http: //www. legal−tools. org/en/doc/5b4aa1/).

appearance of bias was further compounded by Judge Harhoff's statement that he was confronted by a professional and moral dilemma, which the majority considered to be a clear reference to his difficulty in applying the current jurisprudence of the IC-TY. In these circumstances, the majority concluded that the letter, when read as a whole, rebutted the presumption of impartiality. [36]

The dissenting judge of the Special Chamber, Judge Liu Daqun, noted the undoubted impropriety of the Letter. [37] He considered Judge Harhoff's critique of recent ICTY jurisprudence to be "unsubstantiated speculations and insinuations of improper conduct by other colleagues in a fashion that is unbefitting of a Judge". Nevertheless, Judge Liu disagreed with the majority's reasoning and conclusion. Specifically, he believed that the disqualification of a judge cannot be undertaken lightly, and reiterated the high threshold for rebutting the presumption of impartiality attached to a judge. Judge Liu was concerned with the majority's cursory approach in assessing whether the Letter would lead an informed person, with knowledge of all the relevant circumstances, reasonably to apprehend bias on the part of Judge Harhoff in favour of convicting the accused. In this regard, Judge Liu pointed out the majority's failure to properly contextualize and address all surrounding circumstances of Judge Harhoff's statements and limited its considerations simply to the content of the Letter.

In both cases, the personal views of the challenged judges were publicised online. However, the results were different. Comparing the two cases, it may be considered that the situation in the ICTY case was the more serious. The challenged judge at the ICC, Judge Eboe−Osuji, published his blog before he took office and did not mention the guilt or innocence of the accused. Neither did he mention the particular

[36] *Ibid.*

[37] *Ibid.*, Dissenting Opinion of Judge Liu, the following paragraph summarises the dissent, in particular paras. 4−10.

case, but the situation in Sudan and cooperation between the AU and the ICC in general terms. On the other hand, Judge Harhoff was sitting in a particular case, where the accused was charged with participating in a JCE by *inter alia* directing paramilitary forces. Judge Harhoff's Letter explicitly stated that he had always "presumed that it was right to convict leaders for the crimes committed with their knowledge…" and that he was confronted with 'a deep professional and moral dilemma not previously faced'. It is clear that the Letter differs from the ICC judge's blogging. In addition to his dissatisfaction with what he saw as a change in the ICTY jurisprudence, Judge Harhoff further alleged that the change in JCE doctrine came from the ICTY President's pressure on his colleagues. This, he suggested, may form part of a broader American/Israeli plan to curtail JCE and other forms of responsibility. Regardless of whether the ICTY President was actually exerting pressure, there is no doubt that a serious violation of professional ethics was in existence. Furthermore, Judge Harhoff's allegations were not substantiated with any reliable evidence. Had he not been satisfied with the result of deliberations, he should have used proper channels available to him to present any criticism of the recent jurisprudence. On the other hand, the approach adopted by the majority of the judges is also problematic. It jumped to the conclusion without taking into account of the relevant information and Judge Harhoff's previous performance in the Tribunal.

3. 3 Previous involvement in a case related to the accused

The jurisdiction of the *ad hoc* international criminal tribunals is always confined to a specific State or particular area. As a result, all the cases before those tribunals are somehow interrelated or connected. In the *Renzaho* case, the Appeals Chamber of the International Criminal Tribunal of Rwanda ("ICTR") reiterated its established jurisprudence first laid out in *Nahimana* that the judges of the Tribunal are "sometimes involved in trials which, by their very nature, cover overlapping issues". [38]

---

[38] *Renzaho* Appeal Judgement, para. 22, see *supra* note 9.

Rule 15 (C) of the ICTR RPE (also the ICTY RPE) stipulates that a judge who reviews an indictment against an accused shall not be disqualified from sitting in the trial and appeals proceedings concerning the same accused. [39] But, the trial or appeals judgements or decisions in one case may involve other accused in another case. Is it a proper reason for disqualification if a judge sitting in one case involving other accused?

On 20 July 2016, an ICTY accused, Ratko Mladić, filed a motion seeking to disqualify Judge Alphons Orie and Judge Christoph Flugge for judicial bias. One of the bases for the disqualification is that they found Mladić guilty of criminal acts beyond a reasonable doubt in prior cases before this Tribunal. [40] Based on the jurisprudence of the ICTY and ICTR, the President of the ICTY denied the motion. [41] In the "Report pursuant to Rule 15 (B) of the Rules" from Judge Orie, dated 1 August 2016, attached as Annex A to the President Decision, Judge Orie referred to a previous Decision in which the Appeals Chamber held that "findings of criminal responsibility made in a case before the Tribunal are binding only on the accused in a specific case (...). [42] and considered that the Trial Chamber's findings regarding the mere existence and membership of the JCE do not—and cannot—constitute findings of criminal responsibility on the part of any persons who were not charged and con-

---

[39]   Rule 15 (C) of the RPE of the ICTY, see *supra* note 3.

[40]   ICTY, *Prosecutor v. Ratko Mladić*, The Defence Motion Seeking to Disqualify the Honourable Judge Alphons Orie and the Honourable Judge Christoph Flugge under This Trial Chamber's Standard for Judicial Bias, IT-09-92-T, 20 July 2016 (https: //www. legal-tools. org/doc/978e2e/pdf/).

[41]   ICTY, *Prosecutor v. Ratko Mladić*, Decision on Defence Motion Seeking to Disqualify the Honourable Judge Alphons Orie and the Honourable Judge Christoph Flugge, President of the Tribunal, IT-09-92-T, 26 August 2016 (http: //www. icty. org/x/cases/mladic/presdec/en/160826. pdf).

[42]   *Ibid.* "Report pursuant to Rule 15 (B) of the Rules" from Alphons Orie, Presiding Judge of Trial Chamber, 1 August 2016, p. 2. This Report is Annex A attached to the Decision on Defence Motion to Disqualify the Honourable Judge Alphons Orie and the Honourable Judge Christoph, 26 August 2016 (http: // www. icty. org/x/cases/mladic/presdec/en/160826. pdf). In his Report, Judge Orie referred to the quotations from ICTY, *Prosecutor v. Jadranko Prlić et al.*, Decision on Application by the Republic of Croatia for Leave to Appear as Amicus Curiae and to Submit Amicus Curiae Brief, Appeals Chamber, IT-04-74-A, 18 July 2016, para. 9 (http: //www. icty. org/x/cases/prlic/acdec/en/160718. pdf).

victed in this case". [43]

Here, it is also relevant to observe that the ICTR Appeals Chamber in the *Nahimana* case also found that the tribunal judges were sometimes involved in several trials which, by their very nature, cover issues that overlap. It was assumed, in the absence of evidence to the contrary, that, by virtue of their training and experience, tribunal judges would rule fairly on the issues before them, relying solely and exclusively on the evidence adduced in the particular case. The Appeals Chamber agreed with the ICTY Bureau that "a judge is not disqualified from hearing two or more criminal trials arising out of the same series of events, where he is exposed to evidence relating to these events in both cases". [44]

On 10 October 2016, Mladić again challenged the judges dealing with his matters. He filed three separate Motions pursuant to Rule 15 (B), seeking disqualification of Judge Carmel Agius, Judge Theodor Meron and Judge Fausto Pocar from the Appeals Chamber bench hearing his interlocutory appeals. [45] The most relevant to the present discussion is the motion concerning Judge Agius. Mladić sought the voluntary withdrawal or the disqualification of Judge Agius on the grounds of an alleged appearance of bias by reason of prejudgement of his case. [46] He contended that, as a member of the bench in the trial of *Vujadin Popović et al*, [47] Judge Agius made prejudicial statements and findings about him (Mladić) that individually and together

---

[43] *Ibid.*

[44] *Nahimana* Appeal Judgment, para. 78, see *supra* note 8.

[45] There were three Presidential decisions in *Prosecutor v. Ratko Mladić* (case nos. IT—09—92—AR73. 6 & IT—09—92—AR73. 7) on 26 October 2016 in relation to the accused's motions for disqualification of the three judges Agius, Meron and Pocar: ① for Judge Agius: http: //www. icty. org/x/cases/mladic/presdec/en/ 161026_1. pdf; ② for Judge Meron: http: //www. icty. org/x/cases/mladic/presdec/en/161026. pdf; ③ for Judge Pocar: http: //www. icty. org/x/cases/mladic/presdec/en/161026_2. pdf.

[46] *Ibid.*, Decision on Ratko Mladic's Motion for Disqualification of Judge Carmel Agius, President of the Tribunal, para. 7.

[47] ICTY, *Prosecutor v Vujadin Popović* et al, Judgement, Trial Chamber, IT—05—88—T, 10 June 2010 (https: //www. legal—tools. org/en/doc/481867/).

demonstrated prejudgement about his guilt. [48] Mladić added that Judge Agius frequently referred to his involvement or orders, assuming his membership in the JCE, to prove his subordinates' membership therein. [49] Finally, Mladić submitted that Judge Agius had already made findings about his criminal intent in relation to Srebrenica. [50]

On 13 October 2016, pursuant to Rule 15 (B) (iv), the President of the ICTY assigned a judge, to consider Mladić's motion in his place both as Presiding Judge and President of the Tribunal for the purpose of Rule 15 (B) of the RPE. [51] The Acting President first of all pointed out that the Appeals Chamber's jurisprudence had established that determinations of actual bias or unacceptable appearance of bias under Rule 15 should be made on a case—by—case basis. [52] The issue was whether the involvement of Judge Agius in another case, that of *Popovic et al*, and in particular the findings pointed out by Mladić, would lead a reasonable observer, properly informed, to reasonably apprehend bias on the part of Judge Agius when adjudicating Mladić's Interlocutory Appeals. Having carefully reviewed Mladić's Interlocutory Appeals, the Acting President observed that the issues raised there did not require any consideration by the Appeals Chamber of Mladić's individual criminal responsibility. Rather, the subject matter of Mladić's Interlocutory Appeals was procedural and they only required rulings on some specific allegations of violations of fair trial rights in the—then ongoing trial proceedings. Then, the Acting President stated that it was necessary for Mladić to adduce sufficient evidence showing that the substantive issues arising from the *Popovic et al* Trial Judgement were so closely linked to the substan-

---

[48]   Decision on Ratko Mladic's Motion for Disqualification of Judge Carmel Agius, President of the Tribunal, para. 14, see *supra* note 46.

[49]   *Ibid.* , para. 15.

[50]   *Ibid.*

[51]   *Ibid.* , para. 6

[52]   ICTY, *Prosecutor v. Mićo Stanišić and Stojan Župljanin*, Judgement, Appeals Chamber, IT-08-91-A, 30 June 2016, para. 32 (http: //www. icty. org/x/cases/zupljanin_ stanisicm/acjug/en/160630. pdf).

tive issues in his own Interlocutory Appeals so as to cast doubt on the impartiality of Judge Agius. The Acting President was not convinced that any of the relevant findings from the *Popović et al* Trial Judgement would lead a reasonable observer, properly informed, to reasonably apprehend bias on the part of Judge Agius when adjudicating Mladić's Interlocutory Appeals. The Acting President considered that Mladić's argument was insufficient to rebut the presumption of impartiality of Judge Agius to adjudicate Mladić's Interlocutory Appeals. Therefore, Mladić's motion was denied. [53]

It is relevant to note that other international tribunals such as the European Court of Human Right ("ECtHR") have made similar findings. In *Poppe v. The Netherlands*, the ECtHR considered that the work of criminal courts frequently involves judges presiding over various trials in which a number of co-accused are charged. It would therefore render the work of the criminal courts impossible, if by that fact alone, a judge's impartiality could be called into question. The ECtHR applied the objective test and held that:

> The mere fact that a judge has already ruled on similar but unrelated criminal charges or that he or she has already tried a co-accused in separate criminal proceedings is not, in itself, sufficient to cast doubt on that judge's impartiality in a subsequent case. It is, however, a different matter if the earlier judgments contain findings that actually prejudge the question of the guilt of an accused in such subsequent proceedings. [54]

In sum, an international judge could be disqualified if he/she is adjudicating

---

[53] Decision on Ratko Mladic's Motion for Disqualification of Judge Carmel Agius, President of the Tribunal, paras 21–26, see *supra* note 45.

[54] *Poppe v. The Netherlands*, Judgement on Application No. 32271/04, 24 March 2009, para. 26, cited in *Prosecutor v. Radovan Karadžić*, Decision on Defence Motion for a Fair Trial and the Presumption of Innocence or, in the Alternative, a Mistrial, Trial Chamber, IT – 09 – 92 – T, 4 July 2016, para. 11 (http: // www. icty. org/x/cases/mladic/tdec/en/160704. pdf).

the same case both at the trial and appeals stages, and if he/she made a finding in the earlier case on the individual criminal responsibility of the accused. Merely making a statement in the prior case involving the accused does not constitutes enough evidence to rebut the impartiality of the judges.

3. 4 Staff disqualification

Does disqualification also apply to judicial support staff? Whether a staff member or legal officer can be disqualified is a very contentious issue in the international criminal tribunals.

In the *Bizimungo et al.* case before the ICTR, three of the four appellants (Mugenzi, Bicamumpaka and Mugiraneza) filed separate motions to disqualify a Chamber's consultant (legal officer) for his statement at an international symposium in Geneva, Switzerland on 9, 10 and 11 July 2009. This allegedly exhibited bias and displayed a personal view on legal issues relevant to the case. [55] The appellants claimed that "judicial staff" advising judges on legal issues also cannot have an appearance of bias, or actual bias as the impartiality of a Judge may be prejudiced by virtue of his or her association with such staff. [56]

The application reached the Appeals Chamber of the ICTR. There, the judges found that Rule 15 "applies expressly to Judges and does not contemplate the disqualification of Chamber's legal officers or consultants" and that the disqualification of Chambers' legal officers or consultants finds no support in the jurisprudence of the Tribunal. [57] The Appeals Chamber referred to a Panel Report in the *Hartmann* matter at the ICTY. This panel had been appointed to provide an opinion on disqualification of judges and legal staff in connection with a contempt case before the tribunal. It

[55]   ICTR, *Prosecutor v. Casimir Bizimungu et al.* Decision on Appeals Concerning the Engagement of a Chamber Consultant or Legal Officer, Appeals Chamber, ICTR-99-50-AR73. 8, 17 December 2009, para. 2 (https: //www. legal-tools. org/doc/9a74b6/pdf/) ("*Bizimungu* Decision on Appeals Concerning the Engagement of a Chamber Consultant or Legal Officer").

[56]   *Ibid.* , para. 8.

[57]   *Ibid.* , para. 8.

found that a plain reading of Rule 15 showed that it applied solely to judges and did not extend to Chambers' staff, and that the conduct of legal officers was not relevant to determining a judge's impartiality. [58] The Appeals Chamber further noted that in the case at bar, the submissions of Bicamumpaka and Mugiraneza were premised on the erroneous notion that legal officers or consultants play a central role in the judges' deliberations. Judicial decision-making is the sole purview of the judges, and legal officers and consultants play no role in it. Rather, their function is to provide assistance to the judges in terms of legal research and preparing draft decisions, judgements, opinions, and orders in conformity with their instructions. The Appeals Chamber therefore found there to be no merit in Bicamumpaka's and Mugiraneza's assertions that legal officers and consultants must be subject to the same standards of impartiality as the Judges of the Tribunal. [59]

In *Bizimungu et al*, Bicamumpaka accepted that Rule 15 was applicable only to judges, but asserted that the ICTR RPE were not exhaustive in respect of fair trials rights: he claimed that he was entitled to a judgement free of actual bias or the appearance of bias. [60] Mugiraneza argued that to hold that a consultant or a legal officer could never be disqualified would mean that a clearly biased person could participate in the decision of a case and the drafting of its judgement. [61] The Appeals Chamber took the following position: "it follows from this presumption that mere assertions to the effect that a staff member may influence a Judge during deliberations or the adjudication process are not a sufficient basis, in and of themselves, to warrant disqualification of a legal officer or consultant". [62] The Appeals Chamber was not persuaded that the Trial Chamber had committed a discernible error, noting that there could be instances where "a prospective staff member's statements or activities

---

[58] *Ibid.*
[59] *Ibid.*, para. 9.
[60] *Ibid.*, para. 5.
[61] *Ibid.*, para. 6 (referring to Mugiraneza's appeal).
[62] *Ibid.*, para. 10 (referring to Mugiraneza's appeal).

may be so problematic as to either impugn the perceived impartiality of the Judges or the appearance thereof, or, even if this were not the case, the Tribunal's fundamental guarantees of fair trial". [63] This, however, was not such a situation, in fact it fell "far short". [64]

From this part of the reasoning, it can be seen clearly that the Appeals Chamber put the fundamental guarantee of fair trial at the foremost place, while at the same time admitting that a staff member's statements or activities may be so problematic as to affect the impartiality of the judge or the appearance thereof. So, when arranging the work assignment to staff members, the Registrar should carefully scrutinise previous activities to avoid any suspicion of appearance of bias, and also warn them about possible challenges in this regard.

It is here relevant to observe that the ICTR Appeals Chamber in *Hategekimana* also considered that "mere assertions to the effect that a staff member may influence a Judge during deliberations or the adjudication process are not a sufficient basis, in and of themselves" to create in the mind of a reasonable observer, properly informed, an appearance of bias or to rebut the presumption of impartiality of judges. The Appeals Chamber did not find the role of the legal officer in this case to be "so problematic" as to impugn the impartiality of the judges or the appearance thereof. "Therefore, there is no merit to Hategekimana's contention that the Trial Chamber erred in allowing the legal officer to be involved in the drafting process of the Trial Judgement". [65]

---

[63]   *Ibid.* , para. 11 (referring to Mugiraneza's appeal).

[64]   *Ibid.* , para. 11 (referring to Mugiraneza's appeal).

[65]   ICTR, *Prosecutor v. Idelphonse Hategekima*, Judgement, Appeals Chamber, ICTR – 00 – 55B – A, 8 May 2012, para. 20 (https: //www. legal–tools. org/doc/885b2c/pdf/).

4. Some procedural issues

Rule 15 (B) of the ICTY and ICTR RPE governs the procedures for disqualification of judges, and stipulates that:

(i) Any party may apply to the Presiding Judge of a Chamber for the disqualification and withdrawal of a Judge of that Chamber from a trial or appeal upon the above grounds. The Presiding Judge shall confer with the Judge in question and prepare a report which shall include any comments or material provided by the challenged Judge. The Presiding Judge shall present this report to the President. [66]

(ii) Following the report of the Presiding Judge, the President shall, if necessary, appoint a panel of three Judges to report to him its decision on the merits of the application. The panel shall be provided with the report prepared by the Presiding Judge. If the decision is to uphold the application, the President shall assign another Judge to sit in the place of the Judge in question. [67]

In contrast, Article 41 (2) (c) of the ICC Statute provides that "any question as to the disqualification of a judge shall be decided by an absolute majority of the judges", and the challenged judge shall be entitled to present his or her comments but shall not take part in the decision. Article 41 (2) further stipulates that "[t] he Prosecutor or the person being investigated or prosecuted may request the disqualification of a judge". [68]

While procedures for disqualification of judges are different at the ICC and the ICTY, one similarity is apparent: only parties to the case, the prosecution or the de-

---

[66]　Rule 15 B (1) of the RPE of the ICTY, see supra note 4. Before the amendment in 2005, the rule provided that the Presiding Judge shall present this report to the Bureau.

[67]　Rule 15 B (1) of the RPE of the ICTY, see *supra* note 3.

[68]　Article 41 (2) of the ICC Statute, see *supra* note 5.

fence, have the right to request the disqualification of judges. Does it mean that the disqualification must related to a specific case in proceeding? What should a tribunal do if a judge commits misconduct outside the judicial function of the tribunal? Should the President confer with the challenged judge first and should the panel of the three judge or the plenary judges consider the report submitted the presiding judges? Should the parties have the right to appeal if their motion for disqualification fails?

4. 1 The right of parties to seek disqualification

While the ICTY Statute and RPE do not have specific provisions on the judges' alleged misconduct which are not actually related to a specific case, the jurisprudence does provide some guidance. In the *Delalić et al* case, three out of four of the accused submitted a motion pursuant to Rule 15, seeking to disqualify Judge Odio Benito based on her election to the position of Vice-President of Costa Rica. In its decision on this matter, the ICTY Bureau made a distinction between "administrative" and "judicial" issues. [69] Administrative issues relate to "requirements for a person to serve as a Judge of the ICTY and the connected question of what conduct or situations are incompatible with the discharge of judicial functions". [70] Judicial issues, on the other hand, relate to "the grounds for disqualification of a Judge from sitting in a particular case". [71] As discussed earlier, only parties are entitled to initiate disqualification procedures against a judge from sitting in a particular case under Rule 15. The Bureau further determined that "administrative" issues are regulated by Article 13 of the ICTY Statute, which provides that judges must be persons of "high moral character, impartiality and integrity who possess the qualifications required in

---

[69]   ICTY, *Prosecutor v. Zejnil Delalić et al*, Decision of the Bureau on the Motion to Disqualify Judges Pursuant to Rule 15 or in the Alternative that Certain Judges Recuse Themselves, Bureau, IT-96-21-T, 25 October 1999, para. 9 (http: //www. icty. org/x/cases/mucic/acdec/en/91025DQX12987. htm) ("*Delalić et al*, Decision of the Bureau on the Motion to Disqualify Judges Pursuant to Rule 15 or in the Alternative that Certain Judges Recuse Themselves").

[70]   *Ibid.*, para. 6.

[71]   *Ibid.*

their respective countries for appointment to the highest judicial offices". [72] The Bureau also noted that, according to the ICTY Statute, the "terms and conditions of service shall be those of the Judges of the International Court of Justice". [73] The Bureau interpreted this part of the ICTY Statute to mean that judges may not engage in activities incompatible with their judicial function. The Bureau pointed out that the issue of disqualification/recusal is a judicial matter which relates to the right of a judge to sit *in a specific case*. Judges may recuse themselves or be disqualified from hearing a particular case when, pursuant to Sub—rule 15 (A), they have "a personal interest" in or "any association" with the case "which might affect [their] impartiality". [74] If the judge does not fulfill the requirements referred to in Rule 15 (A), he or she is disqualified from hearing that particular case, although he or she is fully entitled to continue to exercise the functions of a judge of the Tribunal and sit in other cases. [75] In this case, the Bureau also noted that the Fourteenth and Seventeenth Plenary decisions in which it was declared that the position of Vice—President of Costa Rica was compatible with the discharge of judicial functions were decisions of an *administrative* nature and that these decisions were "not made with reference to any specific question as to whether Judge Odio Benito was disqualified from sitting in *Celebici*". [76] They therefore denied the motion for disqualification of Judge Odio Benito.

It is clear that if a party wishes to challenge a judge's external activities through disqualification procedures under Rule 15 of the ICTY RPE, that party bears the burden to show that "the activity incompatible with the discharge of judicial functions

---

[72]   Article 13 of the ICTY Statute, see *supra* note 14.

[73]   *Delalić et al*, Decision of the Bureau on the Motion to Disqualify Judges Pursuant to Rule 15 or in the Alternative that Certain Judges Recuse Themselves, para. 7, see *supra* note 69.

[74]   Rule 15 (A) of the ICTY RPE, see *supra* note 4.

[75]   *Delalić et al*, Decision of the Bureau on the Motion to Disqualify Judges Pursuant to Rule 15 or in the Alternative that Certain Judges Recuse Themselves, para. 9, see *supra* note 69.

[76]   *Ibid.* , paras. 12, 13.

has a direct and specific impact upon the impartiality of a Judge *in a particular case* before a Chamber". [77] Thus, the ICTY's jurisprudence has limited the right of the parties to disqualify a judge to a particular case.

However, what if there is misconduct that occurs outside the course of official duties and is of a grave nature that causes or is likely to cause serious harm to the tribunal/court? What if the parties do not lodge a complaint because their case is not directly affected? In these circumstances, who is entitled or entrusted to raise such matters?

The ICC's Statute and Rules seem to provide different procedures for disqualification and removal from the office as a result of serious misconduct occurring outside official duties. Article 46 (1) (a) of the Rome Statute stipulates that a judge, prosecutor, deputy prosecutor, registrar or deputy registrar shall be removed from office where that person is found to have committed "serious misconduct". "Serious misconduct" occurring outside the course of official duties is defined as conduct which is "of a grave nature that causes or is likely to cause serious harm to the standing of the court". [78] If it occurs, "all complaints shall be transmitted to the Presidency, which may also initiate proceedings on its own motion". There seems to be no guidance on who may initiate a complaint or a request for removal from office. Rule 29 of the ICC Rules further stipulates that in the case of a judge, "the question of removal from office shall be put to a vote at a plenary session" and the Presidency shall advise the President of the Bureau of the Assembly of States Parties in writing of any recommendation adopted. According to the Rome Statute's Article 46 (2)(a), a decision as to the removal of a judge shall be made by the Assembly of States Parties by secret ballot by a two-thirds majority upon recommendation adopted by two-thirds

---

[77] *Ibid.*, para. 14.

[78] Rule 24 (1) (b) of the ICC RPE (definition of serious misconduct and serious breach of duty), see *supra* note 6.

majority of the other judges. [79] This procedure is much more complicated. The barriers make removal very difficult, unless the challenged judge commits very serious misconduct or even crimes.

4. 2 The role of the presiding judge

At the ICTY, under Rule 15 (B) (i), when the Presiding Judge received the motion of disqualification, he was required to confer with the judge in question in order to give him an opportunity to be heard. If the challenged judge himself believed that his behavior was not in conformity with the RPE, he could recuse himself. Recusal is the process by which a judge voluntarily withdraws in circumstances in which he or she considers a personal interest or association may affect his or her impartiality. [80] In most situations, the challenged judge is not likely to withdraw easily from a case because of the strong presumption of impartiality.

After conferring with the challenged judge, the Presiding Judge's obligation was to prepare a report including any comments or material provided by him or her. The Presiding Judge was to present this report to the President. When the Presiding Judge and the President of the Tribunal were the same person, this had to be adapted. [81] For instance, further to Mladić's motion for disqualification of Judge Agius, Judge

---

[79] Art. 46 (2) (a) of the ICC Statute, see *supra* note 5.

[80] Rule 15 (A) of RPE of ICTY, see *supra* note 4.

[81] ICTY, *Prosecutor v. Micó Stanišić and Stojan Župlajnanin*, Decision on Motion Requesting Recusal, Acting President, IT-08-91-A, 3 December 2013, para. 21 (https: //www. legal-tools. org/en/browse/record/1c5d4f/); ICTY, *Prosecutor v. Vojislav Šešelj*, Decision on Motion for Disqualification of Judges Fausto Pocar and Theodor Meron from the Appeals Proceedings, Chamber convened by Order of the President, IT-03-67 - R77. 2 - A, 2 December 2009, para. 3 (http: //www. icty. org/x/cases/contempt _ seselj/tdec/en/091202. pdf); ICTY, *Prosecutor v. Vojislav Šešelj*, Decision on Motion for Disqualification, President of the Tribunal, IT-03-67-R77. 2-A, 6 November 2009, para. 5 (http: //www. icty. org/x/cases/contempt_seselj/presdec/en/091106. pdf).

Liu Daqun took the role of Acting President under Rule 15 (B)(iv). [82] He conferred with Judge Agius, the subject of the complaint, about the motion. [83] The Acting President's decision reported that Judge Agius considered the Motion to be "without merit" and that he:

- "firmly reject [ed] any allegation of actual bias";

- did "not believe that the circumstances would lead a reasonable observer properly informed, to reasonably apprehend bias against him";

- considered that "the Tribunal's established jurisprudence supports the conclusion that the fact that the *Popovic et al.* Trial Judgement contains findings regarding Mladić does not rebut the strong presumption of impartiality attached to judges";

- was of the view that "none of the specific findings in the *Popovic et al.* Trial Judgement to which Mladić refers would lead a reasonable observer, properly informed, to reasonably apprehend bias on his part". [84]

If the ICTY President were to appoint a panel of three judges to report to him its decision on the merits of the application, the panel would be provided with a report prepared by the Presiding Judge. It is submitted that such a panel would have the obligation to take into consideration the report and make an informed decision. Unfortunately, the majority of the judges in Judge Harhoff's disqualification case, discussed earlier in this paper, did not follow such a procedure. It will be recalled that a Spe-

---

[82] According to Rule 15 (B)(iv), if the Judge in question is the President, the responsibility of the President in accordance with this paragraph shall be assumed by the Vice-President or, if he or she is not able to act in the application, by the permanent Judge most senior in precedence who is able to act. In this case, President Agius was the Judge in question, therefore, the Vice-President became the Acting President. This Rule was also applicable to Presiding Judge, if he was the Judge in question.

[83] Decision on Ratko Mladic's Motion for Disqualification of Judge Carmel Agius, President of the Tribunal, para. 19, see *supra* note 45.

[84] *Ibid.*, para. 19.

cial Chamber issued a decision in which the Majority, one judge dissenting, upheld a motion by Vojislav Šešelj for the disqualification of Judge Harhoff from the proceedings against him on the basis of the Letter. On 3 September 2013, the Acting President of the Tribunal issued an order, *inter alia*, staying the assignment of another judge to sit in place of Judge Harhoff, and requesting a report from the remaining judges seized of the *Šešelj* case on whether to re—start or continue with the proceedings. [85] On 3 September 2013, the two remaining *Šešelj* judges, including the Presiding Judge, filed a request for clarification of the Decision with the Special Chamber and the Acting President. Judge Harhoff also filed a similar request. [86] On the same date, the Prosecution filed a motion seeking reconsideration and the stay of the Decision. [87] In the Motion, the Prosecution argued that the Majority "abused its discretion by not addressing the contrary report of the Presiding Judge ... who found that the contents of the letter did not cast doubt on Judge Harhoff's impartiality". [88]

The Special Chamber's clarification explained that Rule 15 only provided that the President, or in this instance the Acting President, receive and consider a report prepared by a Presiding Judge of the Trial Chamber prior to deciding whether or not to appoint a panel to consider the merits of a motion for disqualification. [89] It there-

---

[85] ICTY, *Prosecutor v. Vojislav Šešelj*, Order Following Decision of the Panel to Disqualify Judge Frederik Harhoff, President of the Tribunal, IT-03-67-T, 3 September 2013 (http: //www. legal-tools. org/doc/c51c3a/pdf/).

[86] ICTY, *Prosecutor v. Vojislav Šešelj*, Request for Urgent Clarification to the Panel and the Vice President (by the two remaining Judges), IT-03-67-T, 3 September 2013 (https: //www. legal-tools. org/doc/879cb2/pdf/); Request for Clarification of the Panel Decision of 28 August 2013 (by Judge Harhoff), 3 September 2013, cited in Response to Request for Urgent Clarification to the Panel and the Vice President, President, IT-03-67-T, 10 September 2013, fn. 4 (https: //www. legal-tools. org/doc/abbbfe/pdf/).

[87] ICTY, *Prosecutor v. Vojislav Šešelj*, Prosecution Motion for Reconsideration of Decision on Defence Motion for Disqualification Judge Frederik Harhoff and Request for Stay. IT-03-67-T, 3 September 2013 (https: //www. legal-tools. org/doc/04ab97/pdf/).

[88] *Ibid.*, para. 20.

[89] ICTY, *Prosecutor v. Vojislav Šešelj*, Decision on Prosecution Motion for Reconsideration of Decision on Disqualification, Requests for Clarification, and Motion on Behalf of *Stanišić and Župlajnanin*, Chamber Convened by Order of the Vice-President, IT-03-67-T, 7 October 2013, para. 18 (http: //www. icty. org/x/cases/seselj/tdec/en/131007. pdf).

fore held that:

> the Special Chamber convened pursuant to Rule 15 (B) (ii) was not re-
> quired to consider and address the Report in its decision. Furthermore, beyond
> the plain language of Rule 15, a review of the previous decisions by specially
> convened Chambers at the Tribunal did not reveal any established practice of
> taking into consideration the report of a Presiding Judge, or the comments of the
> challenged judge, in the substantive discussion on the merits of a motion for
> disqualification. In light of the Rules and the Special Tribunal's jurisprudence on
> this issue, the Chamber considers that it was not bound to consider the Re-
> port. [90]

It is submitted that both the interpretation and application of Rule 15 by the majority of the judges were wrong and without logic. If the panel of three judges had no
obligation to consider or address the report prepared by the Presiding Judge, why
should the panel be provided with the report? In his dissent, Judge Liu pointed out
that in the impugned Decision, the Majority only addressed and evaluated three isolated sentences from the Letter [91] and "the cursory approach undertaken by the
Majority in its analysis and discussion of the Letter warrant reconsideration of the impugned Decision in order to avoid injustice". [92]

In order to address this matter, in July 2015, the ICTY judges in plenary
changed Rule 15 (B) (1) requesting the Presiding Judge shall in his report "include any comments or material provided by the challenged Judge. The Presiding
Judge shall present this report to the President. " It also requests the panel of three

---

[90]   *Ibid.*, para. 19.

[91]   *Ibid.*, Dissenting Opinion of Judge Liu, para. 4.

[92]   *Ibid.*, para. 6.

judges "shall be provided with the report prepared by the Presiding Judge". [93]

4. 3 Appeal or review

The ICTY Appeals Chamber noted that the Statute and RPE did not provide for an interlocutory appeal to the Appeals Chamber of a decision taken by the Tribunal's Bureau (President) pursuant to Rule 15 (B). Rather, the Appeals Chamber's consideration of whether a trial judge should have been disqualified is limited to an appeal against a conviction or where the issue properly arises in an interlocutory appeal certified by a Trial Chamber. [94] This was also the situation at the ICTR.

Rule 15 (B) was changed in 2005. Comparing the pre and post 2005 versions of the rule, the revised procedure assigned the President of the Tribunal, rather than the Presiding Judge of the chamber, to be the one either to make the decision on his own or refer it for decision. Further, in the latter case, the President referred it not to the Bureau but to a panel of three judges drawn from other Chambers. [95] However, beyond these differences, the language and general procedure of Rule 15 (B) in the two versions was broadly similar. Both provided that the matter may be decided by a lone judge (be it the Presiding Judge or the President) or "if necessary" by a panel of judges (be it a panel of three judges from other Chambers or the Bureau). There was no provision for appeal or review.

In the ICTY's practice, where a decision of the Presiding Judge acting on his own was challenged, it became "necessary" to refer the matter to the Bureau. This would equally apply to the post—2005 procedure under Rule 15 (B). Therefore,

---

[93] Amendments to the Rules of Procedure and Evidence, ICTY, IT/282, 10 July 2015 (http: // www. icty. org/x/file/Legal%20Library/Rules_ procedure_ evidence/150710–it–282–en. pdf).

[94] ICTR, *Prosecutor v. Athanase Seromba*, Decision on Appeal of Bureau Decision, ICTR–01–66–AR, 22 May 2006, para. 4 (http: //cld. unmict. org/assets/Uploads/full – text – dec/2006/Seromba% 20Decision% 20on%20Interlocutory% 20Appeal. pdf). See also ICTY, *Prosecutor v. Vidoje Blagojević et al.* , Decision on Blagojević's Motion for Clarification, Bureau, IT–02–60, 27 March 2003, para. 4, (https: //www. legal – tools. org/en/browse/record/6bc8d7/).

[95] Mohamed Shahabuddeen, *International Criminal Justice at the Yugoslavia Tribunal: A Judge's Recollection* (Oxford University Press, 2012), p. 41.

from 2005—2017 when the ICTY closed, the procedure was that where the President (or the Vice—President) determined that it was not necessary to refer the matter to a panel of judges and decided the matter him or herself, and that decision was challenged, it became "necessary" to refer the matter to a panel of three judges. [96] Rule 15 (B) (iii) clearly stated that there was no interlocutory appeal from a decision by the panel of three judges, which meant that the decision made by the panel of three judges was final. [97] The Appeals Chamber in *Galić* pointed out that:

> Hence, while there is no interlocutory appeal of a decision under Rule 15 (B) of the Rules, the role of the Bureau effectively provides a second course to an accused to have his arguments for disqualification reconsidered in full by an independent panel of judges. Further, the fact that a decision on disqualification cannot be appealed at trial does not necessarily means that the impartiality of a judge cannot be considered in an appeal from a judgement. [98]

This clearly envisioned a specific two—stage process of consideration for a request to disqualify a judge. As the Rule clearly stated, an application for disqualification was to be made to the Presiding Judge of the Chamber seized of the proceedings. The Presiding Judge was then to confer with the judge in question and file a report to the President of the Tribunal, who was, if necessary, to appoint a panel of three judges to report to him its decision on the merits of the application. The panel was to be provided with the report prepared by the Presiding Judge. If the decision was to uphold the application, the President would assign another judge to sit in the

---

[96] ICTY, *Prosecutor v Radovan Karadšić*, Decision on Appeal from Decision on Motion to Disqualify Judge Picard, IT—95—05/18—AR15. 1, 26 June 2009, para. 8 (http: //cld. unmict. org/assets/filings/Decision-on-Appeal-from-Decision-on-Motion-to-Disqualify-Judge-Picard. pdf).

[97] Rule 15 (B) (III) of the ICTY RPE, see *supra* note 4.

[98] *Galić* Appeal Judgement, para. 31, see *supra* note 8.

place of the judge in question. [99]

There were also some exceptions to this rule since it was clearly related to the right of the accused and fair trial. In the *Seromba* case before the ICTR, the complainant, Seromba, did not follow this procedure and filed his claim directly with the Bureau, thereby depriving himself of the review procedure envisioned by the rule. [100] However, when the Bureau denied Seromba's request on 25 April 2006, he filed an appeal. [101] The Appeals Chamber held that "[a] lthough it would have been within the discretion of the Bureau to dismiss Seromba's request as improperly filed", it could not "conclude that it erred in considering the matter in the first instance." [102] In other words, instead of dismissal of Seromba's request and appeal on the ground of improper procedure, both the Bureau and the Appeals Chamber heard his request and appeal.

5. Concluding remarks

Although the parties have the right to seek to disqualify judges in international criminal tribunals, there is a presumption of impartiality and a high threshold to reach in order to rebut the presumption of impartiality, and therefore to disqualify judges. In the history of the international criminal judicial organs, there has only been one judge who was disqualified by a special chamber, and that was with two judges in favour and one against. Even in this case, there were ambiguities and controversial views.

ICTY and ICTR jurisprudence accepted a two-pronged test for judicial bias: actual bias and unacceptable appearance of bias. As for the promotion of human rights causes, the ICTY Appeal Chamber held that personal convictions and opinions

---

[99] Rule 15 B (1) of the ICTY RPE, see *supra* note 4.

[100] ICTR, *Prosecutor v Athanase Seromba*, Decision on Interlocutory Appeal of a Bureau Decision, Appeals Chamber, ICTR – 01 – 66 – AR, 22 May 2006, para. 6. (https: //www. legal – tools. org/en/browse/record/42a814/).

[101] *Ibid.* , para. 2.

[102] *Ibid.*, para. 6.

of judges were not in themselves a basis for inferring a lack of impartiality. Where personal views of judges were publicised, the ICC and ICTY adopted different approaches for situations that were actually rather dissimilar. It is undoubtedly improper for a judge to express his criticisms of jurisprudential developments relevant to the case he was adjudicating, and of the Tribunal President, in an email to a large group of friends. However, as this paper has shown, the way that the matter was handled at the ICTY was problematic. A staff member or legal officer or a consultant supporting judges on legal issues should be exempt from being disqualified. At the ICTY, Rule 15 was held only to apply to judges. Although the decision of the judicial panel was not strictly appealable, in some exceptional cases, appeal were entertained.

In their many years of existence, the procedure at the ICTY and ICTR for disqualification was changed several times to address problems that arose in practice. The experience and lessons in this area will certainly serve as a guidance to future international judicial institutions.

PLUCKING NUMBERS OUT OF THE AIR: IS SENTENCING AT THE ICC AN IMPROVEMENT ON THE ICTY & ICTR?

Professor Suzannah Linton *

1. Plucking numbers out of the air

With 158 persons convicted and sentenced for their participation in international crimes at contemporary international courts and tribunals at time of writing,[1] international sentencing is a now well-mapped area. Yet, this began inauspiciously with the vague provisions of Article 24 of the Statute of the International Criminal Tribunal for the former Yugoslavia ("ICTY"):

1. The penalty imposed by the Trial Chamber shall be limited to imprisonment. In determining the terms of imprisonment, the Trial Chambers shall have recourse to the general practice regarding prison sentences in the courts of the former Yugoslavia.

2. In imposing the sentences, the Trial Chambers should take into account such factors as the gravity of the offence and the individual circumstances of the convicted person.

3. In addition to imprisonment, the Trial Chambers may order the return of

---

* Professor, Law School, Zhejiang Gongshang University, China.

[1] 83 persons at the International Criminal Tribunal for the former Yugoslavia ("ICTY"), 62 at the International Criminal Tribunal for Rwanda ("ICTR"), 9 at the Special Court for Sierra Leone ("SCSL"), and 4 at the International Criminal Court ("ICC") (all last accessed at 6 April 2017). This does not include sentencing for offences against the course of justice and contempt, or cases tried at national or internationalised jurisdictions.

any property and proceeds acquired by criminal conduct, including by means of duress, to their rightful owners.

This was supplemented by Article 7 (3) on superior orders, which provides that this is not a defence but may be considered in mitigation of punishment "if justice so requires" and later buttressed by Rule 101 of the Rules of Procedure of Evidence. [2] These retribution – focused provisions emerged in a barren landscape where there was no system of international criminal justice. The early provisions, described as "general guidelines", [3] drew from the fragmented reality of different practices and approaches to imposition of penalties at the national level, and the distant precedent of the even more unhelpful Nuremberg and Tokyo practice from the 1940s where judges were simply tasked in their statutes to ensure imposition of a just sentence and did not explain the terms that they imposed. A middle way was to require them at least to consider the gravity of the crime and the individual circumstances of the accused, and this is what we see in the ICTY's Article 24 and Rule 101. A year later, in 1994, the provisions of the Rwanda Tribunal ("ICTR") would mirror those of the ICTY, although this court's Statute expressly referred to the need to contribute to "national reconciliation. "[4]

Since the tribunals began operation, and were joined by the Special Court for Sierra Leone ("SCSL"), the International Criminal Court ("ICC"), the Special Tribunal for Lebanon and most recently the Mechanism for International Tribunals ("MICT"), there has developed a wealth of practice on international sentencing. While there is now tribunal – specific and some consistent cross – institutional

---

[2] Rule 101 was adopted on 11 Feb 1994 and then amended four times: on 30 January 1995, 10 July 1998, 1 December 2000, 13 December 2000.

[3] ICTY, *Prosecutor v. Miodrag Jokić*, Judgement on Sentencing Appeal, Appeals Chamber, IT–01–42/1–A, 30 August 2005, para. 6 (https://www. legal–tools. org/en/doc/3cafa2/) ("*Jokić* Judgement on Sentencing Appeal").

[4] Article 23 is the mirror of the ICTY's Article 24, bar the references to the former Yugoslavia.

practice on sentencing, we cannot reasonably speak of a customary international law in the area of sentencing for crimes. There is a continuing diversity at national level which may mean there are not even common general principles beyond the requirements that the sentence must be individualised and proportionate to the crime. Even then, "while national systems generally accept the principle of proportionality, there is significant diversity in their approaches to implementing the principle."[5] Not all States have statutorily mandated maximum and minimum ranges for specified crimes; some have guidelines, others have nothing.[6] The diversity goes beyond that. There are at least 29 countries that maintain a mandatory death penalty for specified offences.[7] In England and Wales, murder is the only offence for which the maximum sentence, life imprisonment, is fixed by law.[8] France, Germany, Italy, Spain and the USA either have minimum or maximum penalties or ranges of penalties and judicial discretion within that.[9] Furthermore, States have different approaches to the function of punishment. Some favour retribution, some favour rehabilitation.

Given that there is disparate practice at the domestic level, it is not surprising that the ICTY and later the ICTR, suffered from the dearth of normative guid-

---

[5] Margaret M deGuzman, "Proportionate Sentencing at the International Criminal Court", in Carsten Stahn (ed.), *The Law and Practice of the International Criminal Court*, Oxford University Press, Oxford, 2014, online version at SSRN available at http://papers.ssrn.com/sol3/papers.cfm? abstract_id = 2423501, last accessed at 1 April 2017 ("deGuzman, 2014"), p. 16. For a review of 23 countries, see Ulrich Sieber, *The Punishment of Serious Crimes: A comparative analysis of sentencing law and practice*, Max - Planck - Institut für ausländisches und internationales Strafrecht, Freiburg i. Br., 2004, vol. 2; also Michael Tonry and Richard S Frase (eds.), *Sentencing and Sanctions in Western Countries*, Oxford University Press, New York, 2011.

[6] Silvia D'Ascoli, *Sentencing in International Criminal Law: The UN ad hoc Tribunals and Future Perspectives for the ICC*, Hart Publishing, Oxford, 2011 (examining England and Wales, France, Germany, Italy, Spain and the USA) ("DAscoli, 2011"); Kai Ambos, *Treatise on International Criminal Law, Vol II: The Crimes and Sentencing*, Oxford University Press, Oxford, 2014 ("Ambos, 2014"), pp. 273-274.

[7] See Cornell Centre on the Death Penalty Worldwide, available at http://www.deathpenaltyworldwide.org/index.cfm, last accessed at 1 April 2017.

[8] See UK Crown Prosecution Service, "Mandatory and Minimum Custodial Sentences", available at http://www.cps.gov.uk/legal/l_to_o/mandatory_and_minimum_custodial_sentences/, last accessed at 1 April 2017.

[9] See D'Ascoli, 2011, chs. 1-2, see *supra* note 6.

ance. Even so, at an institutional level, these bodies have resisted adopting formal guidelines on sentencing, and have been content to leave it to their judges, drawn from all over the world, to respond in the best way they see fit to incorporate meaning into vague notions such as gravity and individual circumstances. Judges would, understandably, draw from their domestic practice in the crafting of tribunal practice.

The result is also not very surprising. Dissatisfaction with sentencing is one of the major reasons that communities in the Balkans and Rwanda cite for their displeasure with the tribunals. [10] Sentencing for international crimes has also long been a very fertile area for "tribunal bashing" by academics. The weakness of the normative sentencing regime, especially the absence of pre—determined ranges of penalties and the perceived arbitrariness and inconsistency arising from extensive judicial discretion, are felt to challenge the fundamental *nulla poena* principle. Ambos, for example, points out that the "*lex certa* component of *nulla poena* is practically ignored in ICL."[11] Three issues have drawn the greatest attention: alleged leniency, [12]

---

[10] See the OSCE, "Public Opinion Survey on Attitudes towards the ICTY and domestic war crimes trials in 2009", available at http://www.osce.org/serbia/40751 and "Attitudes towards war crimes issues, ICTY and the national judiciary in 2012", available at http://www.osce.org/serbia/90422, both last accessed at 14 April 2017. Also see Marko Milanovi ́c, "The Impact of the ICTY on the Former Yugoslavia: An Anticipatory Postmortem", in *American Journal of International Law*, 2016, vol. 110, no. 2, p. 233; Diane Orentlicher, *That Someone Guilty Be Punished: The Impact of the ICTY in Bosnia*, Open Society Justice Initiative and ICTJ, New York, 2010, pp. 51—57. For some reactions to sentences of the ICTR, see Redress and African Rights, *Survivors and Post—Genocide Justice in Rwanda*, Redress and African Rights, London, 2008, pp. 64—71.

[11] Ambos, 2014, p. 272, see *supra* note 6.

[12] For example, Sam Szoke—Burke, "Avoiding Belittlement of Human Suffering: A Retributivist Critique of ICTR Sentencing Practices", in *Journal of International Criminal Justice*, 2012, vol. 10, p. 561; Jens Ohlin, "Proportional Sentences at the ICTY", in Bert Swart et al (eds.), *The Legacy of the International Criminal Tribunal for the Former Yugoslavia*, Oxford University Press, Oxford, 2011, ("Ohlin, 2011") pp. 373—374, 398—399; D' Ascoli, 2011, pp. 49—51, 135, 259, see *supra* note 7; Mark B Harmon and Fergal Gaynor, "Ordinary Sentences for Extraordinary Crimes", in *Journal of International Criminal Justice*, 2007, vol. 5, pp. 683, 711—712; Mark Drumbl, *Atrocity, Punishment and International Law*, Cambridge University Press, New York, 2007, pp. 57—58, 100, 158.

inconsistency, [13] and lack of judicial reasoning or explanation for punishments that were imposed (absence of clarity or transparency). [14] Other grievances are that international sentencing is unpredictable and arbitrary, [15] under-theorised, [16] unduly harsh, [17] and fails to address context and the restorative needs of post-conflict societies. [18] According to Ohlin, "judges have been handing down sentences for war crimes, crimes against humanity, and genocide, with neither a robust system of sentencing procedures nor any coherent theoretical vision of why we are sentencing international criminals in the first place. "[19] An example is the following, from *Gotovina et al.*, where there is much time spent on presenting judicial theories about sentencing, the statutory framework, the practice of the court and the facts of the case, leading up to an abrupt conclusion:

---

[13] The identified inconsistencies range across the treatment of accused who seem to have similar culpability, in the way that chambers identify and evaluate gravity, and aggravating and mitigating factors, between tribunals and in comparison with domestic sentencing practices. See for example, Ohlin, 2011, pp. 373–374, see *supra* note 13; Jennifer Clark, "Zero to Life: Sentencing Appeals at the International Criminal Tribunals for the Former Yugoslavia and Rwanda", in *Georgetown Law Journal*, 2008, vol. 96 ("Clark, 2008"), pp. 1691–1695; Mark A Drumbl, "Collective Violence and Individual Punishment: The Criminality of Mass Atrocity", in *Northwestern University Law Review*, 2005, vol. 99, pp. 582–84.

[14] For example, Barbora Holá, "Consistency and Pluralism of International Sentencing", in Elies van Sliedregt and Sergey Vasiliev (eds.), *Pluralism in International Criminal Law*, Oxford University Press, Oxford, 2014 p. 197 ("Holá, 2014"); Margaret M deGuzman, "Harsh Justice for International Crimes?", in *Yale Journal of International Law*, 2014, vol. 39, no. 1, p. 9 ("deGuzman, 2014"); Ralph Henham, "Developing Contextualized Rationales for Sentencing in International Criminal Trials", in *Journal of International Criminal Justice*, 2007, vol. 5, pp. 760 ("Henham, 2007"); Damien Scalia, "Long-Term Sentences in International Criminal Law: Do they meet the standards set out by the European Court of Human Rights?", in *Journal of International Criminal Justice*, 2011, vol. 9, pp. 682 ("Scalia, 2011"); Ralph Henham, "The Philosophical Foundations of International Sentencing", in *Journal of International Criminal Justice*, 2003, vol. 1, pp. 72 ("Henham, 2003").

[15] Mirko Bagaric and John Morss, "International Sentencing Law: In Search of a Justification and Coherent Framework", in *International Criminal Law Review*, 2006, vol. 6, p. 193.

[16] For example, Jens David Ohlin, "Towards a Unique Theory of International Criminal Sentencing", in Goran Sluiter and Sergey Vasiliev (eds.), *International Criminal Procedure: Towards a Coherent Body of Law*, Cameron May, London, 2009, pp. 382–286; Ambos, 2014, p. 247, see *supra* note 6.

[17] For example, deGuzman, 2014, see *supra* note 5.

[18] For example, Henham, 2007, pp. 80–85, see *supra* note 14.

[19] Ohlin, 2011, p. 375, see *supra* note 12.

The Trial Chamber has considered all the circumstances referred to above and finds that the appropriate sentence with regard to Ante Gotovina is a single sentence of 24 years of imprisonment. [20]

This is the "plucking numbers out of the air" that causes many observers such grief. The judges are not able to explain how they reach the quantum. In the *Gotovina* case, there is no way to understand why the sentence was 24 years, as opposed to 25, 23, 22, 21, 20 or any other term of years.

This present exploration of the evolution of penalties for international crimes focuses on the ICC and the matter of quantum. The points for comparison are therefore the normative framework and judicial practice of the two ad hoc tribunals, with the central question being whether the ICC is an improvement. The statutory framework having already been introduced, we will move immediately to consider the actual practice of the two earlier tribunals (chapter 2). It will be obvious that despite the paucity of the normative framework on quantum of sentence, the chambers have constructed a framework of guidance through their judgements. Reviewing the decisions at both substantive and empirical levels reveals a more coherent and less bleak picture than that painted by critiques such as those cited above. [21] It is true that the absence of formal sentencing guidelines and wide judicial discretion has led to variation, particularly in the early years. However, variation is inevitable in a situation where individualisation of the penalty is an obligation and discretion is in-built. This practice is not absolutely uniform, but there is more consistency than inconsistency

---

[20]   ICTY, *Prosecutor v. Ante Gotovina, Ivan Cermak and Mladen Markac*, Judgement, Trial Chamber, IT-06-90-T, 15 April 2011, para. 2617 (https://www.legal-tools.org/en/doc/7c85bd/) (*"Gotovina et al* Judgement").

[21]   Earlier writers who have challenged the "doom and gloom" assessments include James Meernik and Kimi King, "The Sentencing Determinations of the International Criminal Tribunal for the Former Yugoslavia: An Empirical and Doctrinal Analysis", in *Leiden Journal of International Law*, 2003, vol. 16, p. 717. More recent works will be cited in this paper.

(Holá, Bijleveld and Smeulers have demonstrated different ways to understand consistency;[22] this present author embraces a common—sense understanding of consistency, meaning relative stability and regularity). One extensively researched study has rightly concluded that "a set of sentencing principles is consistently discussed and emphasised by the ICTY and ICTR judges: the most important being the primacy of gravity of crimes in sentence determination and the principles connected to the gravity evaluation: proportionality, gradation and totality. "[23] We can speculate that vocal critiques about perceived anomalies and inadequacies have fed back into the process; the cases do reveal a conscious effort at securing consistency, communicating the approach of the judges, and also determination to do justice in the individual case in line with the scant guidance given and tribunal precedent. There has come to be some predictability in the practice (that is, there is accessibility and foreseeability).

The next section moves on to the core of this paper, a substantive analysis of the ICC's normative framework and sentencing practice. Whether that evolution takes international sentencing sufficiently forward is the central question. The statutory framework is clearly more detailed, and is an improvement. However, there remains extensive discretion with no sentencing guidelines with the same risks of inconsistent results for similar situations. The judgements at the ICC are following the same pattern as those at the ICTY and ICTR. All of the continuing attempts at judicial theorising about sentencing do not obscure the reality that the judges are still not able to explain how they reach the particular penalty imposed. That magic number still seems to be reached in an arbitrary matter, it is still being plucked out of the air.

2. The ICTY and ICTR practice: substantive analysis of sentencing

The judgements do not indicate any judicial discomfort with the exercise of

---

[22] Barbora Holá, Alette Smeulers and Catrien Bijleveld, "Consistency of international sentencing—ICTY and ICTR case study", in *European Journal of Criminology*, 2012, vol. 9 (5) ("Holá et al, 2012"), p. 540.

[23] Barbora Holá, "Sentencing of International Crimes at the ICTY and ICTR: Consistency of Sentencing Case Law", in *Amsterdam Law Forum*, 2012, vol. 4, no. 4 ("Holá, 2012"), p. 22.

broad discretion in determining the appropriate sentence. Tribunal judges in plenary have resisted the adoption of formal sentencing guidelines; they reason that broad judicial discretion arises from the duty of trial judges to individualise the sentence. [24] In line with this and contrary to calls for it to exercise greater supervision[25], the Appeals Chamber of the ICTY and ICTR has been resolute in not imposing formal sentencing guidelines on trial chambers. [26] Appellate judgements have repeatedly pointed out that the regulatory framework does not "constitute binding limitations on a Chamber's discretion to impose a sentence, which must always be decided according to the facts of each particular case. "[27] While some chambers feel their discre-

---

[24]   For example, ICTY, *Prosecutor v Vujadin Popović et al*, Judgement, Appeals Chamber, IT-05-88-A, 30 January 2015, para. 1961 (https://www. legal-tools. org/en/doc/4c28fb/) ("*Popović et al* Appeal Judgement"); ICTY, *Prosecutor v Pavle Strugar*, Judgement, Appeals Chamber, IT-01-42-A, 17 July 2008, para. 335 (https://www. legal-tools. org/doc/981b62/pdf/) ("*Strugar* Appeal Judgement"); ICTY, *Prosecutor v Dragoljub Đorđević et al*, Judgement, Appeals Chamber, IT-05-87/1-A, 27 January 2014, para. 932 (https://www. legal-tools. org/en/doc/e6fa92/) ("*Đorđević* Appeal Judgement"); ICTR, *Prosecutor v. Laurent Semanza*, Judgement, Appeals Chamber, ICTR-97-20-A, 20 May 2005, para. 385 (https://www. legal-tools. org/en/doc/a686fd/) ("*Semanza* Appeal Judgement"); ICTR, *Prosecutor v. Georges Ruggiu*, Judgement and Sentence, Trial Chamber, ICTR-97-32-T, 1 June 2000, para. 61 (https://www. legal-tools. org/en/doc/486d43/) ("*Ruggiu* Judgement and Sentence"); ICTR, *Prosecutor v. Jean Kambanda*, Judgement and Sentence, Trial Chamber, ICTR-97-23-T, 4 September 1998, para. 30 (https://www. legal-tools. org/en/doc/49a299/) ("*Kambanda* Judgement and Sentence"). On the need for appropriately tailored sentencing guidelines, see Holá, 2014, pp. 203-206, see *supra* note 15; Clark, 2008, pp. 1695-1696, see *supra* note 14.

[25]   See for example, Clark, 2008, p. 1695, see *supra* note 13.

[26]   For example, ICTY, *Prosecutor v. Tihomir Blaškić*, Judgement, Appeals Chamber, IT-95-14-A, 29 July 2004, para. 68 (http://www. legal-tools. org/doc/88d8e6/) ("*Blaškić* Appeal Judgement"); ICTY, *Prosecutor v. Radislav Krstić*, Judgement, Appeals Chamber, IT-98-33-A, 19 April 2004, para. 24 (https://www. legal-tools. org/en/doc/86a108/) ("*Krstić* Appeal Judgement"); ICTY, *Prosecutor v Anto Furundžija*, Judgement, Appeals Chamber, IT-95-17/1-A, 21 July 2000, para. 238 (https://www. legal-tools. org/en/doc/660d3f/) ("*Furundžija* Appeal Judgement"); *Prosecutor v Zejnil Delalić et al*, Judgement, Appeals Chamber, IT-96-21-A, 20 February 2001, para. 719 (https://www. legal-tools. org/en/doc/051554/) ("*Delalić et al* Appeal Judgement"). The attempt in cases such as *Imanishimwe* and *Semanza* to establish general sentencing ranges for each specific crime did not take off. Observers have noted that while it is in theory desirable to harmonise sentencing through such guidelines, it is hard to establish an objective hierarchy between underlying acts which are all very serious crimes.

[27]   For example, *Krstić* Appeal Judgement, para. 24, see *supra* note 26.

tion is "unfettered"[28], the correct view must be that of the *Bagilishema* et al. Trial Chamber, that it is "considerable though not unlimited. "[29] Limitations will obviously include working within the regulatory framework and informal guidance provided by the Appeals Chamber in other cases, in line with *Aleksovski*. [30] As the following discussion will demonstrate, that guidance has been considerable and influential, and has contributed towards greater consistency.

The appellate judges have been consistently deferential to trial chambers. For example, in *Simba*, the ICTR Appeals Chamber recalled that whole neither the Statute nor the RPE exhaustively defined the factors which may be considered as mitigating factors, the tribunal's jurisprudence was settled that "what constitutes a mitigating circumstance is a matter for the Trial Chamber to determine in the exercise of its discretion. "[31] Appellate judges have been unwilling to adjust penalties unless there

---

[28] For example, ICTR, *Prosecutor v. Athanase Seromba*, Judgement, Trial Chamber, ICTR-01-66-T, 13 December 2006, para. 376 (https: //www. legal - tools. org/en/doc/e0084d/) ("*Seromba* Judgement") ; ICTR, *Prosecutor v. Georges Rutaganda*, Judgement and Sentence, Trial Chamber, ICTR-96-3-T, 6 December 1999, paras. 458 - 59 (https: //www. legal - tools. org/en/doc/f0dbbb/) ("*Rutaganda* Judgement and Sentence").

[29] ICTR, *Prosecutor v. Théoneste Bagosora et al*, Judgement and Sentence, Trial Chamber, ICTR-98-41-T, 18 December 2008, para. 2263 (https: //www. legal - tools. org/en/doc/6d9b0a/) ("*Bagosora et al* Judgement and Sentence") ; ICTR, *Prosecutor v. Pauline Nyiramasuhuko et al*, Judgement and Sentence, Trial Chamber, ICTR - 98 - 42 - T, 24 June 2011, para. 6188 (https: //www. legal - tools. org/en/doc/e2c881/) ("*Nyiramasuhuko et al* Judgement and Sentence").

[30] ICTY, *Prosecutor v. Zlatko Aleksovski*, Judgement, Appeals Chamber, IT - 95 - 14/1 - T, 24 March 2000, paras. 92-115 (https: //www. legal-tools. org/en/doc/176f05/) ("*Aleksovski* Appeal Judgement").

[31] ICTR, *Prosecutor v. Aloys Simba*, Judgement, Appeals Chamber, ICTR - 01 - 76 - A, 27 November 2007, para. 328 (https: //www. legal-tools. org/en/doc/fc6330/) ("*Simba* Appeal Judgement") ; also ICTR, *Prosecutor v. Théoneste Bagosora et al*, Judgement, Appeals Chamber, ICTR-98-41-A, 14 December 2011, para. 424 (https: //www. legal-tools. org/en/doc/52d501/) ("*Bagosora et al* Appeal Judgement") ; ICTR, *Prosecutor v. Yussuf Munyakazi*, Judgement, Appeals Chamber, ICTR-97-36A, 28 September 2011, para. 174 (https: //www. legal - tools. org/en/doc/48cbd6/) ("*Munyakazi* Appeal Judgement") ; ICTR, *Prosecutor v. Simon Bikindi*, Judgement, Appeals Chamber, ICTR - 01 - 72 - A, 18 March 2010, para. 158 (https: //www. legal-tools. org/doc/e112dd/pdf/) ("*Bikindi* Appeal Judgement") ; ICTR, *Prosecutor v. Siméon Nchamihigo*, Judgement, Appeals Chamber, ICTR - 01 - 63 - A, 18 March 2010, para. 387 (https: //www. legal - tools. org/doc/4b3598/) ("*Nchamihigo* Appeal Judgement") ; ICTY, *Prosecutor v. Dragomir Milosevic*, Judgement, Appeals Chamber, IT-98-29/1-A, 12 November 2009, para. 316 (https: //www. legal-tools. org/en/doc/44327f/) ("*Milošević* Appeal Judgement").

has been a discernible error in the exercise of discretion or failure to follow the law. This approach was explained in the *Blagojević et al* Appeal Judgment:

> Trial Chambers are vested with a broad discretion in determining an appropriate sentence, due to their obligation to individualize penalties to fit the circumstances of the accused and the gravity of the crime. As a rule, the Appeals Chamber will not revise a sentence unless the Trial Chamber has committed a discernible error in exercising its discretion or has failed to follow the applicable law. It is for the appealing party to demonstrate how the Trial Chamber erred in imposing the sentence. [32]

The jurisprudence also clarifies that "discernible error in exercising its discretion" requires proof that the particular trial chamber gave weight to extraneous or irrelevant considerations, failed to accord weight or sufficient weight to relevant considerations, made a clear error as to the facts upon which it exercised its discretion, or demonstrate that its decision was so unreasonable or plainly unjust that the Appeals Chamber is able to infer that the trial chamber must have failed to exercise its

---

[32]　ICTY, *Prosecutor v. Vidoje Blagojević et al*, Judgement, Appeals Chamber, IT-02-60-T, 9 May 2007, para. 321 (https: //www. legal-tools. org/en/doc/c32768/) ("*Blagojević et al* Appeal Judgement"). For more recent jurisprudence, see *Popović et al* Appeal Judgement, para. 1961, see *supra* note 25; *Strugar* Appeal Judgement, para. 336, see *supra* note 24; *Đorđević* Appeal Judgement, para. 932, see *supra* note 25; ICTY, *Prosecutor v. Nikola Šainović et al*, Judgement, Appeals Chamber, IT-05-87-A, 23 January 2014, para. 1798 (https: //www. legal-tools. org/en/doc/81ac8c/) ("*Šainović et al* Appeal Judgement"); *Bagosora et al* Appeal Judgement, para. 419, see *supra* note 31; ICTR, *Prosecutor v. Ephrem Setako*, Judgement, Appeals Chamber, ICTR-04-81-A, 28 September 2011, para. 277 (https: //www. legal-tools. org/doc/e1c09a/) ("*Setako* Judgement"); *Munyakazi* Appeal Judgement, para. 166, see *supra* note 31; ICTR, *Prosecutor v. Tharcisse Renzaho*, Judgement, Appeals Chamber, ICTR-97-31-T, 1 April 2011, para. 606 (https: //www. legal-tools. org/en/doc/0abb32/) ("*Renzaho* Appeal Judgement"); *Nchamihigo* Appeal Judgement, para. 384, see *supra* note 31. For more in depth consideration, see Clark, 2008, see *supra* note 13.

discretion properly. [33]

We should not be misled by this appearance of passivity on the part of the Appeals Chamber. It has not neglected to provide guidance to trial chambers. A review of the footnotes cited in this study reveals how substantial this guidance has actually been. Comparative or consistent sentencing, which calls for judges to be conscious of the sentencing range imposed in other cases in order that similar crimes are punished similarly (like is treated alike), provides an example. At a theoretical level, the Appeals Chamber is obviously in favour of consistency in sentencing, and facilitating this through awareness of other cases. [34] As the Appeals Chamber in the ICTY's *čelebiċ i* case noted, "[o] ne of the fundamental elements in any rational and fair system of criminal justice is consistency in punishment. This is an important reflection of the notion of equal justice. " [35] The appearance of injustice arises where there are substantial inconsistencies in the punishment of different offenders, where the circumstances of the different offences and of the offenders being punished are sufficiently similar that the punishments imposed would, in justice, be expected to be also generally similar. [36]

Despite the assertion that sentences of individuals in like cases should be com-

---

[33] For example, *Šainoviċ et al* Appeal Judgement, para. 1799, see *supra* note 32; ICTY, *Prosecutor v. Ljube Boškoski and Johan Tarčulovski*, Judgement, Appeals Chamber, IT–04–82–T, 19 May 2010, para. 205 (https: //www. legal–tools. org/en/doc/54398a/) ("*Boškoski and Tarčulovski* Appeal Judgement"); ICTY, *Prosecutor v. Momcilo Krajišnik*, Judgement, Appeals Chamber, IT–00–39–A, 17 March 2009, para. 735 (https: //www. legal–tools. org/en/doc/770028/) ("*Krajišnik* Appeal Judgement"); *Popoviċ et al* Appeal Judgement, para. 5, see *supra* note 24; *Bikindi* Appeal Judgement, para. 141, see *supra* note 31.

[34] *Strugar* Appeal Judgement, para. 348, see *supra* note 25; *Prosecutor v. Miroslav Kvočka et al*, Judgement, Appeals Chamber, IT–98–30/1–A, 28 February 2005, para. 681 (https: //www. legal–tools. org/en/doc/006011/) ("*Kvočka et al* Appeal Judgement").

[35] *Delaliċ et al* Appeal Judgement, para. 756, see *supra* note 26. Also, *Popoviċ et al* Appeal Judgement, para. 2093, see *supra* note 24; *Strugar* Appeal Judgement, para. 348, see *supra* note 24; *Nyiramasuhuko et al* Judgement and Sentence, para. 6190, see *supra* note 29.

[36] *Delaliċ et al* Appeal Judgement, para. 756, see *supra* note 26. Also, *Popoviċ et al* Appeal Judgement, para. 2093, see *supra* note 24; *Strugar* Appeal Judgement, para. 348, see *supra* note 24; *Nyiramasuhuko et al* Judgement and Sentence, para. 6190, see *supra* note 29.

parable, sentencing disparity has, as noted earlier, been an active area of criticism of tribunal practice. The judges have not accepted comparative sentencing as a cardinal principle or the sole basis of sentencing because of the realities of difference and the importance of tailoring sentences to the particular situation and the particular individual. In the *čelebići* appellate judgement, the judges declared that "as a general principle such comparison is often of limited assistance… often the differences are more significant than the similarities, and the mitigating and aggravating factors dictate different results. [37] Another leading case providing guidance about the value of comparison with previous cases was *Nikolic*. Here, the Appeals Chamber explained in greater detail why the comparison may not necessarily be a proper avenue to challenge a Trial Chamber's finding in exercising its discretion to impose a sentence. [38] In *Popović*, the Appeals Chamber affirmed the position that any assistance from comparison may be limited, given the Trial Chamber's overriding obligation to tailor a penalty to fit the gravity of the crime and the individual circumstances of the accused. It affirmed that "it is frequently impossible to transpose the sentence in one case mutatis mutandis to another" and so "previous sentencing practice is but one factor among a host of others which must be taken into account when determining the

---

[37] *Kvočka et al* Appeal Judgement, para. 861, see *supra* note 34; ICTY, *Prosecutor v. Mile Mrkšić et al*, Judgement, Trial Chamber, IT–95–13/1–T, 27 September 2007, para. 688 (https://www. legal–tools. org/en/doc/32111c/); *Delalić et al* Appeal Judgement, paras. 719–720, see *supra* note 26; ICTR, *Prosecutor v. Protais Zigiranyirazo*, Judgement, Appeals Chamber, ICTR–01–73–T, 16 November 2009, para. 456 (https://www. legal–tools. org/en/doc/8c455f/) (*"Zigiranyirazo* Judgement and Sentence"); ICTR, *Prosecutor v. Yussuf Munyakazi*, Judgement and Sentence, Trial Chamber, ICTR–97–36A, 5 July 2010, para. 515 (https://www. legal–tools. org/en/doc/9b9ee3/).

[38] ICTY, *Prosecutor v. Dragan Nikolić*, Judgement on Sentencing Appeal, Appeals Chamber, IT–94–2–A, 4 February 2005, paras. 38–39, 41–47, 49–50 (https://www. legal–tools. org/en/doc/5bab22/) (*"Nikolić* Judgement on Sentencing Appeal"). Also relevant are ICTY, *Prosecutor v Milan Babić*, Judgement on Sentencing Appeal, Appeals Chamber, IT–03–72–A, 18 July 2005, para. 32 (https://www. legal–tools. org/en/doc/640374/) (*"Babić* Judgement on Sentencing Appeal"); *Kvočka et al* Appeal Judgement, para. 681, see *supra* note 34; *Furundžija* Appeal Judgement, paras. 249–250, see *supra* note 26.

sentence. " [39] The position is identical at the ICTR. [40]

In their years of adjudication, the ICTY and ICTR chambers regularly cranked out production–line pontifications about sentencing policy and the role of the Trial Chamber, although later cases are much more economical in publicising the Trial Chamber's views of the tribunal's aims and objectives, and that of punishment. They contain a mixture of traditional justifications (retribution and the utilitarian principles of deterrence, incapacitation and rehabilitation), as well as "expressionist" justifications of penal punishment. [41] These are then buttressed by discussion of the gravity of the crime, and aggravating and mitigating factors. Damaška has suggested that the number of goals that the judgements identify in the course of rationalising sentencing is excessive; some of them are contradictory and the message gets diluted. [42] Henham, writing in 2007, identified "incontrovertible" evidence of "confusion and obfuscation on the part of ad hoc tribunals relating to the possible scope and meaning to be accorded to penal justifications. " [43] From general statements, the judgements move to individualise the discussion with a contextual discussion, and then a number

[39]   *Popović et al* Appeal Judgement, para. 1966, see *supra* note 24; *Strugar* Appeal Judgement, para. 349, see *supra* note 24; *Šainović et al* Appeal Judgement, para. 1837, see *supra* note 33; *Prosecutor v. Mile Mrkšić and Veselin Šljivančanin*, Judgement, Appeals Chamber, IT–95–13/1–A, 5 May 2009, para. 415 (https://www. legal–tools. org/en/doc/40bc41/) ("*Mrkšić and Šljivančanin* Appeal Judgement").

[40]   *Semanza* Appeal Judgement, para. 394, see *supra* note 24. More recently, ICTR, *Prosecutor v. Edouard Karemera et al*, Judgement, Appeals Chamber, ICTR–98–44–A, 29 September 2014, para. 701 (https://www. legal–tools. org/en/doc/372a64/) ("*Karemera et al* Appeal Judgement"); ICTR, *Prosecutor v, Emmanuel Rukundo*, Judgement, Appeals Chamber, ICTR–01–70, 20 October 2010, para. 263 (https://www. legal–tools. org/doc/d5b969/); ICTR, *Prosecutor v. Mikaeli Muhimana*, Judgement, Appeals Chamber, ICTR–95–1B–TA, para. 232, 21 May 2007 (https://www. legal–tools. org/en/doc/8b044b/) ("*Muhimana* Appeal Judgement"); ICTR, *Prosecutor v. Ferdinand Nahimana*, Judgement, Appeals Chamber, ICTR–96–11–A, 28 November 2007, para. 1066 (https://www. legal–tools. org/en/doc/04e4f9/) ("*Nahimana* Judgement (Appeal)").

[41]   The general idea is that actions should reflect or express values that underpin the law, see Elizabeth Anderson and Richard Pildes, "Expressive Theories of Law: A General Restatement", in *University of Pennsylvania Law Review*, 2000, vol. 148, p. 1503.

[42]   Mirjan R. Damaška, "What is the Point of International Criminal Justice?", in *Chicago Kent Law Review*, 2008, vol. 83 ("Damaška, 2008"), pp. 329, 331.

[43]   Henham, 2007, p. 69, see *supra* note 14.

is magically pronounced at the end. From the very first cases, *Tadić* and *Akayesu*, there has never any explanation of the mysterious process of how that quantum was reached, for example the extent to which a mitigating or aggravating factor concretely impacted on the final outcome. Discretion is of course not about science, and judicial attempts to justify the choice by way of formulaic verbiage do not detract from this reality.

ICTY and ICTR judges claim a number of objectives when punishing international crimes. These draw in notions of just deserts (just punishment) which is also sometimes described as retribution[44], ending impunity[45], individual and general

[44] For example, ICTY, *Prosecutor v. Radoslav Brđanin*, Judgement, Trial Chamber, IT-99-36-T, 1 September 2004, paras. 2693 (https://www. legal-tools. org/en/doc/4c3228/) ("*Brđanin* Judgement"); ICTY, *Prosecutor v. Momcilo Krajišnik*, Judgement, Trial Chamber, IT-00-39-T, 27 September 2006, para. 1135 (https://www. legal - tools. org/en/doc/62a710/) ("*Krajišnik* Judgement"); *Krajišnik* Appeal Judgement, para. 777, see *supra* note 33; ICTY, *Prosecutor v Dario Kordić and Mario Čerkez*, Judgement, Appeals Chamber, IT-95-14/2-T, 17 December 2004, para. 1075 (https://www. legal-tools. org/en/doc/738211/) ("*Kordić and Čerkez* Appeal Judgement"); *Aleksovski* Appeal Judgement, para. 18, see *supra* note 31; ICTR, *Rutaganda* Judgement and Sentence, paras. 108-109, see *supra* note 28; *Kambanda* Judgement and Sentence, para. 28, see *supra* note 24; ICTR, *Prosecutor v. Omar Serushago*, Sentence, Trial Chamber, ICTR-98-39-T, 5 February 1999, para. 20 (https://www. legal - tools. org/en/doc/e2dddb/) ("*Serushago* Sentence"); *Prosecutor v. Alfred Musema*, Judgement and Sentence, Trial Chamber, ICTR-96-13-T, 27 January 2000, para. 986 (https://www. legal-tools. org/en/doc/1fc6ed/).

[45] For example, *Krajišnik* Judgement, paras. 1134-1138, see *supra* note 44; *Kordić and Čerkez* Appeal Judgement, para. 1081, see *supra* note 44; ICTY, *Prosecutor v Momir Nikolić*, Sentencing Judgement, Trial Chamber, IT - 02 - 60/1 - T, 2 December 2003, paras. 88 - 89 (https://www. legal - tools. org/en/doc/f90842/) ("*Nikolić* Sentencing Judgement"); *Serushago* Sentence, para. 20, see *supra* note 45; *Ruggiu* Judgement and Sentence, para. 33, see *supra* note 24.

deterrence[46] , stigmatisation of conduct[47] , incapacitation of dangerous person[48] , the need to protect society or defend values[49] , reconciliation[50] , and res-

---

[46] For example, ICTY, *Prosecutor v Ramush Haradinaj et al*, Judgement, Trial Chamber, IT−04−84−
T, 3 March 2008, para. 486 (https: //www. legal−tools. org/en/doc/025913/) ; *Kordić and Čerkez* Appeal
Judgement, paras. 1076−1078, see *supra* note 44; *Nikolić* Judgement on Sentencing Appeal, para. 45, see *supra*
note 39; ICTR, *Prosecutor v. Tharcisse Muvunyi*, Judgement and Sentence, Trial Chamber, ICTR−00−55−T, 12
September 2006, para. 135 (https: //www. legal − tools. org/en/doc/fa02aa/) ; ICTR, *Prosecutor v. Siméon
Nchamihigo*, Judgement and Sentence, Trial Chamber, ICTR−01−63−T, 12 November 2008, para. 383 (https: //www. legal−tools. org/en/doc/b3c6e0/) ("*Nchamihigo* Judgement and Sentence") ; ICTR, *Prosecutor
v. Simon Bikindi*, Judgement and Sentence, Trial Chamber, ICTR−01−72−T, 2 December 2008, para. 198 (https: //www. legal − tools. org/doc/4051ba/) (" *Bikindi* Judgement and Sentence ") ; ICTR, *Prosecutor
v. François Karera*, Judgement and Sentence, Trial Chamber, ICTR−01−74−T, 7 December 2007, para. 571
(https: //www. legal−tools. org/en/doc/7bc57f/) ("*Karera* Judgement and Sentence") ; ICTR, *Prosecutor
v. Vincent Rutaganira*, Judgement and Sentence, Trial Chamber, ICTR−95−1C, 14 March 2005, paras. 110,
112 (https: //www. legal − tools. org/doc/cd2a8f/) ("*Rutaganira* Judgement and Sentence") ; *Kambanda*
Judgement and Sentence, para. 28, see *supra* note 24. *Rutaganda* Judgement and Sentence, para. 456, see *supra*
note 29.

[47] For example, ICTY, *Prosecutor v Vidoje Blagojević et al*, Judgement, Trial Chamber, IT−02−60−T,
17 January 2005, para. 81 (https: //www. legal−tools. org/en/doc/7483f2/) ("*Blagojević et al* Judgement") ;
Kordić and Čerkez Appeal Judgement, paras. 1070, 1080, see *supra* note 44; *Nikolić* Sentencing Judgement,
para. 58, see *supra* note 45; *Furundžija* Appeal Judgement, para. 289, see *supra* note 27; ICTR, *Prosecutor
v. Sylvestre Gacumbitsi*, Judgement, Trial Chamber, ICTR − 01 − 64 − 0200/2, 17 June 2004, para. 336 (https: //www. legal−tools. org/doc/b4e8aa/) ; ICTR, *Prosecutor v. Elizaphan Ntakirutimana et al*, Judgement
and Sentence, Trial Chamber, ICTR−96−10−T and ICTR−96−17−T, 21 February 2003, para. 773 (https: //
www. legal−tools. org/en/doc/9a9031/) ("*Ntakirumana et al* Judgement and Sentence") .

[48] For example, *Blagojević et al* Judgement, para. 824, see *supra* note 47; ICTY, *Prosecutor v. Milorad
Krnojelac*, Judgement, Trial Chamber, IT−97−25, −T, 15 March 2002, para. 508 (https: //www. legal−
tools. org/en/doc/1a994b/) ("*Krnojelac* Judgement") .

[49] For example, *Brđanin* Judgement, paras. 1090, 1092, see *supra* note 44; ICTY, *Prosecutor v Tihi-
mor Blaškić*, Judgement, Trial Chamber, IT − 95 − 14 − T, 3 March 2000, para. 61 (https: //www. legal −
tools. org/en/doc/e1ae55/) ("*Blaškić* Judgement") ; *Nchamihigo* Judgement and Sentence, para. 383, see *supra* note 47; *Prosecutor v. Michel Bagaragaza*, Sentencing Judgement, Trial Chamber, ICTR−05−86−T, 17 November 2009, para. 28 (https: //www. legal−tools. org/en/doc/3d2d48/) ("*Bagaragaza* Sentencing Judgement") .

[50] For example, *Blagojević et al* Judgement, para. 82, see *supra* note 47; ICTY, *Prosecutor v. Dražen
Erdemović*, Sentencing Judgement, Trial Chamber, IT−96−22, 5 March 1998, para. 21 (https: //www. legal−
tools. org/doc/92626d/) ; *Seromba* Judgement, para. 376, see *supra* note 28.

toration or maintenance of peace and security[51]. Rehabilitation is sometimes listed but is not a determining factor. [52] The combinations will vary from case to case, including in the way that they are balanced, but it is clear that the judges see deterrence and retribution as the main aims of punishment through imprisonment; the two are quite often twinned together on a parity level. [53] Given that there is diversity in domestic approaches to punishment, some irregularity can be reasonably expected at the international level. Even so, this area illustrates unexpected plurality of views and some unnecessary confusion about core functions of the tribunals, which is not to be explained as being due to discretion or the individualisation of punishment. [54] Holá has referred to this as "considerable disarray. "[55]

---

[51]　For example, ICTY, *Prosecutor v. Milan Babić*, *Sentencing Judgement of Milan Babić*, Trial Chamber I, IT−03−72−T, 29 June 2004, para. 68 (https://www. legal−tools. org/en/doc/1f575a/) ("Sentencing Judgement of *Milan Babić*") ; *Nikolić* Sentencing Judgement, para. 4, see *supra* note 46; *Seromba* Judgement, para. 376, see *supra* note 28.

[52]　For example, *Gotovina et al* Judgement, para. 2598, see *supra* note 20; ICTY, *Prosecutor v. Miroslav Deronjić*, Judgement on Sentencing Appeal, Appeals Chamber, IT−02−61−A, 20 July 2005, paras. 136−137 (https://www. legal−tools. org/en/doc/ba4aa2/) ("*Deronjić* Judgement on Sentencing Appeal") ; *Delalić et al* Appeal Judgement, para. 806, see *supra* note 26; *Kordić and Čerkez* Appeal Judgement, para. 1079, see *supra* note 45; Sentencing Judgement of *Milan Babić*, para. 46, see *supra* note 51; *Bagaragaza* Sentencing Judgement, para. 28, see *supra* note 49; *Nahimana* Judgement (Appeal), para. 1057, see *supra* note 41; *Ruggiu* Judgement and Sentence, para. 33, see *supra* note 24.

[53]　Confirmed by Holá, 2012, see *supra* note 24, p. 7; Jan Philip Book, *Appeal and Sentence*, Berliner Juristische Universitätsschriften: Berlin, 2011, ("Book, 2011") p. 25; Ciara Darmgaard, *Individual Criminal Responsibility for Core International Crimes*, Springer, New York, 2008, pp. 19−20. Examples of the notion of both retribution and deterrence being the main goals or objectives can be found in cases such as ICTY, *Prosecutor v Vujadin Popović* et al, Judgement, Trial Chamber, IT−05−88−T, 10 June 2010, paras. 2128−2129 (https://www. legal−tools. org/en/doc/481867/) ("*Popović* et al Judgement") ; *Popović et al* Appeal Judgement, para. 1966, see *supra* note 25; ICTY, *Prosecutor v. Pavle Strugar*, Judgement, Trial Chamber, IT−01−42−T, 31 January 2005, para. 458 (https://www. legal−tools. org/en/doc/927ba5/) ("*Strugar* Judgement") ; ICTY, *Prosecutor v. Milomir Stakic*, Judgement, Appeals Chamber, IT−97−24−A, 22 March 2006, para. 402 (https://www. legal−tools. org/en/doc/09f75f/) ("*Stakic* Appeal Judgement") ; *Delalić et al* Appeal Judgement, para. 806, see *supra* note 27; *Aleksovski* Appeal Judgement, para. 185, see *supra* note 31; *Nahimana* Judgement (Appeal), para. 1057, see *supra* note 40; *Rutaganda* Judgement and Sentence, para. 456, see *supra* note 28; *Serushago* Sentence, para. 20, see *supra* note 44.

[54]　Also, Holá, 2012, p. 23, see *supra* note 23.

[55]　Holá, 2014, p. 195, see *supra* note 14.

The Statutes and RPE, as discussed earlier, direct the judges to several broad factors to consider in sentencing: ①the gravity of the crime, ②individual circumstances including aggravating and mitigating factors, ③the general practice regarding prison sentences in the courts of the former Yugoslavia and Rwanda, ④credit to be given for the period in detention, if any, pending surrender to the Tribunal or pending trial or appeal; and⑤the extent to which any penalty imposed by a court of any State on the convicted person for the same act has already been served. Other considerations emerging from the caselaw are proportionality of sentencing,[56] capturing the totality of the crime,[57] and expanded discussion on personalised or individualised sentencing[58]. In relation to proportionality, deGuzman has argued that "the sentencing jurisprudence of these tribunals fails to identify a consistent theory of proportionality, whether based in customary international law or otherwise", and there is no consensus on the principles of proportionate punishment. [59] Gravity is the primary consideration: the *Musema* Appeals Chamber held although sentences must be graduated (see later), this "is, however, always subject to the proviso that the

---

[56] For example, *Babić* Judgement on Sentencing Appeal, para. 33, see *supra* note 38; *Kvočka et al* Appeal Judgement, para. 681, see *supra* note 34; ICTY, *Prosecutor v. Goran Jelisić*, Judgement, Appeals Chamber, IT–95–10, 5 July 2001, para. 96 (https: //www. legal-tools. org/doc/477a30/); ICTR, *Prosecutor v. Jean de Dieu Kamuhanda*, Judgement, Appeals Chamber, ICTR–97–23, 19 September 2005, paras. 359, 361 (https: //www. legal-tools. org/en/doc/8ff7cd/) ("*Kamuhanda* Appeal Judgement).

[57] This is a statutory requirement under the RPE. Examples include ICTY, *Prosecutor v. Enver Hadžihasanović and Amira Kubura*, Judgement, Appeals Chamber, IT–01–47–A, 22 April 2008, para. 356 (https: //www. legal-tools. org/en/doc/2705b3/) ("*Hadžihasanović and Kubura* Appeal Judgement"); ICTR, *Prosecutor v. Jean-Paul Akayesu*, Judgement, Appeals Chamber, ICTR–96–4–A, 1 June 2001, para. 416 (https: //www. legal-tools. org/en/doc/c62d06/).

[58] For example, *Popović et al* Appeal Judgement, paras. 1961, 1993, 2039, see *supra* note 24; *Šainović et al* Appeal Judgement, paras. 1837–1839, see *supra* note 32; *Mrkšić and Šljivančanin* Appeal Judgement, para. 415, see *supra* note 39; ICTY, *Prosecutor v Momir Stakić*, Judgement, Appeals Chamber, IT–97–24–A, 22 March 2006, para. 1837 (https: //www. legal-tools. org/en/doc/bfbfcd/) ("*Stakić* Appeal Judgement"); *Nikolić* Judgement on Sentencing Appeal, paras. 19, 45–46, see *supra* note 38; *Blagojević et al* Judgement, para. 832, see *supra* note 47; *Kordić and Čerkez* Appeal Judgement, para. 1087, see *supra* note 44; *Kamuhanda* Appeal Judgement, paras. 351, 357, see *supra* note 56; *Simba* Appeal Judgement, para. 336, see *supra* note 31.

[59] deGuzman, 2014, p. 15, see *supra* note 5.

gravity of the offence is the primary consideration for a Trial Chamber in imposing sentence. "[60]

The ICTY Appeals Chamber in *Kordić & Čerkez* laid out a position that has been applied across the board: "The determination of the gravity of the crime requires a consideration of the particular circumstances of the case, as well as the form and degree of the participation of the accused in the crimes. "[61] Matching the penalty to the gravity of the criminal conduct should be "the overriding obligation in determining sentence. "[62] In its decision in *Blaškić*, the Appeals Chamber suggested several factors to be considered in evaluating gravity. [63] On the link between the gravity of the conduct and the sentence, the ICTR Appeals Chamber in *Nahimana et al.* has affirmed that "the principle of gradation or hierarchy in sentencing requires that the

---

[60]   ICTR, *Prosecutor v. Alfred Musema*, Judgement, Appeals Chamber, ICTR-96-13-A, 16 November 2001, para. 382 (https: //www. legal - tools. org/en/doc/6a3fce/) ("*Musema* Appeal Judgement") ; also *Hadžihasanović and Kubura* Appeal Judgement, para. 321, see *supra* note 57.

[61]   *Kordić and Čerkez* Appeal Judgement, para. 1061, see *supra* note 44 (citing from *Kupreškić*). This principle was approved in cases such as ICTY, *Prosecutor v. Zdravko Tolimir*, Judgement, Appeals Chamber, IT-05-88/2-A, 8 April 2015, para. 633 (https: //www. legal–tools. org/en/doc/010ecb/) ; *Nikolić* Judgement on Sentencing Appeal, para. 18, see *supra* note 38; ICTY, *Prosecutor v. Mitar Vasiljević*, Judgement, Appeals Chamber, IT - 98 - 32 - T, 25 February 2004, para. 156 (https: //www. legal - tools. org/en/doc/ e35d81/) ("*Vasiljević* Appeal Judgement") ; ICTY, *Prosecutor v. Stanislav Galić*, Judgement, Appeals Chamber, IT-98-29-A, 30 November 2006, para. 442 (https: //www. legal–tools. org/en/doc/c81a32/) ("*Galić* Appeal Judgement").

[62]   For example, *Delalić et al* Appeal Judgement, para. 717, see *supra* note 26; *Krnojelac* Judgement, para. 507, see *supra* note 48; ICTY, *Prosecutor v. Predrag Banović*, Sentencing Judgement, Trial Chamber, IT-02-65/1, 28 October 2003, para. 36 (http: //www. legal–tools. org/doc/7323e5/) ; ICTR, *Prosecutor v. Jean de Dieu Kamuhanda*, Judgement and Sentence, Trial Chamber, ICTR-99-54A, 22 January 2004, para. 765 (https: //www. legal–tools. org/doc/4ac346/) ("*Kamuhanda* Judgement and Sentence") ; *Ntakirumana et al* Judgement and Sentence, 2003, para. 883, see *supra* note 48; ICTR, *Prosecutor v. Juvénal Kajelijeli*, Judgement and Sentence, Trial Chamber, ICTR-98-44A, 1 December 2003, para. 163 (https: //www. legal–tools. org/ en/doc/afa827/) ("*Kajelijeli* Judgement and Sentence").

[63]   *Blaškić* Appeal Judgement, para. 68, see *supra* note 27. Trial chambers have also identified such factors, for example, ICTY, *Prosecutor v Stanislav Galić*, Judgement, Trial Chamber, IT-98-29-T, 5 December 2003, para. 758 (https: //www. legal - tools. org/en/doc/eb6006/) ; *Kvočka et al* Appeal Judgement, para. 702, see *supra* note 34.

longest sentences be reserved for the most serious offences. "[64] So, there is consistency about the critical role of gravity (although there are numerous nuanced descriptions of that importance, such as the "primary consideration"[65], the "deciding factor"[66], a "key factor"[67], "litmus test"[68], "a factor of primary importance"[69] and "an essential criterion"[70]). This concept covers gravity *in abstracto* which looks at the objective circumstances such as scale and victims and gravity *in concreto* which looks at the role of the accused in the crime. According to Holá, "ICTY and ICTR judges put primary emphasis in sentence determination on the gravity *in concreto* assessment, i. e. particular circumstances of the case at hand", although there is some confusion and obfuscation of the boundaries between the notions of gravity of crimes and aggravating factors. [71]

At both tribunals, the jurisprudence is consistent that it is for the trial judges to

---

[64]   *Nahimana* Judgement (Appeal), para. 1060, see *supra* note 40. Also see *Kamuhanda* Judgement and Sentence, 2004, para. 760, see *supra* note 62; *Kajelijeli* Judgement and Sentence, 2003, para. 953, see *supra* note 62; ICTR, *Prosecutor v. Mikaeli Muhimana*, Judgement and Sentence, Trial Chamber, ICTR-95-1B-T, 28 April 2005, para. 591 (https://www. legal-tools. org/en/doc/87fe83/) (*Muhimana* Judgement and Sentence).

[65]   For example, *Popović et al* Appeal Judgement, para. 1991, see *supra* note 24; *Đorđević* Appeal Judgement, para. 969, see *supra* note 24; ICTY, *Prosecutor v Milan Lukić and Sredoje Lukić*, Judgement, Appeals Chamber, IT-98-32/1-T, 4 December 2012, para. 649 (https://www. legal-tools. org/en/doc/da785e/); *Gotovina et al* Judgement, para. 2599, see *supra* note 20; ICTY, *Prosecutor v Momcilo Perisić*, Judgement, Trial Chamber, IT-04-81, 6 September 2011, para. 1799 (https://www. legal-tools. org/en/doc/f3b23d/) ("*Perisić* Judgement"); *Delalić et al* Appeal Judgement, para. 73, see *supra* note 26; *Brđanin* Judgement, para. 1094, see *supra* note 44, para. 1094; *Muhimana* Appeal Judgement, para. 233, see *supra* note 40.

[66]   For example, *Nyiramasuhuko et al* Judgement and Sentence, para. 6189, see *supra* note 29; *Nahimana* Judgement (Appeal), para. 1060, see *supra* note 40.

[67]   For example, *Kamuhanda* Appeal Judgement, para. 357, see *supra* note 56.

[68]   For example, *Nikolić* Judgement on Sentencing Appeal, para. 18, see *supra* note 38.

[69]   For example, ICTR, *Prosecutor v Miroslav Deronjić*, Sentencing Judgement, Trial Chamber, IT-02-61-T, 30 March 2004, para. 184 (https://www. legal-tools. org/en/doc/95420f/) ("*Deronjić* Sentencing Judgement"); ICTY, *Prosecutor v Mladen Naletilić and Vinko Martinović*, Judgement, Trial Chamber, IT-98-34-T, 31 March 2003, para. 718 (https://www. legal-tools. org/en/doc/f2cfeb/); ICTR, *Prosecutor v. Joseph Serugendo*, Judgement and Sentence, Trial Chamber, ICTR-05-84-T, 12 June 2006, para. 39 (https://www. legal-tools. org/en/doc/a68054/) ("*Serugendo* Judgement and Sentence").

[70]   For example, *Kambanda* Judgement and Sentence, para, 57, see *supra* note 24.

[71]   Holá, 2012, p. 12, see *supra* note 23.

decide what is or is not an aggravating or mitigating factor, [72] and also that the trial chambers have considerable discretion in relation to the weight to be assigned to factors. [73] This discretion has led to significant differences between cases that are sometimes appear similar, and therefore to consistency concerns. Commentators have noted fundamental differences between cases. An example is "previous good character" where it has sometimes not been accepted at all, sometimes as mitigating, sometimes as aggravating. [74] Appellate guidance has been that the question of whether "certain factors going to a convicted person's character constitute mitigating or aggravating factors depends largely on the particular circumstances of each case." [75] According to one evaluation "aggravating and mitigating circumstances are considered somewhat erratically", with good character, context of the crime, and the age of the accused as examples of factors which go both ways in the jurisprudence. [76]

The explanation is that this is properly a matter of judicial discretion, for a hard and fast rule in matters such as these would lead to conveyor-belt justice. To be fair,

---

[72] For example, *Popović et al* Appeal Judgement, para. 2053, see *supra* note 24; *Šainović et al* Appeal Judgement, para. 1826, see *supra* note 32; *Milošević* Appeal Judgement, para. 316, see *supra* note 31; *Zigiranyirazo* Judgement and Sentence, para. 458, see *supra* note 37; *Bikindi* Judgement and Sentence, para. 449, *supra* 46; *Serugendo* Judgement and Sentence, 2006, para. 40, see *supra* note 69. The jurisprudence is also settled that aggravating factors must be proved beyond reasonable doubt, and mitigating factors on the balance of probabilities.

[73] For example, *Popović et al* Appeal Judgement, para. 2053, see *supra* note 24; *Milošević* Appeal Judgement, para. 316, see *supra* note 31; *Đorđević* Appeal Judgement, para. 305, see *supra* note 24; ICTR, *Prosecutor v Aloys Ntabakuze*, Judgement, Appeals Chamber, ICTR-98-41-T, 8 May 2012, para. 280 (https://www.legal-tools.org/en/doc/281406/) ("*Ntabakuze* Appeal Judgement"); *Bagosora et al* Appeal Judgement, para. 424, see *supra* note 32; *Nahimana* Judgement (Appeal), para. 1038, see *supra* note 40.

[74] Clark, 2008, pp. 1693-1694, see *supra* note 13, citing the ICTY cases of *Babić*, *Tadić*, *Brđanin*, and *Simić et al*.

[75] *Hadžihasanović and Kubura* Appeal Judgement, para. 328, see *supra* note 57; *Babić* Judgement on Sentencing Appeal, para. 49, see *supra* note 38.

[76] Scalia, 2011, p. 682, see *supra* note 14 (footnotes omitted).

at times but not always, the judges are clear about how significant a factor is. [77] As will be seen in this study, two decades of jurisprudence reveal significant commonality in the aggravating and mitigating factors accepted by the chambers. The caselaw also reveals how concepts such as gravity and aggravating factors can overlap, with the risk of unfairly counting factors such as the accused's level of authority twice. There is a consistent line of appellate authority about how there must not be double-counting. Sometimes the guidance has been as simple as "factors considered in establishing the gravity of the crime cannot be considered again as separate aggravating factors" [78] or it is a matter of "some" judicial discretion "as to the rubric under which they treat particular factors. " [79] Sometimes the approach is more concrete, leading to clear guidance such as "discriminatory intent or a discriminatory state of mind for crimes for which such a state of mind is not an element or ingredient can be considered as an aggravating factor" [80] or "a factor considered as an element of the crime

---

[77]　For example, in the ICTY, *Prosecutor v. Dragan Obrenović*, Sentencing Judgement, Trial Chamber, IT-02-60/2-T, 10 December 2003, paras. 116 – 117 (https: //www. legal – tools. org/en/doc/3f6409/) ("*Obrenović* Sentencing Judgement") , the Trial Chamber found that the guilty plea was a significant factor in mitigation of the sentence "due to its contribution to establishing the truth, promoting reconciliation", the "unreserved acceptance" of individual criminal responsibility for his role and because it "spared witnesses from being required to come and testify about painful and traumatic events. " In *Nchamihigo*, the Trial Chamber considered it highly aggravating that this former deputy prosecutor "promoted violence, planned and actively participated in killings, ordered and instigated others to follow suit" and witnesses "testified that because of his position they believed that they could participate in the killings without suffering consequences. Thus he promoted an environment of impunity for mass atrocity", from *Nchamihigo* Judgement and Sentence, para. 391, see *supra* note 46.

[78]　For example, *Popović et al* Appeal Judgement, para. 2019, see *supra* note 24; *Đorđević* Appeal Judgement, para. 936, see *supra* note 24.

[79]　For example, *Hadžihasanović and Kubura* Appeal Judgement, para. 317, see *supra* note 57; *Vasiljević* Judgement, para. 157, see *supra* note 61. Thus, for example, in a case where the conviction has not been under Art 7 (3) or 6 (3) , a trial chamber can choose whether to consider authority under gravity or under aggravating factors.

[80]　For example, *Popović et al* Appeal Judgement, para. 2032, see *supra* note 24; *Blaškić* Appeal Judgement, see *supra* note 26, para. 686; *Vasiljević* Appeal Judgement, paras. 172–173, see *supra* note 61.

cannot also be considered as an aggravating factor" [81] or "the abuse of a position of authority may constitute a distinct aggravating factor in the context of a conviction under Article 7 (1) of the Statute. " [82] The guidance has been extensive. [83] Trial chambers are clearly alert to this issue in theory and in application, yet dissonance is revealed by the extent of litigation on this point. [84]

It is clear from the foregoing that there is some disorderliness, but considerable substantive consistency. The individualisation or tailoring exercise is where the discretion is greatest, and it is here where one would most expect to see chaos, if it does exist. Scrutiny reveals that here too there is no chaos. The situation is one of diversity arising from different factual situations being assessed by different individuals within a system that has come to provide broad parameters. In the jurisprudence, we can regularly find consideration of (not necessarily acceptance of) the following as aggravating factors directly related to the commission of the offence charged and to

---

[81] ICTR, *Prosecutor v. Callixte Nzabonimana*, Judgement, Appeals Chamber, ICTR-98-44D-A, 29 September 2014, para. 464 (https: //www. legal-tools. org/en/doc/a1abb4/); ICTR, *Prosecutor v. Augustin Bizimungu*, Judgement, Appeals Chamber, ICTR-00-56-A, 30 June 2014, para. 380 (https: //www. legal-tools. org/en/doc/2a4ad3/); ICTR, *Prosecutor v. Emmanuel Ndindabahizi*, Judgement, Appeals Chamber, ICTR-01-71-A, 16 January 2007, para. 137 (https: //www. legal-tools. org/en/doc/0f3219/) ("*Ndindabahizi* Appeal Judgement").

[82] For example, *Šainović et al* Appeal Judgement, para. 1812, see *supra* note 32; *Milošević* Appeal Judgement, para. 302, see *supra* note 31; *Stakić* Appeal Judgement, 2006, para. 411, see *supra* note 59.

[83] For example, *Milošević* Appeal Judgement, paras. 306, 309, see *supra* note 31; *Blaškić* Appeal Judgement, para. 695, see *supra* note 26; *Kordić and Čerkez* Appeal Judgement, para. 1089, see *supra* note 44; *Jokić* Judgement on Sentencing Appeal, para. 30, see *supra* note 3; *Deronjić* Judgement on Sentencing Appeal, 2005, para. 12, see *supra* note 52; *Ndindabahizi* Appeal Judgement, para. 137, see *supra* note 81.

[84] For example, ICTY, *Prosecutor v. Fatmir Limaj et al*, Judgement, Trial Chamber, IT-03-66-T, 30 November 2005, para. 731 (https: //www. legal-tools. org/en/doc/4e469a/); *Brđanin* Judgement, paras. 1100-1110, see *supra* note 45; *Blagojević et al* Judgement, para. 840, see *supra* note 47; *Obrenović* Sentencing Judgement, para. 101, see *supra* note 77; ICTR, *Prosecutor v. édouard Karemera and Matthieu Ngirumpatse*, Judgement and Sentence, Trial Chamber, ICTR-98-44-T, 2 February 2012, paras. 1624, 1692, 1706, 1747, 1758 (https: //www. legal-tools. org/en/doc/5b9068/) ("*Karemera et al* Judgement and Sentence").

the offender himself:[85] the accused's abuse of his/her position, influence or authority[86], level of education or professional background[87], duration of the crime[88], scale or large number of victims[89], attacks on places of sanctuary such as churches and hospitals[90], vulnerability of victims[91], public nature of the

---

[85]　Holá has conceptually categorised these factors as either attack—related, offender—role related, victim—related, post—crime conduct—related, proceedings related or falling under the broad category of personal circumstances. See Holá, 2012, pp. 19—22, see *supra* note 23.

[86]　For example, ICTR, *Prosecutor v Nikola Šainović*, Judgement, Trial Chamber, IT—05—87—T, 26 February 2009, para. 1180 (https://www. legal—tools. org/en/doc/9eb7c3/) ("*Šainović* Judgement"); *Perisić* Judgement, para. 1825, see *supra* note 65; *Gotovina et al* Judgement, paras. 2604, 2605, see *supra* note 20; *Milošević* Appeal Judgement, para. 302, see *supra* note 31; *Stakic* Appeal Judgement, para. 411, see *supra* note 53; *Deronjić* Judgement on Sentencing Appeal, 2005, para. 67, see *supra* note 53; *Karemera et al* Judgement and Sentence, 2012, para. 682, see *supra* note 84; *Nyiramasuhuko et al* Judgement and Sentence, paras. 5652, 6196, 6207, see *supra* note 29; ICTR, *Prosecutor v. Athanase Seromba*, Judgement, Appeals Chamber, ICTR—01—66—T, 12 March 2008, para. 230 (https://www. legal—tools. org/en/doc/b4df9d/) ("*Seromba* Appeal Judgement"). Holá *et al*, in their 2011 study, found abuse of position of authority to be an aggravating factor in 58% of cases at the ICTY and 77.5% of cases at the ICTR (*infra* note 159, p. 235).

[87]　For example, ICTY, *Prosecutor v. Blagoje Simić et al*, Judgement, Trial Chamber, IT—95—9—T, 17 October 2003, paras. 1084, 1095, 1108 (https://www. legal—tools. org/en/doc/aa9b81/); *Ntakirumana et al* Judgement and Sentence, 2003, para. 910, see *supra* note 47.

[88]　For example, *Deronjić* Judgement on Sentencing Appeal, 2005, para. 124, see *supra* note 52; *Nyiramasuhuko et al* Judgement and Sentence, para. 6205, see *supra* note 29; ICTR, *Prosecutor v. Eliézer Niyitegeka*, Judgement and Sentence, Trial Chamber, ICTR—96—14—T, 16 May 2003, para. 499 (https://www. legal—tools. org/doc/325567/).

[89]　For example, *Deronjić* Judgement on Sentencing Appeal, 2005, para. 12, see *supra* note 52; *Blaškić* Judgement, paras. 784, 804, see *supra* note 49; *Nyiramasuhuko et al* Judgement and Sentence, paras. 6195, 6205, 6206, see *supra* note 29; *Ndindabahizi* Appeal Judgement, para. 135, see *supra* note 81; *Kambanda* Judgement and Sentence, para. 61, see *supra* note 24. Holá *et al* found that in 25% of ICTY cases and 27.5% of ICTR cases, the number of victims was noted as an aggravating factor (*infra* note 159, at p. 435).

[90]　For example, *Kamuhanda* Appeal Judgement, para. 357, see *supra* note 56; *Ntakirumana et al* Judgement and Sentence, 2003, para. 563, see *supra* note 47; *Karera* Judgement and Sentence, paras. 580, 579, see *supra* note 46.

[91]　For example, *Gotovina et al* Judgement, para. 2603, see *supra* note 20; *Deronjić* Judgement on Sentencing Appeal, 2005, para. 124, see *supra* note 52; *Kordić and čerkez* Appeal Judgement, para. 1088, see *supra* note 44; *Nyiramasuhuko et al* Judgement and Sentence, paras. 6208, 6231, see *supra* note 29; *Muhimana* Judgement and Sentence, 2005, para. 60, see *supra* note 64. Holá *et al* found observations about the special vulnerability of victims in 46% of sentencing cases at the ICTY (p. 435, see *supra* note 158).

crime/humiliation of victim[92] , zeal and sadism/callousness/violent and cruel nature of conduct[93] , lack of genuine remorse[94] , and the effect on the lives of victims[95]. The chambers have taken the view that where discriminatory intent or a discriminatory state of mind is not required for a conviction, it can be considered as an
aggravating factor. [96] Prolonged and systematic involvement in criminal conduct may
also be considered as an aggravating circumstance. [97] An accused's exercise of the
right to remain silent, and not to testify, does not constitute an aggravating circumstance. [98] Inconsistencies have been observed, for example in relation to the disparate handling of the issue of zeal, "voluntariness" and cooperation with the Trial
Chamber[99] in addition to those already identified earlier in this paper. In spite of its

---

[92] For example, ICTY, *Prosecutor v Ranko Češić*, Sentencing Judgement, Trial Chamber, IT–95–10/
1–T, 11 March 2004, paras. 53–54 (https: //www. legal–tools. org/en/doc/c86c07/) ("*Češić* Sentencing
Judgement") ; *Muhimana* Judgement and Sentence, 2005, paras. 608–09, 611, 613, see *supra* note 64.

[93] For example, *Blaškić* Appeal Judgement, para. 686, see *supra* note 26; ICTY, *Prosecutor v Jadranko
Prlić*, Judgement, Trial Chamber, IT–04–74–T, 29 May 2013, para. 1343 (https: //www. legal–tools. org/
en/doc/2daa33/) ("*Prlić* Judgement") ; *Perisić* Judgement, para. 1826, see *supra* note 66; *Nikolić* Judgement
on Sentencing Appeal, paras. 28–30, 40, see *supra* note 38; ICTY, *Prosecutor v. Dusko Tadić*, Judgement, Trial Chamber, IT–94–1–T, 14 July 1997, para. 19 (https: //www. legal–tools. org/en/doc/af6f8c/) ; *Simba*
Appeal Judgement, para. 320, see *supra* note 31; ICTR, *Prosecutor v. Clement Kayishema and Obed Ruzindana*,
Judgement, Appeals Chamber, ICTR–95–1–A, 1 June 2001, para. 351 (https: //www. legal–tools. org/en/
doc/9ea5f4/) ("*Kayishema and Ruzindana* Appeal Judgement").

[94] For example, *Popovi ć et al* Appeal Judgement, para. 2063, see *supra* note 24; *Vasiljević* Appeal
Judgement, para. 177, see *supra* note 61; ICTR, *Prosecutor v. Georges Rutaganda*, Judgement, Appeals Chamber, ICTR–96–3–A, 26 May 2003, para. 590 (https: //www. legal–tools. org/en/doc/40bf4a/) ("*Rutaganda* Appeal Judgement").

[95] For example, *Brđanin* Judgement, para. 1105, see *supra* note 44; *Blagojević et al* Judgement,
para. 845, see *supra* note 47; ICTR, *Prosecutor v. Clement Kayishema and Obed Ruzindana*, Sentence, Trial
Chamber, ICTR–95–1–T, 1 May 1999, para. 16 (https: //www. legal–tools. org/doc/1822e5/).

[96] For example, *Blaškić* Appeal Judgement, para. 695, see *supra* note 26; *Vasiljević* Appeal Judgement,
paras. 171–172, see *supra* note 61; *Semanza* Appeal Judgement, para. 338, see *supra* note 24.

[97] For example, *Popovi ć et al* Appeal Judgement, para. 2038, see *supra* note 24; *Milošević* Appeal
Judgement, para. 304, see *supra* note 31; ICTY, *Prosecutor v. Milan Martić*, Judgement, Appeals Chamber, IT–
95–11, 8 October 2008, para. 340 (https: //www. legal–tools. org/doc/ca5eff/) ; *Hadžihasanović and Kubura*
Appeal Judgement, paras. 350–353, see *supra* note 57.

[98] For example, *Strugar* Judgement, para. 466, see *supra* note 53; *Delalić et al* Appeal Judgement,
para. 783, see *supra* note 26; *Blaškić* Appeal Judgement, para. 687, see *supra* note 26.

[99] *Ibid.*

deferential approach, the Appeals Chamber has had an active role in reviewing complaints about the exercise of discretion in relation to aggravating factors. [100]

The chambers frequently considered the following (not necessarily accepting them) when evaluating mitigating factors: voluntary surrender[101], prior good character[102], confession or guilty pleas[103], duress/necessity[104], low rank or absence of authority[105],

---

[100] See for example the appellate decisions cited in these footnotes.

[101] For example, *Šainović* Judgement, para. 1198, see *supra* note 86; *Perisić* Judgement, para. 1828, see *supra* note 65; *Blaški ć* Appeal Judgement, para. 701, see *supra* note 26; *Seromba* Appeal Judgement, para. 236, see *supra* note 86.

[102] For example, *Br đanin* Judgement, para. 1127, see *supra* note 44; *Semanza* Appeal Judgement, para. 397, see *supra* note 24.

[103] For example, ICTY, *Prosecutor v. Biljana Plavšić*, Sentencing Judgement, Trial Chamber, IT−00−39 & 40/T, 27 February 2003, paras. 70, 73 (https://www. legal−tools. org/en/doc/f60082/) ("*Plavši ć* Sentencing Judgement"); *Nikolić* Judgement on Sentencing Appeal, para. 248, see *supra* note 38; *Bagaragaza* Sentencing Judgement, para. 38, see *supra* note 49; *Rutaganira* Judgement and Sentence, 2005, paras. 147−145, see *supra* note 46; ICTR, *Prosecutor v. Paul Bisengimana*, Judgement and Sentence, Trial Chamber, IC-TR−00−60−T, 13 April 2006, para. 126 (https://www. legal−tools. org/en/doc/694dd8/) ("*Bisengimana* Judgement and Sentence").

[104] For example, ICTY, *Prosecutor v Miroslav Bralo*, Judgement, Trial Chamber, IT−95−17−T, 7 December 2005, para. 53 (https://www. legal − tools. org/en/doc/e10281/) ("*Bralo* Judgement"); ICTY, *Prosecutor v. Darko Mrđa*, Judgement, Trial Chamber, IT−02−59−T, 31 March 2004, paras. 65−68 (https://www. legal−tools. org/doc/d61b0f/) ("*Mrđa* Judgement").

[105] For example, *Prosecutor v. Dusko Tadić*, Judgement in Sentencing Appeals, Appeals Chamber, IT−94−1−A, 26 January 2000, paras. 55−58 (https://www. legal−tools. org/en/doc/853599/) ("*Tadić* Judgement in Sentencing Appeals"); *Setako* Judgement, para. 500, see *supra* note 32; *Ruggiu* Judgement and Sentence, paras. 75−76, see *supra* note 24. Note Holá, 2012, p. 10, see *supra* note 23: "It is not the steadfast rule that all low−ranking defendants automatically receive low sentences and all authorities are automatically punished the most. "

genuine remorse[106] , assistance provided to victims[107] , superior orders[108] , substantial cooperation with the prosecution[109] , good conduct in detention[110] , family and personal circumstances including age and health, [111] and subsequent conduct,

---

[106]   For example, *Kvočka et al* Appeal Judgement, para. 715, see *supra* note 34; *Blaškić* Appeal Judgement, para. 705, see *supra* note 26; ICTR, *Prosecutor v. Juvénal Rugambarara*, Sentencing Judgement, Trial Chamber, ICTR – 00 – 59 – T, 16 November 2007, para. 33 (https: //www. legal – tools. org/doc/37e659/) ("*Rugambarara* Judgement").

[107]   For example, *Kvočka et al* Appeal Judgement, paras. 693, 719–720, see *supra* note 35; *češić* Sentencing Judgement, para. 78, see *supra* note 92; *Nyiramasuhuko et al* Judgement and Sentence, paras. 6232, 6242, see *supra* note 29; *Rugambarara* Judgement, para. 37, see *supra* note 106; *Serugendo* Judgement and Sentence, 2006, paras. 68–69, see *supra* note 70; *Kajelijeli* Judgement and Sentence, 2003, para. 951, see *supra* note 62.

[108]   Tribunal statutes expressly make this available if " justice so requires. " See for example, *Bralo* Judgement, paras. 53–56, see *supra* note 105; *Mrđa* Judgement, paras. 65–68, see *supra* note 104. An example of this not being accepted is in *Rutaganda* Judgement and Sentence, paras. 458 – 459, see *supra* note 28. *Bagosora et al* Judgement and Sentence, para. 2274, see *supra* note 29 (because of " their own senior status and stature in the Rwandan army, the Chamber is convinced that their repeated execution of these crimes as well as the manifestly unlawful nature of any orders they received to perpetrate them reflects their acquiescence in committing them. No mitigation is therefore warranted on this ground. ")

[109]   For example, *Šainović* Judgement, para. 1194, see *supra* note 86; *Jokić* Judgement on Sentencing Appeal, para. 88, see *supra* note 3; *Vasiljević* Appeal Judgement, para. 180, see *supra* note 61; *Obrenović* Sentencing Judgement, paras. 128–129, see *supra* note 78; *Bagaragaza* Sentencing Judgement, para. 39, see *supra* note 49; *Kambanda* Judgement and Sentence, para. 36, see *supra* note 24.

[110]   For example, *Kordić and čerkez* Appeal Judgement, para. 1053, see *supra* note 44; *Bisengimana* Judgement and Sentence, 2006, para. 164, see *supra* note 103.

[111]   For example, *Šainović* Judgement, paras. 1181 – 1182, see *supra* note 86; *Perisić* Judgement, paras. 1833–1834, see *supra* note 66; *Galić* Appeal Judgement, para. 436, see *supra* note 61; *Jokić* Judgement on Sentencing Appeal, see *supra* note 3, paras. 49, 62, 100; *Strugar* Judgement, para. 469, see *supra* note 53; ICTY, *Prosecutor v. Dragoljub Kunarac et al*, Judgement, Appeals Chamber, IT–96–23 & 23/1–A, 12 June 2002, para. 362 (https: //www. legal – tools. org/en/doc/029a09/) ; *Karemera et al* Appeal Judgement, para. 693, see *supra* note 40; *Simba* Appeal Judgement, para. 287, see *supra* note 31; *Ntakirumana et al* Judgement and Sentence, para. 569, see *supra* note 47; *Serugendo* Judgement and Sentence, para. 66, 72, see *supra* note 69; *Simba* Appeal Judgement, para. 287, see *supra* note 31. On the weight to be given to family circumstances, see for example *Nahimana* Judgement (Appeal), para. 1069, see *supra* note 40 (pointing out that the jurisprudence does " not treat it as an important factor, save in exceptional circumstances, the main factor being the gravity of the crimes"). On health, see for example *Šainović et al* Appeal Judgement, para. 1827, see *supra* note 32 (Poor health is mitigating only in exceptional cases).

such as engagement in reconciliation or peace work[112]. Some chambers have held that testing circumstances, such as armed conflict, may mitigate. [113] However, the ICTY Appeals Chamber in *Bralo* dismissed that, reiterating its earlier declaration in *Blaškić* that it saw "neither merit nor logic in recognising the mere context of war itself as a factor to be considered in in the mitigation of the conduct of its participants. "[114] Diminished mental responsibility not amounting to a defence can also be a mitigating factor. [115] Political motivation is not an appropriate factor for mitigation. [116]

Combs has shown how attitudes towards plea agreements and admissions of guilt vary between cases[117] although on balance it seems that lighter sentences are imposed in such situations. [118] The sentence reduction that may be given as a result of human rights violations in the course of the proceedings are not a matter of mitigation, but of the standalone right to a remedy. [119] The cases reveal agreement that the

---

[112]　For example, *Prlić* Judgement, para. 1322, see *supra* note 93; *Perisić* Judgement, para. 1832, see *supra* note 65; *Plavšić* Sentencing Judgement, para. 94, see *supra* note 103; *Babić* Judgement on Sentencing Appeal, para. 59, see *supra* note 38; *Jokić* Judgement on Sentencing Appeal, paras. 89–91, see *supra* note 3; *Obrenović* Sentencing Judgement, para. 143, see *supra* note 77.

[113]　For example, *Prli ć* Judgement, para. 1360, see *supra* note 93; ICTY, *Prosecutor v Enver Hadžihasanović and Amira Kubura*, Judgement, Trial Chamber, IT–01–47–T, 15 March 2006, para. 1248 (https: //www. legal–tools. org/en/doc/8f515a/).

[114]　ICTY, *Prosecutor v Miroslav Bralo*, Judgement on Sentencing Appeal, Appeals Chamber, IT–95–17–A, 2 April 2007, para. 13 (https: //www. legal–tools. org/en/doc/14a169/), citing *Blaškić* Appeal Judgement, para. 711, see *supra* note 26.

[115]　For example, *Delalić et al* Appeal Judgement, para. 590, see *supra* note 26; *Vasiljević* Appeal Judgement, paras. 282–288, see *supra* note 61.

[116]　For example, *Blaškić* Appeal Judgement, para. 711, see *supra* note 26.

[117]　Nancy Combs, "Procuring Guilty Pleas for International Crimes: The Limited Influence of Sentencing Discounts", in *Vanderbilt Law Review*, 2006, vol. 69, pp. 88–100.

[118]　Jenia Iontcheva Turner and Thomas Weigend, "Negotiated Justice", in Goran Sluiter *et al* (eds.), *International Criminal Procedure: Principles and Rules*, Oxford University Press, Oxford, 2013, pp. 1388–1389.

[119]　ICTR, *Prosecutor v. Juvénal Kajelijeli*, Judgement, Appeals Chamber, ICTR–98–44–A, 23 May 2005, paras. 323–324 (https: //www. legal–tools. org/en/doc/2b7d1c/) ("*Kajelijeli* Appeal Judgement"); *Semanza* Appeal Judgement, paras. 325–328, see *supra* note 24. *Jokić* Judgement on Sentencing Appeal, para. 6, see *supra* note 3.

existence of mitigating factors does not automatically imply a reduction of sentence, [120] or preclude the imposition of a sentence of life imprisonment where the gravity of the offence so requires. [121] The weight of each such factor, and the balance between aggravating and mitigating factors, is one that is within the discretion of the trial chambers. [122] This leads to some differences between cases, for example over whether assistance to victims carries any or much weight or could even aggravate, [123] and the weight to be allocated to good conduct in detention. [124] Even so, misapplied judicial discretion can be subjected to review and there are many instances of correction. [125]

Both tribunals have been consistent in how they deal with the statutory obligation to take domestic sentencing practices in the countries of the former Yugoslavia and Rwanda into consideration. All that this means is that while a Trial Chamber must take account of the general practice regarding sentences in these countries, "it is well established in the jurisprudence that the Trial Chamber is not bound by that practice. The Trial Chamber is therefore entitled to impose a greater or lesser sen-

---

[120]   For example, *Babić* Judgement on Sentencing Appeal, para. 44, see *supra* note 38; ICTR, *Prosecutor v. Idelphonse Nizeyimana*, Judgement, Appeals Chamber, ICTR-00-55C-A, 29 September 2014, para. 445 (https: //www. legal - tools. org/en/doc/e1fc66/) ("*Nizeyimana* Appeal Judgement"); *Ntabakuze* Appeal Judgement, para. 280, see *supra* note 74; *Nahimana* Judgement (Appeal), para. 1038, see *supra* note 40; *Kajelijeli* Appeal Judgement, para. 299, see *supra* note 119.

[121]   For example, *Nizeyimana* Appeal Judgement, para. 445, see *supra* note 120; *Ntabakuze* Appeal Judgement, para. 280, see *supra* note 73; ICTR, *Prosecutor v. Dominique Ntawukuriryayo*, Judgement, Appeals Chamber, ICTR - 05 - 82 - T, 14 December 2011, para. 581 (https: //www. legal - tools. org/en/doc/42d81d/) ; *Renzaho* Appeal Judgement, para. 612, see *supra* note 32.

[122]   For example, *Blaškić* Appeal Judgement, paras. 685, 696, see *supra* note 27; *Deronjić* Sentencing Judgement, para. 155, see *supra* note 69; ICTR, *Prosecutor v. Eliézer Niyitegeka*, Judgement, Appeals Chamber, ICTR-96-14-A, 9 July 2004, para. 268 (https: //www. legal-tools. org/en/doc/35cd4f/).

[123]   Holá, 2012, pp. 19-20, see *supra* note 23.

[124]   *Ibid.*, p. 21.

[125]   Closer analysis of appellate revisions to sentences can be found in Clark, 2008, pp. 1703-1713, and the Appendix at pp. 1719-1723, see *supra* note 13.

tence than that which would have been imposed" by those domestic courts. [126] All the trial chambers have to do is to make explicit reference to show that they considered domestic sentencing, they do not have to show that that consideration had any impact on their decision. [127] Even so, as cases have gradually come to be tried in the countries of the former Yugoslavia and Rwanda, their domestic practice has actually become more important in time. Consideration of sentencing by the War Crimes Chamber of the Belgrade District Court in Serbia was conducted in the *Vukovar* Trial Judgement, but it was distinguished on the grounds that those accused were direct perpetrators, unlike the two accused in The Hague. [128] Ideally, there should be no major difference to the quantum imposed in similar cases.

The existence of an accepted hierarchy of international crimes would facilitate more transparent sentencing. There was initially controversy over whether there was such a thing, and if so, which of genocide, crimes against humanity and war crimes was the most serious, which would obviously impact on sentencing. This was particularly notable in the *Erdemović* case at the ICTY[129] and also in early ICTR cases

---

[126] ICTR, *Prosecutor v. Omar Serushago*, Judgement (Appeal against Sentence), Appeals Chamber, IC-TR-98-39-A, 14 February 2000, para. 30 (https://www.legal-tools.org/doc/d23e95/). Other examples of this position include *Nahimana* Judgement (Appeal), para. 1063, see *supra* note 40; *Popović et al* Appeal Judgement, para. 2087, see *supra* note 24; *Boškoski and Tarčulovski* Appeal Judgement, para. 212, see *supra* note 34.

[127] *Semanza* Appeal Judgement, para. 345, see *supra* note 24; *Seromba* Judgement, para. 402, see *supra* note 29.

[128] ICTY, *Prosecutor v. Mile Mrkšić, Miroslav Radić & Veselin Šljivančanin*, IT-95-13/1-T, 27 September 2007, para. 708 (http://www.legal-tools.org/doc/32111c/).

[129] ICTY, *Prosecutor v. Drazen Erdemović*, Judgement: Joint Separate Opinion of Judges McDonald and Vohrah, para. 24, Separate and Dissenting Opinion of Judge Li, Appeals Chamber, IT-96-22-T, 7 October 1997, para. 22 (https://www.legal-tools.org/doc/b618be/) ("*Erdemović* Appeal Judgement").

which stressed genocide as a uniquely serious crime, the "crime of crimes. " [130] The waters have settled, and the dominant position is to describe all as serious violations of international law avoiding the hierarchy issue. [131] Even so, appellate guidance on this has been rather opaque. In *Rutaganda*, the Appeals Chamber noted that the Trial Chamber had "found that the crime of genocide constitutes the 'crime of crimes' which must be taken into account in deciding the sentence" and pointed out at the same time that "there is no hierarchy of crimes under the Statute. " [132] Hierarchy has also been rejected by the Appeals Chamber in *Kayishema & Ruzindana* and Stakić: all three crimes are so serious as to be subject to life imprisonment. [133] Having elsewhere specified that war crimes are not less serious than crimes against humanity, [134] the ICTY Appeals Chamber seemed to suggest a hierarchy in *Krstić*:

> Among the grievous crimes this Tribunal has the duty to punish, the crime
> of genocide is singled out for special condemnation and opprobrium. The crime
> is horrific in its scope; its perpetrators identify entire human groups for extinc-

---

[130]   In the earliest case, *Kambanda*, the Trial Chamber recognised that the Statute did not rank the various crimes hierarchically so in theory they should all draw the same sentences. But, the Chamber "has no doubt that despite the gravity of the violations of Article 3 common to the Geneva Conventions and of the Additional Protocol II thereto, they are considered as lesser crimes than genocide or crimes against humanity. " It was unable to "rank" the two crimes in terms of gravity, both being "crimes which particularly shock the collective conscience", but it concluded that genocide is unique because of its element of dolus specialis (special intent). Thus, "genocide constitutes the crime of crimes, which must be taken into account when deciding the sentence. " *Kambanda* Judgement and Sentence, paras. 12–14, 16, see *supra* note 24.

[131]   See for example, *Mrkšić and Šljivančanin* Appeal Judgement, para. 375, see *supra* note 39; *Rutaganda* Appeal Judgement, para. 590, see *supra* note 94; *Zigiranyirazo* Judgement and Sentence, para. 451, see *supra* note 37; *Bagosora et al* Judgement and Sentence, para. 2263, see *supra* note 29; *Bikindi* Judgement and Sentence, para. 445, see *supra* note 46; *Nchamihigo* Judgement and Sentence, para. 387, see *supra* note 46. See D'Ascoli, 2011, ch. 3, see *supra* note 6, arguing that a ranking would facilitate transparent sentencing.

[132]   *Rutaganda* Appeal Judgement, para. 590, see *supra* note 94.

[133]   *Kayishema and Ruzindana* Appeal Judgement, para. 367, see *supra* note 93; *Stakić* Appeal Judgement, para. 375, see *supra* note 58.

[134]   *Tadić* Judgement in Sentencing Appeals, para. 69, see *supra* note 105; *Furundžija* Appeal Judgement, para. 247, see *supra* note 26.

tion. Those who devise and implement genocide seek to deprive humanity of the manifold richness its nationalities, races, ethnicities and religions provide. This is a crime against all of humankind, its harm being felt not only by the group targeted for destruction, but by all of humanity...The crime of genocide, in particular, is universally viewed as an especially grievous and reprehensible violation. [135]

The nuance is best captured by the *Blagojević & Jokić* Appeal Judgement: "because of their inherently discriminatory character, crimes of genocide and targeted persecutions may thus warrant closer scrutiny." [136] As will be shown in the empirical assessment, the actual sentencing imposed makes it clear that there is a hierarchy in sentencing: genocide convictions consistently draw the heaviest penalties.

Substantive review of the ICTY and ICTR cases also reveals that a number of broadly consistent positions emerge on the relationship between rank or modes of responsibility and sentencing. This is the principle of "gradation", and the practice at the ICTY and ICTR on this issue has been described as a "general principle." [137] The jurisprudence reflects an understanding that there is a hierarchy within modes of responsibility in the liability provisions of the two Statutes. ICTR judgements regularly stated that "[a] t this Tribunal, a sentence of life imprisonment is generally reserved for those who planned or ordered atrocities as well as the most senior authorities." [138] There is agreement at both tribunals that direct perpetration generally warrants a heavier sentence than aiding and abetting. [139] The *Krstić* Appeals Chamber at the ICTY held that "aiding and abetting is a form of responsibility which generally

---

[135]   *Krstić* Appeal Judgement, paras. 36, 275, see *supra* note 26.

[136]   *Blagojević et al* Appeal Judgement, para. 139, see *supra* note 32.

[137]   Holá, 2012, p. 10, see *supra* note 23.

[138]   It is rooted in the *Musema* Appeal Judgement, para. 383, see *supra* note 60.

[139]   Note that this was rejected at the SCSL in the *Taylor* Appeal Judgement, see later discussion on SCSL.

warrants lower sentences than responsibility as a co-perpetrator. "[140] The qualifier "generally" is important to note, and it is here relevant to note a final caveat added by the ICTY Appeals Chamber in *Vukovar*: "the gravity of the underlying crimes remains an important consideration in order to reflect the totality of the criminal conduct. "[141] ICTR jurisprudence is consistent: direct participation of an accused in crimes committed generally attracts a higher sentence than criminal participation by way of aiding and abetting the commission of the crimes. [142] Ohlin, van Sliedregt and Weigend have assessed that the introduction of the joint criminal enterprise ("JCE") doctrine into ICTY caselaw led to the general position that it is to be regarded not as a form of accomplice liability, but as a form of commission, and "aiding and abetting developed into a mode of liability that is considered less blameworthy than participation in a JCE. "[143] The consistent tribunal position became that an indirect participant in a JCE carries greater responsibility than one who merely aids and abets the principal. [144] In support of this is the finding of Werle and Burghardt that the Appeals Chamber has a "policy" of reducing the sentences where it has found erroneous conviction on JCE, "instead of finding mere aiding and abetting. "[145]

Furthermore, there is consensus in the caselaw that leaders and planners

---

[140]   *Krstić* Appeal Judgement, para. 268, see *supra* note 26; more recently, see for example *Popović et al* Appeal Judgement, para. 2104, see *supra* note 24; *Vasiljević* Appeal Judgement, para. 182, see *supra* note 61; ICTR, *Prosecutor v. Gaspard Kanyarukiga*, Judgement, Appeals Chamber, ICTR-02-78-A, 8 May 2012, para. 280 (https://www.legal-tools.org/doc/e6e1c9/).

[141]   ICTY, *Prosecutor v. Mile Mrkšić, Miroslav Radić & Veselin Šljivančanin*, IT-95-13/1-A, para. 407 (http://www.legal-tools.org/doc/40bc41/).

[142]   *Semanza* Appeal Judgement, para. 388, see *supra* note 24, applied *inter alia*, in *Bagaragaza* Sentencing Judgement, para. 42, see *supra* note 50.

[143]   Jens David Ohlin *et al*, "Assessing the Control-Theory", in *Leiden Journal of International Law*, 2013, vol. 26, pp. 741-742.

[144]   ICTR, *Prosecutor v. Milorad Krnojelac*, Judgement, Appeals Chamber, IT-97-25-A, 17 September 2003, para. 73 (https://www.legal-tools.org/en/doc/46d2e5/).

[145]   Gerhard Werle and Boris Burghardt, "Establishing Degrees of Responsibility: Modes of Participation in Article 25 of the ICC Statute", in Elies van Sliedregt and Sergey Vasiliev (eds.), *Pluralism in International Criminal Law*, Oxford University Press, Oxford, 2014 ("Werle and Burghardt, 2014"), p. 15.

should, as a matter of principle, bear heavier responsibility. [146] Even so, there is also agreement that there has to be nuance and this will turn on the facts. [147] A high rank in the military or political field does not, in itself, merit a harsher sentence[148] but a person who abuses or wrongly exercises power deserves a harsher sentence. [149] Consequently, what matters is not the position of authority in itself, but that position coupled with the manner in which the authority is exercised. [150] Evaluating the gravity of the crime in the context of a superior responsibility case involves first looking at the underlying crime committed by the subordinate, and then the superior's own conduct in failing to prevent or punish the underlying crime. [151] On the superior's own conduct, the *Obrenović* Trial Chamber clarified that :

When commanders, through their own actions or inactions, fail in the du-

---

[146] For example, *Babić* Judgement on Sentencing Appeal, para. 80, see *supra* note 39; *Tadić* Judgement in Sentencing Appeals, paras. 55–58, see *supra* note 106; *Nahimana* Judgement (Appeal), para. 500, see *supra* note 41; *Musema* Appeal Judgement, paras. 382–383, see *supra* note 61; *Nchamihigo* Judgement and Sentence, para. 388, see *supra* note 46.

[147] For some observations about the importance of nuance, see *Karera* Judgement and Sentence, para. 583, see *supra* note 46 (noting that life sentences have been imposed on lower ranked individuals who planned or ordered atrocities or participated in the crimes with particular zeal or sadism); and ICTY, *Prosecutor v. Ntagerura et al*, Judgement and Sentence, Trial Chamber, ICTR–99–46, 25 February 2004, para. 815 (http://www.legal–tools.org/doc/60036f/) (noting that the highest penalty "should be reserved for the most serious offenders, such as individuals who planned, led, or ordered a particular criminal act, or individuals who committed crimes with particular cruelty").

[148] For example, *Hadžihasanović and Kubura* Appeal Judgement, para. 320, see *supra* note 58; *Stakić* Appeal Judgement, para. 411, see *supra* note 58; *Deronjić* Sentencing Judgement, para. 195, see *supra* note 69; ICTY, *Prosecutor v Radislav Krstić*, Judgement, Trial Chamber, IT–98–33–T, 2 August 2001, para. 709 (https://www.legal–tools.org/en/doc/440d3a/) ("*Krstić* Judgement"); *Nyiramasuhuko et al* Judgement and Sentence, paras. 5652, 6196, see *supra* note 29.

[149] For example, *Krstić* Judgement, para. 709, see *supra* note 148; *Delalić et al* Appeal Judgement, para. 736, see *supra* note 27; *Rutaganda* Judgement and Sentence, para. 469, see *supra* note 28.

[150] For example, *Hadžihasanović and Kubura* Appeal Judgement, para. 320, see *supra* note 57; *Galić* Appeal Judgement, para. 412, see *supra* note 61; *Babić* Judgement on Sentencing Appeal, para. 80, see *supra* note 38; *Ndindabahizi* Appeal Judgement, para. 136, see *supra* note 81.

[151] For example, *Popović et al* Appeal Judgement, para. 1991, see *supra* note 24; *Perisić* Judgement, para. 1800, see *supra* note 65; *Hadžihasanović and Kubura* Appeal Judgement, para. 313, see *supra* note 57; *Delalić et al* Appeal Judgement, paras. 732, 741, see *supra* note 26.

ty, which stems from their position, training, and leadership skills, to set an example for their troops that would promote the principles underlying the laws and customs of war and thereby—either tacitly or implicitly—promote or encourage the commission of crimes, this may be seen as an aggravating circumstance. [152]

With respect to the flip side, the crimes by subordinates, comparison with sentences imposed on them "may be a factor to be considered" [153] but should not derogate from the Trial Chamber's responsibility to tailor the penalties appropriately.

Not a single ICTY or ICTR judgement has explained the exact role that all their considerations play reaching in the quantum that is actually announced. This is the "plucking numbers out of the air" conundrum. MICT judges have been selected from the tribunals, and unsurprisingly, nothing has changed in relation to sentencing. The MICT Appeals Chamber's first judgement, on the appeal lodged by Augustin Ngirabatware, [154] contains the same approach and reasoning as the others, probably most notably the final ICTR Appeals Chamber judgements in édouard Karemera and Matthieu Ngirumpatse; Ildéphonse Nizeyimana; and Callixte Nzabonimana. While there is broad consistency in approach, the judge are still not able to communicate how they reach the quantum imposed.

3. The ICTY and ICTR practice: empirical analysis of sentencing

Empirical studies add a further dimension to our understanding of practice on sentencing at the ad hoc tribunals. There are a number of *relatively* recent important works that engage is statistical analysis. They include D'Ascoli who in her 2011 man-

---

[152]   *Obrenović* Sentencing Judgement, para. 100, see *supra* note 77 (on the facts, this was not applicable to *Obrenović*).

[153]   *Popović et al* Appeal Judgement, para. 1998, see *supra* note 25; *Strugar* Appeal Judgement, paras. 350–351, see *supra* note 24.

[154]   MICT, *Prosecutor v. Augustin Ngirabatware*, Judgement, Appeals Chamber, MICT-12-29-A, 18 December 2014 (https://www. legal-tools. org/en/doc/16b4ef/).

uscript, *Sentencing in International Criminal Law: The UN Ad Hoc Tribunals and Future Perspectives for the ICC* was able to conclude that "sentences meted out by the ad hoc Tribunals tend to show general patterns of consistency and to satisfy general criteria of legitimacy"; [155] Holá, Bijleveld & Smeulers in "Consistency of international sentencing—ICTY and ICTR case study"; [156] Smeulers, Holá & Van Den Berg in a review of sixty—five years of international justice; [157] and Holá, Smeulers and Bijleveld on "International Sentencing Facts and Figures." [158] They have been conducted over different periods of time, have examined different institutions, used different methods of compiling data, and various approaches to presenting and analysing them. They have generally been hindered in their analysis by the opaqueness of judgements, which explain mechanics but do not show how they reach the quantum imposed, by single sentences imposed further to convictions for multiple crimes, and by sentences for multiple convictions for different types of criminal activity, and different crimes (genocide, crimes against humanity, war crimes). Even so, they are revealing, and generally consistent with each other.

D'Ascoli's statistical analysis, published in 2011, found that the sentences imposed at the ICTY and ICTR were lighter than that imposed by domestic courts, and that the ICTR imposed the heavier sentences among the two. [159]

Considering the inherent seriousness of the crimes and the magnitude—also

---

[155] D'Ascoli, 2011, ch. 4 ("Quantitative Analysis of Sentencing: Data in the Case Law of the ad hoc Tribunals"), p. 1891, see *supra* note 6.

[156] Holá *et al*, 2012, see *supra* note 22.

[157] Alette Smeulers, Barbora Holá and Tom Van den Berg, "Sixty—five years of international criminal justice: the facts and figures", in *International Criminal Law Review*, 2013, vol. 13 (1), p. 21.

[158] Barbora Holá, Alette Smeulers and Catrien Bijleveld, "International Sentencing Facts and Figures: Sentencing Practice at the ICTY and ICTR", in *Journal of International Criminal Justice*, 2011, vol. 9, no. 2, p. 411. A more recent study focused exclusively on the ICTR is by William R Pruitt, "Aggravating and Mitigating Sentencing Factors at the ICTR—An Exploratory Analysis", in *International Criminal Law Review*, 2014, vol. 14, p. 148.

[159] D'Ascoli, 2011, p. 1891, see *supra* note 6.

in numeric terms—of the genocide the ICTR dealt with, we should observe that the Rwanda Tribunal overall imposed adequate sentences. It is not always possible to arrive at the same conclusion as far as the ICTY is concerned. [160]

This study considered 100 trial convictions (70 at the ICTY and 30 before the ICTR), and found a higher concentration of sentences around the range 11—25 years imprisonment (42 cases), 1—10 years imprisonment (32 cases); 51 years—life (14 cases) and 26—50 years imprisonment (12 cases). The average trial sentence was 19.7 years of imprisonment, the average appeal sentence was 17.3 years imprisonment, and the average final sentence was 17.3 years imprisonment. D' Ascoli's study found that for both military and civilians, the lengthiest sentences are associated with the highest leadership levels. Statistically, direct perpetrators received harsher sentences than indirect perpetrators across the different hierarchical levels. As to the factors impacting on sentences, D'Ascoli's work revealed significant and high correlations:

   — between length of sentences and convictions for the crime of genocide;

   — between length of sentences and leadership level (i. e. higher penalties are associated with the highest ranks occupied by the accused in the military or civilian structure);

   — between length of sentences and leadership level associated with type of participation (i. e. harsher sentences are associated with high—ranking perpetrators who were also direct perpetrators);

   — between length of sentences and the following aggravating circumstances: gravity/magnitude of crime, premeditation, willingness in the commission of the crime, superior position, and abuse of authority/trust;

---

[160]　*Ibid.*, Summary of Empirical Findings.

    — between length of sentences and the following mitigating circumstances: family status, remorse, surrender, and guilty plea. [161]

On the other hand, she found insignificant or low correlations in the following:

    — between length of sentences and modes of liability (i. e. convictions entered under para. 1 of Articles 7 ICTY/ 6 ICTR; or under para. 3 of Articles 7 ICTY / 6 ICTR);

    — between length of sentences and type of participation of the accused in the commission of the crime (whether direct/ "dirty hands", or indirect/ "clean hands");

    — between length of sentences and age of the accused (both at the time of the commission of crime and at the time of the sentence);

    — between length of sentences and composition of the judicial bench. [162]

From the 2013 paper of Smeulers, Holá & van den Berg, "Sixty—five years of international criminal justice: the facts and figures", we learn that the overall average of international sentencing, including at internationalised or mixed courts, is 15. 3 years[163]; the average sentence at the ICTY is 15. 9 years, and the average sentence at the ICTR is 22. 6 years[164]. The authors reported that "the sentencing practice seems rather varied and sentences at different courts are quite divergent. The differences among individual courts, however, can be explained by sentencing options, case compositions and prosecutorial strategy. "[165] Statistical data consistently shows that sentencing has been eavier at the ICTR. Based on 2013 data, the ICTR

---

[161] *Ibid.* , summary of ch. 4.

[162] *Ibid.*

[163] Smeulers *et al*, see *supra* note 157 at p. 21.

[164] *Ibid.* , p. 22 (Table 9).

[165] *Ibid.* , p. 21.

imposed 14 life sentences (31. 8%) compared to two life sentences at the ICTY (2. 9%). [166] The quantum of determinate terms is also higher at the ICTR and SCSL than at the ICTY: "The determinate sentences range from 3 years to 40 years at the ICTY; from 6 to 45 years at the ICTR and from 15 to 52 years at the SCSL. The average determinate sentence at the ICTY is 14. 84 years, while at the ICTR and SCSL it is 21. 9 years and 37 years respectively. " [167] These variations, have been explained as follows:

> The high average sentence at the SCSL might be related to the fact that the tribunal is not allowed to render life sentences and dealt only with a very limited number of top—ranking perpetrators. Similarly, the majority of the ICTR defendants were members of government and high ranking organizers of violence convicted to life in prison or lengthy determinate sentences for genocidal killing and/or genocidal violence against victims. The prevalence of genocide convictions at the ICTR could be seen as one of the primary reasons for the more severe ICTR sentences. In contrast, the vast majority of the ICTY defendants were convicted of crimes against humanity and war crimes and the convictions include not only violent crimes such as killing, but also less serious offences such as crimes against property. Initially many more lower ranking hands—on perpetrators who are generally considered less culpable were prosecuted at the ICTY. [168]

As a follow—up to the important work cited above, Holá is presently leading a Dutch—funded empirical study to evaluate to what extent sentencing of international

---

[166]   Barbora Holá and Joris van der Wijk, "Life after Conviction at the International Tribunals: an empirical overview", in *Journal of International Criminal Justice*, 2014, Vol. 12, p. 112.

[167]   *Ibid.*

[168]   Smeulers *et al*, see *supra* note 157 at p. 21.

crimes by international criminal tribunals and domestic courts evolved into consistent practice and how any inconsistencies in international sentencing can be explained. [169] The finalisation of all outstanding work at the tribunals is the ideal opportunity to review the practice in its entirety. [170] Pending the completion of this work, the Holá, Smeulers and Bijleveld paper in the *Journal of International Criminal Justice* on "International Sentencing Facts and Figures", although now 6 years old, offers a particularly helpful and accessible window into the question of the evolution of international sentencing. The following section extracts out *some* of the key findings of their work which go towards issues that we have already identified in this paper. Readers are directed to that paper for a full and reasoned evaluation, and also, importantly, to caveats about the data and analysis. All that will be presented here is a summary of the key findings of Holá, Smeulers and Bijleveld with a view to enhancing appreciation of the previous chapter's substantive analysis.

---

[169]　The project website available at http://cicj. org/research/vertical-inconsistency-of-international-sentencing-case-study-of-bosnia-and-herzegovina-and-rwanda/, last accessed at 1 April 2017, explains that "By combining qualitative legal case file analysis with quantitative regression analysis, it will assess to what extent inconsistency of sentencing of international crimes occurs, as well as identify factors that generate inconsistency. The research is based on a comparative case study of sentencing of international crimes committed in the Former Yugoslavia and Rwanda by various courts at the international and domestic level. "

[170]　It will be particularly important to track how the ICTY sentences match those imposed in the courts of the Balkans, and how the ICTR sentences match those imposed in the courts of Rwanda, and how they all match the sentences imposed by courts exercising universal jurisdiction. This exercise will be particularly insightful since it involves tracking punishment for crimes that are now defined the same way, and often involve individuals involved in the same crime being tried and sentenced at different institutions.

Comparing sentences between ICTY and ICTR (Table 1)

Tribunal	WC	CAH	GEN	CAH + WC	GEN + WC	GEN + CAH	GEN + CAH + WC
ICTY							
Median sentence	9.0	13.0	NA	20.0	NA	NA	35.0
Range	2–20	3–20		6–life			35
No. of cases	18	19	0	33	0	0	1
ICTR							
Median sentence	NA	9.0	20.0	12.0	NA	42.5	55.0
Range		6–15	8–life	12		6–life	25–life
No. of cases	0	4	6	1	0	22	7

Observations:

1. The median ICTY sentence is 15 years, and the median ICTR sentence is 33. 5 years.

2. Contrary to assertions about there being no hierarchy of crimes, the sentence pattern shows heavier sentences imposed for genocide and combinations including genocide, and the lightest sentences for war crimes. This indicates a hierarchy of crimes (genocide, crimes against humanity, war crimes).

3. ICTY convictions for war crimes alone have the shortest sentences. This is followed by crimes against humanity convictions, on their own. The crimes against humanity and war crimes combination is the most common of the ICTY conviction profile. The median sentence for this combination is longer when compared with the median sentences for war crimes and crimes against humanity taken separately.

4. The shortest ICTR sentences were for crimes against humanity, followed by one case where it was a combination with war crimes. Here, the sentences are shorter than at the ICTY. But this picture changes in the matter of genocide convictions: the sentences for genocide are substantially longer. The longest sentences have been handed down to defendants convicted of a combination of genocide, crimes against humanity and war crimes.

5. The authors suggest that harsher ICTR sentences could be linked to the differ-

ent nature of cases tried at that tribunal, compared with the ICTY. The nature of the conflict within which the crimes were committed was different, the crime base was different, there were different prosecution strategies leading to different profiles of cases at the two institutions (the ICTR targeted leaders from the start, the ICTY's initial cases were low ranking accused, and distributed among ethnic groups).

Core criminal activity and sentencing (Table 2)

Tribunal	Killing	Rape	Torture	Violence	Other	Property
ICTY						
Discriminatory	18.0	20.0	17.5	18.0	17.0	20.0
	6–life	20	6–35	5–life	3–40	10–life
Arbitrary	16.0	18.0	15.0	15.0	15.0	12.0
	5–life	12–28	5–28	3–life	7–28	2–40
No. of cases	49	6	25	48	41	24
ICTR						
Discriminatory	40.0	55.0	35.0	55.0	NA	NA
	6–life	25–life	15–life	6–life		
Arbitrary	11.0	NA	12.0	12.0	12.0	NA
	6–15		12	12	12	
No. of cases	40	8	4	19	1	0

Observations:

1. In both tribunals, violent offences draw the heaviest sentences. The heavy sentences imposed for rape are noteworthy in light of the historic neglect of violence against women, but all defendants in this category were convicted for "extensive criminal conduct involving multiple instances of very cruel and deplorable treatment of victims and the cruelty of their acts. "

2. Offences committed with discrimination draw heavier sentences as opposed to random crime. This matches what tribunal judges claim about discriminatory motives adding to the seriousness of a person's actions. Random or arbitrary crime is less harshly sentenced.

3. The lowest sentences at both Tribunals have been handed down to those convicted of crimes that usually do not result in physical damage to victims: "other",

such as taking of hostages, unlawful labour, imprisonment or forcible transfer/deportation 67 and "arbitrary" property crimes.

4. Property crimes, only tried at the ICTY, have drawn heavier sentences in the main because they have been committed in conjunction with other serious acts, for example in the course of forced displacement and killings.

Relevance of modes of responsibility to sentence (Table 3)

Tribunal	Planners	Instigators	Order-givers	Perpetrators	JCE	Aiders	Superiors
ICTY							
Median sentence	25.0	25.0	22.5	18.0	17.0	15.0	9.0
Range	25	7–30	7–life	5–life	6–40	6–35	2–29
No. of Cases	1	3	10	25	25	24	16
ICTR							
Median sentence	32.0	50.0	55.0	50.0	25.0	45.0	55.0
Range	6–life	6–life	6–life	12–life	25	6–life	11–life
No. of Cases	3	14	20	22	1	25	9

Observations:

1. The data reveals different patterns at the two tribunals in this area, and also that the range of sentences imposed by the ICTY is wider than the ICTR.

2. At the ICTY, the highest sentences are imposed on planners, instigators and order givers (median 22. 05 – 25 years). Next are those convicted on the basis of JCE (median of 18 and 17 years). Aiders and abettors receive slightly shorter sentences (median of 15 years). Art 7 (3) convictions get the shortest sentences (median of 9 years).

3. At the ICTR, the highest sentences are imposed on order–givers and superiors (median of 55 years). Instigators and direct perpetrators also receive heavy sentences (median 50 years). Those aiding and abetting are subjected to even lighter sentences, followed by planners. The lowest median is that of a participant in JCE.

4. These differences, the authors suggest, could be due to two features. The first

is that most of the ICTR defendants were convicted of combinations of several modes of liability, such as perpetration, ordering and instigation together, often combined with superior responsibility. The second is that the ICTR deals primarily with cases of killings and violence, as part of genocide. Consequently, the convictions at the ICTR are based on a more homogenous crime base and sentences seem to be not as differentiated as at the ICTY.

Rank and sentencing (Table 4)

Tribunal	High rank	Middle rank	Low rank
ICTY			
Median sentence	20.0	10.0	15.0
Range	3–life	2–life	3–40
No. of cases	21	27	23
ICTR			
Median sentence	55.0	32.0	15.0
Range	25–life	6–life	7–25
No. of cases	10	25	5

Observations:

1. Those of higher rank get heavier sentences at the ICTR (median 55 years) than the ICTY (median 20 years). In both tribunals, those of higher rank receive heavier sentences that those of lower rank, supporting various dicta that this paper has already considered. However, the situation is significantly nuanced.

2. High-ranking defendants receive the heaviest sentences at the ICTY, but the median sentence of low-ranking offenders is five years longer than the median of middle-ranking perpetrators. This could, it is speculated, be due to the individualisation exercise that judges must go through in reaching a sentence, and it is possible that certain case-specific factors such as cruelty, zeal etc. may have led to the imposition of a heavier sentence in those playing a relatively insignificant role due to status.

3. At the ICTR, the median sentences are gradated along the line of defendants' rank. All high-ranking defendants (with one exception) have been sentenced to life imprisonment. Unlike at the ICTY, middle-ranking offenders are subjected to more severe sentences than their low-ranking subordinates/followers.

4. The ICC: statutory framework and practice

4.1   The statutory framework

The sentencing provisions of the 1998 Rome Statute of the ICC emerged from contentious discussions that focused on capital punishment as the ultimate penalty. The generality of the four provisions in Part VII contrasts with the detail of other areas and suggests that States got distracted and consequently failed to settle the purposes and principles that should govern the sentencing for a court that would not be geographically limited in the way that the earlier tribunals were. Significant cleavages about sentencing approaches and practices were glossed over in the light of the need to overcome the significant disputes over whether there could be capital punishment at the ICC, and to a lesser extent, life imprisonment. [171] Thus, the opportunity to build on the legacy of the ICTY and ICTR with a clear vision about the purposes and principles of sentencing, along with concrete guidance going beyond "gravity of the crime", individual circumstances, aggravating and mitigating circumstances, was not maximised. One finds mixed messages, for example when comparing the preamble which stresses deterrence and Rule 145 which stresses retribution. It was eventually settled that imprisonment would be the main penalty and that life would be the maximum tariff. [172]

---

[171]   William A Schabas, *An Introduction to the International Criminal Court*, Cambridge University Press, Cambridge, 2004, p. 140. Alongside imprisonment, the court may also impose a fine (art. 78) , order forfeiture of proceeds, property or assets of crime (art. 77 (2) (b)) and the other is reparations to victims (art. 75).

[172]   Rolf Einar Fife, "Commentary on Article 77, Applicable Penalties", in Otto Triffterer (ed.), *Commentary on the Rome Statute of the International Criminal Court: Observers' Notes, Article by Article*, Nomos Verlagsgesellschaft, Baden-Baden, 1999, p. 990.

Even so, the provisions of the ICC Statute and the four general provisions in the Rules of Procedure and Evidence *do* represent an improvement on the ICTY and IC-TR. From the preamble, we have a now familiar rhetoric of international justice about how "such grave crimes threaten the peace, security and well-being of the world", that they are of concern to the international community as a whole, that they "must not go unpunished", that they must be effectively prosecuted "by taking measures at the national level and by enhancing international cooperation" and that putting an end to impunity contributes "to the prevention of such crimes." The ICC is part of the international community's commitment to "guarantee lasting respect for and the enforcement of international justice." This provides the conceptual framework within which we can view sentencing at the court.

Article 77 of the Statute provides for two penalties, subject to mandatory review: imprisonment for a specified number of years, subject to a 30 year maximum, or in particularly serious cases, a term of life imprisonment (this is to be "justified by the extreme gravity of the crime and the individual circumstances of the convicted person"). [173] This is a compromise provision that balances divergent views on the death penalty, [174] and the opposition of some States to life imprisonment. An improvement this may be, but it is hardly an adequate or helpful sentencing range. It leaves the judges essentially free to pick anything they want in terms of years up to 30, and then life.

Article 78 goes on to repeat the familiar formulation that judges are obliged, in accordance with the Rules of Procedure and Evidence, "take into account such fac-

---

[173] Rule 145 (3) of the ICC Rules of Procedure and Evidence adds that this is to be "as evidenced by the existence of one or more aggravating circumstances." Fines and forfeitures are available in addition to imprisonment.

[174] "In the end, however, predominantly at the insistence of European states, the decision was taken that, despite the sui generis nature of the ICC, the Rome Statute should reflect the trend adopted in the other contemporary mechanisms of international criminal justice on this issue." Steven Freeland, "No longer acceptable: the exclusion of the death penalty under international criminal law", in *Australian Journal of Human Rights*, 2010, vol. 15, no. 2, p. 1, at p. 10.

tors as the gravity of the crime and the individual circumstances of the convicted person. " This is supported by an equally standard provision about deduction of time spent in imprisonment, and a provision dealing with convictions for more than one crime ["the Court shall pronounce a sentence for each crime and a joint sentence specifying the total period of imprisonment ... no less than the highest individual sentence pronounced and shall not exceed 30 years imprisonment or a sentence of life imprisonment in conformity with article 77, paragraph 1 (b)"].

Article 78, which lays out the foundational rule, does not mention an obligation to ensure proportionality of the sentence. The fact that Article 81 (2) (a) provides that "a sentence may be appealed ... on the ground of disproportion between the crime and the sentence" evidences that the judges have not just to consider these two factors of gravity and individualisation, but need to get the balance right. It may be argued that the notion of "crime" in Article 81 (2) suggests that "gravity of the crime" in Article 78 is in fact the dominant factor. However, this sits uncomfortably with Rule 145 (1) (a), discussed below, providing that the "the totality of any sentence ... must reflect the culpability of the convicted person. " The further requirement of Rule 145 (1) (b), also discussed below, to balance all the relevant factors, leads to the conclusion that a proportionate sentence is probably best seen as the *correct balance* that emerges from consideration of the necessary factors such as the gravity of the crime and the individual circumstances of the convicted person. It can be noted here that the *Lubanga* Appeal Chamber observed that the delegates at Rome considered including the qualifiers of "significantly" or "manifestly disproportionate", but ultimately rejected them. "Proportionality is generally measured by the degree of harm caused by the crime and the culpability of the perpetrator and, in this regard, relates to the determination of the length of sentence. " [175] The Chamber's reading is that while proportionality is not mentioned as a principle in Article 78 (1), Rule 145 (1) does in fact provide guidance "on how the Trial Chamber should exercise its discretion in entering a sentence that is proportionate to the crime and reflects the culpability of the convicted person. "

But are the ICC judges more restricted in their discretion, less free to do what they want, than their tribunal counterparts? Rule 145 affords them more help than international judges have ever had in determining the penalty to be imposed on a convicted accused. Judicial discretion is still extensive, but the rule as a whole does represent an improvement taking ICC sentencing towards greater consistency and predictability. Paragraph 1 provides:

In its determination of the sentence pursuant to article 78, paragraph 1, the Court shall:

(a) Bear in mind that the totality of any sentence of imprisonment and fine, as the case may be, imposed under article 77 must reflect the culpability of the convicted person;

(b) Balance all the relevant factors, including any mitigating and aggravating factors and consider the circumstances both of the convicted person and of the crime;

(c) In addition to the factors mentioned in article 78, paragraph 1, give consideration, inter alia, to the extent of the damage caused, in particular the harm caused to the victims and their families, the nature of the unlawful behaviour and the means employed to execute the crime; the degree of participation of

---

[175] ICC, *Prosecutor v. Thomas Lubanga Dyilo*, Judgement on the appeal of Mr Thomas Lubanga Dyilo against his conviction, Appeals Chamber, ICC - 01/04 - 01/06 - A5, 1 December 2014, para. 40 (https: // www. legal-tools. org/en/doc/585c75/) ("*Lubanga* Appeal Judgement") , drawing from Alison Marsten Danner, "Constructing a Hierarchy of Crimes in International Criminal Law Sentencing", in *Virginia Law Review*, 2001, Vol. 87, pp. 437-438.

the convicted person; the degree of intent; the circumstances of manner, time and location; and the age, education, social and economic condition of the convicted person.

The provision goes on to provide that "in addition" to "the factors mentioned above"[176], the judges are to consider mitigating and aggravating factors. Paragraph 2 (a) identifies the following two as illustrative mitigating factors:

i. The circumstances falling short of constituting grounds for exclusion of criminal responsibility, such as substantially diminished mental capacity or duress;

ii. The convicted person's conduct after the act, including any efforts by the person to compensate the victims and any cooperation with the Court.

Paragraph 2 (b) then identifies five aggravating factors and allows for others under the final residual provision:

i. [a] ny relevant prior criminal convictions for crimes under the jurisdiction of the [ICC] or of a similar nature;

ii. abuse of power or official capacity;

iii. commission of the crime where the victim is particularly defenceless;

iv. commission of the crime with particular cruelty or where there were multiple victims;

v. commission of the crime for any motive involving discrimination on any of the grounds referred to in article 21, paragraph 3 [these are gender, age,

---

[176] The *Lubanga* Appeals Chamber clarified that the factors "mentioned above" are those listed in rule 145 (1) (c) and that mitigating and aggravating circumstances, pursuant to rule 145 (2) of the Rules of Procedure and Evidence, are considered as "factors" (*Lubanga* Appeal Judgement, fn. 66, see *supra* note 175).

race, colour, language, religion or belief, political or other opinion, national, ethnic or social origin, wealth, birth or other status];

vi. other circumstances which, although not enumerated above, by virtue of their nature are similar to those mentioned.

Sub—rule (3) provides special guidance to judges when considering life sentences: these may be imposed when justified by the extreme gravity of the crime and the individual circumstances of the convicted person, "as evidenced by the existence of one or more aggravating circumstances."

A substantive issue that arose in *Lubanga* was the relationship between the Article 78 (1) factors and Rule 145 (1) (c). This is about whether certain factors should be treated in the gravity assessment or individual considerations, a balancing exercise that has vexed the judges of the other institutions too. These are not wholly distinct issues, with three possible interpretations of how the two relate to each other in the ICC framework. There, the appellate judges accepted that there were three possible interpretations of that interaction, [177] but the majority found it was not necessary to determine which of the approaches is correct, since "regardless of which interpretation is followed, the issue is whether the Trial Chamber considered all the relevant factors and made no error in the weighing and balancing exercise of these factors in arriving at the sentence." [178] President Song, on the other hand, felt that the appeals judges ought to provide trial judges with more guidance. For him, the correct interpretation was that the Trial Chamber, in assessing the Article 78 (1) factors, is obliged to consider the factors listed in Rule 145 (1) (c). He argued that:

---

[177] The three possible interpretations are: ①the factors of the gravity of the crimes and the individual circumstances of the person can be considered separately from the Rule 145 factors; ②some of the Rule 145 factors are subsumed within the Article 78 factors; ③the Rule 145 factors may be seen as part of, and be taken into account for the purpose of assessing, the Article 78 factors.

[178] *Lubanga* Appeal Judgement, para. 66, see *supra* note 175.

As a general matter, the extent of the damage caused, in particular the harm caused to the victims and their families, the nature of the unlawful behaviour and the means employed to execute the crime; the degree of participation of the convicted person; the degree of intent; and the circumstances of manner, time and location are factors to be considered in the context of the gravity of the crime. However, the age, education, social and economic condition of the convicted person should be considered in the context of the individual circumstances of the convicted person pursuant to article 78 (1) of the Statute. [179]

He therefore suggested that the Trial Chamber should take into account the following three overall factors when determining sentence:

 i. The gravity of the crime pursuant to article 78 (1) of the Statute as informed by those factors identified above in paragraph 3 as set out in rule 145 (1) (c) of the RPE;

 ii. Aggravating and mitigating circumstances pursuant to rule 145 (2) of the RPE;

 iii. The individual circumstances of the convicted person pursuant to article 78 (1) of the Statute as informed by those factors identified above in paragraph 3 as set out in rule 145 (1) (c) of the RPE. [180]

The ICC judges also have to work within the framework of Article 21 on "Applicable Law." This obliges them to follow a prescribed methodology. They must first seek the applicable rules within the Statute and Rules of Procedure and Evidence. If

---

[179] *Lubanga* Appeal Judgement, Partly Dissenting Opinion of Judge Sang-Hyun Song, para. 3, see *supra* note 175.

[180] *Ibid.*, para. 4.

that does not yield the answer, then they can look to applicable treaties and the principles and rules of international law, i. e. customary international law. If that too fails to deliver, they can apply general principles of law found in the legal systems of the world that are applicable to the issue for consideration.

This is certainly more normative guidance than at the ad hoc tribunals. However, the *Lubanga* Appeals Chamber's claim that this represents "a comprehensive scheme for the determination and imposition of a sentence"[181] is overly enthusiastic. ICC judges expressly draw from the practice evolved at the ad hoc tribunals,[182] which they would not need to do if the ICC really had a "comprehensive scheme", and especially in light of the duty to follow the Statute's sources—of—law methodology. It is also obvious that the ICC regime retains much of the extensive judicial discretion at the tribunals that has been so heavily criticised. For Ambos, it "contains the same compromising characteristics ... generality and ambiguity."[183] There is identification of some factors relevant to sentencing but the "sentencing range" is hardly deserving of that moniker. However, Ambos is too harsh, in light of the reality that the sentencing framework will be developed by caselaw, to conclude that it makes "the final sentence highly uncertain and unforeseeable."[184]

4.2 Sentencing practice at the ICC

The ICC has now delivered four sentencing judgements (not including the *Bem-*

---

[181] *Ibid.* , para. 32.

[182] For example, in *Prosecutor v. Germain Katanga*, Decision on Sentence pursuant to Article 76 of the Statute, Trial Chamber, ICC–01/04–01/07, 23 May 2014 (https: //www. legal–tools. org/en/doc/5af172/) ("*Katanga* Decision on Sentence pursuant to Article 76 of the Statute"), the Trial Chamber referenced the ICTY's *Milošević, Hadžihasanović and Kubura, Erdemović, Blagojević and Jokić, Plavšić, Nikolić* and *Strugar* cases as well as the ICTR's *Akayesu, Semanza, Barayagwiza, Kajelijeli, Kambanda*, and *Rugambarara* cases. The *Bemba* Decision on Sentence pursuant to Article 76 of the Statute and the *Al Mahdi* Judgement and Sentence are also replete with ICTY and ICTR references. The first case, *Lubanga*, saw only one ad hoc tribunal case cited (*Nikolić*, cited twice). The SCSL jurisprudence covering convictions for child—soldiering was more frequently cited.

[183] Ambos, 2014, p. 282, see *supra* note 6.

[184] *Ibid.* , p. 281.

ba et al Article 70 matter) [185] and one appellate judgement on sentencing. It is still developing its own practice. The ICC judges understand the Preamble to mean that retribution and deterrence are the primary objectives of punishment at their institution. [186] The *Lubanga* Appeals Chamber has established a clear methodology for the chambers. First, the Trial Chamber must identify and assess the relevant factors in Article 78 (1) and Rule 145 (1) (c) and (2). Then, it is to balance all relevant factors pursuant to Rule 145 (1) (b). "The sentence must be determined by weighing and balancing all the relevant factors. The weight given to an individual factor and the balancing of all relevant factors in arriving at the sentence is at the core of a Trial Chamber's exercise of discretion. " [187] It is to pronounce a sentence for each crime, as well as a joint sentence specifying the total period of imprisonment. The final tally cannot be less than the highest individual sentence. In accordance with Rule 145 (1) (a), the sentence must reflect the culpability of the convicted person.

The Appeals Chamber has also provided guidance on when it will interfere with sentences imposed following a conviction. This provides further insight into what is regarded as an appropriate sentence. This too is consistent with the pre-existing tribunal practice. The sentence will only be interfered with: ①where the exercise of discretion is based on an error of law; ②where the exercise of discretion is exercised on an error of fact; or③where the Trial Chamber's weighing and balancing of relevant factors led to an imposed sentence that was so unreasonable as to amount to an abuse of discretion. [188] Article 83 (2) of the Statute underscores that the impugned sentence must be "materially affected by error of fact or law or procedural error",

---

[185] *Prosecutor v. Jean-Pierre Bemba Gombo et al*, Trial Chamber, ICC-01/05-01/13-2123-Corr, Decision on Sentence pursuant to Article 76 of the Statute, 21 March 2017.

[186] For example, *Katanga* Decision on Sentence pursuant to Article 76 of the Statute, paras. 37-38, see *supra* note 182; ICC, *Prosecutor v. Jean-Pierre Bemba Gombo*, Decision on Sentence pursuant to Article 76 of the Statute, Trial Chamber, ICC-01/05-01/08, 21 June 2016, para. 10 (https://www. legal-tools. org/en/doc/f4c14e/) ("*Bemba* Decision on Sentence pursuant to Article 76 of the Statute").

[187] *Lubanga* Appeal Judgement, para. 1, see *supra* note 175.

[188] *Ibid.* , paras. 3, 36-50.

and the Appeals Chamber considers that the material effect of such an error is only established if the Trial Chamber's exercise of discretion led to a disproportionate sentence. [189]

The approach to the existing jurisprudence of the ad hoc tribunals has been mixed. The first sentencing decision, in *Lubanga*, saw just two references to a single ICTY case but the SCSL's sentencing practice was particularly relevant because of the recruitment or use of child soldiers. [190] The other decisions, following convictions entered in *Katanga*, *Al Mahdi* and *Bemba* have contained extensive references to the sentencing practice of the ad hoc tribunals. There is even consideration of the Cambodian Extraordinary Chambers. [191] However, a cautious approach to comparative sentencing was expressly mandated by the *Lubanga* Appeals Chamber. Citing to the ICTY's *Strugar* Appeal, it took the view that previous sentencing practice is just one of several factors to be taken into account when determining the sentence. Furthermore:

> The value of other sentencing practices is even lower when the reference is to the sentencing practices of another tribunal, as opposed to that of a Trial Chamber of the Court ... even though there are similarities in the sentencing provisions of the Court and those of other international criminal courts and tribunals, the Court has to apply, in the first place, its own Statute and legal instruments. [192]

---

[189] *Ibid.* , para. 4. For criticism of the approach to proportionality, see deGuzman, 2014, see *supra* note 6.

[190] *Ibid.* , paras. 12–15.

[191] See for example, *Bemba* Decision on Sentence pursuant to Article 76 of the Statute, fn. 31, see *supra* note 186. These are, as their title declares, extraordinary chambers in the courts of Cambodia, and not part of an international tribunal.

[192] ICC, *Prosecutor v. Thomas Lubanga Dyilo*, Decision on Sentence Pursuant to Article 76 of the Statute, Trial Chamber, ICC–01/04–01/06, 10 July 2012, paras. 76–77 (https: //www. legal–tools. org/en/ doc/c79996/) ("*Lubanga* Decision on Sentence Pursuant to Article 76 of the Statute").

This was taken up in *Al Mahdi*, where the chamber found that the Defence's arguments about the sentences in other cases were irrelevant, being "based on vastly different circumstances, including the applicable modes of liability and sources of law." [193]

The first sentencing decision in *Lubanga* left observers in the dark as to how the quantum was reached. [194] In *Lubanga*, there was no exposition of a "judicial theory of sentencing" at trial or on appeal. In *Katanga*, Trial Chamber II was slightly more forthcoming, and emphasized three principles: legality, proportionality and individualisation. [195] According to that chamber, sentencing serves two principal functions. Firstly, it has a role in condemning and thus stigmatizing conduct as reprehensible, which is a way to recognize the harm and suffering caused to victims. [196] Secondly, the sentence should dissuade others from committing similar crimes in the future and so is a preventative measure. [197] The sentence should also serve, to some end, the need for justice felt by victims and their close relations/family. The judgement's function is to "give meaning to the sentence pronounced." [198] The *Al Mahdi* Chamber's starting position was influenced by *Katanga* and *Bemba* and the *ad hoc* tribunals:

> With regard to retribution, the Chamber clarifies that it is not to be understood as fulfilling a desire for revenge, but as an expression of the international community's condemnation of the crimes, which, by way of imposition of a proportionate sentence, also acknowledges the harm to the victims and promotes the

---

[193] ICC, *Prosecutor v. Ahmad Al Faqi Al Mahdi*, Judgement and Sentence, Trial Chamber, ICC-01/12-01/15, 27 September 2016, para. 107 (https: //www. legal-tools. org/en/doc/042397/) ("*Al Mahdi* Judgement and Sentence").

[194] See http: //dovjacobs. com/2012/07/10/some-thoughts-on-the-lubanga-sentence-a-throw-of-the-dice/, last accessed at 1 April 2017.

[195] *Katanga* Decision on Sentence pursuant to Article 76 of the Statute, para. 39, see *supra* note 182.

[196] *Ibid.*, para. 38.

[197] *Ibid.*

[198] *Ibid.*, para. 36.

restoration of peace and reconciliation. In respect of deterrence, the Chamber considers that a sentence should be adequate to discourage a convicted person from recidivism (specific deterrence), as well as to ensure that those who would consider committing similar crimes will be dissuaded from doing so (general deterrence). Lastly, the extent to which the sentence reflects the culpability of the convicted person addresses the desire to ease that person's reintegration into society, although, in particular in the case of international criminal law, this goal cannot be considered to be primordial and should therefore not be given any undue weight. [199]

The Prosecution attempted, in *Lubanga*, to inject some objectivity into the mystery of the quantum of sentencing. It proposed that the Trial Chamber should begin with a starting point of 80% of the 30 year maximum term. The rationale was that in order "to avoid inexplicable sentencing discrepancies", the chamber's sentencing policy should presume a "consistent baseline" for sentences, which should not be adjusted on the basis that some crimes are less serious than others. [200] The Trial Chamber rejected this on the grounds that there was no basis in law for this, and in any case, found that it was not a proportionate balance between the crime and sentence. This was not re—litigated before Trial Chamber II in *Katanga*. In *Al Mahdi*, the Prosecution simply proposed a sentencing range between nine and eleven years, having made a commitment to do so in the plea agreement. [201] This was even less scientific than that proposed in *Lubanga*, and has all the elements of arbitrary pulling

---

[199] *Al Mahdi* Judgement and Sentence, para. 67, see *supra* note 193; *Bemba* Decision on Sentence pursuant to Article 76 of the Statute, para. 11, see *supra* note 186; *Katanga* Decision on Sentence pursuant to Article 76 of the Statute, para. 38, see *supra* note 182.

[200] *Lubanga* Decision on Sentence Pursuant to Article 76 of the Statute, para. 92, see *supra* note 192.

[201] ICC, *Prosecutor v. Ahmad Al Faqi Al Mahdi*, Public redacted version of "Prosecution's submissions on sentencing", Prosecution, ICC-01/12-01/15-139-Conf, 22 July 2016, para. 65 (https: //www. legal-tools. org/doc/95421c/).

numbers out of the air. The Prosecution justified this range because:

- the war crime of attacking protected objects under article 8 (2) (e) (iv) of the Statute is inherently serious;
- the attack in this case was particularly serious, given the religious, historical, and cultural significance of the buildings attacked and the manner of the attack, and particularly in light of the motivation of religious discrimination;
- the Accused played an essential role in the commission of the crime;
- the Accused deserves substantial credit for his confession and admitting in detail the facts of the crime, and providing substantial cooperation with the Prosecution's ongoing investigation of the Mali situation. [202]

The Chamber did not engage directly with this, but imposed a sentence of nine years.

In sentencing, the trial chambers in *Lubanga*, *Katanga*, *Al Mahdi* and *Bemba* recognised the significance of gravity in determination of the sentence, and that sentence should also be proportionate to the crime and should reflect the culpability of the person. [203] For Trial Chamber II, gravity is to be analysed quantitatively and qualitatively. [204] The following have been considered (not necessarily accepted) in the gravity evaluation: the purpose behind the prohibited conduct and the impact upon the victims and their families, and also the secondary victims, [205] the large scale

---

[202]   *Ibid.* , para. 66.

[203]   *Ibid.* , para. 36; *Katanga* Decision on Sentence pursuant to Article 76 of the Statute, para. 43, see *supra* note 182; *Bemba* Decision on Sentence pursuant to Article 76 of the Statute, para. 11, see *supra* note 186; *Al Mahdi* Judgement and Sentence, paras. 71-72, see *supra* note 193.

[204]   *Katanga* Decision on Sentence pursuant to Article 76 of the Statute, paras. 42-43, see *supra* note 182.

[205]   *Lubanga* Decision on Sentence Pursuant to Article 76 of the Statute, paras. 38-44, see *supra* note 192; *Katanga* Decision on Sentence pursuant to Article 76 of the Statute, paras. 55-60, see *supra* note 182.

and nature of the crimes, [206] degree of participation and intent of the accused[207] and the discriminatory nature of the crimes. [208] The *Lubanga* decision referred directly to the ICTY's *Nikolic* Appeals Chamber on the prohibition against double-counting factors considered in the gravity evaluation again as aggravating factors. [209] The *Katanga* Trial Chamber considered the vulnerability of the victims, the discriminatory aspect and motives of the attacks in its gravity evaluation, so consciously declined to re-consider them when evaluating aggravating factors.

Al Mahdi is unusual in that the accused was convicted only for his actions against property, the war crime of attacking protected sites (all the ten sites attacked were dedicated to religion and historic monuments, and were not military objectives; all bar one had UNESCO World Heritage site status). Its closest parallel is the Sentencing Decision in *Jokić* at the ICTY, which concerned the shelling of Dubrovnik's historic Old Town. The destruction was in violation of Article 8 (2)(e)(iv) of the ICC Statute, by way of Article 25 (3)(a), and *Al Mahdi* was convicted as a principal, a co-perpetrator. The Trial Chamber followed the jurisprudence of the ICC that this is more blameworthy "generally speaking and all other things being equal. " [210] The quantum of nine years imposed in *Al Mahdi* reflect a number of considerations, but even in September 2016, we still cannot see the mechanics of how that figure, as opposed for example to eight or ten years, was reached. Somewhat more transparent is the *Bemba* decision, which imposed the following terms of imprisonment, permitting some comparison and evaluation:

---

[206] *Lubanga* Decision on Sentence Pursuant to Article 76 of the Statute, paras. 45-50, see *supra* note 193; *Katanga* Decision on Sentence pursuant to Article 76 of the Statute, paras. 46-52, see *supra* note 182.

[207] *Lubanga* Decision on Sentence Pursuant to Article 76 of the Statute, paras. 51-53, see *supra* note 192; *Katanga* Decision on Sentence pursuant to Article 76 of the Statute, paras. 61-69, see *supra* note 183.

[208] *Katanga* Decision on Sentence pursuant to Article 76 of the Statute, paras. 53-54, see *supra* note 183.

[209] *Lubanga* Decision on Sentence Pursuant to Article 76 of the Statute, para. 35, see *supra* note 192.

[210] *Ibid.*, para 58, citing to the *Lubanga* Appeal Judgement, para. 462, see *supra* note 175.

a. Murder as a war crime: 16 years of imprisonment;

b. Murder as a crime against humanity: 16 years of imprisonment;

c. Rape as a war crime: 18 years of imprisonment;

d. Rape as a crime against humanity: 18 years of imprisonment; and

e. Pillaging as a war crime: 16 years of imprisonment.

This allows the observation that rape was considered to deserve a heavier penalty than murder. The 18 year sentence that was ultimately imposed reflected the totality of Bemba's liability.

The *Al Mahdi* Chamber proceeded along the established route in ICC practice: considering (i) the gravity of the crime; (ii) the accused's culpable conduct; and (iii) his individual circumstances, with factoring in of Rule 145 (1)(c) on aggravating and mitigating circumstances. For the Chamber, even if inherently grave, crimes against property are generally of lesser gravity than crimes against persons. Even so, these were globally cherished properties and the targeted buildings were not only religious buildings but had also a symbolic and emotional value for the inhabitants of Timbuktu. [211] In this situation, the crimes were of "significant gravity." [212] *Al Mahdi* had another unusual feature: the parties entered into a plea agreement, pursuant to which the accused accepted his responsibility for the crime charged and provided a detailed account of his actions.

The following have been considered during the individualised aggravating circumstances evaluation (not necessarily accepted): harsh and brutal treatment of the

---

[211] *Ibid.*, para. 79.

[212] *Ibid.*, para. 82.

victims,[213] sexual violence,[214] defencelessness of the victims,[215] discriminatory motives[216], abuse of authority[217]. The *Lubanga* appeal raised the issue of the level of the accused's awareness about certain factors said to be aggravating in order for that to be linked to him. There, the Appeals Chamber upheld the approach of the majority of the Trial Chamber in requiring proof beyond reasonable doubt that child soldiers were subjected to sexual violence or punishment and that this could be attributed to Lubanga in a way that reflected his culpability (i. e. through his intent, awareness or any other form of culpability), without being more concrete than that. [218] The ICC's Rule 145 (2)(b)(ii) requires a Chamber to take into account, as appropriate, abuse of power or official capacity as an aggravating circumstance, and the *Lubanga* Appeals Chamber has expressly endorsed positions laid out in earlier ad hoc tribunal jurisprudence in *Babić*, *Ndindabahizi* and *Deronjic*, to the effect that the consideration of authority in aggravation goes beyond the mere fact of its existence: simply being of a higher rank or position is not determinative; what matters is how it is used, the abuse of that rank or authority. [219]

In the individualised mitigation consideration, the following have been consid-

---

[213]　*Lubanga* Decision on Sentence Pursuant to Article 76 of the Statute, paras. 57–59, see *supra* note 193; *Katanga* Decision on Sentence pursuant to Article 76 of the Statute, para. 71, see *supra* note 182.

[214]　*Lubanga* Decision on Sentence Pursuant to Article 76 of the Statute, paras. 60–76, see *supra* note 193; *Katanga* Decision on Sentence pursuant to Article 76 of the Statute, para. 48, see *supra* note 182. The *Bemba* Decision on Sentence pursuant to Article 76 of the Statute, see *supra* note 187, breaks the aggravation of the sexual violence down into several components: gravity, particularly defenceless victims and particular cruelty. It does this for the murder and pillaging convictions too. Two of the three judges were satisfied that pillaging was committed with particular cruelty while Judge Steiner found it was committed against particularly defenceless victims (both being aggravating factors).

[215]　*Lubanga* Decision on Sentence Pursuant to Article 76 of the Statute, paras. 77–78, see *supra* note 192; *Katanga* considered this in the gravity assessment.

[216]　*Ibid.*, paras. 79–81; *Katanga* considered this in the gravity assessment.

[217]　*Katanga* Decision on Sentence pursuant to Article 76 of the Statute, paras. 72–75, see *supra* note 182.

[218]　*Lubanga* Appeal Judgement, paras. 88–93, see *supra* note 175.

[219]　*Ibid.*, para. 82; followed in *Al Mahdi* Judgement and Sentence, para. 86, see *supra* note 193.

ered (not necessarily accepted) : overall motives and intent, [220] contribution to peace (e. g. disarmament, demobilization, reconciliation) [221] personal or family circumstances, [222] cooperation with the Trial Chamber in general terms, [223] demeanour in court, [224] rights violations during the legal process, [225] and genuine remorse[226]. For the *Katanga* Chamber, cooperation with the Trial Chamber and demeanour in the detention centre, even if completely positive, cannot qualify as a mitigating factor. [227] In *Bemba*, the Trial Chamber did not accept any mitigating circumstances. [228] In that case, a novel argument was put forward: that the penalty should be mitigated because the accused had contributed resources to the trial and reparations process, suffered losses as a result of the depreciation of the frozen and seized assets. [229] In *Al Mahdi*, the Trial Chamber accepted three mitigating circumstances in addition to the admission of guilt and cooperation with the Prosecution: remorse and the empathy that that the accused expressed for the victims, his initial reluctance to commit the crime and the steps he took to limit the damage caused; and even if of limited importance, his good conduct in detention in spite of his "family

---

[220] *Lubanga* Decision on Sentence Pursuant to Article 76 of the Statute, paras. 83-87, see *supra* note 192; *Katanga* considered this in the gravity assessment; *Al Mahdi* Judgement and Sentence, para. 89, see *supra* note 193 (here the consideration was his reluctance to commit the crime and means of execution).

[221] *Katanga* Decision on Sentence pursuant to Article 76 of the Statute, paras. 91 – 115, esp, paras. 106-113, see *supra* note 182; *Bemba* Decision on Sentence pursuant to Article 76 of the Statute, paras. 71-76, see *supra* note 186.

[222] *Katanga* Decision on Sentence pursuant to Article 76 of the Statute, paras. 78-88, see *supra* note 182; *Bemba* Decision on Sentence pursuant to Article 76 of the Statute, paras. 77-78, see *supra* note 186; *Al Mahdi* Judgement and Sentence, paras. 101-102, see *supra* note 193.

[223] *Lubanga* Decision on Sentence Pursuant to Article 76 of the Statute, paras. 88-90, see *supra* note 192; *Al Mahdi* Judgement and Sentence, para. 96, see *supra* note 193; *Bemba* Decision on Sentence pursuant to Article 76 of the Statute, paras. 79-81, see *supra* note 186.

[224] *Katanga* Decision on Sentence pursuant to Article 76 of the Statute, paras. 122-129, see *supra* note 182.

[225] *Bemba* Decision on Sentence pursuant to Article 76 of the Statute, paras. 87-89, see *supra* note 186.

[226] *Ibid.*, para. 121; *Al Mahdi* Judgement and Sentence, paras. 103-105, see *supra* note 193.

[227] *Katanga* Decision on Sentence pursuant to Article 76 of the Statute, para. 129, see *supra* note 182.

[228] *Bemba* Decision on Sentence pursuant to Article 76 of the Statute, para. 93, see *supra* note 186.

[229] *Ibid.*, paras. 82-84.

situation. " In respect of the latter, serious security concerns for his family meant that Al Mahdi had not been able to see them since being transferred to the ICC's jurisdiction. Matters such as age, education, lack of a previous conviction, and lack of a militarised background, were not relevant in this sentencing. [230]

For the *Lubanga* Trial Chamber, the accused's cooperation with the Trial Chamber in light of "some particularly onerous circumstances", was a mitigating factor. [231] This is because Lubanga really did face some significant procedural irregularities. The *Katanga* Chamber noted that personal circumstances including young children were relevant but did not have a major role in mitigation. [232] In terms of the *Al Mahdi* admission of guilt, it seems to have been a weighty factor for the Chamber. The ICC's statutory framework is a "third avenue" (borrowing from Triffterer) between the traditional common law and civil law approaches and draws from the experiences of the ad hoc tribunals, particularly that of the ICTY. The *Al Mahdi* admission was made early, fully and appeared to the judges to be genuine, "led by the real desire to take responsibility for the acts he committed and showing honest repentance. " [233] This admission of guilt, the judgement held:

> Undoubtedly contributed to the rapid resolution of this case, thus saving the Court's time and resources and relieving witnesses and victims of what can be a stressful burden of giving evidence in Court. Moreover, this admission may also further peace and reconciliation in Northern Mali by alleviating the victims' moral suffering through acknowledgement of the significance of the destruction. Lastly, such an admission may have a deterrent effect on others tempted to commit similar acts in Mali and elsewhere. [234]

---

[230] *Al Mahdi* Judgement and Sentence, para. 96, see *supra* note 193.

[231] *Lubanga* Decision on Sentence Pursuant to Article 76 of the Statute, para. 91, see *supra* note 192.

[232] *Katanga* Decision on Sentence pursuant to Article 76 of the Statute, para. 88, see *supra* note 182.

[233] *Al Mahdi* Judgement and Sentence, para. 100, see *supra* note 193.

[234] *Ibid.*, para. 100.

The *Bemba* Trial Chamber drew a line between its gravity considerations and its discretion in considering aggravating factors. In relation to the gravity of the crimes of murder, the Chamber considered the following Rule 145 (1)(c) factors: the extent of damage caused, the nature of the unlawful behaviour, the means employed to execute the crime, and the circumstances of manner, time, and location. The Chamber took the view that the rape and pillaging in this case was of a special nature, and therefore used its discretion to consider the relevant Rule 145 (1)(c) factors (including the nature of the unlawful behaviour and the means employed to execute the crime, and the circumstances of manner, time, and location beyond those considered in relation to the gravity of the crimes), which were not addressed in the gravity consideration. *Bemba* underscored the special status of crimes of a sexual nature, in particular those against children. [235] The additional rape aggravation considerations included:

> Whether the victims were armed; the location of a crime, for example, whether it was committed in places of civilian sanctuary, such as churches and hospitals, or the victims' homes; the victims' ages, particularly in cases of sexual violence; the duration and repeated nature of the acts; the perpetrators' motives; and the violent and humiliating nature of the acts, including their public nature, and any verbal, physical, or other abuse or threats accompanying the crime. [236]

To this end, the Trial Chamber pointed to convincing evidence of victimisation of multiple family members, the young age of many victims, commission of crimes by multiple perpetrators, attacks on persons seeking refuge, attacks on victims in their

---

[235] *Bemba* Decision on Sentence pursuant to Article 76 of the Statute, para. 35, see *supra* note 186.
[236] *Ibid.*, para. 25.

homes and places of sanctuary, the fact that victims were unarmed, the repeated nature of the crimes, the perpetrators' motives, and the violent and humiliating nature of the crimes, including the abuse and threats accompanying the crimes. In its aggravation consideration, the Chamber also drew from expert testimony about the impact of such violence on the direct and indirect victims. The judges pointedly considered the broader context (i. e. in terms of "gender sensitivity") as well as the indirect victims, in particular, family members, who suffered severe and lasting harm. [237] In *Bemba*, the Chamber held, in addition to the general gravity assessment, "the crimes of rape are of utmost, serious gravity. " [238]

The court's jurisprudence on the impact of modes of responsibility has been rather unsettled. Rule 145 requires consideration of the degree of participation of the convicted person; and "the degree of intent", making the mode of responsibility for which the person is convicted relevant to the sentence to be imposed. As at 2013, 75% of the individuals indicted by the ICC were charged and/or confirmed pursuant to one of the modes of liability set forth in Article 25 (3)(a); of the 24 individuals indicted under this provision, 12 were originally charged by the Office of the Prosecutor as co-perpetrators. [239] This is a court where the majority of judges have embraced the "control of the crime" theory, requiring this for co-perpetration. [240] Their jurisprudence has established that there must be clear delineation between commission and the rest (ordering, instigating or aiding and abetting). But on hier-

---

[237] *Ibid.* , para. 32.

[238] *Ibid.* , para. 40.

[239] Women's Initiative for Gender Justice, "Modes of Liability: A Review of the International Criminal Court's Current Jurisprudence and Practice" (Expert Paper 2013), p. 30, available at http: //iccwomen. org/documents/Modes-of-Liability. pdf, last accessed at 1 April 2017.

[240] For example, *Lubanga* Confirmation of Charges Decision, paras. 326, 330, 340, 347; *Lubanga* Decision on Sentence Pursuant to Article 76 of the Statute, paras. 1003 – 1004, see *supra* 192; *Lubanga* Appeal Judgement, paras. 469–473, see *supra* note 175; *Katanga and Chui* Decision on the Confirmation of Charges, para. 525; *Katanga* Decision on Sentence pursuant to Article 76 of the Statute, paras. 1382, 1393–1395, see *supra* note 182. The dissenters to this view have been Judge Fulford, who has left the court, and Judge Van den Wyngaert.

archy between modes of responsibility, there has been cleavage mirroring that which exists in academic writing. [241] Several chambers have taken the view that Article 25 (3) reflects a hierarchy of responsibility, for example the Pre-Trial Chamber in *Mbarushimana*, [242] Pre-Trial Chamber II in the *Ruto* Confirmation Decision, [243] and the *Lubanga* majority. [244] The *Katanga* chamber, Trial Chamber II, stepped away from this, with the view that there is no hierarchy in Article 25 (3), that "a perpetrator of a crime is not always viewed as more reprehensible than an accessory" and "[e] ach mode of liability has different characteristics and legal ramifications which reflect various forms of involvement in criminality. "[245]

The issue of hierarchy between modes of responsibility having been addressed differently in the trial judgements, the two sentencing decisions in *Lubanga* and *Katanga* did not revisit, focusing instead on the case at hand and the conviction entered

---

[241] Against the notion, see Elies van Sliedregt, "Perpetration and Participation in Article 35 (3) ", in Carsten Stahn (ed.), *The Law and Practice of the International Criminal Court*, Oxford University Press, Oxford, 2015, pp. 511-513; James Stewart, "The End of ' Modes of Liability' for International Crimes", in *Leiden Journal of International Law*, 2015, Vol. 25, p. 16. For the notion, see Werle and Burghardt, 2014, see *supra* note 146; Ambos, 2014, pp. 146-147, see *supra* note 6; Gerhard Werle, "Individual criminal responsibility in Article 25 ICC Statute", in *Journal of International Criminal Justice*, 2006, Vol. 5, p. 953, at p. 957.

[242] ICC, *Prosecutor v. Callixte Mbarushimana*, Decision on the confirmation of charges, Pre-Trial Chamber, ICC-01/04-01/10, 16 December 2011, para. 27 (https: //www. legal-tools. org/en/doc/63028f/).

[243] ICC, *Prosecutor v. William Samoei Ruto and Joshua Arap Sang*, Decision on the Confirmation of Charges Pursuant to Article 61 (7)(a) and (b) of the Rome Statute, Pre-Trial Chamber, ICC-01/09-01/ 11, 23 January 2012, para. 254 (https: //www. legal-tools. org/en/doc/96c3c2/).

[244] *Lubanga* Decision on Sentence Pursuant to Article 76 of the Statute, paras. 996, 997-998, see *supra* note 192.

[245] *Katanga* Decision on Sentence pursuant to Article 76 of the Statute, para. 1387, see *supra* note 182. The case did not go on appeal. In support, the Trial Chamber cited to: ①a number of civil law jurisdictions, ②the logic of the provision, ③Claus Roxin, "Crimes as Part of Organized Power Structures", in *Journal of International Criminal Justice*, 2011, vol. 9, p. 202; ④Albin Eser, "Individual Criminal Responsibility", in Antonio Cassese *et al* (eds.), *The Rome Statute of the International Criminal Court: A Commentary*, Oxford University Press, Oxford, 2002, p. 782, ⑤Judge Fulford's separate opinion in the *Lubanga* Trial Judgement, and ⑥Judge Van den Wyngaert's concurring opinion in the *Ngudjolo* Judgement.

against the accused. [246] The sentences do not seem to have been affected by the cleaved views on hierarchy. Even so, the judges did, it is clear, consider the accused's participation, the degree of participation of the convicted person; and "the degree of intent" in reaching sentence. [247] When this issue reached the Appeals Chamber in the matter of *Lubanga*, the guidance to emerge was that there is a hierarchy of blameworthiness in Article 25 (3): ...generally speaking and all other things being equal, a person who is found to commit a crime him—or herself bears more blameworthiness than a person who contributes to the crime of another person or persons. ' [248] This was followed in the recent case of *Al Mahdi*.

The *Bemba* conviction was entered on the basis of command responsibility only. The Trial Chamber held that command responsibility (for which the accused was convicted and sentenced to 18 years imprisonment) is a *sui generis* form of responsibility:

It is not, inherently, a hierarchically lower or higher mode of liability in terms of gravity than commission of a crime under Article 25 (3)(a), or any other mode of liability identified in Article 25 (3)(b) to (e). [249]

The *Bemba* Trial Chamber held that in order to determine an appropriate sentence, gravity must be assessed in concreto, in light of the particular circumstances

---

[246]   In *Lubanga*, this was addressed in the Judgement itself. Judge Fulford's dissent also dealt with this issue, and he rejected the notion of hierarchy of seriousness in principle, and specifically rejected the notion of ordering, soliciting, or inducing a crime (Article 25 (3)(b)) is a less serious form of commission than committing it "through another person" (Article 25 (3)(a), and that the criminality of accessories (Article 25 (3) (c)) is greater than those who participate within a group, see *Lubanga* Decision on Sentence Pursuant to Article 76 of the Statute, Separate Opinion of Judge Adrian Fulford, para. 8. Associating herself with this view, see *Ngudjolo* Judgement, Concurring Opinion of Judge Van den Wyngaert, paras. 23–24, see *supra* note 192.

[247]   *Lubanga* Decision on Sentence Pursuant to Article 76 of the Statute, paras. 52, 59, see *supra* note 193. This is also apparent in the considerations of gravity by the *Katanga* Trial Chamber.

[248]   *Lubanga* Appeal Judgement, para. 462, see *supra* note 175.

[249]   *Bemba* Decision on Sentence pursuant to Article 76 of the Statute, para. 16, see *supra* note 186.

of the case, the gravity of the crimes committed by the subordinates, and the convicted person's culpability. [250] In its analysis, the Chamber distinguished the ICC's Article 28 from its equivalents at the other tribunals, as this particular provision requires a nexus between the commander's failure to exercise proper control over the forces under his effective command and control, or effective authority and control and the crimes. The responsibility of the commander is obviously considerably elevated "when it is established that the crimes would not have been committed, in the circumstances in which they were, had the commander exercised control properly, or the commander exercising control properly would have prevented the crimes. " [251] The *Bemba* Chamber also referred to the consistent practice at the ICTY and ICTR to the effect that a commander who failed and continued to fail to exercise the duties to prevent or repress – which would encourage subordinates to believe that they could commit further crimes with impunity—is generally regarded as being of significantly greater gravity than isolated incidents of such a failure. [252] Furthermore, it observed that in accordance with the principle of gradation used in international sentencing, "high—level leaders, regardless of the mode of liability, generally bear heavier criminal responsibility than those further down the scale" even if they are removed from the direct acts of subordinates. [253]

5. Is sentencing at the ICC an improvement on the ICTY and ICTR?

Seventeen years ago, in 2000, the ICTY Appeals Chamber in *Furundžija* held that it was still "premature to speak of an emerging penal regime" at the international level. In Chapter II of this study, we have seen that in their practice, the judges have in fact developed a "broad pattern of fundamental guidelines" rather than an elaborate sentencing system. [254] Thanks to the role of the Appeals Chambers as levell-

---

[250] *Ibid.*

[251] *Ibid.*, para. 60.

[252] *Ibid.*, para. 17.

[253] *Ibid.*

[254] Book, 2011, p. 29, see *supra* note 53.

er (even if the ICTY – ICTR chamber was not as robust as some would have liked) [255] and cross-chamber and cross-tribunal fertilisation, there are common positions in the jurisprudence and differences can be reasonably understood as being down to judicial discretion. There can be said to be an emerging system of international criminal justice. [256] This is a relatively stable and predictable regime of international sentencing. Put another way, "international criminal law provides for more refined guidelines than has generally been recognised", and there is a "coherent framework" that has in its fundamental principles "attained the status of international law." [257] The tribunal judges have established what Holá has described as the same "algorithm in determining sentences." [258]

Ambos is certainly right in observing that the "history of the sentencing rules in the law of the international criminal tribunals since Nuremberg is the history of a constant improvement of these rules in terms of their precision and foreseeability." [259] This evolution is most obviously seen in the ICC's statutory regime, although much is still left undefined or unaddressed, notably the absence of meaningful sentencing ranges to help guide the judges and indeterminate concepts such as gravity. The ICC judges have used what they have been given in the legal framework and have built on the rich heritage of existing practice. What emerges is also not conveyer-belt justice; the practice is not uniform, but is broadly consistent and follows several regularly emphasised principles. It is built around a structured approach.

It is therefore also clear that the judges at the ICC, like those before them have done, are trying to create a legitimate sentencing framework that blends traditional sentencing approaches with the unique purposes of international justice, and the spe-

---

[255]   *Ibid.* , p. 13; Clark, 2008, pp. 1686–1687, 1694–1695, 1703, 1714, 1718, see *supra* note 13.

[256]   Sergey Valisiev *et al*, "Introduction", in Goran Sluiter *et al* (eds.), *International Criminal Procedure: Principles and Rules*, Oxford University Press, Oxford, 2013, pp. 1–7.

[257]   *Ibid.*, p. 294.

[258]   Holá, 2014, p. 197, see *supra* note 14.

[259]   Ambos, 2014, p. 277, see *supra* note 6.

cificities of their particular institution. The judges are attempting to establish the Court's legitimacy and legal culture within the framework bequeathed to them by the drafters. They are using judicial discretion and individualisation, but also striving for consistency and predictability. The judgements at the ICC, as at the ad hoc tribunals, evidence significant efforts made to explain sentencing *in abstracto* and *in concreto* but they continue to fail to communicate how they settle on the tariff that is imposed. They continue to use verbiage to disguise what remains an arbitrary exercise of discretion. It may well be that without an objective starting point, such as could be provided by tariff guidelines, a transparent and well—communicated process is an impossible task. The Prosecution's attempts to introduce some science into sentencing through suggesting sentence ranges in *Lubanga* and *Al Mahdi* are in fact worthy of more serious consideration. The current approach is clearly not sufficient in making sentencing more transparent: until they can do this, the judges will continue to be seen as "plucking numbers out of the air. "

The ICC is still a penal system in evolution. It would therefore be appropriate to conclude with some further consideration on where we go from here. There are important works going beyond lamenting the perceived shortcomings. Henham has called for international sentencing "to transcend the dynamics of retributivism and deterrence, and engage more directly with victims and the concerns that produce and sustain conflict and social breakdown within victim communities. " [260] D'Ascoli proposes indicative ranges of sentences for each crime taking into account the underlying offence and mode of responsibility and proposing a number of general principles and rules. [261] Ohlin suggests that "the procedural vortex in sentencing" should be filled with "a sui generis theory of punishment...that gives appropriate weight to retributive

---

[260] Henham, 2003, p. 64, see *supra* note 14.

[261] D'Ascoli, 2011, pp. 310–322, see *supra* note 6. She does not provide any indicative ranges.

considerations" [262] and sentencing guidelines. [263] Holá has offered suggestions for the development of "a clear, transparent and consistent sentencing narrative to enable defendants to actually 'see through' sentence determination and understand the level of punishment they are subjected to" [264] as well as appropriately tailored sentencing guidelines. [265] Ambos would like to see a more structured and less discretionary approach that is based on systematisation of international caselaw and comparison of domestic cases dealing with international crimes to craft "guiding principles" or flexible "soft" sentencing guidelines. [266] deGuzman calls for greater leniency and putting forward suggestions for how the ICC judges should understand the goal of crime prevention in determining appropriate sentences and proposing a fresh theory of proportionality. [267]

These are intellectual critiques. The theories and philosophical justifications contained therein play to a narrow academic audience. As noted earlier, the judgements evidence genuine efforts by international judges to communicate judicial reasoning, and a vision or visions about the function of international justice and the role of appropriate punishment at this institution. The judgements evidence efforts to legitimise the ultimate tariff imposed on a convicted person. The reason that the judges are unable to link their reasoning about punishment with the quantum that they impose may lie in the system that has been created, not the judges. Combs has recently argued that the tribunals, including the ICC, are not separate parts of a one single international criminal justice system, but are "discrete bodies designed to take the place of domestic courts when the prosecution of international crimes is not possible

---

[262] Ohlin, 2009, see *supra* note 16.

[263] *Ibid.*, p. 382. He also calls for return the sentencing phase in international trials and an international sentencing commission

[264] Holá, 2012, p. 23, see *supra* note 23.

[265] Holá, 2014, pp. 203–206, see *supra* note 14.

[266] Ambos, 2014, pp. 302–307, see *supra* note 7 footnote references omitted; for his five step approach, inspired by the German tradition, to establishing correct sentencing, see p. 307.

[267] deGuzman, 2014, see *supra* note 5.

in those courts. "[268] She further argues that different tribunals may have different goals, and the adoption of sentencing standards calibrated to the purposes of the particular tribunal are likely unattainable. A better approach, she suggests, is to individualize the principles and purposes of sentencing to reflect local community standards.

The way that sentencing is treated as a rather mechanical process at the ICC suggests that this may well be a court where formal guidelines could gain traction and could work. In any event, judgements are not PhD theses, although many of those that have emerged at the international level certainly have pretensions in that regard. Some observers seem to require that international judges inject an unreasonably elevated level of intellectual rigour into the business of sentencing. Sentencing should in fact take us back to Damaška's primordial question: what is the *point* of international criminal justice?[269] The truth is surely that outside of academia, for the victims and ordinary people affected by the situations at issue who are never going to read let alone digest sentencing judgements, they seek justice, not intellectual abstractions. Most people, whether in Rwanda, Sierra Leone and the Balkans or elsewhere in the world, will be profoundly disinterested in theoretical frameworks and the intellectual demands of judgements that are being made by academics in the search for better sentencing practice. They want to know in lay terms why that particular sentence was imposed. And, it is usually in terms of understanding why a "light" sentence was imposed despite the egregious conduct involved.

The challenge for international courts and tribunals, particularly the ICC as the global court of the now and future, provide justice for a range of constituents, across a range of objectives and through a fair and transparent process. In that, we have to remember that justice and humanity go hand in hand. We should treasure the fact that

---

[268]   Nancy Combs, "Seeking Inconsistency: Advancing Pluralism in International Criminal Sentencing", in *Yale Journal of International Law*, 2016, Vol. 41, p. 1, at p. 24.

[269]   Damaška, 2008, see *supra* note 42.

the process of justice is not one involving or for automatons, and it should not become a mechanical process. Ewald has astutely described the process of sentencing as a "complex psychological process." [270] We do need to facilitate greater consistency and transparency in sentence determination, and in addition to sentencing guidelines at the ICC, one way could be by defining more clearly the parameters around discretion. The rationale for the quantum reached can certainly be better communicated, and there is truth in Ohlin's assertion that "legality is strengthened when objective doctrines, with particular elements, are used to make these determinations regarding relative culpability. The results are likely to be more governed by reasons and less governed by ad hockery." [271] On the other hand, the humanity of the search of justice and the humanity of the result are lost if reduced to a mechanised process of pure logic and theoretical perfection, mathematical equation and utter consistency. In the words of the UK's Justice Cooke, "the exercise of discretion in sentencing must remain in human hands. You cannot program a computer to register the 'feel' of a case, or the impact that a defendant makes upon the sentence." [272]

---

[270] Uwe Ewald, "'Predictably Irrational' —International Sentencing and its Discourse against the Backdrop of Preliminary Empirical Findings on ICTY Sentencing Practices", in *International Human Rights Law Review*, 2010, Vol. 10, p. 389.

[271] Jens Ohlin, "LIJL Symposium: Names, Labels, and Roses", available at http://opiniojuris.org/2012/03/23/ljil-names-labels-and-roses/, last accessed at 1 April 2017.

[272] Cited in Andrew Ashworth, *Sentencing and Criminal Justice*, 4th edn, Oxford University Press, Oxford, 2005, p. 48. For a different perspective, see Streng on the judicial role in German sentencing, and why some discretion is appropriate even in that system: "the judge himself acts as a citizen when determining the punishment, who reflects society's values when assessing the appropriate punishment, whilst keeping within the statutory boundaries. In contrast to a technocratic or an authoritarian criminal law system the judge in our law system relies on values which are coined by his social and professional personality. Under this perception of his role the German judge thus demands for a wide sentencing range, from which he is free to choose a just and fair sanction in accordance to his persuasion": Franz Streng, "Sentencing in Germany—Basic Questions and New Developments", in *German Law Journal*, 2007, Vol. 8, no. 2, p. 154.

FROM THE LEGACY OF THE INTERNATIONAL CRIMINAL TRIBUNAL FOR RWANDA TO THE NEW MODEL OF DISPENSING INTERNATIONAL CRIMINAL JUSTICE: THE INTERNATIONAL RESIDUAL MECHANISM FOR CRIMINAL TRIBUNALS

Roman Boed [*]

1. Introduction

In the context of the conference on the peaceful settlement of international disputes and the functions of international judicial organs, this paper addresses the establishment and impact of the United Nations International Criminal Tribunal for Rwanda ("ICTR", "Rwanda Tribunal", or "Tribunal") and the establishment of the United Nations International Residual Mechanism for Criminal Tribunals ("MICT" or "Mechanism") to carry on the legacy of the tribunals established by the United Nations ("UN") for Rwanda and for the former Yugoslavia ("ICTY" or "Yugoslavia Tribunal"). It has often been said that without justice there can be no lasting peace and it is for this reason, that a discussion of judicial organs is part of a discussion about the peaceful settlement of disputes.

Our shared human history shows that peaceful resolution of disputes has not been the norm of coexistence. It is only since the relatively recent past that the international community has turned to judicial organs to address the failure to settle disputes peacefully. In the 1990s, when the world was confronted with the large–scale atrocities committed during the conflicts in the former Yugoslavia and in Rwanda, the

---

* Legal Officer, United Nations Luternational Criminal Tribunal for Rwanda.

United Nations established two criminal tribunals to apprehend and prosecute the principal alleged perpetrators.

Over two decades later, the establishment of judicial organs to address alleged international crimes does not seem exceptional. During that span of time, the international community has supported the establishment of judicial processes to address grave crimes in Sierra Leone, Cambodia, and Lebanon, for example, as well as of the International Criminal Court, a permanent court with a broad international criminal jurisdiction. But when the ICTR and the ICTY were established in the mid — 1990s, there was very little precedent for adjudicating grave crimes on an international plane. While at the close of the Second World War the Allied Powers established the International Military Tribunal at Nuremberg, planting the seed of international criminal justice as we know it today, the Cold War that followed prevented the polarized international community from responding to mass atrocities collectively. It has been observed that, "[j] ustice was the Cold War's casualty. "[1]

It was the work of the tribunals for the former Yugoslavia and Rwanda that gave a new start to international criminal justice and to the profound development of international criminal law which, in the mid-1990s, was only a nascent discipline. Moreover, the collective experience of the operation of the two Tribunals has led the United Nations to integrate the lessons learned in the design of a new model of administering international criminal justice. This model was embodied in the recent establishment of the Mechanism. This paper provides an overview of the legacy of the Rwanda Tribunal and the innovations introduced to the administration of international criminal justice by the Mechanism, addressing each entity in turn.

2. United Nations International Criminal Tribunal for Rwanda

The Rwanda Tribunal was an international criminal court with a limited jurisdiction. It was established to contribute to securing justice for the victims of the 1994

---

[1] M. Cherif Bassiouni, "From Versailles to Rwanda in Seventy-Five Years: The Need to Establish a Permanent International Court", in *Harvard Human Rights Journal*, 1997, Vol. 10, p. 39 ("Bassiouni").

genocide against the Tutsi in Rwanda, during which Hutu and others who opposed the genocide were also killed. The Tribunal concluded its work after two decades, at the end of 2015. This section provides a brief overview of the tragic events that devastated Rwanda and led to the establishment of the Tribunal and highlights some of the Tribunal's contributions to the development of international criminal justice. [2]

Prior to the independence of Rwanda from Belgium in 1962, members of the minority Tutsi ethnic group dominated the country's political and economic life. [3] During Rwanda's transition to independence, members of the majority Hutu ethnic group assumed political positions and started persecution campaigns against the Tutsis. [4] Consequently, large numbers of Tutsis fled from Rwanda to neighbouring countries from where they periodically launched attacks directed at their homeland, seeking return to power. [5] In response to these attacks, Hutus carried out reprisals against the Tutsis who had remained in Rwanda. [6] For example, in 1963 some 10, 000 Tutsis in Rwanda were killed in response to a military attack by Tutsis exiled in Burundi. [7] These circumstances forced new waves of refugees to flee Rwanda for the safety of neighboring countries.

----

[2] For an overview of the Tribunal's impact in a range of areas of administering international justice, such as management of cases, disclosure, and defence systems, as well as substantive and procedural legal issues, see "A Compendium on the Legacy of the ICTR and the Development of International Law", available at http: //unictr. unmict. org/en/compendium-legacy-ictr-and-development-international-law accessed at 1 August 2017. For a multi - dimensional examination of the Tribunal's legacy, see Sara Kendall and Sarah M. H. Nouwen, "Speaking of Legacy: Toward an Ethos of Modesty at the International Criminal Tribunal for Rwanda", in *American Journal of International Law*, 2016, Vol. 110, p. 212.

[3] See, e. g. , Kingsley Moghalu, *Rwanda's Genocide: The Politics of Global Justice*, Palgrave Macmillan US, New York, 2005, ("Moghalu"), pp. 9–13; Virginia Morris and Michael P. Scharf, *The International Criminal Tribunal for Rwanda*, Transnational Publishers, Ardsley: New York, 1998, vol. 1, pp. 48, 49.

[4] Gerard Prunier, *The Rwanda Crisis*, Columbia University Press, New York, 1995 ("Prunier"), p. 51.

[5] Paul J. Magnarella, *Justice in Africa: Rwanda's Genocide, its Courts, and the UN Criminal Tribunal*, Ashgate, Farnham, 2000, ("Magnarella"), p. 13; Moghalu, see *supra* note 4; p. 13,; Morris and Scharf, see *supra* note 4, p. 50; Prunier, see *supra* note 5, p. 51.

[6] Magnarella, p. 56, *ibid.*

[7] Prunier, see *supra* note 4, p. 56.

The Rwandan Tutsi refugees in Uganda formed the Rwandan Patriotic Front ("RPF"), an organization dedicated to the Tutsis' return home. [8] Between 1990 and 1992, the RPF conducted several attacks against the territory of Rwanda in unsuccessful attempts to seize power. [9] This led to further repression of the Tutsis living in Rwanda who were labelled accomplices of the RPF. [10]

The RPF attacks along with an economic crisis in Rwanda forced the Government of President Habyarimana to meet with the representatives of the RPF to negotiate a cease—fire, return of refugees, power—sharing, and integration of the armed forces. [11] The final of these agreements, known as Arusha Accords after the Tanzanian city where the negotiations were held, was signed in August 1993. [12] Fearing that the implementation of these accords would deprive them of exclusive political power, radical Hutus opposed the Arusha Accords and accused President Habyarimana of being an RPF accomplice. [13]

On 6 April 1994, a plane carrying President Habyarimana, as well as other officials, including the President of Burundi, was shot down on its approach to Kigali. [14] Almost instantly, Hutu soldiers and militias, aided by civilians, started to hunt down and kill Tutsi civilians, moderate politicians, and members of the democratic opposition in the country. [15] The following day, Rwandan government soldiers killed the Rwandan Prime Minister at her home along with ten Belgian soldiers who were assigned to protect her as part of the UN Peacekeeping contingent. [16]

---

[8] Magnarella, see *supra* note 5, p. 15.

[9] *Ibid.*

[10] Alain Destexhe, *Rwanda and Genocide in the Twentieth Century*, Pluto Press, London, 1995, ("Destexhe"), p. 28; Magnarella, see *supra* note 6, p. 15.

[11] Magnarella, see *supra* note 6, p. 17.

[12] *Ibid.*

[13] *Ibid.*

[14] See, e. g., Destexhe, see *supra* note 10, p. 31.

[15] See, e. g., *ibid.*; Magnarella, see *supra* note 5, p. 19; Moghalu, see *supra* note 3, p. 16; Morris and Scharf, see *supra* note 3, p. 53; Prunier, see *supra* note 4, p. 229.

[16] Moghalu, see *supra* note 3, pp. 16, 17.

The violence spread throughout the land with devastating speed: the first six weeks of the massacres claimed 80% of the victims. [17] This rate of killing was an estimated five times that of the Nazi death camps in World War II. [18] The genocidal killings finally ended on 18 July 1994, when the Hutu Government fled from Rwanda to neighboring Congo/Zaire and the RPF established a new government in Kigali. [19] Over 800,000 lives were lost during the genocide which lasted just over three months, making it, it has been argued, the fastest genocide in history. [20] In addition to the killings, it is estimated that over 100,000 women were raped. [21] Most of the victims of these atrocities belonged to the Tutsi ethnic group and included large numbers of civilians, women, children, and the elderly. [22] Of the approximately 930,000 Tutsis living in Rwanda at the beginning of the genocide, only about 130,000 survived. [23]

One week into the genocide, the RPF Representative at the United Nations wrote to the President of the UN Security Council, stating that genocide had been committed against the Rwandan people and requesting that the Security Council immediately set up a tribunal to prosecute those responsible for the massacres. [24] A report of a Special Rapporteur of the UN Commission on Human Rights similarly recommended that those responsible for the massacres in Rwanda be brought before an

---

[17]　Prunier, see *supra* note 4, p. 261.

[18]　*Ibid.*

[19]　Morris and Scharf, see *supra* note 3, p. 58

[20]　See Moghalu, see *supra* note 3, p. 17. Philip Gourevitch estimated that the genocide claimed 333 lives an hour, five and a half lives a minute: Philip Gourevitch, *We Wish to Inform You that Tomorrow We Will Be Killed with Our Families: Stories from Rwanda*, Pan Macmillan, Basingstoke, 1998, p. 133.

[21]　United Nations, "Background Information on Sexual Violence Used as a Tool of War", available at http://www.un.org/en/preventgenocide/rwanda/about/bgsexualviolence.shtml, accessed at 9 June 2017.

[22]　Prunier, see *supra* note 4, p. 248.

[23]　*Ibid.*, pp. 264, 265.

[24]　*Letter Dated 15 December 1999 from the Members of the Independent Inquiry into the Actions of the United Nations during the 1994 Genocide in Rwanda Addressed to the Secretary General*, UN Doc. S/1999/1257, Annex I, p. 68. It has been observed that this was the first time that the issue of possible prosecutions for the events was raised before the Security Council. See Moghalu, see *supra* note 4, p. 20.

international court. [25] Then, toward the end of the genocidal carnage, the Security Council requested the UN Secretary General to establish a commission of experts to determine whether serious breaches of humanitarian law, including genocide, had been committed in Rwanda. [26]

In October 1994, the Commission of Experts reported to the Security Council that genocide, crimes against humanity, and serious breaches of international humanitarian law had been committed. [27] The Commission of Experts strongly recommended that the Security Council ensure that the individuals responsible for these crimes be brought to justice before an independent and impartial international criminal tribunal. [28] Against this background, on 8 November 1994, the Security Council adopted Resolution 955 under Chapter VII of the UN Charter, establishing the Tribunal. [29]

---

[25] *Ibid.*, p. 73.

[26] SC Res. 935, UN Doc. S/RES/935 (1994) (http: //www. legal - tools. org/doc/1594bd/). On the work of the Commission of Experts see generally Bassiouni, see *supra* note 2, p. 46.

[27] *Preliminary Report of the Independent Commission of Experts Established in Accordance with Security Council Resolution* 935 (1994), UN Doc. S/1994/1125, paras. 146–148.

[28] *Ibid.* , para. 150 ("The Commission of Experts strongly recommends that the Security Council take all necessary and effective action to ensure that the individuals responsible for the serious violations of human rights in Rwanda during the armed conflict triggered on 6 April 1994 are brought to justice before an independent and impartial international criminal tribunal. ").

[29] SC Res. 955, UN Doc. S/RES/955 (1994) (http: //www. legal - tools. org/doc/f5ef47/). The resolution passed with 13 votes for, one abstention (China), and one vote against (Rwanda). Though the new Government of Rwanda requested the Secretary General to establish an international tribunal to prosecute those responsible for the events in Rwanda in 1994 (see UN Doc. S/1994/1115), Rwanda ultimately voted against the adoption of Resolution 955. Rwanda objected to the fact that the Tribunal's Statute did not provide for the death penalty and that the temporal jurisdiction of the Tribunal was limited to 1994. See UN Doc. S/PV. 3453, pp. 14–16 (record of the Rwandan Representative's statement following the adoption of Resolution 955 at the 3453rd meeting of the Security Council). For an analysis of the Rwandan vote against Resolution 955, see Payam Akhvan, "The International Criminal Tribunal for Rwanda: The Politics and Pragmatics of Punishment", in *American Journal of International Law*, 1996, Vol. 90, pp. 505–508. See also Victor Peskin, *International Justice in Rwanda and the Balkans: Virtual Trials and Struggle for State Cooperation*, Cambridge University Press, Cambridge, 2008, pp. 153–169; Steven R. Ratner and Jason S. Abrams, *Accountability for Human Rights Atrocities in International Law: Beyond the Nuremberg Legacy*, Oxford University Press, Oxford, 1997, p. 174. Subsequently, Rwanda abolished the death penalty.

The Security Council gave the Tribunal the power to prosecute serious violations of international humanitarian law committed in Rwanda during the calendar year 1994. [30] The serious violations of international humanitarian law included in the jurisdiction of the Tribunal are genocide, that is any of certain acts, such as killing or causing serious harm, committed with the intent to destroy, even in part, a national, ethnic, racial, or religious group; crimes against humanity, that is any of certain violent acts, such as murder, torture, or rape, for example, when committed as part of a widespread or systematic attack against a civilian population; and serious violations of the 1949 Geneva Conventions that aim to protect non—combatants in internal armed conflicts. [31]

The UN General Assembly elected the first group of six judges for a term of four years, from May 1995. [32] Then followed the important work for the judges to draft and adopt the Tribunal's Rules of Procedure and Evidence that would govern the Tribunal's functioning. [33] The Tribunal confirmed the first indictment at the end of November 1995, the first accused arrived in Arusha the following May, and the first trial started in January 1997.

In the twenty years of its existence, the Tribunal indicted 93 individuals, and, by the time of its closure at the end of 2015, concluded cases in respect of all but

---

[30]   Statute of the International Criminal Tribunal for Rwanda, SC Res. 955, annex, art. 1, UN Doc. S/RES/955 (1994) ("ICTR Statute") (http: //www. legal—tools. org/doc/8732d6/).

[31]   Article 3 common to the 1949 Geneva Conventions for the Protection of War Victims (Common Article 3), and of the 1977 Additional Protocol II thereto (Additional Protocol II) (such acts, for example, may be murder, torture, collective punishments, taking of hostages, and the like, when committed in an internal armed conflict against non—combatants). See ICTR Statute, see *supra* note 31, arts. 2–4.

[32]   *Report of the International Criminal Tribunal for the Prosecution of Persons Responsible for Genocide and Other Serious Violations of International Humanitarian Law Committed in the Territory of Rwanda and Rwandan Citizens Responsible for Genocide and Other Such Violations Committed in the Territory of Neighbouring States between 1 January and 31 December 1994*, UN Doc. A/51/399 – S/A996/778 (1996), para. 7 (http: //www. legal—tools. org/doc/36162a/).

[33]   *Ibid.*, para. 27. The Rules of Procedure and Evidence of the Tribunal ("Rules") were adopted on 29 June 1995 and were amended on twenty—three occasions, most recently on 13 May 2015. The Rules are available at http: //unictr. unmict. org/en/documents/rules—procedure—and—evidence, accessed at 13 June 2017.

nine of the indictees who then remained at large. [34] The ICTR prosecutor transferred the cases of the remaining fugitives to Rwanda and to the successor of the Tribunal, the UN International Residual Mechanism for Criminal Tribunals. [35] Subsequently, one of the fugitives was apprehended by the Mechanism and was transferred to Rwanda for trial. [36] The remaining eight fugitives, if they are still alive and are apprehended, will also not escape justice. Rwanda and the Mechanism stand ready to hear their cases when they are apprehended. [37]

During its existence, the Tribunal had before it cases concerning the political, military, business, media, religious, and community leadership of the country. [38] For example, it adjudicated cases of the former Prime Minister of Rwanda and eleven former Ministers as well as the Chairman of the ruling political party. The Tribunal also brought thirteen former military leaders to face justice, including the former Chiefs of Staff of the Army and the Gendarmerie. [39]

The Tribunal's progress through its caseload and the satisfactory completion of its mandate would not have been possible without the cooperation of states. As with all other international courts which lack their own enforcement capacity, the ICTR relied on state cooperation in a wide range of its activities, from investigation of crimes through the enforcement of sentences. Most notably, state cooperation was a

---

[34] See generally *Report on the Completion of the Mandate of the International Criminal Tribunal for Rwanda as at 15 November* 2015, UN Doc. S/2015/884 (2015) ("*ICTR Final Report*"), at http://unictr. unmict. org/en/documents/completion−strategy−reports, accessed at 13 June 2017.

[35] See *ICTR Final Report*, see *supra* note 35, paras. 61, 166, Annex III. See also *Report on the Completion Strategy of the International Criminal Tribunal for Rwanda as at 5 May* 2015, UN Doc. S/2015/340 (2015), para. 13, available at http://unictr. unmict. org/en/documents/completion−strategy−reports, accessed at 13 June 2017.

[36] See http://www. unmict. org/en/news/drc − transfers − ladislas − ntaganzwa − rwanda accessed at 1 August 2017.

[37] See generally *Assessment and Progress Report of the President of the International Residual Mechanism for Criminal Tribunals, Judge Theodor Meron, for the Period from 16 May to 15 November 2016*, paras. 54−57, available at http://www. unmict. org/en/basic−documents/reports, accessed at 13 June 2017.

[38] *ICTR Final Report*, see *supra* note 35, para. 50.

[39] *Ibid.*, Annex I.

crucial component in the apprehension of suspects in Africa, Europe, and North A-
merica and the appearance of the approximately 3,500 witnesses who testified before
the Rwanda Tribunal. [40] State cooperation has been also crucial to the enforcement
of the Tribunal's sentences, as the Tribunal was an *ad hoc* institution that was not
vested with the power to enforce its sentences. [41]

Over the two decades of its functioning, the Tribunal made significant contributions to international criminal justice. While a comprehensive study is beyond the
scope of this paper, a few examples will illustrate the impact of the Tribunal's work
on the development of international criminal law.

Perhaps most significantly, the Tribunal played a foundational role in interpreting and applying the definition of the crime of genocide set out in the Genocide Convention and in confirming that genocide is an international crime for which individual
perpetrators may be held liable. [42] Although genocide has been acknowledged to be
a crime since 1948, prior to the work of the ICTR and the tribunal for the former Yugoslavia, there have been few prosecutions for genocide, none of which was carried
out at an international level. [43]

The Tribunal tackled genocide starting with its first case, *Prosecutor v. Akayesu*,

---

[40] *Ibid.*, para. 54 (noting that with the assistance of national authorities the Tribunal secured the arrest
fugitives from 27 jurisdictions in Africa, Europe, and North America).

[41] In this respect, art. 26 of the Tribunal's Statute provided for enforcement of sentences: "Imprisonment shall be served in Rwanda or any of the States on a list of States which have indicated to the Security Council their willingness to accept convicted persons, as designated by the International Tribunal for Rwanda. Such imprisonment shall be in accordance with the applicable law of the State concerned, subject to the supervision of the
International Tribunal for Rwanda. " The Tribunal had bilateral agreements on the enforcement of sentences with
the following States: Mali, Benin, Swaziland, France, Italy, Sweden, Rwanda, and Senegal. See http: //
unictr. unmict. org/en/documents/bilateral–agreements accessed at 1 August 2017. With the closure of the Tribunal, the supervision of the enforcement of its sentences transferred to the Mechanism. See Statute of the International Residual Mechanism for Criminal Tribunals, SC Res. 1966, Annex, UN Doc. S/RES/1966 (2010)
["MICT Statute"], art. 25 (2) (http: //www. legal–tools. org/doc/e79460/).

[42] William Schabas, "Commentary", in André Klip and Göran Sluiter (eds.), *Annotated Leading Cases of International Criminal Tribunals: The International Criminal Tribunal for Rwanda* 1994–1999, Intersentia,
Amsterdam, 2001, p. 539.

[43] Antonio Cassese, *International Criminal Law*, Oxford University Press, Oxford, 2003, pp. 97, 98.

in which it entered the first ever conviction by an international tribunal for the crime of genocide. [44] Significantly, in that landmark judgement, the Tribunal recognized that rape and sexual violence constitute genocidal acts when committed with the specific intent to destroy a protected group, defining for the first time elements of rape under international law. [45] And with significant impact on the cases that followed and also on the future understanding of the events, the Tribunal held that genocide against Tutsis had occurred in Rwanda in 1994. [46]

Subsequently, the former Prime Minister of Rwanda, Jean Kambanda, pleaded guilty before the Tribunal to genocide counts, acknowledging that genocide had occurred in Rwanda in 1994 and that it was planned at the highest civilian and military levels. [47] This acknowledgement stands against historical revisionism on this issue, as do numerous findings by the Tribunal's Chambers. In one concise yet forceful statement, the Appeals Chamber of the Tribunal wrote that "[t]he fact of the Rwandan genocide is a part of world history, a fact as certain as any other [...]". [48]

---

[44] ICTR, *Prosecutor v. Akayesu*, Judgement, Trial Chamber, ICTR-96-4-T, 2 September 1998 (http://www. legal-tools. org/doc/b8d7bd/). See *Report of the International Criminal Tribunal for the Prosecution of Persons Responsible for Genocide and Other Serious Violations of International Humanitarian Law Committed in the Territory of Rwanda and Rwandan Citizens Responsible for Genocide and Other Such Violations Committed in the Territory of Neighbouring States between 1 January and 31 December 1994*, UN Doc. A/53/429-S/1998/857 (1998), para. 2 (http://www. legal-tools. org/doc/015bf7/).

[45] *Prosecutor v. Akayesu*, see *supra* note 45, paras. 731, 733. See *ICTR Final Report*, see *supra* note 35, para. 57. Significantly, *Akayesu* defined rape as "a physical invasion of a sexual nature under circumstances which are coercive. " *Prosecutor v. Akayesu*, see *supra* note 45, para. 598. This definition dispensed with lack of consent as an element of the crime of rape in circumstances which are coercive, and has been described as a significant breakthrough. See Catharine MacKinnon, "The Recognition of Rape as an Act of Genocide—*Prosecutor v. Akayesu*", in *New England Journal of International and Comparative Law*, 2008, vol. 14, p. 102. The Elements of Crimes stipulated for the crimes defined in the Statute of the International Criminal Court adopted subsequently similarly dispense with lack of consent as an element of sexual violence crimes. See, e. g. , ICC Elements of Crimes, arts. 7 (1)(g)-1, 8 (2)(b)(xxii)-1.

[46] *Prosecutor v. Akayesu*, see *supra* note 45, para. 729.

[47] ICTR, *Prosecutor v. Jean Kambanda*, Case No. ICTR-97-23-S, Judgement and Sentence, Trial Chamber, 4 September 1998 (http://www. legal-tools. org/doc/49a299/).

[48] ICTR, *Prosecutor v. Eduard Karemera et al.* , Decision on Interlocutory Appeal of Decision on Judicial Notice, Appeals Chamber, 16 June 2006, ICTR-98-44-AR73 (C), para. 35 (http://www. legal-tools. org/doc/67d818/).

The *Kambanda* case was also significant for invoking a provision of the Statute of the Tribunal stipulating that: "The official position of any accused person, whether as Head of State or Government or as a responsible government official, shall not relieve such person of criminal responsibility nor mitigate punishment. "[49] The application by the Tribunal of this provision is noteworthy because it runs counter to the traditional recognition of sovereign immunity. Similar provisions are contained in the statutes of other bodies charged with prosecuting international crimes,[50] and the subsequent prosecutions of Slobodan Milošević, the former President of Serbia and the Republic of Yugoslavia, and Charles Taylor, the former President of Liberia, show the pursuit of government leaders for their alleged international crimes. The Tribunal's *Kambanda* case led the way in demonstrating that official position is not a bar to prosecution under international criminal law.

Another key jurisprudential advance was the recognition of criminal responsibility for war crimes committed in internal armed conflicts. Before the establishment of the ICTR and the ICTY, the provisions of the Geneva Conventions that were designed specifically to protect non—combatant victims of internal armed conflicts, Common Article 3 of the 1949 Geneva Conventions and Additional Protocol II thereto, have rarely been enforced in any way, and there had been little precedent for interpreting

---

[49] ICTR Statute, see *supra* note 31, art. 6 (2).

[50] See, e. g. , Statute of the International Criminal Tribunal for the former Yugoslavia, art. 7 (2) (http: //www. legal—tools. org/doc/b4f63b/); Statute of the International Criminal Court, art. 27 (http: // www. legal—tools. org/doc/7b9af9/); Statute of the Special Court for Sierra Leone, art. 6 (2) (http: // www. legal—tools. org/doc/aa0e20/). Referring in part to the precedent from the ICTR, the Preparatory Committee on the Establishment of an International Criminal Court observed that "there was support for the Statute to disallow any plea of official position as Head of State or Government or as a responsible government official; such official position should not relieve an accused of criminal responsibility. " *Report of the Preparatory Committee on the Establishment of an International Criminal Court*, U. N. GAOR, 51st Sess. , Supp. No. 22, U. N. Doc. A/51/ 22 (1996), para. 193 (https: //www. legal—tools. org/doc/e75432/).

and applying them in concrete cases. [51] This is perhaps not surprising, because un-like the provisions applicable to international armed conflicts, Common Article 3 and Additional Protocol II do not prescribe criminal responsibility for breaches of their provisions. [52]

The ICTR Statute was the first international instrument to criminalize serious vi-olations of Common Article 3 and Additional Protocol II and its application by the Tribunal therefore represented a paradigm shift for dealing with serious abuses of vic-

---

[51]　See Roman Boed, "Individual Criminal Responsibility for Violations of Article 3 Common to the Ge-neva Conventions of 1949 and of Additional Protocol II Thereto in the Case Law of the International Criminal Tri-bunal for Rwanda", in *Criminal Law Forum*, 2003, vol. 13, p. 293. See also Theodor Meron, *War Crimes Law Comes of Age*, Oxford University Press, Oxford, 1998, p. 235; Daniel Smith, "New Protections for Victims of International Armed Conflicts: The Proposed Ratification of Protocol II by the United States", in *Military Law Review*, 1988, Vol. 120, p. 65.

[52]　The grave breaches regime set out in the 1949 Geneva Conventions and Additional Protocol I thereto, applicable to international armed conflicts, prescribes effective penal measures, that is criminalization of the of-fences, prosecution or extradition, and punishment. See 1977 Protocol Additional to the Geneva Conventions of 12 August 1949, and Relating to the Protection of Victims of International Armed Conflicts (Protocol I), 1125 UNTS 3, arts. 85–87. See also 1949 Convention for the Amelioration of the Condition of the Wounded and Sick in Armed Forces in the Field (Geneva Convention No. I), 75 UNTS 31, arts. 49, 50; 1949 Convention for the A-melioration of the Condition of Wounded, Sick, and Shipwrecked Members of Armed Forces at Sea (Geneva Con-vention No. II), 75 UNTS 85, arts. 50, 51; 1949 Convention Relative to the Treatment of Prisoners of War (Ge-neva Convention No. III), 75 UNTS 135, arts. 129, 130; 1949 Convention Relative to the Treatment of Civilian Persons in Time of War (Geneva Convention No. IV), 75 UNTS 287, arts. 146, 147. On the grave breaches re-gime, see generally Rudiger Wolfrum, "Enforcement of International Humanitarian Law", in Dieter Fleck (ed.), *The Handbook of Humanitarian Law in Armed Conflicts*, Oxford University Press, Oxford, 1995, pp. 530, 531.

tims of internal armed conflicts. [53] It has been observed, for example, that the fact that the ICTR Statute already contained international norms relating to internal armed conflicts helped overcome reservations of some delegations drafting the statute of the International Criminal Court to include war crimes committed in such conflicts. [54] Numerous states have subsequently adopted legislation criminalizing war crimes committed in internal armed conflicts, providing a path to prosecutions before national

---

[53] In commenting on the Statute, the UN Secretary General reported that the UN Security Council included in the jurisdiction of the Tribunal international instruments regardless of whether they were considered part of customary international law or whether they have customarily entailed the individual criminal responsibility of the perpetrator of the crime. Article 4 of the statute, accordingly, includes violations of Additional Protocol II [...] and for the first time criminalizes common article 3. *Report of the Secretary−General pursuant to Paragraph 5 of the Security Council Resolution* 955 (1994), UN Doc. S/1995/134, para. 12 (http: //www. legal − tools. org/doc/b38d4d/). See also *The Manual of the Law of Armed Conflict*: *UK Ministry of Defence*, Oxford University Press, Oxford, 2004, p. 431 ("This was the first time that the international community had made express provision for individual criminal responsibility for breaches of international law in internal armed conflicts. ").

While the ICTY Statute contains no provisions expressly relating to internal armed conflicts, the ICTY Appeals Chamber held that customary international law imposes criminal liability for serious violations of Common Article 3. See ICTY, *Prosecutor v. Tadić*, Decision on the Defence Motion for Interlocutory Appeal on Jurisdiction, Appeals Chamber, IT−94−1−AR72, 2 October 1995, paras. 134, 135 (http: //www. legal−tools. org/doc/866e17/). See also Laura Perna, *The Formation of the Treaty Law of Non−International Armed Conflicts*, Martinus Nijhoff Publishers, Leiden, 2006, pp. 150, 151 (analyzing this decision).

[54] See Knut Dörmann, "War Crimes under the Rome Statute of the International Criminal Court, with a Special Focus on the Negotiations on the Elements of Crimes" , in *Max Planck Yearbook of UN Law*, Martinus Nijhoff Publishers, Leiden, 2003, vol. 7, p. 341 ("it must be emphasised that the major accomplishment of the Rome Conference with regard to war crimes certainly resides in the inclusion of war crimes committed during non−international armed conflicts. Hesitations by some delegations were overcome due to the fact that the Statute of the International Criminal tribunal for Rwanda included war crimes committed in non−international armed conflict and the ICTY had recognized in its case law the customary nature of individual responsibility for serious violations of international law in such armed conflicts. " *Ibid.*, p. 348 (citation omitted)) ; Darryl Robinson and Herman von Hebel, "War Crimes in Internal Conflicts: Article 8 of the ICC Statute" , in *Yearbook of International Humanitarian Law*, T. M. C. Asser Press, The Hague, 1999, Vol. 2, p. 193.

courts for such crimes. [55]

The judicial work of the Tribunal thus has been significant for the evolution of international criminal justice. The Tribunal has fostered the development of substantive international criminal law and has honed the procedure through which international criminal justice is administered. The experience of the Tribunals for Rwanda and the former Yugoslavia has informed the establishment and functioning of the International Criminal Court as well as other bodies charged with prosecuting international crimes. [56]

While this has been valuable for the progressive development of the international legal order, it was not the reason why the Tribunal was established. As described above, the establishment of the Tribunal was a response to a grave crisis: the Rwandan genocide. The Security Council set up the Tribunal to bring to justice the perpetrators with the conviction that their prosecution would contribute to the national reconciliation and to the restoration and maintenance of peace. [57] And it is in terms of this objective that its overall performance should be assessed.

The Tribunal has been successful in apprehending most of the key suspects and through its work it has exposed those most responsible for the genocide as criminals. Through this process, the extremist ideology that fuelled the genocide has been internationally discredited along with its most dangerous adherents. One Rwandan

---

[55] Jean—Marie Henckaerts and Louise Doswald—Beck, *Customary International Humanitarian Law: Rules*, Cambridge University Press, Cambridge, 2005, p. 553. A study on universal jurisdiction over war crimes conducted at the War Crimes Research Office of the Washington College of Law at American University found that, as of 2013, 58 countries expressly criminalized war crimes committed in non—international armed conflicts. See "Universal Jurisdiction over War Crimes: Overview", available at https: //www. wcl. american. edu/ warcrimes/documents/2013—05—16UJChart. pdf. See also https: //www. wcl. american. edu/warcrimes/2013—05—17UJChart1. xlsx (listing countries and stating the source of relevant legislation). Both accessed at 1 August 2017.

[56] See, e. g. , Adriaan Bos, "The Experience of the Preparatory Committee", in Mauro Politi and Giusepe Nesi (eds.), *The Rome Statute of the International Criminal Court*, Ashgate, Farnham, 2001, pp. 17, 23, 25.

[57] SC Res. 955, UN Doc. S/RES/955 (1994).

commentator observed the following:

By arresting the architects of the genocide, the ICTR deprived the perpetrators of their main leaders. The overarching feeling among survivors is that without such arrests, the former political and military leaders involved in the genocide would have continued to destabilize Rwanda, eliminate witnesses and aggravate the moral suffering of survivors. [58]

Domestic prosecutions could have had a similar effect, but the reality is that many of the leading suspects were hiding in countries that would not extradite them to stand trial in Rwanda where they, until a subsequent change in the law prompted by the ICTR, could have faced the death penalty. [59] Given this, and in the absence of the ICTR, the alternatives would have been domestic prosecutions in the countries where the alleged perpetrators were found or impunity. Generally, with a few exceptions, Rwandans suspected of involvement in the genocide have not been brought to justice in the countries where they settled. This suggests that the likely outcome would have been impunity for those suspected of the greatest involvement in the genocide—the leaders who fled the country—and this would have been a critical obstacle to national reconciliation.

It is in this way that the Tribunal contributed to the national reconciliation and to the restoration and maintenance of peace, as it was charged to do. But it is understood that, as has been noted, reconciliation "cannot come into being with the stroke of a pen. " [60] The Tribunal was limited in the exercise of its duties by its mandate,

---

[58]　Francois-Xavier Nsanzuwera, "The ICTR Contribution to National Reconciliation", in *Journal of International Criminal Justice*, 2005, Vol. 3, p. 948.

[59]　Indeed this was a factor contributing to the Security Council's establishment of the Tribunal. See Michael P. Scharf, "Responding to Rwanda: Accountability Mechanisms in the Aftermath of the Genocide", in *Columbia Journal of International Affairs*, 1999, Vol. 52, p. 628. The accused were transferred to the Tribunal from twenty-four countries. None of them was apprehended in Rwanda.

[60]　Leila Nadya Sadat, "The Contribution of the ICTR to the Rule of Law", in Charles Chernor Jalloh and Alhagi B. M. Marong (eds.), *Promoting Accountability Under International Law for Gross Human Rights Violations in Africa*, Brill, Leiden, 2015 ("Sadat"), p. 128.

and that mandate was for the exercise of judicial functions. Even the most successful completion of such functions can ever be just one of the many steps that a community must take to reach an understanding of what happened, to reconcile, and to move forward. Conscious of this, and limited by its mandate, the Tribunal nevertheless carried out capacity—building and outreach programs aimed at helping Rwanda reconcile and maintain peace in the difficult period after the genocide, alongside its judicial function. [61] For example, the Tribunal set up and operated an information center in Kigali, facilitating access to its jurisprudence and providing information on its activities, and has carried out activities aimed at strengthening the capacity of the Rwandan judiciary. [62]

3. United Nations International Residual Mechanism for Criminal Tribunals

The United Nations Security Council noted the considerable contributions to international criminal justice and accountability for serious international crimes that the Tribunal made as well as its role in the re—establishment of the rule of law in Rwanda. [63] As the work of the Tribunal, and the ICTY, was progressing toward completion, the Security Council decided to establish the International Residual Mechanism for Criminal Tribunals to carry out the essential functions of the Rwanda and Yugo-

---

[61]   For a comprehensive discussion of the capacity—building and outreach efforts of the ICTR, see Adama Dieng, "Capacity—Building Efforts of the ICTR: A Different Kind of Legacy", in *Northwestern Journal of International Human Rights*, 2011, Vol. 9, p. 403.

[62]   *ICTR Final Report*, see *supra* note 35, paras. 142–145. The ICTR outreach efforts included: awareness—raising workshops at grass—roots level in Rwanda for approximately 25, 000 participants, including large numbers of students and teachers from Rwandan schools, youth sensitization and genocide—prevention education in the Great Lakes region, training programs in court procedures, and training programs on legal journalism and ethics. See *ICTR Final Report*, see *supra* note 35, para. 143.

[63]   SC Res. 1966, UN Doc. S/RES/1966 (2010), preamble (3rd recital) (http://www. legal — tools. org/doc/e79460/). See also SC Res. 2256 (2015), UN Doc. S/RES/2256 (2015), para. 2 (http:// www. legal—tools. org/doc/481414/) (acknowledging "the substantial contribution of the ICTR to the process of national reconciliation and the restoration of peace and security, and to the fight against impunity and the development of international criminal justice, especially in relation to the crime of genocide").

slavia Tribunals (collectively "Tribunals") after their closure. [64] This move sought to ensure that the closure of the Tribunals would not result in impunity for the fugitives and that vital functions, such as the protection of victims and witnesses, review of judgements, and supervision of sentences, for example, would continue to be served for as long as necessary. The Security Council deemed that these essential functions would be best performed by a new entity that would be specifically adapted to such a limited, residual purpose.

Indeed, while the ICTR and the ICTY led the way in significant jurisprudential advances, they had been established within a year of each other, at a time when the international community lacked experience with prosecuting and adjudicating international crimes. [65] The cumulative experience of the two Tribunals in adjudicating such crimes and administering international justice over the course of more than two decades informed the Security Council in drawing up the new entity. While designed to continue the ground−breaking work of the ICTR and the ICTY, benefiting from the lessons learned, the Mechanism is founded on a new model of international criminal justice that seeks to foster the highest standards of justice alongside judicial economy and efficiency.

The Security Council established the Mechanism as its new subsidiary organ on 22 December 2010 by way of Resolution 1966, acting under Chapter VII of the UN Charter. [66] The Statute of the Mechanism, as adopted by the Security Council in Resolution 1966, specifies that the Mechanism comprises two branches, one for the ICTR, located in Arusha, and one for the ICTY, located in The Hague. [67] This

---

[64]   SC Res. 1966, see *supra* note 63. On the background to the establishment of the Mechanism, see Thomas Wayde Pittman, "The Road to the Establishment of the International Residual Mechanism for Criminal Tribunals", in *Journal of International Criminal Justice*, 2011, Vol. 9, pp. 798−809; Brigitte Benoit Landale and Huw Llewellyn, "The International Residual Mechanism for Criminal Tribunals: The Beginning of the End for the ICTY and ICTR", in *International Organizations Law Review*, 2011, Vol. 8, pp. 350, 351.

[65]   Sadat, see *supra* note 60, pp. 119, 120.

[66]   SC Res. 1966, see *supra* note 63.

[67]   MICT Statute, see *supra* note 40, art. 3.

structure ensures the presence of the Mechanism and its archives at the respective seats of the ICTR and the ICTY, but does so on the basis of a single, unified entity. [68] This is a notable departure from the ICTR and the ICTY which were individual, self-standing tribunals, each boasting its own judicial, prosecutorial, and administrative structures relying on separate resources. The unified structure of the mechanism avoids inefficiencies resulting from duplication of functions and services as it incorporates shared use of resources across the two branches.

The Mechanism was established for an initial four-year period from 1 July 2012, the date on which it was set to commence functioning in respect of the ICTR. [69] The commencement date in respect of the ICTY was a year later, 1 July 2013. [70] The two Tribunals retained the competence to complete all trials and referral proceedings that were pending before them as of the respective commencement date. [71] They also retained the competence to complete all appellate, review, and contempt proceedings which were instituted prior to the Mechanism's commencement date for the given Tribunal. [72] The Rwanda Tribunal completed its work at the end of 2015 and the Yugoslavia Tribunal is expected to close at the end of 2017. [73]

---

[68]   See, e. g. , Landale and Llewellyn, see *supra* note 64, p. 353.

[69]   SC Res. 1966, see *supra* note 63, para. 1. Following the initial period, the Mechanism functions in two-year period increments, until the Security Council decides otherwise. See SC Res. 1966, see *supra* note 63, para. 17. The Mechanism is subject to prescribed reporting obligations on the progress of its work, with six-monthly progress reports to the Security Council and annual reports to the Security Council and to the General Assembly. *Ibid.* The Security Council reviews the progress of the Mechanism's work toward completing its functions prior to the commencement of each new two-year period of operation. *Ibid.* The Security Council completed its first review of the Mechanism's progress in December 2015. See SC Res. 2256 (2015), UN Doc. S/RES/2256 (2015) (http: //www. legal-tools. org/doc/481414/).

[70]   *Ibid.*

[71]   SC Res. 1966, UN Doc. S/RES/1966 (2010), Annex 2, Transitional Arrangements ("MICT Transitional Arrangements"), art. 1 (1).

[72]   MICT Transitional Arrangements, see *supra* note 71, arts. 2-4.

[73]   *ICTR Final Report*, see *supra* note 35, para. 167; *Assessment and Report of Judge Carmel Agius, President of the International Tribunal for the Former Yugoslavia, Provided to the Security Council Pursuant to Paragraph* 6 *of Security Council Resolution* 1534 (2004) (*period from* 18 *May* 2016 *to* 17 *November* 2016), UN Doc. S/2016/976 (2016), para. 80, available at http: //www. icty. org/en/documents/completion-strategy-and-mict, accessed at 13 June 2017.

There has therefore been overlap between each of the two Tribunals and the Mechanism, with each entity, however, pursuing separate cases in accordance with the Security Council's precise delineation of their respective responsibility during the transitional period. [74]

In a nutshell, the key functions of the Mechanism include:

a. arrest and prosecution of the remaining fugitives indicted by the Rwanda Tribunal;

b. conduct of any remaining appeal proceedings from the two Tribunals or from its own judgements or decisions;

c. conduct of any retrials in instances where the Appeals Chamber orders a new trial;

d. conduct of any trials for contempt of court and false testimony, that is prosecution of individuals who have interfered with the administration of justice and of witnesses who knowingly gave false testimony before the Mechanism or the Tribunals; and also

e. review of final judgements, where a new fact is discovered, that could have been decisive in reaching the original judgement.

The Mechanism is also charged with continuing the protection of victims and witnesses; supervision and enforcement of sentences imposed by the Rwanda and Yu-

---

[74]　In the MICT Transitional Arrangements, the Security Council expressly apportioned the competence of the ICTR, the ICTY, and the Mechanism in respect of trial, appeal, review, and contempt proceedings. See MICT Transitional Arrangements, see *supra* note 71, arts. 1–4. It also specified the transitional responsibility with respect to protection of victims and witnesses and directed the two Tribunals to take all necessary steps to ensure a coordinated transition of all other functions to the Mechanism, including the supervision of sentences, assistance to national authorities, and the management of records and archives. See MICT Transitional Arrangements, see *supra* note 71, arts. 5, 6. The Security Council also specified that, during the transitional period, the President, Judges, Prosecutor, and Registrar of the Mechanism may also hold such offices in the Tribunals and that staff of the Mechanism may also be staff members of the ICTR or the ICTY. MICT Transitional Arrangements, see *supra* note 71, art. 7.

goslavia Tribunals; assistance to national authorities with domestic cases related to the work of the ICTR or the ICTY; monitoring of cases referred by the two Tribunals to national courts; and also the preservation and management of the archives of the two Tribunals.

Based on the founding determination of the Security Council in Resolution 1966 to combat impunity and bring to justice all those indicted by the ICTR and the ICTY, the Statute of the Mechanism specifies that the Mechanism continues the material, territorial, temporal, and personal jurisdiction of the two Tribunals. [75] Notably, given its residual nature, the Mechanism does not have the power to issue new indictments for genocide and other serious violations of international humanitarian law. And, significantly, the Mechanism's power to prosecute is limited to those accused indicted by the ICTR or the ICTY "who are among the most senior leaders suspected of being most responsible" for the substantive crimes within the jurisdiction of the Mechanism. [76] The Statute specifies that consideration in this regard be given to "the gravity of the crimes charged and the level of responsibility of the accused. "[77] In respect of persons indicted by the ICTR or the ICTY who are not among the most senior leaders suspected of being most responsible, the Mechanism has the power to prosecute only in the event that it has exhausted all reasonable efforts to refer such cases to national jurisdictions. [78] Consequently, when apprehended, the Mechanism would prosecute only three of the remaining eight fugitives, with the cases of the oth-

---

[75]   SC Res. 1966, see *supra* note 63, preamble; MICT Statute, see *supra* note 42, art. 1 (1). For a discussion on the continuity of the jurisdiction of the ICTR and the ICTY by the Mechanism, see Gabrielle McIntyre, "The International Residual Mechanism and the Legacy of the International Criminal Tribunals for the Former Yugoslavia and Rwanda", in *Goettingen Journal of International Law*, 2011, Vol. 3, pp. 935–940.

[76]   MICT Statute, see *supra* note 41, art. 1 (2).

[77]   *Ibid.*, art. 1 (2).

[78]   *Ibid.*, art. 1 (3). For the provisions on referral of cases to national jurisdictions, see MICT Statute, see *supra* note 41, art. 6.

ers already having been referred to Rwanda. [79]

So far, the Mechanism has issued over 1,000 judicial decisions and orders, including one appeal judgement. [80] This output represents the sum of the judicial work of the Mechanism to date, including all matters arising from the respective caseloads of the ICTR and the ICTY, notably, in nearly equal numbers. [81] Another interesting observation from the judicial statistics is the rise of the judicial workload, as measured by output of orders and decisions. Whereas in the first year when the Mechanism functioned at both of its branches it issued 79 decisions and orders, last year the output was 405. This rise in the workload is partly attributable to the fact that in 2016 the Mechanism had before it three large cases from the ICTY caseload: a retrial in the *Stanišić and Simatović* case, and two appeals from judgement in the *Karadzic* and *Seselj* cases. The proceedings in these large cases continue and the Mechanism's caseload will increase further in the event of an appeal from judgement in the *Mladic* case which is expected to conclude before the ICTY by the end of 2017.

The trial in the *Stanišić and Simatović* case before the Mechanism is a result of a judgement of the ICTY Appeals Chamber which ordered a retrial in December 2015, upon ruling that an ICTY Trial Chamber had failed to make certain key findings before it had acquitted Jovica Stanišić and Franko Simatović on all counts of the indictment. [82] Stanišić, who was the former Chief of the State Security Service of the Ministry of Interior of the Republic of Serbia, and Simatović, who was a high level advi-

---

[79]   See http: //www. unmict. org/en/cases/searching-fugitives accessed at 1 August 2017. It should be noted, however, that the Mechanism monitors all cases referred to national jurisdictions. See MICT Statute, see *supra* note 41, art. 6 (5). The Mechanism also retains the power to revoke referral before the accused is found guilty or acquitted by a national court, if the conditions for referral are no longer met. See MICT Statute, see *supra* note 41, art. 6 (6).

[80]   As of the end of May 2017, the Mechanism has issued 1, 034 decisions and orders plus one appeal judgement.

[81]   Of the 1, 034 decisions and orders, 461 related to the ICTR caseload and 573 related to the ICTY caseload.

[82]   For information on this case, see http: //www. unmict. org/en/cases/mict-15-96 accessed 1 August 2017.

sor in the security service, were prosecuted before the ICTY for a number of alleged crimes against civilians from Bosnia and Herzegovina and Croatia. Following pre—trial proceedings before the Mechanism, the retrial commenced in June 2017. [83] The Mechanism is also seized of appeals against ICTY trial judgements in the cases of Radovan Karadšić, who was the President of Republika Srpska and who was sentenced by the ICTY to 40 years of imprisonment upon being convicted of genocide, crimes against humanity, and war crimes, and Vojislav Šešelj, a Serb politician who was acquitted by the ICTY. [84]

In addition to these major cases, the Mechanism is also dealing with two requests for review of judgements, and, routinely, it is seized of contempt proceedings, proceedings related to protection of victims and witnesses, access to confidential information, and other matters.

In terms of judicial structure, the Mechanism comprises a Trial Chamber at each of the two branches and an Appeals Chamber that is common to both branches. [85] As the Mechanism was designed to be lean and efficient, there are no standing Chambers. Rather, when a matter comes before the Mechanism, the President of the Mechanism assigns it to a Trial Chamber or the Appeals Chamber to which he then assigns judges from a roster. The President, Judge Theodor Meron, is the only Judge who is present at the Mechanism, whether in Arusha or at The Hague. The other 24 Judges, who were elected by the UN General Assembly, are only on a roster. [86] They receive no salary or any other payment until they exercise functions on behalf of the Mechanism and then they are paid only for the time during

---

[83]　*Prosecutor v. Jovica Stanišić and Franko Simatović*, Case No. MICT–15–96–PT, Scheduling Order, Trial Chamber, 24 May 2017 (http: //www. legal–tools. org/doc/36f7fa/).

[84]　For information on the *Karadšić* case, see http: //www. unmict. org/en/cases/mict–13–55. For information on the *Šešelj* case, see http: //www. unmict. org/en/cases/mict–16–99. Both accessed at 1 August 2017.

[85]　MICT Statute, see *supra* note 41, art. 4 (a).

[86]　*Ibid.*, art. 8 (3).

which they perform Mechanism work. [87] By contrast, judges at the Rwanda and Yugoslavia Tribunals served and were compensated on a full-time basis.

This innovative judicial structure, laid out in the Statute of the Mechanism, seeks to ensure that the Mechanism operates in an efficient and economical manner. By having a roster of expert Judges, all of whom possess the qualifications required in their countries for appointment to the highest judicial office and many of whom have prior experience as judges of the ICTR or the ICTY, the Mechanism is poised to dispose of its caseload in an efficient manner. [88] At the same time, the judges are only called upon when the workload of the Mechanism so demands, ensuring that judicial resources are expended only when and only for as long as necessary. [89] It was not obvious at the outset that judges would be willing to serve under the conditions imposed by the Mechanism Statute. Specifically, the Statute does not envision full-time engagement of the Mechanism judges, besides the President, with judges asked to take on assignments as matters arise. For individual judges this means sporadic assignments that are typically of very limited duration. However, as President Meron recently observed, "[o] n all but very few occasions, Judges have been available and willing to take on assignments for the Mechanism on the terms on which they are offered, thereby supporting the expeditious and efficient completion of judicial work." [90]

The careful use of resources at the Mechanism is further evident in the assignment of judges and the composition of the Chambers. Namely, for most matters at the first instance, the President only assigns a Single Judge to deal with the matter. This

---

[87] MICT Statute, see *supra* note 41, art. 8 (4).

[88] MICT Statute, see *supra* note 41, art. 9. Indeed, presently, twenty of the judges on the roster have prior experience at the ICTR or the ICTY. For a roster of the judges and their background, see http: // www. unmict. org/en/about/judges accessed at 1 August 2017.

[89] MICT Statute, see *supra* note 41, art. 8 (4).

[90] *Remarks of Judge Theodor Meron at the Diplomatic Briefing in The Hague on 17 May* 2017 (on file with the author).

is stipulated in the Statute of the Mechanism, which provides that the President shall assign a Single Judge to deal with any matter at first instance except in the event of a trial of a case concerning substantive crimes within the jurisdiction of the Mechanism or to consider a referral of such a case to a national jurisdiction, in which case the President is to assign three judges to compose a Trial Chamber. [91] To illustrate the significance of this provision, we can look at all the matters that the Mechanism completed in 2016. Of the 91 completed matters, 83 were handled by a Single Judge. This can be compared with the Rwanda and Yugoslavia Tribunals where first–instance matters were handled by Trial Chambers composed of three judges. [92]

The resulting efficient use of judicial resources at the Mechanism is further magnified by a statutory provision relating to assignments of judges to consider appeals. Pursuant to the Mechanism's Statute, where a Single Judge deals with a matter, an appeal from the judge's decision is handled by an Appeals Chamber composed of only three judges. [93] Only in the event of an appeal against a decision of a Trial Chamber composed of three judges does the President assign five judges to the Appeals Chamber to consider the appeal. [94] Given that most first–instance matters at the Mechanism have been assigned to Single Judges, most of the appeals before the Mechanism have been disposed of by three–judge benches of the Appeals Chamber. Again, this can be contrasted with the practice of the Rwanda and Yugoslavia Tribunals where the Appeals Chamber was composed of five judges for each appeal. [95] The Mechanism model, under which judges are compensated on the basis of days spent exercising functions rather than on full–time basis, and which relies on fewer judges per matter by assigning cases to Single Judges and composing smaller Chambers, results in lower expenditures on the judiciary than those incurred by the

---

[91]   MICT Statute, see *supra* note 41, art. 12 (1).

[92]   *Ibid.* , art. 11 (2); ICTY Statute, see *supra* note 51, art. 12 (2).

[93]   MICT Statute, see *supra* note 41, art. 12 (3).

[94]   *Ibid.*

[95]   ICTR Statute, see *supra* note 30, art. 11 (3); ICTY Statute, see *supra* note 51, art. 12 (3).

Rwanda and Yugoslavia Tribunals.

Another special feature of the Mechanism is that the judges work on most matters remotely. The Statute of the Mechanism expressly provides that the judges ' shall only be present at the seats of the branches of the Mechanism as necessary at the request of the President to exercise the functions requiring their presence. ' [96] This is underlined by a provision that the judges who are assigned to exercise functions on behalf of the Mechanism do so, in so far as possible, remotely, away from the seats of the mechanism. [97] By design, the judges of the Mechanism do not maintain an office at either of the branches of the Mechanism, but work from their own premises in their country. It is only when it is necessary for the exercise of their functions on behalf of the Mechanism that judges travel to The Hague or to Arusha to carry out their functions. This reduces the potential expenses of travel, relocation, and office accommodation that would otherwise be attendant in the movement of judges and their performance of duties at one of the branches of the Mechanism.

This economical mode of operation has required the Mechanism to innovate judicial support processes in order to ensure that the judges who are assigned to exercise functions are enabled to perform efficiently, whether working remotely or on site in Arusha or at The Hague. To this end, the Mechanism maintains secure means of communication between the two branches and with each of the judges to enable them to access judicial filings and other necessary materials at any location from which they may be exercising their Mechanism functions. Moreover, the Mechanism has established the Chambers Legal Support Section, to assist the judges in every aspect of the exercise of their functions, wherever performed.

The Chambers Legal Support Section is composed of legal and administrative staff dedicated to assisting the judges in attending to their Mechanism duties such as in their research and drafting and in facilitating their deliberations, for exam-

---

[96] MICT Statute, see *supra* note 41, art. 8 (3).

[97] *Ibid.*

ple. Although leanly staffed, the Chambers Legal Support Section maintains physical presence in Arusha and at The Hague to provide on-site assistance to any judge called to exercise functions at either branch of the Mechanism. At the same time, Chambers staff follow a flexible working method under which every staff member, irrespective of physical location, is available to assist with any matter, whether arising from the Rwanda or the Yugoslavia Tribunal, at any stage of the proceedings, whether first or second instance, and whether assigned to a matter being handled by a judge or judges working remotely or called to one of the seats of the Mechanism. Furthermore, most Chambers staff members are assigned to support judges in respect of diverse matters simultaneously, allowing each staff member to balance the workload through the peaks and troughs of activity in individual matters. This mode of operation enables the Mechanism to maintain modest staffing levels in the Chambers Legal Support Section while providing a high level of legal support services to the judiciary. [98]

4. Conclusion

In sum, the Mechanism represents a new and unique model of administering international criminal justice. Although operating on two continents, it functions as a single organization with common resources serving both branches, as envisioned by the Security Council. In accordance with its Statute, the Mechanism relies on a roster of judges, enabling it to immediately respond to changes in its workload. Moreover, it relies extensively on Single Judges rather than full Trial Chambers, allows and enables judges to work remotely whenever possible, and compensates the judges for the performance of their Mechanism functions rather than on a full-time basis. These aspects of deploying judicial resources, combined with the innovative, dedicated support the Mechanism provides to the judiciary, should result in less costly proceedings while continuing to uphold the highest international standards of justice. In this man-

---

[98]　At time of writing, the current staffing allocation to the Chambers Legal Support Section covering both branches is 22 legal officers and four administrative assistants.

ner, the Mechanism is poised to ensure the legacy of the Rwanda and Yugoslavia Tribunals and serve as a model for further developments in the effective and efficient administration of international criminal justice.

Part II   East – West Perspectives on International Law at Sea

NEW TECHNOLOGY, NEW WEAPONRY AND NEW CHALLENGES UNMANNED MARIAN SYSTEM AND THE APPLICABILITY OF INTERNATIONAL HUMANITARIAN LAW

Judge Liu Daqun [*]

In the whole human history, it is not difficult to find out that the development of technology has great impact on new weaponry and manoeuvrability of warships which revolutionised naval warfare. Every step of improvement of naval warfare depends on the invention of new technology, from sail boat to stream boat, from arrow to cannons, from precision missiles to autonomous weapons. At the present, the naval warfare has come into an era of using more advanced technologies, such as the unmanned marine system (UMS). Generally speaking, unmanned marine system normally is composed of three main parts, Satellite system, unmanned surface/under sea vehicles and weaponry which involve conventional, cyber warfare, autonomous weapons and unmanned aircrafts (drone).

Unmanned marine systems are used for a wide range of military applications, include Mine Counter Measures (MCM), Intelligence, Surveillance and Reconnaissance (ISR), Anti-Submarine Warfare (ASW), and Fast Inshore Attack Craft (FIAC) for combat training.

This paper first discusses the current employment of the UMS in military activities especially on the reconnaissance and surveillance. Then, it explores the future

---

[*] Judge of the United Nation's Mechanism of International Criminal Tribunals, Member of the Permanent Court of Arbitration, Member of the Institute de Droit International. Professor at the Centre of Cooperative Innovation and Judicial Civilization of China's University of Political Science and Law.

usage in actual armed conflicts. For instance, Artificial Intelligence (AI) technology has reached a point where the deployment of such systems is — practically if not legally — feasible within years, not decades, and the stakes are high. Lethal autonomous weapons (LAW) have been described as the third revolution in warfare, after gunpowder and nuclear arms. Thirdly, it will discuss the difference between automated weapons and autonomous weapons and the debate on using those weapons and applicable law. Finally, it will deal with the applicable laws, especially, treaties and international customary law.

1. Employment of new naval warfare weaponry

On January 17, 1991, a small squadron of U. S. Army Apache attack helicopters, dozens of cruise missiles from naval vessels, and a number of F-117 stealth fighters launched the Operation Desert Storm against Iraq's invasion into Kuwait. It was followed by 42 days air bombardment with aircrafts launched from the airbase of neighboring countries as well as from three U. S. aircrafts carries in the Gulf. It was the first non-conventional war; in which new, fairly new, or even experimental weapons were used. The Gulf War displayed much new technology and marked a new era of naval warfare. It is the first time in history, that precision-guided bombs, missiles and drones played a decisive role in war. With the high technology and new weaponry, the United States and its allies critically weakened the fourth-largest army in the world while suffering surprisingly light casualties during the month of the air war. It showed clearly the high-tech weapons would greatly change how wars were fought.

Having established absolute air supremacy from the outset of the war, the allies have been able to hammer Iraq's command centers, supply lines, bunkers, tanks and troops almost at will. A lot of newly invented weaponry was employed during the war, among which only two will be discussed, such as precision weapons like laser-guided bombs and missiles which have greatly enhanced the effectiveness of the attacks and unmanned aircrafts (drones) which was the first time used in an actual armed conflict.

The Tomahawk and the Tomahawk Antiship missile (TASM) are fitted on almost all the naval warships, which are precision weaponry with computer—guidance fired from U. S. combat vessels carrying either 1, 000–lb. warheads or a cluster of 166 soda – can – sized bomblets. The warhead can hit within a few feet of its target. This is one of the backbone attacks of the war. This weapon allowed allied forces to destroy buildings in a very populated area without harming civilians.

Once the missile crosses the shoreline, a more precise guidance method (TERCOM) takes over. It (TERCOM) scans the landscape at set checkpoints, taking altitude readings and comparing them to map data in its own computer memory. The missiles moves at about 700 km. per hour, and can make twists and turns like a radar e-vading fighter plane, all the while skimming over the land at 80 to 200 meters.

After covering up to 1,500 miles, the Tomahawk closes in on its target and a third guidance system then takes over, DSMAC (Digital Scene Matching Area Colla-tor). DSMAC snaps a picture of the target area and compares that data to a version in its own memory. The computer then gives the wings and tail fins a final adjustment and takes the warhead to its target. But rather than flying directly to the target and automatically destroy it, the new version can be programmed to fly around the target area, give commanders a bird's eye view of the battlefield and then be re – pro-grammed for new instructions.

Precision weapons like laser—guided bombs and cruise missiles require pre—in-stalled information and assessment of the result of the bombing. To achieve this aim, drones for the first time were used in collection of information in real warfare. Drone is small, remote—controlled, pilotless plane emerged as a valuable asset in the Gulf War. These remote piloted vehicles resembled oversize model planes and acted as aerial spies.

The U. S. Navy, Marine Corps, and Army used basically two types of drones in the war, the Pointer and the more sophisticated Pioneer. The Pioneer drone (devel-oped by the Israelis and produced in the U. S.) has a range of about 100 miles and flight duration of five hours. It can carry a multitude of sensors including television and communication equipments. The drone is catapulted into the air and when airborne runs on liquid fuel. It is guided by an electronic box with a joystick that the operator uses to turn the plane left or right, up or down in the same way remote—controlled model airplanes works. Each pioneer carries a MYM 400 000 video camera that can take highly detailed pictures from 2 000 feet and transmit them 100 miles away. According to a May 1991 Department of the Navy report, "At least one drone was airborne at all times during Desert Storm."

Comparing with manned aircrafts, drone has a lot of advantages. It is so small that it is difficult for Radar to detect it. Even if detected and fired at, it does not cause the casualties of the pilots. It does not need a long runway to be launched in an aircraft carrier so the aircraft carrier could be smaller and takes as much more drones than manned aircraft. It could stay in the air for a long time and get much more information as possible. During the Gulf War, the drone is mainly employed for the intelligence, surveillance and reconnaissance. Nowadays, drone could carry offensive weapons, like the precision guided missiles, such as the Tomahawk cruise missile and LAW. Systems with a higher degree of autonomy would include drones or unmanned combat aerial vehicles, that can autonomously search, identify and locate enemies but can only engage with a target when authorized by mission command.

Operation Desert Storm is a "new type of war", a war in which technology is king and whoever has the most advanced weapons ultimately wins. Sophisticated technology was used to end the war in a quick and timely manner. That is so called "more tech, less blood." This war is only the first in a long line of wars to come that will use sophisticated technology to defeat the enemy. The advanced weapon technology used in the Gulf War changed the way wars are fought today. That is why the Gulf War is a frontier in history.

Based on this philosophy, all the big powers are devoted to invent new weaponry with the advanced technology after the Gulf War. The great powers competed to build the modern-day battleship. Today, a new arms race may be breaking out, this time with robotic warships. In the naval, the unmanned Lethal Autonomous Weapon System (LAWS) is on the priority agenda for all the big power naval. Unmanned surface (submarine) vehicles (USV) or autonomous surface (submarine) vehicles (ASV) are vehicles that operate on the surface (or under the water) for months at a time without a crew. The unarmed ship was originally conceived as submarine-hunter, but it could emerge as a flexible platform that could fulfill many military roles. On 7 April, 2016, the Sea Hunter, an autonomous unmanned surface vehicle (USV) was launched in Portland, Oregon, U. S. While still in development, it is intended to have offensive capabilities including anti-submarine ordnance. Sea Hunter uses radar and an international ship-tracking program known as the Automatic Identification System (AIS) to find its bearings and dodge other vessels. Boeing's autonomous submarine systems built on the Echo Voyager platform are also being considered for long-range deep-sea military use.

The main reason for not having a "human in the loop" in these systems is the need for rapid response. They have generally been used to protect personnel and installations against incoming projectiles.

China also made great progress in this area. The China Aerospace and Science Technology Corporation, a Chinese defense contractor whose primary strength is in missiles and other aerospace technologies offered the D3000, a stealthy robotic warship designed to operate autonomously for months. The D3000 can either operate by itself, or as part of a larger task force with manned ships.

From available pictures, the D3000 has significant stealth shaping and likely displaces about 100-150 tons. The D3000 is armed with three Type 730 Gatling cannons and anti-ship missile launchers built into its superstructure, and launch tubes above the waterline. Those launch tubes could potentially be used to launch torpedoes, lay mines, or deploy underwater unmanned vehicles.

Using unmanned vessels as a mother ship for more unmanned systems is becoming popular in both defense and civilian applications. In this case, unmanned surface vehicles could extend the sensor net of the D3000, hiding underwater to spot enemy submarines and carriers to call back to the D3000, which, in turn, networks firing solutions to friendly ships and aircraft.

At the present, the unmanned submarine vehicles are often used by big powers. An autonomous underwater vehicle (AUV) is a robot that travels underwater without requiring input from an operator. The oil and gas industry uses AUVs to make detailed maps of the seafloor before they start building subsea infrastructure; pipelines and sub sea completions can be installed in the most cost effective manner with minimum disruption to the environment. The AUV allows survey companies to conduct precise surveys of areas where traditional bathymetric surveys would be less effective or too costly. Also, post—lay pipe surveys are now possible, which includes pipeline inspection. The use of AUVs for pipeline inspection and inspection of underwater man—made structures is becoming more common. A variety of sensors can be affixed to AUVs to measure the concentration of various elements or compounds, the absorption or reflection of light, and the presence of microscopic life. Autonomous underwater vehicles, for example AUV ABYSS, have been used to find wreckages of missing airplanes, e. g. Air France Flight 447. Recently, the Bluefin—21 AUV was used in the search for Malaysia Airlines Flight 370. On January 10, 2018, The government of Malaysia and an American ocean exploration company began a new effort to solve one of history's greatest aviation mysteries: the disappearance of Malaysia Airlines Flight 370 nearly four years ago. Under the agreement, the company will receive nothing if it does not find the missing Boeing 777, which disappeared over the Indian Ocean on March 8, 2014, with 239 people aboard. It is a "no cure, no fee" agreement and it is good opportunity for the company to test its underwater vehicles.

The unmanned underwater vehicles are also used in naval activities. It mainly concentrated on the following areas: Intelligence, surveillance, and reconnaissance, Mine countermeasures, Anti—submarine warfare, Inspection/identification, Oceanography, Communication/navigation network nodes, Payload delivery, Information operations, Time−critical strikes; etc.

2. Difference between automated weapon system and autonomous weapon system

Automated weapon system means the weapons could response to the incoming attacks with already−set human instructions. The oldest automatically−triggered lethal weapon is the land mine, used since at least the 1600s, and naval mines, used since the 1700s. A land mine is an explosive device concealed under or on the ground and designed to destroy or disable enemy targets, ranging from combatants to vehicles and tanks, as they pass over or near it. Such a device is typically detonated automatically by way of pressure when a target steps on it or drives over it, although other detonation mechanisms are also sometimes used. A naval mine is a self−contained explosive device placed under water to damage or destroy surface ships or submarines. Sea mines are deposited and left to wait until they are triggered by the approach of, or contact with, an enemy vessel.

The use of both land and water mines is controversial because of their potential as indiscriminate weapons. They can remain dangerous many years after a conflict has ended, harming civilians and the economy. Anti – personnel mines are banned in many countries by the 1997 Ottawa Treaty, not including the United States, Russia, and much of Asia and the Middle East.

Some current examples are automated "hardkill" active protection systems, such as a radar – guided gun to defend ships that have been in use since the 1970s. Such systems can autonomously identify and attack oncoming missiles, rockets, artillery fire, aircraft and surface vessels within certain distance according to criteria set by the human operator. For instance, USS Ponce of the US already deployed aboard the Navy's Laser Weapon System which concentrates light into a fine point, heating a target until it burns or explodes. The crew of the USS Ponce is allowed to use the laser to defend the ship from actual threats. The laser can fire at different targets in rapid succession. Since shots cost less than a dollar each, double—tapping is probably fine. However, Laser Blind Convention has banned this kind of weapon.

The rail gun is also such kind of weapon which is also called electro magnetism gun or (nostradamus). Railgun is a device that uses electromagnetic force to launch high velocity projectiles, by means of a sliding armature that is accelerated along a pair of conductive rails. It is typically constructed as a weapon and the projectile normally does not contain explosives, relying on the projectile's high speed to inflict damage. It is said that China's naval has set up this weapon on her warship. In early February 2018, pictures of what is claimed to be a Chinese railgun were published online. In the pictures the gun is mounted on the bow of a Type 072III—class landing ship Haiyangshan.

Lethal autonomous weapons (LAWs) are a type of autonomous military robot designed to select and attack military targets (people, installations) without intervention by a human operator. LAWs may operate in the air, on land, on water, under water, or in space. LAWs should not be confused with UCAVs or "combat drones", which are currently remote—controlled by human pilots. (LAWs are considered a subset of combat drones). Even though combat drones can fly autonomously, they do not fire autonomously, but rather by a trained human operator.

Lethal Autonomous weapon systems (LAWS) that kill people, should select and engage targets without further human intervention after programming it. They are designed to allow the weapons to exercise appropriate levels of human judgment over the use of force. The artificial intelligence demonstrates human—level intelligence and concerns the development of computational algorithms suitable for reasoning tasks— that is, problem solving, decision making, prediction, diagnosis, and so forth. Artificial intelligence also involves generalizing or classifying data—what's known as machine learning. And intelligent systems might include computer vision software that aims ultimately to provide meaningful interpretations of images. Functions such as these don't add much excitement to Hollywood movies, but they are of great interest in the development of autonomous weapons. Cruise missiles and remote—controlled drones are in some sense autonomous, and both have been deployed widely in the battlefield. But when people speak of autonomous weapons, they generally mean weapons that have state—of—the—art capabilities in artificial intelligence, robotics, and automatic control and can, independent of human intervention, select targets and decide whether to strike them.

3. Three different views towards autonomous weapons

International community has already put its attention to the regulations of production and deployment of autonomous weapons.

UN Secretary—General Ban Ki—moon took note of "killer robots" in his report on the Protection of Civilians in Armed Conflict issued in November 2013, saying important questions have been raised as to the ability of such systems to operate in accordance with international humanitarian and human rights law. The Secretary — General went on to say: "Although autonomous weapons systems have not yet been deployed and the extent of their development as a military technology remains unclear, discussion of such questions must begin immediately and not once the technology has been developed and proliferated. "

On 14 May 2014 the top United Nations official in Geneva has urged bold action by diplomats at the start of the world body's first ever meeting on Lethal Autonomous Weapons (LAWs), better known as "killer robots," telling them: "You have the opportunity to take pre—emptive action and ensure that the ultimate decision to end life remains firmly under human control. "

Would automated warfare, as some observers claim, minimize collateral damage—or simply result in mass destruction? The answer isn't clear. What's clear is that targeting decisions made by human beings are often extremely bad. To be sure, it's important to discuss the ethics of autonomous weapons and debate whether they should be banned, regulated, or left to develop without restrictions. Dehumanized killing in all its forms is ultimately the issue. Generally speaking, there are three different views towards the autonomous weapons.

3.1 Total ban

In 2014, 87 states sent representatives to a UN conference on LAWs, among which, five States, Cuba, Ecuador, Egypt, Pakistan, and the Vatican submitted statements urging that autonomous weapons systems be banned, while several dozen nations, especially the big military powers are developing military robotics.

In July 2017, at the opening of the International Joint Conference on Artificial Intelligence (IJCAI) in Melbourne, a group of 116 specialists from across 26 countries of the world's leading robotics and artificial intelligence launched a public letter calling on the United Nations to ban the development and use of killer robots. The founders call for the LAWs be added to the list of weapons banned under the UN's convention on certain conventional weapons (CCW) brought into force in 1983, which includes chemical and intentionally blinding laser weapons.

Tesla's Musk, one of the leading person of the signatories of the open letter, has repeatedly warned for the need for pro − active regulation of LAW, calling it is humanity's biggest existential threat. "We do not have long to act. Once this Pandora's box is opened, it will be hard to close."

The letter echoes arguments made since 2013 by the Campaign to Stop Killer Robots, which views autonomous weapons as "a fundamental challenge to the protection of civilians and to ... international human rights and humanitarian law."

The first reason they argued is that the autonomous systems with learning abilities could quickly get beyond their creators' control. They would be a danger to anyone within their immediate reach. Once developed, lethal autonomous weapons will permit armed conflict to be fought at a scale greater than ever, and at timescales faster than humans can comprehend. And autonomous weapons connected to each other via networks, or autonomous agents endowed with artificial intelligence and connected to the Internet, would not be confined to a single geographic territory or to states involved in armed conflict.

Secondly, they believe that no existing weapon can properly be described as an offensive autonomous weapon capable of killing legitimate targets while sparing civilians. Today's artificial intelligence, which cannot reproduce human intelligence and judgment, would pose fundamental challenges to civilian safety if deployed on the battlefield.

Thirdly, it will be disaster if the LAW falls into the hands of terrorists. LAW can be weapons of terror, weapons terrorists use against innocent populations and hacked to behave in undesirable ways. The terrorists in the 21th century are no longen the traditional one with black clothes wrapping all over holding AK47 rifles. They look like ordinary person sitting in an office with a cup of coffee in hands, but they may gain the technology of LAW and create the killing robotics. For instance, the fixed-place sentry gun, developed on behalf of the South Korean government, was the first of its kind with an autonomous system capable of performing surveillance, voice-recognition, tracking and firing with mounted machine gun or grenade launcher. It is not that difficult for the terrorist group to mast this technology and use it for assassination. An autonomous sniper gun could be mounted on a top location and programmed with the facial identification, pattern of expression, gesture recognizing and red light sensors software. Once the gun itself found, identified and verified the target, it will fire automatically and hit the target among thousands of the people.

3.2 In favor

However, there are different views in favor of development of the autonomous weapons. First, the autonomous weapons would commit fewer battlefield atrocities than human beings—and that their development might even be considered morally imperative. The real autonomous weapons with technological advancements should identify permissible targets. They can't maximize chances of military success and minimize the risk of collateral damage today, but someday they might gain those abilities. Advanced autonomous weapons, if ever deployed, should not compromise basic human rights. Applying artificial intelligence to warfare, especially via autonomous weapons, might optimize casualties on the battlefield. Intelligent robotics systems, so the argument goes, could identify targets precisely and efficiently. They could engage in combat in such a way that collateral damage would be minimized—certainly when compared to many missions executed by humans. The weapon's precision concerns only the probability that the weapon will land on that exact spot. No matter it is automated weapons or autonomous weapons, after all, the human chooses that target.

Second, they are confident that LAW and UMS could perform some tasks which seem impossible for human beings. It may outperform humans in some dangerous situations precisely because they are not human. For instance, in a nuclear or chemical warfare, and also in some hazardous environment, in out space, in deep sea bed. They may perform better than humans in the environments where a human combatant may act out of fear or rage.

Thirdly, so much automation has already been integrated into weapons design that banning lethal autonomous weapons seems akin to stopping the development of warfare itself—a practical impossibility. Autonomous weapons have already been accepted into warfare" because modern society has accepted " warfare as a video game. So it's crucial to remember that autonomous weapons technology is an evolving field. Future research and development may make it possible to encode machines with capacities for qualitative judgment that are not possible today. Future technological advancements might allow autonomous weapons to outperform human beings in battlefield situations.

History has showed that a total ban, even if instituted, would likely be ineffective and could not stop the development of new weapons based on new technology and new warfare. For instance, using crossbows was banned by Pope Urban II in 1096; a prohibition that was upheld by Pope Innocent II in 1139. The rebellion forces ignored this ban and used crossbows to defeat the forces of Emperor Frederick II at the Battle of Parma in 1248. In fact, the Holy Roman Emperor was so angry by the violation of the ban. He reportedly ordered his men to cut off the fingers of all crossbowmen captured. Even so, it did not stop the use of crossbows in the battlefields.

Another example is the effort made throughout the 1920s on the limitation of naval armament, when the world's popular mood was peace and disarmament. Treaty for the Limitation of Naval Armament, the Four Power Act (US, UK, France, Italy), the Five Power Treaty (plus Japan) which were to limit the tonnage of warships of big powers, were signed between four or five naval powers. The treaties came into effect as the result of the Washington Disarmament Conference, held by the US in 1921-22. A ten-year agreement fixed the ratio of battleships at 5: 5: 3—that is 525 000 tons for the USA, 525 000 tons for Britain, and 315 000 tons for Japan. During the Second World War, none of those naval powers adhered to the obligation of those treaties and scrambled to have larger warships to gain the superior over the naval warfare in the Second World War.

3. 3 Regulation

Article 35 (1) of the Additional Protocol I to the Geneva Conventions states that "In any armed conflict, the right of the Parties to the conflict to choose methods or means of warfare is not unlimited".

If autonomous weapons systems under effective regulation can prevent mass civilian bloodshed while minimizing collateral damage, they deserve serious consideration as a legitimate technology to be employed during conflict and war.

If the development of fully autonomous lethal weapons would be outlawed—but remote-controlled killing machines, cruise missiles, and other weapons with various levels of automation would not since they have already been in use. In that situation, how could the international community be certain that a remotely controlled weapon deployed in conflict was not entirely controlled by an artificial agent? A weapon's interface need not change according to whether the agent that controls it is human or artificial. And humans could oversee a weapon's actions in either case. But in one case a human would make targeting decisions and in the other case an artificial intelligence would do so.

This is one reason people prefer strong regulation of autonomous weapons over an outright ban on the technology. Regulation would provide the tools necessary for analyzing and understanding increased automation in warfare. It would imply constraints on the development and use of autonomous weapons. And it would strike a blow against dehumanized killing and state—sponsored assassination.

Some states believe that the existing legal regimes are good enough. For instance, the UK Foreign Office, has stated that " [w] e do not see the need for a prohibition" on lethal autonomous weapons because "international humanitarian law already provides sufficient regulation for this area. "

There is no feasible way to ensure that autonomous weapons will never be built. A ban on their development would simply be an invitation to create underground laboratories, which would make it impossible to control the weapons or hold accountable the entities that developed them. What's feasible—through effective international regulation—is to ensure that development of autonomous weapons is analyzed and tracked on a case–by–case basis. Strict rules would govern autonomous weapons' targets, and deployment of the weapons would have to accord with international humanitarian law—if accordance proved impossible, the weapons would never be deployed in the field. Finally, a system must be established for holding accountable any organization that, in creating and deploying autonomous weapons, fails to abide by the regulations that govern them. With or without a ban, effective international legislation is required.

4. Applicable law on new weapons

Article 36 of the Additional Protocol I to the Geneva Conventions of 12 August, 1949, stipulates the application and adoption of new weapons. It says that:

"In the study, development, acquisition or adoption of a new weapon, means or method of warfare, a High Contracting Party is under an obligation to determine whether its employment would, in some or all circumstances, be prohibited by this Protocol or by any other rule of international law applicable to the High Contracting Party. "

Article 36 of Additional Protocol I does not specify in what manner and under what authority reviews of the legality of new weapons are to be constituted. It is the responsibility of each State to adopt legislative, administrative, regulatory and the term "weapon, means or method of warfare" is not defined. A reasonable interpretation has therefore to be applied. Deciding whether an item of equipment is a weapon will be a relatively straightforward process. The term connotes an offensive capability that can be applied to a military object or enemy combatant. Where greater difficulty arises is in defining the term "means or method of warfare". It has been suggested that "method of warfare" is usually understood to mean the way in which weapons are used.

In that way they will include those items of equipment, such as UMS which, whilst they do not constitute a weapon as such, nonetheless have a direct impact on the offensive capability of the force to which they belong. Communications provide a good example of the manner in which the terms in Article 36 can be applied in the face of emerging technologies. Not only do they pass information, they have the capacity to collate, analyses, disseminate, store, retrieve and display information produced in preparation for and in the prosecution of military operations. In considering the compliance of the weapons, methods or means of warfare should also in conformity with a State's legal obligations under international law. The balance must be ensured between military necessity on the one hand and the level of suffering on the other. This is generally referred to as the principle of proportionality. In considering the criteria this balance is paramount. It will impact upon the types of evidence required to conduct a legal review.

In addition, with regard to autonomous weapon systems, reviews should take into account whether the system can comply with other rules relating to the conduct of warfare.

4. 1 Treaty obligations

It is submitted that the principles of international humanitarian law should be applicable to any new weaponry in naval warfare. The principle of humanity, the principle of distinction, the principle of proportionality and the principle of necessary are the basic principles of international humanitarian law. All those principles are embodied in the Hague Conventions and Geneva Conventions and two additional protocols. There are currently 196 countries party to the 1949 Geneva Conventions, including this and the other three treaties. In 1993, the United Nations Security Council adopted a report from the Secretary−General and a Commission of Experts which concluded that the Geneva Conventions had passed into the body of customary international law, thus making them binding on non−signatories to the Conventions whenever they engage in armed conflicts.

In practice, whether new weaponry could be used in compliant with the international humanitarian law depends on the existence of an international treaty prohibiting or limiting the usage of such weaponry. This is also a matter of consideration when conducting review procedure in accordance with the Article 36 of the Additional Protocol I to the Geneva Conventions. As mentioned above, it should be in consistent with the Hague legal systems, Geneva Conventions and other international treaties on the naval warfare. It will necessarily involve an assessment of the restrictions that a treaty may place on types of weapons, as well as prohibitions. The imposition of restrictions will make legal advice necessary on how they might affect the legality of the weapon per se or its intended employment.

Article 35 (2) of the Additional Protocol I to the Geneva Conventions states " it is prohibited to employ weapons, projectiles and material and methods of warfare of a nature to cause superfluous injury or unnecessary suffering. " This is the basic humanitarian law consideration.

Paragraph 3 stipulates that "it is prohibited to employ methods or means of warfare which are intended, or may be expected, to cause widespread, long—term and severe damage to the natural environment". The severe damage to environment has been embodied in the ICC Statute as a war crime.

Geneva Conventions also prohibit employing indiscriminate weapons, means and methods of warfare (i. e. weapons, means and methods of warfare of a nature to strike military objectives and civilians or civilian objects without distinction).

However, it is difficult to see how effective this method is. First, as it is known to all, a treaty only has the binding force upon the contracting party. There is no treaty obligation upon the third parties. If a big power remains outside the treaty regime, there is nothing to do with it. For instance, the Convention on Cluster Munitions (CCM) came into force on 1 August 2010[1], and Convention on the Prohibition of the Use, Stockpiling, Production and Transfer of Anti—Personnel Mines and on their Destruction (Anti – Personnel Mines Convention)[2] has 162 contracting state parties. However, the main states which produce and employ those weapons are not contracting parties. Second, some contracting parties made reservations on the certain treaties, which will reduce the effectiveness of the treaty. Third, even if there is a treaty prohibiting using of certain weapons, the contracting parties is always to circumvent the obligations.

4. 2 Customary international law

In order to solve the problem of treaty obligation, it is necessary to consider the customary international law which is international custom, as evidence of general practice of law found in Article 38 of the Statute of International Court of Justice and adopted by nearly every state in the world. Judge Read in Fisheries case pointed out "Customary international law is the generalization of the practice of States. "[3] If a

---

[1]   United Nations, Treaty Series, Vol. 2688, p. 39;

[2]   The Convention came into force on March 1, 1999. United Nations, Treaty Series, Vol. 2056, p. 211.

[3]   Fisheries Case ICJ Reports, (1951).

norm has become a rule of international customary law, no matter whether a State is a contracting party to a particular treaty enshrined of the norm, the State has to respect the rule. For instance, Common Article 3 of Geneva Conventions has become a rule of international customary law. Even if a State is not a contracting party to the Geneva Conventions, it has to implement this Article. If a weapons has the mass destruction nature, which is a nuclear, radiological, chemical, biological or other weapon that can kill and bring significant harm to a large number of humans or cause great damage to human—made structures, natural structures, or the biosphere, all the state should refrain from employ and use those weapons, regardless of whether they are a contracting parties to a convention.

The principle of humanity is the fundamental principle which should be adhered in any armed conflicts, especially in naval warfare. It includes, but not limited to, the following concepts: In any military attacks, it should not cause excessive damages. All the parties to the conflict should not employ weapons which could cause superfluous injury or unnecessary suffering or large scaled massive destruction. Attacking medical, religious or wounded facilities and persons and UN peace keepers should be forbidden as well as personal or facilities of humanitarian assistance. In the naval warfare, medical ship should no be attacked and wounded, sick and shipwrecked members of armed forces at sea as well of prisoners of war should be well treated. Any attack from the sea should not be directed against religious, educational, artist, science or charity facilities and kindergartens and hospitals. In any circumstance, nuclear facilities and dams should not be the target of the military attack.

As for the principle of distinction, there are two dimensions: personal dimension and material dimension. For the personal dimension, civilian and combatant should be distinct. As for material dimension, there should be a distinction of civilian object and military target.

Additional Protocol I of the Geneva Convention provides traditional criteria for combatants: being commanded by a person responsible for his subordinates; having a fixed distinctive emblem recognizable at a distance; carrying arms openly; and conducting their operations in accordance with the laws and customs of war. Combatants enjoy some privilege. They have the right to participate directly in hostilities'. They should not be prosecuted for killing the adversaries at the battlefield and they are entitled to be treated as prisoner of war. Civilians are those people who do "not take an active part in armed conflict". The protection of the civilian population was governed by The Fourth Geneva Convention.

The Geneva Convention defines Civilians as those who are not combatants, which does no help us a lot. Additional Protocol II stipulates that civilians lose their protection unless and for such time as they take a direct part in hostilities.

When there is a difficult to distinguish combatants and civilians, Presumptions should be in benefit of civilians.

It is submitted that this criterion is still applicable in modern warfare. Although the drone controller or cyber programmer in cyber warfare is not the personal in military sections, so long as they take an active part in armed conflict, they lose the protection as civilians. However, they will enjoy the combatant privilege, since civilian and combatants are mutually exclusive. They are civilians or combatants. There should be no category of the persons between the two.

The purpose of the principle of proportionality is to reduce incidental damage by military operation by balancing the conflicting military and humanitarian interest.

In any armed conflicts, collateral damage is inevitable, but it should be reduced to minimum. This principle implies the obligation for precaution, which means that before any military attack, the commander should be cautious enough, not only to distinguish the targets are civilian or military, but also assess the possible collateral damage, so as to avoid indiscriminate attack.

Principle of Military Necessity requires that no action may be taken which is not military necessary. As early as in 1863, the lieber Code states that "Those measures which are indispensable for securing the ends of the war, and which are lawful according to the modern laws and usages of war". The using of forces should be regulated by the necessity to achieve as quickly as possible the partial or complete submission of the adversary and the forces used should not be greater than needed to achieve the military goals. Anyway, there should be a proper balance between military necessity and humanitarian consideration.

5. Conclusion

It seems unrealistic to have a total ban on the LAW and UMV, since the development of the new technology will inevitably influence the weaponry used in the battlefields and ways and method to engage in armed conflict. The regulation of new weaponry seems to be the most feasible approach. There must be some minimum criteria for the newly created weaponry to enter into the battlefields and to be employed in the armed forces. If those weapons could exercise appropriate levels of human judgment over the use of force and demonstrates human—level intelligence suitable for information gathering, analysis, prediction, diagnosis, balancing the interest, problem solving, decision making, and if they could take all feasible precautions to avoid, and in any event to minimize, incidental loss of civilian life or damage to civilian objects, and with the ability to comply the above mentioned treaty obligations and basic principle of international humanitarian law, there is no reason to have a total ban on those weapons and means of warfare.

THE UPDATED ICRC COMMENTARY ON THE SECOND GENEVA CONVENTION: DEMYSTIFYING THE LAW OF ARMED CONFLICT AT SEA

Bruno Demeyere, Jean–Marie Henckaerts, Heleen Hiemstra and Ellen Nohle *

1. A contemporary interpretation of humanitarian law

The 1949 Geneva Conventions and their 1977 Additional Protocols have passed the test of time in many situations of armed conflict over their respective almost seventy and forty years of applicability. They still constitute the bedrock of international humanitarian law (IHL) and provide fundamental rules protecting persons who are not, or are no longer, taking a direct part in hostilities. These persons include wounded and sick members of armed forces, the shipwrecked, prisoners of war, and civilians. Furthermore, the Conventions foresee the protection of specific categories of persons, such as women and children, the elderly and displaced persons.

In the years following the adoption of the 1949 Geneva Conventions and their 1977 Additional Protocols, the International Committee of the Red Cross (ICRC) published a series of Commentaries that were primarily based on the negotiating his-

* Bruno Demeyere, Jean–Marie Henckaerts and Ellen Nohle are Legal Advisers in the Commentaries Update Unit in the Legal Division of the ICRC, and Heleen Hiemstra is an Associate in this Unit. The authors wish to acknowledge that this article summarizes the key findings of the new Commentary and as such reflects the input of many experts involved in the drafting and review of the Commentary.

tories of these treaties and on prior practice. [1] While these Commentaries undoubtedly retain their historic value, the ICRC decided in 2011 to embark, together with a
number of renowned external experts, on an ambitious project to update the Commentaries, seeking to reflect the significant developments in the application and interpretation of the Conventions and their Additional Protocols in the intervening
years.

The updated Commentaries preserve the format of the original Commentaries,
providing an article—by—article analysis of each of the provisions of the Conventions
and Additional Protocols. Benefiting from decades of practice and legal interpretation
by States (as reflected, for example, in military manuals, national legislation and
official statements), courts and scholars, as well as from research done in the ICRC
Archives (reflecting practices witnessed first—hand by the ICRC in past armed conflicts), however, they do so in a more detailed manner than the original Commentaries. The new Commentaries not only include the ICRC's current interpretations of the
law where they exist, but also indicate where there are divergent views and highlight
issues not yet settled.

To achieve this level of detail and nuance, an elaborate drafting process was put
in place. Besides authoring updated commentaries to one or more articles of the Second Geneva Convention (GC II), contributors (consisting of ICRC staff lawyers
and, importantly, external authors) also read and commented on drafts of updated
commentaries on other provisions. Additionally, an Editorial Committee including

---

[1]   See Jean Pictet (ed.), *Commentary on the Geneva Conventions of 12 August 1949*, Vol. 1: *Geneva
Convention for the Amelioration of the Condition of the Wounded and Sick in Armed Forces in the Field*, ICRC,
Geneva, 1952; Jean Pictet (ed.), *Commentary on the Geneva Conventions of 12 August 1949*, Vol. 2: *Geneva
Convention for the Amelioration of the Condition of Wounded, Sick and Shipwrecked Members of Armed Forces at
Sea*, ICRC, Geneva, 1960; Jean Pictet (ed.), *Commentary on the Geneva Conventions of 12 August 1949*,
Vol. 3: *Geneva Convention relative to the Treatment of Prisoners of War*, ICRC, Geneva, 1960; Jean Pictet
(ed.), *Commentary on the Geneva Conventions of 12 August 1949*, Vol. 4: *Geneva Convention relative to the Pro-
tection of Civilian Persons in Time of War*, ICRC, Geneva, 1958; Yves Sandoz, Christophe Swinarski and Bruno
Zimmermann (eds), *Commentary on the Additional Protocols*, ICRC, Geneva, 1987.

senior ICRC and non-ICRC lawyers reviewed the updated Commentary on GC II as a whole. [2] Finally, a group of over forty peer reviewers representing a large geographic diversity and with significant subject-matter expertise, including naval experts, provided insightful comments and suggestions, greatly contributing to the richness of the analysis found in the final product. After the completion of the updated Commentary on the First Geneva Convention (GC I) in March 2016, the online launch of the updated Commentary on GC II on 4 May 2017 constituted the second milestone of this important project. [3]

The authors of the updated Commentary on GC II followed the same methodology as used for the updated Commentary on GC I. They used the rules of treaty interpretation set out in the Vienna Convention of the Law of Treaties, in particular Articles 31-33, to reflect as accurately as possible the current application and interpretation of GC II. The contributors looked at the ordinary meaning of the terms used in the provisions, their context, the object and purpose of the treaty, and the preparatory work. Additionally, the authors looked at other relevant rules of international law. Since GC II was drafted, many other relevant branches of international law, such as international human rights law and international criminal law, have developed significantly. It is of particular relevance to the topic of armed conflict at sea to assess the impact of the 1982 UN Convention on the Law of the Sea (UNCLOS)[4] as well as a series of treaties adopted under the auspices of the International Maritime Organization (IMO), conferring protection to persons in distress at sea. A treaty must be "interpreted and applied within the framework of the entire legal system pre-

---

[2] The Editorial Committee for the updated Commentary on the Second Geneva Convention consists of Liesbeth Lijnzaad and Marco Sassòli as non-ICRC members, and Philip Spoerri and Knut Dörmann as ICRC members.

[3] The full version is available online at: ihl-databases. icrc. org/ihl/full/GCII-commentary (all internet references were accessed in July 2017). A hard copy of the updated Commentary on the Second Geneva Convention will be published by Cambridge University Press by January 2018.

[4] United Nations Convention on the Law of the Sea, 1833 UNTS 3, 10 December 1982 (entered into force 16 November 1994) (UNCLOS).

vailing at the time of the interpretation". [5] The updated Commentary therefore takes account of how these other fields of law have developed over time, and makes reference to them where relevant.

After this brief overview of the background, scope and methodology of the project to update the Commentaries, [6] this article first situates GC II in its historical context, before addressing the applicability of the Convention and its relationship to other sources of international law. It further describes some of the commonalities and differences between GC I and GC II and their updated Commentaries, as well as highlighting some of the main issues dealt with in the updated Commentary on GC II, including the obligation of parties to an armed conflict to take all possible measures to search for and collect the wounded, sick, shipwrecked and dead at sea, as well as the rules in GC II regulating the protection of hospital ships and coastal rescue craft.

2. Historical background of the Second Geneva Convention[7]

Naval battles have been fought for several thousand years. Yet, when the first Geneva Convention of 1864 was adopted, conferring protection on wounded and sick members of the armed forces, its rules only applied to warfare on land. The eventual inclusion of victims of warfare at sea in humanitarian treaty law was achieved only several decades later through a separate treaty on warfare at sea. [8] The distinction thus established in the protection of victims of armed conflict between warfare on land

---

[5] International Court of Justice, *Advisory Opinion on the Legal Consequences for States of the Continued Presence of South Africa in Namibia (The Namibia Case)*, 21 June 1971, para. 53.

[6] For a more detailed description, see the introduction to the updated Commentary: ICRC, *Commentary on the Second Geneva Convention*, Cambridge University Press, 2017 (ICRC Commentary on GC II), paras 1–66. See also Lindsey Cameron, Bruno Demeyere, Jean-Marie Henckaerts, Eve La Haye and Heike Niebergall-Lackner, "The Updated Commentary on the First Geneva Convention-A New Tool for Generating Respect for International Humanitarian Law", *International Review of the Red Cross*, Vol. 97, No. 900, 2015, pp. 1210–1214; Jean-Marie Henckaerts, "Bringing the Commentaries on the Geneva Conventions and their Additional Protocols into the Twenty-First Century", *International Review of the Red Cross*, Vol. 94, No. 888, 2012.

[7] See ICRC Commentary on GC II, above note 6, Introduction, paras. 79–96.

[8] Hague Convention (III) for the Adaptation to Maritime Warfare of the Principles of the Geneva Convention of 22 August 1864, 29 July 1899 (entered into force 4 September 1900).

and warfare at sea was maintained in 1949 by the adoption of two different Conventions to apply on land and at sea respectively.

The Geneva Convention of 1864 embodied the principle that members of the armed forces who are *hors de combat* must be protected and cared for regardless of their nationality. It would take roughly forty years before States were ready to extend this principle to armed forces at sea. A proposal by the ICRC to include a paragraph in the 1864 Convention stipulating that similar provisions relating to maritime warfare "could be subject of a later Convention" never made it into the final text. [9] Two years later, the Battle of Lissa (1866) in the Adriatic Sea once more reminded States of the need to provide for the protection of wounded, sick, shipwrecked and dead members of the armed forces at sea. [10] Prompted by the needless deaths caused by the lack of care and protection for the sick, wounded and shipwrecked during that battle, a conference in 1868 adopted fifteen "Additional Articles relating to the Conditions of the Wounded in War". These articles addressed issues such as the protection of boats that collect the shipwrecked and wounded, hospital ships and the status of medical personnel. However, the reticence of the major naval powers prevented these articles from entering into force. [11]

In line with the ICRC's repeated calls to adapt the 1864 Geneva Convention to the conditions of warfare at sea, the First Hague Peace Conference of 1899 adopted Hague Convention III, drawing inspiration from the Additional Articles of 1868. Hague Convention III, which entered into force in 1900, was the first treaty to

---

[9]   Article 11 of the draft submitted by the Comité International de Secours aux Militaires Blessés to the 1864 Conference, available in the ICRC Archives under ACICR, A AF 21-3b.

[10]   Pierre Boissier, *History of the International Committee of the Red Cross: From Solferino to Tsushima*, ICRC and Henry Dunant Institute, Geneva, 1985, pp. 190-192.

[11]   ICRC Commentary on GC II, above note 6, Introduction, para. 84. For an overview of the preparation of and debates during and after the 1868 Diplomatic Conference, see P. Boissier, above note 10, pp. 215-225; J. Galloy, *L'inviolabilité des navires-hôpitaux et l'expérience de la guerre 1914-1918*, Sirey, Paris, 1931, pp. 30-47; Christophe Lueder, *La Convention de Genève au point de vue historique, critique et dogmatique*, E. Besold, Erlangen, 1876, pp. 159-198; J. Pictet (ed.), *Commentary on the Second Geneva Convention*, above note 1, pp. 5-10.

protect victims of armed conflict at sea. [12] It was revised in 1907 in light of the new Geneva Convention of 1906 governing land warfare, resulting in the 1907 Hague Convention X on maritime warfare. [13] This convention would remain the governing treaty for the protection of members of armed forces at sea until the adoption of GC II in 1949.

At the International Conference of the Red Cross in 1934, the ICRC was given a mandate to convene a Commission of Experts "to consider in what respect the modification of the Hague Convention of 1907 would appear to be desirable and possible". [14] Convened in Geneva in 1937, the Commission adopted a Draft Revised Maritime Convention, to be considered for adoption by States at the next Diplomatic Conference. [15] Owing to the outbreak of the Second World War, the Diplomatic Conference foreseen for 1940 never took place. After the end of that war, the 1937 Draft Convention served as a basis for the drafting of the Second Geneva Convention of 1949. The revisions made in the years leading up to 1949 were heavily influenced by the experience of the Second World War, which was unparalleled in scope and in the suffering and casualties caused among both combatants and civilians. [16]

---

[12] ICRC Commentary on GC II, above note 6, Introduction, para. 86. For more details, see *Proceedings of the Hague Peace Conferences: The Conference of* 1899, Oxford University Press, Oxford, 1920, pp. 31-44.

[13] ICRC Commentary on GC II, above note 6, Introduction, para. 88. For more details, see *Proceedings of the Hague Peace Conferences: The Conference of* 1907, Vol. 3, Oxford University Press, Oxford, 1920, pp. 305-322. See also J. Galloy, above note 11, pp. 70-90.

[14] ICRC Commentary on GC II, above note 6, Introduction, para. 91. For the full text of that resolution, see *Report Concerning the Revision of the Tenth Hague Convention of* 1907 *for the Adaptation to Maritime Warfare of the Principles of the Geneva Convention of* 1906, 1937, adopted by a Commission of Naval Experts and presented to the 16th International Conference of the Red Cross, London, June 1938 (Document No. 2a) (Naval Expert Report), p. 1, available at: https://library.icrc.org/library/docs/ CDDH/CI_ 1938/CI_ 1938_ DOC02_ ENG. pdf.

[15] ICRC Commentary on GC II, above note 6, Introduction, para. 91. For a detailed overview of all the steps that were undertaken, see Naval Expert Report, above note 14, pp. 1-8.

[16] ICRC Commentary on GC II, above note 6, Introduction, paras. 76, 92.

3. Applicability of the Second Geneva Convention and relationship to other sources of international law

GC II applies in the first place in case of an international armed conflict that takes place wholly or partly at sea. [17] Pursuant to Article 3 common to the four Geneva Conventions, fundamental protections also apply in the event of a non-international armed conflict at sea. While the meaning of the term "sea" is central to determining the applicability of GC II, the latter does not contain a definition of this term. It is commonly understood that the term "sea" is used to distinguish the scope of application of GC II from that of GC I, which applies on land. To avoid a protection gap between the two Conventions, the term "sea" should be interpreted broadly. Thus, for the purpose of determining who deserves the protection of GC II, the term "sea" comprises not only saltwater areas such as the high seas, exclusive economic zones, archipelagic waters, territorial waters and internal waters, but also other bodies of water such as lakes and rivers. [18]

Once wounded, sick and shipwrecked members of the armed forces are put ashore, GC II ceases to apply and these persons immediately benefit from protection under GC I. [19] This principle applies regardless of which "branch" of the armed forces a person belongs to: a member of the air force who is shipwrecked at sea is protected by GC II, as much as a member of the navy who is wounded on land is protected by GC I.

Although persons cannot be simultaneously protected under GC I and GC II, they can benefit from the parallel application of GC II and the Third Convention (GC III). When wounded, sick or shipwrecked members of the armed forces are cared for by enemy medical personnel or on hospital ships of the enemy force, they "fall

---

[17]   *Ibid.*, Art. 4, paras. 935-936.

[18]   *Ibid.*, Art. 12, paras. 1374-1376.

[19]   Geneva Convention (II) for the Amelioration of the Condition of Wounded, Sick and Shipwrecked Members of Armed Forces at Sea of 12 August 1949, 75 UNTS 85 (entered into force 21 October 1950) (GC II), Art. 4.

into enemy hands" and thus become prisoners of war, protected under GC III. [20] Until their recovery, and as long as they remain at sea, they continue to be protected under both GC II and GC III. Wounded and sick prisoners of war who are put ashore are protected simultaneously by GC I and GC III. Once they are recovered, they remain protected under GC III until their final release and repatriation. [21]

Provisions of the Fourth Convention (GC IV) are also relevant in the event of an armed conflict at sea, for the protection of wounded, sick and shipwrecked civilians. GC IV requires, for example, that parties to the conflict assist the shipwrecked and protect them against pillage and ill−treatment, as far as military considerations allow. [22] It also mandates the respect and protection of specially provided vessels on sea used to transport wounded and sick civilians, the infirm and maternity cases. [23]

Moreover, Additional Protocol I, applicable to international armed conflicts, supplements GC II. It provides several definitions relevant to the wounded, sick and shipwrecked at sea. [24] The Protocol also extends the protection of GC II to all civilians who are wounded, sick or shipwrecked, [25] and to other medical ships and craft than those mentioned in GC II. [26] Additional Protocol II, applicable to non−international armed conflicts, complements the provisions of Article 3 of GC II. For example, it prescribes the search for and collection of the wounded, sick and shipw-

---

[20] *Ibid.*, Art. 16.

[21] See ICRC Commentary on GC II, above note 6, Art. 16, para. 1577.

[22] Geneva Convention (IV) relative to the Protection of Civilian Persons in Time of War of 12 August 1949, 75 UNTS 287 (entered into force 21 October 1950), Art. 16.

[23] *Ibid.*, Art. 21.

[24] Protocol Additional (I) to the Geneva Conventions of 12 August 1949, and relating to the Protection of Victims of International Armed Conflicts, 1125 UNTS 3, 8 June 1977 (entered into force 7 December 1978), Art. 8.

[25] Geneva Convention (I) for the Amelioration of the Condition of the Wounded and Sick in Armed Forces in the Field of 12 August 1949, 75 UNTS 31 (entered into force 21 October 1950) (GC I), Art. 22.

[26] *Ibid.*, Art. 23.

recked, and their protection against pillage and ill-treatment. [27]

Finally, it should be mentioned that customary humanitarian law also applies to warfare at sea. In this regard, special mention must be made of the 1994 *San Remo Manual on International Law Applicable to Armed Conflicts at Sea* (San Remo Manual), [28] which, in its own words, is a "contemporary restatement – together with some progressive development – of the law applicable to armed conflicts at sea" and which "has been drafted by an international group of specialists in international law and naval experts". At the time of writing this Commentary, the San Remo Manual is, for the most part, still a valid restatement of customary and treaty international law applicable to armed conflicts at sea. It has been argued, however, that it may be time to consider updating parts of the Manual. [29]

In parallel to these IHL sources, GC II also interacts with other sources of international law regulating activities at sea. This includes the 1982 UNCLOS. The outbreak of an armed conflict at sea does not terminate or suspend the applicability of most provisions of UNCLOS; they remain in operation and apply simultaneously to GC II during an armed conflict. [30] This complementarity is reflected in the updated Commentary on GC II. The term "warship", for example, used several times in GC II, must be interpreted based on the definition provided for in Article 29 of UNCLOS. [31]

There are also a number of treaties adopted under the auspices of the IMO, in

---

[27]   *Ibid.*, Art. 8.

[28]   Louise Doswald-Beck (ed.), *San Remo Manual on International Law Applicable to Armed Conflicts at Sea*, Cambridge University Press, Cambridge, 1995.

[29]   For further details, see ICRC Commentary on GC II, above note 6, Introduction, para. 115.

[30]   *Ibid.*, para. 48. Some UNCLOS provisions are exercised "subject to this Convention and to other rules of international law"; see e. g. Art. 2 (3). This includes GC II, and it is thus possible that the applicability of individual UNCLOS rules that include such a clause is temporarily suspended. ICRC Commentary on GC II, above note 6, Introduction, para. 49.

[31]   *Ibid.*, Art. 14, para. 1520.

particular the Safety of Life at Sea Convention[32] and the Maritime Search and Rescue Convention. [33] With regard to those IMO treaties that do not expressly limit their scope of application by exempting warships, the question arises to what extent and how they apply during an armed conflict that takes place wholly or partly at sea. No clear answer to this question currently exists. Arguably, these IMO treaties are "multilateral law – making treaties" that, based on the International Law Commission's 2011 Draft Articles on the Effect of Armed Conflicts on Treaties,[34] belong to the categories of treaties that may remain in operation during armed conflict, also when this takes place at sea. [35]

3. 1 Commonalities and differences between the First and Second Geneva Conventions

GC II seeks to protect the wounded, sick and shipwrecked members of the armed forces at sea. Similar to the other Geneva Conventions, this is premised on the fundamental principle of respect for the life and dignity of the individual, even, or especially, during armed conflict. This means that victims of armed conflict must in all circumstances be respected and protected; they must be treated humanely and cared for without any adverse distinction based on sex, race, nationality, religion, political opinion or any other similar criteria. [36]

Certain articles common to all four Geneva Conventions are central to the application of the Conventions and to the protections provided therein. For example, common Article 1 deals with the obligation to respect and ensure respect for the Conven-

---

[32] International Convention for the Safety of Life at Sea, 1874 UNTS 3, 1 November 1974 (entered into force 25 May 1980).

[33] International Convention on Maritime Search and Rescue, 1403 UNTS, 27 April 1979 (entered into force 22 June 1985).

[34] United Nations, International Law Commission, Report of the International Law Commission on the Work of Its Sixty–Third Session, *Yearbook of the International Law Commission*, Vol. 2, Part 2, A/66/ 10, 2011.

[35] See ICRC Commentary on GC II, above note 6, Introduction, paras. 51–59.

[36] *Ibid.*, Art. 12, paras. 1417–1424, 1437–1441.

tions in all circumstances. Common Articles 2 and 3 deal with the scope of application of the Conventions, respectively for international and for non – international armed conflicts. The updated Commentary on GC I was an important milestone partly because it included updated commentaries on these articles common to all four Conventions. Nevertheless, even for these common articles, the different contexts to which the Conventions apply have warranted some contextualization in the updated Commentary on GC II, dealing with warfare at sea.

3.2 Contextualization of the updated commentaries on the common articles

Contextualization was sometimes prompted by the existence of complementary rules of international law, outside of IHL, that regulate activities at sea. For example, the updated commentary on Article 2 of GC I notes that the threshold to trigger an international armed conflict is low: "Even minor skirmishes between the armed forces, be they land, air or naval forces, would spark an international armed conflict and lead to the applicability of humanitarian law. "[37] This means that any armed interference in a State's sphere or sovereignty, be it on land, in the air or at sea, may constitute an international armed conflict within the meaning of Article 2. [38] This passage is maintained in the updated commentary on Article 2 of GC II. However, it is elaborated that UNCLOS foresees the innocent passage of foreign ships in the territorial sea of another State, which may include warships. The updated Commentary specifies that such passage does not constitute an international armed conflict. [39]

Some contextualization was also necessary in the updated commentary on common Article 3, regulating non–international armed conflict. The fact that GC II applies at sea entails some practical challenges and raises questions as to how certain

---

[37]   ICRC, *Commentary on the First Geneva Convention*, Cambridge University Press, Cambridge, 2016, Art. 2, para. 237.

[38]   ICRC Commentary on GC II, above note 6, Art. 2, para. 259.

[39]   *Ibid.*

provisions are to be applied. For example, one of the questions the updated Commentary addresses is whether detention in the context of a non-international armed conflict can take place at sea. [40] Article 22 of GC III requires prisoners of war to be interned on land. This applies in international armed conflict, whereas for non-international armed conflict, there is no rule that specifically addresses this issue. However, the updated commentary on Article 3 concludes that, in principle, detention in a non-international armed conflict should also take place on land. [41] Indeed, "the entire system of detention laid down by the Conventions, and in which the ICRC plays a supervisory role, is based on the idea that detainees must be registered and held in officially recognized places of detention accessible, in particular, to the ICRC". [42] Furthermore, if detention in the context of a non-international armed conflict were to take place at sea, the conditions of such detention might be such as to violate the requirement of humane treatment, particularly in cases of prolonged detention. [43]

A further example where the different contexts of warfare on land and warfare at sea warranted the updated commentary on common Article 3 to be contextualized for GC II relates to the right to a fair trial. Common Article 3 prohibits "the passing of sentences and the carrying out of executions without previous judgments pronounced by a regularly constituted court, affording all the judicial guarantees which are recognized as indispensable by civilized peoples". [44] In practice, it seems highly unlikely that a trial at sea can fulfill the minimum fair trial guarantees. To stand trial, therefore, persons would normally have to be transferred to land. [45] Still, the cir-

---

[40] *Ibid.*, Art. 3, para. 741.

[41] *Ibid.*

[42] Jelena Pejic, "Procedural Principles and Safeguards for Internment/Administrative Detention in Armed Conflict and other Situations of Violence", *International Review of the Red Cross*, Vol. 87, No. 858, 2005, p. 385. See also ICRC Commentary on GC II, above note 6, Art. 3, para. 741.

[43] ICRC Commentary on GC II, above note 6, Art. 3, para. 580.

[44] Common Art. 3 to the Geneva Conventions.

[45] ICRC Commentary on GC II, above note 6, Art. 3, para. 696.

cumstances of being at sea may be relevant when assessing the more specific rights stemming from the right to a fair trial. More concretely, for example, the right to be tried within a reasonable time, which is also pertinent in the context of a non-international armed conflict, may require taking into consideration the exceptional circumstances of being at sea. [46]

3. 3 Protection of the shipwrecked

While the basic protection provided for in both Conventions is the same, the scope of persons covered by that protection in GC II is adapted to warfare at sea. The Convention protects not only the wounded and sick, but also the shipwrecked. Thus, the text of common Article 3 is worded slightly differently in GC II compared to the other three Conventions, and this has been reflected in the updated Commentary. [47] Whereas in GC I, GC III and GC IV reference is made only to the "wounded and sick", GC II consistently refers to the "wounded, sick and shipwrecked". For the purpose of common Article 3, a "shipwrecked" person is someone who, as a result of hostilities or their direct effects, is in peril at sea or in other waters and requires rescue. A person would also qualify as shipwrecked where, for example, hostilities adversely affect the ability of those who would normally rescue them to do so in fact. It should be noted that a person in such situations must not commit any hostile acts. [48]

Likewise, Article 12, which establishes the general obligation for States to respect and protect in all circumstances, refers to the "wounded, sick and shipwrecked" in GC II, whereas in GC I it refers only to the "wounded and sick". [49]

3. 4 Protection of hospital ships and coastal rescue craft

Logically, the difference between GC I and GC II also extends to the objects

---

[46]   *Ibid.*, Art. 3, para. 710.

[47]   *Ibid.*, Art. 3, paras. 772-775.

[48]   *Ibid.*, Art. 3, para. 774.

[49]   Note, however, that for legal purposes there is no difference between wounded and sick. *Ibid.*, Art. 12, para. 1378.

that are protected. While ambulances and other land—based medical transports are protected under GC I, [50] medical transports used on water are protected under GC II in equal measure. Recognizing an important means by which its obligations may be implemented, GC II affords protection to hospital ships[51] and coastal rescue craft, [52] as well as to ships chartered for the transport of medical equipment[53] and to medical aircraft. [54]

The operation of hospital ships constitutes one way in which parties to the conflict can carry out their obligation to protect and care for the wounded, sick and shipwrecked at sea. To be able to fulfil this function, hospital ships enjoy special protection "at all times", and they may neither be attacked nor captured. [55] The hospital ship's personnel and crew are likewise accorded special protection, owing to the vital role they play in the ship's performance of its humanitarian functions. [56]

In order to benefit from special protection under GC II, hospital ships must have been "built or equipped...especially and solely with a view to assisting the wounded, sick and shipwrecked, to treating them and to transporting them". [57] It follows that hospital ships may not serve any other than the said humanitarian purpose, and that they lose their protection if they are used to commit acts harmful to the enemy. [58] As noted in the updated commentary on Article 22, it is their exclusively humanitarian function of impartially providing assistance to protected persons that justifies their special protection, [59] but parties to the conflict have the right to control and search

---

[50] GC II, Art. 35.
[51] *Ibid.*, Arts. 22, 24.
[52] *Ibid.*, Art. 27.
[53] *Ibid.*, Art. 38.
[54] *Ibid.*, Art. 39.
[55] *Ibid.*, Art. 22 (1).
[56] *Ibid.*, Art. 36.
[57] *Ibid.*, Art. 22 (1).
[58] *Ibid.*, Art. 34 (1).
[59] ICRC Commentary on GC II, above note 6, Art. 22, para. 1927.

hospital ships to verify that their use conforms to the provisions of GC II. [60] This far–reaching right has been inserted by States into the Geneva Conventions in order to counter the possibility that an enemy's hospital ship may be abused to further military operations.

At present, only a small number of States have military hospital ships, which are not only expensive to operate and maintain but also difficult to protect against attack. [61] The updated commentaries on Articles 33, as well as Articles 18 and 22, point out that one option available to parties seeking to comply with their obligations to respect and protect the shipwrecked, wounded and sick is to transform a merchant vessel into a hospital ship. [62] It is important to note that once a merchant vessel has been transformed into a hospital ship by a party to the conflict, it may not "be put to any other use throughout the duration of hostilities". [63] GC II regulates a variety of aspects pertaining to hospital ships. Two issues in particular have become topical since 1949. First, Article 34 (2) refers, as an example of an "act harmful to the enemy" (which may lead to a loss of protection) , to the requirement that "hospital ships may not possess or use a secret code for their wireless or other means of communication". Thus, in principle, communications to and from hospital ships may never be encrypted, and must be sent in the open. However, due to developments in communication technology, most prominently the use of satellites, encryption is now so common that it is unavoidable as an available technology. As a result, the rule has been challenged in a number of military manuals. This development leads the updated Commentary to conclude that "there is, therefore, a certain trend in international practice whereby the use of satellite communications does not constitute a violation of paragraph 2, even if messages and data are transmitted using encryption". [64]

---

[60]   GC II, Art. 31 (1).

[61]   ICRC Commentary on GC II, above note 6, Art. 22, para. 1928.

[62]   See *ibid.*, para. 1945; Art. 33, para. 2336; Art. 18, para. 1677.

[63]   GC II, Art. 33.

[64]   ICRC Commentary on GC II, above note 6, Art. 34, para. 2403.

The second topical issue pertains to whether hospital ships may be armed, in particular whether they may be armed to the level of being able to defend themselves against incoming attacks (as opposed to relying on other vessels, in particular warships, to defend them). In principle, the arming of hospital ships with weapons other than purely deflective means of defence (such as chaffs and flares) or light individual weapons could be considered an act harmful to the enemy, leading to a loss of protection. [65] Thus, in order to maintain their specially protected status under IHL, the Commentary considers that a party to the conflict may not mount such weapons on a hospital ship. [66]

In addition, GC II affords protection to small craft used by the State or by officially recognized search and rescue organizations. [67] To qualify for protection under Article 27, coastal rescue craft must be employed by a State that is party to the conflict or by lifeboat institutions of a party to the conflict. In the latter case, these institutions must be "officially recognized" for the craft to be protected. This means that the institution in question must have been approved or authorized by a government authority or other public body to perform coastal rescue functions. [68]

Coastal rescue craft have long rendered assistance to those in distress at sea and might be the only vessels available for this purpose to the vast majority of States, which do not have hospital ships. [69] Yet, owing to their small size and speed, at the time of the adoption of GC II, rescue craft were considered difficult to identify and were often suspected of engaging in intelligence—gathering for the enemy. [70] As explained in the updated commentary on Article 27, this generated a reluctance among States to grant them any special protection. The compromise embodied in GC II

---

[65] *Ibid.*, Art. 34, para. 2378.

[66] *Ibid.*, Art. 35, paras. 2419–2421.

[67] GC II, Art. 27.

[68] ICRC Commentary on GC II, above note 6, Art. 27, para. 2194.

[69] *Ibid.*, paras 2149, 2151.

[70] *Ibid.*, Art. 27, paras 2150, 2159.

is to give small craft special protection, but more limited than that afforded to hospital ships. Compared with the eleven articles dedicated to hospital ships, only one deals with coastal rescue craft, namely Article 27.

Coastal rescue craft that satisfy the conditions for protection may not be attacked, captured or otherwise prevented from performing their humanitarian tasks. This protection extends "so far as operational requirements permit". [71] By contrast, the protection afforded to hospital ships is stronger. They "may in no circumstances be attacked or captured, but shall at all times be respected and protected". [72]

Hence, operational considerations by a reasonable commander may justify interference with rescue craft by, *inter alia*, preventing them from performing their humanitarian tasks in a given sea area. Since the reasonableness will, of course, depend on the prevailing circumstances, it is impossible to define the terms in an abstract manner. [73] In this context, it is important to emphasize that this provision cannot be read in isolation from the rules of Additional Protocol I regulating the conduct of hostilities. Thus, coastal rescue craft may only be the object of an attack if they qualify as a "military objective" in the sense of IHL. Finally, there is no mention in GC II of the status of the crew of coastal rescue craft. [74]

With respect to the marking of hospital ships and coastal rescue craft, it is not constitutive of their protection but merely signals their protected status to the parties to the conflict. According to Article 43, all surfaces of the ship or craft shall be white, and one or more dark red crosses shall be displayed on each side of the hull and on the horizontal surfaces. These traditional marking methods, presupposing close physical proximity to allow for visual confirmation of the marking, might not

---

[71] GC II, Art. 27 (1).

[72] *Ibid.*, Art. 22 (1).

[73] See ICRC Commentary on GC II, above note 6, Art. 27, para. 2206.

[74] See *ibid.*, Art. 27, para. 2152, and the commentary on Article 36, Section C. 2. d.

suffice to ensure the proper identification of protected vessels in view of contemporary techniques of naval warfare, such as long—fire and submarine capabilities. It is therefore significant that Article 43 encourages the parties to the conflict to conclude special agreements on the "most modern methods available to facilitate the identification of hospital ships". [75] As noted in the updated commentary on Article 43, there is no reason why such agreements could not also be concluded for coastal rescue craft. [76] Such agreements could be critical to ensure that protected vessels are effectively identified by parties to the conflict and given the protection to which they are entitled in order to be able to carry out their humanitarian work.

4. Substantive obligations under the Second Geneva Convention

Further to the central obligation on the parties to an armed conflict that takes place at sea to respect and protect the wounded, sick and shipwrecked, and to treat them humanely in all circumstances, GC II sets out a number of additional obligations intended to ensure that this core obligation is fulfilled. These include the obligation to take all possible measures to search for and collect the wounded, sick, shipwrecked and dead at sea.

To achieve the protective purpose of GC II, it is paramount that the parties to the armed conflict, after each engagement, take all possible measures to search for and collect casualties. The parties might be the only actors sufficiently close to the victims to search for and collect them. [77] Article 18 thus requires the parties, after each engagement and without delay, to take all possible measures to search for and collect the wounded, sick, shipwrecked and dead at sea, without discriminating between their own and enemy personnel. [78] The good faith interpretation and implementation of this provision is of critical importance in order to achieve the objectives

---

[75]　GC II, Art. 43 (8).

[76]　See ICRC Commentary on GC II, above note 6, Art. 43, para. 2766.

[77]　*Ibid.*, Art. 18, para. 1617.

[78]　*Ibid.*, Art. 18, para. 1618.

of GC II.

The obligation to "take all possible measures" is an obligation of conduct to be carried out with due diligence. [79] All possible measures must be taken "after each engagement" and "without delay". In this respect, Article 18 differs from the parallel provision in GC I, which requires its obligations to be carried out "at all times, and particularly after an engagement". [80] As the updated commentary on Article 18 explains, the different wording reflects the fact that the conditions of warfare at sea, compared to those on land, might make it impossible to carry out search and rescue activities "at all times". [81]

What constitutes "possible measures" in any given case is inherently context-specific. Each organ of the "party to the conflict"-the entity to which the obligation applies-has an obligation, at its own level, to assess in good faith which measures are possible. [82]

Moreover, the updated commentary on Article 18 takes into account the fact that advances in technology and scientific knowledge may influence what measures a party to the conflict can, in practice, take in any given case. Advances in methods of naval warfare since 1949 have resulted in ever longer-distance attack capabilities. A vessel that has launched a weapon from a considerable distance against an enemy warship or aircraft might not be able to implement "without delay" any of the obligations contemplated on the basis of Article 18, since it is not physically present in the vicinity of the casualties. Still, that vessel remains under an obligation to consider what measures are possible in light of the circumstances. This includes considering whether it is possible to take measures such as disclosing the geographic location of the attacked vessel or aircraft with as much precision as possible, not only to its land-based au-

---

[79]　*Ibid.*, Art. 18, para. 1645.

[80]　GC I, Art. 15.

[81]　ICRC Commentary on GC II, above note 6, Art. 18, para. 1653.

[82]　*Ibid.*, Art. 18, paras. 1629-1633.

thorities but also to enemy and neutral vessels or impartial humanitarian organizations capable of conducting search and rescue operations. [83] In this regard, the availability of new technology such as satellites and unmanned aerial platforms can enable a more accurate assessment of the number and location of the shipwrecked, wounded, sick and dead without requiring physical proximity to the attacked vessel or aircraft. [84]

The commentary on Article 18 also describes certain advances in technology and scientific knowledge pertinent to the obligation to search for the dead at sea. There have been considerable developments in underwater technology since 1949 that permit locating and retrieving dead bodies at sea, including remotely operated vehicles with cameras. Moreover, scientific research in marine taphonomy has led to enhanced understanding of the factors that affect human remains in water. The fact that bodies cannot be seen with the naked eye immediately after an engagement no longer means that none can be recovered. [85] The extent to which a party has access to such technology and knowledge may therefore affect the interpretation of the "possible measures" which that party can take in relation to the search for the dead. [86]

The research for the updated Commentary identified a potential dilemma when it comes to the dead at sea: once a warship sinks with enemy members of the armed forces on board, is the enemy still obliged to take all possible measures to search for and collect them? Or does the vessel regain its sovereign immunity, meaning that only the power to which the vessel belongs has the right to retrieve the dead bodies? On this point, the Commentary has reached the conclusion that sunken warships and other ships that sink with their crews constitute war graves, which must be respected. These vessels regain their entitlement to sovereign immunity once they have

---

[83] *Ibid.*, Art. 18, para. 1646.

[84] *Ibid.*, Art. 18, para. 1645.

[85] *Ibid.*, Art. 18, para. 1686.

[86] *Ibid.*, Art. 18, para. 1687.

sunk. [87]

As a measure to comply with both Articles 12 and 18, a party to the conflict "may appeal to the charity" of neutral vessels to help with the rescue effort, as set out in Article 21. The updated commentary on Article 21 notes that, in some situations, the assistance afforded by neutral vessels might be the best or only way of ensuring that as many wounded, sick, shipwrecked or dead persons as possible can be collected. The use of the word "may" in Article 21 implies that making such an appeal is optional. However, there may be cases in which a party may have to make an appeal in order for it to comply with its obligations, such as where it is unable to carry out a rescue itself. [88]

Once collected, the wounded, sick and shipwrecked must receive "adequate care" as soon as possible. [89] This includes providing the medical care and attention required by their condition, as well as other forms of non-medical care, such as provision of food, drinking water, shelter, clothing, and sanitary and hygiene items. The parties are furthermore required to record information that can assist in the identification of the wounded, sick, shipwrecked and dead, and to forward this information to the power on which they depend. This is crucial so that families can be appraised of the fate of their loved ones. Specific obligations pertaining to the dead include respectful and honourable treatment, burial, and respect for their resting place. [90]

With regard to the position of neutral States (i. e., States not party to the international armed conflict), GC II contains a number of provisions regulating their obligations vis-à-vis the persons protected by the Convention. First, when they receive or intern such persons in their territory, they shall apply the provisions of GC II by a-

---

[87] *Ibid.*, Art. 18, para. 1688.

[88] *Ibid.*, Art. 18, para. 1637; Art. 21, para. 1863.

[89] *Ibid.*, Art. 18, paras 1674-1681.

[90] See GC II, Arts. 19 and 20, the latter of which equally deals with burial at sea.

nalogy. [91] Secondly, when such persons are taken on board neutral warships or military aircraft, or are landed in a neutral port with the consent of the local authorities, the Convention stipulates that "where so required by international law" they shall be so guarded that they cannot again take part in operations of war. [92] In view of the scarce and conflicting State practice and literature on this topic, the interpretation of the precise contours of the term "where so required by international law" has proven to be one of the most complex issues the updated Commentary has had to deal with. [93] Undesirable as this may be from the perspective of legal certainty, ultimately, States seem to have retained their freedom of interpretation on this point. [94]

5. Conclusion

Out of the four Geneva Conventions, the Second is the one that probably used to be the least well–known, and that is generally considered to be the most "technical". The updated Commentary on GC II has been written with the benefit of experience and knowledge accrued over the nearly seventy years that have passed since the initial Commentary was published. This experience and knowledge was acquired both in real–life battlefield situations and through the publication of military manuals and scholarly articles. Thus, this Commentary attempts to demystify the Convention's alleged difficulty by filling a critical gap in legal scholarship. By so doing, the updated Commentary provides an important guidance tool for a wide audience, including navies and their commanders and military lawyers, international and national courts, governments and academics.

In comparison with armed conflicts on land, the past decades have not seen many armed conflicts take place at sea (or in other waters). This does not, however, justify complacency. In the event of an armed conflict that takes place wholly or

---

[91] See Art. 4.

[92] GC II, Arts. 15 and 17. A similar rule appears in Art. 40 (3).

[93] ICRC Commentary on GC II, above note 6, Art. 15, paras. 1548–1554; Art. 17, paras. 1605–1611.

[94] *Ibid.*, Art. 17, paras. 1605, 1611.

in part at sea, the provisions of GC II must already be known and their contemporary meaning understood. This understanding must be ensured in peacetime, including through prevention activities such as the training of armed forces and especially naval forces. The Commentary constitutes an easily accessible tool which allows a better understanding of the legal obligations to protect wounded, sick and shipwrecked members of the armed forces at sea.

The updated Commentary on GC II was the second in a series of updated Commentaries to be published by the ICRC in the years to come. Currently, research is ongoing with respect to the protection of prisoners of war (GC III) and the protection of civilians in time of war (GC IV). Updated Commentaries will continue to be published consecutively on these Conventions, as well as on their Additional Protocols I and II, over the coming years.

MAKING AND SHAPING THE LAW OF
ARMED CONFLICT AT SEA

Professor Sandesh Sivakumaran *

1. Introduction

International law is traditionally said to be made by states. The law of armed conflict at sea is part of international law and is likewise seen as being made by states. Certain states themselves take the view that it is states that create international law. In a speech on "The Right of Self−Defence against Imminent Armed Attack in International Law" in 2017, the Australian Attorney−General indicated that "[i] t is vital that States (and their international legal advisers) have the courage to explain and defend their legal positions. Because it is in this way that we ensure that States maintain control over the development of international law. "[1]

In this paper, I explore how the law of armed conflict at sea is made and shaped. Contrary to traditional positivist accounts, I will demonstrate that it is the community of naval warfare lawyers that makes law of armed conflict at sea and it does so through dialogue between its members. The community includes, but is not limited to, states. It also includes international courts and tribunals, the ICRC, expert groups, and others. Through interaction in the selection of issues, during the

---

* Professor of Public International Law, University of Nottingham. This paper is based on my Current Legal Problems Lecture 2017, tailored to the specificities of the law of armed conflict at sea.

[1] Senator the Hon. George Brandis QC, Attorney−General of Australia, "The Right of Self−Defence against Imminent Armed Attack in International Law", 11 April 2017, EJIL: Talk!, available at https: // www. ejiltalk. org/the−right−of−self−defence−against−imminent−armed−attack−in−international−law/#more−15255.

drafting of outputs, and following the publication of the finished product, the community makes and shapes the law of armed conflict at sea. Some members of the community are more influential than others and I will show that actors such as the ICRC and expert groups have had considerable influence in the making and shaping of the law, while states have stepped back and been side-lined.

The paper proceeds in 8 parts. In Part 2, I set out the sources of the law of armed conflict at sea and identify some of the key materials in the field. Part 3 explores the concept of the community of naval warfare lawyers. The community is broken down into its component parts in Part 4, focusing on states, state-empowered entities and non-state actors, while Part 5 analyses the processes through which the community makes and shapes the law. It explores the role of the community in identifying issues to be regulated, the creation of treaties and custom, the drafting of manuals, and the dialogue that occurs following the publication of materials. Part 6 considers the relative absence of states in reacting to materials produced by state-empowered entities and non-state actors and discusses the consequences of this silence for the substance and process of the law of armed conflict at sea. Part 7 considers the particular role played by Asia-Pacific states in making and shaping the law of armed conflict at sea. The paper concludes, in Part 8, with a discussion of how to encourage states to participate in the making and shaping of the law.

2. The sources of the law of armed conflict

The law of armed conflict at sea is part of public international law. Accordingly, the sources of the law of armed conflict at sea are the same as the sources of public international law. According to the classic formulation, the sources are thus treaties, customary international law and general principles of law; and the subsidiary means for determining rules of law are judicial decisions and the teachings of publicists. [2] This Part sets out how the key sources of the law of armed conflict at sea and some of

---

[2] Statute of the International Court of Justice, Article 38 (1).

the most important subsidiary means were developed.

2.1 Conventional law of armed conflict at sea

The principal law of armed conflict at sea conventions include the 1899 and 1907 Hague Conventions, the Second Geneva Convention of 1949, and aspects of the Additional Protocols of 1977. The precise way in which a convention emerges varies from convention to convention. In the case of the Second Geneva Convention, the 1949 Geneva Conventions were concluded by states at the Diplomatic Conference of 1949, which was convened by Switzerland. The International Committee of the Red Cross (ICRC) prepared the drafts of the Geneva Conventions that were put before the 1949 Diplomatic Conference. The drafts had been considered at meetings of national Red Cross societies and Government Experts, and after consultation with a committee of experts. [3] The ICRC drafts had also been considered at the International Conference of the Red Cross in 1948. [4] The ICRC participated at the Diplomatic Conference and was called upon on numerous occasions for its view on particular issues. [5]

2.2 Customary law of armed conflict at sea

On the classical view, the customary law of armed conflict at sea, like customary international law, is made up of state practice and *opinio juris sive necessitatis*. In general terms, state practice refers to consistent and widespread practice by a diverse group of states, while *opinio juris* means that the practice is accepted as law. [6]

In practice, it is nearly impossible for any single individual to undertake the

---

[3] ICRC, *Report on the Work of the Preliminary Conference of National Red Cross Societies for the study of the Conventions and of various problems relative to the Red* Cross (Geneva, July 26-August 3, 1946) (Geneva, 1947); ICRC, *Report on the Work of the Conference of Government Experts for the Study of the Conventions for the Protection of War Victims* (Geneva, April 14-26, 1947) (Geneva, 1947). On the Committee of Experts, see G Best, *War and Law since* 1945 (Clarendon Press, 1994) 93-4.

[4] *Seventeenth International Red Cross Conference* (Stockholm, 1948).

[5] See R Heinsch, 'The International Committee of the Red Cross and the Geneva Conventions of 1949', in R Geiß, A Zimmermann and S Haumer (eds), *Humanizing the Laws of War: The Red Cross and the Development of International Humanitarian Law* (CUP, 2017) 38-9.

[6] *North Sea Continental Shelf* [1969] ICJ Rep 3, para. 77.

first-hand work of identifying and analysing the state practice and *opinio juris* of all states to determine whether a rule of customary international humanitarian law exists. Instead, in reality, we tend to use as a starting point customary rules that have been identified by other bodies. Two, in particular, stand out: the ICRC Customary International Humanitarian Law study and the jurisprudence of the International Criminal Tribunal for the former Yugoslavia (ICTY).

The ICRC Customary International Humanitarian Law study is a two-volume study, in three parts, totalling some 5000 pages. It consists of one volume, which contains a list of 161 rules of customary international humanitarian law together with commentary, and a second volume, in two parts, of supporting practice. The study was drawn up following a request from the International Conference of the Red Cross and Red Crescent to the ICRC, endorsing the recommendation of the Intergovernmental Group of Experts for the Protection of War Victims, to prepare a report on customary rules of international humanitarian law applicable in international and non-international armed conflicts. [7] The study involved some 150 experts from around the world and took nearly 10 years to complete. [8] Although not dealing with the law of armed conflict at sea as such, many of its rules are applicable in that context. [9]

2. 3 Judicial decisions

International courts and tribunals interpret international law and resolve disputes involving questions of international law. The ICTY, for example, has a mandate ' to prosecute persons responsible for serious violations of international humanitarian law

---

[7]　26th International Conference of the International Red Cross and Red Crescent Movement, Geneva, Switzerland, 3 - 7 December 1995, Resolution 1, available at https: //www. icrc. org/eng/resources/documents/resolution/26-international-conference-resolution-1-1995. htm.

[8]　J-M Henckaerts, "Customary International Humanitarian Law: A Response to US Comments" (2007) 89 *IRRC* 473, 474.

[9]　J-M Henckaerts and L Doswald-Beck, *Customary International Humanitarian Law*, *Volume I: Rules* (CUP, 2009) xxxvi.

committed in the territory of the former Yugoslavia'. [10] As such, the jurisprudence of the ICTY has been important for our understanding of international humanitarian law. Today, we cannot fully understand the law of armed conflict, including aspects of the law of armed conflict at sea, unless we have regard for the jurisprudence of international criminal courts and tribunals. The jurisprudence of other courts and tribunals has also proven influential, such as the International Court of Justice and domestic courts.

The identification of custom on the part of international courts and tribunals is of particular importance. With certain exceptions, states tend not to publicly identify the existence of a customary law of armed conflict rule outside the confines of a particular case. By contrast, international courts and tribunals frequently pronounce on the existence or otherwise of a norm of customary international humanitarian law. Whereas the elements that go to the *formation* of customary international humanitarian law are those of states, and perhaps other actors, the *identification* of custom tends to be left to courts, tribunals, the ICRC and expert bodies. The identification of a rule of customary international law can prove constitutive: the rule enters into custom through identification of the rule. The identifier of a customary rule thus can have significant influence.

2. 4 Teachings of publicists

One of the most influential teachings of publicists on the law of armed conflict at sea is the Pictet *Commentary on the* 1949 *Second Geneva Convention*. The commentary was drafted pursuant to the ICRC's mandate "to work for the understanding and dissemination of knowledge of international humanitarian law applicable in armed conflicts and to prepare any development thereof". [11] The Pictet Commentaries have been described by courts and tribunals as "authoritative". [12] And the Commentaries

---

[10]   ICTY Statute, Article 1.

[11]   Statutes, Article 5 (2)(g). ICRC, *Commentary on the Second Geneva Convention* (CUP, 2017).

[12]   *Prosecutor v Tadić*, Appeals Chamber, Judgment, IT-94-1, 15 July 1999, para. 93.

are cited and quoted extensively in judgments. Indeed, the updated *Commentary on the Second Geneva Convention* was cited with approval by a Swedish Court of Appeal shortly after its publication. [13] The influence of the Commentaries extends well beyond judgments. The Head of the Office of International Law of the Australian Commonwealth Attorney—General's Department has indicated that "Government legal advisers frequently avail themselves of the Commentaries in advising their governments on IHL" and has noted that "[t] he frequency with which States refer to the Commentaries in interpreting their obligations demonstrates not only the practical utility of this work, but also the special legitimacy that States, including Australia, accord to the ICRC. "[14]

The weight given to the Commentaries is particularly notable given that they fall into the category of teachings of publicists, and because the Commentaries did *not* in fact represent the official views of the ICRC. [15] Over time, and in practice, the Commentaries have come to be seen as reflecting the ICRC's view.

The work of expert groups has also proven influential. The *San Remo Manual on International Law applicable to Armed Conflicts at Sea*, produced by a group of experts, is of particular importance. It is the leading statement of the law of armed conflict at sea. The military manuals of states published since the adoption of the San Remo Manual draw heavily on it. For example, one chapter of the UK Ministry of Defence Manual notes that "much of the present chapter reflects its content. When appropriate and possible the text of the *San Remo Manual* has been repeated in this

---

[13] *Prosecutor v Omar Sakhanh Haisam*, Svea Court of Appeal, Judgment, 31 May 2017.

[14] J Reid, "Ensuring Respect: The Role of State Practice in Interpreting the Geneva Conventions", ILA Reporter blog, 9 November 2016, available at, http: //ilareporter. org. au/2016/11/ensuring − respect − the−role−of−state−practice−in−interpreting−the−geneva−conventions−john−reid/.

[15] The foreword to the 1960 Commentary on the Second Geneva Convention, for example, provides that, "[a] lthough published by the International Committee of the Red Cross, the Commentary is the personal work of its authors". ICRC, *Commentary II Geneva Convention for the Amelioration of the Condition of the Wounded, Sick and Shipwrecked Members of Armed Forces at Sea* (ICRC 1952) 1.

chapter. "[16] For its part, the Canadian Manual indicates that the chapter on the law relating to the conduct of hostilities at sea is "derived from" the San Remo Manual. [17] Its importance has also been acknowledged by the ICRC and commissions of inquiry. [18]

3. The community of naval warfare lawyers

These key reference points on the law of armed conflict at sea indicate that the law of armed conflict at sea is not made and shaped by states alone, but by a far broader range of actors, what I call the community of naval warfare lawyers. The community consists of those whose core work is the law of armed conflict at sea as well as those who are not strictly speaking naval warfare lawyers but who make pronouncements relating to that body of law.

The community is not a "well—defined identifiable group" with "socially visible boundaries". [19] Members of the community do not need to have "a common goal or vision"; indeed, they can have different interests and points of view. [20] Rather, drawing on literature on communities of practice, the community refers to "participation in an activity system about which participants share understandings concerning what they are doing". [21] The community refers to "intersubjective social structures that constitute the normative and epistemic ground for action" as well as the "real people, who—working via network channels, across national borders, across organizational divides, and in the halls of government—affect political, economic, and so-

---

[16]   UK Ministry of Defence, *Manual on the Law of Armed Conflict* (OUP, 2004), para. 13. 2 (fn omitted).

[17]   Canada, *Law of Armed Conflict* (2001) para. 801. 2.

[18]   J—M Henckaerts and L Doswald—Beck, *Customary International Humanitarian Law*, Volume I; *Rules* (CUP, 2009) xxxvi; Report of the Secretary—General's Panel of Inquiry on the 31 May 2010 Flotilla Incident (September 2011) 88.

[19]   J Lave and E Wenger, *Situated Learning: Legitimate Peripheral Participation* (CUP, 1991) 98.

[20]   E Adler, *Communitarian International Relations* (2005) 21; J Lave and EW Wenger, *Situated Learning: Legitimate Peripheral Participation* (CUP, 1991) 98.

[21]   J Lave and EW Wenger, *Situated Learning: Legitimate Peripheral Participation* (CUP, 1991) 98. See also E Wenger, *Communities of Practice: Learning, Meaning, and Identity* (1998) 72—85.

cial events. "[22] It is related to the interpretive community and the epistemic community. [23]

The community of naval warfare lawyers includes: states; particular international organisations, such as the IMO; certain international courts and tribunals; national courts; the ICRC; expert groups, such as those that drafted the San Remo Manual; and academics working on the law of armed conflict at sea. [24] Although we refer to "states", "courts", and so on, in reality, we are talking about particular individuals who act on behalf of these entities, such as the navy lawyer, the member of the ICRC legal division, and the individual judge. [25]

The precise composition of the community varies depending on the particular subject matter at issue. Indeed, rather than a single community of naval warfare lawyers, there are, in fact, multiple communities. [26] The broader community includes not just naval warfare lawyers *stricto sensu*, but also those actors who periodically make pronouncements related to the subject. For example, with respect to a particular issue, the community might include a UN Human Rights Council commission of inquiry or an ad hoc national expert group looking into a particular situation.

There are also communities within the community. Government legal advisors have their own closed network, as do judges of international and domestic courts. Not all academics play the same role in the community; some are more involved in the interaction among members of the community than others. If we consider some of the

---

[22] E Adler and V Pouliot, "International Practices" (2011) 3 *International Theory* 1, 18. See also E Adler, *Communitarian International Relations* (2005) 14−15.

[23] See eg I Johnstone, "Treaty Interpretation: The Authority of Interpretive Communities" (1990−1) 12 Michigan JIL 371; A Bianchi, "Epistemic Communities", in J d' Aspremont and S Singh (eds), *Fundamental Concepts for International Law* (forthcoming).

[24] On the community of international lawyers, see S Sivakumaran, "Beyond States and Non−State Actors: The Role of State−Empowered Entities in the Making and Shaping of International Law" (2017) 55 *Columbia Journal of Transnational Law* 341, 372.

[25] J Brunnée and SJ Toope, *Legitimacy and Legality in International Law* (CUP, 2010) 61.

[26] M Waibel, "Interpretive Communities in International Law", in A Bianchi et al (eds), *Interpretation in International Law* (2015) 152−60.

expert manuals on the law of armed conflict, some of the same names and states appear, again suggesting a community within the community. [27] There is thus a narrower, core community comprising members whose everyday work relates to the law of armed conflict at sea; and a broader community which includes those who occasionally or periodically engage with it. The community can also be split into the "military law" vision of the law of armed conflict at sea, with its prioritisation of military necessity and the "humanitarian law" vision, with its prioritisation of human dignity. [28] The community can thus be divided in different ways.

The precise composition of the community is critical because the community makes and shapes the law. If an actor is not part of the community, it is far more difficult for it to have a law-making and shaping role. Yet, the community also serves as the gatekeeper. Membership has to be earned through good lawyering and sound argument and new members have to be accepted by existing ones. While the community is a broad one, membership of the community is policed by members who can make it difficult for certain actors to join.

4. Actors within the community

Let me explore the roles of the various members of the community in greater detail.

4. 1 States

States remain important actors in the international community and key makers of international law. This includes the law of armed conflict at sea. It is states that make the conventional law of armed conflict at sea, including the principal treaties in the field, such as the 1899 and 1907 Hague Conventions and the 1949 Geneva Conventions. Likewise, it is the practice and *opinio juris* of states that give rise to customary

---

[27] See G Waschefort, "Africa and International Humanitarian Law: The More Things Change, the More They Stay the Same" (2016) 98 *IRRC* 593, 619.

[28] D Luban, "Military Necessity and the Cultures of Military Law" (2013) 26 *Leiden Journal of International Law* 315.

international law in general, [29] and the customary law of armed conflict at sea. The practice and beliefs of other actors may also be important, but by and large the focus tends to be on the practice and *opinio juris* of states. States thus play the dominant role insofar as the adoption of treaties is concerned and as regards the constituent elements of custom.

However, the picture is more complicated than that description might suggest. Although states remain key makers of international law, in practice, some states do not play much of a role. Furthermore, as will be seen, although the practice and *opinio juris* that goes to the formation of custom are that of states, the identification of custom tends to be left to other actors. Yet, identification of custom is crucial because identification can prove constitutive of a rule of customary international law.

4. 2 State-empowered entities

Although states remain influential actors in law-making, in practice, much of the day-to-day making and shaping of the law of armed conflict, in particular, the interpretation and development of the law, takes place by entities that states have empowered to make and shape the law. These are what Anthea Roberts and I have described as state-empowered entities. [30] State-empowered entities are essentially entities that states have empowered to carry out particular functions. [31] A state-empowered entity is usually created by two or more states and granted authority to make decisions or take actions. However, it can also be an entity that is already in existence, which is subsequently empowered by states to do certain things. State-empowered entities are neither states nor simply vessels through which states act. Equally,

---

[29]   ILC, Second Report on Identification of Customary International Law, by Michael Wood, Special Rapporteur', A/CN. 4/672, 22 May 2014, para. 33.

[30]   A Roberts and S Sivakumaran, "Lawmaking by Nonstate Actors: Engaging Armed Groups in the Creation of International Humanitarian Law" (2012) 37 *Yale Journal of International Law* 107, 116.

[31]   See S Sivakumaran, "Beyond States and Non-State Actors: The Role of State-Empowered Entities in the Making and Shaping of International Law" (2017) 55 *Columbia Journal of Transnational Law* 341, 351-6.

given their empowerment by states, they are not truly non—state actors. Instead, they constitute a category in their own right. [32]

States have empowered a variety of entities to interpret, apply, enforce, or develop the law of armed conflict at sea. States have provided the ICJ with a mandate to decide in accordance with international law disputes that are submitted before it, [33] and those disputes can include disputes relating to the law of armed conflict at sea.

The ICRC's mandate stems from, among other things, its Statutes and the 1949 Geneva Conventions. The Statutes were adopted by the International Conference of the Red Cross and Red Crescent, which includes states parties to the Geneva Conventions, national Red Cross and Red Crescent Societies, the ICRC and the International Federation of the Red Cross and Red Crescent. [34] The Statutes provide that the ICRC is *inter alia* "to work for the understanding and dissemination of knowledge of IHL ... and to prepare any development thereof, [35] though preparing the development of the law is not the same as developing it. The International Conference of the Red Cross and Red Crescent has also requested the ICRC to undertake ad hoc tasks, such as to prepare a report on customary international humanitarian law, [36] which became the Customary International Humanitarian Law study.

---

[32] The notion of empowerment is similar to, but differs from, the notion of delegation in the international relations literature. It does not operate on the basis that States are the "principals" and state—empowered entities the "agents." It is entirely normal for these entities to take on a life of their own and this does not amount to "slippage," Equally, empowerment differs from the principal/trustee relationship, which has been posited as an alternative to the principal/agent model. Unlike the principal/trustee model, the individuals constituting the state—empowered entity are not necessarily chosen because of their expertise or personal reputation and they do not act as trustees in the ordinary sense of the word. See ibid, 351.

[33] ICJ Statute, Article 38 (1).

[34] The Statutes of the International Red Cross and Red Crescent Movement were adopted by the 25th International Conference of the Red Cross in 1986. Article 9 (1) of the Statutes provide that "[t] he members of the International Conference shall be the delegations from the National Societies, from the International Committee, from the Federation and from the States Parties to the Geneva Conventions".

[35] Statutes of the International Red Cross and Red Crescent Movement, art. 2 (g) (emphasis added).

[36] International Conference of the Red Cross and Red Crescent, *Resolutions of the 26th International Conference of the Red Cross and Red Crescent* (1995), Resolution 1.

The Customary study has been hugely influential. It is cited not infrequently as the sole authority for the argument that a particular rule is one of custom. [37] It is understandable why that is the case. If counsel, a judge, government lawyer, or other actor needs to know whether there is a rule of customary international humanitarian law on a particular matter, the ICRC study is useful because it exists and it emanates from a respected body. Realistically, no individual has the time, access to materials and linguistic competence to go through the practice and *opinio juris* of 190 plus states to determine the matter for him or herself. Instead, the study is used as a short cut, as a starting point, to determine whether the purported customary rule does indeed exist. We can take as a starting point the practice compiled in the study, analyse it, and work out for ourselves whether we think that the practice supports the existence of a customary rule. In some cases, I suspect the study will also prove to be the end point, with the decision resting on the conclusions of the study. The identification of custom is important also because, in practice, the identification of a customary rule can serve to crystallize it. The rule becomes one of custom *because* it has been identified as such by an authoritative actor.

As already mentioned, it is states that adopt conventions. However, initial drafts of "Geneva law" that are put before a diplomatic conference are drafted by the ICRC. These initial drafts are influential because the general shape of the agreement— its structure and approach—tends to be retained, with the diplomatic conference making changes (albeit sometimes crucial ones) to specific provisions. It is far more unusual for a diplomatic conference to change the overall design and approach of an agreement. The ICRC thus plays a crucial role insofar as the adoption of Geneva law is concerned.

---

[37] See e. g. Report of the Secretary-General's Panel of Inquiry on the 31 May 2010 Flotilla Incident (September 2011) 88.

4. 3 Non—state actors

Non—state actors also play a role in the making and shaping of the law of armed conflict at sea. When states are unable or unwilling to make and shape the law, when no state—empowered entity has the mandate or opportunity to do so, and where there is a need for the law to be developed, expert groups can play a particularly influential role. Indeed, a perceived need to fill a gap in the law coupled with the inability of states to fill the gap has been the rationale behind the work of several expert groups. For example, the *San Remo Manual on International Law Applicable to Armed Conflicts at Sea* was drafted due to developments in the law since 1913 not being incorporated into treaty law. [38]

A number of reasons explain the particular influence of the work of expert groups, principal amongst which is their actual expertise. The group of experts that drafted the *San Remo Manual* included military lawyers, naval lawyers, government lawyers, ICRC lawyers, and leading academics. [39] In this way, the knowledge and experience of numerous individuals, of various backgrounds, is accumulated and a shared view of the law is presented. If leading figures all take the view that the law is X, it is more difficult, though not impossible, to argue that the law is Y.

Where the composition of the group takes into account geographical distribution, it is likely to be considered more representative and thus potentially more influential than a group that is solely from the global north or global south. It also avoids the criticism that is sometimes directed at individual publicists, namely that a nationalist position is being taken.

The *form* of the work product of the expert group is also important. Manuals of expert groups are particularly useful because they contain black letter law "rules" as well as commentary, with the rules being separated out from the commentary. The rules contain statements of the *lex lata*, with authorities and explanations in the com-

---

[38] *San Remo Manual on International Law Applicable to Armed Conflicts at Sea* (CUP, 1995) 5.

[39] *San Remo Manual*, pp. 46–55.

mentary. They are thus helpful to those who need to know what the law is, as well as those looking for guidance on a particular issue.

When states are not developing the law and there is a gap that needs to be filled, rigorous work by expert groups can usefully fill that gap. This explains why we are in the age of the manual.

5. Process

Although I have divided the community into states, state—empowered entities and non—state actors, that separation is rather artificial. The law is made and shaped through an interactive process *between* members of the community, for example, through dialogue between states, the ICRC, and expert groups. As Brunée and Toope explain: the community "provide [s] the settings in which the knowledge or norms that shape actors' understandings of the world are generated and practices evolve. In turn, it is through actors' participation that these understandings are maintained or shifted. "[40]

The dialogic interaction between members of the community impacts the choice of topics to be discussed and developed, the drafting of the relevant output,[41] as well as the period following publication of the finished product.

5. 1 Choice of issues

Members of the community determine whether an issue is one that requires legal attention. States decide whether to convene a diplomatic conference or initiate another process, following consultation with other states and the ICRC. The ICRC identifies issues that are in need of clarification and convenes expert groups and discusses matters with states. Expert groups identify gaps and fill them through manuals and other publications, sometimes involving states. Thus, there is no single agenda—setter.

5. 2 During the creation of the output

During the drafting of an output, the author of the output tends to engage with

---

[40] J Brunnée and SJ Toope, *Legitimacy and Legality in International Law* (CUP, 2010) 63-4.

[41] By output, I am referring to a treaty, commentary, guidance, etc.

other members of the community of naval warfare lawyers. For example, a diplomatic conference on the law of armed conflict at sea will consist primarily of states. NGOs might participate as observers. The ICRC will always be involved. States' delegations regularly include academics and members of national Red Cross or Red Crescent societies. In the case of the Geneva Conventions, it was the ICRC that produced the drafts that were put before the Diplomatic Conferences. And as part of the initial drafting process, the ICRC consulted with experts, including representatives of states, academics, and others. [42]

Outside the context of Diplomatic Conferences, the ICRC sends drafts of outputs to representative of states, academics and others for their comments. It takes those comments into account when finalizing the output. For example, the ICRC sent a draft of the updated *Commentary on the Second Geneva Convention* to a group of peer reviewers, which included governmental officials, navy lawyers, academics, and representatives of intergovernmental organisations, all acting in an individual capacity. [43] And the Commentary itself incorporates state practice and academic writings. [44]

Expert groups contain state and ICRC representatives, meet with state and ICRC representatives, or send their draft outputs to other members of the community for comments. For example, the rapporteurs and authors, the participants, and the associated experts and observers of the *San Remo Manual* were a mix of academics, state officials and ICRC legal advisers. [45] The outputs draw on state practice, particularly military manuals and academic literature.

---

[42] For example, the ICRC convened meetings of government experts, Red Cross experts and a committee of experts during the drafting of what would become the 1949 Geneva Conventions. See above.

[43] ICRC, *Commentary on the Second Geneva Convention* (ICRC, 2017) xiv–xix. Academic, government and ICRC experts were involved in the preparation of the ICRC Customary International Humanitarian Law study. See J–M Henckaerts and L Doswald–Beck, *Customary International Humanitarian Law*, *Volume I: Rules* (CUP, 2009) xxv–xxx.

[44] See eg the Commentary to Article 12.

[45] *San Remo Manual*, 46–55.

5. 3 Following publication of the finished product

The process does not end with the publication of the output. [46] The dialogic interaction continues even following publication. Following publication of the output, there frequently remains debate as to the meaning of a treaty provision, whether a rule really does reflect customary international law, or whether a statement in a commentary is accurate. Indeed, the weight of an output depends, in large part, on how it is received by the community of naval warfare lawyers. [47]

As states are important actors in the international legal system and key law—makers, how states receive the output is of particular importance. States' acceptance of an output can significantly enhance the authority of that output, in the sense of the weight to be given to it. States' acceptance indicates that the key law—makers accept it, thus imbuing it with greater weight.

An explicit statement of acceptance is uncommon. More common is a state's implicit acceptance through later use of that output. A state might refer to an output such as a court judgment at a later point in time, for example, in pleadings before another court, in official papers, or at a diplomatic conference. States' acceptance of the *San Remo Manual*, for example, can be seen through their incorporation of parts of the *Manual* in their own manuals. [48]

Reactions of states can also take the form of rejection. A state's rejection of an output serves to weaken the authority of that output. Following the rejection, the authority of the output is rendered uncertain and will turn on other reactions. The greater the number of rejections, the more likely it is that the output will not be fol-

---

[46] See J Brunnée and SJ Toope, *Legitimacy and Legality in International Law* (CUP, 2010) 48, noting that "For example, when diplomats return to their capitals after "successfully" concluding a treaty…the hard work of international law has often just begun. " They argue that this is "but a step in the continuing interactions that make, remake or unmake international law. " *Ibid*, 8.

[47] See S Sivakumaran, "Beyond States and Non-State Actors: The Role of State—Empowered Entities in the Making and Shaping of International Law" (2017) 55 *Columbia Journal of Transnational Law* 341, 373–81.

[48] See above, note X.

lowed. Where the output is rejected by only a couple of states, the output will not be authoritative for those states or for like—minded states, but it might retain a certain authoritativeness for others.

The *strength* of states' reactions will also affect the authority of the output. The stronger the disagreement, the more likely it is that the output will be given little weight. For example, in the *Kupreškić* trial judgment, the ICTY held that customary international law prohibited attacks on civilians as a matter of belligerent reprisals. [49] This holding was controversial and leading commentators criticized it. [50] Notably, the UK MoD, in its military manual, explicitly rejected the holding using uncharacteristically strong language. It opined that: "the court's reasoning is unconvincing and the assertion that there is a prohibition in customary law flies in the face of most of the state practice that exists. The UK does not accept the position as stated in this judgment." [51] The ICTY later changed its approach to the issue. [52]

By contrast, the US issued a more ambivalent reaction to the ICRC Customary Study. The US did not purport to reject the Study in its entirety. Rather, it sought to express concerns about the methodology and noted that, "it is not in a position to accept [the Study] without further analysis." [53] It only commented on four rules, although it indicated that further comments would be forthcoming. The US response suggests that it was intended to serve both as a placeholder, reserving its position until such time as it was able to analyse the study further, and as a foundation for any later objection. The US also viewed its response as its contribution to a dialogue a-

---

[49] *Prosecutor v Kupreškić*, IT—95—16—T, Judgment, 14 January 2000, para. 534.

[50] E. g. C Greenwood, "Belligerent Reprisals in the Jurisprudence of the International Criminal Tribunal for the Former Yugoslavia", in H Fischer et al (eds), *International and National Prosecution of Crimes under International Law: Current Developments* (2001) 539; F Kalshoven, "Reprisals and the Protection of Civilians: Two Recent Decisions of the Yugoslavia Tribunal", in LC Vohrah et al (eds), *Man's Inhumanity to Man: Essays in Honour of Antonio Cassese* (2003) 481.

[51] UK Ministry of Defence, *Manual of the Law of Armed Conflict* (2004) 423 fn 62.

[52] *Prosecutor v Martić*, IT—95—11—T, Judgment, 12 June 2007, paras. 464—8.

[53] JB Bellinger III and WJ Haynes II, "A US Government Response to the International Committee of the Red Cross Study *Customary International Humanitarian Law*" (2007) 89 IRRC 443, 444.

mongst relevant actors on the identification of customary rules of international humanitarian law. It expressed the hope that 'the discussion in [its response], as well as
the responses to the Study by other governments and by scholars, will foster a con-
structive, in–depth dialogue with the ICRC and others on the subject.' [54] This
rather ambivalent response, coupled with the considerable use of the Study by a
range of other actors, meant that the response did not significantly affect the weight
afforded to the Study.

Although states do not have a legal obligation to respond, in practice, their reactions can prove important, affecting the weight to be given to an output. Reactions
can confirm the statement of law issued by the entity; or they can reveal that the entity overreached in a particular instance. Reactions of states also frame the debate. Instead of standing alone, any enquiry into the law must consider the output of
the relevant entity together with the responses thereto.

6. State silence and its consequences

6. 1 State silence

There is continued state involvement in the making of treaties. Through state
practice and *opinio juris*, states also continue to participate in the formation of
custom. However, frequently, states do not react to the interpretation, application or
development of the law of state–empowered entities or non–state actors. Only the US,
and to a lesser extent the UK, issued a formal substantive public response to the
ICRC's Customary International Humanitarian Law Study, a major contribution to the
subject.

There are a number of reasons for this relative lack of response. Some states
might be unaware of the output. There might be only a handful of legal advisors in a
state's foreign ministry, and as a result, the state is not in a position to comment. A
state with a single legal advisor at its mission in Geneva would have the nearly impos-

---

[54]   *Ibid*, p. 471.

sible task of covering developments at the ICRC, the periodic International Conferences of the Red Cross and Red Crescent, the WTO, the UN Human Rights Council, the UN human rights treaty bodies, UNHCR, the ILO, and so on. Indeed, there
might not even be a legal advisor at a state's mission in Geneva. Even states with
large numbers of legal advisors might not have the capacity to keep up with, and respond to, outputs from the range of actors. Today, a range of actors make pronouncements on the law of armed conflict, far more than was previously the case. They include the ICRC, international courts and tribunals, UN entities, expert groups and
others. This it is a challenge for any state to keep up to date with developments.

Alternatively, or in addition, states might not consider the output to affect their
interests sufficiently to warrant a reaction. They might wish to keep their options
open, not committing themselves one way or another to a particular position. Or they
might not wish to give prominence to an issue by responding to it, and instead, prefer that the issue dies a natural death. Furthermore, in order to issue a response, a
state might have to agree to a position internally. It might prove difficult, if not impossible, to reach agreement in an inter—departmental process, involving, for example, the Department of Defense, the Department of State, and the Department of
Justice. There are thus very real practical reasons which explain the general lack of
response. But, this relative silence on the part of states has had certain consequences.

6. 2 Consequences: process

The lack of response on the part of states is sometimes taken as acquiescence to
the output. The Special Tribunal for Lebanon has observed that "[t] he combination
of a string of decisions [of international courts and tribunals] ... coupled with the
implicit acceptance or acquiescence of all the international subjects concerned,
clearly indicates the existence of the practice and *opinio juris* necessary for holding

that a customary rule of international law has evolved. "[55] Although states are not under an obligation to react to judgments or make their views known, the actual or imputed knowledge of states coupled with their silence on a string of decisions has been taken as acquiescence. [56] Although the Special Tribunal for Lebanon's observation is not an orthodox account of how customary international law is made, it does seem to reflect the practice of international law.

In light of the relatively few responses of states, the reactions of other members of the community of naval warfare lawyers have taken on particular significance. If other actors within the community accept the output—for example using it and citing it in their own work—this acceptance imbues the output with the additional authority of these other members. Thus, when the *San Remo Manual* is cited in reports of UN and national commissions of inquiry and described as authoritative, [57] the weight to be attached to it increases. The position is no longer one solely of the *Manual* but also of the actors that cite the particular position expressed in it. At the same time, citation of the *Manual* lends credence to the position taken by the entity doing the citing. Or if an international court cites the ICRC Customary International Humanitarian Law study as authority for the existence of a customary rule and then a domestic court cites the study as well as the international court judgment as authority of the customary rule, over time, a shared view of the law can emerge. And this shared view can e-

---

[55]　Case No. CH/AC/2010/02, Decision on Appeal of Pre-Trial Judge's Order regarding Jurisdiction and Standing, para. 47 (Special Tribunal for Lebanon, Nov. 10, 2010).

[56]　On acquiescence and custom, see ILC, Third Report on Identification of Customary International Law, by Michael Wood, Special Rapporteur, A/CN. 4/682, 27 March 2015, paras 19-26. Draft Conclusion 13 (3) of the ILC Draft Conclusions on Subsequent Agreements and Subsequent Practice in relation to the Interpretation of Treaties' provides that "Silence by a party shall not be presumed to constitute subsequent practice under article 31 (3)(b) accepting an interpretation of a treaty as expressed in a pronouncement of an expert treaty body. " A/CN. 4/L. 874, 6 June 2016.

[57]　E. g. The Public Commission to Examine the Maritime Incident of 31 May 2010, The Turkel Commission, Report, Part I; Report of the Secretary-General's Panel of Inquiry on the 31 May 2010 Flotilla Incident (September 2011).

merge with relatively little participation of states. [58] As already noted, once a shared view of the community emerges, it can become very difficult (but not impossible) to challenge it as incorrect some years down the line.

Conversely, if other actors within the community reject the output, this rejection reduces the authority of the output. Rejection by many members of the community casts the output as a product of the author alone and, moreover, one that does not have the acceptance of the broader community. Through acceptance or rejection, the community of naval warfare lawyers influences the authority of outputs.

An additional consequence of the relatively few states that respond is that the reactions of those that do so are given disproportionate weight. When the US responds to the Customary Study, despite being the reaction of a single state, considerable attention is paid to the response (although attention might also be also paid due to the identity of the responding states). Thus, in the same breath that we refer to the Customary Study, we note the US response.

As the process of law—making and shaping becomes more diffuse, states that do have the time and ability to react to the work of members of the community of naval warfare lawyers will exercise a greater influence on law—making and shaping. These will be states with larger numbers of legal advisors and which are able to stay on top of everything that goes on in all the different fora, react to outputs, accept invitations to participate in this and that initiative. It is they who are able to exercise a greater influence in law—making. [59]

6.3 Consequences: substantive rules

Specifically on the law of armed conflict, as Michael N Schmitt has noted, states' reluctance to set out their views on the law of armed conflict, coupled with

---

[58] In the case of the *San Remo Manual*, however, as noted above, certain states have incorporated parts of the *Manual* into their own manuals.

[59] See the associated concern expressed in GR Bandeira Galindo and C Yip, "Customary International Law and the Third World: Do Not Step on the Grass" (2017) 16 *Chinese Journal of International Law* 251, 260-1.

the work of actors such as the ICRC, the ICTY and NGOs, affects the balance be-tween humanity and military necessity that underlies the law of armed conflict. [60] In broad brush terms, state – empowered entities, NGOs, and other membsers of the community tend to push the humanity side of the equation. There is a tendency to find that a norm is one of customary international law or to interpret ambiguity in a text in such a way as to promote humanitarian considerations. By contrast, states tend to interpret silence in a way that promotes operational freedom, [61] and read treaties narrowly. [62] This is, of course, a generalization. There are states that push humani-tarian considerations and publicists that are more constrained in their interpretations of the law. Nonetheless, the position generally holds true.

To be clear, there is nothing wrong with the push and pull between considera-tion of humanity and of military necessity, between states, state—empowered entities, and other members of the community of naval warfare lawyers. Indeed, that push and pull is how the law is made. Ultimately, the creation of the law of armed conflict at sea is a dynamic process involving the members of the community. The relationship is not static but is in a constant state of flux with expansions and contractions, ebbs and flows, and pushes and pulls. It is through this interaction that international law more broadly is made. [63]

However, there is a danger if one category of actor, or several actors in a parti-cular category with a similar view, is silent. It means that one part of the community and one side of the balance is lacking. Insofar as the law of armed conflict at sea is

---

[60]   MN Schmitt, "Military Necessity and Humanity in International Humanitarian Law: Preserving the Delicate Balance" (2010) 50 *Virginia Journal of International Law* 795; MN Schmitt and S Watts, "State *Opinio Juris* and International Humanitarian Law Pluralism" (2015) 92 *International Law Studies* 171.

[61]   See S Watts, "The Updated First Geneva Convention Commentary, DOD's Law of War Manual, and a More Perfect Law of War: Part II", Just Security, 29 July 2016, available at https://www.justsecurity.org/32194/updated−geneva−convention−commentary−dods−law−war−manual−perfect−law−war−part−ii/.

[62]   D Luban, "Military Necessity and the Cultures of Military Law" (2013) 26 *Leiden Journal of International Law* 315, 323.

[63]   See generally J Brunnée and SJ Toope, *Legitimacy and Legality in International Law* (CUP, 2010).

concerned, a potential consequence is for a divergence to emerge between the law on the books and the law as applied at sea. And that would be dangerous because it would call into question the practical reality of the law: "[i] f humanitarian law becomes separated from the everyday experience and practice of professional military forces around the world, it is in danger of being relegated to the remote pursuit of ethereal goals. "[64]

There are signs that this silence of states is changing. Some states seem to be somewhat wary of the law—making and shaping activities of other members of the community. The Attorney—General of Australia has indicated, albeit not in the context of the law of armed conflict, that "We should not abandon the elaboration of legal doctrine to the realm of academia, unmoored from an appreciation of the operational realities confronting executive governments. "[65] And at the International Conference of the Red Cross and Red Crescent, states pushed for a resolution to refer to "the primary role of States in the development of international humanitarian law",[66] and a "State-led" process. [67]

A few states have also started to make their positions clearer on certain law of armed conflict matters. The US DoD and Denmark have recently published military manuals. [68] And Denmark intends to translate its manual into English, which would increase the readership of the manual. US government officials have given speeches

---

[64] MA Newton, "Modern Military Necessity: The Role and Relevance of Military Lawyers" (2007) 12 *Roger Williams University Law Review* 877, 895.

[65] Senator the Hon. George Brandis QC, Attorney—General of Australia, "The Right of Self-Defence against Imminent Armed Attack in International Law", 11 April 2017, EJIL: *Talk!*, available at https://www. ejiltalk. org/the-right-of-self-defence-against-imminent-armed-attack-in-international-law/#more-15255.

[66] Resolution 1 of the 31st International Conference of the Red Cross and Red Crescent, Strengthening Legal Protection for Victims of Armed Conflict.

[67] Resolution 1 of the 32nd International Conference of the Red Cross and Red Crescent, Strengthening International Humanitarian Law Protecting Persons Deprived of their Liberty.

[68] Forsvarsministeriet and Værnsfælles Forsvarskommando, *Militærmanual* (September 2016).

on issues relating to the law of armed conflict, [69] although the content of the spee-ches tend to be rather basic. And there has been some, limited reaction to certain as-pects of the updated ICRC Commentary on the First Geneva Convention, notably on Article 1 common to the four Geneva Conventions of 1949. [70]

7. The role of Asian states

All states are invited to participate at diplomatic conferences on the law of armed conflict and this would include the law of armed conflict at sea. However, a major treaty in the area has not been concluded for years. Furthermore, at a Diplo-matic Conference, some delegations participate more fully than others. Sometimes this might be due to lack of expertise. At other times, a state with a small delegation might not be able to participate fully in the various committees and commissions of the Conference, especially if meetings of the various committees take place in paral-lel.

Insofar as customary international law is concerned, in theory, the practice and *opinio juris* of all states go to its formation. In practice, though, in general public in-ternational law, the situation is often rather different, with the state practice and *opinio juris* being considered, often being that of major western states. The law of armed conflict is perhaps something of an exception in this regard. The ICRC was in-clusive in the practice and *opinio juris* that made up the Customary International Hu-manitarian Study, with the practice of all states considered, including the practice of Asian states.

In the law of armed conflict at sea, just as in the law of armed conflict and pub-

---

[69]   See http: //usnwc. libguides. com/c. php? g=86619&p=557497, last visited, 2019-6-30.

[70]   See J Reid, "Ensuring Respect: The Role of State Practice in Interpreting the Geneva Conventions", ILA Reporter blog, 9 November 2016, available at, http: //ilareporter. org. au/2016/11/ensuring-respect-the-role-of-state-practice-in-interpreting-the-geneva-conventions-john-reid/; Brian J Egan, Legal Advis-er, "International Law, Legal Diplomacy and the Counter-ISIL Campaign", Remarks at the Annual Meeting of the American Society of International Law, available at https: //2009-2017. state. gov/s/l/releases/remarks/255493. htm.

lic international law more generally, there has been a growth in law-making and sha-ping activities of state-empowered entities and non-state actors. If we consider the major pronouncements in the law of armed conflict at sea of the past few decades, al-most all have emerged from these bodies rather than from states: the *San Remo Man-ual*; the Customary International Humanitarian Law study; and the updated *Com-mentary on the Second Geneva Convention*.

There have been some state pronouncements, for example, the publication of detailed military manuals of a few states, including Australia, Canada, Germany, the United Kingdom, and the United States, with a chapter in each on the law of armed conflict at sea. Notably, similar substantive manuals have not tended to be published in recent years by states from the Asian region.

Likewise, the states that do react to outputs of state-empowered entities and non-state actors tend not to be Asian states. Instead, it tends to be the United King-dom, the United States and other major western states. Yet, as noted above, the states that do react can exercise a disproportionate influence. Other states might react internally or confidentially, for example, in confidential bilateral dialogue with the ICRC. However, confidential reactions, whilst potentially influencing the other actor in the dialogue, cannot have a broader more pervasive effect and they inevitably fail to influence other members of the community.

7. Conclusion: encouraging state responses

States are not under an obligation to participate in law-making activities, nor are they required to respond to outputs of state-empowered entities or other actors as a matter of law. However, practice suggests that it is in their own interest to contrib-ute and respond, as appropriate. Should states be silent, the law can develop in a di-rection contrary to that wanted by states. States also need to be more active in the making and shaping of the law of armed conflict at sea in order to ensure that the law remains realistic and that the law on the books is the same as that applied on the seas.

There are things that can be done to encourage state contributions. States should consider issuing comments on behalf of a small number of states, or on behalf of a regional or sub—regional grouping. This is occasionally done, for example, state X issuing comments on a draft output on behalf of states X, Y and Z; or state A issuing a response to a published output on behalf of states of a sub—regional group. Likewise, some like—minded states split up the monitoring of developments of state—empowered entities between them and report back to the group. This enables the workload to be shared and might make responses more manageable. The comments will likely also be given greater weight if a number of states are attached to them. Of course, it will not always be possible, for example, if agreement cannot be reached or if there are diverse positions within the group of states.

States will need to be selective in their comments and responses. It is not a case of commenting on, or responding to, everything or nothing. A state might wish to consider what are, in its view, the major pronouncements coming from state—empowered entities, those that are likely to be influential, or those that particularly affect a state's interests and comment only on those outputs. In this way, the activity becomes more manageable.

States should also give thought to publishing internal legal opinions or memoranda subject to redactions if necessary and after a period of time. States interpret legal rules and take positions on matters of law on a regular basis. However, much of this activity takes place in confidence and behind closed doors, thus not contributing to the interpretation and understanding of the law. Should confidentiality and other sensitivities allow, states should publish their positions, legal opinions and memoranda. This would enable other members of the community to take into account the positions of these states on a particular issue and would increase the input of states in the formation of the law.

States should also be encouraged to make their practices and views available online, for example publishing them on the website of their foreign ministry. Speeches should also be published online. Ease of accessibility makes it more likely that a state-empowered entity will take them into account when formulating a position. And today, the starting point for much research is online. The extent to which the practice and *opinio juris* of particular states are used is affected, in no small part, by the ease of which the materials can be found, the language in which they are written, and the clarity of their content. Publishing materials in English would also contribute to their likely use given the dominance of the English language in international law. However, this imposes costs on states the national language of which is not English. [71]

There are drawbacks to responding. Responding to an output might be perceived as creating a precedent. And if a state does not respond to a later output by the same body, it might be viewed as agreeing with the legal position contained therein. A caveat would assist matters; however, it would remain a concern.

The onus is not only on states to participate in law-making and shaping processes. State-empowered entities, expert groups, and other actors could make the situation more conducive to receiving comments and responses by states. Meetings could take place in locations such as Bangkok or Nairobi, to name but two places, rather than Geneva, in order to enable African and Asian states to send delegations with more legal staff. Alternatively, certain meetings could be live streamed to allow individuals to follow and/or participate remotely. [72] State-empowered entities could extend invitations to comment on drafts to former legal advisors of states. Although their comments would be in an individual capacity and would not constitute state comments, they might nonetheless prove more indicative of state thinking. States' comments should be made available online, even after the output is finalized. [73] Al-

---

[71] See further GR Bandeira Galindo and C Yip, "Customary International Law and the Third World: Do Not Step on the Grass" (2017) 16 *Chinese Journal of International Law* 251, 259.

[72] H Keller and L Grover, "General Comments of the Human Rights Committee and their Legitimacy", in H Keller and G Ulfstein (eds), *UN Human Rights Treaty Bodies: Law and Legitimacy* (CUP, 2012) 184-5.

[73] *Ibid.*

though this is the practice of some entities, such as the ILC, and some states, such as the United States, it is by no means common to all. This allows other actors to take on board states' comments in the longer term, even if they are comments on draft outputs.

States should also consider publishing or revising their manuals. Manuals are used frequently in law–making and shaping activities. They are cited as state practice and/or *opinio juris* in identifying a rule of customary international law. They are used to interpret rules of the law of armed conflict at sea, for example in the updated *Commentary on the Second Geneva Convention*. They are frequently referenced in international and national commissions of inquiry and they influence other states' manuals as well as expert manuals. A manual can have a significant effect on the making and shaping of the law of armed conflict at sea.

"USE OF FORCE" UNDER MARITIME POLICE LAW AND JUS AD BELLUM: DISTINCTION BETWEEN THE RULES OF CONDUCT AND NORMS FOR JUDICIAL PROCEEDINGS

Makoto SETA [*]

1. Introduction

The phrase "use of force" is used in multiple contexts, including law enforcement and military activities. On the seas, where the boundary between the States is not clear, [1] the distinction between these two activities is deemed especially important. A maritime law enforcement (MLE) activity for one State can easily become a military activity for another. In fact, there are some disputes that derive from this differing cognition of one activity. To illustrate, a MLE activity conducted by Canada was characterized as a "use of force" prohibited under Article 2 (4) of the Charter of the United Nations (UN Charter) by Spain. [2] In a similar way, a MLE activity for Japan was criticized as being an illegal use of force that is prohibited under the

---

[*] Falculty member, International College of Arts and Sciences, Yokohama City University, Japan.

[1] This is why the law of maritime delimitation has evolved. Recent publications on the law of the sea tend to have a chapter focusing on maritime delimitation. See, for example, Yoshifumi Tanaka, The International Law of the Sea, 2nd ed. , (2015), pp. 196–228; Malcom D. Evans, *Maritime Boundary Delimitation*, in Donald R. Rothwell, Alex G. O. Elferink, Karen N. Scott, Tim Stephens (eds.), The Oxford Handbook of the Law of the Sea, (2015), pp. 254–279.

[2] *Fisheries Jurisdiction Case (Spain v. Canada)*, *Jurisdiction of the Court*, *Judgment*, *I. C. J. Reports* 1998, p. 432, 465, para. 78.

UN Charter. [3] Moreover, a MLE activity for Suriname was regarded as a violation of the prohibition on "threat of force" for Guyana. [4]

Based on these facts, it can be said that MLE activities and military activities are currently conceptually distinguished. Moreover, it is widely recognized that maritime police law (MPL) and *jus ad bellum* are applied to those activities, respectively. [5] In other words, the proposition that MPL is applied to MLE activities and *jus ad bellum* is applied to military activities is supported by many scholars. [6]

Clearly, a distinction can be found between a MLE activity and a military activity; however, as mentioned in the cases referenced above, this controversial distinction is arguably unclear and seemingly lacks legitimate grounds under general international law. [7] Against this background, this paper reconsiders the relationship between MPL and *jus ad bellum* with focusing on the rules over the use of force and re-

---

[3] See Zou Keyuan, *Disrupting or Maintaining the Marine Legal Order in East Asia*, Chinese Journal of International Law, Vol. 1 (2002), p. 479; With regard to the use of firearm against an unidentified vessel by Japan in 2001, Keyuan argued that "Japan attempted to justify its action by using the argument of self-defense." However, at least in accordance with Japanese municipal law, the measures in question are based on the law on MLE activity.

[4] *Guyana/Suriname*, *Award of the Arbitral Tribunal*, 17 September 2007, para. 445.

[5] In this paper, *jus ad bellum* means "(t) he international law governing when and how military action may lawfully be commenced by one state against another, as set forth in the United Nations Charter (*see especially* Article 2 (4) and Chapters VI and VII) and customary international practice"; Aaron X. Fellmeth and Maurice Horwitz, Guide to Latin in International Law, (2009), 150.

[6] Tom Ruys, *The Meaning of "Force" and the Boundaries of the Jus ad Bellum: Are "Minimal" Use of Force Excluded from UN Charter Article 2 (4)?*, American Journal of International Law, Vol. 108 (2014), p. 201; David H. Anderson, *Some Aspects of the Use of Force in Maritime Law Enforcement*, in Nerina Boschiero et al (eds.), International Courts and Developments of International Law, (2013), p. 234; Olivier Corten, Le droit contre la guerre, (2008), p. 77; Patricia J. Kwast, *Maritime Law Enforcement and the Use of Force: Reflections on the Categorisation of Forcible Action at Sea in the Light of the Guyana/Suriname Award*, Journal of Conflict & Security Law, Vol. 13, No. 1 (2008), p. 62.

[7] In this respect, some commentators have a different view. For example, Gill says "The exercise of routine police powers in enforcing a State's criminal and administrative laws against violations by private individuals, criminal groups and other non-governmental entities, such as merchant ships and fishery vessels, differs both conceptually and in practice from the use of force in the protection and affirmation of rights in the relationship of State to State."; T. D. Gill, "The Forcible Protection, Affirmation and Exercise of Rights by States under Contemporary International Law", *Netherlands Yearbook of International Law*, Vol. 23, (1992), p. 122.

jects the prevailing proposition. For this purpose, Chapter II assesses the historical development of both MPL and *jus ad bellum* and Chapter III clarifies the scope of the two laws. Then, Chapter IV analyzes the relationship between two norms, and finally this paper provides a concluding remark on the basis of the distinction between rules of conduct, which regulate State's activities, and norms for judicial proceedings, which function when leading to a procedural decision in international judicial organs.

2. Historical developments of MPL and *Jus Ad Bellum*

If a clear distinction exists between the scope of application of MPL and *jus ad bellum*, namely that MPL is applied to MLE activities and *jus ad bellum* is applied to military activities, this distinction must inherently exist. In other words, MPL and *jus ad bellum* must have emerged correlatively or must be coordinated, as is the case of recent treaty practices. [8] Without a shared origin or coordination, it is impossible for two norms to be completely distinct in their scope of application. Therefore, this chapter will assess the historical development of MPL and *jus ad bellum*.

2. 1 Historical development of MPL

The origin of MPL dates back to pre–World War II (WWII). Firstly, MPL was found in *the Joint Final Report of the Commission in the Case of the "I'm Alone"* issued in 1935. According to this report, States shall "*use necessary and reasonable force* for the purpose of effecting the objects of boarding, searching, seizing and bringing into port the suspected vessel (emphasis added). "[9] After WWII, the existence of MPL has been confirmed by several precedents, such as the *Red Crusader*, [10] and *the M/V "SAIGA" (No. 2) Case*. It must be noted that in the latter case,

---

[8] An example for coordination of the relationship between rules provided by different treaties is Article 311 (1) of the UNCLOS. It manifestly provides its primacy over the 1958 Geneva Conventions on the law of the sea.

[9] "Joint Final Report of the Commission in the Case of the ' I'm Alone ' ", Reports of International Arbitral Award, Vol. 3 (1935), p. 1615.

[10] *Investigation of certain incidents affecting the British trawler Red Crusader*, Reports of International Arbitral Awards, Vol. 29 (1962), p. 538.

the International Tribunal for the Law of the Sea (ITLOS) said "the use of force must be avoided as far as possible and, where force is unavoidable, it must not go beyond what is reasonable and necessary in the circumstances." [11] Considering that the phrase "use of force" was previously formulated in Article 2 (4) of the UN Charter, the ITLOS arguably distinguished the use of force in the context of MLE activity from that prohibited under the UN Charter.

Aside from this process of establishment through cases, two soft law documents on MPL clarify its content. One is entitled the "Code of Conduct for Law Enforcement Officials" and the other is termed the "Basic Principles on the Use of Force and Firearms by Law Enforcement Officials (the Basic Principles)." As revealed by their nomenclature, these documents generally provide the rules of law enforcement activity and do not limit their scope to the maritime context. Nevertheless, as MLE is also covered by these documents, they are often cited as evidence to establish MPL. [12] Support for this citation may stem from the facts that the documents, especially the Basic Principles, elaborate and clarify the rules of law enforcement, and can be guidelines for officers in general. [13]

Furthermore, recent multilateral treaties tend to incorporate the rules of MPL. To illustrate, Article 22 (1)(f) of the Agreement Relating to the Conservation and Management of Straddling Fish Stocks and Highly Migratory Fish Stocks provides as follows:

The inspecting State shall ensure that its duly authorized inspectors:

---

[11] *The M/V "SAIGA" (No. 2) Case (Saint Vincent and the Grenadines v. Guinea), Judgment of* 1 *July* 1999, paras. 155–156.

[12] Efthymios Papastavridis, *The Use of Force at Sea in the 21ˢᵗ Century: Some Reflections of the Proper Legal Framework (s)*, The Journal of Territorial and Maritime Studies, Vol. 2, (2015), p. 131; Magne Frostad, "Anti-Piracy and the Use of Force: the Cohabitation of the United Nations Convention on the Law of the Sea and the European Convention on Human Rights", Maritime Safety and Environmental Protection in Europe: Multiple Layers in Regulattion and Compliance, (2015), p. 217, footnote 39.

[13] The Basic Principles is composed of eight general provisions and three special provisions with other fifteen rules.

(f) avoid the use of force except when and to the degree necessary to ensure the safety of the inspectors and where the inspectors are obstructed in the execution of their duties. The degree of force used shall not exceed that reasonably required in the circumstances.

Article 8 *bis* (9) of Protocol of 2005 to the Convention for the Suppression of Unlawful Acts against the Safety of Maritime Navigation provides almost identical rules.

Actually, they are treaties drafted to combat specific maritime crimes, such as Illegal, Unreported and Unregulated (IUU) fishing and maritime terrorism; therefore, they do not cover all crimes. Hence, application of the treaties is very limited. Nonetheless, for MPL, which developed through customary international law, it is significant that legally binding instruments stipulate the rules of MPL.

Among recent judgements, the existence of MPL has become quite obvious. For example, in *the M/V "Virginia G" Case*, the ITLOS confirmed the rules of MPL, which derive from precedent, though it did not find a violation of Guinea—Bissau by using excessive force. [14] Furthermore, in *the Arctic Sunrise Case*, the Arbitral Tribunal took a similar position. [15] Therefore, it is now manifest that the customary rules of use of force under MPL are established. [16]

---

[14] *M/V "Virginia G"* (*Panama/Guinea–Bissau*), *Judgment*, *ITLOS Reports* 2014, para. 452.

[15] *The Arctic Sunrise Arbitration* (*Netherlands v. Russia*), *Award on the Merits*, 14th *Aug.* 2015, in International Legal Materials, Vol. 51, No. 1 (2016), para. 191.

[16] Aside from the precedents and documents as shown above, Frostad employs the documents of the IMO which provides the rules relating to the use of force by the privately contracted armed security personnel to examine the use of force under MPL; Frostad, *supra* note 12, pp. 211–214. However, considering that some States, such as UK and Japan, strictly prohibits the use of firearms by private individual, we must be careful on the distinction between use of force by public sector and one by private sector.

2. 2 Historical development of *Jus Ad Bellum*

The limitation of the use of military force was first achieved in the 20th century. [17] After World War I, the League of Nations was established, in part, to restrict war. Article 11 of the Covenant of the League of Nations declares that any war or threat of war is "a matter of concern to the whole League." However, the system of the League of Nations did not prohibit war; Article 12 of the Covenant of the League of Nations provides the following:

The Members of the League agree that, if there should arise between them any dispute likely to lead to a rupture they will submit the matter either to arbitration or judicial settlement or to enquiry by the Council, and they agree in no case to resort to war until three months after the award by the arbitrators or the judicial decision, or the report by the Council...

In this way, the Covenant merely provided a moratorium. [18]

Even under the system of the League of Nations, States pursued a more advanced framework to prohibit war. As a result, the Kellogg–Briand Pact was adopted in 1928, [19] just before the proceedings on "I'm Alone" was initiated. According to Article 1 of the Pact, the contracting parties "condemn recourse to war for the solution of international controversies, and renounce it, as an instrument of national policy in their relations with one another". However, as is often pointed out, though the Pact prohibits war, it does not entirely prohibit the use of force. [20] Accordingly, the

---

[17]   Oliver Dörr, *Use of Force, Prohibition of*, in Rudiger Wolfrum (ed.) , The Max Plank Encyclopedia of Public International Law, Vol. X (2012) , p. 608.

[18]   See Ian Brownlie, International Law and the Use of Force by States, (1963) , pp. 55–65.

[19]   Randall C. H. Lesaffer, *Kellogg–Briand Pact* (1928) , in Rudiger Wolfrum (ed.) , The Max Plank Encyclopedia of Public International Law, Vol. VI (2012) , pp. 579–584.

[20]   Yoram Dinstein, War, Aggression and Self–Defence, 5th ed. , (2011) , p. 87; William K. Lietzau, *Old Laws, New Wars: Jus ad Bellum in an Age of Terrorism*, Max Planck United Nations Yearbook, Vol. 8 (2004) , p. 388.

Pact could not prevent WWII.

Therefore, after WWII, States needed a comprehensive mechanism to prohibit the threat or use of force. For this purpose, Article 2 (4) of the UN Charter was formulated as "All Members shall refrain in their *international relations* from *the threat or use of force* against the territorial integrity or political independence of any state, or in any other manner inconsistent with the Purposes of the United Nations (emphasis added). " In this way, the threat or use of force is generally prohibited with the exceptions of collective security (Article 42 and 43) and self-defense (Article 51). [21] Thus, though the existing *jus ad bellum* is provided in the UN Charter, from its drafting history, it is difficult to find the Charter is affected by MPL, which previously appeared in *the "I'm alone" Case*.

After the adoption of the UN Charter, *jus ad bellum* developed in two courses. First, there is the context of *jus cogens* (peremptory norms). When the UN Charter was adopted, the concept of *jus cogens* was not rooted in international law. Although several scholars acknowledged the existence of *jus cogens* under international law even before WWII, [22] it was not until the drafting history of the Vienna Convention on the Law of Treaties (VCLT) that *jus cogens* under international law appeared as a part of positive law.

In terms of the relationship between *jus ad bellum* and *jus cogens*, traditionally, the former has been recognized as falling within the scope of the latter. For example, Green points out that "*jus cogens* and the *jus ad bellum* share common natural law underpinnings such that one might view them as a perfect conceptual fit. " [23] Moreover, the ILC has the view that the principle of non-use of force is a part of *jus co-*

---

[21] See, for example, Thomas M. Frank, Recourse to Force: State Action against Threats and Armed Attacks, (2002), pp. 2–5.

[22] Lassa F. L. Oppenheim, International Law, 1st ed. , Vol. 1 (1905), p. 528; William Hall, A Treatise of International Law, 8th ed. , (1924), p. 382.

[23] James A. Green, *Questioning the Peremptory Status of the Prohibition of the Use of Force*, Michigan Journal of International Law, Vol. 32 (2011), p. 221.

gens. To illustrate, in its commentary to Article 50 of the Draft of the VCLT, the ILC says "the law of the Charter concerning the prohibition of the use of force in itself constitutes a conspicuous example of a rule in international law having the character of *jus cogens*. "[24]

Pursuant to the second course, the linkage with the concept of aggression makes the content of the use of force more fruitful. Although the phrase "act of aggression" is stipulated in Article 39 of the UN Charter, the definition of "aggression" had not been established. Therefore, with a view to clarify what aggression means, the UN General Assembly (GA) adopted Resolution 3314 (the "Definition of Aggression"). [25] In its preamble, the Resolution firstly acknowledges that "aggression is the most serious and dangerous form of the illegal use of force" and then exemplifies what kinds of action fall within the scope of aggression. More recently, through the amendments of the Rome Statute of International Criminal Court, the crime of aggression, which entail individual responsibility, has been introduced. [26] Now, *jus ad bellum* has become one of the most fundamental and important rules of contemporary international law. [27]

2. 3 Historical development and connection

By comparing the historical development of the two laws, first of all, it can be said that MPL and *jus ad bellum* have completely different origins. It is true that both have been established since the 20th century; however, MPL has been elaborated

---

[24]   *Reports of the International Law Commission to the General Assembly*, Yearbook of International Law Commission 1996, Vol. 2, p. 247.

[25]   Elizabeth Wilmshurst, *Definition of Aggression*, United Nations Audiovisual Library of International Law, p. 1, *available at* <http: //legal. un. org/ avl/ pdf/ ha/ da/ da_ e. pdf> (last visited on 29th Apr. 2016).

[26]   As for the details of the crime of aggression, see Claus Kreß and Leonie von Holtzendorff, *The Kampala Compromise on the Crime of Aggression*, Journal of International Criminal Justice, Vol. 8, No. 5 (2010), pp. 1179−1217.

[27]   Scott points out that "The body of law that seeks to limit recourse to force is of special importance to the system of international law because law represents an attempt to replace anarchy with order. "; Shirley V. Scott, International Law in World Politics: An Introduction, 2nd ed. , (2010), p. 97.

through judicial decisions and recognized as a form of customary international law. [28] In contrast, *jus ad bellum* has developed through treaty practices. [29] Considering these different backgrounds, some may conclude that the origins of these two laws are independent.

Moreover, in the development of these two laws, it is difficult to find how they intertwine prior to *the Fisheries Jurisdiction Case*. On the one hand, *jus ad bellum* developed as a peremptory norm of international law and now entails individual responsibility. On the other hand, discussion asserting that MPL has a character of *jus cogens* is lacking, as is a dialog stating that individuals may owe responsibility for the violation of MPL.

In this way, MPL and *jus ad bellum* are originally and historically separate. In spite of this fact, the separation of applicable scope is well established based on the misunderstanding of the relationship between two laws. Where does this misunderstanding come from? Where is the cross—point of MPL and *jus ad bellum*? One possible answer is found in a close reading of *the Fishery Jurisdiction Case* where the Canadian declaration to accept the ICJ's compulsory jurisdiction is discussed as follows:

(2) I declare that the Government of Canada accepts as compulsory *ipso facto* and without special convention, on condition of reciprocity, the jurisdiction of the International Court of Justice, in conformity with paragraph 2 of Article 36 of the Statute of the Court, until such time as notice may be given to terminate the acceptance, over all disputes arising after the present declaration with regard to situations or facts subsequent to this declaration, other than:

...

---

[28]　Anderson, *supra* note 6, p. 234.

[29]　This fact does not deny that *jus ad bellum* became rules of customary international law, as is confirmed by the ICJ; *Military and Paramilitary Activities in and against Nicaragua (Nicaragua v. United States of America). Merits, Judgment. I. C. J. Reports* 1986, p. 14, 102–103, paras. 193–194.

(*d*) disputes arising out of or concerning *conservation and management meas-ures* taken by Canada with respect to vessels fishing in the NAFO Regulatory Area, as defined in the Convention on Future Multilateral Co-operation in the Northwest Atlantic Fisheries, 1978, and *the enforcement of such measures...* (emphasis added)

In this case, Canada inspected and boarded the Spanish Fishery vessel, *Estai*, with the use of firearms. Against this series of activities, Spain argued that Canada violated international law and brought the case before the ICJ. According to Spain, the Canadian activities violated Article 2 (4) of the UN Charter; therefore, they did not fall within the scope of "the enforcement of such measures" provided in the res-ervation. [30] With respect to this point, however, Canada correctly pointed out that " 'Enforcement' is what it is: it depends on the nature and purpose of the action taken. Whether it is lawful or unlawful is quite a different issue: and it is an issue of merits. " [31] Then, the Court took this Canadian view by arguing that "the use of force authorized by the Canadian legislation and regulations falls within the ambit of what is commonly understood as enforcement of conservation and management meas-ures. " [32]

Thus, the distinction of two activities, namely MLE activity and military activity emerged when deciding jurisdiction of the ICJ. In other words, the issue was trig-gered in response to judicial proceedings not the rules of conduct. It is true that the distinction between police activity and military activity has been argued; however, the arguments basically focused on the scope of *jus ad bellum*. [33] Namely, if an act

---

[30]   *Fisheries Jurisdiction Case, supra* note 2, p. 465, paras. 78–84.

[31]   *Audience publique tenue le mercredi 17 juin 1998, à 10 heures, au Palais de la Paix, sous la présidence de M. Schwebel, président en l' affaire de Ca Compétence en matière de pêcheries (Espagne c. Canada)* (CR 98/14) (1998), para. 52.

[32]   *Ibid.*, p. 466, para. 86.

[33]   Corten, *supra* note 6, p. 71; Mary E. O'Connell, *The Prohibition on the Use of Force*, in Nigel D. White and Christian Henderson (eds.), Research Handbook on International Conflict and Security Law, (2013), p. 102; Robert Kolb, Jus Contra Bellum, 2nd ed., (2009), p. 247.

is labeled as a military activity, that act would fall outside the scope of *jus ad bellum*. Since MPL has not been analyzed in this context, the allocation of application between *jus ad bellum* and MPL has also not been discussed.

Therefore, even though the distinction between MLE activity and military activity or one between police activity and military activity is confirmed,[34] it is not plausible to decide the scope of application of MPL and *jus ad bellum* on the basis of those distinctions. Those distinctions have not been designed for that purpose. The former is deliberated to decide whether Canadian activities fall within its declaration to accept compulsory jurisdiction of the ICJ, and the latter focuses on the scope of *jus ad bellum* with no relation to MPL.

Consequently, it is said that the distinction between MLE activity and military activity and the distinction between MPL and *jus ad bellum* are independent and irrelevant. Although the prevailing formula strongly connects these two distinctions, it is not confirmed from the historical developments of MPL and *jus ad bellum*. Based on this fact, the next chapter will assess the scope and content of MPL and *jus ad bellum*.

3. Scope of MPL and *Jus Ad Bellum*

Because MPL and *jus ad bellum* are rules of conduct, the content of each norm must be examined in order to confirm their scope. Therefore, the content of these two laws is clarified below.

3. 1 Content and scope of MPL

As discussed above, MPL has historically focused on the 'use of force'. Even before WWII, the Committee in *the I'm Alone Case* implied that there are two conditions to use the force: namely, necessity and reasonableness.[35] In *the Red Crusad-*

---

[34] Melzer and Gasteyger points out that " (t) he concept of law enforcement is not defined in international law"; Nile Melzer and Gloria Gaggioli Gasteyger, *Conceptual Distinction and Overlaps between Law Enforcement and the Conduct of Hostilities*, in Terry D. Gill and Dieter Fleck (eds.), The Handbook of the International Law of Military Operations, 2nd ed. , (2015), p. 62.

[35] *"I'm Alone" Case*, *supra* note 9, p. 1615.

er Case, though the Commission of Enquiry has not mentioned the conditions to the use of force, it suggested that force shall not be used beyond the legitimate scope. [36]

Soft law documents provide the conditions in more straightforward manner. For example, Article 3 of the Code of Conduct for Law Enforcement Officials says "Law enforcement officials may use force only when strictly necessary and to the extent required for the performance of their duty." This Article seems to suppose necessity and proportionality as conditions for using force. Furthermore, the Basic Principles elaborates the conditions in detail. Although authoritative decisions were not detailed, less authoritative soft law has elaborated the norm in this manner.

However, in *the M/V "SAIGA" (No. 2) Case*, an authoritative and elaborate judgement was rendered by the ITLOS. As mentioned, the ITLOS stated "the use of force must be avoided as far as possible and, where force is unavoidable, it must not go beyond what is reasonable and necessary in the circumstances." [37] The Court manifestly provided reasonableness and necessity as conditions and at the same time, it held that the use of force must be the last resort. This part of the judgement of *the M/V "SAIGA" (No. 2) Case* was quoted in the following decisions.

In *the Guyana/Suriname Case*, the Arbitral Tribunal referred to this part of the judgement of *the M/V "SAIGA" (No. 2) Case*, and stated that "force may be used in law enforcement activities provided that such force is unavoidable, reasonable and necessary." [38] Moreover, in *the M/V "Virginia G" Case*, the ITLOS confirmed its previous position in *the M/V "SAIGA" (No. 2) Case*. [39] Furthermore, in *the Arctic Sunrise Case*, the Arbitral Tribunal said "ITLOS took account of general international law rules on the use of force in considering the use of force for the arrest of vessel"

---

[36] *Red Crusader Case*, *supra* note 10, p. 538.
[37] *The M/V "SAIGA" (No. 2) Case*, *supra* note 11, paras. 155–156.
[38] *Guyana/Suriname*, *supra* note 4, para. 445.
[39] *M/V "Virginia G"*, *supra* note 14, paras. 359–360.

and quoted part of *the M/V "SAIGA" (No. 2) Case.* [40]

In terms of the conditions to use the force lawfully exercised under MPL, many commentators provide their opinions by analyzing the cases and documents discussed above. [41] It is beyond the scope of this paper to provide all rules and requirements to use force under MPL. However, it must be emphasized that the use of force must be the last resort, as is confirmed in the case law. For example, in *the M/V "SAI-GA" (No. 2) Case*, the ITLOS held as follows:

The normal practice used to stop a ship at sea is first to give an auditory or visual signal to stop, using internationally recognized signals. Where this does not succeed, a variety of actions may be taken, including the firing of shots across the bows of the ship. It is only after the appropriate actions fail that the pursuing vessel may, as a last resort, use force. [42]

Pursuant to this holding, the ITLOS adds the said condition to avoid the use of force as far as possible, and at the same time, it also broadens the utilization of firearms, in the form of warning shot. Thus, it seems difficult to suppose that MPL makes the attempted law enforcement measures illegal. In other words, it is not until measures were taken that the legality of these measures was called into question. Unlike *jus ad bellum*, which prohibits the threat of force as well as the use of force, [43] there is no precedent that recognizes a violation of MPL, without actual use of force. To put it differently, the threat of force cannot constitute a violation of

---

[40] *The Arctic Sunrise Arbitration*, *supra* note 15, para. 191.

[41] Most commentators support that the necessity and reasonableness are one of the conditions. On the other hand, Frostad criticizes the relationship between necessity and reasonableness as being uncertain; Frostad, *supra* note 12, p. 215.

[42] *The M/V "SAIGA" (No. 2) Case*, *supra* note 11, para. 156.

[43] As for the study that focuses on the threat of force, see Nikolas Stürchler, The Threat of Force in International Law, (2007).

MPL.

The scope of MPL has had a recent tendency to expand. As a result, its reach now extends not only to use of force but also to broaden law enforcement measures. For example, in *the M/V "Virginia G" Case*, the ITLOS said "the principle of reasonableness applies generally to enforcement measures under article 73 of the Convention". [44] This principle of reasonableness seems to appear from the requirement of reasonableness for the bond fixed by the Coastal States under Article 73 (2). It is unclear why this requirement can be extended to enforcement measures in general, beyond a price of the bond. However, this conclusion is also supported by the following decision. The Arbitral Tribunal in *the Arctic Sunrise Case* rendered that the Tribunal would examine whether "Russia's measures were carried out in accordance with general principles of reasonableness, necessity, and proportionality", [45] if Russia's measures were formed on a legal basis. [46] As such, although the Scope of MPL has expanded, the threat to use force has not been prohibited.

3. 2 Content and scope of *jus ad bellum*

(1) The UN Charter

Commentators postulate that Article 2 (4) only prohibits military activities and does not cover police activities, even if they are conducted in a foreign territory. [47]

---

[44]   *M/V "Virginia G"*, *supra* note 14, para. 270.

[45]   *The Arctic Sunrise Arbitration*, *supra* note 15, para. 224: Also, the Tribunal states that "Where such measures involve enforcement measures they are subject to the general principles of necessity and proportionality"; *Ibid.*, para. 222.

[46]   In its decision, the Tribunal did not clarify the reason general principles are broadly applied to enforcement measures in general, and the scope of the application is not limited to the use of force. It may be possible to associate this expansion of MPL with the argument that the freedom to protest at the sea is a part of freedom of navigation and therefore this freedom is respected on an equality with human rights; *Ibid.*, paras. 182 and 228. See also Joanna Mossop, *Protests against Oil Exploration at Sea: Lessons from the Arctic Sunrise Arbitration*, The International Journal of Marine and Coastal Law, Vol. 31 (2016), p. 66.

[47]   Albrecht Randelzhofer, *Article 2 (4)*, in Bruno Simma, Daniel-Erasmus Khan, Georg Nolte, and Andreas Paulus (eds.), *The Charter of the United Nations: A Commentary*, 3rd ed., Vol. I, (2012), p. 210.

For example, Rayfuse argues that "International law does not prohibit what are effectively 'police actions'."[48] It is a well–known example that Argentina never claimed a violation of Article 2 (4) in *the Eichmann Case* where the Israel Police compulsorily took Eichmann from Argentina to Israel with the use of firearms.[49] Although military activities are prohibited under the UN Charter, other activities, including police measures, are not. However, this position is not without critics. Guilfoyle argues that "A 'police action' is not something other than a use of force; consent may simply render it not a prohibited use of force."[50] Accordingly, although the use of force in a police action is also covered by *jus ad bellum*, it is justified based on the consent.[51] Therefore, based on his thought, illegal use of force in police activity constitutes a violation of *jus ad bellum*. Because the use of force against private merchant vessels falls within the scope of "armed attacks" which is a significant type of illegal use of force,[52] the use of force against vessels falls within the use of force prohibited by *jus ad bellum*.[53]

This theory is logical and persuasive; however, the fact that a shot against private vessels may fall within the scope of an armed attack, does not necessarily mean that all uses of force against vessels are prohibited by *jus ad bellum*. Moreover, the idea that the use of force against a merchant vessel is basically prohibited by Article 2

---

[48] Rosemary Rayfuse, *Countermeasures and High Seas Fisheries Enforcement*, Netherlands International Law Review, Vol. 51 (2004), p. 74

[49] Corten, *supra* note 6, pp. 68–70; As for the impact of Eichmann Trial, especially on universal jurisdiction, see Makoto Seta, *Expanding the Scope of Universal Jurisdiction through Municipal Law: From Piracy to the Crime of Aggression via Eichmann Trial*, in Morten Bergsmo, Wui Ling Cheah, Tianying Song and Ping Yi (eds.), Historical Origins of International Criminal Law, Vol. IV (2015), pp. 339–366.

[50] Douglas Guilfoyle, Shipping Interdiction and the Law of the Sea, (2009), p. 276.

[51] Article 20 of the Draft Articles on Responsibility of States for Internationally Wrongful Acts provides that "Valid consent by a State to the commission of a given act by another State precludes the wrongfulness of that act in relation to the former State to the extent that the act remains within the limits of that consent."; Yearbook of the International Law Commission, 2001, vol. II, Part Two, (A/CN. 4/SER. A/2001/Add. 1 (Part 2)), p. 27.

[52] *Military and Paramilitary Activities*, *supra* note 29, p. 14, 101, para. 191.

[53] Guilfoyle, *supra* note 50, pp. 273–274.

(4) seems contradict the position of the ITLOS. Recently, in *the M/V "Virginia G" Case*, the Tribunal stated "the use of force in enforcement activities at sea is not generally prohibited",[54] though it might be possible to make a distinction between rules in the exclusive economic zone (EEZ) and in the high seas. [55]

Based on this fact that there definitely are some MLE activities that are not prohibited under *jus ad bellum*, the outer limit of scope of *jus ad bellum* must be delineated. With regard to this point, there are two main grounds to exclude MLE activities from the scope of *jus ad bellum*. One is the condition of "in their international relations" provided in Article 2 (4) of the UN Charter, and the second is the minimum threshold of "force".

Some commentators assert that the exercise of jurisdiction over private persons does not fall within the scope of military activity because the inherent condition in the UN Charter, which is "in their international relations" provided in Article 2 (4). [56] If the phrase is interpreted literally, the threat or use of force against a sovereign State is prohibited, but not against private individual. For example, Milano & Papanicolopulu argue the following:

The limited use of force that may be needed in order to enforce the legislation of the coastal State in maritime areas claimed by it is conceptually different from the use of force in international relations prohibited by article 2 paragraph 4 UN Charter. While in the latter case the use of force is the content and the end of the action by the State, in the former case the use of force is instrumental to another activity,

---

[54] *M/V "Virginia G"*, *supra* note 14, para. 360.

[55] Ruys states that " (a) lthough a coastal state's forcible action against merchant vessels within the maritime zones over which it exercises jurisdiction can reasonably be seen as falling within the law enforcement paradigm, this presumption arguably cannot be extended to forcible action beyond those zones"; Ruys, *supra* note 6, pp. 207–208.

[56] See, for example, Kiara Neri, L' emploi de la force en mer, (2012), pp. 36–37.

consisting in applying the legislation of the coastal State. [57]

However, according to the Definition of Aggression, UN GA Resolution 3314 (XXIX) ,

Any of the following acts, regardless of a declaration of war, shall, subject to and in accordance with the provisions of article 2, qualify as an act of aggression:

…

(d) An attack by the armed forces of a State on the land, sea or air forces, or marine and air fleets of another State; …[58]

Considering that this definition of aggression is widely speared, [59] it might be difficult to acknowledge that use of force against a private individual does not fall within the scope of Article 2 (4). Moreover, Guilfoyle states that " (b) oarding a foreign vessel on the high seas falls within the sphere of ' international rela-tions' . " [60] In addition, in the *Guyana/Suriname Case*, warning against a private sector is labeled as a threat of force under Article 2 (4) , though the character of the

---

[57] Enrico Milano and Irini Papanicolopulu, *State Responsibility in Disputed Areas on Land and at Sea*, Zeitschrift für ausländisches Öffentliches Recht und Völkerrecht, Vol. 71 (2011) , pp. 622−623.

[58] On this point, the representative of Indonesia claimed that "The inclusion of the words ' merchant marine' or ' marine' would be very difficult for his delegation to accept, since it was possible to envisage a situa-tion in the future where a nation aiming to protect its living resources might be accused of committing an act of ag-gression"; Summary Record of the One Hundred and Sixth Meeting, Consideration of the Question of Defining Aggression (A/AC. 134/SR. 106) , p. 24.

[59] For instance, Article 8 *bis* paragraph 2 of the ICC Statute stipulates that "For the purpose of para-graph 1, ' act of aggression' means the use of armed force by a State…. Any of the following acts, regardless of a declaration of war, shall, in accordance with *United Nations General Assembly resolution* 3314 (*XXIX*) of 14 December 1974, qualify as an act of aggression (emphasis added) ": In addition, the ICJ found that some pro-visions of GA Resolution 3314 (XXIX) reflect customary international law; *Military and Paramilitary Activities*, *supra* note 29, p. 14, 103, para. 195.

[60] Guilfoyle, *supra* note 50, pp. 272−273; On the contrary, Ruys argues that "The nationality link is insufficient to automatically characterize such acts as affecting the international relations between states. "; Ruys, *supra* note 6, p. 202.

said private sector is controversial. [61] Furthermore, "unit theory," which gives the flag State a standing to peruse the other States' responsibility for internationally wrongful acts over the ship flying its flag as an injured State, might support the idea that the attack against a private vessel is related to "international relations". [62] This is because, in accordance with "unit theory", the international law of responsibility regards the attack against a merchant vessel not to be an attack against a private person, but a direct attack against the flag State itself. Consequently, when their ships are damaged, States can pursue the responsibility of other States without fulfilling two requirements for exercising diplomatic protection: continuous nationality and exhaustion of local remedies. [63]

Therefore, the object of force, namely, a private individual or sovereign states cannot be a decisive factor by itself, though it helps the characterization of a use of force. Hence, another argument, the condition of minimum threshold of 'force' must be taken into account. This minimum threshold of 'force' has been historically argued. Although it is beyond the scope of this paper to elaborate the threshold, in accordance with previous academic teaching, it is natural to consider that most MLE activities do not reach that threshold. [64] Helmersen argues that "Some, or even all, uses of force against ships based on Articles 105, 110, and 111 can be seen as being too minor to be above the threshold of the prohibition of the use of force, and be outside its scope already on this basis. "[65]

---

[61] Papastavridis emphasizes that Suriname threated to use of force in order to protect its sovereign rights over continental shelf; Papastavridis, *supra* note 12, pp. 131–132.

[62] As for "unite theory", see, for example, *The M/V "SAIGA"* (*No.2*) *Case*, *supra* note 11, para. 106; *The Arctic Sunrise Arbitration*, *supra* note 15, paras. 171–172.

[63] Annemarieke V. Künzli, *A Matter of Interest: Diplomatic Protection and State Responsibility Erga Omnes*, International and Comparative Law Quarterly, Vol. 56, No. 3 (2007), p. 554.

[64] Corten, *supra* note 6, pp. 70–71.

[65] Sondre T. Helmersen, *The Prohibition of the Use of Force as Jus Cogens: Explaining Apparent Derogations*, Netherlands International Law Review, Vol. 66 (2014), p. 179.

(2) Development from the UN Charter

When considering the scope *jus ad bellum*, the evolution after the adoption of the UN Charter must be noted. Once it was commonly understood that *jus ad bellum* was a law that regulates States before an armed conflict occurs, and it does not operate after *jus in bello* is applied. [66] However, the current judge of the ICJ, Sir Christopher Greenwood asserts the following:

The modern *jus ad bellum* applies not only to the act of commencing hostilities but also to each act involving the use of force which occurs during the course of hostilities. Any use of force, even after the outbreak of fighting, is prohibited if it cannot be justified by reference to the right of self—defence recognized in Article 51 of the Charter. [67]

Therefore, according to judge Greenwood, *jus in bello* and *jus ad bellum* are "cumulative and not alternative." [68]

This new cognition of *jus ad bellum* is supported by the ICJ. In *the Nuclear Weapons Advisory Opinion*, the Court said that "a use of force that is proportionate under the law of self—defence, must, in order to be lawful, also meet the requirements of the law applicable in armed conflict." [69] This Court seems to take the po-

---

[66] See, for example, *Commentary*, Syracuse Journal of International Law and Commerce, Vol. 14, No. 4 (1987–1988), pp. 574–578, 582–583, 586, 591, 592 (Frits Kalshoven, Horace B. Robertson, Gert-Jan van Hegelsom); Leslie C. Green, *Comment No. 5 on Mr. Greenwood's Report*, Heintschel von Heinegg (ed.), Visit, Search, Diversion and Capture: the Effect of the United Nations Charter on the Law of Naval Warfare: Reports and Commentaries of the Round-Table of Experts on International Humanitarian Law Applicable to Armed Conflicts at Sea; Bergen, 20–24 September 1991 (1995), p. 1911.

[67] Christopher Greenwood, *The Relationship between jus ad bellum and jus in bello*, Review of International Studies, Vol. 9 (1983), p. 223.

[68] Christopher Greenwood, *jus ad bellum and jus in bello in the Nuclear Weapons Advisory Opinion*, in Laurence B. Chazournes and Philippe Sands (eds.), International Law, the International Court of Justice and Nuclear Weapons, (1999), p. 264.

[69] *Legality of the Threat or Use of Nuclear Weapons*, Advisory Opinion, I. C. J. Reports 1996, p. 226, p. 245, para. 42.

sition that accepts the cumulative application of *jus ad bellum* and *jus in bello*. Actually, Judge Greenwood considers that this opinion accepts the continuing application of *jus ad bellum*. [70]

In addition, in *the Oil Platform Case*, the Court clarifies that whether the object of attack is a legitimate military target shall be into account for the purpose of evaluating the requirement of proportionality for self-defense. [71] It is well known that the rule to define a legitimate military target is incorporated into *jus in bello*. Arguably, this case can be read to admit that the ICJ employed *jus in bello* when evaluating *jus ad bellum*.

In this way, *jus ad bellum* continues to be applied even during an armed conflict in parallel with *jus in bello*. Therefore, in the case of occupation that is regulated by *jus in bello*, [72] *jus ad bellum* plays a role. At the same time, in the case of an occupation, Guilfoyle correctly points out that "military forces may be restricted to a 'policing' use of force paradigm". [73] With this regard, the rule to regulate "policing" use of force is MPL. Given these facts, there may be a situation in which *jus ad bellum* and MPL should be cumulatively applied. [74]

---

[70]   Greenwood, *supra* note 68, p. 258.

[71]   *Oil Platforms* (*Islamic Republic of Iran v. United States of America*), Judgment, *I. C. J. Reports* 2003, p. 161, pp. 186–187, para. 51.

[72]   Giladi argues that both *jus ad bellum* and *jus in bello* work as the law of occupation, though he also doubts the sharp distinction between these two norms in the law of occupation: Rotem Giladi, *The Jus ad Bellum/ Jus in Bello Distinction and the Law of Occupation*, Israel Law Review, Vol. 41, Nos. 1 & 2 (2008), pp. 246–301.

[73]   Douglas Guilfoyle, *The Mavi Marmara Incident and Blockade in Armed Conflict*, British Year Book of International Law, Vol. 81 (2011), p. 210; Yoram Dinstein, The International Law of Belligerent Occupation, (2009), pp. 89–94.

[74]   This conclusion means that *jus in bello* and MPL are also cumulatively applied. Since this point is beyond the scope of this article, it is not elaborated here. However, considering the similar character of these two laws, the relationship between them must carefully delineated. To illustrate, what MPL prohibits can be allowed by *jus in bello*. One possible answer to solve this negative conflict is that *jus in bello* is regarded as *lex specialis* and prevails MPL when it is applied, as is the relationship between human rights law and humanitarian law; see *Legal Consequences of the Construction of a Wall in the Occupied Palestinian Territory*, Advisory Opinion, *I. C. J. Reports* 2004, p. 136, 178, para. 106. As for the relationship between the law of the sea and the laws of war in general, see Robin Churchill and Vaughan Lowe, The Law of the Sea, 3rd ed. , (1999), pp. 421–426.

4. The Relationship between MPL and *Jus Ad Bellum*

4. 1 Reforming the relationship between MPL and *Jus Ad Bellum*

Many commentators to date have analyzed and structured the relationship between MPL and *jus ad bellum*. Therefore, the views of several commentators are summarized below.

The pioneer of this relationship, Kwast, argues that "the distinction between law enforcement and the use of military force serves to identify the applicable international standards that allow the legality of the action to be determined," [75] based on the presumption that there is a legal distinction between MLE activity and military activity. Furthermore, Kwast elaborates in the following manner:

Unlawful forcible law enforcement will not necessarily constitute the use of force in the sense of Article 2 (4) anymore than that lawful use of force will automatically qualify as law enforcement. Rather, to consider the lawfulness of instances of forcible action at sea, the following analytical sequence will apply: ①identifying the relevant aspects of the case; ②classifying the action in question; and ③ determining the applicable legal standards. [76]

In the same vein, Papastavridis argues "*sedes materiae* for the assessment of the legality of the use of force in the course of interception operations are the rules governing law enforcement at sea, as set forth by the previous jurisprudence and as provided in each state's RoEs, and not the rules under the *jus ad bellum*" in his monograph, which focuses on the interceptions of vessels on the high seas. [77] More recently Papastavridis conducted research focusing on the rules of international law o-

---

[75] Kwast, *supra* note 6, p. 62.

[76] *Ibid.*

[77] Efthymios Papastavridis, The Interception of Vessels on the High Seas: Contemporary Challenges to the Legal Order of the Oceans, (2013), p. 72.

ver the use of force at sea. In this research, he lists the three rules of international law which are applicable to the use of force at sea, and contends that the applicable law depends on the circumstances of each case; namely (1) "the law of naval warfare" (*jus in bello*) is applied in the context of armed conflict, (2) "the rules governing law–enforcement" (MPL) is applied in the context of policing operation, and (3) Article 2 (4) and 51 of the UN Charter (*jus ad bellum*) is applied in the case where sovereignty or sovereign rights are related. [78]

Though in a different context, Guilfoyle also takes the view that MPL and *jus ad bellum* are applied separately. Accordingly, when evaluating a shipping interdiction, he asserts that whether the interdiction in question violates Article 2 (4) of the UN Charter (*jus ad bellum*) must be assessed upfront. Then, "the rules governing force during permissible interdictions" are taken into account. [79] Because these rules are a part of MPL, he clearly divides *jus ad bellum* and MPL, and applies the latter to the activities that are legal under the former. A former judge of the ITLOS, Anderson, shows a similar view in the simple manner, by arguing "Drawing the distinction between military activity and law enforcement activity is an important step since the law applicable to the one is different from that applicable to the other. "[80] Furthermore, Neri seems to support this dominant view. She sates that "the fight against illegal activities of private persons will be released from the shackles of the law of the sea and be subject to the law of collective security (translated by the author). "[81]

This conclusion is reached not only by specialists on the law of the sea but also by experts on *jus ad bellum*. They separate application of the law of the sea and the UN Charter, which, in the terminology of the present paper, are MPL and *jus ad*

---

[78] Papastavridis, *supra* note 12, p. 136.

[79] Guilfoyle, *supra* note 50, p. 277.

[80] Anderson, *supra* note 6, p. 241.

[81] On the basis of the terminology of the present paper, "the law of the sea (le droit de la mer) " and "the law of collective security (le droit de la sécurité collective) " are MPL and jus ad bellum, respectively. Neri, *supra* note 56, p. 52.

bellum, respectively. To illustrate, Ruys clarifies the meaning of "force" in Article 2 (4) of the UN Charter and argues the following: "Action that is lawful under the law of the sea will not contravene the Charter framework on the use of force *since the two frameworks have distinct domains of application* (emphasis added). "[82] Similarly, Corten, one of the most distinguished scholars on *jus ad bellum*,[83] confirms the existence of two separate bodies of rules based on case law and practice in his analysis; one is the law of the sea, which governs police measures, and the other is UN Charter, which relates to military action in the State to State relationship. [84]

Far from being identical, the views of these academic scholars on the content of *jus ad bellum* and MPL are considerably divergent, especially with regard to the scope of *jus ad bellum* and the content of MPL. Nevertheless, they uniformly agree that MPL is applied to MLE activity, whereas *jus ad bellum* is applied to military activity. However, as is shown in Chapter II, this proposition seemingly is not based on the historical foundation. Moreover, Chapter III clarifies that there seems to be an overlap between the scope of application of these two laws. Thus, the next section aims to reconsider this proposition and reestablish the relationship between MPL and *jus ad bellum*.

4. 2 Reforming the relationship and its implication

(1) The relationship between MPL and *jus ad bellum*

The majority of commentators who support the proposition that MPL is applied to MLE activity and *jus ad bellum* is applied to military activity rely on the decision of the Arbitral Tribunal in *the Guyana/Suriname Case*. Especially, the Court's finding of "the action mounted by Suriname on 3 June 2000 seemed more akin to a threat of military action rather than a mere law enforcement activity. . . . Suriname's action

---

[82] Ruys, *supra* note 6, p. 202.

[83] Olivier Corten, The Law against War: The Prohibition on the Use of Force in Contemporary International Law, (2010), p. viii.

[84] Corten, *supra* note 6, p. 76.

therefore constituted a threat of the use of force in contravention of the Convention, the UN Charter and general international law. "[85] Although this decision seems to support the prevailing proposition, the Tribunal did not explicitly state that the applicable laws pertaining to military action and law enforcement activity are distinguishable. Rather, the decision derives from the fact that military action generally becomes illegal unless it can be justified under the Chapter VII of the UN Charter. [86] As such, the dominant view is flawed and this paper will demonstrate the better view that MPL and *jus ad bellum* are cumulatively applied to all activities involving the threat or use of force, [87] based on the following three reasons.

First, because of an entirely separate historical development, it is impossible to assume a completely different scope of application. In other words, without any artificial intent, the separation cannot be completed. For example, in the municipal law of most States, the scope of Criminal Procedure Law and Civil Procedure Law is completely separate, because they are designed as such. Meanwhile, with regard to international law, an organization to coordinate international law in that manner does not exist. Therefore, it might be inevitable that some part of MPL and *jus ad bellum* overlap.

Second, an act that violates *jus ad bellum* but not MPL is supposed. [88] The said proposition is based on the fact that MLE and military activity are distinguished,

---

[85]   *Guyana/Suriname*, *supra* note 4, para. 445

[86]   See Guilfoyle, *supra* note 50, p. 276. As for the relationship between the threat of force and the use of force, the ICJ states that "The notions of 'threat' and 'use' of force under Article 2, paragraph 4, of the Charter stand together in the sense that if the use of force itself in a given case is illegal-for whatever reason-the threat to use such force will likewise be illegal. "; *Legality of the Threat or Use of Nuclear Weapons*, *supra* note 69, p. 226, 246, para. 47.

[87]   Rothwell & Stephens seem take a similar view; Donald R. Rothwell and Tim Stephens, The International Law of the Sea, (2010), pp. 418–422.

[88]   More generally, Paddeu argues that "this use of force, lawful as it may be under one rule of international law, may be unlawful under another rule of international law"; Federica I. Paddeu, *Self-Defence as a Circumstance Precluding Wrongfulness: Understanding Article 21 of the Articles on State Responsibility*, British Year Book of International Law, Vol. 86 (2015), p. 42.

and the former is less grave than the latter. Therefore, it is believed that *jus ad bellum* focuses on the military action and MPL prohibits the activities in the wider manner. However, according to the reasoning in *the Guyana/Suriname Case*, which created a precedent for finding a violation of the threat of force, the threat against private individuals would fall within the scope of the threat of force, regardless whether Suriname used force. [89] Therefore, in accordance with precedent, the conduct of Suriname would not constitute a violation of MPL, though it violated *jus ad bellum*. Accordingly, MPL only prohibits actual use of force, whereas *jus ad bellum* does its previous stage, namely, the threat of force. In that sense, *jus ad bellum* may be broader in its application than MPL.

Third, the situation exists where *jus ad bellum* and MPL should be cumulatively applied. Currently, the continuing application of *jus ad bellum* is well established, from the perspective of both academic teachings and case law. [90] Therefore, the use of firearms during armed conflict can be subject to *jus ad bellum*. To illustrate, for the purpose of justifying a gunshot in the occupied area, an occupying State must demonstrate that the gunshot in question does not prevent the State from fulfilling the requirement of proportionality throughout armed conflict. At the same time, an occupying State is obliged to comply with MPL, as in the case of peace time.

Based on this analysis, use of force at sea is legally classified into four types: ①activity that neither violates MPL nor *jus ad bellum*, ②activity that violates MPL but not *jus ad bellum*, ③activity that violates *jus ad bellum* but not MPL, and④activity that violates both MPL and *jus ad bellum*. Among these four types, the result of the second type would be problematic because lawful use of force, namely, the exer-

---

[89] *Supra* note 4.

[90] Aside from Greenwood, Stahn, Gardam and Higgins support the continuing application of *jus ad bellum*: Carsten Stahn, "*Jus ad bellum*", "*jus in bello*" … "*jus post bellum*"? —*Rethinking the Conception of the Law of Armed Force*, European Journal of International Law, Vol. 17, No. 5 (2006), p. 926; Judith Gardam, Necessity, Proportionality and the Use of Force by States, (2004), p. 156; Rosalyn Higgins, Problems and Process: International Law and How We Use It, (1994), pp. 232-233.

cise of self—defence and military activity based on the Security Council (SC) authorization could constitute a violation of MPL. If this is the case, some States might argue that the theory of cumulative application of MPL and *jus ad bellum* is too restrictive. In addition, it is pointed out that the law of the sea should not be understood to contradict with the UN Charter, because the UN Charter has a primacy. [91] However, after reviewing the reasoning of the following two points, the second type of classification cannot be considered a serious problem.

First, according to Article 21 of the Articles on State Responsibility, an exercise of the right of self—defence in conformity with the Charter of the United Nations precludes the wrongfulness of an act of a State. According to the Commentary by the ILC, "Self—defence may justify non—performance of certain obligations other than that under Article 2, paragraph 4, of the Charter of the United Nations, provided that such non—performance is related to the breach of that provision. " [92] Therefore, if a use of force is justified as an exercise of the right of self—defence, that use precludes the wrongfulness that derives from collateral breach of *jus ad bellum*, namely a violation of MPL. [93]

Second, recent SC Resolutions seem to establish the system that is in conformity with MPL. It is evident that the expression "all necessary means" is used with a view to allow member States to use force. [94] However, a literal interpretation of that phrase justifies not only the use of force but also all other violations of international law, including MPL, to the extent it is necessary. Actually, Resolution 678 that authorizes use of force against Iraq seems to allow member States to intrude Iraqi territory aside from the use of force itself. Lowe states that "Resolution 678 gave each one of the States in the 1991 coalition, acting either alone or jointly with some or all of

---

[91]　Rayfuse, *supra* note 48, p. 74.

[92]　Yearbook of the International Law Commission, *supra* note 51, p. 74.

[93]　Paddeu, *supra* note 88, p. 29.

[94]　United Nations, The United Nations and the Iraq—Kuwait Conflict 1990-1996, (1996), p. 22.

the others, the right to take any action, anytime, anywhere, that it considers it necessary or desirable in pursuit of the aim of restoring peace and security in the area". [95] In other words, authorization of the SC precludes the wrongfulness that derive from a violation of MPL, in the same way as self-defence.

Meanwhile, recent SC Resolutions not only justify a violation of MPL, but also require Member States to comply with MPL. For example, against Somali pirates, the SC has adopted several resolutions that allow member States to conduct MLE in the Somali waters, to exercise criminal jurisdiction over the pirate suspects and to take "all necessary means" for that purpose. [96] In addition, these resolutions call upon Member States to comply with "applicable international law including international human rights law. "[97] It is true that the resolutions manifestly refer only to international human rights law. [98] Considering the context of SC Resolutions, MLE activities against Somali pirate, it is reasonable to include MPL into the "applicable international law" provided in SC Resolutions.

(2) The relationship among rules of conduct under international law

The relationship between MPL and *jus ad bellum* can be generalized into the relationships among rules of conduct under international law. As explained, it was once believed that *jus ad bellum* and *jus in bello* are separately applied. In addition, with regard to the relationship between international human rights law and international humanitarian law (*jus in bello*), it was not until *the Israeli Wall Advisory Opinion* in

---

[95]   Vaughan Lowe, *The Iraq Crisis: What Now?*, International and Comparative Law Quarterly, Vol. 52, No. 4 (2003), p. 866.

[96]   See James L. Kateka, *Combating Piracy and Armed Robbery off the Somali Coast and the Gulf of Guinea*, in Lilian del Castillo (ed.), Law of the Sea, From Grotius to the International Tribunals for the Law of the Sea, (2015), pp. 462–463; Anna Petrig, *Piracy*, in Donald R. Rothwell, Alex G. O. Elferink, Karen N. Scott, Tim Stephens (eds.) The Oxford Handbook of the Law of the Sea, (2015), pp. 854–855.

[97]   For example, paragraph 11 of the SC Resolution 1816 (2008).

[98]   Although, paragraph 6 of the SC Resolution 1851 refers to international humanitarian law as well as international human rights law, this inclusive framework was not adopted in the following similar resolutions, such as Resolutions 1897 (2009), 1950 (2010), 2020 (2011), 2077 (2012), 2125 (2013), and 2184 (2014).

2004 that their cumulative application was established. [99] Generally speaking, the applicable scope of the rules of conduct under international law is solely determined by those rules. For example, it is well known that humanitarian law is applied only when an "armed conflict" occurs, whether international or non-international, [100] without any coordination with other bodies of law, such as *jus ad bellum* or international human rights laws. This issue has been hotly debated both academically and in practice since *the Tadić Case* was rendered by the International Tribunal for the Former Yugoslavia (ICTY). [101]

Similarly, the applicable scope of international human rights law, more concretely, human right treaties, is determined by each treaty itself. For example, Article 2 of the International Covenant on Civil and Political Rights (ICCPR) provides "Each State Party to the present Covenant undertakes to respect and to ensure to all individuals within its territory and subject to its jurisdiction the rights recognized in the present Covenant..." Therefore, the meaning of "within its territory and subject to its jurisdiction" has been harshly discussed in the same way as "armed conflict". [102] Then, since the meaning is determined without any reference to the other bodies of law, such as *jus ad bellum* and *jus in bello*, the applicable scope of human rights law also can be determined independently and separately.

Recently, the European Court of Human Rights (ECtHR) has had a tendency

---

[99]   *Supra* note 74.

[100]   Common Article 2 of the 1949 Geneva Conventions provides that the rules in the convention are applied to "all cases of declared war or of any other *armed conflict*... (emphasis added) ". In the same vein, Common Article 3 provides the minimum rules "in the case of *armed conflict* not of an international character... (emphasis added). "

[101]   ICTY, Trial Chamber, Opinion and Judgement, Tadić, Case No. IT-94-1-T (7 May 1997), para. 562.

[102]   See, for example, Marko Milanovic, Extraterritorial Application of Human Rights Treaties: Law, Principles, and Policy, (2011), and Karen da Costa, The Extraterritorial Application of Selected Human Treaties, (2013), pp. 15-92; With regard to US position, Beth Van Schaack, *The United States' Position on the Extraterritorial Application of Human Rights Obligations: Now is the Time for Change*, International Law Studies, Vol. 90 (2014), pp. 20-65.

to apply European Convention on Human Rights (ECHR) to the MLE activities and find violations. For example, in *the Medvedyev Case*, the Grand Chamber held that France violated Article 5 of the ECHR, although, it admits the French measures were in conformity with the law of the sea. [103] More recently, in *the Case of Hassan and Others v. France*, the ECtHR found that the right of Somali pirates were violated by French authorities. [104] Moreover, with regard to the Arctic Sunrise incidents, crewmembers of the vessel brought the case before the EctHR, and the proceeding is currently pending. [105] As shown, the Arbitral Tribunal found that Russia violated the law of the sea, and in the near future, the ECtHR will find the violation of human rights law. It is true that the reparation must be coordinated by the tribunals and courts that found the violation based on the same activities. However, this does not refute the assertion that human rights laws and the law of the sea, especially MPL, are applied cumulatively.

As rules of conduct are omnipresent and each rule decides its applicable scope without coordination with other laws, it is quite natural that some part of their application overlap. From the more macroscopic perspective, not only human rights laws, but also *jus ad bellum* and *jus in bello* may be applied cumulatively with MPL. [106] Moreover, considering the recent increase of new treaties, the fifth law that is applied to the use of force at sea would appear in the not too distant future.

---

[103] *Affaire Medvedyev et autres c. France* (*Requête no* 3394/03), *Arrêt*, 29 *mars* 2010, para. 96 ; Guilfoyle shows his concern on the judgment of the Grand Chamber; Douglas Guilfoyle, *Human Rights Issues and Non-Flag State Boarding of Suspect Ships in International Waters*, in Clive R. Symmons (ed.), Selected Contemporary Issues in the Law of the Sea, (2011), pp. 94-96.

[104] *Affaire Hassan et autres c. France* (*Requête no* 46695/10 *et* 54588/10), *Arrêt*, 4 *déc* 2014, paras. 57-72.

[105] Greenpeace International, *Applications to the European Court of Human Rights*, available at <http://www. greenpeace. org/international/en/campaigns/climate-change/arctic-impacts/Peace-Dove/Arctic-30/European-Court-of-Human-Rights/> (last visited on 29th Apr. 2016).

[106] With regard to the distinction between law enforcement at sea and the exercise of belligerent rights, see Heintschel von Heinegg, "The Difficulties of Conflict Classification at Sea, Distinguishing Incidents at Sea from Hostilities", *International Review of the Red Cross*, Vol. 98 (2016), pp. 449-464.

5. Conclusion

In terms of the relationship between MPL and *jus ad bellum*, this paper has analyzed and rejected the prevailing proposition and concludes that the two laws are applied cumulatively. In addition, it has been clarified that all rules of conduct are applied cumulatively under international law. However, the focus of this paper is limited to use of force at sea and the rules that regulate it. Therefore, the contribution of this paper to public international law is specific in its breadth.

That being said, the implication of this paper has at least one more contribution in the field of public international law in general. This contribution is the clarification of the distinction between rules of conduct and norms for judicial proceedings, which function when leading to a procedural decision in judicial organs like the ICJ. Theoretically speaking, this distinction has existed since the International Courts and Tribunals began their operation. Nevertheless, in the past, international law and the norms of judicial proceedings have been examined only to decide whether the Permanent Court of International Justice and the ICJ has jurisdiction, by interpreting the reservations to the declaration to accept compulsory jurisdiction. One typical example is "conservation and management measures" found in the Canadian declaration. As the Court correctly noted:

In this Judgment, the Court has had to interpret the words of the Canadian reservation in order to determine whether or not the acts of Canada, of which Spain complains, fall within the terms of that reservation, and hence whether or not it has jurisdiction. For this purpose the Court has not had to scrutinize or prejudge the legality of the acts referred to in paragraph 2 (d) of Canada's declaration. [107]

In this way, the issue of rules of conduct and issues of norms for judicial proceedings must be distinguished.

As long as the norms for judicial proceedings only appear in the declaration to

---

[107] *Fisheries Jurisdiction Case*, *supra* note 2, p. 465, para. 85.

accept compulsory jurisdiction, they do not have universal meaning under international law. The meaning of reservations heavily depends on the will of the State that makes the reservation. [108] Moreover, differing meanings of the same word as applied from State to State are irrelevant, because the jurisdiction of the ICJ is applied only to the issues covered by declarations by applicant and respondent. [109] However, under the UNCLOS system, the norms for judicial proceedings are provided directly in the UNCLOS. To illustrate, Articles 288 and 297 first provide the compulsory jurisdiction of the Courts and Tribunals with regard to "interpretation and application" of the UNCLOS. [110] Second, it provides the exceptions for compulsory jurisdiction, such as some marine scientific research, fisheries, and "sea boundary delimitations" under Article 297 and 298. Since the UNCLOS is a treaty, the terms in the UNCLOS must be interpreted in accordance with rules of the VCLT. In addition, the meaning of the same word should be identical to make a treaty stable, independently of the interpreter. To put it differently, basically the phrase "interpretation and application" or "sea boundary delimitations" must be interpreted in the same manner. As a result, it is inevitable for the norms for judicial proceedings to become synchronized to the rules of conduct, though they are distinguishable.

As shown in this paper, the prevailing view that MPL is applied to MLE activity and *jus ad bellum* is applied to military activity is a result of the improper mixture of rules of conduct and the norms for judicial proceedings following *the Fishery Jurisdiction Case*. Considering that the number of judicial proceedings based on the Part XV

---

[108] *Whaling in the Antarctic (Australia v. Japan; New Zealand intervening)*, Judgment, I. C. J. Reports 2014, p. 226, 244, para. 36 ; *Fisheries Jurisdiction Case, Ibid.*, p. 454, para. 48

[109] Hugh Thirlway, The Law and Procedure of the International Court of Justice ; Fifty Years of Jurisprudence, Vol. I, (2013), p. 785.

[110] In the *Chagos Marine Protected Area Case*, the meaning of "interpretation and application of the Convention" was conclusive when deciding whether the arbitral tribunal has a jurisdiction; *Mauritius/United Kingdom, Award of the Arbitral Tribunal*, 18 March, 2015, paras. 306–308.

of the UNCLO has increased, [111] the distinction between rules of conduct and norms for judicial proceedings must be deliberately scrutinized.

---

[111]   Aside from the cases already mentioned, such as *Guyana/Suriname*, *Mauritius/United Kingdom*, *Arctic Sunrise* and *Philippines/China*, currently, the ongoing *"Enrica Lexie"* *Incident* (*Italy v. India*) is initiated on the basis of Part XV of the UNCLOS. As for the *Enrica Lexie Case*, see Angela Del Vecchio, *The Fight against Piracy and the Enrica Lexie Case*, in Lilian del Castillo (ed.) , Law of the Sea, From Grotius to the International Tribunals for the Law of the Sea, (2015) , pp. 397-422.

MARITIME LAW ENFORCEMENT AND THE EXTRATERRITORIAL APPLICATION OF HUMAN RIGHTS AT SEA: AN EXPLORATION OF THE SPATIAL MODEL

Kristof Gombeer *

1. Introduction

States increasingly try to govern maritime spaces beyond the narrow band off their coastlines. Some of these trends were already recognized in the 1982 United Nations Convention on the Law of the Sea (UNCLOS). [1] Thus, for instance, the extent of the territorial sea increased from the common 3 nautical miles to up to 12 nautical miles measured from the baseline. Since UNCLOS it has also been accepted that contrary to some jurisprudence prior to World War II, states exercise sovereignty over their territorial sea in the same way they do over their land territory. [2] Another example is the creation of the right to exercise certain sovereign rights of coastal states in their Exclusive Economic Zone.

Anno 2018, states take their powers at sea even further. Environmental protection, concerns over pollution and illegal fishing, border control, and the fight against piracy, terrorism, modern slavery and smuggling have drawn states further onto the seas. This latest trend is characterised by an increased patrolling by coastal states'

---

* Fellow of the Research Foundation Flanders (FWO), PhD candidate at VU Brussels and Leiden Law School.

[1] United Nations Convention on the Law of the Sea (adopted 10 December 1982, entered into force 16 November 1994) 1833 UNTS 3.

[2] UNCLOS (n 2) art 2. See also: Louis B. Sohn, Kristen Gustafson Juras, John Noyes, Erik Franckx, *Law of the Sea* (2nd edn West 2010) 209-210.

military or coast guard, the use of interceptions on the high seas, and by the use of sophisticated surveillance techniques (e. g. using remotely piloted aircraft, satellite imagery, etc.). This is for example the case in the Mediterranean, where European Union Member States try to control migrant smuggling and illegal trafficking among other things. [3]

Whether or not these new trends in law enforcement are based on the appropriate jurisdictional grounds under UNCLOS or other relevant rules of international law is as such not the focus of this conference paper. Instead the focus lies with analysing the legal protection afforded to those impacted by these new government policies and actions at sea.

Increased law enforcement activities in and the militarisation and surveillance of the seas and oceans indeed raise an important question: Are those affected by these maritime security policies protected by international human rights law? In other words, can human rights apply extraterritorially at sea? In this regard, the European Court of Human Rights in a case concerning law enforcement against drug smugglers held that the special nature of the maritime environment cannot justify an area outside the law where persons are "covered by no legal system capable of affording them enjoyment of rights and guarantees protected by the Convention which the States have undertaken to secure to everyone within their jurisdiction". [4]

This conference paper wants to further the discussion about under which conditions, in the context of these new maritime law enforcement and surveillance trends, a state brings those affected by them within its jurisdiction for human rights purposes. More precisely, it seeks to explore the potential of one of the main tests for the extraterritorial application of human rights: the so-called "spatial model of jurisdiction", which signifies that a state has human rights obligations to those within the ar-

[3] Council of the European Union, *European Union Maritime Security Strategy* (24 June 2014) 11205/ 14.

[4] *Medvedyev v France* App no 3394/03 (ECtHR, 29 March 2010) para. 81.

ea over which it exercises effective control. So far, this model has only been used to assess jurisdiction *on land*, for example in the case of belligerent occupation or control over regimes abroad. This paper asks to which extent this model can also be used *at sea*.

The hypothesis developed here is that *when states exercise effective control over certain areas at sea—even if it concerns certain parts of the high seas—that it can bring those individuals within that area within the jurisdiction of the state for human rights purposes.*

The paper is further structured as follows: Section 2 briefly sketches some of the human rights issues that new trends in maritime governance entail. Subsequently, the paper sets out what jurisdiction for human rights purposes (HR jurisdiction) signifies and amounts to. It illustrates how the concept of HR jurisdiction has so far been applied in the maritime context and what kind of problems and gaps that creates (Section 3). While Section 4 explores the argument of applying the spatial model of HR jurisdiction at sea as a possibility, Section 5 pursues a *prima facie* assessment of whether some EU governance techniques in the Mediterranean might trigger HR jurisdiction pursuant to the spatial model. Section 6 provides some conclusions and elements for further discussion and research.

2. Maritime law enforcement and human rights issues

Human rights can have a normative bearing upon state activities at sea in mainly two ways. Aside from humanitarian considerations already being present in UNCLOS[5], the first avenue is for UNCLOS provisions to be interpreted in light of rel-

---

[5] Tullio Treves, "Human Rights and the Law of the Sea" (2010) 28 (1) Berkeley J. of Int'l Law 3; Bernard Oxman, "Human Rights and the United Nations Convention on the Law of the Sea" (1998) 36 Columbia Journal of Transnational Law 401–402.

evant human rights law norms. [6] A second avenue is for human rights law norms to apply autonomously, i. e. when a state through its actions has triggered the applicability of a human rights law instrument at sea (irrespective of the applicability of certain UNCLOS provisions). This paper focuses its attention on the latter.

Several scenarios in which states engage persons on the high seas have raised human rights concerns. For instance, intercepting and detaining pirates may raise issues under the right to life, the prohibition of torture and inhumane or degrading treatment or punishment, or the right to liberty of person. Halting and arresting drug smugglers may trigger similar human rights concerns. Another example concerns the intercepting and pushing back of migrant vessels which may be limited by the non-refoulement principle and the prohibition of collective expulsion.

The above mentioned examples all involve some sort of direct physical interaction between the agents of the state concerned and the persons affected. Recent trends in maritime policies, however, may raise human rights issues while there actually exists *no direct physical contact between state agents and the persons affected*. One can think of two examples: Firstly, the surveillance of ships via vessel tracking systems and the use of satellite and drone imagery and the sharing of data on the basis thereof might involve data protection issues. Secondly, the monitoring and patrolling of certain maritime routes known for the smuggling of migrants may imply that the search and rescue obligations of the patrolling states or the state responsible for the Search and Rescue Region are assessed in light of the right to life.

For human rights obligations to apply in the first place, however, it has to be established that the persons involved find themselves within the scope of applicability of the human rights treaty binding upon the relevant state. In other words, the vessels

---

[6]   Pursuant to Article 293 UNCLOS or Article 31 (3)(c) of the 1969 Vienna Convention on the Law of Treaties. See also: Irini Papanicolopulu, "International Judges and the Protection of Human Rights at Sea" in Nerina Boschiero, Tullio Scovazzi, Cesare Pitea, Chiara Ragni (eds) *International Courts and the Development of International Law* (Springer 2013) 535.

and the persons on them have to find themselves within the human rights jurisdiction of the state concerned. While this requirement poses no significant problems for our first set of examples (interception, detention) it is not certain whether the second set of examples (remote surveillance, search and rescue) may equally bring the persons affected within the human rights jurisdiction of states. The following section therefore sets out what human rights jurisdiction precisely amounts to and under which conditions persons can be deemed to fall within the jurisdiction of the state for human rights purposes in the maritime context.

3. Human rights jurisdiction at sea: concepts and problems

The litmus test for the applicability of human rights treaties is whether individuals find themselves *within the jurisdiction* of a state. [7] International and regional courts and quasi—judicial bodies have moreover affirmed that human rights treaties can also apply *extraterritorially*. [8] This signifies that, under certain circumstances, states must also protect the human rights of individuals finding themselves *outside* the territory of the state concerned.

3. 1 PIL jurisdiction versus HR jurisdiction

There has been quite an extensive discussion in legal doctrine about what the notion of "within the jurisdiction" amounts to. Does it refer to the classic concept of

---

[7] The phrase "within the jurisdiction" features in several jurisdiction clauses of human rights treaties. Even though some formulations can differ textually, they reflect more or less the same idea. Article 3 CERD ("in territories under their jurisdiction"); Article 6 CERD ("everyone within their jurisdiction"); Article 1 (1) ECHR ("all persons subject to their jurisdiction"); Article 2 (1) CRC ("each child within their jurisdiction"); Article 2 (1) ICCPR ("all individuals within its territory and subject to its jurisdiction"). Note that the ICCPR talks about "territory *and* subject to its jurisdiction". (emphasis added) The UN Human Rights Committee endorses the disjunctive—conjunctive interpretation of this jurisdiction clause stating that "the Covenant applies to anyone within the power or effective control of that State Party, even if not situated within the territory of the State Party." (UN Human Rights Committee (2004), *General Comment No.* 31, at paragraph 10.

[8] ICJ in *Namibia* (1971), in *Construction of a Wall* (2004) and in *Georgia v Russia* (2008); UN Human Rights Committee in *Lopez Burgos* (1981) and in Celiberti (1984); UN Human Rights Committee in *Concluding observations USA* (2014); UN Committee Against Torture in *J. H. A. v Spain* (2008); ECtHR in *Loizidou* (1996), in *Medvedyev* (2010), in *Al—Skeini* (201&), in *Hirsi Jamaa* (2012) and in *N. D. and N. T.* (2017).

jurisdiction of public international law, i. e. the competence to legislate, enforce, and adjudicate?[9] Or does jurisdiction have a different meaning within the context of human rights treaties? The dominant view is that the phrase "within the jurisdiction" signifies the latter and has a particular meaning that can include, but is not limited to the classic concept of jurisdiction under public international law. One could thus−for the sake of clarity−make a distinction between two different notions of the word "jurisdiction": "public international law jurisdiction" (PIL jurisdiction), i. e. referring to the right of a state to prescribe, enforce and adjudicate its laws and regulations, on the one hand, and "human rights jurisdiction" (HR jurisdiction), i. e. when persons find themselves within the authority, power or control of a state, on the other hand. [10]

Legal doctrine has already widely debated what the notion of HR jurisdiction a-mounts to in an extraterritorial context. Some argue that what matters is whether the state is exercising effective control over the individuals concerned. [11] Marko Milanovic, for instance, argues that HR jurisdiction "simply means *actual power*, whether exercised lawfully or not−nothing more and nothing less. "[12] Others have emphasized that mere effective control does not suffice, but that it is the existence of a *specific legal relationship* between the state−duty−bearer and the individual−rights−

---

[9] Cf. *Bankovic v Belgium* App no 52207/99 (ECtHR, 12 December 2001) para 36, 59−61; *Ilascu v Moldova and Russia* App no 48787/99 (ECtHR, 8 July 2004) para. 312.

[10] Every exercise of PIL jurisdiction will normally imply HR jurisdiction, but not every presence of HR jurisdiction implies PIL jurisdiction. It is possible that a person finds himself within the HR jurisdiction of a state even though the later has no legal grounds in PIL to exercise jurisdiction over the person concerned. An example would be the interception and detention of a vessel on the high seas and the people on board without a proper legal basis in UNCLOS or other relevant treaty. Just because that state does not have a legal basis to exercise PIL juris-diction at sea does not mean it cannot have human rights obligations towards those intercepted and detained.

[11] Rick A. Lawson, "Life After Bankovic: On the Extraterritorial Application of the European Conven-tion on Human Rights" in F. Coomans and M. Kamminga (eds), *Extraterritorial Application of Human Rights Treaties* (Intersentia 2004) (talking about a "direct and immediate link" and "control over persons"); Marko Milanovic, *Extraterritorial Application of Human Rights Treaties−Law*, *Principles*, *and Policy* (OUP 2011).

[12] Marko Milanovic (n 11) 41 (emphasis added).

holder which triggers human rights obligations. [13]

3. 2 The personal and spatial models of HR jurisdiction

Despite these disagreements about the precise nature of HR jurisdiction, most commentators agree that two broad models or manifestations of HR jurisdiction can be distinguished in the case law on the extraterritorial applicability of human rights: the spatial model and the personal model. [14] Under the *spatial model* of HR jurisdiction, individuals are *indirectly* brought within the HR jurisdiction of a state when they find themselves within a geographical space under the effective control of a state. Examples include but are not limited to military occupation of a third country or effective control over a region or city. [15] Under the *personal model* of HR jurisdiction, individuals are *directly* brought within the HR jurisdiction of a state when they find themselves personally under the effective control of state agents. Examples include the kidnapping of persons in a foreign country or the detention of persons on board a vessel or aircraft.

3. 3 HR jurisdiction at sea: the limits of the personal model

Within the maritime context, the spatial model has only been applied when it comes to the internal waters and territorial sea of a state. This is because these maritime zones are *de jure* part of the territory of a state, hence bringing those within it by definition within the HR jurisdiction of that state. [16] For HR jurisdiction on the high seas, however, courts and commentators have exclusively relied on the personal

---

[13] Samantha Besson, "The Extraterritoriality of the European Convention on Human Rights: Why Human Rights Depend on Jurisdiction and What Jurisdiction Amounts to" (2012) 25 (4) Leiden J. of Int'l Law 857, 870. Note that for the application of the European Union Charter of Fundamental Rights, for instance, the threshold for its application is the existence of a situation in which EU law is being implemented, i. e. in which there exists a legal relationship based on EU law between the person-right-holder and the state-duty-bearer.

[14] Marko Milanovic (n 11) 118-120; Samantha Besson (n 14) 874-875.

[15] ECtHR in e. g. *Al-Skeini* (2011), *Ilascu* (2004), and *Loizidou* (1996).

[16] Paul Tavernier, "La Cour Européenne des Droits de l'Homme et la Mer" in Daniel-Heywood Anderson, Vincent Bantz, Genevieve Bastid-Burdeau, Mohammed Bedjaoui, Josette Beer-Gabel (eds) *La Mer et Son Droit* (Pedone 2003) 575, 578.

model of jurisdiction to qualify certain scenarios to trigger the applicability of human rights instruments. These cases always involved some form of direct control over the vessels concerned or the people on them. Thus when a state via its agents takes drugs smugglers or migrants on board of one of its state vessels, those persons are brought within the HR jurisdiction of that state. [17] Even when state agents do not take the individuals concerned on board the state vessel, can a state exercise jurisdiction for human rights purposes. In *Xhavara v Italy*, a state vessel maneuvered around and collided with another vessel, causing the latter to capsize. [18] In the *Women on Waves* case, Portugal placed naval ships next to an NGO vessel in order to prevent it from entering Portuguese territorial waters. [19]

But what if there is no direct physical contact between a state and persons at sea whose human rights can be negatively impacted by the former's maritime security policies? Can a migrant in distress on the high seas claim a right to life *vis—à—vis* a coastal state responsible for the search and rescue coordination in a certain area? Can the crew of a merchant vessel involved in shady business rely on data protection and privacy rules prohibiting blanket surveillance techniques? In light of the current case law and doctrinal comments, the answer seems "no". [20] As no physical contact is made which triggers jurisdiction under the personal model, those negatively affected by maritime policies also cannot invoke human rights. Indeed, "without jurisdiction,

---

[17] *Medvedyev v France* App no 3394/03 (ECtHR, 29 March 2010) para 67; *Hirsi Jamaa v Italy* App no 27765/09 (ECtHR, 23 February 2012) para. 81.

[18] *Xhavara v Italy* App no (ECtHR, 2001).

[19] *Women on Waves v Portugal* App no (ECtHR, 2009).

[20] Note that states have certain obligations when it comes to the search and rescue of persons in distress at sea on the basis of legal instruments other than human rights law treaties. Under UNCLOS and the 1979 Maritime Search and Rescue Convention, every captain of a vessel has an obligation to proceed to a person at sea in distress in order to render assistance. Pursuant to those same treaties, coastal states are under an obligation to ensure coordination occurs with a view to the rescue of those in distress within the search and rescue regions for which they bear responsibility. It is, however, unlikely that a refugee producing country would take up the diplomatic protection of boat refugees—the very citizens it tries to persecute—before the International Court of Justice or the International Tribunal for the Law of the Sea against a state failing to provide maritime search and rescue.

there are no human rights applicable and hence no human rights duties. " [21] Itamar Mann has recently called these kinds of scenarios "maritime legal black holes", [22] i. e. when persons are rightless not because a state is violating a person's human rights, but because the relevant state owes no such obligations in the first place because it has no HR jurisdiction.

A few attempts have been made to nonetheless bring these kinds of scenarios within the scope of application of human rights treaties. Some authors argue that effectiveness, *i. e.* "the existence of factual links between a situation (migrants in peril on the high seas) and a state which is aware of the situation and in a position to save their lives" may activate due diligence obligations, *even* when the traditional legal bases for jurisdiction are missing. [23] Others have argued that nearby physical presence—even without physically engaging—can constitute effective control over migrants in distress. [24]

The problem with these suggestions is that they have no *prima facie* basis in positive international law. [25] Like the commentators behind one of the above mentioned ideas state themselves, they look for a paradigm *beyond* the traditional legal bases for

---

[21]   Samantha Besson (n 13) 867.

[22]   Itamar Mann, "Maritime Legal Black Holes: Migration and Rightlessness in International Law" (2018) *Eur. J. Int'l Law* (forthcoming) 14.

[23]   Vassilis Tzevelekos and Elena Katselli, "Migrants at Sea: A Duty to Plural States to Protect (Extraterritorially)?" (2017) 86 Nordic J. Int'l Law 427, 455. Note that some authors argue that the knowledge of a possible threat to life obliges the state to take measures to prevent to the loss of life at sea. See e. g. Lisa—Marie Komp, "The Duty to Assist Persons in Distress: An Alternative Source of Protection against the Return of Migrants and Asylum Seekers to the High Seas?" in Violeta Moreno—Lax and Efthymios Papastavridis (eds), "*Boat Refugees*" *and Migrants at Sea: A Comprehensive Approach* (Brill 2016). One should however clearly distinguish the threshold for triggering jurisdiction from the scope of obligations once such jurisdiction is triggered and human rights law obligations apply.

[24]   Paolo Biondi, "Italy Strikes Back Again: A Push—back's Firsthand Account" (2017) *Border Criminologies*; Martin Faix, "Application of Human Rights to European Union Military Operations: Mission Impossible?" (2013) IV (1) Slovak Yearbook of Int'l Law 28, 43 (asking whether, for example, a military ship exercises effective control already when the affected vessel is in reach of its weaponry or even its operational radius).

[25]   Cf. Itamar Mann (n 22) 28 *in fine* (writing that "the laudable efforts of some lawyers to do so too often risk mixing up *lex lata* and *lex ferenda*, choosing an aspirational analysis of law that cannot be enforced").

jurisdiction. It is unlikely such an argument would survive in a court of law. Similarly, the argument that qualifies sufficient physical proximity as effective control over individuals will unlikely pass the threshold of effective authority and control over persons (personal model of jurisdiction) absent actual physical control over the persons concerned. Both authors, however, implicitly raise an important issue: that states sometimes−despite the absence of direct physical control−may have decisive influence or control over the wider situation in which a vessel and the people on it find themselves.

4. Exploring the spatial model of HR jurisdiction at sea

It is not the contention of this paper to provide a waterproof *lex lata* solution to fill the above mentioned maritime legal black holes. The hypothesis developed here in light of our jurisdiction conundrum is that, under certain circumstances, even the scenarios mentioned above may bring persons within the jurisdiction of a state for human rights law purposes. The underlying thought is that regarding the problem of effective control over persons and vessels on the high seas one should *leave aside the personal model of jurisdiction altogether*. Attention could − contrary to legal wisdoms and intuitions about maritime spaces and PIL jurisdiction on the high seas−instead be directed at the *spatial model* of HR jurisdiction and the idea that coastal states could be said to have effective control over a particular *area* of the high seas, thus *indirectly* bringing persons within that particular area within the HR jurisdiction of a state.

To advance this argument, this section proceeds as follows: Firstly, it shows that there is no compelling reason why the spatial model as applied to *land* cannot also be applied to *seas and oceans* (Subsection 4. 1.). Secondly, on the basis of case law which has identified what amounts to effective control over an area on land (Subsection 4. 2.), it explores what effective control over a maritime area would have to look like in order to trigger HR jurisdiction (Subsection 4. 3). The question investigated boils down to whether the way in which states currently monitor and control maritime areas (e. g. via the use of drones, satellites, real−time data, targeted patrolling) can transform our understanding of what it means to be under the effective control of a government and hence its HR jurisdiction.

4. 1 The spatial model can cover any type of area, whether on land or at sea

There is no principal reason why the spatial model of HR jurisdiction must be limited to effective control over *areas of land and not water*. There actually already exists acceptance of an assumption of *de jure* control over areas of water for human rights purposes: the territorial sea.

One should moreover avoid erroneously applying traditional notions of jurisdiction over maritime areas as established in public international law and the law of the sea in order to assess the concept of jurisdiction for human rights purposes. As already indicated (Section 3. 1.), they have two different meanings. Art 89 UNCLOS tells us indeed that portions of the high seas are not susceptible to state jurisdiction, as "no State may validly purport to subject any part of the high seas to its sovereignty". But applying that rule in the context of establishing jurisdiction for human rights purposes is beside the point, as the notion of jurisdiction for human rights purposes (HR jurisdiction) is different from that one under classic public international law (PIL jurisdiction). *PIL jurisdiction* determines whether a state can exercise its legislative and enforcement powers at sea, for instance, via exercising flag state jurisdiction over fishing vessels flying its flag or by exercising universal criminal jurisdiction over pirates. *HR jurisdiction* determines whether persons find themselves within the actual control of a state which imbues the latter with legal obligations under human rights law. What matters from a human rights law perspective is whether a state is exercising some sort of *effective authority*, *power*, *or control* over an area. Whether the exercise of that control has a basis in law or not, is irrelevant to assess whether a state is exercising effective control and hence HR jurisdiction. This distinction between PIL jurisdiction and HR jurisdiction has already been applied in the maritime context, namely when using the personal model of jurisdiction on the high seas: Vessels on the high seas are indeed under the exclusive jurisdiction of their flag state (Article 92 (1) UNCLOS)(PIL jurisdiction), but when a state exercises effective control over a vessel by stopping it and detaining the people on board—whether it has a legal basis to do so or not pursuant to UNCLOS−it brings those people within the jurisdiction of the state for human rights purposes (HR jurisdiction).

In sum, given the acceptance of the distinction between PIL jurisdiction and HR jurisdiction in the maritime context, and given that HR jurisdiction over maritime spaces (such as a territorial sea) is equally accepted, there is no principal reason why the logic of the spatial model of jurisdiction could not apply to portions of the seas other than the territorial sea: whether a state has a legal basis to do so under domestic, regional, or public international law or not, if a state in one way or another exercises effective control over an area of water on the high seas, it could bring the persons in that area (e. g. smugglers, pirates, migrants, fishers) within the HR jurisdiction of that state.

4. 2 What effective control over an area amounts to

Once it is accepted that the spatial model of HR jurisdiction can be applied as well to maritime zones in general, and to the high seas in particular, the next step is to examine the conditions under which a state can be said to exercise effective control over an area on the high seas. In other words: one has to first identify the threshold criteria for the exercise of spatial control on land and subsequently analyse to which degree those criteria can comparatively be met on the high seas. To this end one needs to clarify what constitutes "effective control over an area".

No treaty or other legal instrument defines what constitutes effective control over an area, and although indicators can be found in for instance the case law of the European Court of Human Rights, the jurisprudence on the subject remains rather casuistic. It should also be recalled that legal doctrine diverges over the question of what it is precisely that triggers HR jurisdiction: while some authors argue the factual power or control is the determining factor, some have argued that there also has to exist some sort of legal relationship or a relation of authority between the state and persons concerned. (*supra* Section 3. 1.) It is thus not a straightforward task to assess which criteria should be taken into account to determine whether a state has effective control over an area.

In the European context, two strands of case law have been developed when contemplating the spatial model of HR jurisdiction. The first type of jurisprudence concerns a state exercising effective control over an area by virtue of exercising control over the actor that is actually in charge on the ground. Examples here are the Russian Federation having control over Transdniestrian separatists in Moldova[26] , or for instance the TRNC authorities in Northern Cyprus surviving by virtue of Turkish support. [27] This jurisprudence, however, does not tell us a lot about which criteria determine whether one controls a physical space; it actually tells us more about criteria to determine whether a state has decisive influence over another state's regime or non–state actors' actions within that physical space. [28]

More interesting for the purpose of developing our hypothesis on spatial HR jurisdiction is the second type of jurisprudence: it concerns assessments of states' effective control of areas abroad, mainly in the context of military occupation. From this case law one indicator that immediately comes to mind is that of *the presence of troops* on the

---

[26] *Ilascu v Moldova and Russia* (n 9) para. 393.

[27] *Cyprus v Turkey* App no 25781/94 (ECtHR, 10 May 2001) para 77. See also: *Al–Skeini v UK* App no 55721/07 (ECtHR, 7 July 2011) para 139 (mentioning 'the extent to which its military, economic and political support for the local subordinate administration provides it with influence and control over the region' as an indicator of effective control over an area).

[28] Note that control or decisive influence by one state over a third state's actions in order to allocate HR jurisdiction may of particular relevance where states try to outsource their law enforcement or border control tasks to a third country, as is for example the case with the Italian and EU policy of funding and training the Libyan coast guard to prevent people from leaving Libyan territorial waters on their way to Europe. See in this vein: Paul Strauch, "When Stopping the Smuggler Means Repelling the Refugee: International Human Rights Law and the European Union's Operation to Combat Smuggling in Libya's Territorial Sea" (2017) 126 (9) Yale Law Journal 2421, 2434–2436.

ground. One might discuss whether the amount of such troops should matter in determining whether a state has effective control over an area, [29] but arguably one should leave some flexibility in this regard in light of additional indicators and the circumstances of the each case. It has moreover been pointed out that control can be exercised temporarily, that control does not have to pertain to every portion of a territory, and it can be exercised over one part without having control over the surrounding areas. [30] One could label this first strand of indicators the "physical power criterion".

Additionally, one must turn back to the disagreement in legal doctrine about whether physical control suffices to constitute effective control over an area and thus indirectly over all persons within that area, or whether there also needs to be some sort of legal relationship between the state−duty−bearer and the person−human rights−holder. In case of the latter, one additional indicator for control over an area might be that a state somehow is trying to govern it by exercising public powers, is laying down rules or otherwise−ad minimum−tries to make an appeal for compliance with certain norms of desired behaviour. [31] One could label this the "governance criterion".

Knowledge of a precarious human rights situation is as such not enough to constitute effective control and thus as a legal basis for HR jurisdiction. Knowledge of a situation may however play a role in two ways: it could arguably be an additional indictor to determine whether a state has physical control over a situation (under the physical power criterion). In the military context, for instance, knowing where a person or target finds itself in a certain area enhances the chances and precision of neutralizing it. Knowledge may, secondly, play a role at the level of assessing the scope of HR ob-

---

[29]   See e. g. *Ilascu v Moldova and Russia* (n 9) para. 355 (the Russian Government submitting that they only had 2000 soldiers on the ground in Moldova compared to the 30000 Turkish soldiers in Cyprus referred to in the *Loizidou* case).

[30]   Robin Geiss and Anna Petrig, *Piracy and Armed Robbery at Sea: The Legal Framework for Counter−Piracy Operations in Somalia and the Gulf of Aden* (OUP 2011) 107 (analyzing the case law of the ECtHR in *Cyprus v Turkey* (2001), *Issa v Turkey* (2004) and *Al−Saadoon v UK* (2009).

[31]   Cf. Samantha Besson (n 13) 864−865.

ligations (e. g. due diligence) once HR jurisdiction is already established.

　　* *Excursion*: In general (i. e. both for the personal model *and* the spatial model of HR jurisdiction), jurisdiction for human rights purposes may be determined on the basis of two main elements: physical control over the person or area (physical power criterion) and/or the extent to which a situation is governed by rules and thus the extent to which there exists a legal relationship between the person affected and the relevant state. In the legal literature one may find some authors emphasizing the former criterion (e. g. Milanovic), while others emphasize the latter (e. g. Besson). One could arguably say the same for human rights law instruments themselves: some seem to take into account actual physical control as an important element (e. g. ECHR, Convention against Torture), while other legal instruments put the emphasis on the existence of a situation being governed by a (specific set of) legal norms (e. g. the European Union Charter of Fundamental Rights). In practice, HR jurisdiction may be based predominantly on one of the two criteria, but a situation triggering HR obligations may also be based on a combination of both. For the sake of analytical representation one could make the following simplified graphical representation of when a situation triggers HR jurisdiction or not:

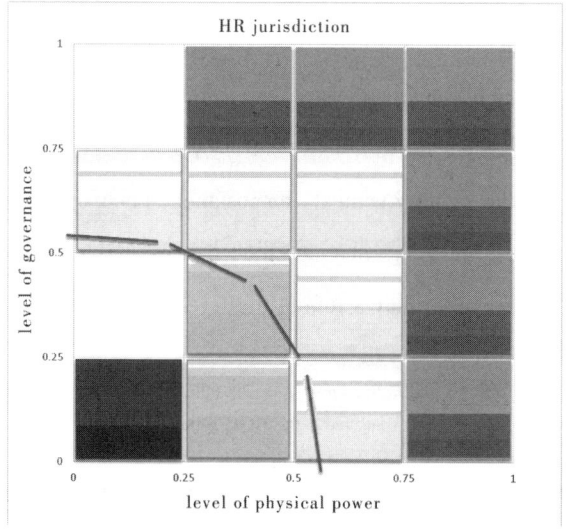

Legend of Situation Triggeling HR Jurisdiction

4. 3 What effective control over an area amounts to at sea

Interestingly, Robin Geiss and Anna Petrig have already explored the issue "effective control over an area" as a model to capture HR jurisdiction at sea. They did so in one particular context, namely when a military or other governmental ship carries out enforcement measures against pirates on the high seas. They argue that:

> "The effective control exercised on board a military ship is simply not confined to the ship itself. Modern military ships have 'long arms' in that they are equipped with technology and weaponry, which give them the capability to exercise control over a wide area beyond their railings. It is, therefore arguable that military ships could be said to exert control over (...) a *delimited geographical area at sea* confined by the ship's operational radius analogous to the common 'control over territory' —criterion (...). " [32]

The inquiry of Geiss and Petrig into the spatial model of HR jurisdiction is, however, limited to one specific scenario, which is the phase of pursuit of pirate ships by naval vessels prior to the actual interception and boarding. [33] The question is whether it is thinkable that states have effective control over an area at sea beyond the immediate context of maritime interception. Geiss and Petrig implicitly hint at that possibility by suggesting that the when several vessels involved in a joint maritime operation are considered cumulatively this may establish a "net of effective overall control over the joint operational area. " [34]

Arguably, the cumulative presence of maritime and aerial assets (warships and smaller patrol vessels; patrol aircraft and helicopters) in a particularly delineated

---

[32]   Robin Geiss and Anna Petrig, *Piracy and Armed Robbery at Sea*: *The Legal Framework for Counter-Piracy Operations in Somalia and the Gulf of Aden* (OUP 2011) 106 (emphasis added).

[33]   *Ibid.*

[34]   Robin Geiss and Anna Petrig (n 32) 108.

zone on the high seas may approximate the presence of troops as required on land in order to talk about effective control over an area. As mentioned above (Subsection 4. 2.) , a high quantity of military or law enforcement personnel is not necessarily required. Nor would it be a deal breaker if the control would only be temporarily exercised (e. g. an operational mandate of a few weeks or months) , that such control was only exercised over certain pockets of the high seas, or that no effective control would be exercised over the remainder of the high seas surrounding the pockets of water covered by the maritime operation. An additional factor is that the use of surveillance techniques (e. g. using Remotely Piloted Aircraft / drones, satellite imagery, under water sensor techniques, etc.) and data analysis (e. g. data on water currents, predictive data on hotspots for illegal fishing, smuggling or trafficking) can contribute to the extent a state can exercise control over a maritime area. Having a comprehensive situational picture and awareness of certain maritime zones and the activity going on in that particular zone, allows a state to more efficiently and effectively undertake enforcement action against persons at sea. Moreover, maritime surveillance in certain areas of the high seas may not only be serve physical control (physical power criterion) but may also be aimed at implementing certain laws and policies hence contributing to−what I have just called for convenience (Subsection 4. 2. *in fine*) −the governance criterion and the existence of a legal relationship.

In a nutshell, a few indicators can be summed up which−taken together−provide a strong indication to consider a state to exercise effective control over an area at sea: the presence of law enforcement or military personnel and assets (war ships, smaller patrol vessels, patrol aircraft, fighter aircraft, helicopters), situational awareness of activities within the targeted area (which could be enhanced through the use of technologies and data sharing) , the aim to seek compliance with certain policies or rules in the targeted area, and actual enforcement action in the targeted area. This exercise of effective control over an area can be temporary as long as there is some continuity to it. The intensity of actual enforcement action in the targeted maritime zone can also vary as there may not always be a direct occasion or reason for enforcement action.

5. Example: EU maritime border surveillance as effective control of an area?

Having identified some criteria which indicate whether a state exercises effective control over an area at sea (i. e. the spatial model of HR jurisdiction at sea), this section looks at certain law enforcement and militarization trends in the Mediterranean Sea. It explores whether some of these maritime enforcement trends may reach the threshold of effective control over a maritime area and would henceforth trigger HR jurisdiction of the relevant state (s) over the persons present in that maritime area.

In 2014, the Council of the European Union adopted the *European Union Maritime Security Strategy* (EU MSS) which aims to protect the EU and its Member States against risks and threats against its maritime security interests. [35] The geographical coverage of the EU MSS includes among other maritime zones "some maritime areas because of their strategic value or potential risk for crisis or instability. "[36] An example of maritime areas of particular interest to the EU are certain pockets of the Mediterranean Sea because they are used for irregular migration towards EU territory. As will be briefly illustrated below, the way in which EU Member States-in cooperation with several EU agencies-try to monitor and control some of these particular zones of the Mediterranean Sea known for irregular migration might come close effective control over an area.

Over the last decade, the EU has created maritime operations in order to assist Member States to monitor and control their external maritime borders against irregular crossings by migrants. Without going too much into detail, these maritime operations always concern specifically delineated portions of the relevant sea. These operations

---

[35] Council of the EU, *European Maritime Security Strategy* (24 June 2014)(hereafter: "EU MSS").
[36] *Ibid.* 4.

have mostly mandates for several months, sometimes years. The pockets of the relevant territorial waters or high seas specifically targeted are then patrolled by maritime vessels and aircraft from the state which hosts the EU mission and from other contributing Member States.

One example is the use of joint maritime operations in the central Mediterranean, which employ staff and assets allowing states to effectively intervene in the targeted areas against migrant smugglers. Operation EUNAVFOR MED Sophia deployed about 1770 troops from several contributing EU Member States and used *inter alia* about 4 naval units and 6 air assets. [37] This operation is currently complemented by Frontex Operation Themis which replaces Frontex Operation Triton and also combines the deployment of border guards from several Member States with patrol vessels and aircraft.

These operations are not blunt, instantaneous acts of coercion. There is a policy and legal framework behind it which aims to protect the strategic economic and security interests of the European Union Member States. Over the last two decades, European legislation has complemented national maritime policies and legislation from areas such as fisheries and environmental protection to areas such as migration control and criminal law enforcement against foreign fighters. Of particular interest for our example concerning the surveillance and control in the central Mediterranean, are the Schengen Borders Code[38], the EUROSUR regulation[39], the Frontex Regula-

---

[37]   European External Action Service, "Assets and deployed units for mission EUNAVFOR MED operation SOPHIA" <https: //eeas. europa. eu/csdp−missions−operations/eunavfor−med−operation−sophia/12215/assets_ en> accessed 10 March 2018.

[38]   Regulation (EU) 2016/399 of the European Parliament and of the Council of 9 March 2016 on a Union Code on the rules governing the movement of persons across borders (Schengen Borders Code).

[39]   Regulation (EU) 2013/1052 of the European Parliament and of the Council of 22 October 2013 establishing the European Border Surveillance System (Eurosur).

tion[40] , the External Sea Borders regulation[41] and several other policy frame-works. As a result of the application of these instruments in the maritime context, the persons affected by maritime surveillance and enforcement measures in these targeted areas may in certain circumstances stand in a legal relationship with the state authorities concerned.

To actually enforce national and EU law, according to a study from the Commission, requires in addition to troops and assets using "technology such as the gathering and analysis of high resolution satellite images, air patrolling, the operation of unmanned platforms, the detection and analysis of underwater sounds. "[42] When the European Commission contemplated the creation of a European Border Surveillance System (EUROSUR) in early 2008, one of the main incentives was to provide Member States "with more timely and reliable information if they are to detect, identify, track and intercept those attempting to enter the EU illegally". [43] In other words, the enhancement of information and of situational awareness on the situation at the external maritime borders is not aimed for the mere sake of information but to increase the effectiveness of actual enforcement activities at sea. Today, state authorities exchange information based on the EUROSUR regulation. An interesting trend in the development of European maritime surveillance and control is the increased use of Remotely Piloted Aircraft (drones) and satellite imagery which can provide a broad coverage and detailed images of targeted areas on demand. [44] During Frontex

---

[40]   Regulation (EU) 2016/1624 of the European Parliament and of the Council of 14 September 2016 on the European Border and Coast Guard.

[41]   Regulation (EU) No 2014/656 of the European Parliament and of the Council of 15 May 2014 establishing rules for the surveillance of the external borders in the context of operational cooperation coordinated by Frontex.

[42]   Commission of the EU, *Towards the integration of maritime surveillance in the EU: A common information sharing environment for the EU maritime domain* (15 October 2009) COM (2009) 538 final, 9.

[43]   Commission of the EU, *Examining the creation of a European Border Surveillance System* (13 February 2008) COM (2008) 68 final, 3.

[44]   *Ibid.* 8.

operations, so-called *EUROSUR Fusion Services* are used which include "vessel detection, monitoring and tracking to anomaly detection, coastal and pre-frontier monitoring, sea weather conditions and nautical charts to different software applications, allowing for instance to calculate the positions of drifting migrant vessels taking into account the type of vessel, sea currents and weather conditions. "[45] The use of EUROSUR services to support enforcement has-in the wording of the European Commission-lead to "success stories" in terms of detections, determining the exact positions of vessels in the targeted area, and subsequent interception. [46] The EU is currently trying to raise the logic of the EUROSUR system to the next level by building and implementing a system called the *Common Information Sharing Environment* (*CISE*) which further integrates the collection and sharing of maritime surveillance information and data by civil and military actors at the national and EU level. [47]

Overall, while EU Member States seem to tick the boxes of some of the above mentioned indicators (Section 4.3.), it is unclear whether the actual deployment of troops and the level of control and enforcement is sufficient in order to constitute an exercise of effective control over certain parts of the central Mediterranean Sea and hence bring the vessels and person on them within those areas within the HR jurisdiction of the relevant EU Member States. To answer this question more confidently, a case by case and more in depth analysis is needed.

6. Conclusion

This conference paper explained that in order for persons at sea to be protected by human rights law, they need to find themselves within the human rights (HR) jurisdiction of a state. Two models were presented as ways to found the applicability of human rights treaties abroad: the personal model of HR jurisdiction and the spatial

---

[45] Commission of the EU, *Joint Staff working document on the implementation of the EU Maritime Security Strategy Action Plan* (22 June 2016) SWD (2016) 217 final, 12.

[46] *Ibid.* 13-14.

[47] See: <http: //www. eucise2020. eu/> accessed 10 March 2018.

model of HR jurisdiction. Because not all scenarios in which persons are negatively affected by maritime law enforcement policies of states can be captured by the personal model of HR jurisdiction, the paper sought to explore the application of the spatial model of HR jurisdiction at sea. According to such a model, it is not necessary for a state to physically intercept a vessel at sea in order to bring the people on board within the HR jurisdiction of the state. Instead, it suffices that those vessels / persons find themselves within a particular area at sea which is under the effective control of the state concerned.

The paper then advanced by asking what kind of criteria determine whether a state has effective control over an area at sea. Based on a preliminary research of case law and the element of effective jurisdiction in the doctrine of historic waters, a few indicators were distilled: the presence of law enforcement or military personnel and assets, situational awareness of activities within the targeted area, the fact that the state concerned seeks compliance with certain policies or rules in the targeted area, and the fact that the state actually undertakes enforcement action in the targeted area. Continuity and intensity of control may also play are role in determining whether the control over the area is effective.

Finally, one specific example was picked out to explore what effective control over an area at sea may look like in practice. Here one could see that the combination of data—based risk assessments, surveillance techniques and overall naval and aerial presence over specific parts of the high seas, namely the European Union's governance of certain zones in the Mediterranean, may meet some of the criteria for effective control over an area at sea.

In sum, maritime surveillance and control may come closer to traditional effective control on land than one might think. Depending on the specifics of the case and the degree of control exercised over the targeted maritime zone, certain surveillance and enforcement policies of a state may bring those persons within that maritime zone within the HR jurisdiction of the state concerned.

THE IMPACT OF MULTILATERAL ECONOMIC SANCTIONS ON COMMERCIAL SHIPPING

Assistant Professor Richard L. Kilpatrick, Jr. *

1. Introduction

Multilateral economic sanctions are increasingly used to achieve the goal of international peace and security. This involves substantial coordination between international policy–makers and private industry. While economic sanctions often focus on restrictions in the banking and finance sectors of the global economy, the maritime shipping industry is also critically impacted. As regulatory regimes evolve to respond to geopolitical developments, the shipping industry must adapt to this changing commercial landscape. This adaptability to regulation is integral for shipping interests, such as shipowners, charterers, cargo owners, and insurers to maintain legal compliance. But sanctions themselves also depend on these commercial actors to generate the intended coercive response.

In recent years, the United Nations Security Council has utilized a variety of maritime sanctions in attempts to pressure Iran and North Korea to abandon nuclear weapons and ballistic missile programs. These have included regulating shipping activities by blacklisting vessels, prohibiting transactions involving certain cargo, authorizing vessel inspections, and even outlawing marine insurance. As these sanctions have created a positive response in Iran, the sanctions have been rolled back, paving the way for renewed shipping activities in that region. Meanwhile, as a diplomatic solution in North Korea has remained elusive, maritime sanctions have increased incre-

---
* Assistant Professor of Business Law, Northeastern Illinois University, College of Business and Management, Chicago, Illinois, USA.

mentally, even approaching a maritime blockade.

With such contemporary geopolitical challenges as the backdrop, this paper explores the interplay between multilateral economic sanctions and shipping practice. It first examines UN Security Council authority to impose measures of economic coercion in accordance with the UN Charter. It then explores recent strategies used by the Security Council to design economic sanctions which regulate shipping activities, particularly in the context of nuclear non—proliferation concerns. The paper then turns to responses within the shipping industry, by considering industry attempts to comply with and adapt to these UN sanctions. For purposes of brevity and clarity, the paper focuses exclusively on multilateral sanctions regimes implemented by UN Security Council Resolutions against Iran and North Korea from 2006 to the present. In an effort to concentrate on universally recognized sanctions practices, it avoids a detailed analysis of supplementary sanctions implemented by national or supranational entities, including the European Union, the United States, or other actors.

2. The UN Security Council and its power to impose economic sanctions

Chapter V of the UN Charter grants the Security Council a central role in maintaining international peace and security. [1] The Security Council is made up of fifteen members, including the five permanent members of China, France, Russia, the United Kingdom, and the United States. [2] The other ten non—permanent members rotate for two—year terms. [3]

While Article 2 (7) of the UN Charter commits UN organs not to "intervene in matters which are essentially within the domestic jurisdiction of any state," the same

---

[1]   Charter of the United Nations And the Statute of the International Court of Justice, Chapter V, available at http://www.un.org/en/charter—united—nations/index.html. Article 24 reads, "In order to ensure prompt and effective action by the United Nations, its Members confer on the Security Council primary responsibility for the maintenance of international peace and security, and agree that in carrying out its duties under this responsibility the Security Council acts on their behalf."

[2]   *Id.*

[3]   *Id.*

document gives substantial power to the Security Council. Despite the limited representation of this exclusive group, under Article 25, " [t] he Members of the United Nations agree to accept and carry out the decisions of the Security Council..."[4]

Under Chapter VI of the UN Charter, in response to disputes that "endanger the maintenance of international peace and security"[5] the Security Council may "recommend appropriate procedures or methods of adjustment. "[6] Acting under this power, the Security Council may issue non – binding recommendatory decisions. However, under its Chapter VII powers, the Security Council has the enhanced authority to "determine the existence of any threat to the peace, or act of aggression and shall make recommendations, or decide what measures shall be taken...to maintain or restore international peace and security. "[7]

Acting pursuant to these Chapter VII powers, once the Security Council identifies a threat to peace, it is deemed to have the power to bind Member States by recommendations and decisions. Articles 40–42 contained in Chapter VII provide specific guidance on these options. [8] Article 40 gives the Security Council the power to "call upon the parties concerned to comply with such provisional measures as it deems necessary or desirable. "[9] Article 41 provides the Security Council with the power to "...decide what measures not involving the use of armed force are to be employed to give effect to its decisions, and it may call upon the Members of the United Nations to apply such measures. " Article 41 further identifies the potential economic coercion as a tool to implement these measures, including the possibility of "complete or partial interruption of economic relations and of rail, sea, air, postal, telegraphic, radio, and other means of communication, and the severance of diplomatic

[4] *Id.* at Art. 25.
[5] *Id.* at Art. 33.
[6] *Id.* at Art. 36.
[7] *Id.* at Art. 39
[8] *Id.* at Arts. 40–41.
[9] *Id.* at Art. 40.

relations. [10] Under Article 42, the Security Council if necessary may consider additional action "by air, sea, or land forces as may be necessary to maintain or restore international peace and security. Such action may include demonstrations, blockade, and other operations by air, sea, or land forces of Members of the United Nations. "[11]

In practice, the Security Council has regularly issued Resolutions relating to issues within its purview. In recent years, relying on these authorities, the Security Council has implemented a global sanctions regime in response to geopolitical developments. [12] Some of these Resolutions have explicitly focused on shipping activities. This has created compliance challenges within the highly mobile and multi-facetted global shipping industry.

3. Security Council strategies for economic sanctions in the maritime sector

Since 2006, the Security Council has issued a number of Resolutions focusing on nuclear non-proliferation concerns in both Iran and North Korea. Both countries have relied significantly on maritime transport to support commercial activity within their territories. Consequently, the Security Council has increasingly utilized regulation of maritime interests as a mechanism to coerce these governments into behavior consistent with international norms.

Between 2006 and 2010, the Security Council issued four different Resolutions relating to Iran's nuclear program that specifically restrict maritime activities. These include the following: UNSC Res 1737 (2006), UNSC Res 1747 (2006), UNSC Res 1803 (2008), and UNSC Res 1929 (2010). A few years after these sanctions were implemented against Iran, diplomacy appeared to prevail in the form of the

---

[10]   *Id.* at Art. 41.

[11]   *Id.* at Art. 42.

[12]   Note that these approaches have been used by the Security Council to respond to developments in Rhodesia, Iraq, Libya, Yugoslavia, Haiti, Sierra Leone, and others. For an overview of these UN sanctions regimes not involving the use of force see, Malcolm Shaw, International Law, at 1241-1251.

Joint Comprehensive Plan of Action (JCPA). [13] Under the JCPA, Iran agreed with the permanent five members of the Security Council plus Germany to halt its nuclear program in exchange for rolling back the UN sanctions. While it remains to be seen whether the end to these sanctions will result in the desired response, there have been no further UN Security Council Resolutions against Iran since 2010.

North Korea has also been the target of many rounds of Security Council economic sanctions since as early as 1993. Since 2013, these Resolutions have increasingly focused on maritime activities, with the Security Council using similar tactics to those employed against Iran. These following recent Resolutions include restrictions on maritime activities involving North Korea: UNSC Res 1718 (2006), UNSC Res 2087 (2013), UNSC Res 2094 (2013), UNSC Res 2270 (2017), UNSC Res 2321 (2016), UNSC Res 2371 (2016), UNSC Res 2375 (2017), UNSC Res 2397 (2017).

3.1 Blacklists of maritime entities and vessels

One of the Security Council's tactics for targeted sanctions is designating certain entities as subject to asset freezes, travel bans, or other financial restrictions. By naming individuals, businesses, and organizations as explicitly subject to Member State prohibitions of financial transactions, the Security Council can avoid applying generalized prohibitions on international commercial transactions across the board. The purpose of this "smart sanctions" approach is to more precisely put pressure on certain individuals and businesses without penalizing the general population or creating humanitarian problems within a sanctioned state.

In recent years, the Security Council has designated a number of shipping businesses or state-controlled maritime assets in its Resolutions, effectively "blacklisting" them by obliging Member States to freeze funds and prohibit other financial

---

[13] See Joint Comprehensive Plan of Action, Vienna, July 14, 2015.

transactions involving them. [14] In the context of Iran, UNSC Res 1929 (2010) explicitly imposes restrictions on maritime assets, including, "the entities of the Islamic Republic of Iran Shipping Lines (IRISL) ...and to any person or entity action on their behalf or at their direction. "[15] Annex III to the same Resolution provides a list of shipping companies designated under the heading, "Entities owned, controlled, or acting on behalf of the Islamic Republic of Iran Shipping Lines (IRISL). " These include shipping companies based in Iran, but also in Belgium. [16]

In addition to these specific references of Iranian maritime assets, UNSC Res 1929 (2010) also imposes broad sanctions on "Iranian—owned or—controlled vessels, including chartered vessels..."[17] The same resolution also utilizes a maritime—specific prohibition of "bunkering services, such as provision of fuel or supplies" to this broadly defined class of vessels. [18] It further requests that Member States communicate any information regarding IRISL attempts to avoid application of the sanctions by "renaming or re—registering" vessels. [19]

Employing similar tactics in the context of nuclear non—proliferation concerns in North Korea, the Security Council has also blacklisted specific vessels and shipping companies. UNSC Res 2270 (2016) names a firm called Ocean Maritime Management as a designated entity subject to asset freezes. [20] The same Resolution's Annex III provides a list of 31 vessels subject to sanctions as "economic resources controlled or operated"[21] by the North Korean government. This list includes the vessel names as well as their International Maritime Organization (IMO) vessel registration num-

---

[14]   See e. g. UNSR Res 1737 (2006) para. 12.

[15]   UNSC Res 1929 (2010) at para 19.

[16]   See e. g. Annex III, para 2, listing IRISL Benelux NV as based in Antwerp Belgium.

[17]   *Id.* at para. 18.

[18]   *Id.* at para. 18.

[19]   *Id.*

[20]   UNSC Res 2270 (2016).

[21]   UNSCR 2270 (2016) para. 23.

bers. [22] The same Resolution further mandates a broad prohibition for "any vessel" to enter the ports of Member States if there is "information that provides reasonable grounds to believe the vessel is owned or controlled, directly or indirectly, by a designated individual or entity..." [23]

3. 2 Prohibitions on vessel registration and insurance coverage

The Security Council has also placed restrictions on registering, re-registering and certifying vessels controlled by sanctioned entities. For example, in the North Korea context, UNSC Res 2270 (2016) prohibits Member States from "registering vessels in the DPRK, obtaining authorization for a vessel to use the DPRK flag, and from owning, leasing, operating, providing any vessel classification, certification or associated service, or insuring any vessel flagged by the DPRK..." [24]

UNSCR Res 2321 (2016) is even more specific. It requires Member States to "de-register any vessel that is owned, controlled, or operated by the DPRK, and further decides that Member States shall not register any such vessel that has been de-registered by another Member State..." [25] It also expands the application of UNSC Res 2270 to include a prohibition on "all leasing, chartering or provision of crew services to the DPRK..." [26]

The Security Council implemented an innovative approach in the Iran context by prohibiting insurance coverage over certain Iranian vessels. UNSC Res 1929 (2010) para 21 specifically calls on Member States to:

---

[22] *Id.* at Annex III. Annex II of the same Resolution, other shipping companies are designated within as subject to asset freezes as well. See e. g. Annex II, para 2, listing Chongchongang Shipping Company as subject to an asset freeze for attempting to directly import an illicit shipment of convention weapons and arms to North Korea in 2013.

[23] *Id.* at para. 22.

[24] UNSC Res 2270 (2016). See also UNSCR 2321 (2016) para 9; UNSC Res 2397 (2017) para. 12.

[25] UNSCR Res 2321 (2016) at para. 22.

[26] UNSC Res 2321 (2016) para. 8.

...prevent the provision of financial services, including insurance or re-insurance...if they have information that provides reasonable grounds to believe that such services, assets or resources could contribute to Iran's proliferation-sensitive nuclear activities, or the development of nuclear weapon delivery systems...[27]

A similar approach was recently utilized in the North Korea context under UNSC Res 2321 (2016), which decides that all Member States.

...shall prohibit their nationals, persons subject to their jurisdiction and entities incorporated in their territory or subject to their jurisdiction from providing insurance or re-insurance services to vessels owned, controlled, or operated, including through illicit means, by the DPRK.... [28]

3.3 Prohibitions on importing and exporting certain cargo

The Security Council Resolutions have also regularly prohibited trade of certain cargo to Iran and North Korea. The most fundamental prohibition covers nuclear technology and military equipment, but the Security Council has slowly applied more comprehensive prohibitions in efforts to enhance diplomatic pressure.

In the Iran context, as early as 2006, the Security Council mandated that Member States take measures to stop "the supply, sale, or transfer directly or indirectly from their territories, or by their nationals or using their flag vessels" of designated goods and equipment that could "...contribute to Iran's enrichment-related, reprocessing or heavy water-related activities, or to the development of nuclear weapon delivery systems..."[29] In enumerating the precise scope of goods prohibited, the UNSC Res 1737 (2006) incorporates a list compiled by the International Atomic En-

---

[27] Para. 21.

[28] UNSC Res 2321 (2016) para. 22.

[29] UNSC Res 1737 (2006) para. 3.

ergy Agency describing materials that could be used for nuclear weapon development purposes. Subsequent resolutions include prohibitions on using vessels flying the flag of a Member State to facilitate Iran's procurement of "any arms or related material. "[30] Likewise, under the same Resolution, Member States are prohibited from procuring banned items from Iran. [31]

Similar Resolutions prohibit transfer of nuclear technology and conventional arms to North Korea. [32] But the current list of prohibited cargo in and out of North Korea is much more comprehensive. Resolutions focusing on prohibiting Member State exports to North Korea have included luxury goods, such as jewelry, precious stones, and even yachts and race cars. [33] More recently, Resolutions have also focused on broad sectorial bans of commodities. In 2017, these included limitations and prohibitions on the supply, sale or transfer of crude oil and other refined petroleum products. [34] Other recent prohibitions include industrial machinery, iron, steel and other metals. [35]

Resolutions also prohibited North Korea from exporting. In a string of Resolutions, the Security Council banned North Korea from selling coal, iron ore, rare earth minerals, precious metals, and seafood. [36] Most recently, it added electrical equipment, machinery, agricultural products, and wood to that list. [37] To define the scope of the prohibition, the Security Council referenced entire chapters of the Harmonized Commodity Description and Coding System, known as the HS Code. [38]

---

[30] UNSC Res 1747 (2006) para 5-6; UNSC Res 1929 (2010) para. 8.

[31] UNSC Res 1747 (2006) para. 7.

[32] See e. g. UNSC Res 1718 (2006) para. 8.

[33] See UNSC Res 1718 (2006) para 8; UNSC Res 2094 (2013), Annex IV.

[34] UNSC Res 2375 (2017).

[35] 2397 (2017) para. 7.

[36] See UNSC Res 2270 (2016) para 29-30; UNSC Res 2231 (2016) para 26-28; UNSC Res 2371 (2017) para. 8.

[37] UNSC Res 2397 (2017) para. 6.

[38] Id.

3. 4 Authorization for cargo inspections and maritime interdiction

To effectuate the cargo bans described above, the Security Council has authorized and required vessel inspections of potential sanctions violators. While acknowledging restrictions on jurisdiction under international law of the sea and customary international law, recent Resolutions have provided Member States with sweeping authority to inspect vessels in their territorial waters and in some circumstances interdict vessels on the high seas.

In the Iran context, under UNSC Res 1803 (2007), the Security Council authorized all States to, "inspect the cargoes to and from Iran, of aircraft and vessels, at their airports and seaports, owned or operated by Iran Air Cargo and Islamic Republic of Iran Shipping Line, provided there are reasonable grounds to believe that the aircraft or vessel is transporting goods prohibited. "[39] This Resolution specifically limits the authorization of such inspections to be in accordance with "national legal authorities and legislation and consistent with international law, in particular the law of the sea..." UNSC Res 1929 (2010) further explains these limits, noting that States "consistent with international law...may request inspections of vessels on the high seas with the consent of the flag State..."

Security Council authorization for vessel inspections in the North Korea context has evolved further. While UNSC Res 1874 (2009) similarly calls on all States to inspect cargo, consistent with international law, when it has "reasonable grounds to believe" the cargo contains prohibited items,[40] it further calls on Member States to inspect such vessels on the high seas "with consent of the flag state. "[41] If that does not work, under UNSC Res 2087 (2013), the UN Security Council Sanctions Committee will issue an "Implementation Assistance Notice" if the vessel "refused to allow an inspection after such an inspection has been authorized by the vessel's Flag

---

[39]　UNSC Res 1803 (2007).

[40]　UNSC Res 1874 (2009) para. 11.

[41]　UNSC Res 1874 (2009) para. 12.

State or if any DPRK−flagged vessel has refused to be inspected..." [42]

UNSC Res 2094 (2013) goes even further. It requires States to inspect " all cargo within or transiting through their territory that has originated in the DPRK, or that is destined for the DPRK, or has been brokered or facilitated by the DPRK or its nationals..." [43] If any vessel refuses inspection after it has been authorized by the flag State (or if it is a DPRK−flagged vessel), the Security Council requires all States to " ...deny such a vessel entry to their ports..." [44]

Under UNSC Res 2375 (2017), if the flag state does not consent to inspection on the high seas and does not direct the vessel to proceed to a convenient port for inspection, then the Sanctions Committee " shall consider designating the vessel" for targeted sanctions. [45] Once designated, the flag state is required to " immediately deregister" the vessel. [46] The Resolution further notes that inspections may only be carried out by " warships and other ships or aircraft clearly marked and identifiable as being on government services. . . " and that inspections are not authorized for vessels " entitled to sovereign immunity under international law. " [47]

Most recently, concerned about illicit North Korean exports facilitated through " deceptive maritime practices," the Security Council under UNSC Res 2397 requires Member States to " seize, inspect, and freeze (impound) any vessel" in its territorial waters, if it has " reasonable grounds to believe" the vessel was involved in prohibited activities. [48]

4. Adapting to life with UN sanctions: shipping industry responses

The Security Council's recent sanctions approaches in the maritime sector have

---

[42]　UNSC Res 2087 (2013) para. 7.

[43]　UNSC Res 2094 (2013) para. 16; See also UNSC Res 2270 (2016) para. 18; UNSC Res 2321 (2016) para. 20.

[44]　UNSC Res 2094 (2013) para. 17.

[45]　UNSC Res 2375 (2017) para. 8.

[46]　UNSC Res 2375 (2017) para. 8.

[47]　UNSC Res 2375 (2017) para. 10.

[48]　UNSCR 2397 (2017) para. 9.

generated substantial discourse among those in the shipping industry. This industry is heavily regulated by international conventions, local laws, and customary practice, so industry participants are relatively used to oversight from national and supranational bodies (including the International Maritime Organization, which is an organ of the United Nations itself). But Security Council sanctions can appear rapidly in response to immediate security crises and may immediately impose burdens on shipping interest to analyze their commercial dealings and ensure compliance. The following is a summary of industry responses to adapt to recent UN sanctions tactics in the maritime sphere.

4. 1 Maritime blacklists

Shipping industry participants must be careful not to engage in financial transactions with designated entities and vessels. While it may seem relatively straight forward to refrain from doing business with these entities by consulting the lists promulgated by the Security Council, as the Resolutions themselves indicate, sanctioned entities regularly attempt to disguise their identity by renaming and re−registering the company or the vessel. This places an enhanced burden on shipping industry participants to engage in thorough "know your customer" inquiries for even basic transactions, such as bunkering services. [49]

These lists of sanctioned entities are also not intended to be exhaustive, as other Resolutions prohibit transactions involving vessels reasonably believed to be linked to sanctioned regimes. This includes not only vessels owned but also those "chartered" by the sanctioned government—adding an additional layer of scrutiny required of industry participants.

4. 2 Vessel registration and insurance prohibitions

Restrictions on renaming and re−registering sanctioned vessels appears to be an issue that would be addressed by Member States. In many cases, it would. For exam-

---

[49]   See UNSC Res 1929 (2010) para. 18.

ple, Singapore, and China are all major flags that utilize governmental offices to o-versee vessel registration within their jurisdictions. For example, the Singapore Registry of Ships is an organ of the Maritime and Port Authority of Singapore, a governmental agency. [50]

Some other major flags are so-called "open registries" or "flags of convenience" that are often utilized by businesses to reduce regulation and costs. [51] Some of the most popular open registries utilize private entities to facilitate their operations. For example, the Republic of the Marshall Islands is one of the top flag states in the world, but its registry is actually controlled by a "privately held maritime and corporate registry service" based in Reston, Virginia, USA. [52] For ship registries of this kind—the Liberian registry is another similar example—the burden of sanctions compliance regarding prohibitions on vessel renaming/re-registration is actually imposed on commercial actors rather than the UN Member States. [53] In this sense, it is the shipping industry itself in the form of privately facilitated registries that must enhance due diligence to ensure that sanctions are properly implemented.

The prohibition on marine insurance coverage on sanctioned vessels has created even more commercial controversy. UNSC Res 1929 (2010) requires Member States to prevent "insurance or re-insurance" over sanctioned vessels in the Iran context. While the precise scope of this Resolution is left undefined, marine insurance providers immediately expressed concern over this mandate, as well as similar mandates imposed under domestic legislation. The uncertainty sparked particular controversy in the United Kingdom, since London has long been home to the world's largest

[50] See Singapore Registry of Ships, Maritime and Port Authority of Singapore, https://www.mpa. gov. sg/web/portal/home/singapore-registry-of-ships.

[51] See H. Edwin Anderson, III "The Nationality of Ships and Flags of Convenience"; Economics, Politics, and Alternatives, 21 Tul. Mar. L. J. 139 (1996).

[52] For more information on the Marshall Islands flag, see the website of International Registries, Inc. at https://www. register-iri. com/index. cfm? action=about.

[53] For more information on the Liberia flag, see the website the Liberian Registry http://www. liscr. com/about-liberian-registry.

marine insurance market.

While the sanctions on marine insurance over Iranian maritime assets remained in place, legal disputes arose concerning the right of insurance companies to terminate coverage over sanctioned vessels. The entire fleet of Islamic Republic of Iran Shipping Line, a specifically designated sanctioned entity under UN Resolutions and UK legislation, was insured as a member of the London-based Steamship Mutual P&I Club. Pursuant to the UK prohibition on marine insurance over IRISL vessels, Steamship Mutual terminated coverage. Coincidently, an IRISL vessel was involved in a collision on the day after cover was terminated. This led to a dispute that went all the way through the UK courts addressing whether or not the insurer had the right to terminate cover at the time. [54] At least one other similar case addressed termination of cover for vessels storing Iranian oil in violation of EU-level sanctions. [55]

In response to such concerns, the insurance industry began promulgating so-called "Sanctions Clauses" for inclusion in policies of marine insurance in order to hedge against the risk of breaching sanctions. [56] These clauses allow early termination of insurance cover and are designed for inclusion in hull insurance policies and P&I Club rules.

In response to the Joint Comprehensive Plan of Action (JCPA) when Iran agreed to halt its nuclear program, many in the shipping industry, particularly in the marine insurance community, eagerly awaited "implementation day" in which trade activities with Iran would normalize. [57] This normalization, however, has been slower than expected. The UN sanctions were implemented at the national and EU level,

---

[54] *IRISL v. Steamship Mutual Underwriting Association* [2010] EWHC 2661.

[55] Arash Shipping v. Groupama [2011] 2 Lloyd's Rep 607.

[56] See e. g. Lloyd's Sanctions Guidance-Sanctions Clauses, October 17, 2014, www. lloyds. com/~/media/files/the% 20market/communications/market% 20bulletins/2012/02/y4560. pdf See Mike Salthouse, Maritime Risk International, "Legacy of the Iran Sanctions Programme for the Shipping Industry" March 21, 2017.

[57] See Helen Kelly and Nidaa Bakhsh, "Insurance Risk to Owners Over Iran Sanctions 'Snapback' ", Lloyd's List, February 2, 2017.

and rolling back the sanctions necessarily involves a legislative response by United States and the European Union, which had imposed sanctions above and beyond those required by the Security Council. The Iran sanctions also have reportedly left a "legacy" in which commercial actors appear hesitant to engage in business with Iran due to fears of the JCPA's impermanence and worries of non—compliance. [58]

This also allowed insurance markets to blossom in places in which the Security Council's decisions were not enforced at the local level. Some industry observers have argued that preventing cover of blacklisted vessels does not actually penalize those operating the vessels at issue, but instead makes it more difficult for third—parties to recover if they suffer injury attributed to the designated vessel. [59] For example, if a sanctioned vessel is not covered by a solvent insurer, casualties such as oil spills or collisions impacting third parties could be catastrophic, ultimately punishing third—parties rather than punishing any political regime.

4. 3 Cargo prohibitions

Cargo prohibitions impact a variety of commercial actors, including shippers and consignees contracting for the sale of goods, commercial vessels carrying cargo in the liner trade and under time and voyage charters, and intermediaries facilitating such transactions. For any of these parties, there is a burden not only to ascertain the i-dentity of the parties to their contracts, but also to engage in vessel—vetting and car-go checking, which becomes increasingly burdensome as sanctions become more comprehensive.

Similar to the approach taken in the marine insurance sector, shipowners and charterers have begun including clauses in their contracts to address the risks of breaching sanctions through the language of their charterparties. Industry organiza-

---

[58]　See Helen Kelly and Nidaa Bakhsh, "Insurance Risk to Owners Over Iran Sanctions ' Snapback' ", Lloyd's List, February 2, 2017.

[59]　See Liz McMahon, "Policing Sanctions Through Insurance Will Hurt Third Parties" Lloyd's List, June 29, 2012.

tions, such as the Baltic and International Maritime Council (BIMCO) and Intertanko have published model clauses designed to allocate such risks. These may be added to standard charterparty forms under a "rider" provision and are also included in the most modern BIMCO form contracts. [60]

For example, one version of a BIMCO "Sanctions Clause for Time Charterparties" reads in relevant part:

...The Owners shall not be obliged to comply with any orders for employment of the Vessel in any carriage, trade or on a voyage which, in the reasonable judgment of the Owners, will expose the Vessel, Owners, managers, crew, the Vessel's insurers, or their re—insurers, to any sanction or prohibition imposed by any State, Supranational or International Governmental Organization...[61]

Such provisions allow a shipowner to refuse orders of a charterer if it believes the orders would subject it to liability for breaching sanctions. While there may be recent cases arising under such language in shipping practice that could shed light on the mechanics of this method of risk allocation, charterparties traditionally include arbitration clauses. Shipping arbitration, at least in the English context, is generally conducted in confidence behind closed doors. Such confidentiality, while commercially favorable for the parties, makes it difficult for observers to track industry practice.

4. 4 Interdiction and inspection

Recent sanctions, particularly in the North Korea context, provide robust authority and responsibility for state actors to engage in vessel inspections both in their territorial waters and even on the high seas with consent of the flag state. While the burden of inspection enforcement remains on UN Member States, it is commercial ac-

---

[60] See e. g. the BIMCO New York Produce and Exchange 2015 Time Charterparty form.

[61] *Id.*

tors who bear the risk of delays and cargo seizures that could result from such inspections. In response to sanctions, industry participants must remain in clear communication with coastal authorities for inspection purposes, while also allocating the risk of commercial delays caused by inspections either through express contract provisions or with insurance coverage designed to hedge against losses suffered by inspection—related delays.

5. Conclusion

While economic sanctions have perhaps become an entrenched part of diplomatic life, they do place commercial entities in the uncomfortable position as an involuntary tool for international policy. It is difficult for shipping interests to track evolving regulations and to comply with them by scrutinizing each transaction they undertake. It is also challenging for them to hedge against the risks of sanctions non—compliance. While frustrations arising out of these problems are understandable, sanctions are a relatively benign alternative to a major military conflict, which of course would be much more commercially disruptive.

**Part III   East-West Perspectives on the Principle of Effec-
tive Control**

REFLECTIONS ON THE JUDICIAL DEVELOPMENT OF EFFECTIVE CONTROL TEST IN THE CONTEXT OF UN PEACE OPERATIONS

Ke Song[*]

1. Introduction

There are serious cases in human rights violation in the context of UN peace operations boomed in the past decades. Among all the cases, many of these have been sent to international courts and tribunals. Reports on human rights and IHL violations of UN military peacekeepers, especially these in form of sexual exploitation and abuse (SEA), have been booming in last decades.[1] The SEA problems have been one of the core concerns of the UN Peace operations.[2] In January 2017, the Sec-

---

* PhD Candidate, University of Edinburgh, School of law, Scotland, UK; (email: ke. song@ ed. ac. uk).
All the websites are as current as of January 30, 2018.

[1] Despite numerous attempts by the UN initiatives and reforms aimed at addressing SEA on peacekeeping operations, such abuse is still prevalent. The number of new allegations of sexual exploitation or sexual abuse received from the departments and offices of the Secretariat and agencies, funds and programmes of the United Nations system totaled 99 in 2015, compared with 80 allegations in 2014. This regrettable increase in the number of new allegations signifies that more needs to be done to reduce the number of allegations and, more importantly, the number of victims affected by sexual exploitation and abuse perpetrated by United Nations personnel. See 2016 Report of the Secretary-General, Special measures for protection from sexual exploitation and sexual abuse, UNGA, A/70/729. "We also recognize that the United Nations often operates in circumstances of heightened risk for sexual exploitation and abuse, where the Organization must take stronger measures to detect, control and prevent behaviour of this kind. " 2017 Special measures for protection from sexual exploitation and abuse: a new approach, Report of the Secretary-General, UNGA, A/71/818.

[2] See e. g. 2017 Special measures for protection from sexual exploitation and abuse: a new approach, Report of the Secretary-General, UNGA, A/71/818; 2016 Report of Special measures for protection from sexual exploitation and sexual abuse, Report of the Secretary-General, UNGA, A/70/729; 2015 Report of the Secretary-General on Special measures for protection from sexual exploitation and sexual abuse, Report of the Secretary-General, UNGA, A/69/779.

retary—General established a diverse High—Level Task Force to develop as a matter of urgency a strategy to achieve visible and measurable improvements in the way the Organization prevents and responds to SEA. As noted by UNSG:

Such acts of cruelty should never take place. Certainly no person serving with the United Nations in any capacity should be associated with such vile and vicious crimes. [3]

In the past a few years, the UN has been taking actions in preventing and punishing the SEAs arising in the UN peace operations. [4] It must be borne in mind that one of the unsolved legal issues in regard to combating against SEAs is on the at-

---

[3] The Secretary—General is committed to the implementation of this strategy and has instructed and expects all his leadership to take immediate action. See Statement of UNSG, Note to Correspondents: The Secretary—General's Report on Special Measures for Protection from Sexual Exploitation and Abuse: A New Approach, https: //www. un. org/sg/en/content/sg/note−correspondents/2017−03−09/note−correspondents−secretary−general%E2%80%99s−report−special.

[4] The most recent actions proposed by UNGA includes: he Assembly is requested to: (a) Take note of my renewed emphasis and actions to address the problem of sexual exploitation and abuse; (b) Take note of steps to introduce victims' assistance support functions at Headquarters and in field locations, including through the victims' rights advocate functions, which will be reported in the next budget cycle of the respective entities; (c) Endorse the revision of the provisions of the Trust Fund in Support of Victims of Sexual Exploitation and Abuse, to allow additional assistance to victims, as might be appropriate and necessary; (d) Endorse the establishment of procedures to withhold reimbursements in the event that investigations are not undertaken, reported on and concluded in a timely manner, and to pay the amounts withheld into the Trust Fund; (e) Endorse the proposal for Member States to receive claims from victims and the related establishment of mechanisms to do so; (f) Endorse, as appropriate under its authority, a Secretary—General's special protocol on preventing sexual exploitation and abuse for the establishment or renewal of any operation where heightened risks exist, as part of the mandates and budgets that are subject to its approval; (g) Endorse the establishment of a system—wide confidential repository of case information to be centralized under the supervision of the Office of the Special Coordinator; (h) Consider proposals to strengthen investigative capacity in sexual exploitation and abuse cases for the Secretariat and its separately administered funds and programmes, as well as across the wider United Nations system; (i) Endorse the principles set forth above for inclusion in the voluntary compact with Member States, for consideration at the high—level meeting; (j) Endorse the extension of the mandate of the Special Coordinator on Improving the United Nations Response to Sexual Exploitation and Abuse to improve United Nations response to sexual exploitation and abuse and support the strengthening of that office. 2017 Special measures for protection from sexual exploitation and abuse: a new approach, Report of the Secretary—General, UNGA A/71/818, 19−20.

tribution of responsibility. The paper will fill this gap by answering the question on how and the extent to which States and international organizations can be held internationally responsible for the conduct of military contingents is determined by the relevant standards of attribution.

It is worth noting that the attribution of responsibility under UN Peace Operation context is *sui generis* in two folds: first, since the wrongful acts are perpetrated by UN military contingents (i. e. peacekeepers), many of which are *de facto* controlled by UN or States. The responsibility is not exclusively about State responsibility in its nature. Instead, it is the responsibility with shared pattern among States and International organizations. Second, the responsibility of international organization (IO), troop-contributing countries (TCCs), and host States may be attributed simultaneously, namely "dual or multiple responsibility", which share the pattern of "responsibility umbrella".

Starting from analyzing the Jurisprudential development of effective control criteria of attribution of responsibility, the paper will conclude that most apposite test is one of "effective control". Therefore, the most important element of attribution is to determine whether "effective control" rests with the UN, TCCs and receiving States. The paper will therefore illustrate the *sui generis* structures and features of UN Peace operations to examine the meaning of "effective control" in this specific context, whereby the specific version, i. e. "*de facto* effective control" test, is proved. It will be argued that the "dual" and "triple" attribution of responsibility to UN or TCCs is possible therein.

2. Jurisprudential development of effective control criteria of attribution of responsibility

How States and international organizations can be held internationally responsible for the conduct of private persons is determined by the relevant standards of attribution? The paper will first examine the tests that have been developed through jurisprudence by various courts and tribunals to determine the questions of attribution of international responsibility, and the implications of these approaches for attribution of wrongful acts of UN military peacekeepers to the UN, host States or the TCCs.

2. 1 Attribution of responsibility of a factual assessment

The reflections of jurisprudence of international courts show that the *factual* exercise of authority, which is based on evidential test, is decisive to attribute the responsibility of international wrongful acts to States or international organizations in concrete cases.

The International Court of Justice (ICJ) in *Nicaragua* case[5] gave a detailed analysis on evidential value of available materials in determining effective control of US on the *contras*. The question of the degree of control of the *contras* whereby the United States had, it is alleged, violated an obligation of international law not to kill, wound or kidnap citizens of Nicaragua. [6] The evidential materials in this case were employed to determine whether the US have *actually* exercised such a degree of control in all fields to justify treating the *contras* as acting on its behalf. In paragraph 109 of that Judgement the ICJ stated that it had to:

[D] etermine [...] whether or not the relationship of the contras to the United States Government was so much one of dependence on the one side and control on the other that it would be right to equate the contras, for legal purposes, with an organ of the United States Government, or as acting on behalf of that Government. [7]

The ICJ in *Territory of the Congo* [8] investigated evidence to examine whether

---

[5] *Military and Paramilitary Activities in and against Nicaragua* (Nicaragua v. United States of America), Merits, Judgment, I. C. J. Reports 1986, pp. 62–65, paras. 109–115.

[6] *Ibid*, paras. 113.

[7] *Ibid*, paras. 109.

[8] *Armed Activities on the Territory of the Congo* (DRC v Uganda), Merits, Judgment, ICJ Report 2005, 168, para. 148–160.

the conduct of violating prohibition against use of force was that of "an organs" of U-ganda;[9] whether that of an entity exercising elements of governmental authority on its behalf;[10] and whether such conduct was "on the instructions of, or under the direction or control of" Uganda. [11] Finally, the ICJ "found that there is no probative evidence by reference to which it has been persuaded that this was the case. "[12]

ICJ in *Genocide* case evaluated the *de facto* status of entities (in this case, the entities is so-called "Scorpions") to decide whether Respondent should be internationally responsible for the wrongful acts. The evidential materials showed that Scorpions were not *de jure* organs of the Respondent. [13] But this does not preclude the possibility to attribute responsibility to State. In this regard, ICJ noted that: "in any event the act of an organ placed by a State at the disposal of another public authority shall not be considered an act of that State if the organ was acting on behalf of the public authority at whose disposal it had been placed. "[14] The ICJ gave affirmation that it is possible in principle to attribute to a State conduct of persons-or groups of persons-who, "while they do not have the legal status of State organs, *in fact* act under such strict control by the State that they must be treated as its organs for pur-

---

[9]   The Court referred to ASR, art. 4: "The conduct of any State organ shall be considered an act of that State under international law, whether the organ exercises legislative, executive, judicial or any other functions, whatever position it holds in the organization of the State, and whatever its character as an organ of the central Government or of a territorial unit of the State. "

[10]   The Court referred to ASR, art. 4: "The conduct of a person or entity which is not an organ of the State under article 4 but which is empowered by the law of that State to exercise elements of the governmental authority shall be considered an act of the State under international law, provided the person or entity is acting in that capacity in the particular instance. "

[11]   The Court referred to ASR, art. 8: "The conduct of a person or group of persons shall be considered an act of a State under international law if the person or group of persons is in fact acting on the instructions of, or under the direction or control of that State in carrying out the conduct. "

[12]   Above n. 8, para. 160.

[13]   *Application of the Convention on the Prevention and Punishment of the Crime of Genocide* (Bosnia and Herzegovina v. Serbia and Montenegro) , Judgment, I. C. J. Reports 2007, p. 43, para. 389.

[14]   *Ibid.*

poses of the necessary attribution leading to the State's responsibility for an internationally wrongful act. " [15]

In sum, the *main* weight of analysis of ICJ in addressing the issue of attribution of responsibility is on evidential test on the *de facto* status of commissioners. It is the *de facto* rather than *de jure* status that determines the attribution of responsibility. Assuming *arguendo* that States have *de jure* effective control over persons, groups of persons or entities, the States can still be exempted from bearing international responsibility, if, as is always the case, the other States or IOs are exercising *de facto* effective control over the persons, groups of persons or entities at the exact timeline. As observed by ICJ in previous case, "it is appropriate to look beyond legal status alone, in order to grasp the *reality* of the relationship between the person taking action, and the State to which he is so closely attached as to appear to be nothing more than its agent. Any other solution would allow States to escape their international responsibility by choosing to act through persons or entities whose supposed independence would be purely fictitious. " [16]

2.2 Applicability of Effective Control test in the UN peace operation context

Apart from evidential test, the attribution of responsibility is under doctrinal limitations, since it always requires proof of a particularly great degree of control over person or entities, a degree of control which the ICJ's judgment employed to attribute the international responsibility. Functioning as the parameter of attribution of international responsibility, such degree of control can be determinative to examine to what extent the State or IOs should be attributed with international responsibility. Then the question may raise, considering the specific nature of the UN peace operation, why effective control test is applicable in this particular context.

In practice, the application of effective control should combine with the *sui ge-*

---

[15] *Ibid.*, para. 391.
[16] *Ibid.*, para. 392.

neris institutional structure of the UN peace operations in concrete cases. It must be borne in mind that jurisprudence of international courts and tribunals are fragmented[17] on the issue of degree of control. On the other hand, legal terms should be variable to adapt to the changing reality. As the Privy Council once put it: "International law was not crystallized [...] but is a living and expanding body. "[18] It may, again, arise the further question whether the jurisprudential coherence of effective control—as the legal parameter in attributing responsibility—is necessary in determining the international responsibility in the peace operation context. [19] It is thus necessary, at the beginning, to examine the origin and development of "effective control", the meaning of this legal term, in order to see why it is specifically applicable in the context of the UN peace operations to attribute international responsibility.

(1) Choice of legal parameter: Effective Control or Overall Control

ICJ *Nicaragua* case

In *Nicaragua* case, with regard to military actions and operations by *contras* involving the use of military force in Nicaragua against the territorial sovereignty and political independence of that State, the Court found that the US born responsibility as a result of its "training, arming, equipping, financing, supplying or otherwise encouraging, supporting and aiding" the *contra* forces. Such responsibility followed from the violation by the US of the obligation not to intervene in the affairs of other States as well as the obligation not to use force in breach of the customary rule of in-

---

[17]   According to the Classification by Philippa Webb, the judicial fragmentation can be broken into two folds: Genuine fragmentation and apparent fragmentation. The former refers to the situation whereby judicial decisions give rise to conflicting developments in the law that are either unconscious due to lack of awareness of other courts' decisions or a conscious departure from existing case law. The latter refers to situation whereby judicial decisions appears to be conflicting, but the variations are due to contextual factors and the underlying legal reasoning can be resolved through clarification and interpretation. See Philippa Webb, *International judicial integration and fragmentation* (Oxford, United Kingdom : Oxford University Press. 2016). p. 12.

[18]   *In re Piracy Jure Gentium* (1934) AC 586, 7 ILR 213, 214 (PC).

[19]   For a comprehensive analysis on the coherence of legal norms in the fragmented system of international law, see Campbell McLachlan, *THE PRINCIPLE OF SYSTEMIC INTEGRATION AND ARTICLE* 31 (3)(C) *OF THE VIENNA CONVENTION*, 54 ICLQ (2005).

ternational law corresponding to Article 2 （4） of the UN Charter.

The Court had then to consider whether some actions by *contras* in breach of international humanitarian law （killing of prisoners, indiscriminate killing of civilians, torture, rape and kidnapping） could be attributed to the US. It answered this question in the negative. It required for such attribution a very exacting test, namely that of "effective control" by the US over *contras*' actions in breach of international humanitarian law, a test the Court held had not been met in the case at bar. By such "effective control", the Court meant that the US should have

"*Directed or enforced* the *perpetration* of the acts contrary to human rights and humanitarian law alleged by the Applicant State. Such acts could well be committed by members of the contras without the control of the United States. For this conduct to give rise to legal responsibility of the United States, it would in principle have to be proven that the State had *effective control* of the military or paramilitary operations in the course of which the alleged violations were committed. （emphasis added） "[20]

According the observation by Antonio Cassese, it seems clear from these words that by "effective control" the Court intended either①the issuance of directions to the contras by the US concerning specific operations （indiscriminate killing of civilians, etc. ）, that is to say, the ordering of those operations by the US, or ②the enforcement by the US of each specific operation of the *contras*, namely forcefully making the rebels carry out those specific operations. [21] Furthermore, there is time restrain for the attribution of responsibility through effective control test: the State should have effective control of the military paramilitary operations in the course of which the alleged violations were committed.

In sum, in the *Nicaragua* case, the jurisprudence of ICJ reflected on the general issue on the attribution of international responsibility for alleged violations by indi-

---

[20] Above n. 5, para. 115.

[21] Antonio Cassese, *The Nicaragua and Tadić Tests Revisited in Light of the ICJ Judgment on Genocide in Bosnia*, 18 The European Journal of International Law （2007）, 653.

viduals and entities. As proposed by ICJ, the effective control served as the most appropriate legal parameter for attributing the responsibility. Nonetheless, it is worth noting that the main weight attribution, as has been said before, lied on evaluation of factual elements.

ICTY *Tadić* case

It must be borne in mind that, in *Tadić* case, the judgement of Appeals Chamber of ICTY was request to answer a question of individual criminal responsibility. In particular, the Appeals Chamber of ICTY was requested to answer the question on whether the conflict was international, as claimed by the Prosecution in its appeal, for the purpose of establishing whether the Trial Chamber could exercise its jurisdiction over those alleged grave breaches of Forth Geneva Convention. In other words, the Appeals Chamber only had to establish whether the prosecutor was right in challenging a Trial Chamber's ruling (under such ruling *Tadić* was not criminally liable under Article 2 of the ICTY Statute for committing grave breaches of the Fourth Geneva Convention, because Article 2 only applies to international armed conflicts whereas that in which *Tadić* was involved was internal. [22]

As proposed by ICTY Appeals Chamber, with regard to the degree of control over actions by organized and hierarchically structured groups, such as military or paramilitary units. In the case of an organized group, the group normally engages in a series of activities. The situation of an organized group is different from that of a single individual performing a specific act on behalf of a State. In the case of an organized group, overall control by the State over the group was sufficient, hence specific instructions were not required for each individual operations. [23] It is apparent that the overall control standard is lower than that of "effective control", since "if it is under the overall control of a State, it must perforce engage the responsibility of that State for its activities, *whether or not each of them was specifically imposed, requested*

---

[22]   ICTY Trial Chamber, *Tadić*, Judgment of 10 August 1995.
[23]   ICTY Appeals Chamber, *Tadić*, Judgment of 15 July 1999, para. 120.

or directed by the State. (emphasis added) " [24] Furthermore, " overall control" resided not only in equipping, financing or training and providing operational support to the group, but also in coordinating or helping in the general planning of its military or paramilitary activity. [25] It should be added that courts have taken a different approach with regard to individuals or groups not organized into military structures. With regard to such individual or groups, courts considered overall or general level of control to be insufficient, but have instead adopted effective control level of control, insisting upon specific instructions or directives aimed at the commission of specific acts, or have required public approval of those acts following their commission. [26]

The judgement of Appeals Chamber has stepped in applying overall control in attributing international responsibility through an expanded interpretation of the overall control criteria. According to the tribunal, the overall control criteria applies both to the situation whereby international law renders any State responsibility for acts in breach of international law performed (i) by individuals having the formal status of organs of a State and (ii) by individuals who make up organized groups subject to the State's control. As observed the ICTY Appeals Chamber, "clearly, the rationale behind this legal regulation is that otherwise, States might easily shelter behind, or use as a pretext, their internal legal system or the lack of any specific instructions in order to disclaim international responsibility. " [27] Therefore, although irrelevant to the seized dispute, the ICTY Appeals Chamber in its judgement, confirmed the applicability of overall control test in attribution of international responsibility, and furtherly exempted out the effective control test that it held to be unpersuasive when attributing States international responsibility the acts of individuals having the formal

---

[24] *Ibid.*, para. 122.
[25] *Ibid.*, paras. 131 & 137.
[26] *Ibid.*, para. 132.
[27] *Ibid.*, para. 123.

status of organs of a State, or becoming organized groups.

ECtHR jurisprudence

The debates on the legality of applying of overall control criteria in attributing State responsibility have been lasting for long. The lower criteria (i. e. overall control) first appeared in ICTY in *Tadi ɛ*, but has been subsequently *revised* in the ECtHR jurisprudence when dealing with the issue of attribution of international responsibility the acts of the individuals having the formal status of organs of a State or organized groups. [28]

In the *Loizidou* judgment, the Court observed that the responsibility of States can be involved by acts and omissions of their authorities which produce effects outside their own territory, where the States exercises *effective control* of an area outside its national territory. And the obligation derives from the fact of such control whether it be exercised directly, through its armed forces, or through a subordinate local administration. [29]

In *Cyprus v. Turkey* case, [30] the ECtHR was requested to decide on the respondent's State's responsibility under the Convention in respect of the alleged violations. [31] Even TRNC is considered as an organized group, the overall control, according to the Court, was still inapplicable there. At paragraph 77, the Court took the view that: "it is to be observed that the Court's reasoning is framed in terms of a broader Statement of principle as regards Turkey's general responsibility under the Convention for the policies and actions of 'TRNC' authorities. Having *effective overall control* over Northern Cyprus, its responsibility cannot be confined to the acts of

---

[28]   See in particular, ECtHR *Cyprus v. Turkey*, Application no. 25781/94, Judgment of 10 May 2001; ECtHR CASE OF ILACU AND OTHERS v. MOLDOVA AND RUSSIA, Application no. 48787/99, Judgment of 8 July 2004, para. 319.

[29]   ECtHR *Loizidou v. Turkey*, Application no. 15318/89, Judgment of 18 December 1996, para. 52.

[30]   Above n. 28. *Cyprus v. Turkey*.

[31]   Above n. 28, *Cyprus v. Turkey*, para. 77.

its own soldiers or officials in Northern Cyprus but must also engaged by virtue of the acts of the local administration which survives by virtue of Turkish military and other support. "[32]

In the subsequent *Ilasu v. Moldova and others v. Moldova and Russia* case, the Court ascertained the strict liability of State for the conduct of their subordinates in the absence of effective control. The Court stipulated that:

A State may also be held responsible even where its agents are acting *ultra vires* or contrary to instructions. Under the Convention, a State's authorities are *strictly* liable for the conduct of their subordinates; they are under a duty to impose their will and cannot shelter behind their inability to ensure that it is respected. [33]

The Court in this case imposed stricter legal parameter than effective control in the attribution of international responsibility. According to the Court, even in the absence of *effective control*, respondent State still owns liability under Article 1 of the ECHR in its power to take and are in accordance with international law to secure to the applicants the rights guaranteed by the Convention. [34]

(2) Separate application of legal parameters: a reflection on ICJ Genocide Judgement

The jurisprudence of the international courts and tribunals, as have been analyzed before, is largely fragmented. The question still remain, whether the "overall control" criteria could be applied to attribute responsibility. From the perspective of law, as has been noted by ICJ in *Genocide* case, the "overall control" test proposed by ICTY in *Tadi* case did not apply in determining State responsibility on two

---

[32] Above n. 28, *Cyprus v. Turkey*, para. 77.

[33] Above n. 28, *Ilasu v. Moldova and others v. Moldova and Russia*, para. 319.

[34] Above n. 28, *Ilasu v. Moldova and others v. Moldova and Russia*, para. 331.

grounds. First, the test had been suggested by the ICTY with respect to the question of determining whether an armed conflict was international and not with regard to the different issue of State responsibility. Second, in any case such expansive application would have overly broadened the scope of State responsibility. Although the ICTY held that overall control criteria are both valid for international humanitarian law and State responsibility, ICJ observed that the ICTY was not called upon in the *Tadié* case, nor is it in general called upon, to rule on question of State responsibility, since its jurisdiction is criminal and extends over persons only. Thus, in that Judgement the ICTY addressed an issue which was not indispensable for the exercise of its jurisdiction, thus giving unpersuasive answer. [35]

According to the ICJ in *Genocide* case, the "overall control" test resorted to in *Tadié*, if it can possibly be applicable when determining whether an armed conflict is international, is "unpersuasive" if used to establish whether a State is responsible for acts performed by armed forces and paramilitary units that are not among its official organs. For the Court, the reason why that test is "unpersuasive" is two folds: ①logic does not require the same test to be adopted in resolving the two issues, which are very different in nature, with the consequence that the degree of a State's involvement in an armed conflict may well differ from that required for State responsibility to arise. ②The "overall control" test overly broadens the scope of responsibility because it goes beyond the three standards set out by the ILC in Article 8 of the

---

[35] " [T] he Court attached the utmost importance to the factual and legal findings made by the ICTY in ruling on the criminal liability of the accused before it, and in the present case, the Court takes fullest account of the ICTY's trial and appellate judgments dealing with the events underlying the dispute. " However, ICJ in this case, declined the reasonableness of the ICTY's legal argumentations on the application of overall control in the attribution of international responsibility by stipulating that "the argument in favour of that test is unpersuasive. " See above n. 13, para. 403, 404.

ASR. [36]

(3) Summary

The Genocide Judgement has been criticized by legal commentators for being unpersuasive. As noted by A. Cassese, any well—founded contestation should assist that judgement on the merits of its holdings. It should not be confined to the flimsy argument that *Tadić* was about the nature of armed conflicts whereas *Nicaragua* revolved around state responsibility and therefore the two different tests may coexist in that they relate to different subject—matter. [37] Furthermore, it is worth noting that Appeals Chamber of ICTY held that the legal criteria (i. e. "overall control" tests) are both valid for international humanitarian law and State responsibility. [38] And both ICTY *Tadić* case and ICJ *Nicaragua* case have proved contradictory jurisprudence. For the ICJ in *Genocide* case, to prove the contrary view which gives a clear division with regard to the applicability between the two notions, the Court has, at least, to prove the contrary State practice and *opinio juris*. Therefore, it might not safe for the Court to conclude that the "overall control" test is inapplicable in attributing State responsibility without taking any practical and legal stand.

However, one particular excerpt of the ICJ *Genocide* judgment, without providing any State practice and *opinio juris* supporting it, is nevertheless reasonable since it is based on the concrete *factual* considerations rather than *legal* doctrines:

It must next be noted that the "overall control" test has the major draw-

---

[36] The Article 8 of the ASR suggested three disjunctive standards for the attribution to a state of conduct of private individuals: ①whether the state has issued instructions to those persons, ②whether the state has directed the persons to do something, or③whether the state has exercised control over those persons. According to the ILC, the instructions, direction or control must relate to the specific conduct that turns out to be in breach of international law. For an authoritative analysis, see above n. 13, para. 404–407; See also above n. 13, 663.

[37] Above n. 21, 663

[38] Above n. 23, para. 118–119, 120, 131, 137.

back of broadening the scope of State responsibility well beyond the fundamental principle governing the law of international responsibility; a State is responsible only for its own conduct, that it to say the conduct of persons acting, on whatever basis, on its behalf. [39]

Therefore, the overall control is insufficient to serve as the legal parameter to fix the internationally responsible bodies for the wrongful acts. Instead, what should be proven is on the effective control test, which can be broken into two folds: first, from the *legal* perspective, the States or IOs should satisfy effective control requirement over the specific wrongful acts of perpetrators during which the wrong was committed. Second, from the perspective of *factual* investigation, the Court should prove that organ of the State or IOs gave the specific instructions or provided the specific direction pursuant to wrongful act acted.

The subsequent analysis will go into both two aspects (i. e. practical and legal aspects) to analyze the applicability of effective control specifically in the context of UN Peace Operations.

3. "Effective control" criteria in UN Peace operations

3. 1 Features of UN peace operations and effective control

Relationship between legal norms and practices is dynamic. The application of legal parameter would appear to be of an evolving nature, in the way that keep the balance between the upholding *status quo* and adapting to the changing policy order. In the words of Jenks, "stability and the protection of acquired rights are essentially functions of any legal system, but no legal system can protect itself against revolution except by providing adequate scope for evolutionary change. " [40] Although effective control has been acknowledged as the legal parameter for the attribution of international responsibility, when it comes to attribution of international responsibility

[39]   See above n. 13, para. 406.

[40]   W. C. Jenks, *The Common Law of Mankind* (Stevens, 1958), at p. 85.

in the context of UN peace operations, the parameter itself should modify in order to adapt to the changing needs of the practices.

Indicating from the UN peace operation practices, it is proposed that the "effective control" criteria should ensure adjustment. Different from the situation in the previous ICJ/ICTY situation, UN military personnel has double identities: on the one hand, they remain an organ of the TCCs, on the other hand, they are also international personnel and thus act as agents of the UN. Such pattern of double identities brings about an interesting interplay between the law on attribution of responsibility to States and to IOs. Furthermore, due to the complexities of the institutions of UN peace operation systems, the attribution of responsibility of wrongful acts of such international personnel in each UN peace operation has been of particular specific nature.

The features of UN peace operations and the implications for attributing international responsibility can be divided into four folds:

i. The possibility of dual responsibility based on the dual identities of UN military contingents. UN contingents, on the one hand, forms part of the State military forces, while on the other hand, they are usually subsidiary organs of the UN. Considering the identity of the perpetrator often ties with the effective control over specific actions, the international responsibility can be attributed, as one aspect of the considerations, by reference to the identities of the UN military contingents; the dual identities of the UN military contingents indicate that the UN or the TPPs may be even simultaneously responsible for the wrongful acts. Furthermore, the receiving State, if at the time of the commission having the effective control over the specific wrongful acts, can also hold the responsibility. Thus in the specific context of UN peace operations, it may also arise the triple international responsibility.

ii. As can be deduced from the UN Peacekeeping practice, the type of command and control exercised by the UN is generally limited to "operational control" and this is not necessarily the same as "effective control". Even proved having generally operational control of the UN peacekeepers, the UN cannot be exempt from taking the responsibility for the wrongful acts, if such specific conduct is under the *de facto* effective control of the UN peace operation. In other words, the general UN peace operation is irrelevant for attribution of the responsibility. It is the *de facto* effective control, whereby the actual control of particular conduct in particular situation matters for the attribution of responsibility.

iii. No UN peace operations will promote the wrongful acts of the military contingents. In the milieu of UN military peacekeeper complicity, the question is not solely who gave orders, but rather who omitted to prevent wrongful acts and to hold perpetrators to account. [41] Therefore, the form of the international responsibility is omission, rather than act. The obligations therein are in the form of responsibility to prevent and punish.

iv. The diverse structures of UN Peace operations system make it more difficult to identify who has the power to order the specific conduct of UN peacekeepers, or who has the capacity to prevent the wrongful acts of the UN peacekeepers. It is important to note again that it is the *de facto* effective control that plays a cardinal role in determining who should hold the international responsibility.

The question may arise, how to apply the *de facto* effective control in the UN concrete peace operations in order to effectively attribute international responsibility.

3. 2 Identity and responsibility in UN peace operations and effective control

(1) Rules on the identity of conductors

First set of rules on the notion of "effective control" test are undoubtedly on the Identity of conductors. These rules answer the question on whose specific actions or omissions shall be considered an act of that State/International Organization under international law. It is a matter of the identity of the perpetrators that has intimate ties

---

[41]   See Róisín Burke, *Attribution of Responsibility: Sexual Abuse and Exploitation, and Effective Control of Blue Helmets*, 16 Journal of International Peacekeeping (2012).

with the matters of attribution of international responsibility. It must be remembered that the drafting rules of ILC specify a wide range of conductors whose actions and omissions are within the purview of international responsibility.

The rules under Articles on State Responsibility (ASR) and Draft Articles on Responsibility of International Organizations (DARIO) on the attribution of responsibility serve as "secondary" rules under general international law, namely, the rules on the remedies in international law, providing detailed customary rules on the attribution of responsibility based on the identities of the conductors.

Article 4 of ASR provides that: "The conduct of any State organ shall be considered an act of that State under international law...An organ includes an person or entity which has that status in accordance with the internal law of the State. " ICJ has also confirmed the rule in categorical terms. In *Difference Relating to Immunity from Legal Process of a Special Rapporteur of the Commission on Human Rights*, it said:

"According to a well—established rule of international law, the conduct of any organ of a State must be regarded as an act of that State. This rule... is of a customary character. "[42]

These type of rules varies according to various situations. Even the ASR and DARIO set out a homogeneous set of rules of attribution, however, the rules governing the State responsibility under ASR could not simply be transposed in full to DARIO (Draft Articles on Responsibility of International organizations)[43], given the distinct nature of IOs, especially in the context of the UN peace operations. [44] Even the notion of "effective control" for State responsibility has been comparatively

---

[42] *Difference Relating to Immunity from Legal Process of a Special Rapporteur of the Commission on Human Rights*, Advisory Opinion, ICJ Reports 1999, p. 62, 87, para. 62.

[43] ILC, DARIO 2011 (UN Doc A/CN. 4/L. 778, 30 May 2011).

[44] A. Pellet, *The definition of Responsibility in International Law*, in J. Crawford, in A. Pellet and S. Olleson (ed.), The Law of International Responsibility, Oxford: Oxford University Press, 2010, 3, 7.

clear, there are still nuances between the attribution of responsibility to IOs and States while the same "effective control" criteria applies therein. As noted by the ILC, attribution of conduct to an IO must rest on different criteria, as "governmental authority" will generally be absent. [45] Moreover, on review of the complexities of UN peace operation system, there is considerably uncertainty as to the degree of control required for it to be "effective".

The Counterpart of Article 4 ASR is Article 6 of DARIO, which is phrased similarly to Article 4 ASR, setting out a general rule on attribution with respect to IOs, provides that: "The conduct of an organ or agent of an international organization in the performance of functions of that organ or agent should be considered as an act of that organization under international law, whatever position the organ or agent holds in respect of the organization. " The ILC commentary to this provision stipulates that: "the conduct is attributable to the international organization when the organ or agent exercises functions that have been given to that organ or agent, and at any event is not attributable when the organ or agent acts in a private capacity. " [46] Identities of conductors serve as one element in the attribution of responsibility. Military contingents deployed as part of a peacekeeping operation form part of a subsidiary organ of the UN. However, in the context of UN peace operations, the military contingents may exercise functions that have been given by TCCs or receiving States, rather than organ or agent of the UN peace operations. Thus, the attribution of responsibility in this context if far more complex than black−letter laws. And the identities of the conductors, is one element but not decisive, in attributing international responsibility in the context of UN Peace Operations.

(2) Rules on attribution of responsibility in the context of dual identities

Military contingents in UN peacekeepers are also, as have been mentioned before, part of the TCCs. Although the basic rule on the attribution of responsibility is

---

[45] DARIO−ILC 2009 Report, UN Doc A/56/10, 2001, p. 63, para. 3.

[46] Commentary on Article 5 DARIO (now Article 6).

applicable for both the States and UN, the dual identity of contingents does not necessarily or undoubtedly result in the dual responsibility for both UN and the TCC. Given the interplay between the law on attribution of responsibility to States and to IOs, Article 7 of DARIO is specially designed to deal with this dilemma. It provides:

> The conduct of an organ of a State or an organ or agent of an international organization that is placed at the disposal of another international organization shall be considered under international law an act of the latter organization if the organization exercises *effective control* over that conduct. (emphasis added). [47]

As can be deduced from above, the central element determining element under Article 7 of DARIO in balancing responsibility for wrongful conduct or omission is where "effective control" rests. As a practical matter, the UNSG has emphasized that "the international responsibility of the United Nations will be limited to the extent of its *effective operation control.* "[48]

The counterpart of Article 7 of DARIO is Article 8 of ASR, which offers the same "effective control" test in the context of State responsibility, following the jurisprudence of ICJ in *Nicaragua* case. As subsequently observed by Cassese, the criteria can be described as:

Three disjunctive standards for the attribution of a state of conduct of private individuals: ①whether the state has issued instructions to those persons, ②whether the state has directed the persons to do something, or③whether the state has exer-

---

[47] DARIO, Art. 7.

[48] UN, Report of the Secretary—General on the United Nations Interim Administration Mission in Kosovo, Report of the Secretary—General, UN Doc S/2008/354, 12 June 2008.

cised control over those persons. [49]

With regard to the notion of "effective control", ICJ in the *Nicaragua* [50] case and *Genocide* [51] case goes beyond mere operational command and requires the giving of specific orders or instructions in each and every action concerned.

In its commentaries to the draft articles, the ILC explains that Article 6 applies when an organ of one international organization is fully seconded to another organization, whereas Article 7 applies when the seconded organ still acts to a certain extent as an organ of the seconding state or as an organ of the seconding organization, since that State remains disciplinary powers and criminal jurisdiction over the members of the national contingents. [52] In practice, however, given the varied mandates and operations of different organizations, and the varying structures and circumstances, to whom specific conduct of the seconded organ is to be attributed is not always clear. [53] As explained by ILC in its commentary, the attribution of conduct to a seconding state or the international organization is based on "the factual control over the specific conduct, in which all factual circumstances and the special context of the case must be taken into account. " In sum, in order to determine whether acts or omissions of troops should be attributed to the UN or TCC, it is essential, at the beginning, based on the factual circumstances of each instance, at what level "effective control" is exercised.

3.3 Summary

As observed by Hersh Lauterpacht in 1933: "There is substance in the view that the existence of a sufficient body of clear rules is not at all essential to the existence of law, and that the decisive test is whether there exists a judge competent to

---

[49]   Above n. 21, 663.

[50]   Above n. 5.

[51]   Above n. 13, 401.

[52]   DARIO, commentary, para. 4.

[53]   Misa Zgonec - Rozej, *Netherlands v. Nuhanovic*; *Netherlands v. Mustafic - Mujic*, 108 Am. J. Int'l L. 509, 515 (2014).

decide upon disputed rights and to command peace. "[54] Furthermore, as noted by ICTY in its very first case, "the 'effective control' test propounded by the International Court of Justice as an exclusive and all—embracing test is at variance with international judicial and State practice: such practice has envisaged State responsibility in circumstances where a lower degree of control than that demanded by the Nicaragua test was exercised. "[55] The legal parameter of effective control should be at variance with the practice of the UN peace operations. Therefore, it is neither identities nor the command structure of the UN peace operations that is cardinal for attributing international responsibility the wrongful acts of the contingents (usually peacekeepers in the UN operations). It is rather, the factual control over the specific conduct, in which all factual circumstances and the special context of the case must be taken into account, combining with the feature of the wrongful acts in the context of peace operations.

4. Wrongful acts in the context of peace operations and effective control

4. 1 Omission

As noted by ECtHR in the *Al—jedda* case, "in interpreting its resolutions, there must be a presumption that the Security Council does not intend to impose any obligation on Member States to breach fundamental principles of human rights. "[56] Therefore, in the context of UN peacekeeping, it is not the act, but the "failing to prevent and punish" would give arise to the responsibility of IOs or States.

It is worth noting that, the ICJ in the *Corfu channel* case first recognized the omission as a form of State responsibility:

---

[54] Hersch Lauterpacht, *The development of international law by the Permanent Court of International Justice* (Longmans, Green. 1934). 432.

[55] The ICTY cited the Stephens case, in this case, the Mexico—United States General Claims Commission attributed to Mexico acts committed by a member of the Mexican "irregular auxiliary" of the army, which lacked both unforms and insignia. To attribute the responsibility, the Commission did not employ the effective control criteria. See above n. 23, para. 125. Referred to *United States v. Mexico* (*Stephens case*), Reports of International Arbitral Awards, vol. IV, pp. 266-267.

[56] *Al—Jedda v. the United Kingdom*, 7 July 2011, Judgment, ECtHR, No. 27021/08, para. 102.

This would certainly not have prevented the Albanian authorities from taking, as they should have done, all necessary steps immediately to warn ships near the danger zone, more especially those that were approaching that zone. In fact, nothing was attempted by the Albanian authorities to prevent the disaster. These grave *omissions* involve the international responsibility of Albania. (Emphasis added) [57]

Judge Winiarski added in his dissenting opinion:

Every State is responsible for an unlawful act, if it has committed that act, or has failed to take the necessary steps to prevent an unlawful act, or has omitted to take the necessary steps to prevent and punish the authors of an unlawful act. Each of these *omissions* involves a State's responsibility in international law, just like the commission of the act itself. [58]

The omission, as the form of wrongful act under international law, has been interpreted by ICJ as " omitted to take the necessary steps to prevent and punish the authors of an unlawful act. " What State is responsible for is therefore not the act of another, which by definition may not be attributed to, but is own act, in the form of an omission. Here, the responsibility enforces the obligation to prevent and punish which international law imposes on the State.

The ICJ jurisprudence on the State responsibility to prevent and punish was, at the beginning, enshrined in the famous *LaGrand case*. ICJ said:

---

[57] *Corfu Channel case*, Judgment of April 9th, 1949: I. C. J. Reports 1949, p. 4, pp. 22–23.

[58] *Corfu Channel case*, Judgment of April 9th, 1949: I. C. J. Reports 1949, p. 4, diss. op. Winiarski, p. 52.

Whereas the international responsibility of a State is engaged by the action of the competent organs and authorities acting in that State, whatever they may be; whereas the United States should take all measures at its disposal to ensure that Walter LaGrand is not executed pending the final decision in these proceedings. [59]

The notion of "effective control" therein refers to the capacity to prevent or punish wrongful acts by a peacekeeper. The IOs, as the subjects of international law, are "international person (s)" and are "capable of possessing international rights and duties."[60] It has been generally acknowledged that IOs should be responsible for their omissions. [61] In the context of the SEA under UN peace operations, the "effective control" criteria specifically refer to the capability to effectively prevent and punish the wrongful acts of peacekeepers. In this regard, it is the "omission" rather than "act" that results in the responsibility of the IOs.

Significant cases in ECtHR and Dutch Courts have clarified the notion of "effective control" in connection with "omission", specifically in the context of UN peace operations, but with the fragmented nature.

4. 2 Fragmented Jurisprudence on "Effective Control" in the Peace Operation Context

(1) ECtHR: Loizidou v. Turkey and Al—Jedda case—Effective Overall Control

In the ECtHR *Loizidou v. Turkey* case, [62] the applicant claimed that Turkey was breaching her right under ECHR, given that Turkish troops had prevented her

---

[59] *LaGrand* (Germany v. United States of America), Provisional Measures, Order of 3 March 1999, I. C. J. Reports 1999, p. 9, at p. 16, para. 28. See also *LaGrand* (Germany v. United States of America), Judgment, I. C. J. Reports 2001, p. 466, at p. 495, para. 81.

[60] See *Reparation for Injuries Suffered in the Service of the United Nations*, 1949, I. C. J. Reports 1949, p. 4, pp. 177.

[61] See F. Larry, *Actions and Omissions*, in James Crawford and S. Olleson (eds.), The Law of International Responsibility, Oxford University Press, 2010, pp. 355–364.

[62] Above n. 29.

from returning to her property in Northern Cyprus. The test set by the ECtHR therein was one of "effective overall control. " It held that Turkey, through the active engagement of large number of Turkish troops in Northern Cyprus, was exercising "effective overall control" over the territory. Therefore, the Court found it not necessary to examine the actual control exercised by the Turkey in the Northern Cyprus. The Court held that Turkey should be responsible for the human rights violation on the basis of the established "territorial control".

In the ECtHR Al—jedda case, the question arose whether the UN exercised "effective command and control" over British forces in Iraq, and therefore whether their conduct could be attributed to the UN arose. The case involved an Iraqi civilian that had been held in prolonged detention in a British ran detention facility in Iraq. The ECtHR referred to Article 7 of DARIO, which sets out the "effective control" test, as the appropriate standard to be applied when an organ of state is placed as the disposal of an IO.

The rationale in these cases cannot apply in the context of the UN peace operations, since the UN, different from sovereign State, usually do not administrate a territory or have the so—called "overall effective control" therein. However, some analogy might be drawn to situations where the UN is transitionally administering a territory, or when the UN is exercising control over local authorities during the peace operation period. [63] It is worth noting that, such criteria is not applicable in majority cases, because the local authorities often do not yield the administrative power to the UN peace operations.

(2) ECtHR: Saramati and Behrami case—Ultimate authority and control.

In the joint case of *Saramati* and *Behrami*, the ECtHR was asked to rule on whether certain TCCs were in breach of their obligations under the ECHR for acts or omissions of their contingents deployed on an operation conducted under UN "aus-

---

[63] See above n. 41, 25.

pices. " The notion employed by the ECtHR, in attributing full responsibility to the UN, was, namely, "ultimate authority and control. "

In *Bahrami* case, the applicant complained his right to life (Article 2 ECHR) had been violated by France, due to the failure of France troops in Kosovo to mark and defuse cluster bombs, despite the knowledge of their location. The omission of French troops in Kosovo has resulted in the death of one of the applicant's children and the serious injuries of another. The applicant in Saramati case claimed that his rights under Article 5 (right to liberty and security), Article 13 (right to an effective remedy) and Article 6 (right to fair trial) ECHR has been violated by France and Norway as he had been detained extra-judicially. [64] Saramati was arrested by UNMIK on order of a Norwegian KFOR Commander, who was later replaced by a Franch KFOR commander. [65]

The Court examined the separate areas of responsibility under the mandate of KFOR and UNMIK to detain persons suspected of criminal offences and de-mine cluster bombs. [66]

The Court concluded that, UNMIK as a UN operation was subsidiary organ of the UN itself. Consequently, its acts were in principle attributable to the UN. The Court ultimately utilized a test of "ultimate authority and control" without elaborating on its reasoning for using a test of "Ultimate authority and control". As often criticized by commentators, the Court did not examine in detail the actual control exercised by the UN and KFOR over specific conduct, as would be necessary under the

---

[64] *Behrami v. France*; *Saramati v. France*, 2 May 2007, Joint Admissibility Decision, ECtHR, Grand Chamber, Nos. 71412/01 and 78166/01.

[65] *Ibid.*, p. 70.

[66] *Ibid.*, p. 121.

"effective control" test. [67]

(3) Supreme Court of Netherlands: *Netherlands v. Nuhanovic* and *Netherlands v. Mustafic Mujic*—Dual Responsibility.

The two cases concerned events in Srebrenica, the town in eastern Bosnia and Herzegovina that was "ethnically cleaned" by Bosnian Serb forces in July 1995. Decided on September 6, 2013, the Dutch Supreme Court held the Government of the Netherlands responsible for the deaths of three men killed by Bosnian Serb forces after the Dutchbat of the peacekeeping mission expelled them from the UN compound in Potocari on July 13, 1995. In doing so, the Court adopted a "dual attribution" approach, finding it possible for both the Netherlands and the United Nations to have effective control over the same wrongful conduct. [68]

Through the creative interpretation of Article 7 of the ASR, the Supreme Court held that more than one party can have effective control over UN troops' conduct and that it is therefore possible for the actions of UN peacekeepers to be attributed to both the United Nations and a contributing State. The ILC has recognized the possibility of dual (or multiple) attribution, [69] but its legal basis has not been firmly established. The Supreme Court considered that Article 7 of the ASR may serve as a legal

---

[67] The reasoning of ECtHR has been criticized by a number of legal commentators for not examining the actual control exercised by the UN and KFOR over specific conduct, thereby giving an obscure impression on the actual criteria in addressing the responsibility therein. See e. g. Sari, Jurisdiction and International responsibility in Peace Support Operations Aurel Sari, *Jurisdiction and International Responsibility in Peace Support Operations: The Behrami and Saramati Cases*, 8 Human Rights Law Review (2008). , 166–68; See also C. Bell, Reassessing Multiple Attribution Caitlin A. Bell, *Reassessing multiple attribution: the international law commission and the Behrami and Saramati decision*, 42 New York University Journal of International Law and Politics (2010). , 534.

[68] *Netherlands v. Nuhanovic*, Sup. Ct. Sept. 6, 2013, No. 12/03324, at http: //www. rechtspraak. nl/ Organisatie/Hoge – aad/OverDeHogeRaad/publicaties/Documents/1 2% 2003324. pdf (Eng. trans.); *Netherlands v. Mustafic–Mujic*, Sup. Ct. Sept. 6, 2013, No. 12/03329, at http: //www. rechtspraak. nl/Organisatie/ Hoge–Raad/OverDeHogeRaad/publicaties/Documents/12%2003329. pdf, para. 3. 11. 3.

[69] Text of the Draft Articles [on Responsibility of International Organizations] with Commentaries, Art. 6, Report of the International Law Commission on the Workoflts Sixty–Third Session 69, 84, UN GAOR, 66th Sess. , Supp. No. 10, UN Doc. A/66/10 & Add. 1 (2011), para. (4).

basis for dual attribution. [70] In this way, the Dutch Supreme Court had disregarded the European Court's jurisprudence on "ultimate overall control", but solely relied on the effective control text in Article 7 of the ASR. It is posited that there is possibility of dual or triple attribution of responsibility to both the UN and TCCs.

The decisions make meaningful contribution to the debate on the accountability of the United Nations, troop-contributing states, and/or individuals for the wrongful conduct of UN peacekeepers. The decisions are important not only for finally awarding remedies to the families of some of the victims of the Srebrenica massacre, but also for reaching significant findings on concept of dual (or multiple) attribution, the criterion for the attribution of peacekeepers' conduct. [71]

(4) Summary

The jurisprudence on attribution of international responsibility in the context of UN peace operations is, in its nature, fragmented. There is significant divergence among courts and tribunals in the reasoning on the same/similar issue. However, the scenarios that the courts and tribunals dealt with are far from similar. It is apparent that the detail the actual control exercised by the UN, TCCs, or receiving States over specific conduct should be examined in order to attribute the responsibility, as would be necessary under the "effective control" test. Such effective control test combining with the factual issues can be termed as *de facto* effective control test. Furthermore, finding it possible for both the TCCs and the United Nations to have effective control over the same wrongful conduct, it is possible to attribute dual responsibility in the UN peace operation context. Even having not been discussed in the previous jurisprudence, if the receiving States failed due diligence obligation to prevent or publish, attribution of responsibility to receiving States is possible. In sum, there might be triple responsibility in the UN operation context, even it is up until now, hypothetical

---

[70] See Zgonec-Rožej Miša, *Netherlands v. Nuhanović*; *Netherlands v. Mustafić-Mujić*, 108 American Journal of International Law (2014). , 512.

[71] See *Ibid*, 511.

in its nature.

5. Conclusion

Examination of the effective tests that have been developed through jurisprudence by various courts and tribunals to determine the questions of attribution of responsibility to States or IOs, including the related provisions under DARIO and ASR on the attribution of State responsibility.

The paper thereby conclude: First, with regard to the possible implications of these approaches for attribution of wrongful acts of UN military peacekeepers to the UN, or the TCCs, the paper conclude that, most apposite test is one of "effective control". In the specific context of UN peace operations, the most important element of attribution is to determine whether "effective control" rests with the UN or TCCs. In particular, "effective control" includes either①the issuance of directions to the UN peacekeepers by the TCCs or UN concerning specific operations, that is to say, the ordering of those operations by the US, or②the enforcement by the UN/TCCs of each specific operation of the UN peacekeepers, namely forcefully making the rebels carry out those specific operations. It must be remembered that the determination of "effective control" is required to consider the specific instructions or enforcements of the UN peace operation missions on the case-by-case basis, based on the evaluation of evidential materials. Thus, the "effective control" test is more of a factual test than a legal doctrine, which can be termed as "*de facto* effective control".

Second, UN peace operations, in any circumstances, never promote the wrongful acts of its contingents. In the milieu of UN military peacekeeper complicity in SEA the question is not solely who gave orders, but rather who omitted to prevent wrongful acts and to hold perpetrators to account. Therefore, the Responsibility under "effective control" criteria are conducts not by "actions", but rather in the form of "omissions."

Third, witnessing the proliferation of courts and tribunals in addressing attribution of responsibility in the UN peace operation contexts, in the core areas of attribution of responsibility, these different international tribunals do share relatively coherent views on this doctrine of effective control. The jurisprudential development of the criteria of attribution of responsibility is moving towards the coherence. Through the analysis of recent jurisprudence on the attribution of responsibility, the paper contends that the "dual" or "multiple attribution" of responsibility to UN, TCCs or receiving States is possible therein. Apart from justified legal grounds, allowing for dual or multiple attribution of conduct would give victims a more effective route for redress, and possibly provide incentive to TCCs, receiving States and the UN to ensure that SEA by UN peacekeepers dealt with properly and that perpetrators are held accountable.

"EFFECTIVE CONTROL", STATE COOPERATION, AND DECLARATIONS UNDER ARTICLE 12 (3) OF THE ROME STATUTE OF THE INTERNATIONAL CRIMINAL COURT

Daley J. Birkett *

1. Introduction

According to the Rome Statute of the International Criminal Court (Rome Statute, ICC Statute), States can accept the ICC's jurisdiction either by becoming Parties to the ICC Statute or by lodging a "declaration" over specific crimes with the Court's Registrar in accordance with Article 12 (3) of the ICC Statute. Article 12 (3) further provides that any State making an *ad hoc* declaration "shall cooperate with the Court without any delay or exception in accordance with Part 9",[1] whose provisions govern the ICC's international cooperation and judicial assistance regime in relation to investigations or prosecutions.

Since the Rome Statute entered into force in 2002, a series of *ad hoc* declarations have been lodged according to Article 12 (3): from Côte D'Ivoire in 2003 (confirmed in 2010 and 2011), from Palestine in 2009 and 2014, from Ukraine in 2014 and 2015, and from purported representatives of Egypt in 2013. In response to the latter declaration, lodged by representatives of the ousted Mohamed Morsi gov-

* Research Associate, Walther Schücking Institute for International Law, University of Kiel (email: dbirkett@wsi.uni-kiel.de). By way of disclosure, the author served as Intern to Judge Anita Ušacka in the Appeals Division of the International Criminal Court at the time she presided over the Judgment on the appeal of Mr Laurent Koudou Gbagbo against the decision of Pre-Trial Chamber I on jurisdiction and stay of the proceedings. This chapter was completed on 31 January 2018. The websites cited herein were current as of this date.

[1] Ome Statute of the International Criminal Court (ICC Statute), 2187 UNTS 90, art. 12.

ernment in 2013, the ICC's Office of the Prosecutor (OTP) referred to the 'legal test of "effective control" ' in determining that "the applicants did not exercise effective control over any part of Egyptian territory, including on the date the declaration was signed. " The OTP therefore concluded that the authority that lodged the declaration was not capable of expressing the consent of Egypt to the exercise of the Court's jurisdiction under Article 12 (3) of the ICC Statute because it lacked "full powers", citing the Vienna Convention on the Law of Treaties.

This chapter critically analyses the law and practice of the ICC in respect of declarations lodged pursuant to Article 12 (3). In particular, the chapter questions the application of the "effective control" test by the OTP in respect of the declaration submitted by purported representatives of Egypt in 2013. The chapter argues that the determination of the OTP in respect of Article 12 (3) declarations must be limited to whether the applicant is able to exercise "full powers" on behalf of the State and refrain from addressing the recognition of governments under international law. However, assuming that the OTP's approach in response to the Egypt communication could be followed in its future practice, the chapter briefly discusses the relevance of the requirement that accepting States "shall cooperate with the Court" in accordance with Part IX of the ICC Statute. The chapter argues that the ability to provide cooperation is critical to the ICC's capacity to successfully investigate and prosecute crimes under its jurisdiction. The chapter concludes that scenarios in which cooperation, and indeed "effective control", might be absent include those where action by the Court could prove most crucial in ending impunity for international crimes. This, in turn, provides a further argument in support of the OTP limiting its determination in respect of Article 12 (3) declarations to whether the applicant possesses "full powers".

2. (Preconditions to the) exercise of jurisdiction

Article 12 of the Rome Statute is titled "Preconditions to the exercise of jurisdiction". [2] According to Articles 12 and 13 of the Rome Statute, only a State or the United Nations Security Council (UNSC) is able to grant jurisdiction to the ICC. A State can accept the ICC's jurisdiction either by becoming a State Party to the ICC Statute or by lodging an "*ad hoc* declaration" over particular crimes with the ICC's Registrar in accordance with Article 12 (3) of the ICC Statute. Article 13 of the Rome Statute provide as follows:

The Court may exercise its jurisdiction with respect to a crime referred to in article 5 in accordance with the provisions of this Statute if:

(a) A situation in which one or more of such crimes appears to have been committed is referred to the Prosecutor by a State Party in accordance with article 14;

(b) A situation in which one or more of such crimes appears to have been committed is referred to the Prosecutor by the Security Council acting under Chapter VII of the Charter of the United Nations; or

(c) The Prosecutor has initiated an investigation in respect of such a crime in accordance with article 15. [3]

Although the Prosecutor may initiate an investigation in respect of the crimes under the Court's subject-matter jurisdiction on her own initiative (or *proprio motu*), this power is subject to the precondition that a State has conferred jurisdiction to the Court by having either (i) ratified or acceded to the Rome Statute; or (ii) submitted an *ad hoc* declaration. The same precondition applies where a State Party refers the situation to the Prosecutor. However, this precondition need not be met if the situation is referred to the Prosecutor by the UNSC. As the title of the provision suggests, it is Article 12 of the Rome Statute that governs these preconditions.

---

[2]　*Ibid.*

[3]　ICC Statute, above n. 1, art. 13.

2. 1 The procedures

Article 12 of the Rome Statute provides as follows:

1. A State which becomes a Party to this Statute thereby accepts the jurisdiction of the Court with respect to the crimes referred to in article 5.

2. In the case of article 13, paragraph (a) or (c), the Court may exercise its jurisdiction if one or more of the following States are Parties to this Statute or have accepted the jurisdiction of the Court in accordance with paragraph 3:

(a) The State on the territory of which the conduct in question occurred or, if the crime was committed on board a vessel or aircraft, the State of registration of that vessel or aircraft;

(b) The State of which the person accused of the crime is a national.

3. If the acceptance of a State which is not a Party to this Statute is required under paragraph 2, that State may, by declaration lodged with the Registrar, accept the exercise of jurisdiction by the Court with respect to the crime in question. The accepting State shall cooperate with the Court without any delay or exception in accordance with Part 9. [4]

Non-Party States to the Rome Statute may thus confer limited jurisdiction to the ICC by lodging a declaration with the Registrar under Article 12 (3) of the Rome Statute. Such a declaration may also serve to give the ICC retroactive jurisdiction. [5] The ICC's temporal jurisdiction is limited to crimes committed after the ICC Statute enters into force for the State ratifying or acceding thereto unless the State has sub-

---

[4] ICC Statute, above n. 1, art. 12.

[5] See Prosecutor v. Laurent Koudou Gbagbo, Judgment on the appeal of Mr Laurent Koudou Gbagbo against thedecision of Pre-Trial Chamber I on jurisdiction and stay of the proceedings, ICC-02/11-01/11-321 (12 Dec. 2012) (Gbagbo Jurisdiction Appeal Judgment), paras. 83-84.

mitted an *ad hoc* declaration with the Court's Registrar in accordance with Article 12 (3) of the Rome Statute. [6]

It is noteworthy that submitting an *ad hoc* declaration leads to the assumption of certain obligations on the part of the "lodging State". Upon lodging a declaration under Article 12 (3), the "lodging State" is obligated to immediately and fully co-operate with the Court in accordance with Part IX of the Rome Statute.

2. 2 The practice

Since the entry into force of the ICC Statute, the Court's Registrar has received a series of declarations lodged pursuant to Article 12 (3): from Côte D'Ivoire in 2003 (confirmed in 2010 and again in 2011); from Palestine in 2009 and 2014; from Ukraine in 2014 and 2015; and from purported representatives of Egypt in 2013. In all four lodging States, it could be argued that effective control over the territory on which certain alleged crimes took place was at issue, if not explicitly disputed, during the lodging process. However, only with respect to the declaration lodged by self-professed representatives of the Arab Republic of Egypt was this factor taken into consideration by any organ of the ICC. The following section critically analyses the practice of the Court in respect of the foregoing four declarations (and confirmations) lodged under Article 12 (3) of the Rome Statute.

(1) Côte D'Ivoire

On 18 April 2003, the then Minister of Foreign Affairs of the Republic of Côte D'Ivoire, Mr Mamadou Bamba, lodged the following declaration with the Court's Registrar:

Pursuant to article 12 (3) of the Statute of the International Criminal Court, the Government of Côte D'Ivoire accepts the jurisdiction of the Court for the purposes

---

[6]   ICC Statute, above n. 1, art. 11 ("1. The Court has jurisdiction only with respect to crimes committed after the entry into force of this Statute. 2. If a State becomes a Party to this Statute after its entry into force, the Court may exercise its jurisdiction only with respect to crimes committed after the entry into force of this Statute for that State, unless that State has made a declaration under article 12, paragraph 3.").

of identifying, investigating and trying the perpetrators and accomplices of acts committed on Ivorian territory since the events of 19 September 2002.

Accordingly, Côte D'Ivoire undertakes to cooperate with the Court without delay or exception in accordance with Part IX of the Statute. This declaration shall be valid for an unspecified period of time and shall enter into effect on being signed. [7]

This declaration was submitted to the ICC at the time when Côte D'Ivoire was under the administration of a "government of national reconciliation" pursuant to the terms of the Linas—Marcoussis Agreement of 24 January 2003. [8] It was Mr Laurent Gbagbo who led this administration until disputed presidential elections took place in late 2010. Both Mr Gbagbo and his opponent, Mr Alessane Ouattara, claimed victory, with the Independent Electoral Commission announcing Mr Ouattara the victor on 2 December 2010 and the Constitutional Council declaring Mr Gbagbo the winner on the following day. [9] It was in this context that Mr Ouattara, on 14 December 2010, sent three near—identical letters to the Court's President, Prosecutor, and Registrar, in which he confirmed the declaration lodged under Article 12 (3) of the Rome Statute by Côte D'Ivoire on 18 April 2003. [10] Mr Ouattara sent a further letter confirming the Article 12 (3) declaration on 3 May 2011. [11] On 4 May 2011, the Constitutional Council, which had previously declared Mr Gbagbo the victor, confirmed Mr Ouattara as the President of Côte d'Ivoire, declaring valid the decisions he had

[7] Prosecutor v. Laurent Koudou Gbagbo, Declaration Accepting the Jurisdiction of the International Criminal Court dated 18 April 2003, ICC–02/11–01/11–129–Anx16–tENG (6 Sep. 2012).

[8] Gbagbo Jurisdiction Appeal Judgment, above n. 5, paras. 48–49. For the text of the Linas—Marcoussis Agreement, see Prosecutor v. Laurent Koudou Gbagbo, Linas Marcoussis Agreement of 24 January 2003, ICC–02/11–01/11–129–Anx17–tENG (11 Oct. 2012).

[9] Gbagbo Jurisdiction Appeal Judgment, above n. 5, paras. 53–54.

[10] Prosecutor v. Laurent Koudou Gbagbo, Letter from Alassane Ouattara to the President of the ICC dated 14 December 2010, ICC–02/11–01/11–129–Anx14–tENG (9 Oct. 2012).

[11] Prosecutor v. Laurent Koudou Gbagbo, Letter from Alassane Ouattara to the Prosecutor of the ICC dated 3 May 2011, ICC–02/11–01/11–129–Anx15–tENG (10 Oct. 2012).

previously taken in this capacity. [12]

On 3 October 2011, the Court's Pre-Trial Chamber III authorised the commencement of an investigation into the Situation in the Republic of Côte D'Ivoire. [13] Mr Gbagbo filed a challenge to the Court's jurisdiction on 29 May 2012, [14] in which he argued, *inter alia*, as follows with respect to the letters of 2 December 2010:

Article 12 (3) is clear: only a "State" can make a declaration accepting the jurisdiction of the Court. For such a declaration to have any legal effect, it must be made by an organ or person competent to bind the State. In this respect, there is no doubt that a Head of State is endowed with such capacity.

[...] The Defence argues, however that Alassane Ouattara could not be considered the legitimate Head of State of Côte D'Ivoire at the time of writing the said letter. The Defence submits that, if the authority of a State representative to bind the State internationally and hence vis-à-vis the Rome Statute is in dispute, the utmost attention must be paid to the legality of the act under domestic law, particularly the Constitution. An international organ such as the Court cannot vest with legal effect within the meaning of its Statute an act emanating from a person who is not *de facto* and *de jure* empowered to bind the State.

[...] Accordingly, the Defence simply moves the Chamber to find that at

---

[12]   Gbagbo Jurisdiction Appeal Judgment, above n. 5, para. 57. For the Decision, see Prosecutor v. Laurent Koudou Gbagbo, Decision of the Constitutional Council No. CI-2011-EP-036/04-05/CC/SG proclaiming Alassane Ouattara President of Côte D'Ivoire, ICC-02/11-01/1 1-129-Anx3-tENG (18 Sep. 2009).

[13]   Situation in the Republic of Côte D'Ivoire, Decision Pursuant to Article 15 of the Rome Statute on the Authorisation of an Investigation into the Situation in the Republic of Côte D'Ivoire, ICC - 02/11 - 14 (3 Oct. 2011).

[14]   Prosecutor v. Laurent Koudou Gbagbo, Corrigendum of the challenge to the jurisdiction of the International Criminal Court on the basis of articles 12 (3), 19 (2), 21 (3), 55 and 59 of the Rome Statute filed by the Defence for President Gbagbo (ICC-02/11-01/11-129), ICC-02/11-01/11-129-Corr-tENG (29 May 2012) (Gbagbo Jurisdiction Challenge).

the time of writing the 14 December 2010 letter, Alassane Ouattara was not *de facto* and *de jure* President of the country within the meaning of the Ivorian constitution. [15]

As to the letter of 3 May 2011, the Defence for Mr Gbagbo asked the Court to disregard it based in part on "Mr Ouattara's lack of official capacity on 3 May 2011", [16] which the Defence argued deprived the letter of "any legal effect". [17]

On 15 August 2012, ICC Pre—Trial Chamber I dismissed the Defence's challenge to the Court's jurisdiction, [18] finding it "unnecessary to address the validity of the letters of 14 December 2010 and 3 May 2011 or the question of the capacity of Mr Ouattara to bind Côte D'Ivoire on those particular dates." [19] In short, the Pre—Trial Chamber found that the ICC had jurisdiction over all alleged crimes committed since 19 September 2002 based on the declaration of 18 April 2003. [20] Notably, however, Pre—Trial Chamber I opined as follows with respect to the subsequent letters confirming the Article 12 (3) declaration:

[...] while not necessary from a legal point of view, these letters, together with the subsequent statements and continuous cooperation of Côte D'Ivoire with the Court, are further evidence that Côte D'Ivoire has accepted the exercise of jurisdiction of the Court in relation to the situation [.] [21]

---

[15]   *Ibid.*, paras. 93–94, 98 (footnotes omitted).

[16]   Gbagbo Jurisdiction Challenge, above n. 14, para. 101.

[17]   *Ibid.*

[18]   Prosecutor v. Laurent Koudou Gbagbo, Decision on the "Corrigendum of the challenge to the jurisdiction of the International Criminal Court on the basis of articles 12 (3), 19 (2), 21 (3), 55 and 59 of the Rome Statute filed by the Defence for President Gbagbo (ICC–02/11–01/11–129) ", ICC–02/11–01/11–212 (15 Aug. 2012) (Gbagbo Jurisdiction Decision).

[19]   *Ibid.*, para. 66.

[20]   Gbagbo Jurisdiction Decision, above n. 14, para. 65.

[21]   Gbagbo Jurisdiction Decision, above n. 14, para. 66.

The Appeals Chamber did not address Pre-Trial Chamber I's finding, which it found to be *obiter dicta*, on appeal. [22] At no stage of the Article 12 (3) declaration process did any organ of the Court make a determination as to whether Mr Gbagbo or Mr Ouattara exercised "effective control" over the territory of Côte D'Ivoire, despite the supposedly disputed status of the presidency at the time the letters of 14 December 2010 and 3 May 2011 were sent. The Court avoided this issue by focusing on the earlier declaration.

(2) Palestine[23]

On 21 January 2009, Mr Ali Khashan, the then Minister of Justice of the Government of Palestine, submitted a declaration to the ICC's Registrar, which provides as follows, in relevant part:

In conformity with Article 12, paragraph 3 of the Statute of the International Criminal Court, the Government of Palestine hereby recognizes the jurisdiction of the Court for the purpose of identifying, prosecuting and judging the authors and accomplices of acts committed on the territory of Palestine since 1 July 2002.

As a consequence, the Government of Palestine will cooperate with the

---

[22] Gbagbo Jurisdiction Appeal Judgment, above n. 5, paras. 91–92.

[23] For an engaging debate concerning the relationship between Palestine and the ICC, including discussion of its Article 12 (3) declarations, see, *inter alia*, Yaël Ronen, ICC Jurisdiction over Acts Committed in the Gaza Strip: Art. 12 (3) of the ICC Statute and Non-state Entities, 8 Journal of International Criminal Justice (2010), 3; Yuval Shany, In Defence of Functional Interpretation of Article 12 (3) of the Rome Statute: A Response to Yaël Ronen, 8 Journal of International Criminal Justice (2010), 329; Alain Pellet, The Palestinian Declaration and the Jurisdiction of the International Criminal Court, 8 Journal of International Criminal Justice (2010) 981; Malcolm N Shaw QC, The Article 12 (3) Declaration of the Palestinian Authority, the International Criminal Court and International Law, 9 Journal of International Criminal Justice (2011), 301; Andreas Zimmermann, Palestine and the International Criminal Court *Quo Vadis*? Reach and Limits of Declarations under Article 12 (3), 11 Journal of International Criminal Justice (2013), 303; Eugene Kontorovich, Israel/Palestine-The ICC's Uncharted Territory, 11 Journal of International Criminal Justice (2013), 979; Yaël Ronen, Israel, Palestine and the ICC-Territory Uncharted but Not Unknown, 12 Journal of International Criminal Justice (2014), 7.

Court without delay or exception, in conformity with Chapter IX of the Statute.

This declaration, made for an indeterminate duration, will enter into force upon its signature. Material supplementary to and supporting this declaration will be provided shortly in a separate communication. [24]

On 3 April 2012, after having initiated a preliminary examination in order to determine whether there was a reasonable basis to proceed with an investigation, the Office of the Prosecutor (OTP) determined that the preconditions to the exercise of jurisdiction under Article 12 of the Rome Statute had not been met. [25] The OTP reasoned as follows:

[...] competence for determining the term "State" within the meaning of article 12 rests, in the first instance, with the United Nations Secretary General who, in case of doubt, will defer to the guidance of General Assembly. The Assembly of States Parties of the Rome Statute could also in due course decide to address the matter in accordance with article 112 (2)(g) of the Statute.

[...] In interpreting and applying article 12 of the Rome Statute, the Office has assessed that it is for the relevant bodies at the United Nations or the Assembly of States Parties to make the legal determination whether Palestine qualifies as a State for the purpose of acceding to the Rome Statute and thereby enabling the exercise of jurisdiction by the Court under article 12 (1). The Rome Statute provides no authority for the Office of the Prosecutor to adopt a method to define the term "State" under article 12 (3) which would be at variance with that established for the purpose of article 12 (1). [26]

---

[24] Declaration recognizing the Jurisdiction of the International Criminal Court (21 Jan. 2009) (www. legal-tools. org/doc/d9b1c6/).

[25] Office of the Prosecutor, Situation in Palestine (3 Apr. 2012) (www. legal-tools. org/doc/f5d6d7/) (OTP Palestine Determination).

[26] *Ibid.*, paras. 5-6.

The OTP did, however, explicitly accept the possibility that it could, in future, consider allegations of crimes within the Court's jurisdiction committed in Palestine, should the United Nations or the Assembly of States Parties "resolve the legal issue" or should the Security Council confer it with jurisdiction under Article 13 of the Rome Statute. [27]

On 1 January 2015, Palestine tendered a second declaration recognising the jurisdiction of the Court in accordance with Article 12 (3) of the Rome Statute, thereby affording the OTP the opportunity to further consider alleged crimes under the jurisdiction of the ICC committed on its territory. [28] The second Palestinian declaration was signed and lodged with the Court's Registrar by Palestinian President, Mr Mahmoud Abbas. [29] Worded in similar terms to its earier declaration, Palestine recognised the Court's jurisdiction over alleged international crimes "committed in the occupied Palestinian territory, including East Jerusalem, since June 13, 2014. "[30] As with the first declaration, Palestine agreed to cooperate immediately and fully with the Court under Part IX of the Rome Statute and stated that the declaration was valid upon signature for an unspecified period of time. [31] Notably, Palestine then acceded to the Rome Statute on 2 January 2015, with the treaty entering into force for Palestine on 1 April 2015. [32]

On this occasion, the OTP determined that Palestine's status before the United Nations rendered it competent to lodge a declaration under Article 12 (3) of the

---

[27]   OTP Palestine Determination, above n. 25, para. 8.

[28]   Declaration Accepting the Jurisdiction of the International Criminal Court (31 December 2014) (www. legal—tools. org/doc/60aff8/) (2015 Palestine Declaration).

[29]   *Ibid.*

[30]   2015 Palestine Declaration, above n. 28.

[31]   *Ibid.*

[32]   OTP, Report on Preliminary Examination Activities (2015) (12 Nov. 2015) (www. legal —tools. org/doc/ac0ed2/) (2015 OTP Report), para. 45.

Rome Statute. [33] The OTP reasoned, in relevant part, as follows:

> The Office considers that, since Palestine was granted observer State status in the UN by the UNGA, it must be considered a "State" for the purposes of accession to the Rome Statute (in accordance with the "all States" formula). Additionally, as the Office has previously stated publicly, the term "State" employed in article 12 (3) of the Rome Statute should be interpreted in the same manner as the term "State" used in article 12 (1). Thus, a State that may accede to the Rome Statute may also lodge a declaration under article 12 (3). [...] For the Office, the focus of the inquiry into Palestine's ability to accede to the Rome Statute has consistently been the question of Palestine's status at the UN. The UNGA Resolution 67/19 [granting Palestine "non—member observer State" status in the UN] is therefore determinative of Palestine's ability to accede to the Statute pursuant to article 125, and equally, its ability to lodge an article 12 (3) declaration. [34]

As with Côte D'Ivoire, again the OTP did not enter into an analysis of 'effective control' over the territory on which the alleged crimes under the Court's jurisdiction took place. Instead, the OTP refrained from undertaking such an analysis and, as is argued, properly limited its assessment to the question of statehood as determined by the United Nations.

(3) Ukraine[35]

Ukraine has also lodged two declarations with the Registrar of the Court accep-

---

[33] *Ibid.*, paras. 52–53.

[34] 2015 OTP Report, above n. 32, paras. 52–53.

[35] For an excellent analysis of Ukraine's relationship with the ICC, including declarations lodged thereby under Article 12 (3) of the Rome Statute, see Iryna Marchuk, Ukraine and the International Criminal Court: Implications of the Ad Hoc Jurisdiction Acceptance and Beyond, 49 Vanderbilt Journal of Transnational Law (2016), 323.

ting ICC jurisdiction in accordance with Article 12 (3) of the Rome Statute. On 9 A-pril 2014, the Embassy of Ukraine to the Kingdom of the Netherlands notified the ICC Registrar that such a declaration, made by the Parliament of Ukraine (*Verkhov-na Rada*), [36] had entered into force on 25 February 2014. [37] According to the am-bassadorial communiqué, by this declaration, "Ukraine hereby recognizes the juris-diction of the Court for the purpose of identifying, prosecuting and judging the au-thors and accomplices of acts committed on the territory of Ukraine within the period 21 November 2013-22 February 2014. "[38]

On 8 September 2015, the Minister for Foreign Affairs of Ukraine, Mr Pavlo Klimkin, informed the ICC's Registrar that the *Verkhovna Rada* of Ukraine had a-dopted a second Resolution, on 4 February 2017, granting jurisdiction to the Court under the auspices of Article 12 (3) of the Rome Statute. [39] In accordance with the second declaration, Ukraine recognised the jurisdiction of the Court "for the pur-pose of identifying, prosecuting and judging the perpetrators and accomplices of acts committed in the territory of Ukraine since 20 February 2014. "[40] The second de-claration therefore served to extend the ICC's temporal jurisdiction over alleged inter-national crimes committed in Ukraine as the first declaration was confined to a limit-

---

[36]   Declaration of the Verkhovna Rada of Ukraine to the International Criminal Court on the recognition of the jurisdiction of the International Criminal Court by Ukraine over crimes against humanity, committed by senior officials of the state, which led to extremely grave consequences and mass murder of Ukrainian nationals during peaceful protests within the period 21 November 2013-22 February 2014 (25 February 2014) (www. legal-tools. org/doc/1a65fa/) (2014 Ukraine Declaration).

[37]   Embassy of Ukraine to the Kingdom of the Netherlands, Letter dated 9 April 2014 (9 April 2014) (www. legal-tools. org/doc/eec0cf/).

[38]   *Ibid.*

[39]   Declaration of the Verkhovna Rada of Ukraine on the recognition of the jurisdiction of the Internation-al Criminal Court by Ukraine over crimes against humanity and war crimes committed by senior officials of the Russian Federation and leaders of terrorist organizations "DNR" and "LNR," which led to extremely grave con-sequences and mass murder of Ukrainian nationals (4 February 2015) (www. legal-tools. org/doc/b53005/) (2015 Ukraine Declaration).

[40]   *Ibid.*

ed period (21 November 2013 – 22 February 2014). [41] The reason for the second declaration was explained in the Declaration of the *Verkhovna Rada*, which is appended to the communiqué. [42] According to the *Verkhovna Rada*:

Starting from 20 February 2014 there is an ongoing Russian Federation's and Russia supported militant – terrorists' armed aggression against Ukraine, during which a part of the territory of an independent and sovereign state of Ukraine – the Autonomous Republic of Crimea and the city of Sevastopol – was annexed, parts of Donetsk and Luhansk regions of Ukraine were occupied, thousands of Ukrainian nationals, including children, were killed, thousands of people were injured, the infrastructure of the whole region was destroyed and hundreds of thousands of people were forced to flee from their homes. [43]

Unlike the 2014 declaration, the 2015 Ukrainian declaration was made for an indefinite period of time. As with the first, Ukraine confirmed its obligation to cooperate with the Court under Part IX of the Rome Statute in its second declaration under Article 12 (3). [44]

The analysis conducted by the OTP as to the capacity of the individuals who lodged the first and second declarations with the Court's Registrar was brief and uncontroversial:

Ukraine is not a State Party to the Rome Statute. However, pursuant to the two article 12 (3) declarations lodged by the Government of Ukraine on 17 April 2014 and 8 September 2015, respectively, the Court may exercise jurisdiction over Rome Statute crimes committed on the territory of Ukraine from 21 November 2013 onwards. Ukraine's acceptance of the exercise of jurisdiction by the ICC was made, in both cases, on the basis of declarations of the Verkhovna Rada of Ukraine (the Par-

---

[41] 2014 Ukraine Declaration, above n. 36. See also 2015 OTP Report, above n. 32, paras. 107–108.

[42] 2015 Ukraine Declaration, above n. 39.

[43] *Ibid.*

[44] 2015 Ukraine Declaration, above n. 39.

liament of Ukraine), urging acceptance of the exercise of jurisdiction by the Court in respect of crimes allegedly committed during the relevant periods. [45]

Thus, although the territory on which some of the alleged crimes under ICC jurisdiction occurred was arguably beyond Ukraine's effective control (to a lesser or greater extent, the Autonomous Republic of Crimea and parts of the Donetsk and Luhansk regions) on the dates on which the declarations were lodged, there was no dispute as to the capacity of the respective Ukrainian representatives to bind Ukraine under international law.

(4) Egypt

According to the determination by the OTP concerning the communication received in relation to Egypt:

On 13 December 2013, lawyers acting on behalf of, among others, the Freedom and Justice Party ("the applicants"), submitted to the Registrar of the ICC ("ICC" or the "Court") documents seeking to accept the exercise of jurisdiction by the ICC pursuant to article 12 (3) of the Rome Statute ("Statute") with respect to alleged crimes committed on the territory of the State of Egypt from 1 June 2013. [46]

The analysis of the OTP was split into two parts, the latter labelled "further analysis". [47] The first part of the OTP's factual and legal analysis led it to determine that:

[...] the purported declaration submitted to the Registrar on 13 December 2013, was not submitted, as a matter of international law, by any person with the requisite authority or bearing "full powers" to represent the State of Egypt

---

[45] 2015 OTP Report, above n. 32, para. 81.

[46] OTP, The determination of the Office of the Prosecutor on the communication received in relation to Egypt (8 May 2014) (www. legal-tools. org/doc/2945cd/) (OTP Egypt Determination).

[47] *Ibid.*

for the purpose of expressing the consent of that State to the exercise of jurisdiction by the Court. In short, the applicants lacked locus standi to seize the Court's jurisdiction pursuant to article 12 (3) of the Rome Statute. [48]

As to the further analysis, the OTP first affirmed that only the United Nations Security Council or a State can confer jurisdiction upon the Court and that "the Statute provides no authority for it to adopt a method to define the term 'State' under article 12 (3), which would be at variance with that established for the purpose of article 12 (1)." [49] The OTP then confirmed its conclusion that the applicants lacked both the requisite authority and the full powers to represent Egypt both on the date on which the declaration was signed and on the date the applicants submitted the communication to the Court's Registrar. [50] The third paragraph of the OTP's further analysis turned to the representatives of Egypt before the United Nations, as follows:

The UN Protocol List indicates that a new Head of State (Mr. Adly Mansour), Head of Government (Mr. Hazem El Beblawi) and Minister of Foreign Affairs (Mr. Nabil Fahmy) were appointed in July 2013. Furthermore, on 5 December 2013, the UN General Assembly accepted without a vote, the credentials of the Egyptian delegation, led by current Foreign Minister, Mr. Nabil Fahmy. This is a clear indication that none of the UN Member States considered representatives of Dr Mohamed Morsi to be the representatives of the State of Egypt at the UN in lieu of the delegation whose credentials were recognized. Because the UN Secretary – General acts as depositary of the Statute, this also means that, from July 2013 onwards, Dr Morsi would not have been able to deposit an instrument of accession to the Statute on behalf of the State of Egypt, had he sought to do so. Although, the lawyers for the applicants argued that the African Union's decision to suspend Egypt's participation

---

[48] OTP Egypt Determination, above n. 46.

[49] OTP Egypt Determination, above n. 46, para. 1.

[50] OTP Egypt Determination, above n. 46, para. 2.

in its activities indicated that there has been a collective refusal of recognition of the new government, which took power on 3 July 2013, the Office concluded that this did not equate to continued recognition of Dr Morsi as the Egyptian Head of State. [51]

The OTP could have opted to end its analysis at that stage, leaving the determination to the United Nations General Assembly, as it did in respect of the declarations lodged by Palestine under Article 12 (3) of the Rome Statute. However, the fourth paragraph of the OTP's further analysis continued as follows:

In accordance with the legal test of "effective control," the entity which is in fact in control of a State's territory, enjoys the habitual obedience of the bulk of the population, and has a reasonable expectancy of permanence, is recognized as the government of that State under international law. Application of that test, on both the date that the purported declaration was signed and the date it was submitted, lead to the conclusion that Dr Morsi was no longer the governmental authority with the legal capacity to incur new international legal obligations on behalf of the State of E-gypt. The information available indicates that, at all material times, the applicants did not exercise effective control over any part of Egyptian territory, including on the date the declaration was signed. Nor would it be consistent with the "effective control" test to have one putative authority exercising effective control over the territory of a State, and the other competing authority retaining international treaty—making capacity. [52]

In the fifth and final paragraph of its further analysis with respect to the communication received in relation to Egypt, the OTP concluded as follows:

Based on these considerations, the Office has determined that the purported declaration submitted to the Registrar on 13 December 2013, was not sub-

---

[51] OTP Egypt Determination, above n. 46, para. 3 (footnotes omitted).
[52] OTP Egypt Determination, above n. 46, para. 4.

mitted, as a matter of international law, by any person with the requisite authority or bearing "full powers" to represent the State of Egypt for the purpose of expressing the consent of that State to the exercise of jurisdiction by the Court. [53]

3. The "effective control" test and Article 12 (3) declarations

The OTP did not enter into an effective control analysis with respect to the declarations lodged in accordance with Article 12 (3) of the Rome Statute by Côte D'Ivoire, Palestine, or Ukraine. Nor did the respective Pre—Trial Chambers and Appeals Chamber regarding Côte D'Ivoire's declaration and communiqués confirming acceptance of the jurisdiction of the Court. It was therefore only as regards the communication received from alleged representatives of the Arab Republic of Egypt that the OTP discussed whether the party lodging such a declaration exercised effective control over the State territory on which crimes under ICC jurisdiction were alleged to have taken place. This is despite the fact that, in respect of Côte D'Ivoire, effective control over the State's territory was arguably contested at the time of the letters sent by Mr Alessane Ouattara to ICC officials on 14 December 2010 and 4 May 2011. As regards Palestine, when its representatives lodged its two declarations under Article 12 (3), effective control over the territory on which the crimes were alleged to have occurred was also arguably disputed. Finally, in respect of Ukraine, as noted above, the Ukrainian Parliament acknowledged that Crimea and parts of parts of the Donetsk and Luhansk regions were occupied at the time it transmitted its second declaration to the Court.

This is not to say that the OTP ought to have entered into such an analysis in respect of the respective declarations lodged by Côte D'Ivoire, Palestine, and Ukraine. Rather, it is argued that the OTP correctly limited its analysis in these in-

---

[53] OTP Egypt Determination, above n. 46, para. 5.

stances to the determination of the United Nations General Assembly and to whether the lodging party possessed the requisite "full powers" to bind the lodging State under international law.

3. 1 Application of the test by the OTP in relation to the Egypt communication

Michael Kearney has argued, replying to discussion of the OTP's application of the test of effective control by Eugene Kontorovich that an effective control test "does not exist as a matter of international law" as regards the recognition of governments. [54] Rather, in Kearney's opinion, government recognition is better viewed a political process and the OTP's application of an effective control test was misplaced. [55]

When lawyers acting on behalf of, among others, the Freedom and Justice Party of Dr Mohamed Morsi attempted to lodge a declaration with the ICC, the question of Egypt's statehood was not at issue. The OTP therefore need not have made recourse to a test of effective control, which has been explicitly considered by some States in the context of their recognition of States. For example, in 1976, the United States Department of State wrote as follows: " In [reaching its judgment as to whether to recognise another an entity as a State], the United States has traditionally looked to the establishment of certain facts. These facts include effective control over a clearly defined territory [...] ". [56]

Kearney proposes that the OTP might have based its reference to "effective con-

---

[54]   Eugene Kontorovich, Guest Post: Effective Control and Accepting ICC Jurisdiction (4 August 2014), response by Michael Kearney dated 8. 04. 2014 at 12: 19 pm EST (www. opiniojuris. org/2014/08/04/guest-post-effective-control-accepting-icc-jurisdiction/). The author has verified that this response was authored by Dr Michael Kearney, who is, at the time of writing, Senior Lecturer in Law at the University of Sussex.

[55]   *Ibid.*

[56]   Eleanor C. McDowell, Contemporary Practice of the United States Relating to International Law, 71 AJIL (1977), 337, citing Notice posted in Dept. of State Press Relations Office on Nov. 1, 1976, in response to a question raised in a news briefing of Oct. 22, 1976. See also Thomas D. Grant, The Recognition of States: Law and Practice in Debate and Evolution (2007), 6

trol" in this context on a 1980 decision by the Government of the United Kingdom to no longer recognise governments. [57] Instead, such status was to be inferred from relations between the UK Government and the new regime. [58] According to Colin Warbrick, quoting Lord Carrington, the then UK Secretary of State for Foreign and Commonwealth Affairs:

Among the factors that would influence the quality of the relations with the new authority would be the British Government's assessment of: "Whether they are able of themselves to exercise effective control of the territory of the State concerned and seem likely to do so". The thrust of the statement was that effectiveness would generally be a necessary precondition for governmental status, but it would not necessarily be a guarantee of 'normal Government to Government' relations. [59]

Articles 2 (1)(c) and 7 (1) of the Vienna Convention on the Law of Treaties, to which the OTP refers in its consideration of the purported Article 12 (3) declaration lodged by Dr Morsi's representatives, provide as follows:

Article 2 [...]

1. For the purposes of the present Convention: [...]

(c) "Full powers" means a document emanating from the competent authority of a State designating a person or persons to represent the State for negotiating, adopting or authenticating the text of a treaty, for expressing the consent of the State to be bound by a treaty, or for accomplishing any other act with respect to a treaty; [...]

Article 7 [...]

1. A person is considered as representing a State for the purpose of adop-

---

[57] Kearney, above n. 54, referring to Colin Warbrick, Recognition of Governments, 56 Modern LR (1993), 92.

[58] Warbrick, above n. 57, 92.

[59] Warbrick, above n. 57, 92, citing HL Deb vol 408, cols 1121–1122, 28 April 1980 (Lord Carrington).

ting or authenticating the text of a treaty or for the purpose of expressing the consent of the State to be bound by a treaty if:

(a) He produces appropriate full powers; or

(b) It appears from the practice of the States concerned or from other circumstances that their intention was to consider that person as representing the State for such purposes and to dispense with full powers. [60]

Having concluded that, under international law, the applicants were not in possession of the requisite "full powers" to act on behalf of the State of Egypt, "either on the date the declaration was signed or on the date it was submitted to the Registrar", [61] the OTP was not required to enter into an effective control analysis. Indeed, by applying this test to a situation in which statehood was by no means contested, the OTP's analysis introduces uncertainty into the Article 12 (3) declaration process. Instead, it is argued that the OTP ought to limit its consideration in this context to determination by the United Nations.

The present author finds it difficult to disagree with Michael Kearney, who, contrasting the response of the OTP to the declarations from representatives of Palestine and Egypt, doubts how "on the one hand the OTP is adamant that under the law of the Rome Statute it cannot establish the existence of a state, while on the other hand it is fully capable of engaging with the far murkier question of establishing the existence of a government". [62]

3. 2 State cooperation and Article 12 (3) declarations

Notwithstanding, should the OTP follow a similar approach to that adopted with respect to the Egypt communication in its future practice, the requirement that accepting States "shall cooperate with the Court" in accordance with Part IX of the

---

[60]   Vienna Convention on the Law of Treaties, 888 UNTS 999.

[61]   OTP Egypt Determination, above n. 46, para. 2.

[62]   Kearney, above n. 54.

ICC Statute must be taken into consideration. The capacity to provide cooperation is essential to the Court's ability to effectively investigate and prosecute the crimes under its jurisdiction, whether conferred under Article 12 (3) of the ICC Statute or otherwise. Without cooperation, the Court is unable to, among other things, preserve and collect evidence, question persons under investigation, and protect victims and witnesses. [63] The ability to cooperate ought therefore to be factored into any effective control analysis, should the OTP continue to follow such an approach in the future. However, this is not to say that the OTP should persist with an effective control analysis. As argued above, the OTP ought to leave such questions to determination by the United Nations.

Further, when taking into account the lodging State's ability to cooperate, it ought to be borne in mind that situations in which cooperation (and indeed effective control) might be lacking include those where action by the Court could prove vital in ending impunity for crimes under its jurisdiction. It is argued that this consideration, in turn, provides an additional argument for the OTP to limit its determination with respect to future Article 12 (3) declarations to whether the applicant possesses "full powers" to bind the lodging State, as evidenced by the determination of the United Nations General Assembly.

4. Conclusion

This chapter has sought to argue that the OTP, when considering declarations lodged with the Court's Registrar according to Article 12 (3) of the Rome Statute, ought not to enter into an analysis of whether the lodging entity exercises "effective control" over territory. Rather, the Court should leave any determination of competing governmental claims to the United Nations General Assembly. This body is a much more suitable entity than a criminal court for the resolution of such claims. The OTP should limit its assessment to whether the applicants possess the requisite "full

---

[63] On which, see Olympia Bekou and Daley J. Birkett (eds.), Cooperation and the International Criminal Court: Perspectives from Theory and Practice (2016).

powers" to bind the State they seek to represent in lodging the *ad hoc* declaration. If, however, the OTP continues to apply the effective control test, consideration should be paid to the ability of the lodging party to cooperate with the Court, a crucial requirement enabling the fulfilment of its mandate.

EXTRATERRITORIAL OBLIGATION TO PREVENT AND THE CONCEPT OF EFFECTIVE CONTROL: AN ANALYSIS OF THE INTERNATIONAL LAW COMMISSION'S DRAFT ARTICLES ON THE PREVENTION AND PUNISHMENT OF CRIMES AGAINST HUMANITY

Ezéchiel Amani Cirimwami *

Abstract

This paper concerns the International Law Commission's Draft Articles on the Prevention and Punishment of Crimes Against Humanity and, in particular, the State obligation to prevent crimes against humanity in "any territory under its jurisdiction" found in Draft Article 4. The newly formulated wording seen in Draft Article 4 is a departure from the language used in earlier versions where the obligation to prevent crimes against humanity binds a State to "any territory under its jurisdiction or control". Unfortunately, the deletion of control in the most recent version of Draft Article 4 is not clearly explained in its accompanying Commentary. This paper assesses the merit of the new phrasing by examining whether the concept of control can be interpreted as a test for determining jurisdiction over activities carried out in other territory. It concludes that, in line with Draft Article 4, jurisdiction has to be broadly interpreted to encompass those situations in which State only exercises a factual power,

---

 * Ezéchiel Amani Cirimwami is a PhD candidate with the Faculty of Law and Criminology at the Vrije Universiteit Brussel. Former Deputy Public Prosecutor, he is currently a Permanent Judge in the Democratic Republic of the Congo. I am grateful to the colleagues Derek Inman and Balingene Kahombo for the comments on an earlier draft of this paper. Email: Ezechiel. Cirimwami. Amani@ vub. be.

authority or control over a particular territory. Therefore, as opposed to simply referring to legal competence, effective control over a foreign territory appears as a requisite in order to prove jurisdiction over it. The assessment relies principally on the basis of the materials relied upon in the commentary to Draft Articles but is also supported by international human rights jurisprudence and related sources.

1. Introduction

In 2017, the International Law Commission (hereinafter the "ILC") adopted, on first reading, the Draft Articles on the Prevention and Punishment of Crimes Against Humanity (hereinafter the "Draft Articles") as well as the accompanying Commentaries. [1] The ILC had been engaged in the consideration of this topic since 2014, with Mr. Sean D. Murphy as the Special Rapporteur. [2]

Draft Article 4, which relates to the duty to prevent crimes against humanity, makes it clear that States must undertake to prevent crimes against humanity in any "territory under its jurisdiction". [3] The newly formulated wording of Draft Article 4 is a departure from the language used in earlier versions where the obligation to prevent crimes against humanity binds States to any "territory under its jurisdiction or control". [4] By using the conjunction "or" one notes that jurisdiction was used as an alternative to control. Clearly, the drafters had two scenarios in mind: One where certain territory was under the jurisdiction of a State and the other, where certain ter

---

[1]   ILC 2017 Draft Articles on the Prevention and Punishment of Crimes Against Humanity, with Commentaries.

[2]   ILC Report, Sixty-Ninth session (1 May-2 June and 3 July-4 August 2017), Supplement No 10 (A/69/10), para. 266.

[3]   "Article 4 [4] Obligation of prevention

1. Each State undertakes to prevent crimes against humanity, in conformity with international law, including through:

(a) effective legislative, administrative, judicial or other preventive measures in any territory under its jurisdiction; [...] "

[4]   ILC 2015 Draft Articles on the Prevention and Punishment of Crimes Against Humanity, with Commentaries provisionally adopted at the Sixty-seventh session, Supplement No 10 (A/70/10), chap. Ⅶ, sect. C., art. 4, para. 1 (a) (referring to "any territory under its jurisdiction or control").

ritory was under its control. [5] Hence, jurisdiction and control were presupposed to be mutually exclusive, the main difference between those situations being the presence of legal competence or thereof. [6]

Unfortunately, the change of language seen in the recently revised Draft Article 4 is not clearly explained in its accompanying Commentary. The only way to understand the reason for this change is by referring to the Commentary of Draft Article 6 (Establishment of National Jurisdiction)[7], which was adopted by the ILC in 2016. The 6th Commentary *in fine* reveals the ILC's intention to review Draft Article 4 in an effort to ensure a consistency in terminology:

Draft article 6, paragraph 1 (a), requires that jurisdiction be established when the offence occurs in the State's territory, a type of jurisdiction often referred to as "territorial jurisdiction". Rather than refer solely to a State's "territory", the Commission considered it appropriate to refer to territory "under [the State's] jurisdiction", which is intended to encapsulate the territory *de jure* of the State, as well as territory under its jurisdiction or *de facto* control. Such terminology aligns with the formulations used by relevant treaties in the field. The text of draft article 4 will need to be revisited in the future to ensure consistency in terminology). [8]

---

[5] María L. Piqué, "Beyond Territory, Jurisdiction, and Control: Towards a Comprehensive Obligation to Prevent Crimes Against Humanity", in Morten Bergsmo and Tianying Song (eds), On the Proposed Crimes Against Humanity Convention (Torkel Opsahl Academic EPublisher 2014), 151.

[6] *Ibid.*; Ezéchiel A. Cirimwami and Stefaan Smis, "Le régime des obligations positives de prévenir et de poursuivre à défaut d'extrader ou de remise prévues dans le texte des projets d'articles sur les crimes contre l'humanité provisoirement adoptés par la Commission du droit international", Revue Québécoise de droit international (2017) [forthcoming].

[7] ILC 2016 Draft Articles on the Prevention and Punishment of Crimes Against Humanity, with Commentaries provisionally adopted at its Sixty-Eighth Session, Supplement No. 10 (A/71/10), chap. VII, sect. C., art. 6, para. 1 (a):

"1. Each State shall take the necessary measures to establish its jurisdiction over the offences covered by the present draft articles in the following cases:

(a) when the offence is committed in any territory under its jurisdiction or on board a ship or aircraft registered in that State".

[8] See Commentary on Draft Article 6 (corresponding to the newly Draft Article 7), ILC 2016 Draft Articles, *Ibid*, 280, para. 6.

Jurisdiction clauses, such as Draft Article 4, are tools that are used to establish the scope of States' obligations under a particular treaty. In human rights treaties, jurisdiction clauses, as the one highlighted above, have been broadly interpreted as referring to a particular kind of factual power, authority, or control that a State has over a territory and, consequently, over persons in that territory. [9] Hence, control has been used as a requisite in order to prove the existence of jurisdiction.

However, when reading the commentaries on Draft Article 4 what remains unclear is how to determine which situations would result in the applicability of the term "any territory under its jurisdiction", particularly when the State is operating abroad. The ILC Commentaries have just indicated that such formulation covers the "territory of a State", but also covers "activities carried out in other territory under the State's jurisdiction". [10] The ILC noted that it covers situations in which a State is exercising *de facto* jurisdiction, even though it lacks *de jure* jurisdiction, and used the case of unlawful intervention, occupation and annexation as an example by referring to the advisory opinion by the International Court of Justice in the case concerning the *Legal Consequences for States of the Continued Presence of South Africa in Namibia (South West Africa) notwithstanding Security Council Resolution* 276 (1970) (hereinafter, the *Namibia* case). [11] In that advisory opinion, the Court, after holding South Africa responsible for having created and maintained a situation which the Court declared illegal and finding that South Africa had an obligation to withdraw its administration from Namibia, nevertheless attached certain legal consequences to the *de facto* control of South Africa over Namibia. [12]

The overall purpose of this paper is to provide a detailed analysis of Draft Article

---

[9] Marko Milanović, "From Compromise to Principle: Clarifying the Concept of State Jurisdiction in Human Rights Treaties", 8 Human Rights Law Review 3 (2008), 417-418.

[10] See above n. 1, para. 18 of the commentary to Draft Article 4.

[11] Legal Consequences for States of the Continued Presence of South Africa in Namibia (South West Africa) notwithstanding Security Council Resolution 276 (1970), Advisory Opinion, ICJ Reports 1971, 16.

[12] *Ibid* at 54, para. 118. About the legal consequence, see below, n. 39.

4 in an effort to determine how the concept of control can be interpreted as a test for determining jurisdiction of State over a particular territory. In doing so, the paper will investigate whether or not the effective control test can be used to determine if a State has an extraterritorial obligation to prevent crimes against humanity.

2. Understanding "any territory under its jurisdiction": when effective control engages States outside their borders.

As mentioned above, this paper will examine the role that effective control plays in the determination of the extraterritorial obligation to prevent crimes against humanity. Under the Draft Articles, the obligation to prevent is found in Articles 2 and 4. On the one hand, Draft Article 2 contains a general obligation to prevent crimes against humanity, whether or not it is committed in time of armed conflict. On the other hand, Draft Article 4 places an obligation on the State party to take special, legislative, administrative, judicial or other effective preventive measures in any "territory under its jurisdiction", and to cooperate with other States, relevant intergovernmental organizations and, as appropriate, other organizations, to prevent crimes against humanity.

In order to clarify the scope of the obligations laid down in Draft Articles 2 and 4, it is necessary to first analyze the wording of these provisions, in particular the binding nature of the "undertaking to prevent" crimes against humanity (A) and the normative scope of this obligation to prevent within territory under the jurisdiction of the State (B).

2. 1 The binding nature of the "undertaking to prevent" crimes against humanity

The Draft Articles adopted by the ILC are not, and will most likely not be, the only international instrument obliging States to take certain steps to prevent the commission of crimes it seeks to prohibit. Many other instruments include a similar obligation but in different forms. [13] An early but significant example of an obligation to prevent is found in the 1948 Convention on the Prevention and Punishment of the Crime of Genocide (Genocide Convention), which states: "The Contracting Parties confirm that genocide, whether committed in time of peace or in time of war, is crime under international law which they undertake to prevent and punish". [14] In the case concerning the *Application of the Convention on the Prevention and Punishment of the Crime of Genocide (Bosnia and Herzegovina v. Serbia and Montenegro)*, the International Court of Justice (ICJ) analysed the meaning of "undertake to prevent" as contained in Article 1 of the Genocide Convention. At the provisional measures phase, the ICJ determined that undertaking in Article 1 imposes "a clear obligation" on the two parties "to do all in their power to prevent the commission of any such acts in the future". [15] At the merits phase, the ICJ described such an undertaking as "a formal promise ... not merely hortatory or purposive ..." [16]

In that regard, one could try to understand the binding nature of "undertaking to prevent" crimes against humanity set out in Draft Articles 2 and 4 in light of the

---

[13]   See, for example, the Convention against Torture and Other Cruel, Inhuman or Degrading Treatment or Punishment, GA Res. 46, UN GAOR, 39th Sess. , Supp. No. 51, UN Doc. A/39/51, 10 December 1984, 1465 UNTS 85 (hereinafter CAT), art. 2, para. 1 ("Each State Party shall take effective legislative, administrative, judicial or other measures to prevent acts of torture in any territory under its jurisdiction") ; Convention on the Prevention and Punishment of Crimes against Internationally Protected Persons, including Diplomatic Agents (New York, 14 December 1973), UNTS vol. 1035, No. 15410 at 167, art. 4 ("States Parties shall co-operate in the prevention of the crimes set forth in article 2, particularly by: (a) taking all practicable measures to prevent preparations in their respective territories for the commission of those crimes within or outside their territories") ; International Convention on the Suppression and Punishment of the Crime of Apartheid (New York, 30 November 1973), UNTS vol. 1015, No. 14861 at 243, art. IV: ("The States Parties to the present Convention undertake ... (a) To adopt any legislative or other measures necessary to suppress as well as to prevent any encouragement of the crime of apartheid and similar segregationist policies or their manifestations and to punish persons guilty of that crime").

[14]   Convention on the Prevention and Punishment of the Crime of Genocide, New York, 9 December 1948, 78 UNTS 277, art. I.

[15]   Application of the Convention on the Prevention and Punishment of the Crime of Genocide (Bosnia & Herzegovina v. Yugoslavia), Order on Provisional Measures, I. C. J. Reports 1993, p. 3, at p. 22.

[16]   Application of the Convention on the Prevention and Punishment of the Crime of Genocide (Bosnia and Herzegovina v. Serbia and Montenegro), Judgment, I. C. J. Reports 2007, para. 162.

developments that have emerged from the jurisprudence surrounding the aforementioned Genocide Convention. However, this methodology calls for some caution. The content of the obligation to prevent varies from one instrument to another, according to the wording of the relevant provisions, and depending on the nature of the acts to be prevented. This assertion has been confirmed by the ICJ in the case mentioned above, where the ICJ advised that its decision does not purport to establish a general jurisprudence applicable to all cases where a treaty instrument, or other binding legal norm, includes an obligation for States to prevent certain acts. [17] Therefore, the decision does not allow, in and of itself, the extension of the binding nature or the scope of the obligation to prevent genocide to crimes against humanity.

The ILC, for its part, noted that undertaking to prevent crimes against humanity, as formulated in paragraph 1 of Draft Article 4, is intended to be legally binding upon States. [18] Therefore, the words "undertake to" in Draft Article 4 remain an obligation analogous to the interpretation provided by ICJ where "the ordinary meaning of the word 'undertake' is to give a formal promise, to bind or engage oneself, to give a pledge or promise, to agree, to accept an obligation". [19]

This general obligation to prevent manifests itself in two ways: First, an obligation by the State not to commit such acts through its own organs, or persons over whom they have control such that their conduct is attributable to the State under international law. Second, an obligation for the State to employ any reasonable means at its disposal, when necessary, appropriate, and lawful, to prevent persons or groups not directly under their authority from committing such acts. [20]

---

[17] *Ibid*, para. 429.

[18] See above n. 10.

[19] See above n. 16, para. 162.

[20] *Ibid*. , para. 430; see also Bruno Simma, "Genocide and the International Court of Justice," in Christoph Safferling and Eckart Conze (eds) , *The Genocide Convention Sixty Years After its Adoption* (ZMC Asser Press, 2010) , 259 and 262.

2. 2 The scope of the obligation to prevent crimes against humanity

The scope of States' positive obligations to prevent crimes against humanity is shaped by Draft Article 4, which asserts that such obligations are meant to be observed within each State Party's "territory under its jurisdiction". [21]

In several human rights treaties that contain provisions similar to those found in Draft Article 4, the provisions are utilised to define the territorial scope of the obligations of States under the said treaties. [22] Moreover, the way those words have been interpreted within human rights treaties by international, regional and domestic bodies has had a major impact on their extraterritorial applicability. [23]

Whereas all the rights enshrined in human rights conventions are applicable within a State's territory, it is not always the case when the State is operating abroad. In those situations, the number of enforceable rights "may be limited by the

---

[21] The negative obligation that implicitly stems from Draft Articles 2 and 4 is to refrain from committing crimes against humanity, which does not have territorial limits. In line with the criteria set by the ICJ in the Genocide case, the prohibition to commit crimes against humanity may be inferred from the object and purpose of the Proposed Convention, from some specific provisions regarding State responsibility and the obligation to prevent, and from the characterization of crimes against humanity as "international crimes". In turn, Draft Article 4 imposes on States Parties the obligation to prevent crimes against humanity. In addition, even if the worldwide scope of the prohibition against crimes against humanity was questioned, those crimes committed by a State acting abroad would, as Professor Luban notes, simultaneously constitute war crimes, and therefore, they would amount to international crimes anyway. See David Luban, "A Theory of Crimes Against Humanity", 29 Yale Journal of International Law (2004), 94.

[22] For a review of all the uses of the word 'jurisdiction' in human rights treaties, see, e. g. Marko Milanović, above n. 9; Michael J. Dennis, Application of Human Rights Treaties Extraterritorially in Times of Armed Conflict and Military Occupation, 99 AJIL (2005); Ralph Wilde, Legal " Black Hole" ?: Extraterritorial State Action and International Treaty Law on Civil and Political Rights, 26 MJIL (2005), 739; Sigrun Skogly, Beyond National Borders: States' Human Rights Obligations in International Cooperation (Intersentia 2006); Mark Gibney and Sigrun Skogly (eds), Universal Human Rights and Extraterritorial Obligations (University of Pennsylvania Press 2010); Ralph Wilde, Compliance with Human Rights Norms Extraterritorially: " Human Rights Imperialism" ?, in: Laurence Boisson de Chazournes and Marcelo Kohen (eds), International Law and the Quest for its Implementation, Liber Amicorum Vera Gowlland – Debbas (Brill/Martinus Nijhoff 2010), ch. 16; Marko Milanović, Extraterritorial Application of Human Rights Treaties: Law, Principles, and Policy (OUP 2011); Karen da Costa, The extraterritorial application of selected human rights treaties, v. 11 (Leiden; Boston: Martinus Nijhoff Publishers, 2013).

[23] Michal Gondek, The Reach of Human Rights in a Globalising World: Extraterritorial Application of Human Rights Treaties, (Antwerp: Intersentia, 2009), 126–131 and 367.

scope of the State's authority or control in the circumstances". [24] Therefore, importance must be placed in deconstructing the phrase "territory under its jurisdiction" used in Draft article 4 and analysis must be performed on the way it impacts the scope of States' obligations to prevent crimes against humanity.

Under general international law, jurisdiction is often understood as the legal competence of the State and has been defined in numerous ways, such as: "the legal power conferred or recognized by international law to a State to submit persons, property and activities to its legal order" [25]; " [t] he capacity of a State under international law to prescribe or to enforce a rule of law" [26]; or, "to regulate the conduct of physical and legal persons, and to enforce such regulations". [27] As noted by Milanović, that "jurisdiction" is not a unitary concept, as it encompasses at least two, and possibly three, distinct sets of powers. [28] The jurisdiction to prescribe – also termed legislative jurisdiction or *compétence normative*–is the State's authority to make or prescribe legal rules. The jurisdiction to enforce – executive jurisdiction or *compétence d'exécution*–is the State's authority to apply or enforce the rules that it has previously prescribed. Finally, there is the State's adjudicatory, curial or judicial jurisdiction, which refers to the power of its courts to settle legal disputes, though this type of jurisdiction may safely be subsumed under the State's prescriptive and enforcement jurisdiction. [29] In essence, a State's jurisdiction is derived from, or an

---

[24] John Cerone, "Jurisdiction and Power: The Intersection of Human Rights Law and the Law of Non–International Armed Conflict in an Extraterritorial Context", 40 Israel Law Review (2007), 437.

[25] Jean Salomon (ed), Dictionnaire de droit international public (Bruxelles : Bruylant, 2001), 220 and 625.

[26] Michal Gondek, above n. 23, 47; Marko Milanović, above n. 9, 36: "Jurisdiction is the authority of the state, based in and limited by international law, to regulate the conduct of persons, both natural and legal, by means of its own domestic law".

[27] María L. Piqué, above n. 5, 149.

[28] Marko Milanović, above n. 9, 420; see also O'Keefe, "Universal Jurisdiction: Clarifying the Basic Concept", 2 Journal of International Criminal Justice 735 (2004), 736.

[29] Marko Milanović, ibid.

aspect of, its sovereignty and its right to regulate its own public affairs. [30] From the standpoint of public international law, the jurisdictional competence of a State is primarily territorial[31]. Therefore, in line with Draft Article 4, jurisdiction refers to the meaning of the term derived from the general principles of international law: legal competence or authority to make and enforce the law. Hence, States would be under the obligation to import crimes against humanity into their domestic criminal law, and to establish their competence—through the necessary legislation—in order to investigate, prosecute and punish crimes against humanity whether they are committed in their own territory, or by their nationals, or if the victim is a national of that State. The text of the Draft Articles does not exclude the exercise of any criminal jurisdiction established by a State in accordance with its national law. [32]

However, jurisdiction could mean something other than the legal competence. On the one hand, the jurisdiction of Draft Article 4 could refer only to the space in which the State is empowered to exercise its competence, i. e. its sovereign

---

[30]   See, for example, Ian Brownlie, Principles of Public International Law, 6th ed. , (Oxford: Oxford University Press, 2003), 297; Antonio Cassese, International Law, 2nd ed. , (Oxford: Oxford University Press, 2005), 49.

[31]   While the jurisdiction of States is primarily territorial, it may sometimes be exercised outside the national territory (see Legal Consequences of the Construction of a Wall in the Occupied Palestinian Territory, Advisory Opinion of 9 July 2004, ICJ Reports 2004 at 136, para. 109). The European Court of Human Rights ("ECtHR"), seems to have chosen this interpretation of "jurisdiction" in its 2001 Bankovic decision. See, Bankovic and Others v. Belgium and Others, 2001–XII 333 Eur. Ct. H. R. , para 59: " [F] rom the standpoint of public international law, the jurisdictional competence of a State is primarily territorial. While international law does not exclude a State's exercise of jurisdiction extra–territorially, the suggested bases of such jurisdiction (including nationality, flag, diplomatic and consular relations, effect, protection, passive personality and universality) are, as a general rule, defined and limited by the sovereign territorial rights of the other relevant States. " See the references that the ECtHR makes to scholars supporting this point of view, including some of the most famous textbooks on international law by Oppenheim, Dupuy (P. M.) and Brownlie. For information, more generally on territorial jurisdiction, see the "all time classic" work of F. A. Mann, "The Doctrine of Jurisdiction in International Law", 1 Collected Courses of The Hague Academy of International 111 (1964); F. A. Mann, "The Doctrine of International Jurisdiction Revisited after Twenty Years" 186 Collected Courses of The Hague Academy of International 9 (1985); M. Akehurst, "Jurisdiction in International Law", 46 British Yearbook of International Law 145 (1972). But see also, Marko Milanović, above n. 9, 423.

[32]   See ILC 2017 Draft Articles, above no. 1, Draft Article 7 (3).

territory, and exceptionally other territories (military occupation, lease, etc.). [33] The ILC seems to have followed this reading in its commentary on Draft Article 7, which relates to the establishment of national jurisdiction, and expressly considered jurisdiction in Draft Article 4 as encapsulating the "territory *de jure* of the State", as well as "other territory under its jurisdiction":

(6) ... Rather than refer solely to a State's "territory", the Commission considered it appropriate to refer to territory "under [the State's] jurisdiction" which, as was the case for draft article 4, is intended to encapsulate the territory *de jure* of the State, as well as other territory under its jurisdiction. [34]

This reading tends to equate jurisdiction to territory albeit the two terms are not synonymous. Thus, it cannot be supported within the context of Draft Article 4 the fact that the ILC chose the wording "territory under its jurisdiction" no longer allows jurisdiction to be regarded as a territory for the simple reason that this would be redundant. Hence, in the presence of two possible readings of a text, it seems reasonable to reject the one which leads to redundancy in favor of that which confers a full scope on each word. [35]

On the other hand, it could also be argued that jurisdiction in Draft Article 4 has a different meaning, closer to the one contained within human rights conventions where such provisions are very common. From this viewpoint, jurisdiction should not be exclusively understood from the framework of general international law—legal competence—but should also include "a particular kind of factual power, authority or

---

[33] Jean Salmon (ed), Dictionnaire de droit international public (Bruxelles : Bruylant, 2001), p. 624; Guillaume Grisel, *Application extraterritoriale du droit international des droits de l'homme* (Bale : Helbing Lichtenhahn, 2010), 50-51.

[34] ILC 2017 Draft Articles, see above 1, 6th commentary on Draft article 7.

[35] See American jurisprudence, Us *vs* Pan, Award of 27 June 1993, 7 Ann. Dig. (1993-34), 225, 257 (*Us-pan Claims Comm's*), reference cited by Guillaume Grisel, above n. 30, 61 and footnote 176.

control that a State has over a territory, and consequently over persons in that territory". [36] In this case, jurisdiction would be a broader concept than legal competence since it would also include the exercise of pure, factual authority, or control, which would serve as a condition for assessing the existence of a particular obligation of a State regarding a particular victim – or potential victim – of a human rights violation simply because of his or her presence in a certain territory. [37] Therefore, the purpose served by this meaning of jurisdiction is to determine the applicability of a human rights treaty to the particular conduct of a State, with the legality or illegality of that conduct being irrelevant. [38]

It is worthwhile observing that in the *Namibia* Advisory Opinion referred to by the ILC commentary to Draft Article 4, the ICJ stated that South Africa, which at the time was unlawfully occupying Namibia, was:

[…] accountable for any violations […] of the rights of the people of Namibia. The fact that South Africa no longer has any title to administer the Territory does not release it from its obligations and responsibilities under international law towards other States in respect of the exercise of its powers in relation to this Territory. Physical control of a territory, and not sovereignty or legitimacy of title, is the basis of State liability for acts affecting other States. [39]

Interestingly, the ICJ established the principle that territorial control, rather than the enjoyment of territorial sovereignty (legal title) alone, should be the basis

---

[36] Marko Milanović, above n. 9, 428.

[37] See also Gondek, above n. 23, p. 16, who differentiates between both meanings of "jurisdiction", one of them being "the legal competence of a State to legislate, adjudicate and enforce the law" ("jurisdiction" as it is understood in international criminal law) and the other being "a given location" ("jurisdiction" as it is used in human rights treaties).

[38] María L. Piqué, above n. 5, 151.

[39] Namibia Advisory Opinion, above n. 11, 54, para. 118.

for the operation of State obligations in general. [40]

Furthermore, this broad reading in the *Namibia* case paved the way for later decisions in the field of human rights law by human rights bodies. In this regard, two considerations have emerged. The first of these is that State obligation should not be limited to situations where a State enjoys legal title or competence. This is the basic underpinning of extraterritorial applicability. The second is that the particular concept of "physical control over territory" as a basis for determining where obligations should subsist despite the lack of legal competence has been adopted in later human rights decisions, notably those made in interpreting the meaning of "jurisdiction". [41] For example, in General Comment No. 2, the Committee against Torture (CAT) interpreted Article 2 (1) of the 1984 Convention against Torture and Other Cruel, Inhuman or Degrading Treatment or Punishment (Convention against Torture) [42] in this manner:

Article 2, paragraph 1, [...] includes all areas where the State party exercises, directly or indirectly, in whole or in part, *de jure* or *de facto* effective control, in accordance with international law. [43]

This approach was later reaffirmed by the Human Rights Committee (HRC) in

---

[40]   See also, Ralph Wilde, "Human Rights beyond Borders at the World Court: The Significance of the International Court of Justice's Jurisprudence on the Extraterritorial Application of International Human Rights Law Treaties", 12 Chinese JIL (2013), 661.

[41]   *Ibid*, 662.

[42]   Convention against Torture, art. 2, para. 1: "Each State Party shall take effective legislative, administrative, judicial or other measures to prevent acts of torture in any territory under its jurisdiction". According to the commentary of the ILC, this has inspired the wording of Draft Article 4 (See the 13th commentary on Draft Article 4).

[43]   See Committee against Torture, General Comment No. 2 on the implementation of article 2, paragraph 4, in Official Records of the General Assembly, Sixty—Third Session, Supplement No. 44, U. N. Doc. A/63/44 (2007), annex VI, para 16.

General Comment No. 31, [44] where they stated that a State Party was compelled to respect and ensure human rights to anyone within the power or effective control of that State Party, even if not situated within the territory of the State Party. [45] Moreover, the European Court of Human Rights (ECtHR) has taken a similar approach in the *Loizidou*[46] and *Cypriot*[47] cases. In *Loizidou*, the ECtHR has used the effective control test to determine whether a State Party to the Convention was under the (positive) obligation to secure the rights and freedoms of the European Convention for the Protection of Human Rights and Fundamental Freedoms (ECHR)[48] in an occupied territory. [49] Specifically, the ECtHR applied this test vis-à-vis alleged human rights violations in Cyprus and found that Turkey was indeed exercising effective control, which could be exercised "directly, through its armed forces, or through a subordinate local administration". [50] In the decision on the Merits, [51] the ECtHR maintained this position although it changed the test slightly to "effective overall control". [52] This ruling was reaffirmed in *Cypriot* where the ECtHR had to determine whether human rights violations in Northern Cyprus were capable of falling within the jurisdiction of Turkey under the ECHR even though they had occurred outside its national territory. Turkey was again held liable for human rights violations committed in the territory over which it had effective overall control. [53] Finally, at

---

[44]   Human Rights Committee, General Comment No. 31, The Nature of the General Legal Obligation Imposed on States Parties to the Covenant, adopted on 29 March 2004 (2187th meeting), CCPR/C/21/Rev. 1/Add. 13 (General Comments).

[45]   *Ibid.* , para. 10

[46]   ECtHR, Loizidou v Turkey (1997) 23 EHRR 513.

[47]   ECtHR, Case of Cyprus v. Turkey, Judgment, 10 May 2001, Reports of Judgments and Decisions 2001–IV 172. For a detailed analysis, see Michal Gondek, 2009, *supra* note 23 at pp. 126–131.

[48]   Council of Europe, European Convention for the Protection of Human Rights and Fundamental Freedoms, as amended by Protocols Nos. 11 and 14, 4 November 1950, ETS 5.

[49]   Loizidou v. Turkey, Preliminary Objections, 23 March 1995, Series A, No. 310.

[50]   *Ibid.*, para. 62.

[51]   Loizidou v. Turkey, Judgment, 18 December 1996, Reports 1996–VI.

[52]   *Ibid.*, para. 56.

[53]   See, ...above no. 47, 77–78.

the Inter – American level, the Inter – American Commission on Human Rights (IACHR) noted that:

the exercise of its jurisdiction over acts with an extra-territorial locus will not only be consistent with, but required by, the norms which pertain [...]. Given that individual rights inhere simply by virtue of a person's humanity each American State is obliged to uphold the protected rights of any person subject to its jurisdiction. While this most commonly refers to persons within a state's territory, it may, under given circumstances, refer to conduct with an extraterritorial locus where the person concerned is present in the territory of one state, but subject to the control of another state – usually through the acts of the latter's agents abroad. In principle, the inquiry turns not on the presumed victim's nationality or presence within a particular geographic area, but on whether, under the specific circumstances, the State observed the rights of a person subject to its authority and control. [54]

Thus, given the fact that every person is entitled to individual rights, American States are obliged to uphold the protected rights, contained within the American Declaration of the Rights and Duties of Man, [55] of any person under its authority and control, even if the State Party is acting beyond its national boundaries. [56]

In case of extraterritoriality, effectiveness in the exercised control is a precondition for jurisdiction. It is a criterion that allows an assessment of whether a primary

---

[54] IACHR, Coard et al. v. the United States, Report No. 109/99, Case No. 10. 951, 29 September 1999, para. 37.

[55] Inter-American Commission on Human Rights (IACHR), American Declaration of the Rights and Duties of Man, 2 May 1948.

[56] See also, IACHR, Rafael Ferrer – Mazorra et al. (United States), Report No. 51/01, Case No. 9903, 4 April 2001, IACHR Annual Report, 2000, OEA/Ser. L/V/II. 111, Doc. 20 rev. , para. 178; Saldano case (Argentina), Report No. 38/99, 11 March 1999, in IACHR Annual Report, 1998, OEA/Ser. L/V/II. 102, Doc. 6 rev. , paras. 15-20.

human rights obligation exists for the State. [57] Given this, in order to determine whether States have an extraterritorial obligation to prevent crimes against humanity, jurisdiction, as is written in Draft Article 4, should be broadly interpreted as is in human rights law, where it encompasses those situations where States exercise some kind of factual power over a territory without any legal competence. As such, "effective control" appears as the criterion for determining whether that State is under the obligation to prevent crimes against humanity regarding acts that take place beyond its territory and that is required to prove the existence of jurisdiction. [58]

Therefore, it is within this interpretation that the scope of Draft Article 4 reaches situations[59] where State has control over a territory even if it does not have jurisdiction over it–due, for instance, to illegal military operations that are being performed in another State's territory–and *vice versa*, where a State, although having jurisdiction over a territory, does not have control. For example, jurisdiction without control could arise in situations such as the one depicted by the ECtHR in its decision in the *Ilaşcu and Others v. Moldova and Russia* case. [60] In this case, the Court acknowledged that the Moldovan government did not exercise authority (control) over Transnistria because of its secession. Even in the absence of effective control over that region, the Court found Moldova to be under a positive obligation "to take the

---

[57]   See Vassilis P. Tzevelekos, "Reconstructing the Effective Control Criterion in Extraterritorial Human Rights Breaches: Direct Attribution of Wrongfulness, Due Diligence, and Concurrent Responsibility", 36 Michigan JIL 129 (2014), 142.

[58]   This effective control test is over an area or a territory. It should not be confused with the role it plays in the law of State responsibility (attribution of wrongful act) as the effective control, in this case, is utilised to assert that certain acts fall within the jurisdiction of a State. Even though both jurisdiction and attribution can be based on the same set of facts, the two questions are regulated by different bodies of law and ought to be treated separately. The concept of jurisdiction stems from the framework of the primary law. In contrast, attribution in international law is regulated by the secondary rules of international responsibility. In fact, this evaluation can only be done after it has been demonstrated that the State had jurisdiction regarding its obligation to prevent crimes against humanity.

[59]   About those situations, see also María L. Piqué, above n. 5, 154–5.

[60]   See, Ilaşcu v. Moldova, Judgment, 8 July 2004, Application No. 48787/99, Reports of Judgments and Decisions 2004–VII at para 330–331.

diplomatic, economic, judicial or other measures that it is in its power to take and are in accordance with international law to secure to the applicants the rights guaranteed by the [ECHR] ". According to Draft Article 4, Moldova would be under the obligation to prevent the commission of crimes against humanity in the Transnistrian region independently of who commits the crimes. On the other hand, control without jurisdiction could arise in situations such as the one portrayed by the ICJ in the *Armed Activities on the Territory of the Congo* case. [61] In that case, the ICJ found that Uganda was the occupying power in Ituri, which is located in the Democratic Republic of the Congo, at the relevant time and that it was under the obligation to "secure respect for the applicable rules of international human rights law and international humanitarian law, to protect the inhabitants of the occupied territory against acts of violence, and not to tolerate such violence by any third party". [62] Hence, in line with proposed interpretation of Draft Article 4 outlined above, a State Party in Uganda's situation would also be under the obligation to prevent the commission of crimes against humanity against the inhabitants of Ituri, notwithstanding who is perpetrating those crimes.

3. Concluding remarks

The ILC Draft Articles on the Prevention and Punishment of Crimes Against Humanity establish a clear obligation upon States to prevent crimes against humanity in any territory under its jurisdiction. When it comes to interrogating the relationship between the extraterritorial obligation to prevent crimes against humanity and effective control, this paper has one simple conclusion: the notion of "jurisdiction" in Draft Article 4 has to be broadly interpreted, also referring to a power that States exercise over a territory and its inhabitants. This power is a question of fact, actual authority, and control. Thus, as an alternative to legal competence over a foreign territory, ef-

---

[61] Armed Activities on the Territory of the Congo (Democratic Republic of the Congo v. Uganda), Judgment, 19 December 2005, ICJ. Reports 2005.

[62] *Ibid.*, 168 and 178.

fective control appears as a requisite in order to prove the existence of a State's jurisdiction over that territory. It is therefore a *de facto* jurisdiction. In other words, the "effective control" is a criterion for determining whether that State is under the primary obligation to prevent crimes against humanity regarding acts that take place beyond its own territory.